THE CLA
WO

A Di

The Natural History of Religion

A Dissertation on the Passions and *The Natural History of Religion* were first published in 1757 in a volume entitled *Four Dissertations*, the last philosophical work written by Hume. The *Natural History* is an original work on religion as a natural phenomenon. It discusses ways in which human nature gives rise to religious belief and devotion. It is the only major work devoted exclusively to the subject of religion that Hume lived to see through the press himself. In his *Dissertation on the Passions*, Hume revisits his theory of the passions first presented in Book 2 of *A Treatise of Human Nature*. He identifies the issues of chief importance to him and clarifies and revises many passages in the *Treatise*.

The last edition of both works seen through the press by Hume appeared in 1772. It provides the copy-text for the present edition, but all substantive changes to the text planned by Hume before his death are taken into account. The editor's historical introduction discusses the genesis, revision, publishing history, and reception of these works, which went into nine editions at the author's hand. Annotations provide information about Hume's sources, allusions, citations, and terminology. Biographical sketches of all of the individuals mentioned by Hume in the work are supplied in a separate appendix. Two bibliographies list the works cited by Hume and by the editor, and a bibliographical history of work on the passions is provided. Hume's original index to these texts is reproduced, and a separate, comprehensive index is provided by the editor. The critical apparatus charts all substantive variations between editions and reports all editorial revisions.

Tom L. Beauchamp is Professor of Philosophy and Senior Research Scholar at Georgetown University, Washington DC. He is one of the General Editors of the Clarendon Hume. He is co-author of *Principles of Biomedical Ethics* (1979, 5th edn 2001), *Hume and the Problem of Causation* (1981), and *A History and Theory of Informed Consent* (1986), and editor of the Clarendon editions of David Hume's *An Enquiry concerning the Principles of Morals* (1998) and *An Enquiry concerning Human Understanding* (2000).

THE CLARENDON EDITION OF THE WORKS OF DAVID HUME

General Editors of the Philosophical Works

Tom L. Beauchamp David Fate Norton M. A. Stewart

DAVID HUME

A Dissertation on the Passions

The Natural History of Religion

A CRITICAL EDITION

EDITED BY
TOM L. BEAUCHAMP

CLARENDON PRESS · OXFORD

OXFORD
UNIVERSITY PRESS

Great Clarendon Street, Oxford OX2 6DP

Oxford University Press is a department of the University of Oxford.
It furthers the University's objective of excellence in research, scholarship,
and education by publishing worldwide in

Oxford New York

Auckland Cape Town Dar es Salaam Hong Kong Karachi
Kuala Lumpur Madrid Melbourne Mexico City Nairobi
New Delhi Shanghai Taipei Toronto

With offices in

Argentina Austria Brazil Chile Czech Republic France Greece
Guatemala Hungary Italy Japan Poland Portugal Singapore
South Korea Switzerland Thailand Turkey Ukraine Vietnam

Oxford is a registered trade mark of Oxford University Press
in the UK and in certain other countries

Published in the United States
by Oxford University Press Inc., New York

First published 2007
First published in paperback 2009

British Library Cataloguing in Publication Data

Data available

Library of Congress Cataloging in Publication Data

Hume, David, 1711–1776.
[Of the passions]
A dissertation on the passions; The natural history of religion:
a critical edition/David Hume; edited by Tom L. Beauchamp.
p.cm.—(The Clarendon edition of the works of David Hume)
Includes bibliographical references and index.
ISBN: 978–0–19–925188–9 (alk. paper)
1. Emotions (Philosophy)—History—Early works to 1800.
2. Religion—Philosophy—Early works to 1800. I. Beauchamp, Tom L. II. Hume, David, 1711–1776.
Natural history of religion. III. Title. IV. Series: Hume, David, 1711–1776. Works. 1998. B1493.O3 2006
128′.37—dc22 2006017201

Typeset by Laserwords Private Limited, Chennai, India
Printed in Great Britain
by
The MPG Group

ISBN 978–0–19–925188–9 (hbk.); 978–0–19–957574–9 (pbk.)

1 3 5 7 9 10 8 6 4 2

PREFACE

The two works in this volume were originally published as 'dissertations'. They were published in 1757, together with two other dissertations, in a small book entitled *Four Dissertations*. Hume abandoned this title in 1758 when he incorporated all four dissertations into his collected philosophical, political, economic, and literary works entitled *Essays and Treatises on Several Subjects*. He continued to revise the writings in this collection until his death in 1776. Hume extracted the bulk of *A Dissertation on the Passions* from book 2 of *A Treatise of Human Nature*. *The Natural History of Religion* was an original work, and is the only major work devoted exclusively to the subject of religion that Hume published in his lifetime.

This volume is one of several comprising the Clarendon Hume. The plan for a critical edition of Hume's philosophical, political, and literary works was initiated in 1975 during meetings of the Hume Society at the University of Wisconsin. A year later, at the Bicentennial Hume Congress in Montreal, consultation with Hume scholars set the stage for what would become the Clarendon Hume. Work began on this particular volume in 1980. The entire series adopts modern editing techniques to establish authoritative texts. The substantive variants created by Hume's steady course of revisions are all recorded, and techniques of bibliographical and historical scholarship are used to correct the texts, present their histories, and trace their intellectual backgrounds.

The principles governing the Clarendon Hume were formulated in consultation with my co-editors of the series, David Fate Norton and M. A. Stewart. They made numerous recommendations for improvement, as did Mark Box. The dedication, support, and critical scrutiny of these colleagues merit the strongest possible acknowledgement. I am also indebted to Peter Millican for thoughts about how to structure this and other Clarendon Hume volumes.

A. Wayne Colver, Sadao Ikeda, T. E. Jessop, Peter Nidditch, and W. B. Todd previously published material pertaining to the bibliographical schema included in the Introduction to this volume. Their pioneering work has been meticulously corrected and augmented for this volume, as for the volumes of Hume's *An Enquiry concerning Human Understanding* and *An Enquiry concerning the Principles of Morals*, by Professor Stewart. Nidditch's unpublished work on Hume's essays, which the Oxford University Press passed on to the co-editors of the Clarendon Hume for preparation of the volume of Hume's Essays, has been useful in constructing a few formal features of the critical apparatus in the present volume.

Innumerable research assistants and librarians in Europe, the United States, and Japan have worked diligently to provide information that would render this edition reliable and comprehensive. Librarians and curators at eight institutions merit special acknowledgement: the British Library, the National Library of Scotland, the Library of Congress, the Beinecke Library at Yale University, the Milton S. Eisenhower Library at the Johns Hopkins University, McGill University Libraries, the Harry Ransom Library at the University of Texas at Austin, and the Woodstock Library and Lauinger Library at Georgetown University.

Philosophy editor Peter Momtchiloff has been exceptionally attentive to the needs of this edition and supportive in seeing the work through the process of critical review. Angela Griffin, Robert Ritter, Charlotte Jenkins, Jenni Craig, Jean van Altena, and Rupert Cousens contributed sound editorial advice and corrections that improved the volume. My administrative assistant, Moheba Hanif, mastered the rules of this edition and the Oxford University Press, for which she deserves both admiration and commendation.

The US National Endowment for the Humanities and McGill University contributed funds to support the early stages of this project. The Graduate School, the Department of Philosophy, and the Kennedy Institute of Ethics at Georgetown University were generous with sabbatical leaves and financial support. The constant support and good will of Wayne Davis will always be remembered.

Tom L. Beauchamp

Chilmark, Massachusetts, and Washington, DC
January 2007

CONTENTS

ABBREVIATIONS AND CONVENTIONS

Abstract	*An Abstract of . . . A Treatise of Human Nature*
ann.	the annotation(s) at [the following point]
Appx.	Appendix to *EPM*, designated by appendix number and paragraph number
B	The Biographical Appendix in this edition contains a biography of this person
c.	century *or* centuries
Cat.	Catalogue of Hume's References
Dial.	'A Dialogue' (published with *EPM*), designated by paragraph numbers
Dialogues	*Dialogues concerning Natural Religion*
DP	*A Dissertation on the Passions*
EHU	*An Enquiry concerning Human Understanding*
EPM	*An Enquiry concerning the Principles of Morals*
ETSS	*Essays and Treatises on Several Subjects*
Letters	*Letters of David Hume* (ed. Greig)
New Letters	*New Letters of David Hume* (ed. Klibansky and Mossner)
NHR	*The Natural History of Religion*
RL	Reference List
THN	*A Treatise of Human Nature*

INTRODUCTION: A HISTORY OF TWO DISSERTATIONS

Four Dissertations (1757) was the last philosophical book written and seen through the press by Hume. The first of the four dissertations was *The Natural History of Religion* (*NHR*) and the second was *Of the Passions* (retitled in 1758 *A Dissertation on the Passions* (*DP*)). The *Natural History* and Hume's earlier work on religious topics—primarily Sections 10–11 of *An Enquiry concerning Human Understanding*—together elicited more philosophical commentary from his contemporaries than any other of his works published in his lifetime. His *Dissertation on the Passions*, by contrast, received little attention.

This Introduction discusses the genesis, revision, and reception of these two dissertations, which went into nine editions at the author's hand. The first section surveys pertinent features of Hume's life and philosophical development. The second examines his emergence as an essayist and its import for *Four Dissertations*. The third section treats the history of the editions from 1757 to the posthumous edition of 1777. This history includes the origins of *A Dissertation on the Passions* in *A Treatise of Human Nature* (*THN*). The fourth section reports bibliographical details on all volumes published from 1757 to 1777. In Section 5, the portions of the *Treatise* that Hume retained in *A Dissertation on the Passions* are displayed, using parallel columns. The sixth and seventh sections detail the reception of the two dissertations in journals, pamphlets, and other publications prior to Hume's death in 1776.

1. HUME'S EARLY LIFE AND PHILOSOPHY

Birth of a Philosopher

Hume recorded the salient facts surrounding his birth in his small autobiography, 'My Own Life': 'I was born the 26 of April 1711, O.S. [old style] at Edinburgh. I was of a good family both by Father and Mother. My Father's Family is a Branch of the Earl of Home's or Hume's; and my Ancestors had been Proprietors of the Estate, which my Brother possesses, for several

Generations.'[1] Hume's early years were spent in Edinburgh and Ninewells, in the family home here mentioned. His father died when Hume was two years of age (1713), and his devout mother, Katherine, reared her three children in the family home. With her, Hume would have attended the Church of Scotland at Chirnside parish church, where his uncle by marriage (Revd George Home of Broadhaugh) was pastor. However, little reliable information is available regarding the formation and nature of Hume's religious convictions as a child.

Hume was a 10-year-old youth when he entered the University in Edinburgh during the 1721–2 session.[2] His studies included Latin, Greek, logic and metaphysics, natural philosophy and, almost certainly, mathematics. His family hoped that he would choose a career in law, a path he briefly considered. He notes in 'My Own Life' that 'My studious Disposition, my Sobriety, and my Industry gave my Family a Notion that the Law was a proper Profession for me: But I found an unsurmountable Aversion to every thing but the pursuits of Philosophy and general Learning.'[3]

In the spring of 1734 Hume wrote a letter containing information about his early philosophical reflections. He reported that, at age 18, he arrived at a 'new Scene of Thought, which transported me beyond Measure, & made me, with an Ardor natural to young men, throw up every other Pleasure or Business to apply entirely to it'.[4] Hume may here be reflecting back on some early philosophical thoughts that evolved into his three-volume work *A Treatise of Human Nature* (1739–40), although this link cannot be documented. As the title of this work indicates, and, as he states in this letter, Hume had by 1734 'resolved to make [human nature] my principal Study'.[5] This ambition was likely the genesis of *A Dissertation on the Passions*.

Hume began as a youth to reflect on religion and on answers to many questions that had been posed by philosophical theologians:

Tis not long ago that I burn'd an old Manuscript Book, wrote before I was twenty; which contain'd, Page after Page, the gradual Progress of my Thoughts on that head [namely, arguments about religion]. It begun with an anxious Search after

[1] 'My Own Life' 1; *Letters*, 1: 1 ('The Life of David Hume, Esq. Written by Himself', cited by par. no. and also the page no. in *Letters of David Hume*, 1: 1–7; abbreviated *Letters*).

[2] Edinburgh University matriculation register, 1704–62 (Edinburgh University Library, MS Da), p. 62. This information is based on the research of M. A. Stewart and Michael Barfoot.

[3] 'My Own Life' 3; *Letters*, 1: 1.

[4] Spring 1734, to an unnamed doctor, *Letters*, 1: 13–14. On the early origins of the *Treatise*, see also *Letters*, 1: 187. A historical account of Hume's early philosophy is provided by David Fate Norton in the Introduction ('Historical Account') to the Clarendon Hume edition of the *Treatise*. Parts of the present edition of *DP* are indebted to Norton's research on the *Treatise*.

[5] Spring 1734, to an unnamed doctor, *Letters*, 1: 16.

Arguments, to confirm the common Opinion: Doubts stole in, dissipated, return'd, were again dissipated, return'd again; and it was a perpetual Struggle of a restless Imagination against Inclination, perhaps against Reason. . . . What danger can ever come from ingenious Reasoning & Enquiry? The worst speculative Sceptic ever I knew, was a much better Man than the best superstitious Devotee & Bigot. I must inform you, too, that this was the way of thinking of the Antients on this Subject.[6]

In August 1734 Hume journeyed to France in order to write free of distractions. He reports in his autobiography that 'During my retreat in France, first at Reims, but chiefly at La Fleche in Anjou, I composed my *Treatise of Human Nature*. After passing three years very agreeably in that country, I came over to London in 1737.'[7] Apparently Hume had completed a draft of the *Treatise* by the time he visited London in the autumn of 1737. Because *A Dissertation on the Passions* is drawn primarily from the second book of the *Treatise*, most of the passages in this small dissertation date from this period. Consequently, Hume probably drafted the bulk of its philosophical theses by September 1738 when a contract for publication of the *Treatise* was signed.

The Treatise*'s Ill Fortune and Later Work on the Passions*

Hume's contemporaries regarded the *Treatise* as enigmatic and difficult. It did not fare well in reviews and sales.[8] Hume came to regret his decision to publish it in the form in which it appeared, but he judged that errors of

6 10 Mar. 1751, to Gilbert Elliot of Minto, *Letters*, 1: 154. Some of Hume's early notes about religion have been preserved, though it is uncertain in which years they were drafted. See 'Hume's Early Memoranda', ed. E. C. Mossner. These memoranda, or reading notes, were initially brought to public attention in the 1840s by John Hill Burton, *Life and Correspondence of David Hume*, 1: 95–6, 124–35. Corrections to Burton's and Mossner's representations are found in M. A. Stewart, 'The Dating of Hume's Manuscripts'. Stewart shows that these holograph notes were likely compiled after publication of *THN*. See, further, on the connection between Bayle's writings and Hume's early notes (and their dating), Jean-Paul Pittion, 'Hume's Reading of Bayle: An Inquiry into the Source and Role of the Memoranda'; Fernando A. Bahr, 'Pierre Bayle en los "Early Memoranda" de Hume'; and Lothar Kreimendahl, 'Humes frühe religionsphilosophische Interessen im Lichte seiner "Early Memoranda"'.

7 'My Own Life' 5; *Letters*, 1: 2.

8 See Hume's comment on complaints of obscurity and difficulty in *Abstract*, Pref. 2. See, further, the anonymous reviews of *A Treatise of Human Nature* in *The History of the Works of the Learned*, 2 (Nov. 1739), 353–90, and (Dec. 1739), 391–404; *Göttingische Zeitungen von gelehrten Sachen* [succeeding title, after 1753: *Göttingische Anzeigen von gelehrten Sachen*], 2 (7 Jan. 1740), 9–12; *Bibliotheque raisonnée des ouvrages des savans de l'Europe*, 24 (Apr.–June 1740), 324–55; *Nouvelle bibliotheque, ou histoire litteraire*, 6 (July 1740), 291–316, and 7 (Sept. 1740), 44–63; and *Bibliotheque raisonnée des ouvrages des savans de l'Europe*, 26 (Apr.–June 1741), 411–27 (this journal reviewed vols. 1–2 and vol. 3 separately). English translations of the second, third, and fourth reviews listed above (by, respectively, Manfred Kuehn; David Fate Norton and Mary J.

style, youthful expression, and failures to revise difficult passages, more than philosophical lapses or incorrect philosophical principles, were to blame for the work's lack of success.[9] He decided in the early 1740s to correct these defects and to 'cast . . . anew'[10]—that is, wholly recompose in a more accessible manner—the *Treatise*'s principal doctrines. He almost completely recomposed the ideas in book 1 (probably in 1745–7), and published the work in 1748 as *Philosophical Essays concerning Human Understanding*. He changed the title of this work in 1758 to *An Enquiry concerning Human Understanding*. Book 3 of the *Treatise* was heavily recast in style and focus (probably in 1749–50), and was published in 1751 as *An Enquiry concerning the Principles of Morals*. After many deletions and a few additions, book 2 was abbreviated and restructured, then published in 1757 as 'Of the Passions', soon changed in title to *A Dissertation on the Passions*. Hume described it as one of the 'small pieces' that he included with *The Natural History of Religion*.[11]

Hume expressly distanced himself from the *Treatise* in late 1775. His statement was printed in January 1776 as an 'Advertisement' to be placed in copies of unsold editions as well as in copies of new editions of *Essays and Treatises on Several Subjects* (*ETSS*).[12] He declared the *Treatise* a 'juvenile work' by comparison to his later publications, and expressed a hope 'that

Norton; and David Fate Norton and Rebecca Pates) are found in J. Fieser (ed.), *Early Responses to Hume's Metaphysical and Epistemological Writings*.

Several *announcements, advertisements*, and *notices* were issued prior to these *reviews*, some including critical appraisal, and some in the same journals listed in this note. For the full array of attention to the *Treatise*, see the Introduction ('Historical Account') by D. F. Norton in the Clarendon Hume Edition, esp. sects. 6–7.

[9] See Mar. or Apr. 1751, to Gilbert Elliot of Minto, *Letters*, 1: 158; Feb. 1754, to John Stewart, *Letters*, 1: 187. These letters to Elliot and Stewart were written in the period in which Hume was mining bk. 2 of the *Treatise* to create *DP*, often word for word. Whatever the precise scope of his concern about the style and manner of the *Treatise*, he cannot have meant the very passages from bk. 2 that he was at the time planning to keep in a verbatim form. Hume's statements do not preclude the possibility that he had some *philosophical* reasons for disenchantment with the *Treatise*, not merely stylistic concerns. Even in his famous statement that 'The philosophical Principles are the same in both' the *Treatise* and in his later philosophy (*Letters*, 1: 158), the scope of 'philosophical principles' is unclear. Hume presumably means that he retained the same general philosophical viewpoint and the same general principles, but not an identity of philosophical substance, use of example, or argument. As he matured he seemed to become increasingly attached to the view that he retained the same philosophical principles or doctrines, modifying only his presentation, style, topic, examples, and the like.

[10] 'My Own Life' 8; *Letters*, 1: 3.

[11] 'My Own Life' 13; *Letters*, 1: 5.

[12] See sect. 4 of the editor's introduction to the Clarendon Edition of *An Enquiry concerning Human Understanding*; and A. Wayne Colver, 'A Variant of Hume's Advertisement Repudiating the Treatise'. This Advertisement is Hume's first published acknowledgement of authorship of the *Treatise*, and is difficult to interpret because he does not disavow, renounce, or repudiate the *Treatise* as a whole; nor does he reject its doctrines or principles.

the following Pieces may alone be regarded as containing [my] philosophical sentiments and principles'.[13] *A Dissertation on the Passions* and *The Natural History of Religion* appear to be two of these 'Pieces', because they are two of the four main philosophical works in *Essays and Treatises on Several Subjects* that Hume identified (by specific volume) as the portion to which the Advertisement was to be appended.[14]

Hume's discontent with the *Treatise* was apparent before he published his *Dissertation on the Passions* and *Natural History*. By 1740 he expressed concerns about some of his 'errors' in correspondence with Francis Hutcheson,[15] and in 1754 he said, 'I shall acknowledge . . . a very great Mistake in Conduct, viz my publishing at all the Treatise of human Nature. . . . Above all, the positive Air, which prevails in that Book, & which may be imputed to the Ardor of Youth, so much displeases me, that I have not Patience to review it.'[16]

Despite this anguish over some features of the *Treatise*, the second book on the passions seems never to have been the subject of Hume's uneasiness; nor did his critics focus on it. The fact that Hume retained many passages from book 2 without substantive modifications—by contrast to his near total recasting of the other two books—may indicate a general satisfaction with at least some of his work on the passions. Nonetheless, as reported below, roughly 88 per cent of the material on the passions in the second book of the *Treatise* was abandoned in drafting *A Dissertation on the Passions*. (The figure is 85 per cent of book 2 if the material on liberty and necessity is excluded from the calculation.[17]) Hume's dissatisfaction with the *Treatise*'s style or manner may have played some role in his decision to present *A Dissertation on the Passions* as a revision that eliminated what he disliked.

Hume's personal assessment of *A Treatise of Human Nature*, its public reception, and its commercial failure jointly had a lasting impact. The book never reappeared in print in the eighteenth century. *A Dissertation on the Passions*, by contrast, enjoyed eight new editions at Hume's hand.

[13] Advertisement, 1777 (*ETSS*). In a letter of 26 Oct. 1775 (*Letters*, 2: 301; with a correction in a letter of 13 Nov. 1775, *Letters*, 2: 304), Hume gave instructions to his printer, William Strahan, to prefix his Advertisement to the second volume of *ETSS* (1772) and to earlier editions in the warehouse. The second volume included *An Enquiry concerning Human Understanding, A Dissertation on the Passions, An Enquiry concerning the Principles of Morals*, and *The Natural History of Religion*.

[14] 13 Nov. 1775, to William Strahan, *Letters*, 2: 304.

[15] 16 Mar. 1740, to Francis Hutcheson, *Letters*, 1: 38–9.

[16] Feb. 1754, to John Stewart, *Letters*, 1: 187.

[17] *Of liberty and necessity* is discussed in *THN* 2.3.1.1–2.3.2.8. This material is comparable to *EHU* 8. If this material on liberty and necessity is excluded from bk. 2 of *THN*, approximately 56,700 words remain, of which approximately 8,500 are carried into *DP*.

2. FROM ESSAYS TO ENQUIRIES

Rather than reworking the *Treatise*, Hume began the 1740s by publishing moral and political essays.[18] These essays mark the beginning of Hume's move from the model of an all-embracing philosophical system with interlocking parts to a more approachable style in which attention is focused on individual topics. In an *Advertisement* placed in the first book of these essays, he described their nature and independence:

> MOST of these ESSAYS were wrote with a View of being publish'd as WEEKLY-PAPERS, and were intended to comprehend the Designs both of the SPECTATORS and CRAFTSMEN.... THE READER must not look for any Connexion among these ESSAYS, but must consider each of them as a Work apart.[19]

Soon there appeared a second edition of this work, and then a companion (second) volume of new essays.[20] A few essays contain criticisms of religious beliefs, religious wars, superstition, speculative doctrines, religious intolerance, priestly pretension and ambition, and the character of the clergy. Hume's comments critical of religion are sprinkled across the following essays: 'Whether the British Government Inclines More to Absolute Monarchy, or to a Republic', 'Of Parties in General', 'Of the Parties of Great Britain', 'Of Superstition and Enthusiasm', 'Of the Rise and Progress of the Arts and Sciences', and (from 1748) 'Of National Characters'. Excepting a few comments in the *Treatise*, these essays are Hume's initial forays into published criticism of religion and clerical affairs.

The essay style was known to Hume through writings of essayists such as Michel de Montaigne, Francis Bacon, John Dryden, Joseph Addison, and Alexander Pope. His commitment to the essay was still in place when he wrote *Four Dissertations*. However, some events in 1745 that have a bearing on his thoughts about religion need to be considered before we attend to these four dissertations.

A Letter from a Gentleman (1745)

In 1745 Hume's career aspirations came into conflict with local family loyalties and politics, causing him a personal disappointment.[21] In 1744–5

[18] The first group was published in 1741 as *Essays Moral and Political*.

[19] *Essays, Moral and Political*, 1741 edn., pp. iii, v; repeated in the 1742 edn.

[20] *Essays, Moral and Political*, vol. 2 (1742).

[21] For the relevant history, including previously unpublished historical data, see M. A. Stewart, *The Kirk and the Infidel*; Roger L. Emerson, 'The "Affair" at Edinburgh and the "Project" at

he hoped to become Professor of Pneumaticks and Moral Philosophy at Edinburgh. Revd William Wishart (1692–1753), Principal of the university, and other academic figures[22] stood in opposition to Hume's election to the position. Part of the job description required that the chair-holder teach the truth of Christian monotheism and allied doctrines. The central obstacle was Hume's alleged scepticism about religion and morality and the fact that he would teach young students.[23] Wishart assembled an account of several theses in books 1 and 3 of the *Treatise*, often reorganizing Hume's own words to sabotage his candidacy by demonstrating that his writings rendered him unsuited for the chair. Wishart's complete disregard of book 2 of the *Treatise* indicates that Hume's work on the passions was not among the material that his detractors found offensive.

Hume then 'composed in one Morning'[24] a letter of reply. It was sent to former Lord Provost John Coutts (1699–1751), who, with Henry Home (1696–1782; later Lord Kames),[25] had promoted Hume's candidacy. Home apparently edited and adapted Hume's swiftly composed letter (possibly also expanding or revising it), combined it with the statement of charges against the *Treatise*, and published it under the title *A Letter from a Gentleman to his Friend in Edinburgh*. The work seems to have been published neither at Hume's initiative nor with his approval or editing. Nonetheless, Hume's objectives in sending the letter to Coutts are clear. He wanted to defend the philosophy of the *Treatise* against zealous critics, especially those who accused it of a dangerous scepticism.[26]

The charges made against Hume, together with his responses, bear on the history and interpretation of the *Natural History*. His critics left no public doubt about their disapproval of the sceptical import of Hume's views or about their belief that his philosophy constituted a threat to religion and morals. The airing of these issues left Hume with little to

Glasgow'; Richard Sher, 'Professors of Virtue'; and David Norton, Introduction ('Historical Account') to the Clarendon Hume Edition of the *Treatise*, sect. 8, pp. 521–6.

[22] Notably William Leechman (1706–85), Professor of Divinity at Glasgow, and Francis Hutcheson (1694–1746), Professor of Philosophy at Glasgow.

[23] See 4 Aug. 1744, to William Mure; and 25 Apr. 1745, to Matthew Sharpe, *Letters*, 1: 55–60.

[24] *A Letter from a Gentleman* 41.

[25] In the 1730s Home was aware of Hume's drafting of the *Treatise*, forwarded a copy of vols. 1 and 2 to Francis Hutcheson, and suggested a strategy to increase its sales in Scotland. See Hume's letters of 2 Dec. 1737, to Henry Home, *New Letters*, 1–3; 4 June 1739 and 1 July 1739, to Henry Home, *New Letters*, 5–7; and 6 Apr. 1739, to Pierre Desmaizeaux [Des Maizeaux], *Letters*, 1: 29–30. Home was a Scottish lawyer and legal historian raised to the bench in 1752, as Lord Ordinary of the Court of Session. He became Lord Kames upon this appointment. Below he is often referred to as Kames rather than Home.

[26] 13–15 June 1745, to Henry Home, *New Letters*, 14–15.

lose by publishing his views on religion. Indeed, he had something to gain; he could use his philosophical writings as an indirect reply to his opponents. His *Philosophical Essays concerning Human Understanding* (that is, *An Enquiry concerning Human Understanding*) seem to contain elements of such a response.

Religion in the First Enquiry: the Philosophical Essays *of 1748*

The style and topical focus of the essayist are maintained as Hume moves past the two first volumes of popular 'moral and political' essays to the *Philosophical Essays* and then to his *Enquiry concerning the Principles of Morals*. The essay style is evident in both, though the topics are more thematically related and the collection has an increased internal coherence, by contrast to the earlier volumes of essays.

The *Philosophical Essays*—i.e. The First Enquiry—contains two sections attentive to religion: Section 10, 'Of Miracles' (on the foundations of revealed religion), and Section 11, 'Of a Particular Providence and of a Future State' (on the foundations of natural religion). In the first, Hume holds that evidence adduced for miracles and testimony in support of miracles are suspect. In the second, he presents a dialogue that debates whether Epicurus presented a serious threat to political authorities and to social morality and religion. Hume presents Epicurus as a model of scepticism concerning the possibility of a natural, or philosophical, theology.

Both sections provoked responses from Hume's peers. Soon the essay on miracles became the most extensively criticized of his published writings. The hostile reception of this essay increased his reputation as a sceptic, especially about religion. This reputation was in place by the time he published the *Natural History*.

Religion in the Second Enquiry: the Moral Essays of 1751

Hume's Second Enquiry places morality on a secular footing, implicitly divorcing religion and morality. This stratagem was not lost on Hume's critics. For example, James Balfour of Pilrig (1705–95), a member of the gentry and a committed Presbyterian, wrote an anonymous monograph in which he scolded Hume for obviously incorrect claims about morality and religion.[27] Hume's moral theses and perspectives on the character of

[27] *A Delineation of the Nature and Obligation of Morality. With Reflexions upon Mr. Hume's Book, intitled, An Inquiry concerning the Principles of Morals*, esp. pp. 27, 33 ff., 79, 137 ff., 159, 162, 174.

the clergy were also challenged by Robert Clayton (1695–1758), bishop of Clogher.[28]

Hume's moral theory, though not overtly anti-religious, conveyed to his contemporaries a scepticism about divine authority over morals. His views regarding the foundations of morals in human nature therefore had the effect of furthering his reputation as a sceptic and an infidel writer.

Hume's Changes of Title (1753–7)

A decade after publishing *Philosophical Essays concerning Human Understanding*, Hume changed the wording in its title from *Essays* to *Enquiry* (*An Enquiry concerning Human Understanding*). The title already given to *An Enquiry concerning the Principles of Morals* apparently inspired this change. Both works were originally conceived as a group of essays.[29] Hume's conception of his new work as collections of essays endured for several years.[30]

However, investing heavily in the words *book, essay, enquiry*, and *treatise* in the interpretation of Hume's changes of titles can be as misleading as it is rewarding. Hume never analysed the precise meaning of his titles or explained why he changed them, and some changes of title may have derived from the marketing objectives of booksellers. All that can be asserted with confidence is that Hume's changes of title seem to reflect an evolving conception of his writings that may be intermixed with marketing strategies. In the 1740s he had laboured in his publishing ventures as an essayist, only to emerge, in the mid-1750s, with a collection of diverse works. In 1757 he used yet another term in his title when he published *Four Dissertations*.

Four Dissertations fits squarely into the pattern of Hume's literary development through this period. *The Natural History* has the same general character as the Enquiries, except that the constituent topics were not (in the first edition) separately identified, but presented as a continuous narrative. *Of the Passions* has the character of a book of the *Treatise* pared down to the scope of a single narrative, by contrast to a group of essays. The term

[28] *Some Thoughts on Self-Love, Innate-Ideas, Free-Will, Taste, Sentiment, Liberty and Necessity, etc. Occasioned by reading Mr. Hume's Works.*

[29] Hume referred to the contents of *EPM* as 'these Essays' in his first edition (1751, p. 110 n.). He changed this wording (in the 1751 errata) to 'this Enquiry'. His original words were apparently no mistake. In the only other reference to *EPM* in the 1st edn., Hume refers to the book as containing 'Essays' rather than 'Sections' (1751, p. 55 n., changed in the errata). Hume seems to have originally conceived *EPM*, like *EHU*, as a group of independent essays on related subjects.

[30] When *Four Dissertations* was published in 1757, it carried a bookseller's advertisement for *ETSS* that listed *Philosophical Essays concerning Human Understanding* (as 'VOL. II').

Dissertation may serve as a catch-all to reflect the diversity of the collection, or it may indicate that Hume was still engaged in some degree of literary experiment, conceived originally as one form of the more extended essay.

3. A HISTORY OF THE NINE EDITIONS

The first section of this Introduction described Hume's decision to recast parts of book 2 of his *Treatise* in the form of *A Dissertation on the Passions*. An Editorial Appendix (pp. 172–204) treats the nature of Hume's corrections as he revised the editions of both *A Dissertation on the Passions* and the *Natural History*. The present section examines the drafting, printing, and publishing of the editions.

Drafting the Manuscripts

The date of composition of the *Natural History* cannot be fixed with precision. Drafting, by contrast to note-taking of the sort found in Hume's early memoranda, was probably not begun before Hume finished *An Enquiry concerning Human Understanding* in 1748.

In the spring of 1749 Hume was in London. He departed by early summer for Ninewells, where he entered into an intense stretch of work on *An Enquiry concerning the Principles of Morals* (1751), *Political Discourses* (1752), and *Dialogues concerning Natural Religion* (a posthumous publication, but under revision in the early 1750s and possibly completed in draft by 1751). Though scant evidence exists of his activities during this period, it is probable that Hume began to work on the *Natural History*, and possibly completed it, between 1749 and 1752. His *Dialogues* are concerned with different aspects of religion, and some of the same sources may have been consulted for both works. There is an occasional overlap of subject-matter, possibly reflecting parallel research. Parts of the *Natural History*, then, may have been written or revised as parts of the *Dialogues* were written or revised.

No later than 24 September 1752, Hume was labouring on his *History of England* (1754–61) and correcting the fourth edition (1753) of *Essays, Moral and Political*.[31] In his autobiography he recorded some major events of the period:

> In 1752, the Faculty of Advocates chose me their Librarian, an office from which I received little or no emolument, but which gave me the command of a large library.

[31] 24 Sept. 1752, to Adam Smith, *Letters*, 1: 167–8.

I then formed the plan of writing the History of England; but being frightened with the notion of continuing a narrative through a period of 1700 years, I commenced with the accession of the House of Stuart.[32]

On the one hand, the massive task of writing a history of England presumably would leave Hume with little time for other projects. On the other hand, the large library of the Faculty of Advocates would possibly have facilitated work on the *Natural History*, which is among his most copiously footnoted volumes. Based on the available evidence, a reasonable presumption is that Hume completed the bulk of the *Natural History* by late 1752, and then polished it for publication between 1752 and 1755 (see the letter of 1755 quoted immediately below). Hume's practice of concentrating almost wholly on a particular project suggests that he may have written *The Natural History of Religion* in a few weeks or months during the period just identified.

The earliest known reference to the completed manuscripts of both the *Natural History* and *A Dissertation on the Passions* is found in a letter Hume wrote in June 1755 to his bookseller, Andrew Millar (1707–68):

There are four short Dissertations, which *I have kept some Years by me, in order to polish them as much as possible*. One of them is that which Allan Ramsay[33] mentiond to you. Another of the Passions; a third of Tragedy; a fourth, some Considerations previous to Geometry & Natural philosophy. The whole, I think, wou'd make a Volume a fourth less than my Enquiry;[34] as nearly as I can calculate: But it wou'd be proper to print it in a larger Type, in order to bring it to the same Size & Price. I wou'd have it publish'd about the new Year; I offer you the Property for fifty Guineas, payable at the Publication. You may judge, by my being so moderate in my Demands, that I do not propose to make any Words about the Bargain. It wou'd be more convenient for me to print here; especially one of the Dissertations, where there is a good deal of Literature, but as the Manuscript is distinct & accurate, it wou'd not be impossible for me to correct it, tho' printed at London. I leave it to your Choice; tho' I believe, that it might be as cheaply & conveniently & safely executed here. However, the Matter is pretty near indifferent to me.[35]

Millar accepted the offer and sent the dissertations to a London printer (Bowyer), who farmed it out to another firm (Emonson). In the year of publication, Hume described his *Four Dissertations* thus: 'Some of these Dissertations are Attempts to throw Light upon the most Profound

[32] 'My Own Life' 11; *Letters*, 1: 4.

[33] The painter and friend of Hume's. The dissertation is *The Natural History of Religion*.

[34] *An Enquiry concerning the Principles of Morals*, the only work to carry the title 'Enquiry' at the time.

[35] 12 June 1755, to Andrew Millar, *Letters*, 1: 223 (italics added).

Philosophy: Others contain a greater Mixture of polite Literature, & are wrote in a more easy Style & Manner.'[36] These dissertations helped consolidate and complete his remaining projects. The work on religion rounded out his work on this subject, and the work on the passions brought to fruition the final part of his projected recasting of the *Treatise*.

From Four to Three to Five to Four Dissertations

Four Dissertations has its own curious history, including the writing of a Dedication to the Revd John Home, late-placed in many copies of the work.[37] The history of this dedication is to be treated elsewhere in detail in the Clarendon Hume Editions. However, the essentials about *Four Dissertations* as they bear on *The Natural History of Religion* and *A Dissertation on the Passions* require attention here.

Some events transpired almost immediately upon Hume's initial transmission of the manuscript. Seventeen years later he recounted the main lines of this story to his printer, William Strahan (1715–85):[38]

I am told by a Friend, that Dr Millar said to him, there was a Bookseller in London, who had advertisd a new Book, containing, among other things, two of my suppress'd Essays. These I suppose are two Essays of mine, one on Suicide another on the Immortality of the Soul, which were printed by Andrew Millar about seventeen years ago, and which from my abundant Prudence I suppress'd and woud not now wish to have revivd. I know not if you were acquainted with this Transaction. It was this: I intended to print four Dissertations, the natural History

[36] Letter of 27 Feb. 1757, to an unknown correspondent (held in the Lilly Library, University of Indiana).

[37] See Hume's correspondence regarding the dedication: 20 Jan. 1757, to Andrew Millar, *Letters*, 1: 239–40; Feb. or Mar. 1757, to Adam Smith, *Letters*, 1: 245–6; and 22 July 1757, to the Abbé Le Blanc, *Letters*, 1: 261.

[38] Though not the printer of *Four Dissertations*, Strahan had earlier printed several volumes of Hume's and was the printer of all editions of *ETSS* from 1758 to 1777. Millar and Strahan were both Scots who had created firms in London. Millar maintained a close association with Edinburgh bookseller Alexander Kincaid, with whom he co-published some of Hume's works (see the editions of *ETSS*, 1758–72, for Kincaid—and also 1758–77, for A. Donaldson). Millar remained Hume's London bookseller until Millar died in 1768; thereafter Thomas Cadell became Hume's London bookseller (see editions of *ETSS*, 1768–77). Details of the history of Hume's relationship with his printers and booksellers and the nature of the printing and bookselling industries are set out in the Introduction to the Clarendon Hume Edition of *EPM*. See also notes below on Bowyer and Emonson.

See, further, J. A. Cochrane, *Dr. Johnson's Printer*; Colin Clair, *A History of Printing in Britain*; P. M. Handover, *Printing in London*; Alvin Kernan, *Printing Technology, Letters, & Samuel Johnson*; Richard Sher, 'The Book in the Scottish Enlightenment'; H. R. Plomer, G. H. Bushnell, and E. R. McC. Dix, for The Bibliographical Society, *A Dictionary of the Printers and Booksellers who were at Work in England, Scotland and Ireland from 1726 to 1775*.

of Religion, on the Passions, on Tragedy, and on the metaphysical Principles of Geometry. I sent them up to Mr Millar; but before the last was printed,[39] I happend to meet with Lord Stanhope,[40] who was in this Country, and he convincd me, that either there was some Defect in the Argument or in its perspicuity; I forget which; and I wrote to Mr Millar, that I would not print the Essay; but upon his remonstrating that the other Essays woud not make a Volume, I sent him up these two, which I had never intended to have publishd. They were printed; but it was no sooner done than I repented; and Mr Millar and I agreed to suppress them at common Charges, and I wrote a new Essay on the Standard of Taste, to supply their place. Mr Millar assurd me very earnestly that all the Copies were suppress'd, except one.[41]

As this letter indicates, when Hume proposed publishing only three dissertations, Millar protested that the three would not constitute an adequately sized volume. Hume's two essays 'Of Suicide' and 'Of the Immortality of the Soul' ('which I had never intended to have publishd') were sent up to be substituted in the place of the essay on geometry. These essays were printed for Millar (perhaps to be published under the title *Five Dissertations*), folded in sheets with the remaining three essays, and made ready for publication (presumably completed in time for the edition to be suppressed by early Feb. 1756).

A few copies were circulated prior to distribution for sale.[42] Hume eventually decided to suppress the two late additions, and they were cut physically, leaving a few page stubs immediately following page 200. Some of the stubs retain tiny fragments of the print. The five dissertations were in this manner trimmed to three, but the essay 'Of the Standard of Taste' was then bound in after page 200 (its half-title counted as p. 201).[43]

In the above letter to Strahan, Hume gave as the explanation for the suppression of these two essays his 'abundant Prudence' and his having 'repented'.[44] It is unclear whether Hume suppressed the two essays because

[39] There was an initial setting, some time later than June 1755, with a view to publication early in 1756, which got, at most, no further than quire I, because Hume withdrew the essay on geometry before the setting had reached that point.

[40] The essay on geometry was withdrawn before being set in type on the advice of Philip Stanhope (1717–86), 2nd Earl Stanhope and prominent mathematician. This essay has been lost.

[41] 25 Jan. 1772, to William Strahan, *Letters*, 2: 253.

[42] See Hume's correspondence of 27 May 1756, to Andrew Millar, *Letters*, 1: 232 (regarding a copy given to Andrew Mitchell), and 23 May 1764, to Andrew Millar, *Letters*, 1: 444–5 (regarding a copy given to John Wilkes).

[43] 'Of the Standard of Taste' had been printed in late 1756 for the purpose of replacing the cancelled matter ('Of Suicide' and 'Of the Immortality of the Soul'), and had been completed in time for launching the edition early in 1757. The interpolated dedication to John Home (printed Hume) had proofs that were being corrected in Jan. 1757.

[44] 25 Jan. 1772, to William Strahan, *Letters*, 2: 253.

he was dissatisfied with their content, was acting on the persuasive advice of a friend, took seriously the critical reactions of some initial readers of the circulated copies, was pressured (along with his bookseller) by powerful clergy and public officials, or some combination of these reasons.[45]

Two Cancels in the Natural History

Hume at some point during the printing of his dissertations determined to make two substantive changes in *The Natural History of Religion.* Some scholars have maintained that religious sensitivities and social pressures explain why he made these late changes, but his motives are not transparent.

Shortly after publication of *Four Dissertations*, Hume commented in a letter to Adam Smith on alterations made to the *Natural History*. It is unclear which particular changes he has in mind:

> You have read all the Dissertations in Manuscript; but you will find that on the natural History of Religion somewhat amended in point of Prudence. I do not apprehend, that it will much encrease the Clamour against me. . . .
>
> Did you ever hear of such Madness & Folly as our Clergy have lately fallen into? For my Part, I expect that the next Assembly will very solemnly pronounce the Sentence of Excommunication against me: But I do not apprehend it to be a Matter of any Consequence.[46]

Hume's two late, substantive changes in the *Natural History* were both in Section 6 (6.8 and 6.12). Physical evidence of two revisions was once contained in a bound copy of the dissertations. Although now lost, the variants were recorded from corrections found on uncancelled leaves in the Advocates' Library copy during preparation of the 1875 edition of Hume's philosophical works, edited by T. H. Green and T. H. Grose.[47] The variants, as Green and Grose recorded them, are as follows:

[45] An incautious but influential interpretation of Hume's motivation is found in E. C. Mossner, 'Hume's *Four Dissertations*' (and restated in briefer form in Mossner's *Life of David Hume*). In this article Mossner also treats the two cancels that are discussed immediately below.

[46] Feb. or Mar. 1757, to Adam Smith, *Letters*, 1: 245–6. Hume is referring to the fact that an attempt by some prominent evangelicals to bring a discussion of Hume's writings before the General Assembly of the Church of Scotland in 1756 had failed in committee. Hume's information that the matter would be raised again in 1757 proved to be wrong. It remains unclear what role, if any, these investigations played in Hume's decisions about both the choice of essays and altered passages in the *Natural History*. See Hume's correspondence with Allan Ramsay, June 1755, *Letters* 1: 224.

[47] See *Philosophical Works of David Hume*, 4: 331–2; see also 'A History of the Editions' (by Grose), 3: 15–84. Grose believed that he had inspected proof-sheets, though they could have been uncancelled leaves marked with revisions. Grose does not assert that the revisions were in Hume's hand.

Uncancelled State (passage 1): Thus the deity, whom the vulgar Jews conceived only as the God of *Abraham, Isaac*, and *Jacob*, became their *Jehovah* and Creator of the world.
Revised State (passage 1): Thus, notwithstanding the sublime ideas suggested by *Moses* and the inspired writers, many vulgar *Jews* seem still to have conceived the supreme Being as a mere topical deity or national protector.

Uncancelled State (passage 2): Were there a religion (and we may suspect Mahomatanism of this inconsistence) which sometimes painted the Deity in the most sublime colours, as the creator of heaven and earth; sometimes degraded him so far to a level with human creatures as to represent him wrestling with a man, walking in the cool of the evening, showing his back parts, and descending from heaven to inform himself of what passes on earth . . .[48]
Revised State (passage 2): [the following is substituted for the portion after the semicolon above:] sometimes degraded him nearly to a level with human creatures in his powers and faculties . . .

These changes have no clear connection to prudential amendment. The modifications made in passage 1 may have derived from a change of mind on Hume's part about the best way to express complicated reflections on Judaism, its history, and the distinction between its prophets and vulgar Jews. The revised passage is not manifestly more prudent or less offensive than the original. The changes in passage 2 could have derived from Hume's desire to bring his description more in line with Islamic religious beliefs. Hume's opening lines seem to call for a passage with content distinctly aligned with the religion of the Prophet Muhammad, rather than the biblical passages[49] to which he alludes in the original version.

Hume states in his letter to Smith that he had prudential goals in making some changes, but all such prudential amendments could have been made on the manuscript prior to typesetting. They could have occurred at any place in *The Natural History of Religion* on more than one occasion in its history of changes. *The Natural History of Religion* had been in print for a year before the suicide and immortality essays were typeset, and remained in that state after these two essays were suppressed and 'Of the Standard of Taste' was delivered and set in type.

[48] Green and Grose report that, in passage 2, the pen in the proof was drawn through everything from the first 'as' to 'earth'; and for 'so far' the word 'nearly' was substituted in the margin (4: 332).

[49] The representations of the deity in the original version of passage 2 are found in Genesis 3 and 32 and Exodus 33.

Some commentators have maintained that these two leaves were cancelled as a result of the threats of prosecution that Hume mentioned in his letter to Smith, and by forms of intimidation from latitudinarian English theologian (later bishop) William Warburton (1698–1777) directed at Hume's bookseller, Millar.[50] Warburton wrote on 14 February 1756 to the Revd Thomas Balguy that he thought Hume was 'afraid of a prosecution' and had 'suppressed' the volume,[51] but this opinion is neither impartial nor substantiated by evidence. Warburton also wrote a letter to Millar, on 7 February 1757, criticizing the *Natural History* as an attempt to establish atheism, but this letter was too late to have affected publication.[52]

It has never been established that a credible threat of force served as a coercive influence on Hume or on his bookseller—or, if there was such an influence, that there was a connection between this threat and the changes made in the two controversial passages. Hume's two changes to the text offer little, if anything, in the way of a substantive change that would satisfy his critics. The changes clearly did nothing to mollify Warburton, who persisted in his attempts to convince Millar to suppress the work.[53]

If Hume's unencumbered desire had been to publish the cancelled portions, an editor should restore these cancellations to the text under the guidelines of a proper account of the final intention of the author. Some of Hume's editors have chosen this course.[54] However, the cancelled portions are not restored in the text of this edition. In most essentials, Hume himself restored the proof-sheet version of passage 1 in his 1764 edition and thereafter retained it in all editions. (See *NHR* 6.8 in the present edition.) By contrast, the changed text of passage 2 became part of the canon of the author's work, and he perpetuated this passage through many revised editions in which he had ample opportunity to restore the text to its original form or to any other form. Hume studied and amended this work over a

[50] See William Rose, Review of *Essays on Suicide and Immortality*; Mossner, 'Hume's *Four Dissertations*', 39–43; and J. C. A. Gaskin, *Hume's Philosophy of Religion*, 4–5.

[51] Warburton MS letters (Harry Ransom Humanities Research Center, University of Texas at Austin; bound, uncatalogued), vol. 2, no. 32. Mossner (*Life of David Hume*, 323) comments on the contents of this letter and offers a historical explanation of its importance.

[52] *A Selection from Unpublished Papers of the Right Rev. William Warburton*, 309. 7 Feb. 1757 is the advertised date of publication of *Four Dissertations*. For further details, see sect. 7 of this Introduction below, on 'William Warburton [and Richard Hurd]'.

[53] Ibid. Warburton proposed that Hume was attempting to establish 'naturalism', which entailed 'atheism'. Warburton's correspondence with Millar, and Hume's with Smith, present no evidence that the changes identified by Grose played a role in Warburton's reaction, or that they figured in Hume's prudential amendments.

[54] Richard Wollheim (ed.), *David Hume: On Religion*, 58–9; Hume, *Natural History of Religion*, ed. Fieser, xxxii, 32–4; Antony Flew (ed.), *David Hume: Writings on Religion*, 138–9.

twenty-year period, and it is reasonable to infer that he was satisfied with the passage and knew what he wished to convey to the reader.

The Incorporation of Four Dissertations *into* Essays and Treatises

Four Dissertations was published on 7 February 1757. Hume recalled its early reception: 'I published at London my Natural History of Religion, along with some other small pieces: its public entry was rather obscure, except only that Dr. Hurd wrote a pamphlet against it.'[55] Even before publication,[56] plans were laid to present his philosophy in a new format of collected works that included a consolidated index. The way was paved for this new edition, published in 1758, by a rapidly prepared reissue of the extant duodecimo editions of Hume's works in 1753 (under the common title *Essays and Treatises on Several Subjects*) and their piecemeal replacement by new editions up to 1756. *Four Dissertations*, before the assimilation of its components into the 1758 collected works, was in format a companion volume to this duodecimo set, and in a number of libraries is bound uniformly with it.

Hume had told Millar late in 1756 that he was interested in an updated edition that incorporated his four new dissertations: 'I am extremely desirous to have these four Volumes, with that which you will publish this Winter [the *Four Dissertations*] brought into a Quarto Volume.'[57] Here we see Hume's early vision of the integration of *Four Dissertations* into his revised post-*Treatise* writings. The edition of 1758 would realize this objective. It included the second editions of all four works in *Four Dissertations*.

The Collected Works of 1758

Hume made numerous changes in both the *Natural History* and the *Dissertation on the Passions* in preparation for the 1758 edition. One change was an attempt to communicate to readers the structure and integrity of the *Natural History*. Hume decided to add titles to each section, which

[55] 'My Own Life' 13; *Letters*, 1: 5. In the final two sections of this Introduction, it is pointed out that Hume's *Four Dissertations* was not as ignored as he here implies. Several reviews, pamphlets, and articles were published, and in some cases they drew responses from other writers. Hurd's pamphlet is discussed below, pp. cxii–cxxvi. Hurd also published a measured criticism of the third dissertation in *Four Dissertations*, 'Of Tragedy'. See his *Q. Horatii Flacci Epistolae ad Pisones, et Augustum: with an English Commentary and Notes*, 3rd edn., corrected and enlarged (London, 1757), note to line 103 of *Ars poetica*.

[56] See 4 Dec. 1756, to Andrew Millar, *Letters*, 1: 236. This letter shows Hume and Millar having discussions about a future unified octavo collection, ahead of the new publication.

[57] 4 Dec. 1756, to Andrew Millar, *Letters*, 1: 236.

he loosely called 'chapters'.[58] This change was possibly in response to a suggestion in a review of *Four Dissertations* in the *Critical Review* (see below, pp. cxviii–cxx). He stated his objectives in a letter to Strahan:

I find it has been often objected to My natural History of Religion, that it wants order. That I may obviate that Objection, I am resolv'd to prefix the enclosd Contents to it. . . . These are the Titles of the several Sections. I should likewise desire, that the Title of each Section be prefixed to the Section. This will help the Reader to see the Scope of the Discourse.[59]

Hume also instructed Strahan about how to integrate the material from *Four Dissertations* into his collected works:

I have receiv'd the two first Sheets of the Quarto Edition of my philosophical Writings; and am very well satisfy'd with it. Please only to tell the Compositor, that he always employ a Capital after the Colons. Here follow a few Alterations, which I desire you to make on the last published Volume of four Dissertations which are to be inserted in different Places of the Quarto Volume. . . .

Please to get a Copy of the Dissertations from Mr Millar and make these Alterations. Observe also that the two Dissertations, which are to be inserted among the Essays, are to be entitled Essays. The other two are to be inserted in the Places as directed.[60]

Hume placed an 'Advertisement' at the beginning of the 1758 edition (p. iii) to announce the scattering of *Four Dissertations* throughout the volume:

What in former Editions was called *Essays moral and political*, is here entitled *Essays, moral, political, and literary, Part* 1. *The political Discourses* form the *second Part*. What in former Editions was called, *Philosophical Essays concerning human Understanding*, is here entitled *An Enquiry concerning human Understanding*. The *four Dissertations* lately published are dispersed thro' different Parts of this Volume.

In this restructuring, 'Of the Passions' was retitled *A Dissertation on the Passions*. It was placed between *An Enquiry concerning Human Understanding*

[58] Beinecke Library (Yale University), Osborn files, folder 7729, letter from Hume to either Andrew Millar or William Strahan, 25 June 1757: 'I fancy it will not be necessary to print the Contents of *the Natural History of Religion* on the Title Page of it: It will be sufficient that the Contents of each Chapter be prefix'd to it: And as there must be a general Table of Contents for the whole Volume; the Contents of the *natural History* will there find their Place.' This letter was written in anticipation of a new edition of the items contained in *Four Dissertations*. The corrections were incorporated into the text tradition.

[59] 25 May 1757, to William Strahan, *Letters*, 1: 250–1.

[60] 18 Apr. 1757, to William Strahan, *Letters*, 1: 247. All substantive changes made in 1758 are listed in the Editorial Appendix.

and *An Enquiry concerning the Principles of Morals,* with the *Natural History* following these three treatises. Through the titles and placement of the first three treatises, Hume recaptured the arrangement of topics in the three books of the *Treatise*, possibly at the cost of dismantling any integrity he may have envisioned for the *Four Dissertations.*[61] With these four additions, Hume's post-*Treatise* philosophy became fixed in structure for the remainder of his life. That is, the 1758 edition created a permanent canon and arrangement of Hume's philosophical, political, and literary writings published after 1740—excepting, if applicable under these categories, his *History of England*, posthumous works, and various essays subsequently deleted or added.

Hume carefully attended to punctuation, spelling, the use of contractions, and choice of language in the 1758 and later editions. Although he often made substantial changes, most changes were word substitutions, small clarifications and deletions, and stylistic improvements, together with attempts to improve the quality of argument.[62] These corrections and the dating of the types of change that were introduced in *ETSS* are discussed in the Introductions and Editorial Appendices to *An Enquiry concerning the Principles of Morals* and *An Enquiry concerning Human Understanding* in the Clarendon Hume. These corrections need no additional review here, but changes in the 1767 and 1768 editions and their relation to the 1764, 1770, and later editions do need attention.

The Editions from 1760 to 1770

Hume made a concentrated attempt to reduce inconsistent usage in the 1767 and 1768 editions. The 1767 edition introduced numerous modifications to the 1764 edition, and the 1768 edition extensively revised that of 1767.

However, almost all of the corrections made in 1768 vanished during preparation of the 1770 edition. It is likely that Hume prepared his changes for the printer of the 1770 edition using a copy of an edition other than

[61] On the possibility that the *Four Dissertations* had more integrity than has generally been attributed to this volume, see John Immerwahr, 'Introduction' to his facsimile edition of the 1757 *Four Dissertations*, and his 'Hume's *Dissertation on the Passions*'. Hume had, of course, originally envisioned a different collection of essays, and it seems unlikely that he had a philosophical vision that integrally linked geometry, religion, and the passions. Any integrity he might have envisioned, at some point in its history of shifting contents, could have been a consequence of fortuitous circumstances.

[62] See, e.g., comments on the nature of the changes in correspondence of 24 Sept. 1752, to Adam Smith, *Letters*, 1: 167–9; 15 Mar. 1753, to James Balfour, *Letters*, 1: 172–4; 20 June 1758, to William Strahan, *Letters*, 1: 282–3; 4 Sept. 1771, to William Strahan, *Letters*, 2: 249–50; and 2 Jan. 1772, to William Strahan, *Letters*, 2: 251–2.

that of 1768.[63] One possible explanation is that he used the 1767 edition, in preparing the 1770 edition. However, the hypothesis that Hume used the 1767 edition as the basis for the 1770 edition is disconfirmed by available evidence. Collation of both the formal and the substantive variants shows that the majority of the changes entered in the 1767 edition, like those entered in the 1768 edition, were lost in 1770. Although the bulk of these differences involve small changes of punctuation and style that do not affect Hume's philosophical positions, such revision of the text was important to him, and many of the 1767 and 1768 changes do not appear to be of the sort that he would have abandoned intentionally. It is therefore unlikely that the 1770 edition descended directly from that of 1767 or 1768.

Though it seems odd that the corrections in the 1767 and 1768 editions were abandoned, collation of the editions indicates that the 1764 edition was probably the edition from which, after corrections by Hume, the 1770 edition was printed. The salient facts concerning formal and substantive changes in the editions of the *Natural History* and the *Dissertation on the Passions* from 1764 to 1770 are these:[64] Ninety-six formal and substantive changes (14 in *DP* and 82 in *NHR*) were introduced in 1767 and carried over to the 1768 edition; all ninety-six were omitted in 1770, and did not reappear in 1772. That is, 100 per cent of the changes introduced in 1767 and retained in 1768 were lost in the 1770 and 1772 editions. Moreover, eighty-nine additional changes (22 in *DP* and 67 in *NHR*) were introduced in 1768. Only one of these eighty-nine changes appears in the 1770 edition. (In addition, one change that occurred in 1767 was removed in 1768, and later reappeared in 1770.) These facts strongly support the conclusion that Hume did not prepare the edition of 1770 from either the edition of 1767 or the edition of 1768.

Collation further shows that there are 112 instances in the *Dissertation on the Passions* and the *Natural History* (16 in *DP* and 96 in *NHR*) of words and forms that *appeared in the 1764 edition*, were changed in 1767 to a different word or form, and then *reappeared in the 1770 edition*. The correlation between the 1764 and the 1770 editions is continuous, throughout *ETSS*, in the manner expected when one edition has served as the basis for another.

[63] The 1768 edn., which was printed for multiple booksellers, was a beautifully polished, 2-vol. quarto and the first to display Hume's portrait as a frontispiece. It was the only copy of *Essays and Treatises* to survive Hume in the Hume Library (Norton and Norton, *David Hume Library*, 104, no. 653). It is conceivable that he did not wish to mark up this edition.

[64] These figures are compiled from collation of both accidental and substantive variants, with typographical errors excluded. All figures here mentioned are for *DP* and *NHR* combined, and for these two works only. However, the *pattern* of changes does not significantly vary in other works in *ETSS*.

Collation also shows that the 1760 edition is very unlikely to be the edition from which the 1770 edition was corrected. Not even a single change in this edition (in the *Dissertation on the Passions* and the *Natural History*), when discontinued in 1764, reappeared in the 1770 edition.

The 1772 Copytext and 1777 Changes

Almost as soon as Hume received copies of the 1770 edition, he began to make corrections for the edition of 1772,[65] the last edition he saw through the press. Hume reported that he had examined his work for this edition 'carefully *five times over*'.[66] He also remarked on the quality, and the probable finality, of his corrections:

> This is the last time I shall probably take the pains of correcting that work, which is now brought to as great a degree of accuracy as I can attain; and is probably much more labour'd . . . than any other production in our Language. This Power, which Printing gives us, of continually improving and correcting our Works in successive Editions, appears to me the Chief Advantage of that Art.[67]

Hume's correspondence shows an earnest concentration on and satisfaction with the 1772 edition.[68] His attention to this edition strongly recommended it as the copytext for this critical edition, a choice that is compatible with a qualified acceptance of the post-1772 substantive changes that were introduced in the posthumous 1777 edition.[69] The 1777 edition was not published until more than a year after Hume's death. Strahan solicited corrections in a letter of 12 April 1776. On 20 April Hume informed Strahan that 'My Body sets out to-morrow by Post for London; but whether it will arrive there is somewhat uncertain. . . . I bring up my philosophical Pieces corrected, which will be safe, whether I dye by the Road or not.'[70] Sensitive to Hume's declining health and interested in securing an adequate body of revisions, Strahan promptly implemented some of his changes.[71]

[65] 21 Jan. 1771, to William Strahan, *Letters*, 2: 233–5: 'I shall read over several times this new Edition; and send you a corrected Copy by some safe hand.'

[66] 11 Mar. 1771, to William Strahan, *Letters*, 2: 235 (italics added).

[67] 25 Mar. 1771, to William Strahan, *Letters*, 2: 239.

[68] 4 Sept. 1771, to William Strahan, *Letters*, 2: 250.

[69] See the Editorial Appendix, pp. 172–204.

[70] 20 Apr. 1776, to William Strahan, *Letters*, 2: 315. For Strahan's request, see Hume MSS, National Library of Scotland, MS 23157 (and, further, Ian C. Cunningham, 'The Arrangement of the Royal Society of Edinburgh's David Hume Manuscripts').

[71] J. H. Burton (ed.), *Letters of Eminent Persons Addressed to David Hume*, 102–4.

4. A BIBLIOGRAPHICAL SCHEMA OF THE NINE EDITIONS

English Editions in Hume's Lifetime

Hume saw eight editions of *A Dissertation on the Passions* and *The Natural History of Religion* through the press, and then prepared copy for a ninth. This section presents bibliographical information about their printing and publishing histories.[72] French and German editions published in Hume's lifetime are treated in less detail near the end of this section.

The English-language editions were all printed on laid paper, normally unwatermarked, with the exception of the edition of 1770, for which separate details are provided below. The chain lines in the octavo volumes are vertical, and in the duodecimo and quarto horizontal. In all editions, there are catchwords on each text page except the last, with minor inconsistencies of practice on Contents pages and on pages immediately preceding the titles of major divisions. In the transcriptions of the title-pages, lower-case 's', whether roman or italic, is to be read as long 's' if it is not the last letter of a word, and as long 's' within a ligature if it occurs in the combination 'st'.

1757

Title. FOUR | DISSERTATIONS. | I. THE NATURAL HISTORY OF RELIGION. | II. OF THE PASSIONS. | III. OF TRAGEDY. | IV. OF THE STANDARD OF TASTE. | BY | DAVID HUME, Esq. | (Floral ornament) | LONDON, | Printed for A. MILLAR, in the Strand. | MDCCLVII.

Collation. 12°: π1 A^2(A1 + a^4) B^{12} C^{12}(±C12) D^{12}(±D1) E–I^{12} K^{12} (–K5–12) L^{12}(±) M^8 [\$6 (–aiii–iv +C12) signed]; 127 leaves; pp. [*2*] i–vii *viii* [*2*] *1* 2–240.

Contents. $\pi1^r$ half-title; $\pi1^v$, bookseller's announcement; $A1^r$ title as above, verso blank; $a1^r$–$a4^r$ TO The Reverend Mr. Hume; $a4^v$ blank; $A2^r$ half-title,

[72] The bibliographical descriptions for English-language editions on matters of collation, contents, variant states, and notes derive from the research of M. A. Stewart. A useful additional source for some types of information is Chuo University Library, *David Hume and the Eighteenth Century British Thought*. Where the editions of *DP* and *NHR* are common to *EHU* and *EPM*, they have already been described in the Introductions to the Clarendon Editions of *EHU* and *EPM*. Some of the reports in those two volumes are revised here in the light of further bibliographical analysis. Work on the advertisements in British newspapers and periodicals was facilitated by the research of Mark Box and Jane Roscoe.

verso blank; B1^r–F11^r text; F11^v blank; F12^r half-title, verso blank; G1^r–I7^r text; I7^v blank; I8^r half-title, verso blank; I9^r–K4^v text; L1^r half-title, verso blank; L2^r–M8^v text; M8^v ERRATA (3 1/4 lines).

Text:[73] *NHR*, Introduction (pp. 1–2); I (pp. 3–9); II (pp. 10–15); III (pp. 16–23); IV (pp. 24–34); V (pp. 35–41); VI (pp. 42–50); VII (pp. 51–3); VIII (pp. 54–7); IX (pp. 58–64); X (pp. 65–7); XI (pp. 68–71); XII (pp. 72–93); XIII (pp. 94–102); XIV (pp. 103–11); XV (pp. 112–17); *DP*, Sect. I (pp. 121–31); II (pp. 132–56); III (pp. 157–62); IV (pp. 163–9); V (pp. 170–2); VI (pp. 173–81); Of Tragedy (pp. 185–200); Of the Standard of Taste (pp. 203–40).

Two issues. The collation formula supplied above is an idealization. Some copies deviate from it in detail, particularly in the ordering of the early leaves, but the primary distinction is between a first issue that lacks the added quire 'a' within the preliminary gathering *A*,[74] and a second issue that contains the added quire. These are more than variant 'states', because each form of presentation was the result of a deliberate publishing decision. From Hume's correspondence it appears that quire 'a' was printed and inserted, but then withdrawn, immediately prior to publication, so that the work was initially published without that addition; then, within a few weeks, the remaining stock was issued with quire 'a' restored.[75] This is borne out by the physical condition of the Newhailes copy, still in its paper covers, where two distinct sets of stitching holes are visible in quire 'a'.[76] A majority of the surviving copies examined have quire 'a' inserted. It is impossible to prove that some copies lacking quire 'a' were not in circulation as pre-publication copies before the additional quire was printed; likewise, where the stitching evidence is not visible, it is impossible to prove that some copies that contain quire 'a' were not already in circulation before quire 'a' was removed.

[73] Details supplied under the heading 'Text' relate solely to contents designated as 'text' in the preceding formula. Pages other than those explicitly designated 'text' are not included.

[74] Specimen instances are National Library of Scotland, MS 509; King's College Library, Cambridge, F. 22. 27; Trinity College Library, Cambridge, Sraffa 91; Cambridge University Library, Keynes W. 4. 10; Dr Williams's Library, London, 5602. D. 5; Belfast Central Library, 828 HUME; Harvard University Library, EC7S H8823. 757fa; University of Missouri (Columbia) Library, Special Collections; Newberry Library, Chicago, Case B 243. 4202; University of Texas, Harry Ransom Library, Am H882 757 f.

[75] Quire 'a' carries the dedication to his kinsman John Home ('the Reverend Mr. Hume'), which Hume dated 3 Jan. 1757. On 20 Jan. Hume wrote to Millar asking for work on the dedication to be temporarily suspended (*Letters*, 1: 240). By the next post he apparently withdrew the dedication completely, and two posts or four days later, on his own information (*Letters*, 1: 243, to William Mure of Caldwell), retracted this withdrawal. On 1 Feb. he wrote to Strahan in the belief that the publication of the dedication was going ahead (*Letters*, 1: 241); and when he learned that he had been too late, he issued instructions 'that the Dedication shall still be publish'd' (*Letters*, 1: 243).

[76] National Library of Scotland, Nha. Misc. 243. Quire 'a' is unopened.

Minor variants. In some copies of leaf B5^{r} (p. 9), the first letter 'l' of the first word 'lative' (i.e. 'specu-/lative') has either slipped or been entirely lost.[77]

Binding variants. Leaf π1 is sometimes lost, or wrongly positioned among the preliminary leaves; in one instance[78] it has been found bound into the back of the book. Quire 'a' is sometimes bound after leaf *A*1–2, commonly but not exclusively where the gathering *A* has been wrongly folded so that its leaves are in reverse order.[79] None of these variations constitutes a separate state.

Production.[80] Probably 500 copies.[81] Emonson's partnership papers record costs of £23. 12*s*. for 12½ sheets at 1 Apr. 1756.[82]

[77] No evidence has been found to support William B. Todd's claims ('David Hume. A Preliminary Bibliography', 200) that the lost letter was subsequently restored or that at G6^{r} (p. 131) the first word 'lancing' had a variant form 'Iancing', rather than dirty type.

[78] Trinity College Library, Cambridge, R.W. 27. 52.

[79] e.g. King's College Library, Cambridge, F. 22. 26; Trinity College Library, Cambridge, R.W. 27. 52; Bishop Hurd's Library, Hartlebury Castle, Eb. 5.

[80] Hume reported that William Bowyer the younger (1699–1777) was the printer of *Four Dissertations* (1 Feb. 1757, to William Strahan, *Letters*, 1: 240–1). The printer's ornaments in *Four Dissertations* all show up in Bowyer's ornament stock (see Keith Maslen (ed.), *The Bowyer Ornament Stock*), inspected for this edition by M. A. Box. The Bowyer Ledgers, in the possession of the Grolier Club, New York, are now too fragile to be handled, but may be consulted on a microfiche jointly published by the Bibliographical Society, London, and the Bibliographical Society of America (1991). The record for this volume is at ledger B, p. 600, below a higher entry dated 29 Dec. 1755. The report contained in Keith Maslen and John Lancaster (eds.), *The Bowyer Ledgers*, entry 4107, is inaccurate.

[81] Hume's claim in a letter to William Mure, probably of February 1757 (*Letters*, 1: 243), that Bowyer had 'opend his Sale, & dispos'd of 800 Copies' is inconsistent with the frequency of the dedication in the many surviving copies. Hume may have misread his information, including the figure. Bowyer's ledger records the provision of 8 + 2 reams of paper, which he then tallied as ten; a 'printer's ream' was 500 sheets, ten reams totalling 5,000. Bowyer's setting this out as an arithmetical addition shows that the provision was in two stages. The proportion 8:2 matches the ratio of sheets that would have been completed at the time that Hume withdrew the dissertation on Geometry (B–I is eight sheets, and represents the first stage of composition) to the number that would be used in completing the setting to the end of the two new pieces before those were withdrawn (K–L is two sheets, and represents a second, later stage), so that each copy of the 'five' dissertations prior to the provision of title-page and other preliminaries used up ten sheets. The original sheets up to the end of the third dissertation were retained when the final fourth dissertation and preliminary pages were added in late 1756 or early 1757 (new sheet L and sheet M representing a third stage) and when the dedication was added as a final stage. It is therefore a reasonable inference that the print run was from the outset 500.

[82] Bodleian Library, MS Eng. misc. c. 141, fo. 176^{r}. Bowyer had a partnership with James Emonson that lasted from 10 Oct. 1754 to 4 July 1757. (See Keith Maslen, *An Early London Printing House at Work*, Appendix, pp. 245–8.) Emonson's record of the present business shows signs of revision over time, probably originating with a record of 10 sheets at 1 Apr. 1756, then expanding to 12½, with the ½ possibly added later. This confirms Bowyer's record of an initial expenditure of no more than 10 reams. The additional paper and printing, added to the original ledger entry at a later time, was for two cancels, the new fourth dissertation, a title-page and its conjugate half-title, a preliminary half-title with perhaps an original conjugate leaf, and the late

Publication. 7 Feb. 1757. Price 3*s*. bound.[83]

Note. Quires L and M, representing the text of 'Of the Standard of Taste', were printed in late 1756 to replace cancelled matter that had previously occupied K5ʳ–L12ᵛ ('Of Suicide' and 'Of the Immortality of the Soul'). Several copies of the cancelled leaves existed in Hume's lifetime.[84] Only one set is now known to survive, retained and amended by Hume himself and bound into a copy of the published text that was sent to William Strahan as one of Hume's posthumous manuscripts under the terms of his will (National Library of Scotland, MS 509).[85]

1758

Title. ESSAYS | AND | TREATISES | ON | SEVERAL SUBJECTS. | BY | DAVID HUME, Esq; | (Rule) | A NEW EDITION. | (Rule) | (Floral ornament) | (Double rule) | LONDON: | Printed for A. MILLAR, in the STRAND; | AND | A. KINCAID and A. DONALDSON, at EDINBURGH. | (Short rule) | M.DCC.LVIII.

additional quire 'a'. The bill was not finally settled by Millar until some time after July 1757 (fos. 97–9).

83 *The Daily Advertiser*, nos. 8135–6 and 8141 (7–8 and 14 Feb. 1757), p. 1. *The Public Advertiser*, nos. 6955 ff. (8–15 Feb. 1757), p. 1. *The London Evening-Post*, no. 4566 (10–12 Feb. 1757), p. 3 (see also no. 4560 (27–9 Jan. 1757), prelim. advertisement 'Next month will be publish'd'). *The Scots Magazine*, 19 (Feb. 1757), p. 112, 'New Books'. *The Gentleman's Magazine*, 27 (Feb. 1757), p. 94, 'Catalogue of Books', entry 18. *The London Magazine*, 26 (Jan.–Feb. 1757), p. 104, 'Monthly Catalogue', entry 57. *Caledonian Mercury*, no. 5496 (22 Mar. 1757) (in advertisement for Maitland), p. 3. *Scots Magazine*, 19 (June 1757), pp. 293–4, reprints '*Mr* Hume'*s dedication of his* Four Dissertations, *which were published, at London, in the beginning of February*'.

The book was advertised again late in 1757, with unexplained 'publication' dates: *The London Evening-Post*, nos. 4683–5 (10–12, 12–15, 15–17 Nov. 1757) ('*This Day was publish'd*'). *The Public Advertiser*, nos. 7192–4 (12, 14–15 Nov. 1757), p. 4 ('*This Day is publish'd*'). *The Gentleman's Magazine*, 27 (Nov./Dec. 1757), p. 605, Register of 'Books published in November and December', entry 18.

The advertisements in *The Whitehall Evening-Post* (nos. 1883–5, 1888, and 1896) listed below under the 1758 edn. inform readers that Hume's *Essays and Treatises* is available in a 5-vol. set for 15*s*. This advertisement suggests that the 1757 *Four Dissertations* was marketed as if it were a fifth volume in the 1753–6 *Essays and Treatises* (and not marketed merely as an independent publication).

84 23 May 1764, to Andrew Millar, *Letters*, 1: 444–5; and 25 Jan. 1772, to William Strahan, *Letters*, 2: 252–4.

85 Todd's contention ('David Hume', 201) that the stubs of this copy provide evidence of a second cancellation—of leaves 5–8 of a reimposed quire K^8—is incorrect. The fragments of letterpress surviving on the verso of what Todd believed to be a new leaf K5 are of K9, the original conjugate leaf of the surviving K4.

Collation. 4°: *A*⁴ B–3Y⁴ 3Z² [$2 (–*A*1–2, 3E2, 3Z2) signed; sig. 2R2 misnumbered R2]; 274 leaves; pp. *i–v* vi–viii *1–2* 3–539 *540* (96 misnumbered 6 in some copies, 184 misnumbered 182).

Contents. *A*1^r title, verso blank; *A*2^r ADVERTISEMENT; *A*2^v bookseller's announcement; *A*3^r–4^v THE CONTENTS; B1^r half-title, verso blank; B2^r–U1^v text; U2^r half-title, verso blank; U3^r–2N4^v text; 2O1^r half-title, verso blank; 2O2^r–3E1^v text; 3E2^r half-title, verso blank; 3E3^r–3Y1^r text (3R1^v blank); 3Y1^v blank; 3Y2^r–3Z2^r INDEX; 3Z2^v ERRATA (15½ lines).

Text: *Essays, Moral, Political, and Literary* (pp. 3–280); *EHU* (pp. 283–375); *DP*, Sect. I (pp. 376–9); II (pp. 379–87); III (pp. 387–9); IV (pp. 389–91); V (pp. 391–2); VI (pp. 392–4); *EPM* (pp. 397–489); *NHR*, Introduction (pp. 491–2); Sect. I, That polytheism was the primary religion of men (pp. 492–4); II, Origin of polytheism (pp. 494–5); III, The same subject continued (pp. 496–8); IV, Deities not considered as creators or formers of the world (pp. 498–502); V, Various forms of polytheism: allegory, hero-worship (pp. 502–4); VI, Origin of theism from polytheism (pp. 504–7); VII, Confirmation of this doctrine (pp. 507–8); VIII, Flux and reflux of polytheism and theism (pp. 508–9); IX, Comparison of these religions, with regard to persecution and toleration (pp. 509–11); X, With regard to courage or abasement (p. 512); XI, With regard to reason or absurdity (pp. 513–14); XII, With regard to doubt or conviction (pp. 514–21); XIII, Impious conceptions of the divine nature in most popular religions of both kinds (pp. 521–4); XIV, Bad influence of most popular religions on morality (pp. 525–7); XV, General corollary from the whole (pp. 527–9).

Variant issue. An additional sheet (*) was printed in March 1760, to make available to purchasers of the 1758 edition two new essays which Hume was adding to the 1760 edition of *ETSS*. It is paginated to duplicate the numbers 187–9, 265–9, with the impracticable advice that the new pp. 187–9 (*1^r–2^r) are to be placed after the existing p. 186, and the new pp. 265–9 (*2^v–4^v) after p. 264. In copies in which it survives, it is more often bound at the end of the *Essays*, after p. 280, between gatherings N and O.

Production. 750 copies, printed October 1757 (68½ sheets at £1. 1*s*., total £71. 18*s*. 6*d*.; index, 9*s*.). 750 copies of the two new essays, printed March 1760 (1 sheet at £1. 1*s*.).[86]

[86] British Library, Add. MS 48800, fos. 102, 108. It is not known why Strahan added an additional charge for the index. One speculative possibility is that he was employing someone to help with its preparation.

Publication. Around 13–15 April 1758. Price 15*s*. bound.[87]

1760

Title (Vol. 3). ESSAYS | AND | TREATISES | ON | SEVERAL SUBJECTS. | By DAVID HUME, Esq; | VOL. III. | Containing an ENQUIRY concerning | HUMAN UNDERSTANDING. | (Rule) | A NEW EDITION. | (Double rule) | LONDON: | Printed for A. MILLAR, in the Strand; | AND | A. KINCAID and A. DONALDSON, at Edinburgh. | MDCCLX.

Collation. 12°: A^2 B–N^{12} O^6 [$6 (–*A*1–2, O4–6) signed; $1 (–*A*1), VOL. III.]; 152 leaves; pp. *i–iv 1–2* 3–299 *300.*

Contents. *A*1^r title as above, verso blank; *A*2^{r-v} THE CONTENTS OF THE THIRD VOLUME; B1^r half-title, verso blank; B2^r–O6^r text (C2^v, C10^v, E9^v, E12^v, H7^v, H11^v, O6^v blank).

Text: *EHU* (pp. 3–250); *DP*, Sect. I (pp. 251–9); II (pp. 260–80); III (pp. 281–5); IV (pp. 285–90); V (pp. 291–3); VI (pp. 293–9).

Title (Vol. 4). ESSAYS | AND | TREATISES | ON | SEVERAL SUBJECTS. | By DAVID HUME, Esq; | VOL. IV. | Containing an ENQUIRY concerning | the PRINCIPLES of MORALS. | (Rule) | A NEW EDITION. | (Double rule) | LONDON: | Printed for A. MILLAR, in the Strand; | AND | A. KINCAID and A. DONALDSON, at Edinburgh. | MDCCLX.

Collation. 12°: A^4 B–P^{12} Q^8 [$6 (–*A*1–4, Q5–6) signed; $1 (–*A*1) VOL. IV.]; 180 leaves; pp. *i–viii 1–2* 3–352.

Contents. *A*1^{r-v} blank; *A*2^r title, verso blank; *A*3^r–4^r THE CONTENTS OF THE FOURTH VOLUME; *A*4^v blank; B1^r half-title, verso blank; B2^r–Q8^v text (D7^v, D12^v, F3^v, G10^v, H7^v, I12^v, K8^v, L3^v, M6^v blank).

Text: *EPM* (pp. 3–251, including A dialogue); *NHR*, Introduction (pp. 253–4); Sect. I, That polytheism was the primary religion of men

[87] *Whitehall Evening-Post*, nos. 1883–5, 1888, and 1896 (13–15, 15–18, 20–2, and 25–7 Apr.; 2–4 May 1758), p. 4; see also no. 1874 (23–5 Mar. 1758 ('*Next Month will be published*')). *Public Advertiser*, nos. 9798–9800 and 9802–3 (13–15, 17–18 Apr. 1758). *London Evening-Post*, no. 4747 (8–11 Apr. 1758) (see also 23–5 and 28–30 Mar. 1758 ('Next month will be publish'd')). *Scots Magazine*, 20 (Apr. 1758), p. 222. *Edinburgh Magazine*, 2 (May 1758), p. 84. *Caledonian Mercury*, no. 5683 (30 May 1758), p. 3 (and listed among books for sale, no. 5679 (20 May 1758), p. 3).

Price information is also in advertisements for Hume's *History* and for other edns. of *ETSS*: *London Chronicle*, 15 (28–31 Jan.; 23–5 Feb.; 28 Apr.–1 May; 24–6, 29–31 May; 31 May–2 June; 2–5 June 1764), pp. 104, 192, 416, 503, 517, 523, 532. *Public Advertiser*, nos. 9207 (3 May 1764), and 9235–7 (5–7 June 1764). *London Evening-Post*, nos. 5653, 5667, 5679, 5705–7, 5709–11 (26–8 Jan.; 25–8 Feb.; 24–7 Mar.; 24–6, 26–9, 29–31 May; 2–5, 5–7, 7–9 June 1764).

(pp. 255–60); II, Origin of polytheism (pp. 261–5); III, The same subject continued (265–71); IV, Deities not considered as creators or formers of the world (pp. 272–82); V, Various forms of polytheism: allegory, hero-worship (pp. 282–8); VI, Origin of theism from polytheism (pp. 288–95); VII, Confirmation of this doctrine (pp. 295–8); VIII, Flux and reflux of polytheism and theism (pp. 298–301); IX, Comparison of these religions, with regard to persecution and toleration (pp. 301–6); X, With regard to courage or abasement (pp. 307–9); XI, With regard to reason or absurdity (pp. 309–12); XII, With regard to doubt or conviction (pp. 312–32); XIII, Impious conceptions of the divine nature in most popular religions of both kinds (pp. 332–41); XIV, Bad influence of most popular religions on morality (pp. 341–8); XV, General corollary from the whole (pp. 348–52).

Watermarks. Sheets *A* and O of vol. 4 show a fleur-de-lys watermark in some copies.[88]

Production. 1,000 copies, printed March 1760 (4 vols., 61 sheets at £1. 10*s*., total £91. 10*s*.).[89]

Publication. Around 19–22 April 1760. Price 12*s*. bound (4 vols.).[90]

1764

Title. ESSAYS | AND | TREATISES | ON | SEVERAL SUBJECTS. | By DAVID HUME, Esq; | VOL. II. | CONTAINING | An ENQUIRY concerning HUMAN | UNDERSTANDING. | An ENQUIRY concerning the PRINCIPLES of | MORALS. | AND | The NATURAL HISTORY of RELIGION. | (Rule) | A NEW EDITION. | (Double rule) | LONDON: | Printed for A. MILLAR, in the Strand; | AND | A. KINCAID and A. DONALDSON, at Edinburgh. | MDCCLXIV.

[88] Bodleian Library, 26782 f. 11 and Vet A5 f. 2618; National Library of Scotland, Hall 133. i; King's College Library, Cambridge, F. 22. 29.

[89] British Library, Add. MS 48800, fo. 108.

[90] *Whitehall Evening-Post*, nos. 2198–2200 and 2202–4 (17–19, 19–22, 22–4, and 26–9 Apr.; 29 Apr.–1 May; 1–3 May 1760), see also nos. 2191, 2193, and 2195 (1–3, 5–8, 10–12, Apr. 1760 ('*Speedily will be publish'd*')). *London Evening-Post*, nos. 5068–9 (26–9 Apr.; 29 Apr.–1 May 1760); see also nos. 5066–7 (22–4, 24–6 Apr. 1760 ('*Speedily will be publish'd*')). *London Chronicle*, 17–19 (Apr. 1760), p. 384.

Price information is also in advertisements for Hume's *History* or other edns. of *ETSS*: *London Evening-Post*, nos. 5653, 5667, 5679, 5705–7, and 5709–11 (26–8 Jan.; 25–8 Feb.; 24–7 Mar.; 24–6, 26–9, 29–31 May; 2–5, 5–7, 7–9 June 1764). *London Chronicle*, 15 (28–31 Jan.; 23–5 Feb.; 24–6, 29–31 May; 31 May–2 June; 2–5 June 1764), pp. 104, 192, 503, 517, 523, 532. *Public Advertiser*, nos. 9207 and 9235–7 (3 May 1764; 5–7 June 1764).

Collation. 8°: *A*^{4} B–2I^8 2K^4 [$4 (–*A*1–4, 2K3–4) signed; $1 Vol. II.]; 256 leaves; pp. *i–viii 1–2* 3–503 *504* (89 unnumbered in some copies, 469 misnumbered 699).

Contents. *A*1^r half-title, verso blank; *A*2^r title as above, verso blank; *A*3^r–4^r THE CONTENTS OF THE SECOND VOLUME; *A*4^v blank; B1^r half-title, verso blank; B2^r–P7^r text (C3^v, F1^v, I2^v, I5^v, L2^v blank); P7^v blank; P8^r half-title, verso blank; Q1^r–2I3^r text (Q4^v, R4^v, S8^v, T4^v, U7^v, 2A3^v, 2B1^v, 2B6^v blank); 2I3^v blank; 2I4^r–2K4^r INDEX; 2K4^v blank.

Text: *EHU* (pp. 3–184); *DP*, Sect. I (pp. 185–91); II (pp. 191–206); III (pp. 206–10); IV (pp. 210–14); V (pp. 214–15); VI (pp. 216–21); *EPM* (pp. 225–414); *NHR*, Introduction (pp. 415–16); Sect. I, That polytheism was the primary religion of men (pp. 416–20); II, Origin of polytheism (pp. 421–4); III, The same subject continued (pp. 424–9); IV, Deities not considered as creators or formers of the world (pp. 429–36); V, Various forms of polytheism: allegory, hero-worship (pp. 436–40); VI, Origin of theism from polytheism (pp. 440–5); VII, Confirmation of this doctrine (pp. 445–7); VIII, Flux and reflux of polytheism and theism (pp. 447–9); IX, Comparison of these religions, with regard to persecution and toleration (pp. 449–53); X, With regard to courage or abasement (pp. 453–5); XI, With regard to reason or absurdity (pp. 455–8); XII, With regard to doubt or conviction (pp. 458–71); XIII, Impious conceptions of the divine nature in most popular religions of both kinds (pp. 471–7); XIV, Bad influence of most popular religions on morality (pp. 477–82); XV, General corollary from the whole (pp. 482–5).

Production. 1,000 copies, printed May 1764 (2 vols., 68 sheets at £1. 10*s*., total £102; index, 10*s*. 6*d*.).[91]

Publication. Late May to early June 1764. Price 12*s*. bound (2 vols.).[92]

[91] British Library, Add. MS 48800, fo. 128. Although Strahan recorded 68 sheets per copy of this edition of *ETSS*, each of which would generate 8 leaves or 16 pages, the whole work requires the use of only 67 sheets.

[92] *London Chronicle*, 15 (24–6, 29–31 May; 2–5 June 1764), pp. 503, 517, 532 (also vol. 15 (27–9 Mar.; 28 Apr.–1 May; 24–6 May; 31 May–2 June 1764), pp. 300, 416, 503, 523 ('Speedily will be published'), in advertisements for Hume's *History*). *London Evening-Post*, nos. 5709–11 (2–5, 5–7, 7–9 June 1764) (also nos. 5679 and 5705 (24–7 Mar.; 24–6 May 1764) ('Speedily will be publish'd'), in advertisement for Hume's *History*). *Public Advertiser*, nos. 9235–7 (5–7 June 1764) (also no. 9207 (3 May 1764) ('Speedily will be published'), in advertisement for Hume's *History*, and prelim. advertisement on 30 May 1764 ('Next month')). A letter from Andrew Millar to Hume of 26 Nov. 1764 (*Letters*, 2: 354) states that the edition was 'published in May'.

1767

Title. ESSAYS | AND | TREATISES | ON | SEVERAL SUBJECTS. | By DAVID HUME, Esq; | VOL. II. | CONTAINING | An ENQUIRY concerning HUMAN | UNDERSTANDING. | An ENQUIRY concerning the PRINCIPLES of | MORALS. | AND | The NATURAL HISTORY of RELIGION. | (Rule) | A NEW EDITION. | (Double rule) | LONDON: | Printed for A. MILLAR, in the Strand; | AND | A. KINCAID, and A. DONALDSON, at Edinburgh. | MDCCLXVII.

Collation. 8°: A^4 B–2I^8 2K^4 [$4 (–*A*1–4, 2K3–4) signed; $1 VOL. II.]; 256 leaves; pp. *i–viii 1–2* 3–503 *504*.

Contents. *A*1^r half-title, verso blank; *A*2^r title as above, verso blank; *A*3^r–4^r THE CONTENTS OF THE SECOND VOLUME; *A*4^v blank; B1^r half-title, verso blank; B2^r–P7^r text (C3^v, F1^v, I2^v, I5^v, L2^v blank); P7^v blank; P8^r half-title, verso blank; Q1^r–2I3^r text (Q4^v, R4^v, S8^v, T4^v, U7^v, 2A3^v, 2B1^v, 2B6^v blank); 2I3^v blank; 2I4^r–2K4^r INDEX; 2K4^v blank.

Text: *EHU* (pp. 3–184); *DP*, Sect. I (pp. 185–91); II (pp. 191–206); III (pp. 206–10); IV (pp. 210–14); V (pp. 214–15); VI (pp. 216–21); *EPM* (pp. 225–414); *NHR*, Introduction (pp. 415–16); Sect. I, That polytheism was the primary religion of men (pp. 416–20); II, Origin of polytheism (pp. 421–4); III, The same subject continued (424–9); IV, Deities not considered as creators or formers of the world (pp. 429–36); V, Various forms of polytheism: allegory, hero-worship (pp. 436–40); VI, Origin of theism from polytheism (pp. 440–5); VII, Confirmation of this doctrine (pp. 445–7); VIII, Flux and reflux of polytheism and theism (pp. 447–9); IX, Comparison of these religions, with regard to persecution and toleration (pp. 449–53); X, With regard to courage or abasement (pp. 453–5); XI, With regard to reason or absurdity (pp. 455–8); XII, With regard to doubt or conviction (pp. 458–71); XIII, Impious conceptions of the divine nature in most popular religions of both kinds (pp. 471–7); XIV, Bad influence of most popular religions on morality (pp. 477–82); XV, General corollary (pp. 482–5).

Note. In at least one copy, *A*1 has been folded back behind *A*4.[93]

Watermarks. Sheets *A* and 2K have been found with fleur-de-lys watermark; countermark (initials) not identified.

93 e.g. Edinburgh University Library, E.B. .1924.

Production. 1,000 copies, printed September 1766 (2 vols., 67 sheets at £1. 10*s*., total £100. 10*s*.).[94]

Publication. Around late January 1767. Price 12*s*. bound (2 vols.).[95]

1768

Title. ESSAYS | AND | TREATISES | ON | SEVERAL SUBJECTS. | BY DAVID HUME, ESQ. | VOL. II. | CONTAINING | An ENQUIRY concerning HUMAN | UNDERSTANDING. | An ENQUIRY concerning the PRINCIPLES of | MORALS. | AND | The NATURAL HISTORY of RELIGION. | (Rule) | A NEW EDITION. | (Double rule) | LONDON: | Printed for A. MILLAR, | A. KINCAID, J. BELL, and A. DONALDSON, in Edinburgh. | And sold by T. CADELL, in the Strand. | MDCCLXVIII.

Collation. Royal 4°: A^2 B–$3U^4$ $3X^2$ [\$2 (–*A*1–2, 3X2) signed; \$1 (–*A*1) VOL. II.]; 264 leaves; pp. *i–iv 1–2* 3–509 *510–24*.

Contents. *A*1^r title, verso blank; *A*2^{r-v} THE CONTENTS OF THE SECOND VOLUME; B1^r half-title, verso blank; B2^r–2G4^r text; 2G4^v blank; 2H1^r half-title, verso blank; 2H2^r–3T2^v text; 3T3^r–3X2^v INDEX.

Text: *EHU* (pp. 3–191); *DP*, Sect. I (pp. 192–9); II (pp. 199–215); III (pp. 216–19); IV (pp. 219–23); V (pp. 224–5); VI (pp. 225–31); *EPM* (pp. 233–431); *NHR*, Introduction (pp. 432–3); Sect. I, That polytheism was the primary religion of men (pp. 433–8); II, Origin of polytheism (pp. 438–41); III, The same subject continued (pp. 441–6); IV, Deities not considered as creators or reformers of the world (pp. 447–54); V, Various forms of polytheism: allegory, hero-worship (pp. 454–9); VI, Origin of theism from polytheism (pp. 459–64); VII, Confirmation of this doctrine (pp. 464–6); VIII, Flux and reflux of polytheism and theism (pp. 466–9); IX, Comparison of these religions, with regard to persecution and toleration (pp. 469–73); X, With regard to courage or abasement (pp. 473–5); XI, With regard to reason or absurdity (pp. 475–8); XII, With regard to doubt or conviction (pp. 478–93); XIII, Impious conceptions of the divine nature in most popular religions of both kinds (pp. 493–9); XIV, Bad influence of

[94] British Library, Add. MS 48800, fo. 137.

[95] This 'new Edition' of *ETSS* was announced in advertisements for Hume's *History: London Evening-Post*, nos. 6123–5 (24–7 Jan. 1767), p. 2 (repeated 27 Feb.–1 Mar. 1767, p. 2, and 30 Apr.–2 May 1767, p. 3). *Gazetteer and New Daily Advertiser*, no. 11,825 (28 Jan. 1767), p. 1.

Price information is also in three advertisements for other works by Hume: *Public Advertiser*, no. 11,567 (23 Nov. 1771), p. 1. *Gazetteer and New Daily Advertiser*, no. 13,162 (9 May 1771), p. 1, and repeated in no. 13,210 (3 July 1771), p. 1.

most popular religions on morality (pp. 499–504); XV, General corollary (pp. 504–8).

Production. 500 copies, printed January 1768 (2 vols., 139½ sheets at 15*s.*, total £104. 12*s.* 6*d.*; index 15*s.* 6*d.*).[96]

Publication. No information on date. Price £1. 16*s.* bound (2 vols.).[97]

Other information. In January 1776, Strahan printed 250 copies of an additional leaf to be inserted in the remaining stock of this volume. This leaf carried an early version of the 'Advertisement' that was prefixed to the 1777 edn. of *ETSS*, vol. II.[98] No copies of this extra leaf in the 1768 *ETSS* have been discovered.

1770

Title (Vol. 3). ESSAYS | AND | TREATISES | ON | SEVERAL SUBJECTS. | By DAVID HUME, Esq; | VOL. III. | CONTAINING | An ENQUIRY concerning HUMAN | UNDERSTANDING. | AND | A DISSERTATION on the PASSIONS. | (Rule) | A NEW EDITION. | (Double rule) | LONDON: | Printed for T. CADELL (Successor to Mr. MILLAR) | in the Strand; and | A. KINCAID and A. DONALDSON, at Edinburgh. | (Short rule) | MDCCLXX.

Collation. Sm. 8°: A^2 B–T^8 U^6 [\$4 (–*A*1–2, U4) signed; \$1 (–*A*1), VOL. III.]; 152 leaves; pp. *i–iv 1–2* 3–298 *299–300* (152 misnumbered 2 in some copies).

Contents. *A*1^r title, verso blank; *A*2^{r-v} THE CONTENTS OF THE THIRD VOLUME; B1^r half-title, verso blank; B2^r–T5^r text; T5^v blank; T6^r–U5^v NOTES TO THE THIRD VOLUME; U6^{r-v} blank.

Text: *EHU* (pp. 3–231); *DP*, Sect. I (pp. 232–41); II (pp. 241–62); III (pp. 262–6); IV (pp. 266–72); V (pp. 272–4); VI (pp. 274–81).

[96] British Library, Add. MS 48800, fo. 138.

[97] Price information is in advertisements for Hume's *History*, other edns. of *ETSS*, and 'The Life of David Hume': *London Evening-Post*, nos. 6603–4 (27 Feb.–1 Mar.; 1–3 Mar. 1770; 8–11 Mar. 1777), p. 2. *Public Advertiser*, no. 11,567 (23 Nov. 1771), p. 1. *General Evening Post*, no. 5940 (7 Nov. 1771), p. 3; no. 6158 (30 Mar.–1 Apr. 1773), p. 3; and no. 6766 (10–13 May 1777), p. 2. *Gazetteer and New Daily Advertiser*, no. 12,795 (5 Mar. 1770), p. 4; no. 13,162 (9 May 1771), p. 1. *London Chronicle*, 41 (8–11 Mar. 1777), p. 239. See also the advertisement in Hume's *Essays and Treatises on Several Subjects*, 1772 edn., 2: 535.

[98] British Library, Add. MS 48801 (Strahan's General Expenses book covering forty-three years), fo. 68; and 26 Oct. 1775, to William Strahan, *Letters*, 2: 301.

Watermarks. Sheets B–P, R: Britannia; countermark GR, crowned. Sheets *A*, Q, S–U: Garden of Holland ('Maid of Dort'); countermark LVG.

Note. The blank leaf U6 is frequently removed or used as a pastedown, but occasionally survives intact.[99]

Title (Vol. 4). ESSAYS | AND | TREATISES| ON | SEVERAL SUBJECTS. | By DAVID HUME, Esq; | VOL. IV. | CONTAINING | An ENQUIRY concerning the PRINCIPLES | of MORALS; | AND | The NATURAL HISTORY of RELIGION. | (Rule) | A NEW EDITION. | (Double rule) | LONDON: | Printed for T. CADELL (Successor to Mr. MILLAR) | in the Strand; and | A. KINCAID and A. DONALDSON, at Edinburgh. | (Short rule) | MDCCLXX.

Collation. Sm. 8°: A^2 B–2A^8 2B^2 [$4 (–*A*1–2, 2B2) signed; $1 (–*A*1) VOL. IV.]; 188 leaves; pp. *i–iv 1–2* 3–371 *372*.

Contents. *A*1^r title, verso blank; *A*2^{r-v} THE CONTENTS OF THE FOURTH VOLUME; B1^r half-title, verso blank; B2^r–Y5^r text; Y5^v blank; Y6^r–2A1^r NOTES; 2A1^v blank; 2A2^r–2B2^r INDEX; 2B2^v blank.

Text: *EPM* (pp. 3–236, including A dialogue); *NHR*, Introduction (pp. 237–8); Sect. I, That polytheism was the primary religion of men (pp. 239–44); II, Origin of polytheism (pp. 245–9); III, The same subject continued (pp. 249–55); IV, Deities not considered as creators or formers of the world (pp. 255–65); V, Various forms of polytheism: allegory, hero-worship (pp. 265–71); VI, Origin of theism from polytheism (pp. 271–8); VII, Confirmation of this doctrine (pp. 278–81); VIII, Flux and reflux of polytheism and theism (pp. 281–4); IX, Comparison of these religions, with regard to persecution and toleration (pp. 284–9); X, With regard to courage or abasement (pp. 289–91); XI, With regard to reason or absurdity (pp. 292–5); XII, With regard to doubt or conviction (pp. 295–312); XIII, Impious conceptions of the divine nature in most popular religions of both kinds (pp. 312–17); XIV, Bad influence of most popular religions on morality (pp. 317–24); XV, General corollary (pp. 325–9).

Watermarks. Sheets B–M, 2B: Garden of Holland ('Maid of Dort'); countermark LVG. Sheets *A*, N–2A: Lion; countermark GR, crowned.

Production. 1,000 copies, printed October 1770 (4 vols., 87½ sheets at £1. 3*s*., total £100. 12*s*. 6*d*.; index £1. 1*s*.).[100]

[99] e.g. Aberdeen University Library, S.B. 1924 E^2.

[100] British Library, Add. MS 48801, fo. 35.

Publication. Between 23 January and 3 July 1771. Price 14*s.* bound (4 vols.).[101]

Other information. In January 1776, Strahan printed 500 copies of an additional leaf to be inserted in the remaining stock of this volume. This leaf carried an early version of the 'Advertisement' that was prefixed to the 1777 edition of *ETSS*, vol. II.[102] The only known copies of this extra leaf in the 1770 *ETSS* have been bound in error into vol. I.[103]

1772

Title. ESSAYS | AND | TREATISES | ON | SEVERAL SUBJECTS. | By DAVID HUME, Esq; | VOL. II. | CONTAINING | An ENQUIRY concerning HUMAN | UNDERSTANDING; | A DISSERTATION on the PASSIONS; | An ENQUIRY concerning the PRINCIPLES | of MORALS; | AND | The NATURAL HISTORY of RELIGION. | (Rule) | A NEW EDITION. | (Double rule) | LONDON: | Printed for T. CADELL, in the Strand: and | A. KINCAID, and A. DONALDSON, at Edinburgh. | MDCCLXXII.

Collation. 8°: *A*^{4} B–2L^8 2M^4 [$4 (–*A*1–4, 2M3–4) signed; $1 (–*A*1), VOL. II.]; 272 leaves; pp. *i–viii 1–2* 3–533 *534–536.*

*Contents. A*1^r half-title, verso blank; *A*2^r title, verso blank; *A*3^r–4^r THE CONTENTS OF THE SECOND VOLUME; *A*4^v blank; B1^r half-title, verso blank; B2^r–P6^v text (B8^v, D1^v, E2^v, I3^v, I6^v, N4^v blank); P7^r half-title, verso blank; P8^r–2H6^r text (Q3^v, R3^v, S6^v, T2^v, X5^v, Z8^v, 2A6^v, 2B2^v, 2B8^v blank); 2H6^v blank; 2H7^r–2L2^r NOTES TO THE SECOND VOLUME; 2L2^v blank; 2L3^r–2M3^r INDEX; 2M3^v blank; 2M4^{r-v} bookseller's announcements.

Text: *EHU* (pp. 3–183); *DP*, Sect. I (pp. 185–91); II (pp. 191–206); III (pp. 206–10); IV (pp. 210–14); V (pp. 214–15); VI (pp. 215–20); *EPM*

[101] *Gazetteer and New Daily Advertiser*, no. 13,073 (23 Jan. 1771), p. 1 ('In a few days will be published'); no. 13,162 (9 May 1771), p. 1 ('This day is published'); and 13,210 (3 July 1771), p. 1 ('This day is published'). Publication may have been unexpectedly delayed, but it is possible that the edition was published a few days after 23 Jan. and not advertised as such for 3 months.

Price information is also in advertisements for Hume's *History* and 'The Life of David Hume': *Public Advertiser*, no. 11,567 (23 Nov. 1771), p. 1. *General Evening Post*, no. 6158 (30 Mar.–1 Apr. 1773), p. 3; no. 6766 (10–13 May 1777), p. 2. *London Chronicle*, 33 (25–7 Feb. 1773), p. 195; and 41 (8–11 Mar. 1777), p. 239. *London Evening-Post*, no. 8577 (8–11 Mar. 1777), p. 2.

[102] British Library, Add. MS 48801, fo. 68; and 26 Oct. 1775, to William Strahan, *Letters*, 2: 301.

[103] A. Wayne Colver, private copy (see Colver, 'A Variant of Hume's Advertisement Repudiating the Treatise'); and Liverpool University Library, Fraser 832.

(pp. 223–406); *NHR*, Introduction (pp. 407–8); Sect. I, That polytheism was the primary religion of men (pp. 408–12); II, Origin of polytheism (pp. 413–16); III, The same subject continued (pp. 416–21); IV, Deities not considered as creators or formers of the world (pp. 421–8); V, Various forms of polytheism: allegory, hero-worship (pp. 428–32); VI, Origin of theism from polytheism (pp. 432–8); VII, Confirmation of this doctrine (pp. 438–9); VIII, Flux and reflux of polytheism and theism (pp. 440–2); IX, Comparison of these religions, with regard to persecution and toleration (pp. 442–6); X, With regard to courage or abasement (pp. 446–7); XI, With regard to reason or absurdity (pp. 447–50); XII, With regard to doubt or conviction (pp. 450–63); XIII, Impious conceptions of the divine nature in popular religions of both kinds (pp. 463–7); XIV, Bad influence of popular religions on morality (pp. 467–72); XV, General corollary (pp. 472–5).

Production. 1,000 copies, printed November 1771 (2 vols., 69½ sheets at £1. 10*s*., total £104. 5*s*.).[104]

Publication. No later than May 1772. Price 12*s*. (2 vols.).[105]

Other information. In January 1776, Strahan printed 500 copies of an additional leaf to be inserted in the remaining stock of this volume. This leaf carried an early version of the 'Advertisement' that was prefixed to the 1777 edition of *ETSS*, vol. II.[106] No copies of this leaf of the 1772 *ETSS* have been discovered.

1777

Title. ESSAYS | AND | TREATISES | ON | SEVERAL SUBJECTS. | By DAVID HUME, Esq; | VOL. II. | CONTAINING | An ENQUIRY concerning HUMAN | UNDERSTANDING; | A DISSERTATION on the PASSIONS; | An ENQUIRY concerning the PRINCIPLES | of MORALS; | AND | The NATURAL HISTORY of RELIGION. | (Rule) |

[104] British Library, Add. MS 48801, fo. 52.

[105] 3 June 1772, to Thomas Cadell, *Letters* 2: 262 (and compare 27 Feb. 1772, William Strahan to Hume, in *Letters of David Hume to William Strahan*, ed. G. B. Hill, 244; and 7 Feb. 1772, to Benjamin Franklin, *New Letters*, 194).

Price information is found in advertisements for Hume's *History* and 'The Life of David Hume': *London Chronicle*, 33, no. 2530 (25–7 Feb. 1773), p. 195; and 41, no. 3161 (8–11 Mar. 1777), p. 239. *London Evening-Post*, no. 8577 (8–11 Mar. 1777), p. 2. *General Evening Post*, no. 6158 (30 Mar.–1 Apr. 1773), p. 3; no. 6766 (10–13 May 1777), p. 2.

[106] British Library, Add. MS 48801, fo. 68; and 26 Oct. 1775, to William Strahan, *Letters*, 2: 301.

A NEW EDITION. | (Double rule) | LONDON: | Printed for T. CADELL, in the Strand: and | A. DONALDSON, and W. CREECH, at Edinburgh. | MDCCLXXVII.

Collation. 8°: A^4 B–2L^8 [$4 (–A1, 3–4) signed; $1 (–A1), VOL. II.]; 268 leaves; pp. *i–viii 1–2* 3–527 *528* (92 misnumbered 2 in some copies, 191 misnumbered 189, 192 misnumbered 129).

Contents. A1^r title, verso blank; A2^r ADVERTISEMENT, verso blank; A3^r–4^r THE CONTENTS OF THE SECOND VOLUME; A4^v blank; B1^r half-title; verso blank; B2^r–P2^v text (B8^v, C5^v, D6^v, H7^v, I2^v, M8^v blank); P3^r half-title, verso blank; P4^r–2C7^v text (P7^v, Q3^v, R6^v, S2^v, U5^v, Y8^v, Z6^v, 2A6^v, 2B4^v blank); 2C8^r half-title, verso blank; 2D1^r–2H3^r text; 2H3^v blank; 2H4^r–2K7^r NOTES TO THE SECOND VOLUME; 2K7^v blank; 2K8^r–2L8^r INDEX; 2L8^v bookseller's announcement.

Text: *EHU* (pp. 3–175); *DP*, Sect. I (pp. 177–83); II (pp. 183–98); III (pp. 198–202); IV (pp. 202–6); V (pp. 206–7); VI (pp. 207–12); *EPM* (pp. 215–398); *NHR*, Introduction (pp. 401–2); Sect. I, That polytheism was the primary religion of men (pp. 402–6); II, Origin of polytheism (pp. 407–10); III, The same subject continued (pp. 410–15); IV, Deities not considered as creators or formers of the world (pp. 415–22); V, Various forms of polytheism: allegory, hero-worship (pp. 422–6); VI, Origin of theism from polytheism (pp. 426–32); VII, Confirmation of this doctrine (pp. 432–3); VIII, Flux and reflux of polytheism and theism (pp. 434–6); IX, Comparison of these religions, with regard to persecution and toleration (pp. 436–40); X, With regard to courage or abasement (pp. 440–1); XI, With regard to reason or absurdity (pp. 441–4); XII, With regard to doubt or conviction (pp. 444–57); XIII, Impious conceptions of the divine nature in popular religions of both kinds (pp. 457–61); XIV, Bad influence of popular religions on morality (pp. 461–6); XV, General corollary (pp. 466–9).

Production. 1,000 copies, printed September 1777 (2 vols., 69½ sheets at £1. 10*s*., total £104. 5*s*.).[107]

Publication. January or early February 1778. Price 12*s*. (2 vols.).[108]

[107] British Library, Add. MS 48815, fo. 8.

[108] Registered at Stationers' Hall, Stationers' Co. Records, entry book of copies, 10 Jan. 1778, p. 99, s.v. Wm. Strahan. Advertised: *Public Advertiser*, no. 13,518–20 (5–7 Feb. 1778), p. 1 (see also 13,529 (18 Feb. 1778), p. 1, in advertisement for Hume's *History*). *Edinburgh Advertiser*, 29, no. 1489 (3–7 Apr. 1778), p. 222 (the latter apparently for Edinburgh release by Donaldson).

Notes. 1. This edition published posthumously. 2. The 'ADVERTISEMENT' prefixed to the 1777 edition, vol. II, is the one mentioned above in 'other information' about the editions of 1768, 1770, and 1772.[109]

French Translations in Hume's Lifetime[110]

1758–60 5-vol. Collection. (8°). Amsterdam, J. H. Schneider. Volumes 3–4 have *Œuvres philosophiques de Mr. D. Hume* on the half-title. Volume 5 bears the half-title *Œuvres de Mr. Hume*.
Contents:

Vols. 1–2 (1758)—*Essais philosophiques sur l'entendement humain, par Mr. Hume, avec les quatre philosophes du même auteur*.[111] Traduit par Jean-Bernard Mérian.
Vol. 3 (1759)—*Histoire naturelle de la religion traduit de l'Anglois de Mr. D. Hume avec un examen critique et philosophique de cet ouvrage*. Traduit par Jean-Bernard Mérian.
Vol. 4 (1759)—*Dissertations sur les passions, sur la tragédie, sur la règle du goût*. Traduit par Jean-Bernard Mérian.
Vol. 5 (1760)—*Essais de morale ou Recherches sur les principes de la morale*. Traduit par Jean-Baptiste-René Robinet.[112]

Notes: 1. In 1758, the first and second volumes were published as a two-volume set (lacking the general title *Œuvres philosophiques de Mr. D. Hume*).

[109] See British Library, Add. MS 48801, fo. 68; and 26 Oct. 1775, to William Strahan, *Letters*, 2: 301.

[110] Only French editions containing translations of *The Natural History of Religion* and *A Dissertation on the Passions* are considered in this section. Archaic French has been retained in the entries. Other volumes of the Clarendon Hume contain additional information on French editions of other works by Hume. See also Chuo University Publications, *David Hume and the Eighteenth Century British Thought*; T. E. Jessop, *A Bibliography of David Hume and of Scottish Philosophy*, 10–11; *Letters*, ed. Greig, vol. 2, Appendix B; and C. A. Rochedieu, *Bibliography of French Translations of English Works 1700–1800*. None of these sources has complete or entirely correct information on the French editions.

[111] 'Les Quatre philosophes' are Hume's four essays *The Epicurean, The Stoic, The Platonist*, and *The Sceptic*.

[112] According to numerous sources, 'Mlle de la Chaux' (her first name is never mentioned) was a third translator involved in one or more volumes in this 5-vol. collection—or perhaps in some later French publication of a work by Hume. This attribution appears to have its roots in an interpretation, or misinterpretation, of some comments by Denis Diderot in *Ceci n'est pas un conte*—in particular, Naigeon's edn. of this work. However, there is no credible or consistent evidence to show that Mlle de la Chaux had a role as translator in any given French translation of a work by Hume. Diderot appears to be writing fiction rather than literary history. See Laurence Bongie, *Diderot's Femme Savante*, in the series Studies on Voltaire and the Eighteenth Century (Oxford: Voltaire Foundation at the Taylor Institution, 1977). The editor of the present volume consulted widely with French and American rare books librarians in search of additional information, only to reach a conclusion fundamentally similar to that of Bongie.

2. In 1759, the third and fourth volumes were each issued individually (collective title-page lacking), but also issued, bound together, under the general title of *Œuvres philosophiques de M. D. Hume*, 2 vols. in 1 (8°), numbered 'tome troisieme' and 'tome quatrieme'. These two volumes are, in effect, a translation by Mérian of *Four Dissertations*.[113] 3. In 1760, the fifth volume was issued individually, with the half-title *Œuvres de Mr. Hume*. 4. The preface in vol. 1 was written by Jean-Henri-Samuel Formey.

1761, 1764 *Œuvres de Mr. Hume*, 2ᵉ édition (8°): 1. (1764)—*Essais moraux et politiques*. 2ᵉ ed.; 2. (1761)—*Essais philosophiques sur l'entendement humain*. 2ᵉ ed. Amsterdam, J. H. Schneider.

Note: Only these two volumes were issued with 2nd edn. specified on special title-pages. These two volumes were also issued in a newly packaged and reordered 5-vol. set. Schneider may have meant 'second edition' to refer to his 'new' *Œuvres de Mr. Hume*, not merely to individual volumes. The 5-vol. Schneider edition then became:[114]

Vol. 1 (1764, 2ᵉ édition)—*Essais moraux et politiques*. (All new material and translations, with the exception of 'Les Quatre philosophes', which was formerly in vol. 2 of the 1st edn.)
Vol. 2 (1761, 2ᵉ édition)—*Essais philosophiques sur l'entendement humain*. (Complete in 1 vol.; formerly in vols. 1 and 2 of the 1st edn.)
Vol. 3 (1759)—*Histoire naturelle de la religion*. (No new edn. or vol. no. change.)
Vol. 4 (1759)—*Dissertations sur les passions sur la tragédie sur la règle du goût*. (No new edn. or vol. no. change.)
Vol. 5 (1760)—*Essais de morale ou Recherches sur les principes de la morale*. (No new edn. or vol. no. change.)

Notes: 1. Although what is essentially a new volume (vol. 1) is here added to the prior Schneider collection, it remains a collection in 5 vols. 2. Volume numbers were assigned, at the point of publication, to vols. 1–2,

[113] See, further, Hume's letter to William Robertson, 12 Mar. 1759, *Letters*, 1: 301. This letter discusses a potential French edition and names a translator of *The Natural History of Religion*. However, there is no trace of this translation.

[114] Copies at Fondren Library, Rice University, B 1459 .F5 1758 v.1–5 (set of vols. 1–5); Rare Book, Manuscript, and Special Collections Library, Duke University, E H921EU (set of vols. 1–5); Old Building B1F, Keio University (Japan), EC@11B@7925@1–4 (set of vols. 1–5; 3–4 bound together); Rare Book Division, McGill University Libraries (set of vols. 1–5): B1459 M47 1759 (set of vols. 1–4 only; 3–4 bound together); Bibliothèque Nationale: Notice n° FRBNF30628405 (set of vols. 1–2 only); Emmanuel D'Alzon Library, Assumption College (B1459 .F5 1764, vol. 1 only).

and retained for the other 3 vols.[115] 3. Half-title of vol. 2 wanting in at least one copy.[116]

1764 *Œuvres philosophiques de M. D. Hume*. Nouvelle edition. 6 vols. (8°). London: David Wilson.[117]

This collection is a reissue by Wilson of Schneider's editions, once designated *Œuvres philosophiques de Mr. D. Hume*, with new title-pages and containing the 2 vols. in a 2nd edn. that Schneider had issued in 1761 and 1764 (see above), but with some content rearranged.

1. Les huits premiers Essais sur l'entendement humain.
2. Les quatre derniers Essais sur l'entendement humain [continued] et les quatre philosophes.
3. L'histoire naturelle de la religion. (Includes 'A Monsieur Hume, auteur de la tragédie de Douglas'.)
4. Les Dissertations sur les passions, sur la tragédie & sur la règle du goût.
5. Les Recherches sur les principes de la morale [with 'A Dialogue'].
6. Les Essais moraux & politiques.

Notes: 1. These volumes are found bound together in various patterns: 6 vols. in 2; 6 vols. in 3; 6 vols. in 4; 6 vols. in 5. 2. Some volumes are mixed with volumes from the earlier editions of Schneider (above) to create sets. 3. The 1764 *Essais moraux et politiques* is vol. 6 in this collection, though it was placed as vol. 1 by Schneider in his '2nd edn.'; the 'nouvelle edn.' of 1764 is, from this perspective, identical in material to that in Schneider's volumes.

1767 *Pensées philosophiques, morales, critiques, littéraires et politiques de M. Hume*. London . . . Paris: Veuve Duchesne (12°). Selections extracted from Hume's works, trans. Jean-Auguste Jullien (De Boulmiers). The Seconde Partie, pp. 81–121, contains selected portions of *A Dissertation on the Passions*, without mention of this title. The editor excerpted pieces of Hume's text and reorganized them under new headings that depart from

[115] Schneider wrote to Hume on 5 Dec. 1763 (National Library of Scotland MS, unpublished, as quoted in *Letters*, 2: 344) that he would soon publish a 'sixth volume of the first edition and the "first" [vol.] of the second edition'. The 'sixth volume' (here vol. 1) is presumably *Essais moraux & politiques*; and the first (here vol. 2) is presumably *Essais philosophiques sur l'entendement humain*. Schneider also reports in this letter that (in the first edition) vols. 1–4 were translated in Berlin and vol. 5 in Paris.

[116] Fondren Library, Rice University, B1459 .F5 1761.

[117] David Wilson was a friend of Andrew Millar's from London bookselling circles. Hume reported to Millar that he saw Wilson in Paris and presented him to Lord Hertford in the same year this edition was published (3 Sept. 1764, to Millar, *Letters*, 1: 465).

the original order. Approximately one-half of *A Dissertation on the Passions* was excerpted and translated. The general practice was to translate entire sentences or paragraphs, but there is some brief paraphrasing to connect excerpted portions. The preface and translator's notes (pp. iii, 26) indicate that all of *The Natural History of Religion* and the bulk of four sections of *EHU* (4, 9, 10, and 11) were excluded from the collection due to the danger of Hume's conclusions about religion. See n. 140 below.

German Translations in Hume's Lifetime[118]

1759. *Vier Abhandlungen: 1. Die natürliche Geschichte der Religion; 2. Von den Leidenschaften; 3. Vom Trauerspiel; 4. Von der Grundregel des Geschmacks. Aus dem Englischen übersetzt.* Quedlingsburg and Leipzig, Andreas Franz Biesterfeld. A translation of *Four Dissertations*; translator reported in several sources to be Friedrich Gabriel Resewitz, but these reports are unconfirmed.

5. TREATISE PASSAGES PRESERVED IN *A DISSERTATION ON THE PASSIONS*

The first three works in the second half of *Essays and Treatises on Several Subjects* bear titles that are effectively identical to the three Books of *A Treatise of Human Nature*, when Hume's shifting language of 'Book', 'Essay', 'Enquiry', and 'Dissertation' is stripped away:

In the *Treatise*	In *Essays and Treatises* [second half]
Of the *Understanding*	... concerning Human *Understanding*
Of the *Passions*	... on the *Passions*
Of *Morals*	... concerning ... *Morals*[119]

Did Hume retain not only the book titles of the *Treatise*, but also large blocks of text in the exact language of the *Treatise*? This hypothesis is testable by computer collation. Collations performed for this edition by comparing the *Treatise* with *An Enquiry concerning Human Understanding*

[118] See, further, Günter Gawlick and Lothar Kreimendahl, *Hume in der Deutschen Aufklärung*. There were numerous reviews in German periodicals of both *Four Dissertations* and *Vier Abhandlungen*. These reviews are catalogued, and some discussed, ibid. 74–7 and 202 ff.

[119] *The Natural History of Religion* is the sole work in the second half of *ETSS* to stand outside this threefold division. However, *NHR* is, like the others, a work on human nature; it may for this reason have been grouped with the other three treatises. Other possible reasons for the grouping are *NHR*'s length and the need to equalize the size of the first and second parts of *ETSS*.

and *An Enquiry concerning the Principles of Morals* are presented in other volumes of the Clarendon Hume. These collations indicate that there is *not* a significant carry-over of passages in the two Enquiries.[120] However, a substantial carry-over does occur in *A Dissertation on the Passions*, which was essentially created from the text of the *Treatise*.

A Dissertation on the Passions (1757 edn.) contains approximately 10,500 words, by contrast to the approximately 61,400 words in the second book of the *Treatise* (or 56,700 words if the material on liberty and necessity is excepted). Hume added several entirely new paragraphs and short passages to *A Dissertation on the Passions*. Approximately 2,850 words, or 27.5 per cent, of the work was new and did *not* derive directly from the *Treatise*. Thus, when composing *A Dissertation on the Passions*, Hume included approximately 7,550 words—or 12 per cent of *THN* 2—and excluded approximately 53,850 words—or 88 per cent of *THN* 2 (alternatively, 49,150 words, or 85 per cent, if the material on liberty and necessity is set aside).

All variations between these two works are shown below by shading. Additions in *A Dissertation on the Passions* appear as shaded text of the 1st (1757) edition; italics are represented by '/' for the beginning and '\' for the end. Text common to both works is free of shading.

This presentation follows the precise order of sections and paragraphs in the *Dissertation*, while displaying corresponding book, part, section, and paragraph(s) of the 1739 *Treatise*. No reference is provided to the page numbers of any edition of either work. Every word of the 1757 *Dissertation* is retained, so that the reader can see exactly what was added to the *Treatise* remnants. By contrast, only two types of passage are retained from the *Treatise*: (1) those that are shared in common with the *Dissertation* (displaying variants), and (2) relatively short segments of the *Treatise* that were omitted in the *Dissertation* but that are helpful for understanding Hume's editing, rewriting, or transitions.

[120] *EHU* carries over approximately 122 sentences or sentence fragments (including footnotes and quotations from other authors) from *Treatise*, bks. 1 and 2, the *Abstract* of the *Treatise*, and *A Letter from a Gentleman*. (However, passages from *LG* may have been copied from a pre-existing draft of *EHU*.) These sentences—the preserved remnants of the three works—appear in *EHU* 2, 3, 4, 5, 6, 7, 8, and 12, of which sects. 5 and 8 are the only ones to borrow a significant percentage of sentences from the earlier works. However, the sentences borrowed comprise but a small percentage of the sentences in each section. *EPM* carries over approximately 74 sentences or sentence fragments drawn from eleven sections of *Treatise*, bks. 2 and 3. They appear in seven sections and one appendix of *EPM*. These comparisons confirm that only a small amount of text is carried over from *THN* to *EHU* and *EPM*. Approximately 8 per cent of the text in *EHU* (including new words added to fill out partially recast sentences), and approximately 4 per cent of the text in EPM (including new words added to fill out partially recast sentences) derive from *THN*.

In these comparisons it is considered a purely typographical convention that the 1757 edition had the first word of each paragraph in either all large capitals (in the case of all *section* openers) or a combination of large and small capitals (in the case of *paragraph* openers). To facilitate comparison and reading, letters in these words have been converted to initial capital followed by lower-case letters. Capitalization elsewhere in the text has *not* been altered. In effect, a distinction is recognized between typographical conventions and capitalization practices.

The system of shading shows some, but not all, differences in accidentals. Differences of *punctuation and italicization* are shaded; differences of *capitalization for the first letter of a word and orthography* are not shaded. Thus, 'Any'–'any', 'Tho'–'tho', and 'Beauty'–'beauty' are not shaded, despite the capitalization differences in the texts; likewise, 'establish'd'–'established', 'surprizing'–'surprising', 'ethicks'–'ethics', and 'oftner'–'oftener' are not shaded. The difference between ''Tis' and 'It is' is also interpreted under this no-shading convention.

A Treatise of Human Nature—Book 2	A Dissertation on the Passions—1757
Of the Passions.	/Of the Passions\.
	SECT. I
	[1.1] 1. Some objects produce immediately an agreeable sensationtion, by the original structure of our organs, and are thence denominated GOOD; as others, from their immediate disagreeable sensation, acquire the appellation of EVIL. Thus moderate warmth is agreeable and good; excessive heat painful and evil.
	[1.2] Some objects again, by being naturally conformable or contrary to passion, excite an agreeable or painful sensation; and are thence called /Good\ or /Evil\.

The punishment of an adversary, by gratifying revenge, is good; the sickness of a companion, by affecting friendship, is evil.

[1.3] 2. All good or evil, whence-ever it arises, produces various passions and affections, according to the light, in which it is surveyed.[121]

[Immediately below: *THN* 2.3.9.5–12 (in *Of the direct passions*) is compared to *DP* 1.4–10.]

[2.3.9.5] When good is certain or probable, it produces JOY. When evil is in the same situation there arises GRIEF or SORROW.	[1.4] When good is certain or very probable, it produces JOY: When evil is in the same situation, there arises GRIEF or SORROW.
[2.3.9.6] When either good or evil is uncertain, it gives rise to FEAR or HOPE, according to the degrees of uncertainty on the one side or the other.	[1.5] When either good or evil is uncertain, it gives rise to FEAR or HOPE, according to the degrees of uncertainty on one side or the other.
[2.3.9.7] DESIRE arises from good consider'd simply, and AVERSION is deriv'd from evil. The WILL exerts itself, when either the good or the absence of the evil may be attain'd by any action of the mind or body.	[1.6] DESIRE arises from good considered simply; and AVERSION, from evil. The WILL exerts itself, when either the presence of the good or absence of the evil may be attained by any action of the mind or body.
[2.3.9.9] None of the direct affections seem to merit our particular attention, except hope and fear, which we shall here endeavour to account for. 'Tis evident that the very same event, which by its certainty wou'd produce grief or	[1.7] 3. None of these passions seem to contain any thing curious or remarkable, except /Hope\ and /Fear\, which, being derived from the probability of any good or evil, are mixt passions, that merit our attention.

[121] Cf. these three introductory paragraphs in *DP* to *THN* 2.1.1.4 and 2.3.9.3–4.

joy, gives always rise to fear or hope, when only probable and uncertain. In order, therefore, to understand the reason why this circumstance makes such a considerable difference, we must reflect on what I have already advanc'd in the preceding book concerning the nature of probability.

[2.3.9.10] Probability arises from an opposition of contrary chances or causes, by which the mind is not allow'd to fix on either side, but is incessantly tost from one to another, and at one moment is determin'd to consider an object as existent, and at another moment as the contrary. The imagination or understanding, call it which you please, fluctuates betwixt the opposite views; and tho' perhaps it may be oftner turn'd to the one side than the other, 'Tis impossible for it, by reason of the opposition of causes or chances, to rest on either. The /pro\ and /con\ of the question alternately prevail; and the mind, surveying the object in its opposite principles, finds such a contrariety as utterly destroys all certainty and establish'd opinion.

[1.8] Probability arises from an opposition of contrary chances or causes, by which the mind is not allowed to fix on either side; but is incessantly tost from one to another, and in one moment is determined to consider an object as existent, and in another moment as the contrary. The imagination or understanding, call it which you please, fluctuates betwixt the opposite views; and tho' perhaps it may be oftener turned to one side than the other, it is impossible for it, by reason of the opposition of causes or chances, to rest on either. The /pro\ and /con\ of the question alternately prevail; and the mind, surveying the objects in their opposite causes, finds such a contrariety as utterly destroys all certainty or established opinion.

[2.3.9.11] Suppose, then, that the object, concerning whose reality we are doubtful, is an object either of desire or aversion, 'tis evident, that, according as the mind turns itself either to the one side or the other, it must feel a

[1.9] Suppose, then, that the object, concerning which we are doubtful, produces either desire or aversion; it is evident, that, according as the mind turns itself to one side or the other, it must feel a momentary impression of joy or

momentary impression of joy or sorrow. An object, whose existence we desire, gives satisfaction, when we reflect on those causes, which produce it; and for the same reason excites grief or uneasiness from the opposite consideration: So that as the understanding, in all probable questions, is divided betwixt the contrary points of view, the affections must in the same manner be divided betwixt opposite emotions.

[2.3.9.12] Now if we consider the human mind, we shall find, that with regard to the passions, 'tis not of the nature of a wind-instrument of music, which in running over all the notes immediately loses the sound after the breath ceases; but rather resembles a string-instrument, where after each stroke the vibrations still retain some sound, which gradually and insensibly decays. The imagination is extreme quick and agile; but the passions are slow and restive: For which reason, when any object is presented, that affords a variety of views to the one, and emotions to the other; tho' the fancy may change its views with great celerity; each stroke will not produce a clear and distinct note of passion, but the one passion will always be mixt and confounded with the other. According as the probability inclines to good or evil, the passion of joy or sorrow predominates in the composition:

sorrow. An object, whose existence we desire, gives satisfaction, when we think of those causes, which produce it; and for the same reason, excites grief or uneasiness, from the opposite consideration. So that, as the understanding, in probable questions, is divided betwixt the contrary points of view, the heart must in the same manner be divided betwixt opposite emotions.

[1.10] Now, if we consider the human mind, we shall observe, that, with regard to the passions, it is not like a wind-instrument of music, which, in running over all the notes, immediately loses the sound when the breath ceases; but rather resembles a string-instrument, where, after each stroke, the vibrations still retain some sound, which gradually and insensibly decays. The imagination is extremely quick and agile; but the passions, in comparison, are slow and restive: For which reason, when any object is presented, which affords a variety of views to the one and emotions to the other; tho' the fancy may change its views with great celerity; each stroke will not produce a clear and distinct note of passion, but the one passion will always be mixt and confounded with the other. According as the probability inclines to good or evil, the passion

Because the nature of probability is to cast a superior number of views or chances on one side; or, which is the same thing, a superior number of returns of one passion; or since the dispers'd passions are collected into one, a superior degree of that passion. That is, in other words, the grief and joy being intermingled with each other, by means of the contrary views of the imagination, produce by their union the passions of hope and fear.

of grief or joy predominates in the composition; and these passions, being intermingled by means of the contrary views of the imagination, produce by the union the passions of hope or fear.

[At this point five paragraphs of *THN* (2.3.9.13–17) were skipped over (but four of the five were subsequently revised and used at *DP* 1.21–4). Immediately below: *THN* 2.3.9.18–29 is compared to *DP* 1.11–20.]

[2.3.9.18] As the hypothesis concerning hope and fear carries its own evidence along with it, we shall be the more concise in our proofs. A few strong arguments are better than many weak ones.

[1.11] 4. As this theory seems to carry its own evidence along with it, we shall be more concise in our proofs.

[2.3.9.19] The passions of fear and hope may arise when the chances are equal on both sides, and no superiority can be discover'd in the one above the other. Nay, in this situation the passions are rather the strongest, as the mind has then the least foundation to rest upon, and is toss'd with the greatest uncertainty. Throw in a superior degree of probability to the side of grief, you immediately see that passion diffuse itself over the composition, and tincture it

[1.12] The passions of fear and hope may arise, when the chances are equal on both sides, and no superiority can be discovered in one above the other. Nay, in this situation the passions are rather the strongest, as the mind has then the least foundation to rest upon, and is tost with the greatest uncertainty. Throw in a superior degree of probability to the side of grief, you immediately see that passion diffuse itself over the composition, and tincture it into

into fear. Encrease the probability, and by that means the grief, the fear prevails still more and more, till at last it runs insensibly, as the joy continually diminishes, into pure grief. After you have brought it to this situation, diminish the grief, after the same manner that you encreas'd it; by diminishing the probability on that side, and you'll see the passion clear every moment, 'till it changes insensibly into hope; which again runs, after the same manner, by slow degrees, into joy, as you encrease that part of the composition by the encrease of the probability. Are not these as plain proofs, that the passions of fear and hope are mixtures of grief and joy, as in optics 'tis a proof, that a colour'd ray of the sun passing thro' a prism, is a composition of two others, when, as you diminish or encrease the quantity of either, you find it prevail proportionably more or less in the composition? I am sure neither natural nor moral philosophy admits of stronger proofs.

[2.3.9.20] Probability is of two kinds, either when the object is really in itself uncertain, and to be determin'd by chance; or when, tho' the object be already certain, yet 'tis uncertain to our judgment, which finds a number of proofs on each side of the question. Both these kinds of probabilities cause fear and hope; which can only

fear. Encrease the probability, and by that means the grief; the fear prevails still more and more, till at last it runs insensibly, as the joy continually diminishes, into pure grief. After you have brought it to this situation, diminish the grief, by a contrary operation to that, which encreased it, to wit, by diminishing the probability on the melancholy side; and you will see the passion clear every moment, till it changes insensibly into hope; which again runs, by slow degrees, into joy, as you encrease that part of the composition, by the encrease of the probability. Are not these as plain proofs, that the passions of fear and hope are mixtures of grief and joy, as in optics it is a proof, that a coloured ray of the sun, passing thro' a prism, is a composition of two others, when, as you diminish or encrease the quantity of either, you find it prevail proportionably, more or less, in the composition?

[1.13] 5. Probability is of two kinds; either when the object is itself uncertain, and to be determined by chance; or when, tho' the object be already certain, yet is it uncertain to our judgment, which finds a number of proofs or presumptions on each side of the question. Both these kinds of probability cause fear and hope; which proceed from that property, in which they agree, /viz\. the uncertainty and fluctuation they bestow on the imagination by that contrariety of views, which is common to both.

must proceed from that property, in which they agree; to wit, the uncertainty and fluctuation which they bestow on the passion, by that contrariety of views, which is common to both.

[2.3.9.21] 'Tis a probable good or evil, that commonly produces hope or fear; because probability, being a wavering and unconstant method of surveying an object, causes naturally a like mixture and uncertainty of passion. But we may observe, that wherever from other causes this mixture can be produc'd, the passions of fear and hope will arise, even tho' there be no probability; which must be allow'd to be a convincing proof of the present hypothesis.

[1.14] 6. It is a probable good or evil, which commonly causes hope or fear; because probability, producing an inconstant and wavering survey of an object, occasions naturally a like mixture and uncertainty of passion. But we may observe, that, wherever, from other causes, this mixture can be produced, the passions of fear and hope will arise, even tho' there be no probability.

[2.3.9.22] We find that an evil, barely conceiv'd as /possible\, does sometimes produce fear; especially if the evil be very great. A man cannot think of excessive pains and tortures without trembling, if he be in the least danger of suffering them. The smallness of the probability is compensated by the greatness of the evil; and the sensation is equally lively, as if the evil were more probable. One view or glimpse of the former, has the same effect as several of the latter.

[1.15] An evil, conceived as barely /possible\, sometimes produces fear; especially if the evil be very great. A man cannot think of excessive pain and torture without trembling, if he runs the least risque of suffering them. The smallness of the probability is compensated by the greatness of the evil.

[2.3.9.23] But they are not only possible evils, that cause fear, but even some allow'd to be /impossible\; as when we tremble on the

[1.16] But even /impossible\ evils cause fear; as when we tremble on the brink of a precipice, tho' we know ourselves to be in perfect

brink of a precipice, tho' we know ourselves to be in perfect security, and have it in our choice whether we will advance a step farther. This proceeds from the immediate presence of the evil, which influences the imagination in the same manner as the certainty of it wou'd do; but being encounter'd by the reflection on our security, is immediately retracted, and causes the same kind of passion, as when from a contrariety of chances contrary passions are produc'd.

security, and have it in our choice, whether we will advance a step farther. The immediate presence of the evil influences the imagination and produces a species of belief; but being opposed by the reflection on our security, that belief is immediately retracted, and causes the same kind of passion, as when, from a contrariety of chances, contrary passions are produced.

[2.3.9.24] Evils, that are /certain\, have sometimes the same effect in producing fear, as the possible or impossible. Thus a man in a strong prison well-guarded, without the least means of escape, trembles at the thought of the rack, to which he is sentenc'd. This happens only when the certain evil is terrible and confounding; in which case the mind continually rejects it with horror, while it continually presses in upon the thought. The evil is there fix'd and establish'd, but the mind cannot endure to fix upon it; from which fluctuation and uncertainty there arises a passion of much the same appearance with fear.

[1.17] Evils, which are/certain\, have sometimes the same effect as the possible or impossible. A man, in a strong prison, without the least means of escape, trembles at the thoughts of the rack, to which he is sentenced. The evil is here fixed in itself; but the mind has not courage to fix upon it; and this fluctuation gives rise to a passion of a similar appearance with fear.

[2.3.9.25] But 'tis not only where good or evil is uncertain, as to its /existence\, but also as to its /kind\, that fear or hope arises. Let one be told by a person, whose

[1.18] 7. But it is not only where good or evil is uncertain as to its /existence\, but also as to its /kind\, that fear or hope arises. If any one were told, that one of veracity he cannot doubt of , that one of his sons is suddenly kill'd, 'tis evident the passion this event wou'd occasion, wou'd not settle into pure grief, till he got certain information, which of his sons he had lost. Here there is an evil certain, but the kind of it uncertain: Consequently the fear we feel on this occasion is without the least mixture of joy, and arises merely from the fluctuation of the fancy betwixt its objects. And tho' each side of the question produces here the same passion, yet that passion cannot settle, but receives from the imagination a tremulous and unsteady motion, resembling in its cause, as well as in its sensation, the mixture and contention of grief and joy. . . .

his sons is suddenly killed; the passion, occasioned by this event, would not settle into grief, till he got certain information, which of his sons he had lost. Tho' each side of the question produces here the same passion; that passion cannot settle, but receives from the imagination, which is unfixt, a tremulous, unsteddy motion, resembling the mixture and contention of grief and joy.

[2.3.9.27] Thus all kinds of uncertainty have a strong connexion with fear, even tho' they do not cause any opposition of passions by the opposite views and considerations they present to us. A person, who has left his friend in any malady, will feel more anxiety upon his account, than if he were present, tho' perhaps he is not only incapable of giving him assistance, but likewise of judging of the event of his sickness. In this case, tho' the principal object of the passion, /viz\. the life or death of his friend, be to him equally uncertain when present as when absent; yet there are a thousand little circumstances

[1.19] 8. Thus all kinds of uncertainty have a strong connexion with fear, even tho' they do not cause any opposition of passions, by the opposite views, which they present to us. Should I leave a friend in any malady, I should feel more anxiety upon his account, than if he were present; tho' perhaps I am not only incapable of giving him assistance, but likewise of judging concerning the event of his sickness. There are a thousand little circumstances of his situation and condition, which I desire to know; and the knowledge of them would prevent that fluctuation and uncertainty, so nearly allied to fear.

of his friend's situation and condition, the knowledge of which fixes the idea, and prevents that fluctuation and uncertainty so near ally'd to fear. Uncertainty is, indeed, in one respect as near ally'd to hope as to fear, since it makes an essential part in the composition of the former passion; but the reason, why it inclines not to that side, is, that uncertainty alone is uneasy, and has a relation of impressions to the uneasy passions.

[2.3.9.28] 'Tis thus our uncertainty concerning any minute circumstance relating to a person encreases our apprehensions of his death or misfortune.

/Horace\ has remark'd this phænomenon.

/Ut assidens implumibus pullus avis
Serpentium allapsus timet,
Magis relictis; non, ut adsit, auxili
Latura plus presentibus\.

[2.3.9.29] But this principle of the connexion of fear with uncertainty I carry farther, and observe that any doubt produces that passion, even tho' it presents nothing to us on any side but what is good and desireable. A virgin, on her bridal-night goes to bed full of fears and apprehensions, tho' she expects nothing but pleasure of the highest kind, and what she has long wish'd for. The newness and greatness of the

[no ¶] /Horace\ has remarked this phænomenon:

/Ut assidens implumibus pullus avis
Serpentum allapsus timet,
Magis relictis; non, ut adsit, auxili
Latura plus præsentibus\.

[1.20] A virgin on her bridal-night goes to bed full of fears and apprehensions, tho' she expects nothing but pleasure. The confusion of wishes and joys, the newness and greatness of the unknown event, so embarrass the mind, that it knows not in what image or passion to fix itself.

event, the confusion of wishes and joys, so embarrass the mind, that it knows not on what passion to fix itself; from whence arises a fluttering or unsettledness of the spirits, which being, in some degree, uneasy, very naturally degenerates into fear.

[At this point Hume went back to earlier paragraphs of *THN* 2.3.9. Immediately below: *THN* 2.3.9.14–17 is compared to *DP* 1.21–4.]

[2.3.9.14] When the contrary passions arise from objects entirely different, they take place alternately, the want of relation in the ideas separating the impressions from each other, and preventing their opposition. Thus when a man is afflicted for the loss of a law-suit, and joyful for the birth of a son, the mind running from the agreeable to the calamitous object, with whatever celerity it may perform this motion, can scarcely temper the one affection with the other, and remain betwixt them in a state of indifference.

[2.3.9.15] It more easily attains that calm situation, when the same event is of a mixt nature, and contains something adverse and something prosperous in its different circumstances. For in that case, both the passions, mingling with each other by means of the relation, become mutually destructive, and leave the mind in perfect tranquillity.

[1.21] 9. Concerning the mixture of affections, we may remark, in general, that when contrary passions arise from objects no way connected together, they take place alternately. Thus when a man is afflicted for the loss of a law-suit, and joyful for the birth of a son, the mind, running from the agreeable to the calamitous object; with whatever celerity it may perform this motion, can scarcely temper the one affection with the other, and remain betwixt them in a state of indifference.

[1.22] It more easily attains that calm situation, when the /same\ event is of a mixt nature, and contains something adverse and something prosperous in its different circumstances. For in that case, both the passions, mingling with each other by means of the relation, often become mutually destructive, and leave the mind in perfect tranquillity.

[2.3.9.16] But suppose, in the third place, that the object is not a compound of good or evil, but is consider'd as probable or improbable in any degree; in that case I assert, that the contrary passions will both of them be present at once in the soul, and instead of destroying and tempering each other, will subsist together, and produce a third impression or affection by their union.

[2.3.9.17] Upon the whole, contrary passions succeed each other alternately, when they arise from different objects: They mutually destroy each other, when they proceed from different parts of the same: And they subsist both of them, and mingle together, when they are deriv'd from the contrary and incompatible chances or possibilities, on which any one object depends. The influence of the relations of ideas is plainly seen in this whole affair. If the objects of the contrary passions be totally different, the passions are like two opposite liquors in different bottles, which have no influence on each other. If the objects be intimately connected, the passions are like an/alcali\ and an/acid\, which, being mingled, destroy each other. If the relation be more imperfect, and consists in the contradictory views of the same object, the passions are like oil and vinegar, which, however

[1.23] But suppose, that the object is not a compound of good and evil, but is considered as probable or improbable in any degree; in that case, the contrary passions will both of them be present at once in the soul, and instead of ballancing and tempering each other, will subsist together, and by their union, produce a third impression or affection, such as hope or fear.

[1.24] The influence of the relations of ideas (which we shall afterwards explain more fully) is plainly seen in this affair. In contrary passions, if the objects be /totally different\, the passions are like two opposite liquors in different bottles, which have no influence on each other. If the objects be intimately/connected\, the passions are like an /alcali\ or an /acid\, which, being mingled, destroy each other. If the relation be more imperfect, and consists in the /contradictory\ views of the /same\ object, the passions are like oil and vinegar, which, however mingled, never perfectly unite and incorporate.

mingled, never perfectly unite and incorporate.

[1.25] The effect of a mixture of passions, when one of them is predominant and swallows up the other, shall be explained afterwards.

SECT. II

[2.1] 1. Besides those passions above-mentioned, which arise from a direct pursuit of good and aversion to evil, there are others of a more complicated nature, and imply more than one view or consideration. Thus /Pride\ is a certain satisfaction in ourselves, on account of some accomplishment or possession, which we enjoy: /Humility\, on the other hand, is a dissatisfaction with ourselves, on account of some defect or infirmity.[122]

[2.2] /Love\ or /Friendship\ is a complacency in another, on account of his accomplishments or services: /Hatred\, the contrary.[123]

[At this point Hume moved to earlier parts of *THN* 2. Immediately below: *THN* 2.1.2.4; 2.2.1.3; and 2.1.4.2–5 are compared to *DP* 2.3–9. (The first and last of these paragraphs of *THN* are in the section

122 Cf. this paragraph to *THN* 2.1 (*Of pride and humility*), esp. 2.1.1.4.

123 Cf. this paragraph to *THN* 2.2 (*Of love and hatred*).

***Of pride and humility: their objects and causes*; the middle portion is taken from the section *Experiments to confirm this system*.)]**

[2.1.2.4] We must, therefore, make a distinction betwixt the cause and the object of these passions; betwixt that idea, which excites them, and that to which they direct their view, when excited. Pride and humility, being once rais'd, immediately turn our attention to ourself...

[2.2.1.3] But tho' the object of love and hatred be always some other person, 'tis plain that the object is not, properly speaking, the /cause\ of these passions, or alone sufficient to excite them.

[2.3] 2. In these two sets of passions, there is an obvious distinction to be made betwixt the /object\ of the passion and its /cause\. The object of pride and humility is self: The cause of the passion is some excellence in the former case; some fault, in the latter. The object of love and hatred is some other person: The causes, in like manner, are either excellencies or faults.

[2.4] With regard to all these passions, the causes are what excite the emotion; the object is what the mind directs its view to when the emotion is excited. Our merit, for instance, raises pride; and it is essential to pride to turn our view on ourself with complacency and satisfaction.

[2.5] Now as the causes of these passions are very numerous and various, tho' their object be uniform and simple; it may be a subject of curiosity to consider, what that circumstance is, in which all these various causes agree; or, in other words, what is the real, efficient cause of the passion. We shall begin with pride and humility.

[2.1.4.2] In order to this we must reflect on certain properties of human nature, which tho' they have a mighty influence on every operation both of the understanding

[2.6] 3. In order to explain the causes of these passions, we must reflect on certain properties, which, tho' they have a mighty influence on every operation, both of the and passions, are not commonly much insisted on by philosophers. The /first\ of these is the association of ideas, which I have so often observ'd and explain'd. 'Tis impossible for the mind to fix itself steadily upon one idea for any considerable time; nor can it by its utmost efforts ever arrive at such a constancy. But however change able our thoughts may be, they are not entirely without rule and method in their changes. The rule, by which they proceed, is to pass from one object to what is resembling, contiguous to, or produc'd by it. When one idea is present to the imagination, any other, united by these relations, naturally follows it, and enters with more facility by means of that introduction.

[2.1.4.3] The /second\ property I shall observe in the human mind is a like association of impressions. All resembling impressions are connected together, and no sooner one arises than the rest immediately follow. Grief and disappointment give rise to anger, anger to envy, envy to malice, and malice to grief again, till the whole circle be compleated. In like manner our temper, when elevated with joy, naturally throws itself into love, generosity, pity, courage, pride, and the other resembling affections.

[2.1.4.4] In the /third\ place, 'tis observable of these two kinds of

understanding and passions, are not commonly much insisted on by philosophers. The first of these is the /association \ of ideas, or that principle, by which we make an easy transition from one idea to another. However uncertain and changeable our thoughts may be, they are not entirely without rule and method in their changes. They usually pass with regularity, from one object, to what resembles it, is contiguous to it, or produced by it. [<Note> See philosophical Essays. Essay iii. <End of note>] When one idea is present to the imagination; any other, united by these relations, naturally follows it, and enters with more facility, by means of that introduction.

[2.7] The /second\ property, which I shall observe in the human mind, is a like association of impressions or emotions. All /resembling\ impressions are connected together; and no sooner one arises, than the rest naturally follow. Grief and disappointment give rise to anger, anger to envy, envy to malice, and malice to grief again. In like manner, our temper, when elevated with joy, naturally throws itself into love, generosity, courage, pride, and other resembling affections.

[2.8] In the /third\ place, it is observable of these two kinds of association, that they very much assist and forward each other, and that the transition is more easily made where they both concur in the same object. Thus a man, who, by any injury from another, is very much discompos'd and ruffled in his temper, is apt to find a hundred subjects of discontent, impatience, fear, and other uneasy passions; especially if he can discover these subjects in or near the person, who was the cause of his first passion. Those principles, which forward the transition of ideas, here concur with those, which operate on the passions; and both uniting in one action, bestow on the mind a double impulse. The new passion, therefore, must arise with so much greater violence, and the transition to it must be render'd so much more easy and natural.

association, that they very much assist and forward each other, and that the transition is more easily made, where they both concur in the same object. Thus, a man, who, by any injury from another, is very much discomposed and ruffled in his temper, is apt to find a hundred subjects of hatred, discontent, impatience, fear, and other uneasy passions; especially, if he can discover these subjects in or near the person, who was the object of his first emotion. Those principles, which forward the transition of ideas, here concur with those, which operate on the passions; and both, uniting in one action, bestow on the mind a double impulse.

[2.1.4.5] Upon this occasion I may cite the authority of an elegant writer, who expresses himself in the following manner. "As the fancy delights in every thing that is great, strange, or beautiful, and is still more pleas'd the more it finds of these perfections in the /same\ object, so it is capable of receiving a new satisfaction by the assistance of another sense. Thus any continu'd sound, as the music of birds, or a fall of waters, awakens every moment the mind of the beholder,

[2.9] Upon this occasion, I may cite a passage from an elegant writer, who expresses himself in the following manner. [<Note> Addison, Spectator, No 412.[124] <End of note>] "As the fancy delights in every thing, that is great, strange, or beautiful, and is still the more pleased the more it finds of these perfections in the/same\ object, so it is capable of receiving new satisfaction by the assistance of another sense. Thus, any continued sound, as the music of

[124] Addison, *Spectator*, no. 412, was quoted, but not cited by title or author, in *THN* 2.1.4.5.

and makes him more attentive to the several beauties of the place, that lie before him. Thus if there arises a fragrancy of smells or perfumes, they heighten the pleasure of the imagination, and make even the colours and verdure of the landscape appear more agreeable; for the ideas of both senses recommend each other, and are pleasanter together than when they enter the mind separately: As the different colours of a picture, when they are well disposed, set off one another, and receive an additional beauty from the advantage of the situation." In these phænomena we may remark the association both of impressions and ideas, as well as the mutual assistance they lend each other.

birds, or a fall of waters, awakens every moment the mind of the beholder, and makes him more attentive to the several beauties of the place, that lie before him. Thus, if there arises a fragrancy of smells or perfumes, they heighten the pleasure of the imagination, and make even the colours and verdure of the landscape appear more agreeable; for the ideas of both senses recommend each other, and are pleasanter together than where they enter the mind separately: As the different colours of a picture, when they are well disposed, set off one another, and receive an additional beauty from the advantage of the situation." In these phænomena, we may remark the association both of impressions and ideas; as well as the mutual assistance these associations lend to each other.

[2.10] 4. It seems to me, that both these species of relation have place in producing /Pride\ or /Humility\, and are the real, efficient causes of the passion.

[2.11] With regard to the first relation, that of ideas, there can be no question. Whatever we are proud of, must, in some manner, belong to us. It is always /our\ knowledge, /our\ sense, beauty, possessions, family, on which we value ourselves. Self, which is the /object\ of the passion, must still be related to that quality or circumstance, which /causes\ the passion. There must be a connexion betwixt them; an easy transition of the imagination; or a facility of the conception in passing from one to the other. Where this connexion is wanting, no object can either excite pride or humility; and the more you weaken the connexion, the more you weaken the passion.

[2.12] 5. The only subject of enquiry is, whether there be a like relation of impressions or sentiments, wherever pride or humility is felt; whether the circumstance, which causes the passion, produces antecedently a sentiment similar to the passion; and whether there be an easy transfusion of the one into the other.

[Hume here appears to return to the point in *THN* at which he had previously stopped (at the end of *THN* 2.1.4.5). Immediately below: *THN* 2.1.5.1 (in *Of the influence of these relations on pride and humility*) is compared to *DP* 2.13.]

[2.1.5.1] These principles being establish'd on unquestionable experience, I begin to consider how we shall apply them, by revolving over all the causes of pride and humility, whether these causes be regarded, as the qualities, that operate, or as the subjects, on which the qualities are plac'd. In examining these /qualities\ I immediately find many of them to concur in producing the sensation

[2.13] The feeling or sentiment of pride is agreeable; of humility, painful. An agreeable sensation is, therefore, related to the former; a painful, to the latter. And if we find, after examination, that every object, which produces pride, produces also a separate pleasure;and every object, that causes humility, excites in like manner a separate uneasiness; we must allow, in that case, that the present theory

of pain and pleasure, independent of those affections, which I here endeavour to explain. Thus the beauty of our person, of itself, and by its very appearance, gives pleasure, as well as pride; and its deformity, pain as well as humility. A magnificent feast delights us, and a sordid one displeases. What I discover to be true in some instances, I /suppose\ to be so in all; and take it for granted at present, without any farther proof, that every cause of pride, by its peculiar qualities, produces a separate pleasure, and of humility a separate uneasiness.

is fully proved and ascertained. The double relation of ideas and sentiments will be acknowledged incontestible.

[At this point Hume moved to *THN* 2.1.7 (*Of vice and virtue*) and 2.1.8 (*Of beauty and deformity*). Immediately below: *THN* 2.1.7.2 and 2.1.7.5–2.1.8.6 are compared to *DP* 2.14–20.]

[2.1.7.2] To begin with VICE and VIRTUE, which are the most obvious causes of these passions; 'twou'd be entirely foreign to my present purpose to enter upon the controversy, which of late years has so much excited the curiosity of the publick, /whether these moral distinctions be founded on natural and original principles, or arise from interest and education\.

[2.14] 6. To begin with personal merit and demerit, the most obvious causes of these passions; it would be entirely foreign to our present purpose to examine the foundation of moral distinctions. It is sufficient to observe, that the foregoing theory concerning the origin of the passions may be defended on any hypothesis.

[2.1.7.5] ... The most probable hypothesis, which has been ad vanc'd to explain the distinction betwixt vice and virtue, and the origin of moral rights and obligations, is, that from a primary

[no ¶] The most probable system, which has been advanced to explain the difference betwixt vice and virtue, is, that either from a primary constitution of nature, or from a sense of public or private

constitution of nature certain characters and passions, by the very view and contemplation, produce a pain, and others in like manner excite a pleasure. The uneasiness and satisfaction are not only inseparable from vice and virtue, but constitute their very nature and essence. To approve of a character is to feel an original delight upon its appearance. To disapprove of it is to be sensible of an uneasiness. The pain and pleasure, therefore, being the primary causes of vice and virtue, must also be the causes of all their effects, and consequently of pride and humility, which are the unavoidable attendants of that distinction.

[2.1.7.6] But supposing this hypothesis of moral philosophy shou'd be allow'd to be false, 'tis still evident, that pain and pleasure, if not the causes of vice and virtue, are at least inseparable from them. A generous and noble character affords a satisfaction even in the survey; and when presented to us, tho' only in a poem or fable, never fails to charm and delight us. On the other hand cruelty and treachery displease from their very nature; nor is it possible ever to reconcile us to these qualities, either in ourselves or others. Thus one hypothesis of morality is an undeniable proof of the foregoing system, and the other at worst agrees with it.

interest, certain characters, upon the very view and contemplation, produce uneasiness; and others, in like manner, excite pleasure. The uneasiness and satisfaction, produced in the spectator, are essential to vice and virtue. To approve of a character, is to feel a delight upon its appearance. To disapprove of it, is to be sensible of an uneasiness. The pain and pleasure, therefore, being, in a manner, the primary source of blame or praise, must also be the causes of all their effects; and consequently, the causes of pride and humility, which are the unavoidable attendants of that distinction.

[2.15] But supposing this theory of morals should not be received; it is still evident, that pain and pleasure, if not the sources of moral distinctions, are at least inseparable from them. A generous and noble character affords a satisfaction even in the survey; and when presented to us, tho' only in a poem or fable, never fails to charm and delight us. On the other hand, cruelty and treachery displease from their very nature; nor is it possible ever to reconcile us to these qualities, either in ourselves or others. Virtue, therefore, produces always a pleasure distinct from the pride or self-satisfaction, which attends it: Vice, an uneasiness separate from the humility or remorse.

[2.1.7.7] But pride and humility arise not from these qualities alone of the mind, which, according to the vulgar systems of ethicks, have been comprehended as parts of moral duty, but from any other that has a connexion with pleasure and uneasiness. Nothing flatters our vanity more than the talent of pleasing by our wit, good humour, or any other accomplishment; and nothing gives us a more sensible mortification than a disappointment in any attempt of that nature. No one has ever been able to tell what /wit\ is, and to shew why such a system of thought must be receiv'd under that denomination, and such another rejected. 'Tis only by taste we can decide concerning it, nor are we possest of any other standard, upon which we can form a judgment of this kind. Now what is this /taste\, from which true and false wit in a manner receive their being, and without which no thought can have a title to either of these denominations? 'Tis plainly nothing but a sensation of pleasure from true wit, and of uneasiness from false, without our being able to tell the reasons of that pleasure or uneasiness. The power of bestowing these opposite sensations is, therefore, the very essence of true and false wit; and consequently the cause of that pride or humility, which arises from them.

[2.16] But a high or low conceit of ourselves arises not from those qualities alone of the mind, which, according to common systems of ethics, have been defined parts of moral duty; but from any other, which have a connexion with pleasure or uneasiness. Nothing flatters our vanity more than the talent of pleasing by our wit, good humour, or any other accomplishment; and nothing gives us a more sensible mortification, than a disappointment in any attempt of that kind. No one has ever been able to tell precisely, what /wit\ is, and to shew why such a system of thought must be received under that denomination, and such another rejected. It is by taste alone we can decide concerning it; nor are we possest of any other standard, by which we can form a judgment of this nature. Now what is this /taste\, from which true and false wit in a manner receive their being, and without which no thought can have a title to either of these denominations? It is plainly nothing but a sensation of pleasure from true wit, and of disgust from false, without our being able to tell the reasons of that satisfaction or uneasiness. The power of exciting these opposite sensations is, therefore, the very essence of true or false wit; and consequently, the cause of that vanity or mortification, which arises from one or the other.

[2.1.8.1] . . . But / beauty\ of all kinds gives us a peculiar delight and satisfaction; as /deformity\ produces pain, upon whatever subject it may be plac'd, and whether survey'd in an animate or inanimate object. If the beauty or deformity, therefore, be plac'd upon our own bodies, this pleasure or uneasiness must be converted into pride or humility, as having in this case all the circumstances requisite to produce a perfect transition of impressions and ideas. These opposite sensations are related to the opposite passions. The beauty or deformity is closely related to self, the object of both these passions. No wonder, then our own beauty becomes an object of pride, and deformity of humility.

[2.17] 7. Beauty of all kinds gives us a peculiar delight and satisfaction; as deformity produces pain, upon whatever subject it may be placed, and whether surveyed in an animate or inanimate object. If the beauty or deformity belong to our own face, shape, or person, this pleasure or uneasiness is converted into pride or humility; as having in this case all the circumstances requisite to produce a perfect transition, according to the present theory.

[2.1.8.2] . . . we may conclude, that beauty is nothing but a form, which produces pleasure, as deformity is a structure of parts, which conveys pain; and since the power of producing pain and pleasure make in this manner the essence of beauty and deformity, all the effects of these qualities must be deriv'd from the sensation; and among the rest pride and humility, which of all their effects are the most common and remarkable.

[2.18] It would seem, that the very essence of beauty consists in its power of producing pleasure. All its effects, therefore, must proceed from this circumstance: And if beauty is so universally the subject of vanity, it is only from its being the cause of pleasure.

[2.1.8.3] This argument I esteem just and decisive; but in order to give greater authority to the present reasoning, let us suppose it false for a moment, and see what will follow. 'Tis certain, then, that if the power of producing pleasure and pain forms not the essence of beauty and deformity, the sensations are at least inseparable from the qualities, and 'tis even difficult to consider them apart.

[2.1.8.5] Concerning all other bodily accomplishments we may observe in general, that whatever in ourselves is either useful, beautiful, or surprising, is an object of pride; and it's contrary, of humility. Now 'tis obvious, that every thing useful, beautiful or surprising, agrees in producing a separate pleasure, and agrees in nothing else. The pleasure, therefore, with the relation to self must be the cause of the passion.

[2.19] Concerning all other bodily accomplishments, we may observe in general, that whatever in ourselves is either useful, beautiful, or surprizing, is an object of pride; and the contrary, of humility. These qualities agree in producing a separate pleasure; and agree in nothing else.

[2.1.8.6] Thus we are vain of the surprising adventures we have met with, the escapes we have made, and dangers we have been expos'd to. Hence the origin of vulgar lying; where men without any interest, and merely out of vanity, heap up a number of extraordinary events, which are either the fictions of their brain, or if true, have at least no connexion with themselves. Their fruitful invention supplies them with a variety of adventures; and

[2.20] We are vain of the surprizing adventures which we have met with, the escapes which we have made, the dangers to which we have been exposed; as well as of our surprising feats of vigour and activity. Hence the origin of vulgar lying; where men, without any interest, and merely out of vanity, heap up a number of extraordinary events, which are either the fictions of their brain; or, if true, have no connexion with themselves. Their

where that talent is wanting, they appropriate such as belong to others, in order to satisfy their vanity.

fruitful invention supplies them with a variety of adventures; and where that talent is wanting, they appropriate such as belong to others, in order to gratify their vanity: For betwixt that passion, and the sentiment of pleasure, there is always a close connexion.

[At this point Hume skipped over three paragraphs of *THN* (viz. 2.1.8.7–9) and moved to *THN* 2.1.9 (*Of external advantages and disadvantages*) and 2.1.10 (*Of property and riches*). Immediately below: *THN* 2.1.9.1, 2.1.9.6–2.1.10.3 is compared to *DP* 2.21–32.]

[2.1.9.1] But tho' pride and humility have the qualities of our mind and body, that is /self\, for their natural and more immediate causes, we find by experience, that there are many other objects, which produce these affections, and that the primary one is, in some measure, obscur'd and lost by the multiplicity of foreign and extrinsic. We found a vanity upon houses, gardens, equipages, as well as upon personal merit and accomplishments; and tho' these external advantages be in themselves widely distant from thought or a person, yet they considerably influence even a passion, which is directed to that as its ultimate object. This happens when external objects acquire any particular relation to ourselves, and are associated or connected with us. A beautiful fish in the ocean, an animal in a desart, and indeed any thing that neither belongs, nor is related to

[2.21] 8. But tho' pride and humility have the qualities of our mind and body, that is, of self, for their natural and more immediate causes; we find by experience, that many other objects produce these affections. We found vanity upon houses, gardens, equipage, and other external objects; as well as upon personal merit and accomplishments. This happens when external objects acquire any particular relation to ourselves, and are associated or connected with us. A beautiful fish in the ocean, a well proportioned animal in a forest, and indeed any thing, which neither belongs nor is related to us, has no manner of influence on our vanity; whatever extraordinary qualities it may be endowed with, and whatever degree of surprize and admiration it may naturally occasion. It must be someway associated with us, in order to touch our pride. Its idea must hang, in

us, has no manner of influence on our vanity, whatever extraordinary qualities it may be endow'd with, and whatever degree of surprize and admiration it may naturally occasion. It must be some way associated with us in order to touch our pride. Its idea must hang in a manner, upon that of ourselves; and the transition from the one to the other must be easy and natural.

a manner, upon that of ourselves; and the transition from one to the other must be easy and natural.

[2.1.9.6] This will appear still more evidently in particular instances. Men are vain of the beauty of their country, of their county, of their parish. Here the idea of beauty plainly produces a pleasure. This pleasure is related to pride. The object or cause of this pleasure is, by the supposition, related to self, or the object of pride. By this double relation of impressions and ideas, a transition is made from the one impression to the other.

[2.22] Men are vain of the beauty either of /their\ country, or /their\ county, or even of /their\ parish. Here the idea of beauty plainly produces a pleasure. This pleasure is related to pride. The object or cause of this pleasure is, by the supposition, related to self, the object of pride. By this double relation of sentiments and ideas, a transition is made from one to the other.

[2.1.9.7] Men are also vain of the temperature of the climate, in which they were born; of the fertility of their native soil; of the goodness of the wines, fruits or victuals, produc'd by it; of the softness or force of their language; with other particulars of that kind. These objects have plainly a reference to the pleasures of the senses, and are originally consider'd as agreeable to the feeling, taste or hearing. How is

[2.23] Men are also vain of the temperature of the climate, in which they are born; of the fertility of their native soil; of the goodness of the wines, fruits, or victuals, produced by it; of the softness or force of their language, with other particulars of that kind. These objects have plainly a reference to the pleasures of the senses, and are originally considered as agreeable to the feeling, taste, or hearing. How could they become causes

it possible they cou'd ever become objects of pride, except by means of that transition above-explain'd?

of pride, except by means of that transition above explained?

[2.1.9.8] There are some, that discover a vanity of an opposite kind, and affect to depreciate their own country, in comparison of those, to which they have travell'd. These persons find, when they are at home, and surrounded with their countrymen, that the strong relation betwixt them and their own nation is shar'd with so many, that 'tis in a manner lost to them; whereas their distant relation to a foreign country, which is form'd by their having seen it and liv'd in it, is augmented by their considering how few there are who have done the same. For this reason they always admire the beauty, utility and rarity of what is abroad, above what is at home.

[2.24] There are some, who discover a vanity of an opposite kind, and affect to depreciate their own country, in comparison of those, to which they have travelled. These persons find, when they are at home, and surrounded with their countrymen, that the strong relation betwixt them and their own nation is shar'd with so many, that it is in a manner lost to them; whereas, that distant relation to a foreign country, which is formed by their having seen it, and lived in it, is augmented by their considering how few have done the same. For this reason, they always admire the beauty, utility, and rarity of what they have met with abroad, above what they find at home.

[2.1.9.9] Since we can be vain of a country, climate or any inanimate object, which bears a relation to us, 'tis no wonder we are vain of the qualities of those, who are connected with us by blood or friendship. Accordingly we find, that the very same qualities, which in ourselves produce pride, produce also in a lesser degree the same affection, when discover'd in persons related to us. The beauty, address, merit, credit and honours of their kindred are carefully

[2.25] Since we can be vain of a country, climate, or any inanimate object, which bears a relation to us; it is no wonder we should be vain of the qualities of those, who are connected with us by blood or friendship. Accordingly we find, that any qualities, which, when belonging to ourself, produce pride, produce also, in a less degree, the same affection, when discovered in persons, related to us. The beauty, address, merit, credit, and honours of their kindred are carefully displayed by

display'd by the proud, as some of the most considerable sources of their vanity.

the proud, and are considerable sources of their vanity.

[2.1.9.10] As we are proud of riches in ourselves, so to satisfy our vanity we desire that every one, who has any connexion with us, shou'd likewise be possest of them, and are asham'd of any one, that is mean or poor, among our friends and relations. For this reason we remove the poor as far from us as possible; and as we cannot prevent poverty in some distant collaterals, and our forefathers are taken to be our nearest relations; upon this account every one affects to be of a good family, and to be descended from a long succession of rich and honourable ancestors.

[2.26] As we are proud of riches in ourselves, we desire, in order to gratify our vanity, that every one, who has any connexion with us, should likewise be possest of them, and are ashamed of such as are mean or poor among our friends and relations. Our forefathers being conceived as our nearest relations; every one naturally affects to be of a good family, and to be descended from a long succession of rich and honourable ancestors.

[2.1.9.11] I have frequently observ'd, that those, who boast of the antiquity of their families, are glad when they can join this circumstance, that their ancestors for many generations have been uninterrupted proprietors of the same portion of land, and that their family has never chang'd its possessions, or been transplanted into any other county or province. I have also observ'd, that 'tis an additional subject of vanity, when they can boast, that these possessions have been transmitted thro' a descent compos'd entirely of males, and that the honours and fortune

[2.27] Those, who boast of the antiquity of their families, are glad when they can join this circumstance, that their ancestors, for many generations, have been uninterrupted proprietors of the /same\ portion of land, and that their family has never changed its possessions, or been transplanted into any other county or province. It is an additional subject of vanity, when they can boast, that these possessions have been transmitted thro' a descent, composed entirely of males, and that the honours and fortune have never past thro' any female. Let us endeavour to explain

have never past thro' any female. Let us endeavour to explain these phænomena by the foregoing system.

[2.1.9.12] 'Tis evident, that when any one boasts of the antiquity of his family, the subjects of his vanity are not merely the extent of time and number of ancestors, but also their riches and credit, which are suppos'd to reflect a lustre on himself on account of his relation to them. He first considers these objects; is affected by them in an agreeable manner; and then returning back to himself, thro' the relation of parent and child, is elevated with the passion of pride, by means of the double relation of impressions and ideas. Since therefore the passion depends on these relations, whatever strengthens any of the relations must also encrease the passion, and whatever weakens the relations must diminish the passion. Now 'tis certain the identity of the possession strengthens the relation of ideas arising from blood and kindred, and conveys the fancy with greater facility from one generation to another, from the remotest ancestors to their posterity, who are both their heirs and their descendants. By this facility the impression is transmitted more entire, and excites a greater degree of pride and vanity.

these phænomena from the foregoing theory.

[2.28] When any one values himself on the antiquity of his family, the subjects of his vanity are not merely the extent of time and number of ancestors (for in that respect all mankind are alike) but these circumstances, joined to the riches and credit of his ancestors, which are supposed to reflect a lustre on himself, upon account of his connexion with them. Since therefore the passion depends on the connexion, whatever strengthens the connexion must also encrease the passion, and whatever weakens the connexion must diminish the passion. But it is evident, that the sameness of the possessions must strengthen the relation of ideas, arising from blood and kindred, and convey the fancy with greater facility from one generation to another; from the remotest ancestors to their posterity, who are both their heirs and their descendants. By this facility, the sentiment is transmitted more entire, and excites a greater degree of pride and vanity.

[2.1.9.13] The case is the same with the transmission of the honours and fortune thro' a succession of males without their passing thro' any female. 'Tis a quality of human nature, which we shall consider [<Note> Part II. sect. 2. <End of note>] afterwards, that the imagination naturally turns to whatever is important and considerable; and where two objects are presented to it, a small and a great one, usually leaves the former, and dwells entirely upon the latter. As in the society of marriage, the male sex has the advantage above the female, the husband first engages our attention; and whether we consider him directly, or reach him by passing thro' related objects, the thought both rests upon him with greater satisfaction, and arrives at him with greater facility than his consort. 'Tis easy to see, that this property must strengthen the child's relation to the father, and weaken that to the mother. For as all relations are nothing but a propensity to pass from one idea to another, whatever strengthens the propensity strengthens the relation; and as we have a stronger propensity to pass from the idea of the children to that of the father, than from the same idea to that of the mother, we ought to regard the former relation as the closer and more considerable. This is the reason why children commonly bear their father's name,

[2.29] The case is the same with the transmission of the honours and fortune, thro' a succession of males, without their passing thro' any female. It is an obvious quality of human nature, that the imagination naturally turns to whatever is important and considerable; and where two objects are presented, a small and a great, it usually leaves the former, and dwells entirely on the latter.

[no ¶] This is the reason, why children commonly bear their father's name, and are esteemed to be of a nobler or meaner birth, according to /his\ family. And tho' the

and are esteem'd to be of nobler or baser birth, according to /his\ family. And tho' the mother shou'd be possest of a superior spirit and genius to the father, as often happens, the /general rule\ prevails, notwithstanding the exception, according to the doctrine above-explain'd. Nay even when a superiority of any kind is so great, or when any other reasons have such an effect, as to make the children rather represent the mother's family than the father's, the general rule still retains such an efficacy that it weakens the relation, and makes a kind of break in the line of ancestors. The imagination runs not along them with facility, nor is able to transfer the honour and credit of the ancestors to their posterity of the same name and family so readily, as when the transition is conformable to the general rules, and passes from father to son, or from brother to brother.

mother should be possest of superior qualities to the father, as often happens, the /general rule\ prevails, notwithstanding the exception, according to the doctrine, which shall be explained afterwards. Nay, even when a superiority of any kind is so great, or when any other reasons have such an effect, as to make the children rather represent the mother's family than the father's, the general rule still retains an efficacy, sufficient to weaken the relation, and make a kind of breach in the line of ancestors. The imagination runs not along them with the same facility, nor is able to transfer the honour and credit of the ancestors to their posterity of the same name and family so readily, as when the transition is conformable to the general rules, and passes thro' the male line, from father to son, or from brother to brother.

[2.1.10.1] But the relation, which is esteem'd the closest, and which of all others produces most commonly the passion of pride, is that of /property\. This relation 'twill be impossible for me fully to explain before I come to treat of justice and the other moral virtues. 'Tis sufficient to observe on this occasion, that property may be defin'd, /such a relation betwixt a person and an object as permits him, but forbids any other, the free use and

[2.30] 9. But /property\, as it gives us the fullest power and authority over any object, is the relation, which has the greatest influence on these passions.

[Explanatory n. 3 in *DP* occurs at this point, beginning in the 1760 edn. It has been incorporated for comparative purposes and collated immediately below, using the 1760 edn. of *DP*:]

That property is a species of /relation\, which produces a

possession of it, without violating the laws of justice and moral equity\. If justice, therefore, be a virtue, which has a natural and original influence on the human mind, property may be look'd upon as a particular species of /causation\; whether we consider the liberty it gives the proprietor to operate as he please upon the object, or the advantages, which he reaps from it. 'Tis the same case, if justice, according to the system of certain philosophers, shou'd be esteem'd an artificial and not a natural virtue. For then honour, and custom, and civil laws supply the place of natural conscience, and produce, in some degree, the same effects. This in the mean time is certain, that the mention of the property naturally carries our thought to the proprietor, and of the proprietor to the property; which being a proof of a perfect relation of ideas is all that is requisite to our present purpose. A relation of ideas, join'd to that of impressions, always produces a transition of affections; and therefore, whenever any pleasure or pain arises from an object, connected with us by property, we may be certain, that either pride or humility must arise from this conjunction of relations; if the foregoing system be solid and satisfactory. And whether it be so or not, we may soon satisfy ourselves by the most cursory view of human life.

connexion between the person and the object is evident: The imagination passes naturally and easily from the consideration of a field to that of the person, whom it belongs to. It may only be asked, how this relation is resolveable into any of those three, viz. /causation, contiguity\ and /resemblance\, which we have affirmed to be the sole connecting principles among ideas. To be the proprietor of any thing is to be the sole person, who, by the laws of society, has a right to dispose of it, and to enjoy the benefit of it. This right has at least a tendency to procure the person the exercise of it; and in fact does commonly procure him that advantage. For rights which had no influence, and never took place, would be no rights at all. Now a person who disposes of an object, and reaps benefit from it, both produces, or may produce, effects on it, and is affected by it. Property therefore is a species of /causation\. It enables the person to produce alterations on the object, and it supposes that his condition is improved and altered by it. It is indeed the relation the most interesting of any, and occurs the most frequently to the mind.

[2.1.10.2] Every thing belonging to a vain man is the best that is any where to be found. His houses, equipage, furniture, cloaths, horses, hounds, excel all others in his conceit; and 'tis easy to observe, that from the least advantage in any of these, he draws a new subject of pride and vanity. His wine, if you'll believe him, has a finer flavour than any other; his cookery is more exquisite; his table more orderly; his servants more expert; the air, in which he lives, more healthful; the soil he cultivates more fertile; his fruits ripen earlier and to greater perfection: Such a thing is remarkable for its novelty; such another for its antiquity: This is the workmanship of a famous artist; that belong'd once to such a prince or great man: All objects, in a word, that are useful, beautiful or surprizing, or are related to such, may, by means of property, give rise to this passion. These agree in giving pleasure, and agree in nothing else. This alone is common to them; and therefore must be the quality that produces the passion, which is their common effect. As every new instance is a new argument, and as the instances are here without number, I may venture to affirm, that scarce any system was ever so fully prov'd by experience, as that which I have here advanc'd.

[2.31] Every thing, belonging to a vain man, is the best that is any where to be found. His houses, equipage, furniture, cloaths, horses, hounds, excel all others in his conceit; and it is easy to observe, that, from the least advantage in any of these, he draws a new subject of pride and vanity. His wine, if you will believe him, has a finer flavour than any other; his cookery is more exquisite; his table more orderly; his servants more expert; the air, in which he lives, more healthful; the soil, which he cultivates, more fertile; his fruits ripen earlier, and in greater perfection: Such a thing is remarkable for its novelty; such another for its antiquity: This is the workmanship of a famous artist; that belonged once to such a prince or great man. All objects, in a word, which are useful, beautiful, or surprizing, or are related to such, may, by means of property, give rise to this passion. These all agree in giving pleasure. This alone is common to them; and therefore must be the quality, that produces the passion, which is their common effect. As every new instance is a new argument, and as the instances are here without number; it would seem, that this theory is sufficiently confirmed by experience.

[2.1.10.3] If the property of any thing, that gives pleasure either by its utility, beauty or novelty, produces also pride by a double relation of impressions and ideas; we need not be surpriz'd, that the power of acquiring this property, shou'd have the same effect....

[2.32] Riches imply the power of acquiring whatever is agreeable; and as they comprehend many particular objects of vanity, necessarily become one of the chief causes of that passion.

[2.33] 10. Our opinions of all kinds are strongly affected by society and sympathy, and it is almost impossible for us to support any principle or sentiment, against the universal consent of every one, with whom we have any friendship or correspondence. But of all our opinions, those, which we form in our own favour; however lofty or presuming; are, at bottom, the frailest, and the most easily shaken by the contradiction and opposition of others. Our great concern, in this case, makes us soon alarmed, and keeps our passions upon the watch: Our consciousness of partiality still makes us dread a mistake: And the very difficulty of judging concerning an object, which is never set at a due distance from us, nor is seen in a proper point of view, makes us hearken anxiously to the opinions of others, who are better qualified to form just opinions concerning us. Hence that strong love of fame,[125] with which all mankind are possest. It is in order to

[125] See *THN* 2.1.11 (*Of the love of fame*) and the comparison immediately below of material from this section. Compare the present paragraph in *DP* (2.33) to *THN* 2.1.11.1.

fix confirm their favourable opinion of themselves, not from any original passion, that they seek the applauses of others. And when a man desires to be praised, it is for the same reason, that a beauty is pleased with surveying herself in a favorable looking-glass, and seeing the reflexion of her own charms.

[At this point Hume omitted the material from *THN* 2.1.10.3 through 2.1.11.10. Immediately below: *THN* 2.1.11.11–13 is compared to *DP* 2.34–40.]

[2.1.11.11] Among these phænomena we may esteem it a very favourable one to our present purpose, that tho' fame in general be agreeable, yet we receive a much greater satisfaction from the approbation of those, whom we ourselves esteem and approve of, than of those, whom we hate and despise. In like manner we are principally mortify'd with the contempt of persons, upon whose judgment we set some value, and are, in a great measure, indifferent about the opinions of the rest of mankind. But if the mind receiv'd from any original instinct a desire of fame, and aversion to infamy, fame and infamy wou'd influence us without distinction; and every opinion, according as it were favourable or unfavourable, wou'd equally excite that desire or aversion. The judgment of a fool is the judgment of another person, as well as that of a

[2.34] Tho' it be difficult in all points of speculation to distinguish a cause, which encreases an effect, from one, which solely produces it; yet in the present case the phænomena seem pretty strong and satisfactory in confirmation of the foregoing principle.

[2.35] We receive a much greater satisfaction from the approbation of those, whom we ourselves esteem and approve of, than of those, whom we contemn and despise.

wise man, and is only inferior in its influence on our own judgment.

[2.1.11.12] We are not only better pleas'd with the approbation of a wise man than with that of a fool, but receive an additional satisfaction from the former, when 'tis obtain'd after a long and intimate acquaintance. This is accounted for after the same manner.

[2.36] When esteem is obtained after a long and intimate acquaintance, it gratifies our vanity in a peculiar manner.

[2.37] The suffrage of those, who are shy and backward in giving praise, is attended with an additional relish and enjoyment, if we can obtain it in our favour.

[2.38] Where a great man is nice in his choice of favourites, every one courts with greater earnestness his countenance and protection.

[2.1.11.13] The praises of others never give us much pleasure, unless they concur with our own opinion, and extol us for those qualities, in which we chiefly excel. . . .

[2.39] Praise never gives us much pleasure, unless it concur with our own opinion, and extol us for those qualities, in which we chiefly excel.

[2.40] These phænomena seem to prove, that the favourable opinions of others are regarded only as authorities, or as confirmations of our own opinion. And if they have more influence in this subject than in any other, it is easily accounted for from the nature of the subject.

[At this point Hume returned to *THN* 2.1.6 (*Limitations of this system*). Immediately below: *THN* 2.1.6.3, 2.1.6.7, and 2.1.6.4, respectively, are compared to *DP* 2.41–3.]

[2.1.6.3] Here then is the first limitation, we must make to our general position, /that every thing related to us, which produces pleasure or pain, produces likewise pride or humility\. There is not only a relation requir'd, but a close one, and a closer than is requir'd to joy.

[2.41] 11. Thus few objects, however related to us, and whatever pleasure they produce, are able to excite a great degree of pride or self-satisfaction; unless they be also obvious to others, and engage the approbation of the spectators. What disposition of mind so desirable as the peaceful, resigned, contented; which readily submits to all the dispensations of providence, and preserves a constant serenity amidst the greatest misfortunes and disappointments? Yet this disposition, tho' acknowledged to be a virtue or excellence, is seldom the foundation of great vanity or self-applause; having no brilliant or exterior lustre, and rather cheering the heart, than animating the behaviour and conversation. The case is the same with many other qualities of the mind, body, or fortune; and this circumstance, as well as the double relations above mentioned, must be admitted to be of consequence in the production of these passions.

[2.1.6.7] 4. The fourth limitation is deriv'd from the inconstancy of the cause of these passions, and from the short duration of its connexion with ourselves. What is casual and inconstant gives but little joy, and less pride. We

[2.42] A second circumstance, which is of consequence in this affair, is the constancy and duration of the object. What is very casual and inconstant, beyond the common course of human affairs, gives little joy, and less pride. We are not much satisfy'd with the thing itself; and are still less apt to feel any new degrees of self-satisfaction upon its account. We foresee and anticipate its change by the imagination; which makes us little satisfy'd with the thing: We compare it to ourselves, whose existence is more durable; by which means its inconstancy appears still greater. It seems ridiculous to infer an excellency in ourselves from an object, which is of so much shorter duration, and attends us during so small a part of our existence. 'Twill be easy to comprehend the reason, why this cause operates not with the same force in joy as in pride; since the idea of self is not so essential to the former passion as to the latter.

are not much satisfied with the thing itself; and are still less apt to feel any new degree of self-satisfaction upon its account. We foresee and anticipate its change; which makes us little satisfied with the thing itself: We compare it to ourselves, whose existence is more durable; by which means its inconstancy appears still greater. It seems ridiculous to make ourselves the object of a passion, on account of a quality or possession, which is of so much shorter duration, and attends us during so small a part of our existence.

[2.1.6.4] 2. The second limitation is, that the agreeable or disagreeable object be not only closely related, but also peculiar to ourselves, or at least common to us with a few persons. 'Tis a quality observable in human nature, and which we shall endeavour to explain afterwards, that every thing, which is often presented, and to which we have been long accustom'd, loses its value in our eyes, and is in a little time despis'd and neglected.

[2.43] A third circumstance, not to be neglected, is, that the objects, in order to produce pride or self-value, must be peculiar to us, or at least, common to us with a few others. The advantages of sun-shine, weather, climate, &c. distinguish us not from any of our companions, and give us no preference or superiority. The comparison, which we are every moment apt to make, presents no inference to our advantage; and we still remain, notwithstanding these enjoyments, on a level with all our friends and acquaintance.

[At this point Hume moved to *THN* 2.1.8.8 (mid-paragraph), in the section *Of beauty and deformity*. Immediately below: *THN* 2.1.8.8–9 is compared to *DP* 2.44–5.]

[2.1.8.8] ... Now as health and sickness vary incessantly to all men, and there is none, who is /solely\ or /certainly\ fix'd in either, these accidental blessings and calamities are in a manner separated from us, and are never consider'd as connected with our being and existence. And that this account is just appears hence, that wherever a malady of any kind is so rooted in our constitution, that we no longer entertain any hopes of recovery, from that moment it becomes an object of humility; as is evident in old men, whom nothing mortifies more than the consideration of their age and infirmities. They endeavour, as long as possible, to conceal their blindness and deafness, their rheums and gouts; nor do they ever confess them without reluctance and uneasiness. And tho' young men are not asham'd of every head-ach or cold they fall into, yet no topic is so proper to mortify human pride, and make us entertain a mean opinion of our nature, than this, that we are every moment of our lives subject to such infirmities. This sufficiently proves that bodily pain and sickness are in themselves proper causes of humility; tho' the custom of estimating every thing by comparison more than by its intrinsic

[2.44] As health and sickness vary incessantly to all men, and there is no one, who is solely or certainly fixed in either; these accidental blessings and calamities are in a manner separated from us, and are not considered as a foundation for vanity or humiliation. But wherever a malady of any kind is so rooted in our constitution, that we no longer entertain any hopes of recovery, from that moment it damps our self-conceit; as is evident in old men, whom nothing mortifies more than the consideration of their age and infirmities. They endeavour, as long as possible, to conceal their blindness and deafness, their rheums and gouts; nor do they ever avow them without reluctance and uneasiness. And tho' young men are not ashamed of every head-ach or cold which they fall into; yet no topic is more proper to mortify human pride, and make us entertain a mean opinion of our nature, than this, that we are every moment of our lives subject to such infirmities. This proves, that bodily pain and sickness are in themselves proper causes of humility; tho' the custom of estimating every thing, by comparison, more than by its intrinsic worth and value, makes us overlook those calamities, which we find incident

worth and value, makes us overlook these calamities, which we find to be incident to every one, and causes us to form an idea of our merit and character independent of them.

to every one, and causes us to form an idea of our merit and character, independent of them.

[2.1.8.9] We are asham'd of such maladies as affect others, and are either dangerous or disagreeable to them. Of the epilepsy; because it gives a horror to every one present: Of the itch; because it is infectious: Of the king's-evil; because it commonly goes to posterity. Men always consider the sentiments of others in their judgment of themselves.

[2.45] We are ashamed of such maladies as affect others, and are either dangerous or disagreeable to them. Of the epilepsy; because it gives a horror to every one present: Of the itch; because it is infectious: Of the king's evil; because it often goes to posterity. Men always consider the sentiments of others in their judgment of themselves.

[At this point Hume continued to draw upon *THN* 2.1.6. Immediately below: *THN* 2.1.6.8–9 is compared to *DP* 2.46–7.]

[2.1.6.8] 5. I may add as a fifth limitation, or rather enlargement of this system, that /general rules\ have a great influence upon pride and humility, as well as on all the other passions. Hence we form a notion of different ranks of men, suitable to the power or riches they are possest of; and this notion we change not upon account of any peculiarities of the health or temper of the persons, which may deprive them of all enjoyment in their possessions. This may be accounted for from the same principles, that explain'd the influence of general rules on the understanding. Custom readily carries us beyond the just bounds in our passions, as well as in our reasonings.

[2.46] A fourth circumstance, which has an influence on these passions, is /general rules\; by which we form a notion of different ranks of men, suitable to the power or riches of which they are possest; and this notion is not changed by any peculiarities of the health or temper of the persons, which may deprive them of all enjoyment in their possessions. Custom readily carries us beyond the just bounds in our passions, as well as in our reasonings.

[2.1.6.9] It may not be amiss to observe on this occasion, that the influence of general rules and maxims on the passions very much contributes to facilitate the effects of all the principles, which we shall explain in the progress of this treatise. For 'tis evident, that if a person full-grown, and of the same nature with ourselves, were on a sudden transported into our world, he wou'd be very much embarrass'd with every object, and wou'd not readily find what degree of love or hatred, pride or humility, or any other passion he ought to attribute to it. The passions are often vary'd by very inconsiderable principles; and these do not always play with a perfect regularity, especially on the first trial. But as custom and practice have brought to light all these principles, and have settled the just value of every thing; this must certainly contribute to the easy production of the passions, and guide us, by means of general establish'd maxims, in the proportions we ought to observe in preferring one object to another. This remark may, perhaps, serve to obviate difficulties, that may arise concerning some causes, which I shall hereafter ascribe to particular passions, and which may be esteem'd too refin'd to operate so universally and certainly, as they are found to do.

[2.47] It may not be amiss to observe on this occasion, that the influence of general rules and maxims on the passions very much contributes to facilitate the effects of all the principles or internal mechanism, which we here explain. For it seems evident, that, if a person full-grown, and of the same nature with ourselves, were on a sudden transported into our world, he would be very much embarrassed with every object, and would not readily determine what degree of love or hatred, of pride or humility, or of any other passion should be excited by it. The passions are often varied by very inconsiderable principles; and these do not always play with perfect regularity, especially on the first tryal. But as custom or practice has brought to light all these principles, and has settled the just value of every thing; this must certainly contribute to the easy production of the passions, and guide us, by means of general established rules, in the proportions, which we ought to observe in prefering one object to another. This remark may, perhaps, serve to obviate difficulties, that may arise concerning some causes, which we here ascribe to particular passions, and which may be esteemed too refined to operate so universally and certainly, as they are found to do.

SECT. III

[3.1] 1. In running over all the causes, which produce the passion of pride or that of humility; it would readily occur, that the same circumstance, if transferred from ourself to another person, would render him the object of love or hatred,[126] esteem or contempt. The virtue, genius, beauty, family, riches, and authority of others beget favourable sentiments in their behalf; and their vice, folly, deformity, poverty, and meanness excite the contrary sentiments. The double relation of impressions and ideas[127] still operates on these passions of love and hatred; as on the former of pride and humility. Whatever gives a separate pleasure or pain, and is related to another person or connected with him, makes him the object of our affection or disgust.

[3.2] Hence too injury or contempt is one of the greatest sources of hatred; services or esteem of friendship.

[3.3] 2. Sometimes a relation to ourself excites affection towards any person. But there is always here implied a relation of sentiments, without which the other relation would have no influence.

[126] See *THN* 2.2 (*Of love and hatred*), esp. 2.2.1 (*Of the objects and causes of love and hatred*). See, further, the comparisons below from this part of *THN*.

[127] The expression 'double relation of impressions and ideas' appears several times in *THN*, sometimes using the examples of both love and hatred and pride and humility. See, e.g., *THN* 2.2.2.9 and 2.2.2.28.

[3.4] A person, who is related to us, or connected with us, by blood, by similitude of fortune, of adventures, profession, or country, soon becomes an agreeable companion to us; because we enter easily and familiarly into his sentiments and conceptions: Nothing is strange or new to us: Our imagination, passing from self, which is ever intimately present to us, runs smoothly along the relation or connexion, and conceives with a full sympathy the person, who is nearly related to self. He renders himself immediately acceptable, and is at once on an easy footing with us: No distance, no reserve has place, where the person introduced is supposed so closely connected with us.

[3.5] Relation has here the same influence as custom or acquaintance, in exciting affection; and from like causes. The ease and satisfaction, which, in both cases, attend our intercourse or commerce, is the source of the friendship.

[At this point Hume moved to *THN* 2.2.6 (*Of benevolence and anger*). Immediately below: *THN* 2.2.6.3 is compared to *DP* 3.6.]

[2.2.6.3] The passions of love and hatred are always follow'd by, or rather conjoin'd with benevolence and anger. 'Tis this conjunction, which chiefly distinguishes these affections from pride and humility.

[3.6] 3. The passions of love and hatred are always followed by, or rather conjoined with, benevolence and anger. It is this conjunction, which chiefly distinguishes these affections from pride and humility.

For pride and humility are pure emotions in the soul, unattended with any desire, and not immediately exciting us to action. But love and hatred are not compleated within themselves, nor rest in that emotion, which they produce, but carry the mind to something farther. Love is always follow'd by a desire of the happiness of the person belov'd, and an aversion to his misery: As hatred produces a desire of the misery and an aversion to the happiness of the person hated. So remarkable a difference betwixt these two sets of passions of pride and humility, love and hatred, which in so many other particulars correspond to each other, merits our attention.

For pride and humility are pure emotions in the soul, unattended with any desire, and not immediately exciting us to action. But love and hatred are not compleat within themselves, nor rest in that emotion, which they produce; but carry the mind to something farther. Love is always followed by a desire of happiness to the person beloved, and an aversion to his misery: As hatred produces a desire of the misery, and an aversion to the happiness of the person hated. These opposite desires seem to be originally and primarily conjoined with the passions of love and hatred. It is a constitution of nature, of which we can give no farther explication.

[3.7] 4. Compassion frequently arises, where there is no preceding esteem or friendship; and compassion is an uneasiness in the sufferings of another. It seems to spring from the intimate and strong conception of his sufferings; and our imagination proceeds by degrees, from the lively idea, to the real feeling of another's misery.[128]

[3.8] Malice and envy also arise in the mind without any preceding hatred or injury; tho' their tendency is exactly the same with that of anger and ill-will. The comparison of ourselves with others seems the source of envy and malice. The

[128] Cf. this paragraph to *THN* 2.2.7 (*Of compassion*), esp. 2.2.7.1.

more unhappy another is, the more happy do we ourselves appear in our own conception.[129]

[3.9] 5. The similar tendency of compassion to that of benevolence, and of envy to anger, forms a very close relation betwixt these two sets of passions; tho' of a different kind from that insisted on above. It is not a resemblance of feeling or sentiment, but a resemblance of tendency or direction. Its effect, however, is the same, in producing an association of passions. Compassion is seldom or never felt without some mixture of tenderness or friendship; and envy is naturally accompanied with anger or ill-will. To desire the happiness of another, from whatever motive, is a good preparative to affection: And to delight in another's misery almost unavoidably begets aversion towards him.[130]

[3.10] Even where interest is the source of our concern, it is commonly attended with the same consequences. A partner is a natural object of friendship; a rival of enmity.[131]

[3.11] 6. Poverty, meanness, disappointment, produce contempt and dislike: But when these misfortunes are very great, or are

[129] Cf. this paragraph to *THN* 2.2.8 (*Of malice and envy*), esp. 2.2.8.6–12.

[130] Cf. this paragraph to *THN* 2.2.7–9 (*Of compassion; Of malice and envy*; and *Of the mixture of benevolence and anger with compassion and malice*).

[131] Cf. this paragraph to *THN* 2.2.9.7–9.

represented to us in very strong colours, they excite compassion, and tenderness, and friendship. How is this contradiction to be accounted for? The poverty and meanness of another, in their common appearance, gives us uneasiness, by a species of imperfect sympathy; and this uneasiness produces aversion or dislike, from the resemblance of sentiment. But when we enter more intimately into another's concerns, and wish for his happiness, as well as feel his misery, friendship or good-will arises, from the similar tendency of the inclinations.[132]

[3.12 first appeared in the 1777 edn. and therefore is omitted here.]

[3.13] 7. In respect, there is a mixture of humility, along with the esteem or affection: In contempt, a mixture of pride.[133]

[3.14] The amorous passion is usually compounded of complacency in beauty, a bodily appetite, and friendship or affection. The close relation of these sentiments is very obvious, as well as their origin from each other, by means of that relation. Were there no other phænomenon to reconcile as to the present theory, this alone, methinks, were sufficient.[134]

[132] Cf. this paragraph to *THN* 2.2.9.10–16.

[133] On these themes of respect and contempt, cf. *THN* 2.2.10 (*Of respect and contempt*). Hume discusses 'a mixture of humility or pride' at *THN* 2.2.10.8.

[134] Cf. *THN* 2.2.11 (*Of the amorous passion, or love betwixt the sexes*). The presentation at *DP* 3.14 may be an abbreviated version of *THN* 2.2.11.1.

SECT. IV

[4.1] 1. The present theory of the passions depends entirely on the double relations of sentiments and ideas, and the mutual assistance, which these relations lend to each other. It may not, therefore, be improper to illustrate these principles by some farther instances.

[4.2] 2. The virtues, talents, accomplishments, and possessions of others make us love and esteem them: Because these objects excite a pleasant sensation, which is related to love; and having also a relation or connexion with the person, this union of ideas forwards the union of sentiments, according to the foregoing reasoning.

[At this point Hume may have taken a sentence from *THN* 2.2.2.11 (*Experiments to confirm this system*). Immediately below: *THN* 2.2.2.11 is compared to *DP* 4.3.]

[2.2.2.11] Fifth Experiment. To give greater authority to these experiments, let us change the situation of affairs as much as possible, and place the passions and objects in all the different positions, of which they are susceptible. Let us suppose, beside the relations above-mention'd, that the person, along with whom I make all these experiments, is closely connected with me either by blood or friendship.

[4.3] But suppose, that the person, whom we love, is also related to us, by blood, country, or friendship; it is evident, that a species of pride must also be excited by his accomplishments and possessions; there being the same double relation, which we have all along insisted on. The person is related to us, or there is an easy transition of thought from him to us; and the sentiments, excited by his advantages and virtues, are agreeable, and consequently related to pride. Accordingly we find, that people are naturally vain of the good qualities or high fortune of their friends and countrymen.

[4.4] 3. But it is observable, that, if we reverse the order of the passions, the same effect does not follow. We pass easily from love and affection to pride and vanity; but not from the latter passions to the former, tho' all the relations be the same. We love not those related to us on account of our own merit; tho' they are naturally vain on account of our merit. What is the reason of this difference? The transition of the imagination to ourselves, from objects related to us, is always very easy; both on account of the relation, which facilitates the transition, and because we there pass from remoter objects to those which are contiguous. But in passing from ourselves to objects, related to us; tho' the former principle forwards the transition of thought, yet the latter opposes it; and consequently there is not the same easy transfusion of passions from pride to love as from love to pride.[135]

[4.5] 4. The virtues, services, and fortune of one man inspire us

[135] Cf. this paragraph to *THN* 2.2.2.13 ff.

readily with esteem and affection for another related to him. The son of our friend is naturally entitled to our friendship: The kindred of a very great man value themselves, and are valued by others, on account of that relation. The force of the double relation is here fully displayed.

[At this point Hume moved to *THN* 2.2.8 (*Of malice and envy*). Immediately below: *THN* 2.2.8.13–19 is compared to *DP* 4.6–11.]

[2.2.8.13] 'Tis worthy of observation concerning that envy, which arises from a superiority in others, that 'Tis not the great disproportion betwixt ourself and another, which produces it; but on the contrary, our proximity. A common soldier bears no such envy to his general as to his sergeant or corporal; nor does an eminent writer meet with so great jealousy in common hackney scriblers, as in authors, that more nearly approach him. It may, indeed, be thought, that the greater the disproportion is, the greater must be the uneasiness from the comparison. But we may consider on the other hand, that the great disproportion cuts off the relation, and either keeps us from comparing ourselves with what is remote from us, or diminishes the effects of the comparison. . . .

[4.6] 5. The following are instances of another kind, where the operation of these principles may still be discovered. Envy arises from a superiority in others; but it is observable, that it is not the great disproportion betwixt us, which excites that passion, but on the contrary, our proximity. A great disproportion cuts off the relation of the ideas, and either keeps us from comparing ourselves with what is remote from us, or diminishes the effects of the comparison.

[2.2.8.15] To confirm this we may observe, that the proximity in the degree of merit is not alone

[4.7] A poet is not apt to envy a philosopher or a poet of a different kind, of a different nation,

sufficient to give rise to envy, but must be assisted by other relations. A poet is not apt to envy a philosopher, or a poet of a different kind, of a different nation, or of a different age. All these differences prevent or weaken the comparison, and consequently the passion.

or of a different age. All these differences, if they do not prevent, at least weaken the comparison, and consequently the passion.

[2.2.8.16] This too is the reason, why all objects appear great or little, merely by a comparison with those of the same species. A mountain neither magnifies nor diminishes a horse in our eyes; but when a /Flemish\ and a /Welsh\ horse are seen together, the one appears greater and the other less, than when view'd apart.

[4.8] This too is the reason, why all objects appear great or little, merely by a comparison with those of the same species. A mountain neither magnifies nor diminishes a horse in our eyes: But when a /Flemish\ and a /Welsh\ horse are seen together, the one appears greater and the other less, than when viewed apart.

[2.2.8.17] From the same principle we may account for that remark of historians, that any party in a civil war always choose to call in a foreign enemy at any hazard rather than submit to their fellow-citizens. /Guicciardin\ applies this remark to the wars in /Italy\, where the relations betwixt the different states are, properly speaking, nothing but of name, language, and contiguity. Yet even these relations, when join'd with superiority, by making the comparison more natural, make it likewise more grievous, and cause men to search for some other superiority, which may be attended with no relation, and by that means may have a less sensible influence on the imagination.

[4.9] From the same principle we may account for that remark of historians, that any party, in a civil war, or even factious division, always choose to call in a foreign enemy at any hazard rather than submit to their fellow-citizens. /Guicciardin\ applies this remark to the wars in /Italy\; where the relations betwixt the different states are, properly speaking, nothing but of name, language, and contiguity. Yet even these relations, when joined with superiority, by making the comparison more natural, make it likewise more grievous, and cause men to search for some other superiority, which may be attended with no relation, and by that means, may have a less sensible influence

The mind quickly perceives its several advantages and disadvantages; and finding its situation to be most uneasy, where superiority is conjoin'd with other relations, seeks its repose as much as possible, by their separation, and by breaking that association of ideas, which renders the comparison so much more natural and efficacious. When it cannot break the association, it feels a stronger desire to remove the superiority; and this is the reason why travellers are commonly so lavish of their praises to the /Chinese\ and /Persians\, at the same time, that they depreciate those neighbouring nations, which may stand upon a foot of rivalship with their native country.

on the imagination. When we cannot break the association, we feel a stronger desire to remove the superiority. This seems to be the reason, why travellers, tho' commonly lavish of their praises to the /Chinese\ and /Persians\, take care to depreciate those neighbouring nations, which may stand upon a footing of rivalship with their native country.

[2.2.8.18] These examples from history and common experience are rich and curious; but we may find parallel ones in the arts, which are no less remarkable. Shou'd an author compose a treatise, of which one part was serious and profound, another light and humorous, every one wou'd condemn so strange a mixture, and wou'd accuse him of the neglect of all rules of art and criticism. These rules of art are founded on the qualities of human nature; and the quality of human nature, which requires a consistency in every performance, is that which renders the mind incapable of passing in a moment from one passion and disposition to a quite

[4.10] 6. The fine arts afford us parallel instances. Should an author compose a treatise, of which one part was serious and profound, another light and humourous; every one would condemn so strange a mixture, and would blame him for the neglect of all rules of art and criticism.

different one. Yet this makes us not blame Mr. /Prior\ for joining his /Alma\ and his /Solomon\ in the same volume; tho' that admirable poet has succeeded perfectly well in the gaiety of the one, as well as in the melancholy of the other. Even supposing the reader shou'd peruse these two compositions without any interval, he wou'd feel little or no difficulty in the change of passions: Why, but because he considers these performances as entirely different, and by this break in the ideas, breaks the progress of the affections, and hinders the one from influencing or contradicting the other?

[no ¶] Yet we accuse not /Prior\ for joining his /Alma\ and /Solomon\ in the same volume; tho' that amiable poet has succeeded perfectly in the gaiety of the one, as well as in the melancholy of the other. Even suppose the reader should peruse these two compositions without any interval, he would feel little or no difficulty in the change of the passions. Why? but because he considers these performances as entirely different; and by that break in the ideas, breaks the progress of the affections, and hinders the one from influencing or contradicting the other.

[2.2.8.19] An heroic and burlesque design, united in one picture, wou'd be monstrous; tho' we place two pictures of so opposite a character in the same chamber, and even close by each other, without any scruple or difficulty.

[4.11] An heroic and burlesque design, united in one picture, would be monstrous; tho' we place two pictures of so opposite a character in the same chamber, and even close together, without any scruple.

[4.12] 7. It needs be no matter of wonder, that the easy transition of the imagination should have such an influence on all the passions. It is this very circumstance, which forms all the relations and connexions amongst objects. We know no real connexion betwixt one thing and another. We know only, that the idea of one thing is associated with that of another, and that the imagination makes an easy transition betwixt them. And as the easy transition of ideas, and that of sentiments mutually assist each other; we might beforehand expect, that this principle must have a mighty influence on all our internal movements and affections. And experience sufficiently confirms the theory.[136]

[At this point Hume moved to *THN* 2.2.2 (*Experiments to confirm this system*). Immediately below: *THN* 2.2.2.8–9 is compared to *DP* 4.13.]

[2.2.2.8] Most fortunately all this reasoning is found to be exactly conformable to experience, and the phænomena of the passions. Suppose I were travelling with a companion thro' a country, to which we are both utter strangers; 'tis evident, that if the prospects be beautiful, the roads agreeable, and the inns commodious, this may put me into good humour both with myself and fellow-traveller. But as we suppose, that this country has no relation either to myself or friend, it can never be the immediate cause of pride or love; and therefore if I found not the passion on some other object, that bears either of us a closer relation, my emotions are rather to be consider'd as the overflowings of an elevate or humane disposition, than as an establish'd passion. The

[4.13] For, not to repeat all the foregoing instances: Suppose, that I were travelling with a companion thro' a country, to which we are both utter strangers; it is evident, that, if the prospects be beautiful, the roads agreeable, and the fields finely cultivated; this may serve to put me in good humour, both with myself and fellow-traveller. But as the country has no connexion with myself or friend, it can never be the immediate cause either of self-value or of regard to him: And therefore, if I found not the passion on some other object, which bears to one of us a closer relation, my emotions are rather to be considered as the overflowings of an elevated or humane disposition, than as an established passion. But supposing the agreeable prospect before us to be surveyed either

[136] Cf. this paragraph to *THN* 2.2.8.20.

case is the same where the object produces uneasiness.

[2.2.2.9] Fourth Experiment. Having found, that neither an object without any relation of ideas or impressions, nor an object, that has only one relation, can ever cause pride or humility, love or hatred; reason alone may convince us, without any farther experiment, that whatever has a double relation must necessarily excite these passions; since 'tis evident they must have some cause. But to leave as little room for doubt as possible, let us renew our experiments, and see whether the event in this case answers our expectation.

from his country-seat or from mine; this new connexion of ideas gives a new direction to the sentiment of pleasure, proceeding from the prospect, and raises the emotion of regard or vanity, according to the nature of the connexion. There is not here, methinks, much room for doubt or difficulty.

[At this point Hume may have pulled words and concepts from parts of *THN* 2.3.3 (*Of the influencing motives of the will*). Immediately below: *THN* 2.3.3.1–2, 8, is compared to *DP* 5.1–2.]

[2.3.3.1] . . . I shall endeavour to prove /first\, that reason alone can never be a motive to any action of the will; and /secondly\, that it can never oppose passion in the direction of the will.

[2.3.3.2] The understanding exerts itself after two different ways, as it judges from demonstration or probability; as it regards the abstract relations of our ideas, or those relations of objects, of which experience only gives us

SECT. V

[5.1] 1. It seems evident, that reason, in a strict sense, as meaning the judgment of truth and falshood, can never, of itself, be any motive to the will, and can have no influence but so far as it touches some *passion* or affection. /Abstract relations\ of ideas are the object of curiosity, not of volition. And /matters of fact\, where they are neither good nor evil, where they neither excite desire nor aversion, are totally indifferent; and whether known or unknown, whether

information. I believe it scarce will be asserted, that the first species of reasoning alone is ever the cause of any action. As it's proper province is the world of ideas, and as the will always places us in that of realities, demonstration and volition seem, upon that account, to be totally remov'd, from each other.

[2.3.3.8] . . . Hence it proceeds, that every action of the mind, which operates with the same calmness and tranquillity, is confounded with reason by all those, who judge of things from the first view and appearance. Now 'tis certain, there are certain calm desires and tendencies, which, tho' they be real passions, produce little emotion in the mind, and are more known by their effects than by the immediate feeling or sensation. These desires are of two kinds; either certain instincts originally implanted in our natures, such as benevolence and resentment, the love of life, and kindness to children; or the general appetite to good, and aversion to evil, consider'd merely as such. When any of these passions are calm, and cause no disorder in the soul, they are very readily taken for the determinations of reason, and are suppos'd to proceed from the same faculty, with that, which judges of truth and falshood. Their nature and principles have been suppos'd

mistaken or rightly apprehended, cannot be regarded as any motive to action.

[5.2] 2. What is commonly, in a popular sense, called reason, and is so much recommended in moral discourses, is nothing but a general and a calm passion, which takes a comprehensive and distant view of its object, and actuates the will, without exciting any sensible emotion. A man, we say, is diligent in his profession from reason; that is, from a calm desire of riches and a fortune. A man adheres to justice from reason; that is, from a calm regard to a character with himself and others.

the same, because their sensations are not evidently different.[137]

[2.3.3.9] Beside these calm passions, which often determine the will, there are certain violent emotions of the same kind, which have likewise a great influence on that faculty. When I receive any injury from another, I often feel a violent passion of resentment, which makes me desire his evil and punishment, independent of all considerations of pleasure and advantage to myself, When I am immediately threaten'd with any grievous ill, my fears, apprehensions, and aversions rise to a great height, and produce a sensible emotion.

[5.3] 3. The same objects, which recommend themselves to reason in this sense of the word, are also the objects of what we call passion, when they are brought near to us, and acquire some other advantages, either of external situation, or congruity to our internal temper; and by that means, excite a turbulent and sensible emotion. Evil, at a great distance, is avoided, we say, from reason: Evil, near at hand, produces aversion, horror, fear, and is the object of passion.[138]

[At this point Hume moved to the end of *THN* 2.3.3 and then began a new section at 2.3.4 (*Of the causes of the violent passions*). Immediately below: *THN* 2.3.3.10–2.3.6.9 is compared to *DP* 5.4–6.19, the end of *DP*. (2.3.5 is entitled *Of the effects of custom*, and 2.3.6 is entitled *Of the influence of the imagination on the passions*.)]

[2.3.3.10] The common error of metaphysicians has lain in ascribing the direction of the will entirely to one of these principles, and supposing the other to have no influence. Men often act knowingly against their interest: For which reason the view of the greatest possible good does not always influence them. Men often

[5.4] 4. The common error of metaphysicians has lain in ascribing the direction of the will entirely to one of these principles, and supposing the other to have no influence. Men often act knowingly against their interest: It is not therefore the view of the greatest possible good which always influences them. Men often

[137] Calm passions are the subject of *THN* 2.3.3.8–10.

[138] Though there are no good matches of words or phrases, *DP* 5.3 may be a recasting of *THN* 2.3.3.9.

counter-act a violent passion in prosecution of their interests and designs: 'Tis not therefore the present uneasiness alone, which determines them. In general we may observe, that both these principles operate on the will; and where they are contrary, that either of them prevails, according to the /general\ character or /present\ disposition of the person. What we call strength of mind, implies the prevalence of the calm passions above the violent; tho' we may easily observe, there is no man so constantly possess'd of this virtue, as never on any occasion to yield to the sollicitations of passion and desire. From these variations of temper proceeds the great difficulty of deciding concerning the actions and resolutions of men, where there is any contrariety of motives and passions.

[2.3.4.1] . . . The same good, when near, will cause a violent passion, which, when remote, produces only a calm one. As this subject belongs very properly to the present question concerning the will, we shall here examine it to the bottom, and shall consider some of those circumstances and situations of objects, which render a passion either calm or violent.

counteract a violent passion, in prosecution of their distant interests and designs: It is not therefore the present uneasiness alone, which determines them. In general, we may observe, that both these principles operate on the will; and where they are contrary, that either of them prevails, according to the general character or present disposition of the person. What we call /strength of mind\ implies the prevalence of the calm passions above the violent; tho' we may easily observe, that there is no person so constantly possest of this virtue, as never, on any occasion, to yield to the sollicitation of violent affections and desires. From these variations of temper proceeds the great difficulty of deciding concerning the future actions and resolutions of men, where there is any contrariety of motives and passions.

SECT. VI

[6.1] 1. We shall here enumerate some of those circumstances, which render a passion calm or violent, which heighten or diminish any emotion.

[2.3.4.2] 'Tis a remarkable property of human nature, that any emotion, which attends a passion, is easily converted into it, tho' in their natures they be originally different from, and even contrary to each other. 'Tis true; in order to make a perfect union among passions, there is always requir'd a double relation of impressions and ideas; nor is one relation sufficient for that purpose. But tho' this be confirm'd by undoubted experience, we must understand it with its proper limitations, and must regard the double relation, as requisite only to make one passion produce another. When two passions are already produc'd by their separate causes, and are both present in the mind, they readily mingle and unite, tho' they have but one relation, and sometimes without any. The predominant passion swallows up the inferior, and converts it into itself. The spirits, when once excited, easily receive a change in their direction; and 'tis natural to imagine this change will come from the prevailing affection. The connexion is in many respects closer betwixt any two passions, than betwixt any passion and indifference.

[6.2] It is a property in human nature, that any emotion, which attends a passion, is easily converted into it; tho' in their natures they be originally different from, and even contrary to each other. It is true, in order to cause a perfect union amongst passions, and make one produce the other, there is always required a double relation according to the theory above delivered. But when two passions are already produced by their separate causes, and are both present in the mind, they readily mingle and unite; tho' they have but one relation, and sometimes without any. The predominant passion swallows up the inferior, and converts it into itself. The spirits, when once excited, easily receive a change in their direction; and it is natural to imagine, that this change will come from the prevailing affection. The connexion is in many cases closer betwixt any two passions, than betwixt any passion and indifference.

[2.3.4.3] When a person is once heartily in love, the little faults and caprice of his mistress, the jealousies and quarrels, to which that commerce is so subject; however

[6.3] When a person is once heartily in love, the little faults and caprices of his mistress, the jealousies and quarrels, to which that commerce is so subject; however unpleasant and related to anger and hatred; are yet found to give additional force to the prevailing passion. 'Tis a common artifice of politicians, when they wou'd affect any person very much by a matter of fact, of which they intend to inform him, first to excite his curiosity; delay as long as possible the satisfying it; and by that means raise his anxiety and impatience to the utmost, before they give him a full insight into the business. They know that his curiosity will precipitate him into the passion they design to raise, and assist the object in its influence on the mind. A soldier advancing to the battle, is naturally inspir'd with courage and confidence, when he thinks on his friends and fellow-soldiers; and is struck with fear and terror, when he reflects on the enemy. Whatever new emotion, therefore, proceeds from the former naturally encreases the courage; as the same emotion, proceeding from the latter, augments the fear; by the relation of ideas, and the conversion of the inferior emotion into the predominant. Hence it is that in martial discipline, the uniformity and lustre of our habit, the regularity of our figures and motions, with all the pomp and majesty of war, encourage ourselves and allies; while the same objects in the enemy strike terror into us, tho' agreeable and beautiful in themselves.

unpleasant they be, and rather connected with anger and hatred; are yet found, in many instances, to give additional force to the prevailing passion. It is a common artifice of politicians, when they would affect any person very much by a matter of fact, of which they intend to inform him, first to excite his curiosity; delay as long as possible the satisfying it; and by that means raise his anxiety and impatience to the utmost, before they give him a full insight into the business. They know, that his curiosity will precipitate him into the passion, which they purpose to raise, and will assist the object in its influence on the mind. A soldier, advancing to battle, is naturally inspired with courage and confidence, when he thinks on his friends and fellow-soldiers; and is struck with fear and terror, when he reflects on the enemy. Whatever new emotion, therefore, proceeds from the former naturally encreases the courage; as the same emotion proceeding from the latter, augments the fear. Hence in martial discipline, the uniformity and lustre of habit, the regularity of figures and motions, with all the pomp and majesty of war, encourage ourselves and our allies; while the same objects in the enemy strike terror into us, tho' agreeable and beautiful in themselves.

[6.4] Hope is, in itself, an agreeable passion, and allied to friendship and benevolence; yet is it able sometimes to blow up anger, when that is the predominant passion. /Spes addita suscitat iras\. Virg.

[2.3.4.4] Since passions, however independent, are naturally transfus'd into each other, if they are both present at the same time; it follows, that when good or evil is plac'd in such a situation, as to cause any particular emotion, beside its direct passion of desire or aversion, that latter passion must acquire new force and violence.

[2.3.4.5] This happens, among other cases, whenever any object excites contrary passions. For 'tis observable that an opposition of passions commonly causes a new emotion in the spirits, and produces more disorder, than the concurrence of any two affections of equal force. This new emotion is easily converted into the predominant passion, and encreases its violence, beyond the pitch it wou'd have arriv'd at had it met with no opposition. Hence we naturally desire what is forbid, and take a pleasure in performing actions, merely because they are unlawful. The notion of duty, when opposite to the passions, is seldom able to overcome them; and when it fails of that effect, is apt rather

[6.5] 2. Since passions, however independent, are naturally transfused into each other, if they are both present at the same time; it follows, that when good or evil is placed in such a situation as to cause any particular emotion, besides its direct passion of desire or aversion, that latter passion must acquire new force and violence.

[6.6] 3. This often happens, when any object excites contrary passions. For it is observable, that an opposition of passions commonly causes a new emotion in the spirits and produces more disorder than the concurrence of any two affections of equal force. This new emotion is easily converted into the predominant passion, and in many instances, is observed to encrease its violence, beyond the pitch, at which it would have arrived, had it met with no opposition. Hence we naturally desire what is forbid, and often take a pleasure in performing actions, merely because they are unlawful. The notion of duty, when opposite to the passions, is not always able to overcome them; and when it

to encrease them, by producing an opposition in our motives and principles.

fails of that influence, is apt rather to encrease and irritate them, by producing an opposition in our motives and principles.

[2.3.4.6] The same effect follows whether the opposition arises from internal motives or external obstacles. The passion commonly acquires new force and violence in both cases. The efforts, which the mind makes to surmount the obstacle, excite the spirits and inliven the passion.

[6.7] 4. The same effect follows, whether the opposition arises from internal motives or external obstacles. The passion commonly acquires new force in both cases. The efforts, which the mind makes to surmount the obstacle, excite the spirits, and enliven the passion.

[2.3.4.7] Uncertainty has the same influence as opposition. The agitation of the thought; the quick turns it makes from one view to another; the variety of passions, which succeed each other, according to the different views: All these produce an agitation in the mind, and transfuse themselves into the predominant passion.

[6.8] 5. Uncertainty has the same effect as opposition. The agitation of the thought, the quick turns which it makes from one view to another, the variety of passions, which succeed each other, according to the different views: All these produce an agitation in the mind; and this agitation transfuses itself into the predominant passion.

[2.3.4.8] There is not in my opinion any other natural cause, why security diminishes the passions, than because it removes that uncertainty, which encreases them. The mind, when left to itself, immediately languishes; and in order to preserve its ardour, must be every moment supported by a new flow of passion. For the same reason, despair, tho' contrary to security, has a like influence.

[6.9] Security, on the contrary, diminishes the passions. The mind, when left to itself, immediately languishes; and in order to preserve its ardour, must be every moment supported by a new flow of passion. For the same reason, despair, tho' contrary to security, has a like influence.

[2.3.4.9] 'Tis certain nothing more powerfully animates any affection, than to conceal some part of its object by throwing it into a kind of shade, which at the same time that it shews enough to pre-possess us in favour of the object, leaves still some work for the imagination. Besides that obscurity is always attended with a kind of uncertainty; the effort, which the fancy makes to compleat the idea, rouzes the spirits, and gives an additional force to the passion.

[6.10] 6. Nothing more powerfully excites any affection than to conceal some part of its object, by throwing it into a kind of shade, which, at the same time, that it shows enough to prepossess us in favour of the object, leaves still some work for the imagination. Besides, that obscurity is always attended with a kind of uncertainty; the effort, which the fancy makes to compleat the idea, rouzes the spirits, and gives an additional force to the passion.

[2.3.4.10] As despair and security, tho' contrary to each other, produce the same effects; so absence is observ'd to have contrary effects, and in different circumstances either encreases or diminishes our affections. The /Duc de la Rochefoucault\ has very well observ'd, that absence destroys weak passions, but encreases strong; as the wind extinguishes a candle, but blows up a fire. Long absence naturally weakens our idea, and diminishes the passion: But where the idea is so strong and lively as to support itself, the uneasiness, arising from absence, encreases the passion, and gives it new force and violence. . . .

[6.11] 7. As despair and security, tho' contrary, produce the same effects; so absence is observed to have contrary effects, and in different circumstances, either encreases or diminishes our affection. /Rochefoucault\ has very well remarked, that absence destroys weak passions, but encreases strong; as the wind extinguishes a candle, but blows up a fire. Long absence naturally weakens our idea, and diminishes the passion: But where the passion is so strong and lively as to support itself, the uneasiness, arising from absence, encreases the passion, and gives it new force and influence.

[2.3.5.2] When the soul applies itself to the performance of any action, or the conception of any object, to which it is

[6.12] 8. When the soul applies itself to the performance of any action, or the conception of any object, to which it is not accustom'd, there is a certain unpliableness in the faculties, and a difficulty of the spirit's moving in their new direction. As this difficulty excites the spirits, 'tis the source of wonder, surprize, and of all the emotions, which arise from novelty; and is in itself very agreeable, like every thing, which inlivens the mind to a moderate degree. But tho' surprize be agreeable in itself, yet as it puts the spirits in agitation, it not only augments our agreeable affections, but also our painful, according to the foregoing principle, /that every emotion, which precedes or attends a passion, is easily converted into it\. Hence every thing, that is new, is most affecting, and gives us either more pleasure or pain, than what, strictly speaking, naturally belongs to it. When it often returns upon us, the novelty wears off; the passions subside; the hurry of the spirits is over; and we survey the objects with greater tranquillity.

[2.3.6.1] 'Tis remarkable, that the imagination and affections have a close union together, and that nothing, which affects the former, can be entirely indifferent to the latter. . . .

[2.3.6.2] Any pleasure, with which we are acquainted, affects us more than any other, which we own to be superior, but of whose nature we are wholly ignorant. Of

not accustomed, there is a certain unpliableness in the faculties, and a difficulty of the spirits moving in their new direction. As this difficulty excites the spirits, it is the source of wonder, surprize, and of all the emotions, which arise from novelty; and is in itself very agreeable, like every thing, which inlivens the mind to a moderate degree. But tho' surprise be agreeable in itself, yet as it puts the spirits in agitation, it not only augments our agreeable affections, but also our painful, according to the foregoing principle. Hence every thing, that is new, is most affecting, and gives us either more pleasure or pain, than what, strictly speaking, should naturally follow from it. When it often returns upon us, the novelty wears off; the passions subside; the hurry of the spirits is over; and we survey the object with greater tranquillity.

[6.13] 9. The imagination and affections have a close union together. The vivacity of the former, gives force to the latter. Hence the prospect of any pleasure, with which we are acquainted, affects us more than any other pleasure, which we may own superior, but of whose nature we are /wholly\ ignorant. Of the one we can form a particular and determinate idea: The other, we

the one we can form a particular and determinate idea: The other we conceive under the general notion of pleasure; . . .

conceive under the general notion of pleasure.

[2.3.6.5] Any satisfaction, which we lately enjoy'd, and of which the memory is fresh and recent, operates on the will with more violence, than another of which the traces are decay'd, and almost obliterated. From whence does this proceed, but that the memory in the first case assists the fancy, and gives an additional force and vigour to its conceptions? The image of the past pleasure being strong and violent, bestows these qualities on the idea of the future pleasure, which is connected with it by the relation of resemblance.

[6.14] Any satisfaction, which we lately enjoyed, and of which the memory is fresh and recent, operates on the will with more violence, than another of which the traces are decayed and almost obliterated.

[2.3.6.6] A pleasure, which is suitable to the way of life, in which we are engag'd, excites more our desires and appetites than another, which is foreign to it. This phænomenon may be explain'd from the same principle.

[6.15] A pleasure, which is suitable to the way of life, in which we are engaged, excites more our desires and appetites than another, which is foreign to it.

[2.3.6.7] Nothing is more capable of infusing any passion into the mind, than eloquence, by which objects are represented in their strongest and most lively colours. We may of ourselves acknowledge, that such an object is valuable, and such another odious; but 'till an orator excites the imagination, and gives force to these ideas, they may

[6.16] Nothing is more capable of infusing any passion into the mind, than eloquence, by which objects are represented in the strongest and most lively colours.

have but a feeble influence either on the will or the affections.

[2.3.6.8] But eloquence is not always necessary. The bare opinion of another, especially when inforc'd with passion, will cause an idea of good or evil to have an influence upon us, which wou'd otherwise have been entirely neglected. This proceeds from the principle of sympathy or communication; and sympathy, as I have already observ'd, is nothing but the conversion of an idea into an impression by the force of imagination.

[no ¶] The bare opinion of another, especially when inforced with passion, will cause an idea to have an influence upon us, tho' that idea might otherwise have been entirely neglected.

[2.3.6.9] 'Tis remarkable, that lively passions commonly attend a lively imagination. In this respect, as well as others, the force of the passion depends as much on the temper of the person, as the nature or situation of the object.

[6.17] It is remarkable, that lively passions commonly attend a lively imagination. In this respect, as well as others, the force of the passion depends as much on the temper of the person, as on the nature or situation of the object.

[6.18] What is distant, either in place or time, has not equal influence with what is near and contiguous.[139]

[6.19] I pretend not here to have exhausted this subject. It is sufficient for my purpose, if I have made it appear, that, in the production and conduct of the passions, there is a certain regular mechanism, which is susceptible of as accurate a disquisition, as the laws of motion, optics,

[139] See *THN* 2.3.7 (*Of contiguity and distance in space and time*).

hydrostatics, or any part of natural philosophy.

Notes

The 1757 notes are shown in the text as compared above. Note 3, found at 2.30 of the critical edition of *DP*, occurred only in those editions published from 1760 to 1777. This note bears a strong resemblance to *THN* 2.1.10.1, to which it is collated above (at *THN* 2.1.10.1/*DP* 2.30), using the text of the 1760 edn. of *DP*. Note 4 in editions of *DP* published from 1760 to 1777, as well as in the present critical edition, was note 3 in the 1757 edn. This note is compared immediately below with a fragment of *THN* 2.2.12 (*Of the love and hatred of animals*), which Hume may have consulted when writing this note.

[2.2.12.5] The affection of parents to their young proceeds from a peculiar instinct in animals, as well as in our species.	[Note 4] The affection of parents to children seems founded on an original instinct. The affection towards other relations depends on the principles here explained.

6. REVIEWS OF *FOUR DISSERTATIONS*

Hume's philosophy was critically examined during his lifetime in books, monographs, reviews, notices, pamphlets, and articles. *Four Dissertations* roused even more interest among reviewers than had his earlier philosophical works. In this section reviews of *Four Dissertations* as a whole are featured. Assessment of *A Dissertation on the Passions* appeared exclusively in these reviews; this work received little notice after the British reviews (1757) and the French translation (1759). The *Natural History*, by contrast, received extensive attention. Reviews and commentary concerned exclusively with this dissertation are the subject of the next section (section 7).

In both sections attention is restricted to those commentators who assessed these two dissertations in English-language publications during Hume's lifetime (though it is worth noting that the markedly critical préface to the 1767 French edition of Hume's writings entitled *Pensées philosophiques, morales, critiques, littéraires et politiques de M. Hume* contains a revealing and judgemental treatment of Hume's personal qualities and philosophy by one French source[140]). Hume's eighteenth-century reception in countries such as France, Germany, the Netherlands, and Italy is still under investigation.[141]

Rose's Review in The Monthly Review (1757)

William Rose (1719–86) wrote a review of *Four Dissertations* that was published anonymously in February 1757.[142] Rose praises Hume for 'a delicacy of sentiment, an original turn of thought, a perspicuity, and often an elegance, of language, that cannot but recommend his writings to every Reader of taste'. However, Rose laments

[140] This preface discusses why *The Natural History of Religion* and four sections of *EHU* (4 (almost all paragraphs), 9, 10, and 11) were excluded from the edition: 'In this preface we . . . have omitted all that could bring doubt into the mind and trouble the conscience. The essays on the *Natural History of Religion* and *On Miracles* have been totally suppressed, and we have adopted only that which appears to conform to Christian morality. . . . The quarrel that has arisen between J. J. Rousseau and Mr. Hume is one of the reasons we have undertaken this edition. . . . By presenting the moral theory of Mr. Hume to the eyes of the public, it can compare this theory with that of Mr. Rousseau and then judge which of these two is the guilty party' (pp. iii, x; see also p. 26 n.).

The front matter in other French editions is occasionally illuminating. Also of interest, regarding the reception in France, are letters between Hume and Charles de Brosses and between de Brosses and Diderot regarding Hume's *Natural History of Religion* and de Brosses's *Le cultee des dieux fétiches* (1760). This last argues that fetishism was the first religion. The third part of the work contains a comparison of Hume's views with those of de Brosses. Diderot called Hume's book to de Brosses's attention and engaged in active correspondence about its contents. Hume later corresponded with de Brosses. Details of this congenial correspondence and de Brosses's synthesis of Hume's work are examined in three articles by Madeleine David: 'Lettres inédites de Diderot et de Hume écrites de 1755 à 1763 au président de Brosses'; 'Histoire des religions et philosophie au XVIIIe siècle'; and 'Le Président de Brosses historien des religions et philosophie'.

[141] For examples, see the evidence of the reception in German reviews and books (1739–1800) in M. Kuehn, 'Hume in the *Göttingische Anzeigen*', and G. Gawlick and L. Kreimendahl, *Hume in der deutschen Aufklärung*. For some French reactions to the material on religion in *Four Dissertations*, see Frank Manuel, *The Eighteenth Century Confronts the Gods*, 168–83.

[142] Rose, Review of *Four Dissertations, Monthly Review*, 16 (Feb. 1957), 122–39. All parenthetical page references are to this source. The Reference List contains additional bibliographical information on this and other reviews discussed below.

that such a genius should employ his abilities in the manner he frequently does. In his attacks upon the religion of his country, he acts not the part of an open and generous enemy, but endeavours to weaken its authority by oblique hints, and artful insinuations. In this view his works merit little, if any, regard; and few Readers, of just discernment ... will envy him any honours his acuteness, or elegance, can possibly obtain, when they are only employed in filling the mind with the uncomfortable fluctuations of scepticism, and the gloom of infidelity. (p. 122)

Rose presents several excerpts from and summaries of the dissertations. Noting that the *Natural History* 'takes up near half the volume' (p. 131), Rose devotes eleven of his eighteen pages (pp. 122–33) to this dissertation, concentrating on the following parts: Introduction, 9.6, 11.2–5, 12.6, and 15.1–13. Rose offers the opinion that the *Natural History* 'abounds with shrewd reflections, and just observations, upon human nature: mixed with a considerable portion of that sceptical spirit, which is so apparent in all his works; and with some insinuations, artfully couched, against the Christian religion' (p. 133).

Rose dedicates a ten-line paragraph to 'Of the Passions' (pp. 133–4). He reports that Hume's design is to show that the passions can be explained in terms of a 'regular mechanism' and to defend the theory of the 'double relations of sentiments and ideas'. He assesses the essay as 'extremely ingenious' and deserving of careful perusal. There is no negative appraisal.

Rose also devotes a paragraph to 'Of Tragedy', and five pages to 'Of the Standard of Taste' (pp. 134–9). The latter he also finds an 'ingenious dissertation'.

Anonymous Review in The Critical Review (1757)

An extensive review of *Four Dissertations* appeared almost immediately upon its publication in February 1757.[143] The reviewer begins with the *Natural History*, noting that 'the ingenious Mr. Hume' has a strong power of pleasing and persuading. The reader is warned 'to be [on] guard, to separate the truth of what is advanced from the manner of delivering it', because Hume has the 'power to mislead and betray' (pp. 97–8). There follows a detailed summary of the contents of this dissertation. The reviewer is not much concerned with evaluating the work, though there is an occasional negative comment, such as 'Mr. *Hume*'s remark bears perhaps a little too hard on the orthodox, and devotee'. There is also the occasional positive

[143] Anonymous, two-part review of *Four Dissertations*: *Critical Review*, 3 (Feb. 1757), 97–107 (Mar. 1957), 209–16. All parenthetical references are to pages in this source.

comment, such as 'The truth of this observation is evident . . . but perhaps never better express'd than by our author' (pp. 103, 106).

The reviewer concludes Part 1 of the review by observing that, despite many 'remarks pertinent and just, we do not meet with that novelty, or force of argument which we expected from an author of such distinguished abilities: Nor can we indeed perceive *quo tendit*, to what use or purpose this dissertation [*NHR*] was written. A deficiency in our author's arrangement of his notions, and a want of method and connection is also visible throughout the whole, occasioned perhaps by some castration of the original.' (The latter comment may be a knowing allusion to the 1756–7 controversy over the publishing of *NHR*, discussed above and below on pp. xxii–xxvii, cxxiii–cxxvi.)

Regarding 'Of the Passions', the reviewer proposes a specific interpretation (by contrast to the paraphrase-style utilized for the *Natural History*). The opening comment is that 'Mr. Hume's second dissertation . . . was written, (as we are informed by himself at the conclusion of it) with a design to prove, that "in the production and conduct of the passions there is a certain regular mechanism"'. The reviewer judges that this is 'an assertion our readers will perhaps consider as rather paradoxical, and call upon Mr. *Hume* for much more convincing proofs than any he has produced in the essay before us, which in our opinion contains nothing new or entertaining on the occasion' (p. 209).

There follow several passages quoted from *A Dissertation on the Passions* (1.7–10, 1.12, 2.6–8, 2.15, 2.36–9, 4.8). The passages are presented as 'specimens' of Hume's manner of treating the subject. The reviewer finds that on the topics of the causes of pride and humility and the connection to pleasure and uneasiness, 'we must allow, in that case, that the present theory is fully proved and ascertained. The double relation of ideas and sentiments will be acknowledged incontestable. Our author is pretty diffuse in his discussion of this point. What he says of the vain man has more of truth than novelty in it' (p. 211).

In a general conclusion the reviewer insists that Hume's ideas were developed long ago: '[S]urely there need [be] no Mr. *Hume*, the great philosopher, to acquaint us with discoveries made so long ago, and so often repeated. This whole dissertation . . . appears to us very trite and superficial; and unworthy of so eminent a writer' (p. 212). The reviewer also expresses disappointment with 'Of Tragedy': 'Instead of an essay on the construction of several parts of the drama which we expected, we meet only with a cold philosophical enquiry' (p. 212). The fourth dissertation is judged 'almost' as disappointing as the third. Hume is said to conclude 'with the philosopher of old, that all we know is, that we know nothing' (p. 213). Nonetheless, the reviewer summons up a positive appraisal of the fourth dissertation, judging Hume a man who 'knows what a delicate taste is. . . . This short dissertation is indeed in our opinion much the best of the four' (p. 214).

Anonymous Review in The Literary Magazine (1757)

A third review of *Four Dissertations* appeared in December 1757.[144] The review begins positively: 'The public curiosity will no doubt be greatly excited by these essays, from a gentleman who has before contributed both to their pleasure and instruction' (p. 32). Nonetheless, the reviewer judges that 'The Natural History of Religion' offers 'few or no positions, that are not to be found in other writers on this subject'. He isolates for close examination Hume's theses about polytheism as the natural religion of the unenlightened heathen world. The reviewer suggests that although Hume 'has exhibited in a very probable light' the history of the operations of the mind (for example, hopes and fears) in the development of religion, it was 'to be wished, that his talents had been employed on all occasions to serve the cause of religion' (p. 32).

This short treatment of the first dissertation is followed by a longer discussion of the dissertation 'Of the Passions'. The reviewer finds the work 'clear and perspicuous' with an elegant style, but again does 'not perceive any thing new' (p. 32). Lengthy passages are quoted from *DP* 1.7–10, 2.6–8 to illustrate the nature of Hume's 'philosophy and stile' (p. 33). No critical commentary follows, but the reviewer does venture the opinion that 'there is one new position in this Dissertation, which appears somewhat surprising from one, who in general seems to think with precision'. This uncommon passage is one in which Hume notes that 'no one has ever been able to tell precisely, what *wit* is' (*DP* 2.16). The reviewer disputes the claim, holding that wit has long been 'very justly defined'. He offers a crude definition, which proclaims wit to be a matter of 'judgment and not taste'. The reviewer takes this position to be contrary to Hume's (pp. 33–4).

Hume's third dissertation, on tragedy, is also said to be founded upon 'principles that have been already subscribed to by many elegant *English* writers' (p. 34); and the fourth dissertation, on the standard of taste, is praised as 'elegant and entertaining', though judged disappointing in not providing a more 'fixed and immutable' standard of taste (p. 35).

The review concludes, abruptly, with a generous overall assessment of the volume:

[144] Anonymous, Review of *Four Dissertations, Literary Magazine*, 2 (Dec. 1757), 32–6. All parenthetical references are to pages in this source.

Upon the whole, the literary world is greatly indebted to Mr. *Hume*: he thinks more for himself than almost any of his cotemporaries; and commonly with elegance and precision; insomuch that he bids very fair to be considered by posterity among the few classics of this age; notwithstanding his *Latitudinarian* sentiments in religious matters. (p. 36)

This review is the last of the appraisals in English-language publications during Hume's lifetime of his dissertation on the passions.

7. THE RECEPTION OF *THE NATURAL HISTORY OF RELIGION*

Additional commentary on the *Natural History* appeared in books, pamphlets, and journals. It was criticized for its appeal to imagination rather than reason, for holding that polytheism is the origin of religion, for interpreting the ancients improperly, and for suggesting that mythology is tantamount to real religious belief.

This section, like its predecessor, is confined to sources published in English during Hume's lifetime.

A Postscript on Mr. Hume's Natural History of Religion, in Caleb Fleming's Three Questions Resolved (1757)[145]

An anonymously published monograph, written by Caleb Fleming (1698–1779), contains forty-nine pages devoted to three questions: What is religion?; What is the Christian religion?; and What is the Christian Catholic Church? A six-page postscript ('P.S.') is devoted entirely to Hume's *Natural History of Religion*. The author assumes (though both works were published in 1757) that the reader has a general familiarity with *Four Dissertations*, which is neither cited nor mentioned by name in the review.

The author begins with a summary of Hume's search for principles of human nature and his views on the historical transition from polytheism to monotheism. The author counters that 'If the history of *Moses* be authentic, men degenerated from true theism to idolatry.... The primary religion of the new world, peopled by *Noah* and his family, surely could not be polytheism and idolatry' (p. 51). However, when addressing the subject of the nature of true theism, the author seems to accept Hume's 'charming

[145] Caleb Fleming, *Three Questions Resolved ... Wherein Popery is Proved to Have no Claim ... With A Postscript on Mr.* Hume*'s Natural History of Religion*, pp. 50–6 (the title of the postscript appears only on the title-page of the larger work). All parenthetical page references are to this source.

description' centred on monotheism and to construe it and other descriptions as drawn from 'genuine christianity'. The author quotes several passages from the *Natural History* (Introduction, 1.1, 6.12, and 9.1) to support this interpretation (p. 51).

The author then discusses 'some very uncommon observations' made in Hume's dissertation: (1) 'religion and idolatry have one and the same origin' (*NHR* 8.1); (2) there is (or was) a universal polytheism, and yet also a tendency to rise from polytheism to theism (*NHR* 10); and (3) 'the origin of idolatry or polytheism' is in 'the active imagination of men' (*NHR* 8.1). 'But in truth', the author says, Hume's 'idea of the religion of mankind, does not intend more, than the superstition which has arisen from depravity.' After extensive quotation (drawn from *NHR* 11.3, 13.6, 14.5, and 14.8), the author implies that Hume's arguments, properly conceived, show that superstition is not a primary principle in human nature, and that 'the principles of genuine theism and religion, must have their origin in human nature' (pp. 52–5).

With this interpretation in place, the writer offers 'the following conclusions':

Mr. *Hume*'s fundamental principles are manifestly wrong. He has called the superstition of the world, *a natural history of the religion of mankind*. He has affirmed a natural tendency in man to rise out of idolatry into religion. He has strangely declared, that religion and superstition, theism and polytheism have one and the same origin; and this no better than the imagination.... Notwithstanding these sophisms, Mr. *Hume* has finely exposed superstition and popery: professeth himself an advocate of pure theism. And so far as he is a theist, he cannot be an enemy to genuine christianity. (p. 56)

William Warburton [and Richard Hurd], Remarks on Mr. David Hume's Essay on the Natural History of Religion (1757)

The assessments of Hume's work in *Four Dissertations* reported thus far were overshadowed by a detailed and impassioned critique in a lengthy pamphlet written primarily by William Warburton (1698–1779).[146] Warburton was an influential but combative figure who directed criticism at Bayle, Chubb, Collins, Bolingbroke, Crousaz, Hume, Mandeville, Tindal,

[146] Warburton (and Hurd), *Remarks on Mr. David Hume's Essay on the Natural History of Religion*, published anonymously. According to a letter of the Revd Thomas Birch [to Sir David Dalrymple], dated 27 Sept. 1757, 'Mr. Hume's Natural History of Religion has had no notice taken of it here [i.e. London] except in a pamphlet containing a few Remarks upon it address'd to Dr. Warburton' (Beinecke Library, Yale University, Osborn files, folder 1290).

Toland, Voltaire, and many others. Warburton's anonymously published critique was prepared from comments he had jotted in the margin of Hume's dissertation. Warburton's associate, friend, and biographer, the Revd Richard Hurd (1720–1808), polished and augmented these marginalia for anonymous publication.[147]

Warburton's commentary is entitled *Remarks*, because it is organized as twenty-one 'Remarks' on every major dimension of Hume's dissertation. In Warburton's estimate, Hume is inconsistent and insincere. He has distorted the sources he used in his citations and has ignored the most vital periods in the history of religion and the most substantive features of religion. The critique is caustic and scornful.

Warburton maintains that Hume's purpose in the *Natural History* is 'to establish Naturalism on the ruins of Religion': 'The sum of all' that Hume teaches is 'That that Religion, of which he professes himself a follower, and which has its *foundation in Reason*, is *Naturalism*: and, That that Religion which *all mankind* follow . . . is nothing but *Superstition* and *Fanaticism*, having *its origin in human Nature*; that is, in the imagination and the passions only.' 'Naturalism', for Warburton, implies deism: namely, 'the belief of a God, the Creator and Physical Preserver, but not moral Governor of the World'.[148] From this perspective, Hume lacks a genuine theism and true religion. However, Warburton holds that Hume is closer to real religion in *NHR* than he was in *An Enquiry concerning Human Understanding*, Section 11, where he was 'in the dregs of Atheism when he wrote his Epicurean arguments against the being of a God. Sometime or other he may come to his senses. A few animadversions on the *Essay* before us may help him forwards.'[149]

Warburton judges that Hume is writing a *history* and insists that this 'history' (1) excludes all the historical evidence that supports genuine religion, and (2) offers little in the way of historical evidence to support its anti-religious views. The reason behind the first assertion (1) is that because Hume lacks Christian conviction, he does not accept biblical history, which is the primary source of evidence to counter his theses. Instead of examining real religion—which '*reforms men's lives, purifies their hearts, inforces moral*

[147] Hurd reported the relevant history in *A Discourse, By Way of General Preface to the Quarto Edition of Bishop Warburton's Works; containing some Account of the Life, Writings, and Character of the Author*, 78–82. See n. 157 below.

[148] Though 'naturalism' here implies deism, it had no single meaning in the eighteenth century (and may have meant more than deism even to Warburton). In Richard Baxter's earlier use of the term, it refers principally to 'Heathens and Idolaters', not to deists (*The Reasons of the Christian Religion* 2.2, 'Of the several Religions which are in the world').

[149] Warburton, *Remarks*, Remarks 1 and 3.

duties, and secures obedience to the laws of the civil magistrate'—Hume tends to look at superstitious and fanatical beliefs and at that '*adulterate species of Religion, which inflames faction, animates sedition, and prompts rebellion*'. Warburton's second general finding (2) is that Hume should either reason a priori (from the nature of things) to support his historical claims—such as the claim that polytheism pre-dates theism—or reason a posteriori from 'antient testimony' that is powerful enough to refute biblical history. However, Warburton judges, 'Our honest Philosopher does neither. He insists chiefly on antient testimony, but is as silent concerning the Bible as if no such book had ever been written.'[150]

Warburton surmises that Hume's aversion to miracles and revelation explains the positions he takes on divine providence and pagan beliefs. Here is a typical Warburton appraisal:

> 'The Getes' (says our Historian [Hume]) 'affirmed Zamolxis their Deity . . . and asserted the worship of all other nations to be addressed to fictions and chimæras' [*NHR* 7.3]. This assertion contradicts all Antiquity, as well as the very nature and genius of Paganism itself. But what of that? It served . . . the purpose to which all his patriot endeavours tend, the discredit of Revelation.[151]

Warburton submits that Hume has elevated the importance of *ceremonies* and *dogmas*, while degrading *faith*. This emphasis results in an improper treatment of similarities and differences between religions such as the Jewish and Egyptian faiths. Since Hume sees the differences entirely in terms of 'frivolous' dogmas, his analysis is 'nothing more than this, whether mankind should fall down before a dog, a cat, or a monkey, or whether he should worship the God of the Universe[,] . . . [a] curious specimen of our Author's ideas concerning *Faith* and *Ceremonies*'.[152]

Warburton uses two strategies to criticize Hume. First, he argues that Hume has improperly interpreted the classical and modern writers that he cites as authorities. Warburton challenges Hume's appeals to Herodotus, Pliny, Varro, Xenophon, Rutilius, Cicero, Machiavelli, and the Chevalier Ramsay.[153] Second, Warburton attempts to show that Hume contradicts himself as he shifts from one topic to the next.

An example of the distance between Hume and Warburton on the psychology of religion is found in Hume's argument that there is 'a kind of contradiction' between two principles of human nature that nourish religious belief (*NHR* 13.1–3). On the one hand, there is 'an anxious fear of future events' that frames actions of the deity as perverse, wicked, and in need of

150 Ibid., Remarks 2 and 3. 151 Ibid., Remarks 4–7. 152 Ibid., Remarks 8–9.
153 Ibid., Remarks 7, 10, 12–13, 15, 17.

appeasement. On the other hand, praise and eulogy lead to ascription to the deity of every virtue and excellence. From this perspective, the religionist accepts 'opposite principles'. In response, Warburton concludes that 'Thus has this wretched man misrepresented and calumniated those two simple principles . . . , namely *Fear*, and *Love*. . . . *Fear* kept the Religionist from evil . . . [and] *Love inclined him to virtuous practice*'.[154]

To find contradictions, Warburton sometimes distils Hume's meaning to what Warburton takes to be its true essence: '*Nothing*, says our Philosopher, *is more destructive to the interest of superstition, than a manly steady virtue*: Which in plainer English is, "None will be so free from Superstition as the most hardened Rogue".' (The italicized portion is close to a direct quotation from *NHR* 14.8; the interpretation in quotation marks is Warburton's gloss.)

In his concluding 'Remark', Warburton says that Hume attempts to screen himself from public contempt by taking 'shelter in the dark umbrage of *Scepticism*. These are his concluding words. "The whole is a riddle, an ænigma, an inexplicable mystery. Doubt, uncertainty, suspence of judgment appear the only result of our most accurate scrutiny."' On Warburton's reckoning, Hume finds that even sceptical doubt about religion would be difficult to sustain unless we set 'the *Religionists a quarrelling*' and then make an escape '*into the calm, though obscure, regions of philosophy*' (cf. *NHR* 15.13). Warburton proclaims this strategy Hume's 'last effort to defend his *dogmatical* nonsense with *scepticism* still more nonsensical. . . . For the sake of this beloved object, *deliberate doubt*, there is no mischief he is not ready to commit. . . . And all of this for the selfish and unnatural lust of *escaping*. . . . But here we have earthed him; rolled up in the Scoria of a *dogmatist* and *Sceptic*, run down together.'[155]

Hume wrote in his autobiography that Hurd was the author of this 'pamphlet': 'Dr Hurd wrote a Pamphlet against it, with all the illiberal Petulance, Arrogance, and Scurrility, which distinguishes the Warburton-ian School. This Pamphlet gave me some Consolation for the otherwise indifferent Reception of my Performance.'[156] One might think that any

[154] Ibid., Remark 16. [155] Ibid., Remark 21.

[156] 'My Own Life' 13; *Letters*, 1: 5. In 'My Own Life' 9 (four paragraphs prior to the above quotation; *Letters*, 1: 3), Hume relates a story about an event that occurred in either 1749 or 1750:

My Bookseller, A. Millar, informed me, that my former Publications (all but the unfortunate Treatise) were beginning to be the Subject of Conversation, that the Sale of them was gradually encreasing, and that new Editions were demanded. Answers, by Reverends and Right Reverends, came out two or three in a Year: And I found by Dr. Warburtons Railing, that the Books were beginning to be esteemed in good Company.

For an example of 'Dr. Warburton's railing', made public after both he and Hume had died, see Warburton, *Letters from a Late Eminent Prelate*, 10. For other statements about *EHU* that

'consolation' Hume found in Warburton's monograph would have been undercut had he known that Warburton attempted to manipulate him into the belief that Hurd was the author of the volume. However, there is more to the story than Hume mentions in his autobiography.

Years later Hurd recalled the writing and the attempted deception of Hume:

> [Hume's *Natural History*] came out early in 1757, and falling into the hands of Dr. Warburton, provoked him, by its uncommon licentiousness, to enter on the margin, as he went along, such remarks as occurred to him. And when that was too narrow to contain them all, he put down the rest on loose scraps of paper. . . . [I]n a letter from Cambridge, he [Warburton] wrote the following. . . . 'I will now . . . finish my skeleton. . . . It will make no more than a pamphlet. . . . The address will remove it from me; the author, a gentleman of Cambridge, from you; and the secrecy of printing, from us both.'
>
> Mr. Hume in particular . . . was the first to fall into the trap. He was much hurt, and no wonder, by so lively an attack upon him, and could not help confessing it in what he calls his *own Life*.[157]

Hurd may have been more deceived than deceiver. Hume apparently believed from an early date that Hurd was not the primary author of the pamphlet, and that Warburton was. Shortly after the pamphlet was published, Hume wrote to Millar that

> I am positively assurd, that Dr. Warburton wrote that Letter to himself which you sent me; and indeed the Style discovers him sufficiently. I shou'd answer him; but he attacks so small a Corner of my Building, that I can abandon it without drawing great Consequences after it. . . . At present, nothing coud tempt me to take the Pen in hand, but Anger, of which I feel myself incapable, even upon this Provocation.[158]

Hume had apparently only been keeping up the pretence that Warburton's remarks had been composed 'by a Gentleman of Cambridge in a Letter'.

Thomas Stona's Remarks upon The Natural History of Religion (1758)

An anonymous 159-page monograph on idolatry and religion that begins with a treatment of Hume's *Natural History* appeared in 1758. It was presented as written by 'S.T.'—apparently reversed initials standing for Thomas

Warburton withheld from publication, see *A Selection from Unpublished Papers of the Right Rev. William Warburton*, pp. 309–15.

157 Hurd, *A Discourse, By Way of General Preface to the Quarto Edition of Bishop Warburton's Works*, pp. 79–82.

158 3 Sept. 1757, to Andrew Millar, *Letters*, 1: 265. See also Hume's mention of Hurd in a letter of June 1757, to William Strahan, *Letters*, 1: 252.

Stona (1727/8–92).[159] The unit devoted to Hume uses a semi-dialogue style structured as private letters to and from 'Theophilus' and 'Acasto' on ideas advanced by Hume.

Acasto's letter to Theophilus is brief: He does 'not pretend to be a judge of the merits of this performance; but must confess, that the air of freedom which enlivens every part of it, delighted me extremely'. Though a self-proclaimed lover of literary liberty, Acasto enquires whether readers should be protected 'from the abuses of the *freethinker*', whose views will be 'entirely repugnant to the profession of the Mosaic history'. Acasto requests that Theophilus examine Hume's book to see if he has fairly assessed religious belief and human nature in 'its primitive state' (pp. 2–3).

In response, Theophilus offers an 'abstract' of Hume's *Natural History* (p. 4). It consists of a two-page quotation that concentrates on the thesis that historically the popular religion in most countries has been polytheism or idolatry. Hume's views are respectfully criticized on the grounds that polytheism was not the first religion and that persons in early cultures were capable of reasoning about the existence of God and reaching conclusions about monotheism:

> The works of the creation . . . have been the perpetual testimony of the existence of a God, and reason is the medium with which the human creature, from the very first period of its being, hath been furnished to discover it: . . . and from that reflection must have been immediately led to conclude, that this beauteous scene of things must certainly have been created by a being infinitely superior in wisdom and power to man. . . . [M]ankind were as able to discover the existence of a God in the remotest ages of antiquity, as at present. (pp. 6–8)

Even 'the illiterate ancient' was capable of generating such reflection, which was 'the offspring of its reason', not 'the monster of its fears' that Hume proclaims (pp. 8, 13). Hume is faulted for unjustly presuming that reason was inferior in ancient times to its modern manifestations. He is also accused of lacking evidence for his claims about reflective life in ancient cultures and about ancient religious texts: 'So whether theism or polytheism was the primary religion of mankind, can be determined upon no other authority, than revelation; and if *that* is excluded by this author, then the solution of this question can be only founded on conjecture, and that side

[159] *Remarks upon the Natural History of Religion By Mr. Hume. With Dialogues on Heathen Idolatry and the Christian Religion* (1758). Published anonymously ('by S.T.'). All parenthetical page references are to this source. 'Remarks upon the *Natural History of Religion* By Mr. Hume' is on pp. 1–30. It is followed by two units of dialogues, pp. 30–106 ('Dialogue on Idolatry', with brief mention of *NHR*) and pp. 106–59 ('Dialogue on the Christian Religion'). Authorship is attributed to Stona by John Nichols, *Literary Anecdotes of the Eighteenth Century*, 2: 717.

of it which is supported by the greatest degree of probability have a right to our assent' (p. 18).

Theophilus proceeds to examine what is known about ancient cultures to demonstrate which hypothesis, his or Hume's, is most reasonable and best grounded in established fact. Theophilus argues that the pyramids of Egypt, the ancient 'magnificent cities', and the great systems of justice in the ancient world provide sufficient evidence of cultures advanced in the use of reason and possessing a commitment to theism (pp. 18–22). Various classical writers mentioned by Hume are cited in support of this conclusion. These include Pliny (*Natural History*), Herodotus, Xenophon, Plutarch, and Homer. Stona may have been using a strategy of turning Hume's own appeals to classical authority against him in order to prove that 'theism was the primary religion of mankind' (pp. 23–7).

William Rose's Reply to Stona's 'Remarks' in The Monthly Review (1758)

William Rose criticized Stona's assessment of Hume.[160]

> The Author of these Remarks, &c. appears to be a friend to religion and freedom of enquiry; but he has advanced nothing, in our opinion, that can give the judicious reader any high idea of his discernment or acuteness. His remarks upon Mr. Hume's Natural History of Religion are extremely superficial, and scarce contain any thing that deserves particular notice.

Rose faults Stona for quoting classical authors without clear evidentiary purpose and for having no convincing evidence or arguments about polytheism among primitive persons.

Review of Hume and Stona in The Critical Review (1758)

Stona's 'Remarks' were the subject of a lengthy, anonymous article that appeared in *The Critical Review*.[161] The author of these remarks begins by allowing that 'Few writers have been more admired, more opposed, and misrepresented than' Hume, a man of 'sound judgment, and fine imagination' (p. 411). In the case of Stona's book, Hume is said to have

[160] Rose, Review of 'Remarks upon the Natural History of Religion By Mr. Hume. With Dialogues on Heathen Idolatry, and the Christian Religion By S.T.', *The Monthly Review*, 19 (1758), 532–3; published anonymously.

[161] Anonymous, Review of 'Remarks upon the Natural History of Religion, by Mr. Hume. *With dialogues on heathen idolatry, and the Christian religion*', *The Critical Review*, 6 (Nov. 1758), 411–18. All parenthetical page references are to this source.

been 'attacked with the candour and good breeding of a gentleman, with the erudition of a scholar; but, if we may draw a comparison, with a capacity, a closeness, and precision inferior to his [Hume's] own' (p. 412).

The reviewer suggests a reversal of Stona's probability assessment: 'Before any considerable progress was made in the arts of society, and man's care was engrossed by an attention to the necessities, the weakness, and the wants of his nature, we think it improbable he should be equally affected with the beauty, the order, and the wisdom which appears in the universe' (p. 414). Like Rose, this reviewer holds that Stona has no plausible explanation for the rise of either philosophical theology or idolatry and polytheism. Overall, Stona's work is said to be 'a work of learning, taste, and merit... and an elegant and liberal turn of sentiment, without, perhaps, the strongest powers of the discussive faculty' (p. 418).

François Marie Arouet de Voltaire, Philosophical Dictionary, 'Religion' (1764)[162]

In the 'Second Question' of a wide-ranging article on religion, Voltaire (1694–1778) critically assesses Hume's theory that polytheism was the first religion. Though he identifies Hume only by description ('one of the most profound metaphysicians'), Section 1 of *NHR* is clearly the object of his enquiry.[163]

Voltaire argues that 'people began by acknowledging a single God, and that later human weakness led to the adoption of several' (p. 438). Voltaire's reasoning is predicated both on speculation about the nature of ancient villages 'before large towns were built' and on a psychological theory of human behaviour in the face of natural dangers:

> It is quite natural that a village, frightened by thunder, afflicted by the loss of its harvests, mistreated by the neighboring village, sensing an invisible power everywhere, should soon say: 'There is some being above us which works our good and ill.'
>
> It seems impossible to me that it said: 'There are two powers'. For why several? In all things people begin with the simple, the complex comes later, and with superior enlightenment one often comes back to the simple at last. This is the course of the human mind. (p. 438)

[162] Voltaire, *Philosophical Dictionary*, trans. Gay, 'Religion', 'Second Question', 2: 438–42. All parenthetical page references are to this translation. This book was originally published in French (Geneva, 1764).

[163] Voltaire mentions theses unique to *NHR*. Moreover, in 1786 F. X. Swediaur (1748–1824) included in his *Philosophical Dictionary* some freely edited excerpts from both Hume (*NHR* 1.2–8) and Voltaire (*Philosophical Dictionary*, 'Religion', part of the 'Second Question'). The selection by Voltaire—entitled 'Polytheism not the Primary Religion of Mankind' (3: 26–30)—was revised, and it was stated specifically that Voltaire is criticizing Hume's views in the *Natural History of Religion*.

Oswald's Appeal to Common Sense in Behalf of Religion (1766–1772)

The Revd James Oswald (1703–93) wrote *An Appeal to Common Sense in Behalf of Religion* as a defence of religion against sceptics and infidels.[164] Oswald's appeals to 'the authority of common sense' and to *reason*, which for him is the functional equivalent of common sense, were aimed at the protection of what he calls 'primary truths' that are known with 'indubitable certainty'.[165]

Hume's views on religion are repudiated at several points. He is presented as one among several philosophers, commencing with Descartes, who make improper assumptions about the need to provide epistemic warrant for foundational truths, or 'first principles' of metaphysics, morals, and religion. Hume's views in *The Natural History of Religion* are judged little more than selective historical reports of the *prejudices* and *passions* present in various religious traditions. Oswald acknowledges that truly 'nonsensical' views about religion have been held by many peoples, but he maintains that these can be distinguished from the 'obvious truths' of religion and morality. Oswald thinks that the particular opinions that Hume chooses to report are 'the disgrace of the human kind'. He judges that Hume's theories built on these reports contain 'absurd and dangerous paradoxes'.

Oswald also holds that 'in his dissertation on the passions, [Hume] presents us with a view of the judgment we form of our own merit in such a variety of instances, so weak, so childish, so absolutely false and silly, that we would gladly disavow it if we could. But there is no resisting the truth of facts. The ideas we form of ourselves are indeed as unworthy of rational beings, as those we form of God.'[166]

Duncan Shaw's Appendix: Hume on the Rise of Idolatry (1776)

Duncan Shaw (1725–95) wrote a history of religion and comparative religion that contains an appendix on Hume.[167] The appendix is divided into two 'numbers'. 'Number 1' (pp. 247–67) is entitled 'An Examination of the Sentiments of David Hume, Esq; with respect to the Origin of Priests'; here Shaw criticizes Hume's essay 'Of Superstition and Enthusiasm'. 'Number 2'

[164] *An Appeal to Common Sense in Behalf of Religion*, 2 vols. Vol. 1 was published in 1766 as a complete work.

[165] Ibid. See 1: 8–10, 17–18, 26–7, 40–1, 66–7; and the opening pages of vol. 2.

[166] Ibid., vol. 1, bk. 6, ch. 4; vol. 2, bk. 1, ch. 4.

[167] Shaw, *A Comparative View of the Several Methods of Promoting Religious Instruction: From the Earliest Down to the Present Time*, vol. 2, appx. 2. All parenthetical page references are to this source. This book was published early in 1776; a review appeared in the *London Review* in Feb. 1776.

(pp. 268–302) is entitled 'An Examination of the Account given by David Hume Esq; of the Rise of Idolatry, in his Essay, entitled, The Natural History of Religion'. Attention below is confined to the second number.

Shaw criticizes Hume's treatment of idolatry and polytheism. He views Hume as mistaken in treating the two notions as effectively identical. Shaw describes Hume's historical claims as 'laboured' (p. 270), yet lacking in good evidence:

> Is it not well enough known, that the most antient histories we have, one only excepted, do not lead us very far back?—They can therefore authorize no conclusion with respect to the state of Religion in earlier times. . . . At what precise time Polytheism began to gain footing, it must be difficult, if at all possible to determine, for want of antient historical records. . . . (pp. 275, 282)

Shaw maintains that the only history providing a short account of religion from its inception is the history 'written by Moses' (p. 294). Shaw insists that Hume's dismissal of Mosaic history lacks justification and that from its credible testimony 'nothing can be more evident than that Adam was a Theist' who would 'instill his own notions of the Deity into the minds of his Children' (p. 295). Shaw also maintains that Hume is inconsistent in assuming that the biblical Adam could have reasoned to a single creator from his awareness of order in the universe. If Adam had these powers, Shaw reasons, then the priority of monotheism over polytheism would be apparent:

> By the manner in which Mr. Hume introduces this observation concerning Adam, he would seem to insinuate, that the *full* perfection of his faculties at his creation, was one of the chief causes that enabled him to derive his notions of the Creator of all things, and particularly to infer his unity, from the contemplation of his works. From thence may it not be asked, why might not the rest of mankind, when they arrive at the full exercise of their faculties, have done the same? (p. 277)

Shaw maintains that even if one asserts, for argument's sake, that the order of nature did not sufficiently impress the ancients to lead them to monotheism, the unity of God might still be discovered from 'some other principle', such as feelings that would naturally arise from 'a sense of derived existence and conscious dependence' or other forms of awareness of causal dependence (pp. 285–6). After primitive humans experienced perplexity over such matters, they would 'probably' be led to discover the being and character of the Author of nature. It would then be but a short step to an appreciation of the grandeur of the universe and the unity of a Being superior to humankind (pp. 289–93). Shaw concludes that Hume has not exhausted the plausible hypotheses that might be explored in opposition to his arguments for the priority of polytheism, and that his history is therefore not as *natural* as he imagines it to be (p. 302).

Hume's *Essays and Treatises on Several Subjects* was, from at least 1758 until his death, the work on which he staked his reputation as a philosopher. Unlike the *Treatise*—the only other source of his philosophical reputation during this period—*Essays and Treatises* was a commercial success through many editions. We shall never know how many copies were sold or read in Hume's lifetime, but we do know that *A Dissertation on the Passions* and *The Natural History of Religion* were core works in his representation of his philosophy in the last eighteen or so years of his life. Assuming that he received assorted reactions from friends, peers, and booksellers, the published commentary that has been reviewed in this section is probably but a small part of the story of the reception of these two dissertations, as Hume experienced it.

A NOTE ON THE TEXT

The Natural History of Religion and *A Dissertation on the Passions* were published in 1757 as Dissertation 1 and Dissertation 2 in *Four Dissertations*. The title of the second dissertation was 'Of the Passions', the same title as Book 2 of *A Treatise of Human Nature*, from which this dissertation descended. *A Dissertation on the Passions* became the title in 1758, when it and *The Natural History of Religion* were placed in the collection *Essays and Treatises on Several Subjects* (*ETSS*).

The last edition of all the works in this collection seen through the press under Hume's supervision appeared in 1772. This edition is the copytext for the present critical edition. The posthumous edition of 1777 has been consulted for evidence of late authorial changes and has generally been followed when the changes are substantive, but not when they are purely formal. A history of Hume's editions of these two works, with bibliographical data, is provided in the Introduction.

The text was initially prepared from a photocopy of the 1772 edition of *ETSS* in the Hume collection of the Department of Rare Books and Special Collections, McGill University Libraries.[1] This copy has been inspected for printing or photocopying vagaries by collating it with three originals of the 1772 edition privately acquired by the editor. Two of these privately acquired copies and seven additional copies obtained from libraries[2] were optically (or 'mechanically') collated against one of the other privately acquired copies. This work was carried out by use of a McLeod Portable Collator.[3] David Fate Norton and his associates performed these collations of the 1772 copies either at his office or at the Colgate Collection of the Department of Rare Books and Special

[1] Shelf mark: B1455 1772 v.2 c.1.

[2] Special Collections Divisions of the following libraries provided copies: Chuo University, Tokyo (Vault); Folger Shakespeare Library, Washington, DC (shelf mark: B1455 1772 Cage); Guy W. Bailey/David W. Howe Library, University of Vermont (shelf mark: B1455, 1772); Harry Ransom Humanities Research Center, University of Texas at Austin (shelf mark: B1455, 1772); Bancroft Library, University of California, Berkeley (shelf mark: B1455, 1772, v.2); New York State Library, University of the State of New York, Albany, NY (shelf mark: B1455, 1772 v.2); McGill University, copy 2 (shelf mark: B1455 1772 v.2 c.2). The editor has inspected, but not collated, additional copies of the 1772 edition from the National Library of Scotland, the British Library, and the Honnold Library, Claremont.

[3] Randall McLeod, 'Collator in a Handbag'.

Collections, McGill University Libraries. Several variants were discovered in copies of the 1772 edition of *ETSS*, but none were in *DP* or *NHR*.[4] All differences appear to have been generated by imperfect inking or type problems (breakages of type or slippage in the position of the type during printing).

No cancels were discovered in a physical examination by the editor of six bound copies of the 1772 edition. There were, however, cancels in the 1757 edition that bear on the substance of the text of *NHR*. The nature of these cancels and the reasons for not restoring original readings in the present edition are discussed in the Editor's Introduction to this volume (pp. xxiv–xxvii).

Variants in the several editions of *DP* and *NHR* were collected over a ten-year period by both visual collation and computer collation. Two independent visual collations were performed against the copytext, and multiple computer collations were performed by comparing the copytext to all other editions published from 1757 to 1777. Apparent substantive variants were verified by consulting the original printed texts, and computer files were corrected whenever mistakes of entry were detected. Using this procedure, each file of each edition was checked for accuracy at least three times after the initial collation was completed. The accuracy of the computer file of the copytext was corroborated by sixteen independent computer comparisons with the corrected computer files of the other editions. After this work was completed and a full critical apparatus of substantive variants was constructed, texts of all editions were again collated (this time for both formal and substantive variants) using the program Collate developed by Peter Robinson at the Oxford Computing Centre. All variants discovered by this method were compared against the variants produced by the previous methods, and all discrepancies eliminated after consulting the original printed texts.

The Advertisement, or notice, that Hume published late in life in *ETSS* is not included in this volume. It expressed some of his views about the importance of his later works, including those in this volume. This Advertisement is included in the Clarendon Hume Edition of *An Enquiry concerning Human Understanding*.[5]

[4] The variants found in vol. 2 of the 1772 *ETSS* are reported in the volumes of *EHU* and *EPM* in the Clarendon Hume.

[5] The Advertisement was printed in Jan. 1776 in three formats to be placed in the unsold copies of the 1768, 1770, and 1772 edns. No copies of the versions printed for insertion in the edns. of 1768 and 1772 have been discovered.

The Editorial Appendix explains the rationale behind the choice of copytext and the acceptance of substantive changes from the 1777 and other editions, as well as the methods used to convert the copytext into the critical text. This Appendix also contains a brief account of editorial policy with regard to substantive emendation, correction of errors, and the like. The Editorial Appendix reports all emendations to the notes and text, without exception. A more extensive account of editorial policy is found in the Clarendon Hume Edition of *An Enquiry concerning Human Understanding*.

All references made by Hume in his footnotes (which were endnotes in some editions) have been checked against appropriate early modern editions of the sources. Numbers have been corrected if Hume or his compositor introduced *errors* into the citation of units such as page, book, and chapter numbers. Hume's earlier editions sometimes contain the correct numbering; other sources that warrant these corrections appear in the works listed in the Catalogue or the Reference List. Occasionally Hume's numbering was correct for one or more of the editions of his day, but the numbering systems in those editions are today obsolete. If such a *conflict* (by contrast to an *error*) of numbering systems occurs, Hume's numbering is retained in the text, and today's conventional numbering is provided in the annotations. An exception to this rule is made in the case of Hume's two references to Sextus Empiricus. Hume apparently used the rare and idiosyncratic edition edited by P. and J. Chouët (see Cat.). To avoid confusion, Hume's numbering has been changed in these two references to the standard numbering. His original numbers are provided in the annotations. (See, further, n. 6 in the Editorial Appendix, which explains the problem of 'incorrect' quotations.)

The Annotations also provide precise references that expand the information in Hume's spare footnotes; volumes, books, chapters, sections, lines, verses, and the like are supplied wherever feasible.[6] The text itself is never so expanded. More generally, no editorial intrusions appear in the text itself. The only exception is that numbers are placed in the margin at the head of each paragraph in order to establish a universal reference system that allows precise citation without use of page numbers.

[6] There had been published, in some cases, several editions of the works cited in Hume's footnotes (see the Catalogue on pp. 264–70), and these editions varied in organization and numbering. These variations can be subtle and confusing. For example, Locke's numbering in his fifth and final edition of the *Essay* (the most widely reprinted edition) is different from the numbering in the fourth edition, on which the critical edition of Locke and references in the present edition of Hume are based.

A
DISSERTATION
ON
THE
PASSIONS

SECTION 1

1 1. SOME objects produce immediately an agreeable sensation, by the original structure of our organs, and are thence denominated GOOD; as others, from their immediate disagreeable sensation, acquire the appellation of EVIL. Thus moderate warmth is agreeable and good; excessive heat painful and evil.

2 Some objects again, by being naturally conformable or contrary to passion, excite an agreeable or painful sensation; and are thence called *Good* or *Evil.* The punishment of an adversary, by gratifying revenge, is good; the sickness of a companion, by affecting friendship, is evil.

3 2. All good or evil, whence-ever it arises, produces various passions and affections, according to the light in which it is surveyed.

4 When good is certain or very probable, it produces JOY: When evil is in the same situation, there arises GRIEF or SORROW.

5 When either good or evil is uncertain, it gives rise to FEAR or HOPE, according to the degree of uncertainty on one side or the other.

6 DESIRE arises from good considered simply; and AVERSION, from evil. The WILL exerts itself, when either the presence of the good or absence of the evil may be attained by any action of the mind or body.

7 3. None of these passions seem to contain any thing curious or remarkable, except *Hope* and *Fear*, which, being derived from the probability of any good or evil, are mixed passions, that merit our attention.

8 Probability arises from an opposition of contrary chances or causes, by which the mind is not allowed to fix on either side; but is incessantly tossed from one to another, and is determined, one moment, to consider an object as existent, and another moment as the contrary. The imagination or understanding, call it which you please, fluctuates between the opposite views; and though perhaps it may be oftener turned to one side than the other, it is impossible for it, by reason of the opposition of causes or chances, to rest on either. The *pro* and *con* of the question alternately prevail; and the mind, surveying the objects in their opposite causes, finds such a contrariety as destroys all certainty or established opinion.

9 Suppose, then, that the object, concerning which we are doubtful, produces either desire or aversion; it is evident, that, according as the mind turns itself to one side or the other, it must feel a momentary impression of joy or sorrow. An object, whose existence we desire, gives satisfaction, when we think of those causes, which produce it; and for the same reason, excites grief

or uneasiness from the opposite consideration. So that, as the understanding, in probable questions, is divided between the contrary points of view, the heart must in the same manner be divided between opposite emotions.

10 Now, if we consider the human mind, we shall observe, that, with regard to the passions, it is not like a wind instrument of music, which, in running over all the notes, immediately loses the sound when the breath ceases; but rather resembles a string-instrument, where, after each stroke, the vibrations still retain some sound, which gradually and insensibly decays. The imagination is extremely quick and agile; but the passions, in comparison, are slow and restive: For which reason, when any object is presented, which affords a variety of views to the one and emotions to the other; though the fancy may change its views with great celerity; each stroke will not produce a clear and distinct note of passion, but the one passion will always be mixed and confounded with the other. According as the probability inclines to good or evil, the passion of grief or joy predominates in the composition; and these passions being intermingled by means of the contrary views of the imagination, produce by the union the passions of hope or fear.

11 4. As this theory seems to carry its own evidence along with it, we shall be more concise in our proofs.

12 The passions of fear and hope may arise, when the chances are equal on both sides, and no superiority can be discovered in one above the other. Nay, in this situation the passions are rather the strongest, as the mind has then the least foundation to rest upon, and is tossed with the greatest uncertainty. Throw in a superior degree of probability to the side of grief, you immediately see that passion diffuse itself over the composition, and tincture it into fear. Encrease the probability, and by that means the grief; the fear prevails still more and more, till at last it runs insensibly, as the joy continually diminishes, into pure grief. After you have brought it to this situation, diminish the grief, by a contrary operation to that, which encreased it, to wit, by diminishing the probability on the melancholy side; and you will see the passion clear every moment, till it changes insensibly into hope; which again runs, by slow degrees, into joy, as you encrease that part of the composition, by the encrease of the probability. Are not these as plain proofs, that the passions of fear and hope are mixtures of grief and joy, as in optics it is a proof, that a coloured ray of the sun, passing through a prism, is a composition of two others, when, as you diminish or encrease the quantity of either, you find it prevail proportionably, more or less, in the composition?

13 5. Probability is of two kinds; either when the object is itself uncertain, and to be determined by chance; or when, though the object be already

certain, yet it is uncertain to our judgment, which finds a number of proofs or presumptions on each side of the question. Both these kinds of probability cause fear and hope; which must proceed from that property, in which they agree; namely, the uncertainty and fluctuation which they bestow on the passion, by that contrariety of views, which is common to both.

14 6. It is a probable good or evil, which commonly causes hope or fear; because probability, producing an inconstant and wavering survey of an object, occasions naturally a like mixture and uncertainty of passion. But we may observe, that, wherever, from other causes, this mixture can be produced, the passions of fear and hope will arise, even though there be no probability.

15 An evil, conceived as barely *possible*, sometimes produces fear; especially if the evil be very great. A man cannot think of excessive pain and torture without trembling, if he runs the least risque of suffering them. The smallness of the probability is compensated by the greatness of the evil.

16 But even *impossible* evils cause fear; as when we tremble on the brink of a precipice, though we know ourselves to be in perfect security, and have it in our choice, whether we will advance a step farther. The immediate presence of the evil influences the imagination and produces a species of belief; but being opposed by the reflection on our security, that belief is immediately retracted, and causes the same kind of passion, as when, from a contrariety of chances, contrary passions are produced.

17 Evils, which are *certain*, have sometimes the same effect as the possible or impossible. A man, in a strong prison, without the least means of escape, trembles at the thoughts of the rack, to which he is sentenced. The evil is here fixed in itself; but the mind has not courage to fix upon it; and this fluctuation gives rise to a passion of a similar appearance with fear.

18 7. But it is not only where good or evil is uncertain as to its *existence*, but also as to its *kind*, that fear or hope arises. If any one were told that one of his sons is suddenly killed; the passion, occasioned by this event, would not settle into grief, till he got certain information which of his sons he had lost. Though each side of the question produces here the same passion; that passion cannot settle, but receives from the imagination, which is unfixed, a tremulous unsteady motion, resembling the mixture and contention of grief and joy.

19 8. Thus all kinds of uncertainty have a strong connexion with fear, even though they do not cause any opposition of passions, by the opposite views, which they present to us. Should I leave a friend in any malady, I should feel more anxiety upon his account, than if he were present; though perhaps I am not only incapable of giving him assistance, but likewise of

judging concerning the event of his sickness. There are a thousand little circumstances of his situation and condition, which I desire to know; and the knowledge of them would prevent that fluctuation and uncertainty, so nearly allied to fear. HORACE has remarked this phænomenon.

> Ut assidens implumibus pullis avis
> Serpentium allapsus timet,
> Magis relictis; non, ut adsit, auxilî
> Latura plus præsentibus.

20 A virgin on her bridal-night goes to bed full of fears and apprehensions, though she expects nothing but pleasure. The confusion of wishes and joys, the newness and greatness of the unknown event, so embarrass the mind, that it knows not in what image or passion to fix itself.

21 9. Concerning the mixture of affections, we may remark, in general, that when contrary passions arise from objects nowise connected together, they take place alternately. Thus when a man is afflicted for the loss of a law-suit, and joyful for the birth of a son, the mind, running from the agreeable to the calamitous object; with whatever celerity it may perform this motion, can scarcely temper the one affection with the other, and remain between them in a state of indifference.

22 It more easily attains that calm situation, when the *same* event is of a mixed nature, and contains something adverse and something prosperous in its different circumstances. For in that case, both the passions, mingling with each other by means of the relation, often become mutually destructive, and leave the mind in perfect tranquillity.

23 But suppose, that the object is not a compound of good and evil, but is considered as probable or improbable in any degree; in that case, the contrary passions will both of them be present at once in the soul, and instead of balancing and tempering each other, will subsist together, and by their union, produce a third impression or affection, such as hope or fear.

24 The influence of the relations of ideas (which we shall explain more fully afterwards) is plainly seen in this affair. In contrary passions, if the objects be *totally different*, the passions are like two opposite liquors in different bottles, which have no influence on each other. If the objects be intimately *connected*, the passions are like an *alcali* and an *acid*, which, being mingled, destroy each other. If the relation be more imperfect, and consist in the *contradictory* views of the *same* object, the passions are like oil and vinegar, which, however mingled, never perfectly unite and incorporate.

25 The effect of a mixture of passions, when one of them is predominant, and swallows up the other, shall be explained afterwards.

SECTION 2

1 1. BESIDES those passions above-mentioned, which arise from a direct pursuit of good and aversion to evil, there are others which are of a more complicated nature, and imply more than one view or consideration. Thus *Pride* is a certain satisfaction in ourselves, on account of some accomplishment or possession, which we enjoy: *Humility*, on the other hand, is a dissatisfaction with ourselves, on account of some defect or infirmity.

2 *Love* or *Friendship* is a complacency in another, on account of his accomplishments or services: *Hatred*, the contrary.

3 2. In these two sets of passion, there is an obvious distinction to be made between the *object* of the passion and its *cause*. The object of pride and humility is self: The cause of the passion is some excellence in the former case; some fault, in the latter. The object of love and hatred is some other person: The causes, in like manner, are either excellencies or faults.

4 With regard to all these passions, the causes are what excite the emotion; the object is what the mind directs its view to when the emotion is excited. Our merit, for instance, raises pride; and it is essential to pride to turn our view on ourselves with complacency and satisfaction.

5 Now as the causes of these passions are very numerous and various, though their object be uniform and simple; it may be a subject of curiosity to consider, what that circumstance is, in which all these various causes agree; or, in other words, what is the real efficient cause of the passion. We shall begin with pride and humility.

6 3. In order to explain the causes of these passions, we must reflect on certain principles, which, though they have a mighty influence on every operation, both of the understanding and passions, are not commonly much insisted on by philosophers. The first of these is the *association* of ideas, or that principle, by which we make an easy transition from one idea to another. However uncertain and changeable our thoughts may be, they are not entirely without rule and method in their changes. They usually pass with regularity, from one object, to what resembles it, is contiguous to it, or produced by it.[1] When one idea is present to the imagination, any other, united by these relations, naturally follows it, and enters with more facility, by means of that introduction.

[1] See *Enquiry concerning Human Understanding*, Section 3.

7 The *second* property, which I shall observe in the human mind, is a like association of impressions or emotions. All *resembling* impressions are connected together; and no sooner one arises, than the rest naturally follow. Grief and disappointment give rise to anger, anger to envy, envy to malice, and malice to grief again. In like manner, our temper, when elevated with joy, naturally throws itself into love, generosity, courage, pride, and other resembling affections.

8 In the *third* place, it is observable of these two kinds of association, that they very much assist and forward each other, and that the transition is more easily made, where they both concur in the same object. Thus, a man, who, by any injury received from another, is very much discomposed and ruffled in his temper, is apt to find a hundred subjects of hatred, discontent, impatience, fear, and other uneasy passions; especially, if he can discover these subjects in or near the person, who was the object of his first emotion. Those principles, which forward the transition of ideas, here concur with those which operate on the passions; and both, uniting in one action, bestow on the mind a double impulse.

9 Upon this occasion I may cite a passage from an elegant writer, who expresses himself in the following manner:[2] "As the fancy delights in every thing, that is great, strange, or beautiful, and is still the more pleased the more it finds of these perfections in the *same* object, so it is capable of receiving new satisfaction by the assistance of another sense. Thus, any continued sound, as the music of birds, or a fall of waters, awakens every moment the mind of the beholder, and makes him more attentive to the several beauties of the place, that lie before him. Thus, if there arises a fragrancy of smells or perfumes, they heighten the pleasure of the imagination, and make even the colours and verdure of the landscape appear more agreeable; for the ideas of both senses recommend each other, and are pleasanter together than when they enter the mind separately: As the different colours of a picture, when they are well disposed, set off one another, and receive an additional beauty from the advantage of the situation." In these phænomena, we may remark the association both of impressions and ideas; as well as the mutual assistance these associations lend to each other.

10 4. It seems to me, that both these species of relation have place in producing *Pride* or *Humility*, and are the real, efficient causes of the passion.

11 With regard to the first relation, that of ideas, there can be no question. Whatever we are proud of must, in some manner, belong to us. It is always

[2] Addison, *Spectator*, No. 412.

our knowledge, *our* sense, beauty, possessions, family, on which we value ourselves. Self, which is the *object* of the passion, must still be related to that quality or circumstance, which *causes* the passion. There must be a connexion between them; an easy transition of the imagination; or a facility of the conception in passing from one to the other. Where this connexion is wanting, no object can either excite pride or humility; and the more you weaken the connexion, the more you weaken the passion.

12 5. The only subject of enquiry is, whether there be a like relation of impressions or sentiments, wherever pride or humility is felt; whether the circumstance, which causes the passion, previously excites a sentiment similar to the passion; and whether there be an easy transfusion of the one into the other.

13 The feeling or sentiment of pride is agreeable; of humility, painful. An agreeable sensation is, therefore, related to the former; a painful, to the latter. And if we find, after examination, that every object, which produces pride, produces also a separate pleasure; and every object, which causes humility, excites in like manner a separate uneasiness; we must allow, in that case, that the present theory is fully proved and ascertained. The double relation of ideas and sentiments will be acknowledged incontestable.

14 6. To begin with personal merit and demerit, the most obvious causes of these passions; it would be entirely foreign to our present purpose to examine the foundation of moral distinctions. It is sufficient to observe, that the foregoing theory concerning the origin of the passions may be defended on any hypothesis. The most probable system, which has been advanced to explain the difference between vice and virtue, is, that either from a primary constitution of nature, or from a sense of public or private interest, certain characters, upon the very view and contemplation, produce uneasiness; and others, in like manner, excite pleasure. The uneasiness and satisfaction, produced in the spectator, are essential to vice and virtue. To approve of a character, is to feel a delight upon its appearance. To disapprove of it, is to be sensible of an uneasiness. The pain and pleasure, therefore, being, in a manner, the primary source of blame or praise, must also be the causes of all their effects; and consequently, the causes of pride and humility, which are the unavoidable attendants of that distinction.

15 But supposing this theory of morals should not be received; it is still evident that pain and pleasure, if not the sources of moral distinctions, are at least inseparable from them. A generous and noble character affords a satisfaction even in the survey; and when presented to us, though only in a poem or fable, never fails to charm and delight us. On the other hand, cruelty and treachery displease from their very nature; nor is it

possible ever to reconcile us to these qualities, either in ourselves or others. Virtue, therefore, produces always a pleasure distinct from the pride or self-satisfaction which attends it: Vice, an uneasiness separate from the humility or remorse.

16 But a high or low conceit of ourselves arises not from those qualities alone of the mind, which, according to common systems of ethics, have been defined parts of moral duty; but from any other, which have a connexion with pleasure or uneasiness. Nothing flatters our vanity more than the talent of pleasing by our wit, good-humour, or any other accomplishment; and nothing gives us a more sensible mortification, than a disappointment in any attempt of that kind. No one has ever been able to tell precisely, what *wit* is, and to show why such a system of thought must be received under that denomination, and such another rejected. It is by taste alone we can decide concerning it; nor are we possessed of any other standard, by which we can form a judgment of this nature. Now what is this *taste*, from which true and false wit in a manner receive their being, and without which no thought can have a title to either of these denominations? It is plainly nothing but a sensation of pleasure from true wit, and of disgust from false, without our being able to tell the reasons of that satisfaction or uneasiness. The power of exciting these opposite sensations is, therefore, the very essence of true or false wit; and consequently, the cause of that vanity or mortification, which arises from one or the other.

17 7. Beauty of all kinds gives us a peculiar delight and satisfaction; as deformity produces pain, upon whatever subject it may be placed, and whether surveyed in an animate or inanimate object. If the beauty or deformity belong to our own face, shape, or person, this pleasure or uneasiness is converted into pride or humility; as having in this case all the circumstances requisite to produce a perfect transition, according to the present theory.

18 It would seem, that the very essence of beauty consists in its power of producing pleasure. All its effects, therefore, must proceed from this circumstance: And if beauty is so universally the subject of vanity, it is only from its being the cause of pleasure.

19 Concerning all other bodily accomplishments, we may observe in general, that whatever in ourselves is either useful, beautiful, or surprizing, is an object of pride; and the contrary of humility. These qualities agree in producing a separate pleasure; and agree in nothing else.

20 We are vain of the surprizing adventures which we have met with, the escapes which we have made, the dangers to which we have been exposed;

as well as of our surprizing feats of vigour and activity. Hence the origin of vulgar lying; where men, without any interest, and merely out of vanity, heap up a number of extraordinary events, which are either the fictions of their brain; or, if true, have no connexion with themselves. Their fruitful invention supplies them with a variety of adventures; and where that talent is wanting, they appropriate such as belong to others, in order to gratify their vanity: For between that passion, and the sentiment of pleasure, there is always a close connexion.

21 8. But though pride and humility have the qualities of our mind and body, that is, of self, for their natural and more immediate causes; we find by experience, that many other objects produce these affections. We found vanity upon houses, gardens, equipage, and other external objects; as well as upon personal merit and accomplishments. This happens when external objects acquire any particular relation to ourselves, and are associated or connected with us. A beautiful fish in the ocean, a well-proportioned animal in a forest, and indeed, any thing, which neither belongs nor is related to us, has no manner of influence on our vanity; whatever extraordinary qualities it may be endowed with, and whatever degree of surprize and admiration it may naturally occasion. It must be someway associated with us, in order to touch our pride. Its idea must hang, in a manner, upon that of ourselves; and the transition from one to the other must be easy and natural.

22 Men are vain of the beauty either of *their* country, or *their* county, or even of *their* parish. Here the idea of beauty plainly produces a pleasure. This pleasure is related to pride. The object or cause of this pleasure is, by the supposition, related to self, the object of pride. By this double relation of sentiments and ideas, a transition is made from one to the other.

23 Men are also vain of the happy temperature of the climate, in which they are born; of the fertility of their native soil; of the goodness of the wines, fruits, or victuals, produced by it; of the softness or force of their language, with other particulars of that kind. These objects have plainly a reference to the pleasures of sense, and are originally considered as agreeable to the feeling, taste, or hearing. How could they become causes of pride, except by means of that transition above explained?

24 There are some, who discover a vanity of an opposite kind, and affect to depreciate their own country, in comparison of those, to which they have travelled. These persons find, when they are at home, and surrounded with their countrymen, that the strong relation between them and their own nation is shared with so many, that it is in a manner lost to them; whereas, that distant relation to a foreign country, which is formed by their having

seen it, and lived in it, is augmented by their considering how few have done the same. For this reason, they always admire the beauty, utility, and rarity of what they met with abroad, above what they find at home.

25 Since we can be vain of a country, climate, or any inanimate object, which bears a relation to us; it is no wonder we should be vain of the qualities of those, who are connected with us by blood or friendship. Accordingly we find, that any qualities which, when belonging to ourselves, produce pride, produce also, in a less degree, the same affection, when discovered in persons, related to us. The beauty, address, merit, credit, and honours of their kindred are carefully displayed by the proud, and are considerable sources of their vanity.

26 As we are proud of riches in ourselves, we desire, in order to gratify our vanity, that every one, who has any connexion with us, should likewise be possessed of them, and are ashamed of such as are mean or poor among our friends and relations. Our forefathers being regarded as our nearest relations; every one naturally affects to be of a good family, and to be descended from a long succession of rich and honourable ancestors.

27 Those, who boast of the antiquity of their families, are glad when they can join this circumstance, that their ancestors, for many generations, have been uninterrupted proprietors of the *same* portion of land, and that their family has never changed its possessions, or been transplanted into any other county or province. It is an additional subject of vanity, when they can boast, that these possessions have been transmitted through a descent, composed entirely of males, and that the honours and fortune have never passed through any female. Let us endeavour to explain these phænomena from the foregoing theory.

28 When any one values himself on the antiquity of his family, the subjects of his vanity are not merely the extent of time and number of ancestors (for in that respect all mankind are alike) but these circumstances, joined to the riches and credit of his ancestors, which are supposed to reflect a lustre on himself, upon account of his connexion with them. Since therefore the passion depends on the connexion, whatever strengthens the connexion must also encrease the passion, and whatever weakens the connexion must diminish the passion. But it is evident, that the sameness of the possessions must strengthen the relation of ideas, arising from blood and kindred, and convey the fancy with greater facility from one generation to another; from the remotest ancestors to their posterity, who are both their heirs and their descendants. By this facility, the sentiment is transmitted more entire, and excites a greater degree of pride and vanity.

29 The case is the same with the transmission of the honours and fortune, through a succession of males, without their passing through any female. It is an obvious quality of human nature, that the imagination naturally turns to whatever is important and considerable; and where two objects are presented, a small and a great, it usually leaves the former, and dwells entirely on the latter. This is the reason, why children commonly bear their father's name, and are esteemed to be of a nobler or meaner birth, according to *his* family. And though the mother should be possessed of superior qualities to the father, as often happens, the *general rule* prevails, notwithstanding the exception, according to the doctrine, which shall be explained afterwards. Nay, even when a superiority of any kind is so great, or when any other reasons have such an effect, as to make the children rather represent the mother's family than the father's, the general rule still retains an efficacy, sufficient to weaken the relation, and make a kind of breach in the line of ancestors. The imagination runs not along them with the same facility, nor is able to transfer the honour and credit of the ancestors to their posterity of the same name and family so readily, as when the transition is conformable to the general rule, and passes through the male line, from father to son, or from brother to brother.

30 9. But *property*, as it gives us the fullest power and authority over any object, is the relation, which has the greatest influence on these passions.[3]

31 Every thing, belonging to a vain man, is the best that is any where to be found. His houses, equipage, furniture, cloaths, horses, hounds, excel all others in his conceit; and it is easy to observe, that, from the least advantage in any of these, he draws a new subject of pride and vanity. His wine, if you will believe him, has a finer flavour than any other; his cookery is more exquisite; his table more orderly; his servants more expert; the air, in which he lives, more healthful; the soil, which he cultivates, more fertile; his fruits ripen earlier, and to greater perfection: Such a thing is remarkable for its

[3] That property is a species of *relation*, which produces a connexion between the person and the object is evident: The imagination passes naturally and easily from the consideration of a field to that of the person, to whom it belongs. It may only be asked, how this relation is resolvable into any of those three, *viz. causation, contiguity*, and *resemblance*, which we have affirmed to be the only connecting principles among ideas. To be the proprietor of any thing is to be the sole person, who, by the laws of society, has a right to dispose of it, and to enjoy the benefit of it. This right has at least a tendency to procure the person the exercise of it; and in fact does commonly procure him that advantage. For rights which had no influence, and never took place, would be no rights at all. Now a person who disposes of an object, and reaps benefit from it, both produces, or may produce, effects on it, and is affected by it. Property therefore is a species of *causation*. It enables the person to produce alterations on the object, and it supposes that his condition is improved and altered by it. It is indeed the relation the most interesting of any, and occurs the most frequently to the mind.

novelty; such another for its antiquity: This is the workmanship of a famous artist; that belonged once to such a prince or great man. All objects, in a word, which are useful, beautiful, or surprizing, or are related to such, may, by means of property, give rise to this passion. These all agree in giving pleasure. This alone is common to them; and therefore must be the quality, that produces the passion, which is their common effect. As every new instance is a new argument, and as the instances are here without number; it would seem, that this theory is sufficiently confirmed by experience.

32 Riches imply the power of acquiring whatever is agreeable; and as they comprehend many particular objects of vanity, necessarily become one of the chief causes of that passion.

33 10. Our opinions of all kinds are strongly affected by society and sympathy, and it is almost impossible for us to support any principle or sentiment, against the universal consent of every one, with whom we have any friendship or correspondence. But of all our opinions, those, which we form in our own favour; however lofty or presuming; are, at bottom, the frailest, and the most easily shaken by the contradiction and opposition of others. Our great concern, in this case, makes us soon alarmed, and keeps our passions upon the watch: Our consciousness of partiality still makes us dread a mistake: And the very difficulty of judging concerning an object, which is never set at a due distance from us, nor is seen in a proper point of view, makes us hearken anxiously to the opinions of others, who are better qualified to form just opinions concerning us. Hence that strong love of fame, with which all mankind are possessed. It is in order to fix and confirm their favourable opinion of themselves, not from any original passion, that they seek the applauses of others. And when a man desires to be praised, it is for the same reason, that a beauty is pleased with surveying herself in a favourable looking-glass, and seeing the reflection of her own charms.

34 Though it be difficult, in all points of speculation, to distinguish a cause, which encreases an effect, from one, which solely produces it; yet in the present case the phænomena seem pretty strong and satisfactory in confirmation of the foregoing principle.

35 We receive a much greater satisfaction from the approbation of those whom we ourselves esteem and approve of, than of those whom we contemn and despise.

36 When esteem is obtained after a long and intimate acquaintance, it gratifies our vanity in a peculiar manner.

37 The suffrage of those, who are shy and backward in giving praise, is attended with an additional relish and enjoyment, if we can obtain it in our favour.

38 Where a great man is delicate in his choice of favourites, every one courts with greater earnestness his countenance and protection.

39 Praise never gives us much pleasure, unless it concur with our own opinion, and extol us for those qualities, in which we chiefly excel.

40 These phænomena seem to prove, that the favourable suffrages of the world are regarded only as authorities, or as confirmations of our own opinion. And if the opinions of others have more influence in this subject than in any other, it is easily accounted for from the nature of the subject.

41 11. Thus few objects, however related to us, and whatever pleasure they produce, are able to excite a great degree of pride or self-satisfaction; unless they be also obvious to others, and engage the approbation of the spectators. What disposition of mind so desirable as the peaceful, resigned, contented; which readily submits to all the dispensations of providence, and preserves a constant serenity amidst the greatest misfortunes and disappointments? Yet this disposition, though acknowledged to be a virtue or excellence, is seldom the foundation of great vanity or self-applause; having no brilliancy or exterior lustre, and rather cheering the heart, than animating the behaviour and conversation. The case is the same with many other qualities of the mind, body, or fortune; and this circumstance, as well as the double relations above-mentioned, must be admitted to be of consequence in the production of these passions.

42 A second circumstance, which is of consequence in this affair, is the constancy and durableness of the object. What is very casual and inconstant, beyond the common course of human affairs, gives little joy, and less pride. We are not much satisfied with the thing itself; and are still less apt to feel any new degree of self-satisfaction upon its account. We foresee and anticipate its change; which makes us little satisfied with the thing itself: We compare it to ourselves, whose existence is more durable; by which means its inconstancy appears still greater. It seems ridiculous to make ourselves the object of a passion, on account of a quality or possession, which is of so much shorter duration, and attends us during so small a part of our existence.

43 A third circumstance, not to be neglected, is, that the objects, in order to produce pride or self-value, must be peculiar to us, or at least, common to us with a few others. The advantages of sun-shine, good weather, a happy climate, *&c.* distinguish us not from any of our companions, and give us no preference or superiority. The comparison, which we are every moment apt to make, presents no inference to our advantage; and we still remain, notwithstanding these enjoyments, on a level with all our friends and acquaintance.

44 As health and sickness vary incessantly to all men, and there is no one, who is solely or certainly fixed in either; these accidental blessings and calamities are in a manner separated from us, and are not considered as a foundation for vanity or humiliation. But wherever a malady of any kind is so rooted in our constitution, that we no longer entertain any hope of recovery, from that moment it damps our self-conceit, as is evident in old men, whom nothing mortifies more than the consideration of their age and infirmities. They endeavour, as long as possible, to conceal their blindness and deafness, their rheums and gouts; nor do they ever avow them without reluctance and uneasiness. And though young men are not ashamed of every head-ach or cold which they fall into; yet no topic is more proper to mortify human pride, and make us entertain a mean opinion of our nature, than this, that we are every moment of our lives subject to such infirmities. This proves, that bodily pain and sickness are in themselves proper causes of humility; though the custom of estimating every thing, by comparison, more than by its intrinsic worth and value, makes us overlook those calamities, which we find incident to every one, and causes us to form an idea of our merit and character, independent of them.

45 We are ashamed of such maladies as affect others, and are either dangerous or disagreeable to them. Of the epilepsy; because it gives a horror to every one present: Of the itch; because it is infectious: Of the king's evil; because it often goes to posterity. Men always consider the sentiments of others in their judgment of themselves.

46 A fourth circumstance, which has an influence on these passions, is *general rules*; by which we form a notion of different ranks of men, suitably to the power or riches of which they are possessed; and this notion is not changed by any peculiarities of the health or temper of the persons, which may deprive them of all enjoyment in their possessions. Custom readily carries us beyond the just bounds in our passions, as well as in our reasonings.

47 It may not be amiss to observe on this occasion, that the influence of general rules and maxims on the passions very much contributes to facilitate the effects of all the principles or internal mechanism, which we here explain. For it seems evident, that, if a person full-grown, and of the same nature with ourselves, were on a sudden transported into our world, he would be much embarrassed with every object, and would not readily determine what degree of love or hatred, of pride or humility, or of any other passion should be excited by it. The passions are often varied by very inconsiderable principles; and these do not always play with perfect regularity, especially on the first trial. But as custom or practice has brought to light all these principles, and has settled the just value of every thing; this must certainly

contribute to the easy production of the passions, and guide us, by means of general established rules, in the proportions, which we ought to observe in preferring one object to another. This remark may, perhaps, serve to obviate difficulties, that may arise concerning some causes, which we here ascribe to particular passions, and which may be esteemed too refined to operate so universally and certainly, as they are found to do.

SECTION 3

1 1. In running over all the causes, which produce the passion of pride or that of humility; it would readily occur, that the same circumstance, if transferred from ourselves to another person, would render him the object of love or hatred, esteem or contempt. The virtue, genius, beauty, family, riches, and authority of others beget favourable sentiments in their behalf; and their vice, folly, deformity, poverty, and meanness excite the contrary sentiments. The double relation of impressions and ideas still operates on these passions of love and hatred; as on the former of pride and humility. Whatever gives a separate pleasure or pain, and is related to another person or connected with him, makes him the object of our affection or disgust.

2 Hence too injury or contempt towards us is one of the greatest sources of our hatred; services or esteem, of our friendship.

3 2. Sometimes a relation to ourselves excites affection towards any person. But there is always here implied a relation of sentiments, without which the other relation would have no influence.[4]

4 A person, who is related to us, or connected with us, by blood, by similitude of fortune, of adventures, profession, or country, soon becomes an agreeable companion to us; because we enter easily and familiarly into his sentiments and conceptions: Nothing is strange or new to us: Our imagination, passing from self, which is ever intimately present to us, runs smoothly along the relation or connexion, and conceives with a full sympathy the person, who is nearly related to self. He renders himself immediately acceptable, and is at once on an easy footing with us: No distance, no reserve has place, where the person introduced is supposed so closely connected with us.

5 Relation has here the same influence as custom or acquaintance, in exciting affection; and from like causes. The ease and satisfaction, which, in both cases, attend our intercourse or commerce, is the source of the friendship.

6 3. The passions of love and hatred are always followed by, or rather conjoined with, benevolence and anger. It is this conjunction, which chiefly distinguishes these affections from pride and humility. For pride and humility are pure emotions in the soul, unattended with any desire, and

[4] The affection of parents to children seems founded on an original instinct. The affection towards other relations depends on the principles here explained.

not immediately exciting us to action. But love and hatred are not compleat within themselves, nor rest in that emotion, which they produce; but carry the mind to something farther. Love is always followed by a desire of happiness to the person beloved, and an aversion to his misery: As hatred produces a desire of the misery, and an aversion to the happiness of the person hated. These opposite desires seem to be originally and primarily conjoined with the passions of love and hatred. It is a constitution of nature, of which we can give no farther explication.

7 4. Compassion frequently arises, where there is no preceding esteem or friendship; and compassion is an uneasiness in the sufferings of another. It seems to spring from the intimate and strong conception of his sufferings; and our imagination proceeds by degrees, from the lively idea to the real feeling of another's misery.

8 Malice and envy also arise in the mind without any preceding hatred or injury; though their tendency is exactly the same with that of anger and ill-will. The comparison of ourselves with others seems to be the source of envy and malice. The more unhappy another is, the more happy do we ourselves appear in our own conception.

9 5. The similar tendency of compassion to that of benevolence, and of envy to anger, forms a very close relation between these two sets of passions; though of a different kind from that which was insisted on above. It is not a resemblance of feeling or sentiment, but a resemblance of tendency or direction. Its effect, however, is the same, in producing an association of passions. Compassion is seldom or never felt without some mixture of tenderness or friendship; and envy is naturally accompanied with anger or ill-will. To desire the happiness of another, from whatever motive, is a good preparative to affection; and to delight in another's misery almost unavoidably begets aversion towards him.

10 Even where interest is the source of our concern, it is commonly attended with the same consequences. A partner is a natural object of friendship; a rival of enmity.

11 6. Poverty, meanness, disappointment, produce contempt and dislike: But when these misfortunes are very great, or are represented to us in very strong colours, they excite compassion, and tenderness, and friendship. How is this contradiction to be accounted for? The poverty and meanness of another, in their common appearance, gives us uneasiness, by a species of imperfect sympathy; and this uneasiness produces aversion or dislike, from the resemblance of sentiment. But when we enter more intimately into another's concerns, and wish for his happiness, as well as feel his misery, friendship or good-will arises, from the similar tendency of the inclinations.

12 A bankrupt, at first, while the idea of his misfortunes is fresh and recent, and while the comparison of his present unhappy situation with his former prosperity operates strongly upon us, meets with compassion and friendship. After these ideas are weakened or obliterated by time, he is in danger of compassion and contempt.

13 7. In respect, there is a mixture of humility, with the esteem or affection: In contempt, a mixture of pride.

14 The amorous passion is usually compounded of complacency in beauty, a bodily appetite, and friendship or affection. The close relation of these sentiments is very obvious, as well as their origin from each other, by means of that relation. Were there no other phænomenon to reconcile us to the present theory, this alone, methinks, were sufficient.

SECTION 4

1 1. THE present theory of the passions depends entirely on the double relations of sentiments and ideas, and the mutual assistance, which these relations lend to each other. It may not, therefore, be improper to illustrate these principles by some farther instances.

2 2. The virtues, talents, accomplishments, and possessions of others, make us love and esteem them: Because these objects excite a pleasing sensation, which is related to love; and as they have also a relation or connexion with the person, this union of ideas forwards the union of sentiments, according to the foregoing reasoning.

3 But suppose, that the person, whom we love, is also related to us, by blood, country, or friendship; it is evident, that a species of pride must also be excited by his accomplishments and possessions; there being the same double relation, which we have all along insisted on. The person is related to us, or there is an easy transition of thought from him to us; and the sentiments, excited by his advantages and virtues, are agreeable, and consequently related to pride. Accordingly we find, that people are naturally vain of the good qualities or high fortune of their friends and countrymen.

4 3. But it is observable, that, if we reverse the order of the passions, the same effect does not follow. We pass easily from love and affection to pride and vanity; but not from the latter passions to the former, though all the relations be the same. We love not those who are related to us, on account of our own merit; though they are naturally vain on account of our merit. What is the reason of this difference? The transition of the imagination to ourselves, from objects related to us, is always easy; both on account of the relation, which facilitates the transition, and because we there pass from remoter objects, to those which are contiguous. But in passing from ourselves to objects, related to us; though the former principle forwards the transition of thought, yet the latter opposes it; and consequently there is not the same easy transfusion of passions from pride to love as from love to pride.

5 4. The virtues, services, and fortune of one man inspire us readily with esteem and affection for another related to him. The son of our friend is naturally entitled to our friendship: The kindred of a very great man value themselves, and are valued by others, on account of that relation. The force of the double relation is here fully displayed.

6 5. The following are instances of another kind, where the operation of these principles may still be discovered. Envy arises from a superiority in others; but it is observable, that it is not the great disproportion between us, which excites that passion, but on the contrary, our proximity. A great disproportion cuts off the relation of the ideas, and either keeps us from comparing ourselves with what is remote from us, or diminishes the effects of the comparison.

7 A poet is not apt to envy a philosopher, or a poet of a different kind, of a different nation, or of a different age. All these differences, if they do not prevent, at least weaken the comparison, and consequently the passion.

8 This too is the reason, why all objects appear great or little, merely by a comparison with those of the same species. A mountain neither magnifies nor diminishes a horse in our eyes: But when a FLEMISH and a WELSH horse are seen together, the one appears greater and the other less, than when viewed apart.

9 From the same principle we may account for that remark of historians, that any party, in a civil war, or even factious division, always choose to call in a foreign enemy at any hazard, rather than submit to their fellow-citizens. GUICCIARDIN applies this remark to the wars in ITALY; where the relations between the different states are, properly speaking, nothing but of name, language, and contiguity. Yet even these relations, when joined with superiority, by making the comparison more natural, make it likewise more grievous, and cause men to search for some other superiority, which may be attended with no relation, and by that means, may have a less sensible influence on the imagination. When we cannot break the association, we feel a stronger desire to remove the superiority. This seems to be the reason, why travellers, though commonly lavish of their praise to the CHINESE and PERSIANS, take care to depreciate those neighbouring nations, which may stand upon a footing of rivalship with their native country.

10 6. The fine arts afford us parallel instances. Should an author compose a treatise, of which one part was serious and profound, another light and humorous; every one would condemn so strange a mixture, and would blame him for the neglect of all rules of art and criticism. Yet we accuse not PRIOR for joining his *Alma* and *Solomon* in the same volume; though that amiable poet has perfectly succeeded in the gaiety of the one, as well as in the melancholy of the other. Even suppose the reader should peruse these two compositions without any interval, he would feel little or no difficulty in the change of the passions. Why? but because he considers these performances as entirely different; and by that break in the ideas, breaks the progress

of the affections, and hinders the one from influencing or contradicting the other.

11 An heroic and burlesque design, united in one picture, would be monstrous; though we place two pictures of so opposite a character in the same chamber, and even close together, without any scruple.

12 7. It needs be no matter of wonder, that the easy transition of the imagination should have such an influence on all the passions. It is this very circumstance, which forms all the relations and connexions among objects. We know no real connexion between one thing and another. We only know, that the idea of one thing is associated with that of another, and that the imagination makes an easy transition between them. And as the easy transition of ideas, and that of sentiments mutually assist each other; we might before-hand expect, that this principle must have a mighty influence on all our internal movements and affections. And experience sufficiently confirms the theory.

13 For, not to repeat all the foregoing instances: Suppose, that I were travelling with a companion through a country, to which we are both utter strangers; it is evident, that, if the prospects be beautiful, the roads agreeable, and the fields finely cultivated; this may serve to put me in good-humour, both with myself and fellow-traveller. But as the country has no connexion with myself or friend, it can never be the immediate cause either of self-value or of regard to him: And therefore, if I found not the passion on some other object, which bears to one of us a closer relation, my emotions are rather to be considered as the overflowings of an elevated or humane disposition, than as an established passion. But supposing the agreeable prospect before us to be surveyed either from his country-seat or from mine; this new connexion of ideas gives a new direction to the sentiment of pleasure, derived from the prospect, and raises the emotion of regard or vanity, according to the nature of the connexion. There is not here, methinks, much room for doubt or difficulty.

SECTION 5

1 1. It seems evident, that reason, in a strict sense, as meaning the judgment of truth and falsehood, can never, of itself, be any motive to the will, and can have no influence but so far as it touches some passion or affection. *Abstract relations* of ideas are the object of curiosity, not of volition. And *matters of fact*, where they are neither good nor evil, where they neither excite desire nor aversion, are totally indifferent; and whether known or unknown, whether mistaken or rightly apprehended, cannot be regarded as any motive to action.

2 2. What is commonly, in a popular sense, called reason, and is so much recommended in moral discourses, is nothing but a general and a calm passion, which takes a comprehensive and a distant view of its object, and actuates the will, without exciting any sensible emotion. A man, we say, is diligent in his profession from reason; that is, from a calm desire of riches and a fortune. A man adheres to justice from reason; that is, from a calm regard to public good, or to a character with himself and others.

3 3. The same objects, which recommend themselves to reason in this sense of the word, are also the objects of what we call passion, when they are brought near to us, and acquire some other advantages, either of external situation, or congruity to our internal temper; and by that means, excite a turbulent and sensible emotion. Evil, at a great distance, is avoided, we say, from reason: Evil, near at hand, produces aversion, horror, fear, and is the object of passion.

4 4. The common error of metaphysicians has lain in ascribing the direction of the will entirely to one of these principles, and supposing the other to have no influence. Men often act knowingly against their interest: It is not therefore the view of the greatest possible good which always influences them. Men often counteract a violent passion, in prosecution of their distant interests and designs: It is not therefore the present uneasiness alone, which determines them. In general, we may observe, that both these principles operate on the will; and where they are contrary, that either of them prevails, according to the general character or present disposition of the person. What we call *strength of mind* implies the prevalence of the calm passions above the violent; though we may easily observe, that there is no

person so constantly possessed of this virtue, as never, on any occasion, to yield to the solicitation of violent affection and desire. From these variations of temper proceeds the great difficulty of deciding with regard to the future actions and resolutions of men, where there is any contrariety of motives and passions.

SECTION 6

1 1. WE shall here enumerate some of those circumstances, which render a passion calm or violent, which heighten or diminish any emotion.

2 It is a property in human nature, that any emotion, which attends a passion, is easily converted into it; though in their natures they be originally different from, and even contrary to each other. It is true, in order to cause a perfect union among passions, and make one produce the other, there is always required a double relation, according to the theory above delivered. But when two passions are already produced by their separate causes, and are both present in the mind, they readily mingle and unite; though they have but one relation, and sometimes without any. The predominant passion swallows up the inferior, and converts it into itself. The spirits, when once excited, easily receive a change in their direction; and it is natural to imagine, that this change will come from the prevailing affection. The connexion is in many cases closer between any two passions, than between any passion and indifference.

3 When a person is once heartily in love, the little faults and caprices of his mistress, the jealousies and quarrels, to which that commerce is so subject; however unpleasant they be, and rather connected with anger and hatred; are yet found, in many instances, to give additional force to the prevailing passion. It is a common artifice of politicians, when they would affect any person very much by a matter of fact, of which they intend to inform him, first to excite his curiosity; delay as long as possible the satisfying of it; and by that means raise his anxiety and impatience to the utmost, before they give him a full insight into the business. They know, that this curiosity will precipitate him into the passion, which they purpose to raise, and will assist the object in its influence on the mind. A soldier, advancing to battle, is naturally inspired with courage and confidence, when he thinks on his friends and fellow-soldiers; and is struck with fear and terror, when he reflects on the enemy. Whatever new emotion therefore proceeds from the former, naturally encreases the courage; as the same emotion proceeding from the latter, augments the fear. Hence in martial discipline, the uniformity and lustre of habit, the regularity of figures and motions, with all the pomp and majesty of war, encourage ourselves and our allies; while the same objects in the enemy strike terror into us, though agreeable and beautiful in themselves.

4 Hope is, in itself, an agreeable passion, and allied to friendship and benevolence; yet is it able sometimes to blow up anger, when that is the predominant passion. "Spes addita suscitat iras." VIRG.

5 2. Since passions, however independent, are naturally transfused into each other, if they be both present at the same time; it follows, that when good or evil is placed in such a situation as to cause any particular emotion, besides its direct passion of desire or aversion, this latter passion must acquire new force and violence.

6 3. This often happens, when any object excites contrary passions. For it is observable, that an opposition of passions commonly causes a new emotion in the spirits, and produces more disorder than the concurrence of any two affections of equal force. This new emotion is easily converted into the predominant passion, and in many instances, is observed to encrease its violence, beyond the pitch, at which it would have arrived, had it met with no opposition. Hence we naturally desire what is forbid, and often take a pleasure in performing actions, merely because they are unlawful. The notion of duty, when opposite to the passions, is not always able to overcome them; and when it fails of that effect, is apt rather to encrease and irritate them, by producing an opposition in our motives and principles.

7 4. The same effect follows, whether the opposition arise from internal motives or external obstacles. The passion commonly acquires new force in both cases. The efforts, which the mind makes to surmount the obstacle, excite the spirits, and enliven the passion.

8 5. Uncertainty has the same effect as opposition. The agitation of the thought, the quick turns which it makes from one view to another, the variety of passions which succeed each other, according to the different views: All these produce an emotion in the mind; and this emotion transfuses itself into the predominant passion.

9 Security, on the contrary, diminishes the passions. The mind, when left to itself, immediately languishes; and in order to preserve its ardour, must be every moment supported by a new flow of passion. For the same reason, despair, though contrary to security, has a like influence.

10 6. Nothing more powerfully excites any affection than to conceal some part of its object, by throwing it into a kind of shade, which, at the same time that it shows enough to prepossess us in favour of the object, leaves still some work for the imagination. Besides that obscurity is always attended with a kind of uncertainty; the effort, which the fancy makes to compleat the idea, rouzes the spirits, and gives an additional force to the passion.

11 7. As despair and security, though contrary, produce the same effects; so absence is observed to have contrary effects, and in different circumstances,

either encreases or diminishes our affection. ROCHEFOUCAULT has very well remarked, that absence destroys weak passions, but encreases strong; as the wind extinguishes a candle, but blows up a fire. Long absence naturally weakens our idea, and diminishes the passion: But where the affection is so strong and lively as to support itself, the uneasiness, arising from absence, encreases the passion, and gives it new force and influence.

12 8. When the soul applies itself to the performance of any action, or the conception of any object, to which it is not accustomed, there is a certain unpliableness in the faculties, and a difficulty of the spirits moving in their new direction. As this difficulty excites the spirits, it is the source of wonder, surprize, and of all the emotions, which arise from novelty; and is, in itself, agreeable, like every thing which enlivens the mind to a moderate degree. But though surprize be agreeable in itself, yet, as it puts the spirits in agitation, it not only augments our agreeable affections, but also our painful, according to the foregoing principle. Hence every thing, that is new, is most affecting, and gives us either more pleasure or pain, than what, strictly speaking, should naturally follow from it. When it often returns upon us, the novelty wears off; the passions subside; the hurry of the spirits is over; and we survey the object with greater tranquillity.

13 9. The imagination and affections have a close union together. The vivacity of the former gives force to the latter. Hence the prospect of any pleasure, with which we are acquainted, affects us more than any other pleasure, which we may own superior, but of whose nature we are *wholly* ignorant. Of the one we can form a particular and determinate idea: The other we conceive under the general notion of pleasure.

14 Any satisfaction, which we lately enjoyed, and of which the memory is fresh and recent, operates on the will with more violence, than another of which the traces are decayed and almost obliterated.

15 A pleasure, which is suitable to the way of life, in which we are engaged, excites more our desire and appetite than another, which is foreign to it.

16 Nothing is more capable of infusing any passion into the mind, than eloquence, by which objects are represented in the strongest and most lively colours. The bare opinion of another, especially when enforced with passion, will cause an idea to have an influence upon us, though that idea might otherwise have been entirely neglected.

17 It is remarkable, that lively passions commonly attend a lively imagination. In this respect, as well as in others, the force of the passion depends as much on the temper of the person, as on the nature and situation of the object.

18 What is distant, either in place or time, has not equal influence with what is near and contiguous.

19 I pretend not to have here exhausted this subject. It is sufficient for my purpose, if I have made it appear, that, in the production and conduct of the passions, there is a certain regular mechanism, which is susceptible of as accurate a disquisition, as the laws of motion, optics, hydrostatics, or any part of natural philosophy.

INTRODUCTION

1 As every enquiry, which regards religion, is of the utmost importance, there are two questions in particular, which challenge our attention, to wit, that concerning its foundation in reason, and that concerning its origin in human nature. Happily, the first question, which is the most important, admits of the most obvious, at least, the clearest solution. The whole frame of nature bespeaks an intelligent author; and no rational enquirer can, after serious reflection, suspend his belief a moment with regard to the primary principles of genuine Theism and Religion. But the other question, concerning the origin of religion in human nature, is exposed to some more difficulty. The belief of invisible, intelligent power has been very generally diffused over the human race, in all places and in all ages; but it has neither perhaps been so universal as to admit of no exception, nor has it been, in any degree, uniform in the ideas, which it has suggested. Some nations have been discovered, who entertained no sentiments of Religion, if travellers and historians may be credited; and no two nations, and scarce any two men, have ever agreed precisely in the same sentiments. It would appear, therefore, that this preconception springs not from an original instinct or primary impression of nature, such as gives rise to self-love, affection between the sexes, love of progeny, gratitude, resentment; since every instinct of this kind has been found absolutely universal in all nations and ages, and has always a precise determinate object, which it inflexibly pursues. The first religious principles must be secondary; such as may easily be perverted by various accidents and causes, and whose operation too, in some cases, may, by an extraordinary concurrence of circumstances, be altogether prevented. What those principles are, which give rise to the original belief, and what those accidents and causes are, which direct its operation, is the subject of our present enquiry.

SECTION 1

That Polytheism Was the Primary Religion of Men

1 It appears to me, that, if we consider the improvement of human society, from rude beginnings to a state of greater perfection, polytheism or idolatry was, and necessarily must have been, the first and most ancient religion of mankind. This opinion I shall endeavour to confirm by the following arguments.

2 It is a matter of fact incontestable, that about 1700 years ago all mankind were polytheists. The doubtful and sceptical principles of a few philosophers, or the theism, and that too not entirely pure, of one or two nations, form no objection worth regarding. Behold then the clear testimony of history. The farther we mount up into antiquity, the more do we find mankind plunged into polytheism. No marks, no symptoms of any more perfect religion. The most ancient records of human race still present us with that system as the popular and established creed. The north, the south, the east, the west, give their unanimous testimony to the same fact. What can be opposed to so full an evidence?

3 As far as writing or history reaches, mankind, in ancient times, appear universally to have been polytheists. Shall we assert, that, in more ancient times, before the knowledge of letters, or the discovery of any art or science, men entertained the principles of pure theism? That is, while they were ignorant and barbarous, they discovered truth: But fell into error, as soon as they acquired learning and politeness.

4 But in this assertion you not only contradict all appearance of probability, but also our present experience concerning the principles and opinions of barbarous nations. The savage tribes of America, Africa, and Asia are all idolaters. Not a single exception to this rule. Insomuch, that, were a traveller to transport himself into any unknown region; if he found inhabitants cultivated with arts and sciences, though even upon that supposition there are odds against their being theists, yet could he not safely, till farther enquiry, pronounce any thing on that head: But if he found them ignorant and barbarous, he might before-hand declare them idolaters; and there scarcely is a possibility of his being mistaken.

5 It seems certain, that, according to the natural progress of human thought, the ignorant multitude must first entertain some groveling and

familiar notion of superior powers, before they stretch their conception to that perfect Being, who bestowed order on the whole frame of nature. We may as reasonably imagine, that men inhabited palaces before huts and cottages, or studied geometry before agriculture; as assert that the Deity appeared to them a pure spirit, omniscient, omnipotent, and omnipresent, before he was apprehended to be a powerful, though limited being, with human passions and appetites, limbs and organs. The mind rises gradually, from inferior to superior: By abstracting from what is imperfect, it forms an idea of perfection: And slowly distinguishing the nobler parts of its own frame from the grosser, it learns to transfer only the former, much elevated and refined, to its divinity. Nothing could disturb this natural progress of thought, but some obvious and invincible argument, which might immediately lead the mind into the pure principles of theism, and make it overleap, at one bound, the vast interval which is interposed between the human and the divine nature. But though I allow, that the order and frame of the universe, when accurately examined, affords such an argument; yet I can never think, that this consideration could have an influence on mankind, when they formed their first rude notions of religion.

6 The causes of such objects, as are quite familiar to us, never strike our attention or curiosity; and however extraordinary or surprizing these objects in themselves, they are passed over, by the raw and ignorant multitude, without much examination or enquiry. ADAM, rising at once, in paradise, and in the full perfection of his faculties, would naturally, as represented by MILTON, be astonished at the glorious appearances of nature, the heavens, the air, the earth, his own organs and members; and would be led to ask, whence this wonderful scene arose. But a barbarous, necessitous animal (such as man is on the first origin of society), pressed by such numerous wants and passions, has no leisure to admire the regular face of nature, or make enquiries concerning the cause of those objects, to which, from his infancy, he has been gradually accustomed. On the contrary, the more regular and uniform, that is, the more perfect nature appears, the more is he familiarized to it, and the less inclined to scrutinize and examine it. A monstrous birth excites his curiosity, and is deemed a prodigy. It alarms him from its novelty; and immediately sets him a trembling, and sacrificing, and praying. But an animal, compleat in all its limbs and organs, is to him an ordinary spectacle, and produces no religious opinion or affection. Ask him, whence that animal arose; he will tell you, from the copulation of its parents. And these, whence? From the copulation of theirs. A few removes satisfy his curiosity, and set the objects at such a distance, that he entirely loses sight of them. Imagine not, that he will so much as start the

question, whence the first animal; much less, whence the whole system or united fabric of the universe arose. Or, if you start such a question to him, expect not, that he will employ his mind with any anxiety about a subject, so remote, so uninteresting, and which so much exceeds the bounds of his capacity.

7 But farther, if men were at first led into the belief of one Supreme Being, by reasoning from the frame of nature, they could never possibly leave that belief, in order to embrace polytheism; but the same principles of reason, which at first produced and diffused over mankind, so magnificent an opinion, must be able, with greater facility, to preserve it. The first invention and proof of any doctrine is much more difficult than the supporting and retaining of it.

8 There is a great difference between historical facts and speculative opinions; nor is the knowledge of the one propagated in the same manner with that of the other. An historical fact, while it passes by oral tradition from eye-witnesses and contemporaries, is disguised in every successive narration, and may at last retain but very small, if any, resemblance of the original truth, on which it was founded. The frail memories of men, their love of exaggeration, their supine carelessness; these principles, if not corrected by books and writing, soon pervert the account of historical events; where argument or reasoning has little or no place, nor can ever recall the truth, which has once escaped those narrations. It is thus the fables of HERCULES, THESEUS, BACCHUS are supposed to have been originally founded in true history, corrupted by tradition. But with regard to speculative opinions, the case is far otherwise. If these opinions be founded on arguments so clear and obvious as to carry conviction with the generality of mankind, the same arguments, which at first diffused the opinions, will still preserve them in their original purity. If the arguments be more abstruse, and more remote from vulgar apprehension, the opinions will always be confined to a few persons; and as soon as men leave the contemplation of the arguments, the opinions will immediately be lost and be buried in oblivion. Whichever side of this dilemma we take, it must appear impossible, that theism could, from reasoning, have been the primary religion of human race, and have afterwards, by its corruption, given birth to polytheism and to all the various superstitions of the heathen world. Reason, when obvious, prevents these corruptions: When abstruse, it keeps the principles entirely from the knowledge of the vulgar, who are alone liable to corrupt any principle or opinion.

SECTION 2

Origin of Polytheism

1 If we would, therefore, indulge our curiosity, in enquiring concerning the origin of religion, we must turn our thoughts towards polytheism, the primitive religion of uninstructed mankind.

2 Were men led into the apprehension of invisible, intelligent power by a contemplation of the works of nature, they could never possibly entertain any conception but of one single being, who bestowed existence and order on this vast machine, and adjusted all its parts, according to one regular plan or connected system. For though, to persons of a certain turn of mind, it may not appear altogether absurd, that several independent beings, endowed with superior wisdom, might conspire in the contrivance and execution of one regular plan; yet is this a merely arbitrary supposition, which, even if allowed possible, must be confessed neither to be supported by probability nor necessity. All things in the universe are evidently of a piece. Every thing is adjusted to every thing. One design prevails throughout the whole. And this uniformity leads the mind to acknowledge one author; because the conception of different authors, without any distinction of attributes or operations, serves only to give perplexity to the imagination, without bestowing any satisfaction on the understanding. The statue of Laocoon, as we learn from Pliny, was the work of three artists: But it is certain, that, were we not told so, we should never have imagined, that a groupe of figures, cut from one stone, and united in one plan, was not the work and contrivance of one statuary. To ascribe any single effect to the combination of several causes, is not surely a natural and obvious supposition.

3 On the other hand, if, leaving the works of nature, we trace the footsteps of invisible power in the various and contrary events of human life, we are necessarily led into polytheism and to the acknowledgment of several limited and imperfect deities. Storms and tempests ruin what is nourished by the sun. The sun destroys what is fostered by the moisture of dews and rains. War may be favourable to a nation, whom the inclemency of the seasons afflicts with famine. Sickness and pestilence may depopulate a kingdom, amidst the most profuse plenty. The same nation is not, at the same time, equally successful by sea and by land. And a nation, which now triumphs over its enemies, may anon submit to their more prosperous arms. In short,

the conduct of events, or what we call the plan of a particular providence, is so full of variety and uncertainty, that, if we suppose it immediately ordered by any intelligent beings, we must acknowledge a contrariety in their designs and intentions, a constant combat of opposite powers, and a repentance or change of intention in the same power, from impotence or levity. Each nation has its tutelar deity. Each element is subjected to its invisible power or agent. The province of each god is separate from that of another. Nor are the operations of the same god always certain and invariable. To-day he protects: To-morrow he abandons us. Prayers and sacrifices, rites and ceremonies, well or ill performed, are the sources of his favour or enmity, and produce all the good or ill fortune, which are to be found amongst mankind.

4 We may conclude, therefore, that, in all nations, which have embraced polytheism, the first ideas of religion arose not from a contemplation of the works of nature, but from a concern with regard to the events of life, and from the incessant hopes and fears, which actuate the human mind. Accordingly, we find, that all idolaters, having separated the provinces of their deities, have recourse to that invisible agent, to whose authority they are immediately subjected, and whose province it is to superintend that course of actions, in which they are, at any time, engaged. JUNO is invoked at marriages; LUCINA at births. NEPTUNE receives the prayers of seamen; and MARS of warriors. The husbandman cultivates his field under the protection of CERES; and the merchant acknowledges the authority of MERCURY. Each natural event is supposed to be governed by some intelligent agent; and nothing prosperous or adverse can happen in life, which may not be the subject of peculiar prayers or thanksgivings.[1]

5 It must necessarily, indeed, be allowed, that, in order to carry men's attention beyond the present course of things, or lead them into any inference concerning invisible intelligent power, they must be actuated by some passion, which prompts their thought and reflection; some motive, which urges their first enquiry. But what passion shall we here have recourse to, for explaining an effect of such mighty consequence? Not speculative curiosity surely, or the pure love of truth. That motive is too refined for such gross apprehensions; and would lead men into enquiries concerning

[1] "Fragilis & laboriosa mortalitas in partes ista digessit, infirmitatis suæ memor, ut portionibus quisquis coleret, quo maxime indigeret." PLIN. lib. 2. cap. 7. So early as HESIOD's time there were 30,000 deities. Opera & dies, lib. 1. ver. 252. But the task to be performed by these seems still too great for their number. The provinces of the deities were so subdivided, that there was even a god of *Sneezing*. See ARIST. Probl. Section 33. cap. 7. The province of copulation, suitably to the importance and dignity of it, was divided among several deities.

the frame of nature, a subject too large and comprehensive for their narrow capacities. No passions, therefore, can be supposed to work upon such barbarians, but the ordinary affections of human life; the anxious concern for happiness, the dread of future misery, the terror of death, the thirst of revenge, the appetite for food and other necessaries. Agitated by hopes and fears of this nature, especially the latter, men scrutinize, with a trembling curiosity, the course of future causes, and examine the various and contrary events of human life. And in this disordered scene, with eyes still more disordered and astonished, they see the first obscure traces of divinity.

SECTION 3

The Same Subject Continued

1 WE are placed in this world, as in a great theatre, where the true springs and causes of every event are entirely concealed from us; nor have we either sufficient wisdom to foresee, or power to prevent those ills, with which we are continually threatened. We hang in perpetual suspence between life and death, health and sickness, plenty and want; which are distributed among the human species by secret and unknown causes, whose operation is oft unexpected, and always unaccountable. These *unknown causes*, then, become the constant object of our hope and fear; and while the passions are kept in perpetual alarm by an anxious expectation of the events, the imagination is equally employed in forming ideas of those powers, on which we have so entire a dependence. Could men anatomize nature, according to the most probable, at least the most intelligible philosophy, they would find, that these causes are nothing but the particular fabric and structure of the minute parts of their own bodies and of external objects; and that, by a regular and constant machinery, all the events are produced, about which they are so much concerned. But this philosophy exceeds the comprehension of the ignorant multitude, who can only conceive the *unknown causes* in a general and confused manner; though their imagination, perpetually employed on the same subject, must labour to form some particular and distinct idea of them. The more they consider these causes themselves, and the uncertainty of their operation, the less satisfaction do they meet with in their researches; and, however unwilling, they must at last have abandoned so arduous an attempt, were it not for a propensity in human nature, which leads into a system, that gives them some satisfaction.

2 There is an universal tendency among mankind to conceive all beings like themselves, and to transfer to every object, those qualities, with which they are familiarly acquainted, and of which they are intimately conscious. We find human faces in the moon, armies in the clouds; and by a natural propensity, if not corrected by experience and reflection, ascribe malice or good-will to every thing, that hurts or pleases us. Hence the frequency and beauty of the *prosopopœia* in poetry; where trees, mountains and streams are personified, and the inanimate parts of nature acquire sentiment and passion. And though these poetical figures and expressions gain not on

the belief, they may serve, at least, to prove a certain tendency in the imagination, without which they could neither be beautiful nor natural. Nor is a river-god or hamadryad always taken for a mere poetical or imaginary personage; but may sometimes enter into the real creed of the ignorant vulgar; while each grove or field is represented as possessed of a particular *genius* or invisible power, which inhabits and protects it. Nay, philosophers cannot entirely exempt themselves from this natural frailty; but have oft ascribed to inanimate matter the horror of a *vacuum*, sympathies, antipathies, and other affections of human nature. The absurdity is not less, while we cast our eyes upwards; and transferring, as is too usual, human passions and infirmities to the deity, represent him as jealous and revengeful, capricious and partial, and, in short, a wicked and foolish man, in every respect but his superior power and authority. No wonder, then, that mankind, being placed in such an absolute ignorance of causes, and being at the same time so anxious concerning their future fortune, should immediately acknowledge a dependence on invisible powers, possessed of sentiment and intelligence. The *unknown causes*, which continually employ their thought, appearing always in the same aspect, are all apprehended to be of the same kind or species. Nor is it long before we ascribe to them thought and reason and passion, and sometimes even the limbs and figures of men, in order to bring them nearer to a resemblance with ourselves.

3 In proportion as any man's course of life is governed by accident, we always find, that he encreases in superstition; as may particularly be observed of gamesters and sailors, who, though, of all mankind, the least capable of serious reflection, abound most in frivolous and superstitious apprehensions. The gods, says Coriolanus in Dionysius,[2] have an influence in every affair; but above all, in war; where the event is so uncertain. All human life, especially before the institution of order and good government, being subject to fortuitous accidents; it is natural, that superstition should prevail every where in barbarous ages, and put men on the most earnest enquiry concerning those invisible powers, who dispose of their happiness or misery. Ignorant of astronomy and the anatomy of plants and animals, and too little curious to observe the admirable adjustment of final causes; they remain still unacquainted with a first and Supreme Creator, and with that infinitely perfect spirit, who alone, by his almighty will, bestowed order on the whole frame of nature. Such a magnificent idea is too big for their narrow conceptions, which can neither observe the beauty of the work, nor comprehend the grandeur of its author. They suppose their deities,

[2] Lib. 8.

however potent and invisible, to be nothing but a species of human creatures, perhaps raised from among mankind, and retaining all human passions and appetites, together with corporeal limbs and organs. Such limited beings, though masters of human fate, being, each of them, incapable of extending his influence every where, must be vastly multiplied, in order to answer that variety of events, which happen over the whole face of nature. Thus every place is stored with a crowd of local deities; and thus polytheism has prevailed, and still prevails, among the greatest part of uninstructed mankind.[3]

4 Any of the human affections may lead us into the notion of invisible, intelligent power; hope as well as fear, gratitude as well as affliction: But if we examine our own hearts, or observe what passes around us, we shall find, that men are much oftener thrown on their knees by the melancholy than by the agreeable passions. Prosperity is easily received as our due, and few questions are asked concerning its cause or author. It begets cheerfulness and activity and alacrity and a lively enjoyment of every social and sensual pleasure: And during this state of mind, men have little leisure or inclination to think of the unknown invisible regions. On the other hand, every disastrous accident alarms us, and sets us on enquiries concerning the principles whence it arose: Apprehensions spring up with regard to futurity: And the mind, sunk into diffidence, terror, and melancholy, has recourse to every method of appeasing those secret intelligent powers, on whom our fortune is supposed entirely to depend.

5 No topic is more usual with all popular divines than to display the advantages of affliction, in bringing men to a due sense of religion; by subduing their confidence and sensuality, which, in times of prosperity, make them forgetful of a divine providence. Nor is this topic confined merely to modern religions. The ancients have also employed it. "Fortune has never liberally, without envy," says a Greek historian,[4] "bestowed an

[3] The following lines of Euripides are so much to the present purpose, that I cannot forbear quoting them:

Οὐκ ἔστιν οὐδὲν πιστόν, οὔτ' εὐδοξία,
Οὔτ' αὖ καλῶς πράσσοντα μὴ πράξειν κακῶς.
Φύρουσι δ' αὖθ' οἱ θεοὶ πάλιν τε καὶ πρόσω,
Ταραγμὸν ἐντιθέντες, ὡς ἀγνωσίᾳ
Σέβωμεν αὐτούς.

Hecuba.

"There is nothing secure in the world; no glory, no prosperity. The gods toss all life into confusion; mix every thing with its reverse; that all of us, from our ignorance and uncertainty, may pay them the more worship and reverence."

[4] Diod. Sic. lib. 3.

unmixed happiness on mankind; but with all her gifts has ever conjoined some disastrous circumstance, in order to chastize men into a reverence for the gods, whom, in a continued course of prosperity, they are apt to neglect and forget."

6 What age or period of life is the most addicted to superstition? The weakest and most timid. What sex? The same answer must be given. "The leaders and examples of every kind of superstition," says STRABO,[5] "are the women. These excite the men to devotion and supplications, and the observance of religious days. It is rare to meet with one that lives apart from the females, and yet is addicted to such practices. And nothing can, for this reason, be more improbable, than the account given of an order of men among the GETES, who practiced celibacy, and were notwithstanding the most religious fanatics." A method of reasoning, which would lead us to entertain a bad idea of the devotion of monks; did we not know by an experience, not so common, perhaps, in STRABO's days, that one may practice celibacy, and profess chastity; and yet maintain the closest connexions and most entire sympathy with that timorous and pious sex.

[5] Lib. 7.

SECTION 4

Deities Not Considered as Creators or Formers of the World

1 THE only point of theology, in which we shall find a consent of mankind almost universal, is, that there is invisible, intelligent power in the world: But whether this power be supreme or subordinate, whether confined to one being, or distributed among several, what attributes, qualities, connexions, or principles of action ought to be ascribed to those beings; concerning all these points, there is the widest difference in the popular systems of theology. Our ancestors in EUROPE, before the revival of letters, believed, as we do at present, that there was one supreme God, the author of nature, whose power, though in itself uncontroulable, was yet often exerted by the interposition of his angels and subordinate ministers, who executed his sacred purposes. But they also believed, that all nature was full of other invisible powers; fairies, goblins, elves, sprights; beings, stronger and mightier than men, but much inferior to the celestial natures, who surround the throne of God. Now, suppose, that any one, in those ages, had denied the existence of God and of his angels; would not his impiety justly have deserved the appellation of *atheism*, even though he had still allowed, by some odd capricious reasoning, that the popular stories of elves and fairies were just and well-grounded? The difference, on the one hand, between such a person and a genuine theist is infinitely greater than that, on the other, between him and one that absolutely excludes all invisible intelligent power. And it is a fallacy, merely from the casual resemblance of names, without any conformity of meaning, to rank such opposite opinions under the same denomination.

2 To any one, who considers justly of the matter, it will appear, that the gods of all polytheists are no better than the elves or fairies of our ancestors, and merit as little any pious worship or veneration. These pretended religionists are really a kind of superstitious atheists, and acknowledge no being, that corresponds to our idea of a deity. No first principle of mind or thought: No supreme government and administration: No divine contrivance or intention in the fabric of the world.

3 The CHINESE, when[6] their prayers are not answered, beat their idols. The deities of the LAPLANDERS are any large stone which they meet with of an extraordinary shape.[7] The EGYPTIAN mythologists, in order to account for animal worship, said, that the gods, pursued by the violence of earth-born men, who were their enemies, had formerly been obliged to disguise themselves under the semblance of beasts.[8] The CAUNII, a nation in the Lesser ASIA, resolving to admit no strange gods among them, regularly, at certain seasons, assembled themselves compleatly armed, beat the air with their lances, and proceeded in that manner to their frontiers; in order, as they said, to expel the foreign deities.[9] "Not even the immortal gods," said some GERMAN nations to CÆSAR, "are a match for the SUEVI."[10]

4 Many ills, says DIONE in HOMER to VENUS wounded by DIOMEDE, many ills, my daughter, have the gods inflicted on men: And many ills, in return, have men inflicted on the gods.[11] We need but open any classic author to meet with these gross representations of the deities; and LONGINUS[12] with reason observes, that such ideas of the divine nature, if literally taken, contain a true atheism.

5 Some writers[13] have been surprized, that the impieties of ARISTOPHANES should have been tolerated, nay publicly acted and applauded by the ATHENIANS; a people so superstitious and so jealous of the public religion, that, at that very time, they put SOCRATES to death for his imagined incredulity. But these writers do not consider, that the ludicrous, familiar images, under which the gods are represented by that comic poet, instead of appearing impious, were the genuine lights, in which the ancients conceived their divinities. What conduct can be more criminal or mean, than that of JUPITER in the AMPHITRYON? Yet that play, which represented his gallante exploits, was supposed so agreeable to him, that it was always acted in ROME by public authority, when the state was threatened with pestilence, famine, or any general calamity.[14] The ROMANS supposed, that, like all old letchers, he would be highly pleased with the recital of his former feats of prowess and vigour, and that no topic was so proper, upon which to flatter his vanity.

6 The LACEDEMONIANS, says XENOPHON,[15] always, during war, put up their petitions very early in the morning, in order to be before-hand with their enemies, and, by being the first solicitors, pre-engage the gods in their

[6] Père LE COMTE. [7] REGNARD, Voïage de LAPONIE.

[8] DIOD. SIC. lib. 1. LUCIAN. de sacrificiis. OVID alludes to the same tradition, Metam. lib. 5. l. 321. So also MANILIUS, lib. 4.

[9] HERODOT. lib. 1. [10] CÆS. Comment. de bello Gallico, lib. 4. [11] Lib. 5. 381.

[12] Cap. 9. [13] Père BRUMOY, Théâtre des GRECS; & FONTENELLE, Histoire des oracles.

[14] ARNOB. lib. 7. [15] De LACED. rep.

favour. We may gather from SENECA,[16] that it was usual, for the votaries in the temples, to make interest with the beadle or sexton, that they might have a seat near the image of the deity, in order to be the best heard in their prayers and applications to him. The TYRIANS, when besieged by ALEXANDER, threw chains on the statue of HERCULES, to prevent that deity from deserting to the enemy.[17] AUGUSTUS, having twice lost his fleet by storms, forbad NEPTUNE to be carried in procession along with the other gods; and fancied, that he had sufficiently revenged himself by that expedient.[18] After GERMANICUS's death, the people were so enraged at their gods, that they stoned them in their temples; and openly renounced all allegiance to them.[19]

7 To ascribe the origin and fabric of the universe to these imperfect beings never enters into the imagination of any polytheist or idolater. HESIOD, whose writings, with those of HOMER, contained the canonical system of the heathens;[20] HESIOD, I say, supposes gods and men to have sprung equally from the unknown powers of nature.[21] And throughout the whole theogony of that author, PANDORA is the only instance of creation or a voluntary production; and she too was formed by the gods merely from despight to PROMETHEUS, who had furnished men with stolen fire from the celestial regions.[22] The ancient mythologists, indeed, seem throughout to have rather embraced the idea of generation than that of creation or formation; and to have thence accounted for the origin of this universe.

8 OVID, who lived in a learned age, and had been instructed by philosophers in the principles of a divine creation or formation of the world; finding, that such an idea would not agree with the popular mythology, which he delivers, leaves it, in a manner, loose and detached from his system. "Quisquis fuit ille Deorum:"[23] Whichever of the gods it was, says he, that dissipated the chaos, and introduced order into the universe. It could neither be SATURN, he knew, nor JUPITER, nor NEPTUNE, nor any of the received deities of paganism. His theological system had taught him nothing upon that head; and he leaves the matter equally undetermined.

9 DIODORUS SICULUS,[24] beginning his work with an enumeration of the most reasonable opinions concerning the origin of the world, makes no mention of a deity or intelligent mind; though it is evident from his history, that he was much more prone to superstition than to irreligion.

[16] Epist. 41. [17] QUINT. CURTIUS, lib. 4. cap. 3. DIOD. SIC. lib. 17.

[18] SUETON. in vita AUG. cap. 16. [19] Id. in vita CAL. cap. 5.

[20] HERODOT. lib. 2. LUCIAN. JUPITER confutatus, de luctu, SATURN. *&c.*

[21] Ὡς ὁμόθεν γεγάασι θεοὶ θνητοί τ' ἄνθρωποι. HESIOD, Opera & dies, l. 108.

[22] Theog. l. 570. [23] Metamorph. lib. 1. l. 32. [24] Lib. 1.

And in another passage,[25] talking of the ICHTHYOPHAGI, a nation in INDIA, he says, that, there being so great difficulty in accounting for their descent, we must conclude them to be *aborigines*, without any beginning of their generation, propagating their race from all eternity; as some of the physiologers, in treating of the origin of nature, have justly observed. "But in such subjects as these," adds the historian, "which exceed all human capacity, it may well happen, that those, who discourse the most, know the least; reaching a specious appearance of truth in their reasonings, while extremely wide of the real truth and matter of fact."

10 A strange sentiment in our eyes, to be embraced by a professed and zealous religionist![26] But it was merely by accident, that the question concerning the origin of the world did ever in ancient times enter into religious systems, or was treated of by theologers. The philosophers alone made profession of delivering systems of this kind; and it was pretty late too before these bethought themselves of having recourse to a mind or supreme intelligence, as the first cause of all. So far was it from being esteemed profane in those days to account for the origin of things without a deity, that THALES, ANAXIMENES, HERACLITUS, and others, who embraced that system of cosmogony, passed unquestioned; while ANAXAGORAS, the first undoubted theist among the philosophers, was perhaps the first that ever was accused of atheism.[27]

11 We are told by SEXTUS EMPIRICUS,[28] that EPICURUS, when a boy, reading with his preceptor these verses of HESIOD,

> Eldest of beings, *chaos* first arose;
> Next *earth*, wide-stretch'd, the *seat* of all.

[25] Id. ibid.

[26] The same author, who can thus account for the origin of the world without a Deity, esteems it impious to explain from physical causes, the common accidents of life, earthquakes, inundations, and tempests; and devoutly ascribes these to the anger of JUPITER or NEPTUNE. A plain proof, whence he derived his ideas of religion. See lib. 15. p. 364. ex edit. RHODOMANNI.

[27] It will be easy to give a reason, why THALES, ANAXIMANDER, and those early philosophers, who really were atheists, might be very orthodox in the pagan creed; and why ANAXAGORAS and SOCRATES, though real theists, must naturally, in ancient times, be esteemed impious. The blind, unguided powers of nature, if they could produce men, might also produce such beings as JUPITER and NEPTUNE, who being the most powerful, intelligent existences in the world, would be proper objects of worship. But where a supreme intelligence, the first cause of all, is admitted, these capricious beings, if they exist at all, must appear very subordinate and dependent, and consequently be excluded from the rank of deities. PLATO (de leg. lib. 10.) assigns this reason for the imputation thrown on ANAXAGORAS, namely his denying the divinity of the stars, planets, and other created objects.

[28] Adversus mathem. lib. 10.

The young scholar first betrayed his inquisitive genius, by asking, "And chaos whence?" but was told by his preceptor, that he must have recourse to the philosophers for a solution of such questions. And from this hint Epicurus left philology and all other studies, in order to betake himself to that science, whence alone he expected satisfaction with regard to these sublime subjects.

12 The common people were never likely to push their researches so far, or derive from reasoning their systems of religion; when philologers and mythologists, we see, scarcely ever discovered so much penetration. And even the philosophers, who discoursed of such topics, readily assented to the grossest theory, and admitted the joint origin of gods and men from night and chaos; from fire, water, air, or whatever they established to be the ruling element.

13 Nor was it only on their first origin, that the gods were supposed dependent on the powers of nature. Throughout the whole period of their existence they were subjected to the dominion of fate or destiny. "Think of the force of necessity," says Agrippa to the Roman people, "that force, to which even the gods must submit."[29] And the Younger Pliny,[30] agreeably to this way of thinking, tells us, that amidst the darkness, horror, and confusion, which ensued upon the first eruption of Vesuvius, several concluded, that all nature was going to wrack, and that gods and men were perishing in one common ruin.

14 It is great complaisance, indeed, if we dignify with the name of religion such an imperfect system of theology, and put it on a level with later systems, which are founded on principles more just and more sublime. For my part, I can scarcely allow the principles even of Marcus Aurelius, Plutarch, and some other Stoics and Academics, though much more refined than the pagan superstition, to be worthy of the honourable appellation of *theism*. For if the mythology of the heathens resemble the ancient European system of spiritual beings, excluding God and angels, and leaving only fairies and sprights; the creed of these philosophers may justly be said to exclude a deity, and to leave only angels and fairies.

[29] Dionys. Halic. lib. 6. [30] Epist. lib. 6.

SECTION 5

Various Forms of Polytheism: Allegory, Hero-Worship

1 But it is chiefly our present business to consider the gross polytheism of the vulgar, and to trace all its various appearances, in the principles of human nature, whence they are derived.

2 Whoever learns by argument, the existence of invisible intelligent power, must reason from the admirable contrivance of natural objects, and must suppose the world to be the workmanship of that divine being, the original cause of all things. But the vulgar polytheist, so far from admitting that idea, deifies every part of the universe, and conceives all the conspicuous productions of nature, to be themselves so many real divinities. The sun, moon, and stars, are all gods according to his system: Fountains are inhabited by nymphs, and trees by hamadryads: Even monkies, dogs, cats, and other animals often become sacred in his eyes, and strike him with a religious veneration. And thus, however strong men's propensity to believe invisible, intelligent power in nature, their propensity is equally strong to rest their attention on sensible, visible objects; and in order to reconcile these opposite inclinations, they are led to unite the invisible power with some visible object.

3 The distribution also of distinct provinces to the several deities is apt to cause some allegory, both physical and moral, to enter into the vulgar systems of polytheism. The god of war will naturally be represented as furious, cruel, and impetuous: The god of poetry as elegant, polite, and amiable: The god of merchandize, especially in early times, as thievish and deceitful. The allegories, supposed in Homer and other mythologists, I allow, have often been so strained, that men of sense are apt entirely to reject them, and to consider them as the production merely of the fancy and conceit of critics and commentators. But that allegory really has place in the heathen mythology is undeniable even on the least reflection. Cupid the son of Venus; the Muses the daughters of Memory; Prometheus, the wise brother, and Epimetheus the foolish; Hygieia or the goddess of health descended from Æsculapius or the god of physic: Who sees not, in these, and in many other instances, the plain traces of allegory? When a god is supposed to preside over any passion, event, or system of actions, it is almost

unavoidable to give him a genealogy, attributes, and adventures, suitable to his supposed powers and influence; and to carry on that similitude and comparison, which is naturally so agreeable to the mind of man.

4 Allegories, indeed, entirely perfect, we ought not to expect as the productions of ignorance and superstition; there being no work of genius, that requires a nicer hand, or has been more rarely executed with success. That *Fear* and *Terror* are the sons of Mars is just; but why by Venus?[31] That *Harmony* is the daughter of Venus is regular; but why by Mars?[32] That *Sleep* is the brother of *Death* is suitable; but why describe him as enamoured of one of the Graces?[33] And since the ancient mythologists fall into mistakes so gross and palpable, we have no reason surely to expect such refined and longspun allegories, as some have endeavoured to deduce from their fictions.

5 Lucretius was plainly seduced by the strong appearance of allegory, which is observable in the pagan fictions. He first addresses himself to Venus as to that generating power, which animates, renews, and beautifies the universe: But is soon betrayed by the mythology into incoherencies, while he prays to that allegorical personage to appease the furies of her lover Mars: An idea not drawn from allegory, but from the popular religion, and which Lucretius, as an Epicurean, could not consistently admit of.

6 The deities of the vulgar are so little superior to human creatures, that, where men are affected with strong sentiments of veneration or gratitude for any hero or public benefactor, nothing can be more natural than to convert him into a god, and fill the heavens, after this manner, with continual recruits from among mankind. Most of the divinities of the ancient world are supposed to have once been men, and to have been beholden for their *apotheosis* to the admiration and affection of the people. The real history of their adventures, corrupted by tradition, and elevated by the marvellous, became a plentiful source of fable; especially in passing through the hands of poets, allegorists, and priests, who successively improved upon the wonder and astonishment of the ignorant multitude.

7 Painters too and sculptors came in for their share of profit in the sacred mysteries; and furnishing men with sensible representations of their divinities, whom they cloathed in human figures, gave great encrease to the public devotion, and determined its object. It was probably for want of these arts in rude and barbarous ages, that men deified plants, animals, and even brute, unorganized matter; and rather than be without a sensible object of worship, affixed divinity to such ungainly forms.

[31] Hesiod, Theog. l. 933. [32] Id. ibid. & Plutarch. in vita Pelop. [33] Iliad, 14. 263.

Could any statuary of SYRIA, in early times, have formed a just figure of APOLLO, the conic stone, HELIOGABALUS, had never become the object of such profound adoration, and been received as a representation of the solar deity.[34]

8 STILPO was banished by the council of AREOPAGUS, for affirming that the MINERVA in the citadel was no divinity; but the workmanship of PHIDIAS, the sculptor.[35] What degree of reason must we expect in the religious belief of the vulgar in other nations; when ATHENIANS and AREOPAGITES could entertain such gross conceptions?

9 These then are the general principles of polytheism, founded in human nature, and little or nothing dependent on caprice and accident. As the *causes*, which bestow happiness or misery, are, in general, very little known and very uncertain, our anxious concern endeavours to attain a determinate idea of them; and finds no better expedient than to represent them as intelligent, voluntary agents, like ourselves; only somewhat superior in power and wisdom. The limited influence of these agents, and their great proximity to human weakness, introduce the various distribution and division of their authority; and thereby give rise to allegory. The same principles naturally deify mortals, superior in power, courage, or understanding, and produce hero-worship; together with fabulous history and mythological tradition, in all its wild and unaccountable forms. And as an invisible spiritual intelligence is an object too refined for vulgar apprehension, men naturally affix it to some sensible representation; such as either the more conspicuous parts of nature, or the statues, images, and pictures, which a more refined age forms of its divinities.

10 Almost all idolaters, of whatever age or country, concur in these general principles and conceptions; and even the particular characters and provinces, which they assign to their deities, are not extremely different.[36] The GREEK and ROMAN travellers and conquerors, without much difficulty, found their own deities every where; and said, This is MERCURY, that VENUS; this MARS, that NEPTUNE; by whatever titles the strange gods might be denominated. The goddess HERTHA of our SAXON ancestors seems to be no other, according to TACITUS,[37] than the *Mater Tellus* of the ROMANS; and his conjecture was evidently just.

[34] HERODIAN. lib. 5. JUPITER AMMON is represented by CURTIUS as a deity of the same kind, lib. 4. cap. 7. The ARABIANS and PESSINUNTIANS adored also shapeless unformed stones as their deity. ARNOB. lib. 6. So much did their folly exceed that of the EGYPTIANS.

[35] DIOG. LÆRT. lib. 2.

[36] See CÆSAR of the religion of the GAULS, de bello Gallico, lib. 6.

[37] De moribus GERM.

SECTION 6

Origin of Theism from Polytheism

1 THE doctrine of one supreme Deity, the author of nature, is very ancient, has spread itself over great and populous nations, and among them has been embraced by all ranks and conditions of men: But whoever thinks that it has owed its success to the prevalent force of those invincible reasons, on which it is undoubtedly founded, would show himself little acquainted with the ignorance and stupidity of the people, and their incurable prejudices in favour of their particular superstitions. Even at this day, and in EUROPE, ask any of the vulgar, why he believes in an omnipotent creator of the world; he will never mention the beauty of final causes, of which he is wholly ignorant: He will not hold out his hand, and bid you contemplate the suppleness and variety of joints in his fingers, their bending all one way, the counterpoise which they receive from the thumb, the softness and fleshy parts of the inside of his hand, with all the other circumstances, which render that member fit for the use, to which it was destined. To these he has been long accustomed; and he beholds them with listlessness and unconcern. He will tell you of the sudden and unexpected death of such a one: The fall and bruise of such another: The excessive drought of this season: The cold and rains of another. These he ascribes to the immediate operation of providence: And such events, as, with good reasoners, are the chief difficulties in admitting a supreme intelligence, are with him the sole arguments for it.

2 Many theists, even the most zealous and refined, have denied a *particular* providence, and have asserted, that the Sovereign mind or first principle of all things, having fixed general laws, by which nature is governed, gives free and uninterrupted course to these laws, and disturbs not, at every turn, the settled order of events by particular volitions. From the beautiful connexion, say they, and rigid observance of established rules, we draw the chief argument for theism; and from the same principles are enabled to answer the principal objections against it. But so little is this understood by the generality of mankind, that, wherever they observe any one to ascribe all events to natural causes, and to remove the particular interposition of a deity, they are apt to suspect him of the grossest infidelity. "A little philosophy," says Lord BACON, "makes men atheists: A great deal reconciles them to

religion." For men, being taught, by superstitious prejudices, to lay the stress on a wrong place; when that fails them, and they discover, by a little reflection, that the course of nature is regular and uniform, their whole faith totters, and falls to ruin. But being taught, by more reflection, that this very regularity and uniformity is the strongest proof of design and of a supreme intelligence, they return to that belief, which they had deserted; and they are now able to establish it on a firmer and more durable foundation.

3 Convulsions in nature, disorders, prodigies, miracles, though the most opposite to the plan of a wise superintendent, impress mankind with the strongest sentiments of religion; the causes of events seeming then the most unknown and unaccountable. Madness, fury, rage, and an enflamed imagination, though they sink men nearest to the level of beasts, are, for a like reason, often supposed to be the only dispositions, in which we can have any immediate communication with the Deity.

4 We may conclude, therefore, upon the whole, that, since the vulgar, in nations, which have embraced the doctrine of theism, still build it upon irrational and superstitious principles, they are never led into that opinion by any process of argument, but by a certain train of thinking, more suitable to their genius and capacity.

5 It may readily happen, in an idolatrous nation, that, though men admit the existence of several limited deities, yet is there some one God, whom, in a particular manner, they make the object of their worship and adoration. They may either suppose, that, in the distribution of power and territory among the gods, their nation was subjected to the jurisdiction of that particular deity; or reducing heavenly objects to the model of things below, they may represent one god as the prince or supreme magistrate of the rest, who, though of the same nature, rules them with an authority, like that which an earthly sovereign exercises over his subjects and vassals. Whether this god, therefore, be considered as their peculiar patron, or as the general sovereign of heaven, his votaries will endeavour, by every art, to insinuate themselves into his favour; and supposing him to be pleased, like themselves, with praise and flattery, there is no eulogy or exaggeration, which will be spared in their addresses to him. In proportion as men's fears or distresses become more urgent, they still invent new strains of adulation; and even he who outdoes his predecessor in swelling up the titles of his divinity, is sure to be outdone by his successor in newer and more pompous epithets of praise. Thus they proceed; till at last they arrive at infinity itself, beyond which there is no farther progress: And it is well, if, in striving to get farther, and to represent a magnificent simplicity, they run not into inexplicable mystery, and destroy the intelligent nature of their deity, on

which alone any rational worship or adoration can be founded. While they confine themselves to the notion of a perfect being, the creator of the world, they coincide, by chance, with the principles of reason and true philosophy; though they are guided to that notion, not by reason, of which they are in a great measure incapable, but by the adulation and fears of the most vulgar superstition.

6 We often find, amongst barbarous nations, and even sometimes amongst civilized, that, when every strain of flattery has been exhausted towards arbitrary princes, when every human quality has been applauded to the utmost; their servile courtiers represent them, at last, as real divinities, and point them out to the people as objects of adoration. How much more natural, therefore, is it, that a limited deity, who at first is supposed only the immediate author of the particular goods and ills in life, should in the end be represented as sovereign maker and modifier of the universe?

7 Even where this notion of a supreme deity is already established; though it ought naturally to lessen every other worship, and abase every object of reverence, yet if a nation has entertained the opinion of a subordinate tutelar divinity, saint, or angel; their addresses to that being gradually rise upon them, and encroach on the adoration due to their supreme deity. The Virgin *Mary*, ere checked by the reformation, had proceeded, from being merely a good woman, to usurp many attributes of the Almighty: God and St. Nicholas go hand in hand, in all the prayers and petitions of the Muscovites.

8 Thus the deity, who, from love, converted himself into a bull, in order to carry off Europa; and who, from ambition, dethroned his father, Saturn, became the Optimus Maximus of the heathens. Thus, the God of Abraham, Isaac, and Jacob, became the supreme deity or Jehovah of the Jews.

9 The Jacobins, who denied the immaculate conception, have ever been very unhappy in their doctrine, even though political reasons have kept the Romish church from condemning it. The Cordeliers have run away with all the popularity. But in the fifteenth century, as we learn from Boulainvilliers,[38] an Italian *Cordelier* maintained, that, during the three days, when Christ was interred, the hypostatic union was dissolved, and that his human nature was not a proper object of adoration, during that period. Without the art of divination, one might foretel, that so gross and impious a blasphemy would not fail to be anathematized by the people. It was the occasion of great insults on the part of the Jacobins; who now got some recompence for their misfortunes in the war about the immaculate conception.

[38] Histoire abregée, p. 499.

10 Rather than relinquish this propensity to adulation, religionists, in all ages, have involved themselves in the greatest absurdities and contradictions.

11 HOMER, in one passage, calls OCEANUS and TETHYS the original parents of all things, conformably to the established mythology and tradition of the GREEKS: Yet, in other passages, he could not forbear complimenting JUPITER, the reigning deity, with that magnificent appellation; and accordingly denominates him the father of gods and men. He forgets, that every temple, every street was full of the ancestors, uncles, brothers, and sisters of this JUPITER; who was in reality nothing but an upstart parricide and usurper. A like contradiction is observable in HESIOD; and is so much the less excusable, as his professed intention was to deliver a true genealogy of the gods.

12 Were there a religion (and we may suspect MAHOMETANISM of this inconsistence) which sometimes painted the Deity in the most sublime colours, as the creator of heaven and earth; sometimes degraded him nearly to a level with human creatures in his powers and faculties; while at the same time it ascribed to him suitable infirmities, passions, and partialities, of the moral kind: That religion, after it was extinct, would also be cited as an instance of those contradictions, which arise from the gross, vulgar, natural conceptions of mankind, opposed to their continual propensity towards flattery and exaggeration. Nothing indeed would prove more strongly the divine origin of any religion, than to find (and happily this is the case with CHRISTIANITY) that it is free from a contradiction, so incident to human nature.

SECTION 7

Confirmation of this Doctrine

1 It appears certain, that, though the original notions of the vulgar represent the Divinity as a limited being, and consider him only as the particular cause of health or sickness; plenty or want; prosperity or adversity; yet when more magnificent ideas are urged upon them, they esteem it dangerous to refuse their assent. Will you say, that your deity is finite and bounded in his perfections; may be overcome by a greater force; is subject to human passions, pains, and infirmities; has a beginning, and may have an end? This they dare not affirm; but thinking it safest to comply with the higher encomiums, they endeavour, by an affected ravishment and devotion, to ingratiate themselves with him. As a confirmation of this, we may observe, that the assent of the vulgar is, in this case, merely verbal, and that they are incapable of conceiving those sublime qualities, which they seemingly attribute to the Deity. Their real idea of him, notwithstanding their pompous language, is still as poor and frivolous as ever.

2 That original intelligence, say the Magians, who is the first principle of all things, discovers himself *immediately* to the mind and understanding alone; but has placed the sun as his image in the visible universe; and when that bright luminary diffuses its beams over the earth and the firmament, it is a faint copy of the glory, which resides in the higher heavens. If you would escape the displeasure of this divine being, you must be careful never to set your bare foot upon the ground, nor spit into a fire, nor throw any water upon it, even though it were consuming a whole city.[39] Who can express the perfections of the Almighty? say the Mahometans. Even the noblest of his works, if compared to him, are but dust and rubbish. How much more must human conception fall short of his infinite perfections? His smile and favour renders men for ever happy; and to obtain it for your children, the best method is to cut off from them, while infants, a little bit of skin, about half the breadth of a farthing. Take two bits of cloth,[40] say the Roman Catholics, about an inch or an inch and a half square, join them by the corners with two strings or pieces of tape about sixteen inches long, throw this over your head, and make one of the bits of cloth lie upon your

[39] Hyde, de Relig. veterum Persarum.

[40] Called the Scapulaire.

breast, and the other upon your back, keeping them next your skin: There is not a better secret for recommending yourself to that infinite Being, who exists from eternity to eternity.

3 The GETES, commonly called immortal, from their steady belief of the soul's immortality, were genuine theists and unitarians. They affirmed ZAMOLXIS, their deity, to be the only true god; and asserted the worship of all other nations to be addressed to mere fictions and chimeras. But were their religious principles any more refined, on account of these magnificent pretensions? Every fifth year they sacrificed a human victim, whom they sent as a messenger to their deity, in order to inform him of their wants and necessities. And when it thundered, they were so provoked, that, in order to return the defiance, they let fly arrows at him, and declined not the combat as unequal. Such at least is the account, which HERODOTUS gives of the theism of the immortal GETES.[41]

[41] Lib. 4.

SECTION 8

Flux and Reflux of Polytheism and Theism

1 It is remarkable, that the principles of religion have a kind of flux and reflux in the human mind, and that men have a natural tendency to rise from idolatry to theism, and to sink again from theism into idolatry. The vulgar, that is, indeed, all mankind, a few excepted, being ignorant and uninstructed, never elevate their contemplation to the heavens, or penetrate by their disquisitions into the secret structure of vegetable or animal bodies; so far as to discover a supreme mind or original providence, which bestowed order on every part of nature. They consider these admirable works in a more confined and selfish view; and finding their own happiness and misery to depend on the secret influence and unforeseen concurrence of external objects, they regard, with perpetual attention, the *unknown causes*, which govern all these natural events, and distribute pleasure and pain, good and ill, by their powerful, but silent, operation. The unknown causes are still appealed to on every emergence; and in this general appearance or confused image, are the perpetual objects of human hopes and fears, wishes and apprehensions. By degrees, the active imagination of men, uneasy in this abstract conception of objects, about which it is incessantly employed, begins to render them more particular, and to clothe them in shapes more suitable to its natural comprehension. It represents them to be sensible, intelligent beings, like mankind; actuated by love and hatred, and flexible by gifts and entreaties, by prayers and sacrifices. Hence the origin of religion: And hence the origin of idolatry or polytheism.

2 But the same anxious concern for happiness, which begets the idea of these invisible, intelligent powers, allows not mankind to remain long in the first simple conception of them; as powerful, but limited beings; masters of human fate, but slaves to destiny and the course of nature. Men's exaggerated praises and compliments still swell their idea upon them; and elevating their deities to the utmost bounds of perfection, at last beget the attributes of unity and infinity, simplicity and spirituality. Such refined ideas, being somewhat disproportioned to vulgar comprehension, remain not long in their original purity; but require to be supported by the notion of inferior mediators or subordinate agents, which interpose between mankind and their supreme deity. These demi-gods or middle beings,

partaking more of human nature, and being more familiar to us, become the chief objects of devotion, and gradually recall that idolatry, which had been formerly banished by the ardent prayers and panegyrics of timorous and indigent mortals. But as these idolatrous religions fall every day into grosser and more vulgar conceptions, they at last destroy themselves, and, by the vile representations, which they form of their deities, make the tide turn again towards theism. But so great is the propensity, in this alternate revolution of human sentiments, to return back to idolatry, that the utmost precaution is not able effectually to prevent it. And of this, some theists, particularly the JEWS and MAHOMETANS, have been sensible; as appears by their banishing all the arts of statuary and painting, and not allowing the representations, even of human figures, to be taken by marble or colours; lest the common infirmity of mankind should thence produce idolatry. The feeble apprehensions of men cannot be satisfied with conceiving their deity as a pure spirit and perfect intelligence; and yet their natural terrors keep them from imputing to him the least shadow of limitation and imperfection. They fluctuate between these opposite sentiments. The same infirmity still drags them downwards, from an omnipotent and spiritual deity, to a limited and corporeal one, and from a corporeal and limited deity to a statue or visible representation. The same endeavour at elevation still pushes them upwards, from the statue or material image to the invisible power; and from the invisible power to an infinitely perfect deity, the creator and sovereign of the universe.

SECTION 9

Comparison of these Religions, with regard to Persecution and Toleration

1 POLYTHEISM or idolatrous worship, being founded entirely in vulgar traditions, is liable to this great inconvenience, that any practice or opinion, however barbarous or corrupted, may be authorized by it; and full scope is given, for knavery to impose on credulity, till morals and humanity be expelled from the religious systems of mankind. At the same time, idolatry is attended with this evident advantage, that, by limiting the powers and functions of its deities, it naturally admits the gods of other sects and nations to a share of divinity, and renders all the various deities, as well as rites, ceremonies, or traditions, compatible with each other.[42] Theism is opposite both in its advantages and disadvantages. As that system supposes one sole Deity, the perfection of reason and goodness, it should, if justly prosecuted, banish every thing frivolous, unreasonable, or inhuman from religious worship, and set before men the most illustrious example, as well as the most commanding motives, of justice and benevolence. These mighty advantages are not indeed overbalanced, (for that is not possible) but somewhat diminished, by inconveniencies, which arise from the vices and prejudices of mankind. While one sole object of devotion is acknowledged, the worship of other deities is regarded as absurd and impious. Nay, this unity of object seems naturally to require the unity of faith and ceremonies, and furnishes designing men with a pretence for representing their adversaries as profane, and the objects of divine as well as human vengeance. For as each sect is positive that its own faith and worship are entirely acceptable to the Deity, and as no one can conceive, that the same being should be pleased with different and opposite rites and principles; the several sects fall naturally

[42] VERRIUS FLACCUS, cited by PLINY, lib. 28. cap. 2. affirmed, that it was usual for the ROMANS, before they laid siege to any town, to invocate the tutelar deity of the place, and by promising him greater honours than those he at present enjoyed, bribe him to betray his old friends and votaries. The name of the tutelar deity of ROME was for this reason kept a most religious mystery; lest the enemies of the republic should be able, in the same manner, to draw him over to their service. For without the name, they thought, nothing of that kind could be practiced. PLINY says, that the common form of invocation was preserved to his time in the ritual of the pontifs. And MACROBIUS has transmitted a copy of it from the secret things of SAMMONICUS SERENUS.

into animosity, and mutually discharge on each other that sacred zeal and rancour, the most furious and implacable of all human passions.

2 The tolerating spirit of idolaters, both in ancient and modern times, is very obvious to any one, who is the least conversant in the writings of historians or travellers. When the oracle of DELPHI was asked, *What rites or worship was most acceptable to the gods?* "Those which are legally established in each city," replied the oracle.[43] Even priests, in those ages, could, it seems, allow salvation to those of a different communion. The ROMANS commonly adopted the gods of the conquered people; and never disputed the attributes of those local and national deities, in whose territories they resided. The religious wars and persecutions of the EGYPTIAN idolaters are indeed an exception to this rule; but are accounted for by ancient authors from reasons singular and remarkable. Different species of animals were the deities of the different sects among the EGYPTIANS; and the deities being in continual war, engaged their votaries in the same contention. The worshippers of dogs could not long remain in peace with the adorers of cats or wolves.[44] But where that reason took not place, the EGYPTIAN superstition was not so incompatible as is commonly imagined; since we learn from HERODOTUS,[45] that very large contributions were given by AMASIS towards rebuilding the temple of DELPHI.

3 The intolerance of almost all religions, which have maintained the unity of God, is as remarkable as the contrary principle of polytheists. The implacable narrow spirit of the JEWS is well known. MAHOMETANISM set out with still more bloody principles; and even to this day, deals out damnation, though not fire and faggot, to all other sects. And if, among CHRISTIANS, the ENGLISH and DUTCH have embraced the principles of toleration, this singularity has proceeded from the steady resolution of the civil magistrate, in opposition to the continued efforts of priests and bigots.

4 The disciples of ZOROASTER shut the doors of heaven against all but the MAGIANS.[46] Nothing could more obstruct the progress of the PERSIAN conquests, than the furious zeal of that nation against the temples and images of the GREEKS. And after the overthrow of that empire, we find ALEXANDER, as a polytheist, immediately re-establishing the worship of the BABYLONIANS, which their former princes, as monotheists, had carefully abolished.[47] Even the blind and devoted attachment of that conqueror to the GREEK superstition hindered not but he himself sacrificed according to the BABYLONISH rites and ceremonies.[48]

[43] XENOPH. Memor. lib. 1. [44] PLUTARCH. de ISID. & OSIRIDE. [45] Lib. 2. sub fine.
[46] HYDE, de Relig. vet. PERSARUM. [47] ARRIAN. de exped. lib. 3. Id. lib. 7.
[48] Id. ibid.

5 So sociable is polytheism, that the utmost fierceness and antipathy, which it meets with in an opposite religion, is scarcely able to disgust it, and keep it at a distance. Augustus praised extremely the reserve of his grandson, Caius Cæsar, when this latter prince, passing by Jerusalem, deigned not to sacrifice according to the Jewish law. But for what reason did Augustus so much approve of this conduct? Only, because that religion was by the Pagans esteemed ignoble and barbarous.[49]

6 I may venture to affirm, that few corruptions of idolatry and polytheism are more pernicious to society than this corruption of theism,[50] when carried to the utmost height. The human sacrifices of the Carthaginians, Mexicans, and many barbarous nations,[51] scarcely exceed the inquisition and persecutions of Rome and Madrid. For besides, that the effusion of blood may not be so great in the former case as in the latter; besides this, I say, the human victims, being chosen by lot, or by some exterior signs, affect not, in so considerable a degree, the rest of the society. Whereas virtue, knowledge, love of liberty, are the qualities, which call down the fatal vengeance of inquisitors; and when expelled, leave the society in the most shameful ignorance, corruption, and bondage. The illegal murder of one man by a tyrant is more pernicious than the death of a thousand by pestilence, famine, or any undistinguishing calamity.

7 In the temple of Diana at Aricia near Rome, whoever murdered the present priest, was legally entitled to be installed his successor.[52] A very singular institution! For, however barbarous and bloody the common superstitions often are to the laity, they usually turn to the advantage of the holy order.

[49] Sueton. in vita Aug. cap. 93.

[50] *Corruptio optimi pessima.*

[51] Most nations have fallen into this guilt of human sacrifices; though, perhaps, that impious superstition has never prevailed very much in any civilized nation, unless we except the Carthaginians. For the Tyrians soon abolished it. A sacrifice is conceived as a present; and any present is delivered to their deity by destroying it and rendering it useless to men; by burning what is solid, pouring out the liquid, and killing the animate. For want of a better way of doing him service, we do ourselves an injury; and fancy that we thereby express, at least, the heartiness of our good-will and adoration. Thus our mercenary devotion deceives ourselves, and imagines it deceives the deity.

[52] Strabo, lib. 5. Sueton. in vita Cal.

SECTION 10

With regard to Courage or Abasement

1 From the comparison of theism and idolatry, we may form some other observations, which will also confirm the vulgar observation, that the corruption of the best things gives rise to the worst.

2 Where the Deity is represented as infinitely superior to mankind, this belief, though altogether just, is apt, when joined with superstitious terrors, to sink the human mind into the lowest submission and abasement, and to represent the monkish virtues of mortification, penance, humility, and passive suffering, as the only qualities which are acceptable to him. But where the gods are conceived to be only a little superior to mankind, and to have been, many of them, advanced from that inferior rank, we are more at our ease in our addresses to them, and may even, without profaneness, aspire sometimes to a rivalship and emulation of them. Hence activity, spirit, courage, magnanimity, love of liberty, and all the virtues which aggrandize a people.

3 The heroes in paganism correspond exactly to the saints in popery and holy dervises in Mahometanism. The place of Hercules, Theseus, Hector, Romulus, is now supplied by Dominic, Francis, Anthony, and Benedict. Instead of the destruction of monsters, the subduing of tyrants, the defence of our native country; whippings and fastings, cowardice and humility, abject submission and slavish obedience, are become the means of obtaining celestial honours among mankind.

4 One great incitement to the pious Alexander in his warlike expeditions was his rivalship of Hercules and Bacchus, whom he justly pretended to have excelled.[53] Brasidas, that generous and noble Spartan, after falling in battle, had heroic honours paid him by the inhabitants of Amphipolis, whose defence he had embraced.[54] And in general, all founders of states and colonies among the Greeks were raised to this inferior rank of divinity, by those who reaped the benefit of their labours.

5 This gave rise to the observation of Machiavel,[55] that the doctrines of the Christian religion (meaning the catholic; for he knew no other) which recommend only passive courage and suffering, had subdued the spirit of

[53] Arrian. passim. [54] Thucyd. lib. 5. [55] Discorsi, lib. 6.

mankind, and had fitted them for slavery and subjection. An observation, which would certainly be just, were there not many other circumstances in human society which controul the genius and character of a religion.

6 BRASIDAS seized a mouse, and being bit by it, let it go. "There is nothing so contemptible," said he, "but what may be safe, if it has but courage to defend itself."[56] BELLARMINE patiently and humbly allowed the fleas and other odious vermin to prey upon him. "We shall have heaven," said he, "to reward us for our sufferings: But these poor creatures have nothing but the enjoyment of the present life."[57] Such difference is there between the maxims of a GREEK hero and a CATHOLIC saint.

[56] PLUTARCH. Apophth.

[57] BAYLE, Article BELLARMINE.

SECTION 11

With regard to Reason or Absurdity

1 HERE is another observation to the same purpose, and a new proof that the corruption of the best things begets the worst. If we examine, without prejudice, the ancient heathen mythology, as contained in the poets, we shall not discover in it any such monstrous absurdity, as we may at first be apt to apprehend. Where is the difficulty in conceiving, that the same powers or principles, whatever they were, which formed this visible world, men and animals, produced also a species of intelligent creatures, of more refined substance and greater authority than the rest? That these creatures may be capricious, revengeful, passionate, voluptuous, is easily conceived; nor is any circumstance more apt, among ourselves, to engender such vices, than the licence of absolute authority. And in short, the whole mythological system is so natural, that, in the vast variety of planets and worlds, contained in this universe, it seems more than probable, that, somewhere or other, it is really carried into execution.

2 The chief objection to it with regard to this planet, is, that it is not ascertained by any just reason or authority. The ancient tradition, insisted on by heathen priests and theologers, is but a weak foundation; and transmitted also such a number of contradictory reports, supported, all of them, by equal authority, that it became absolutely impossible to fix a preference amongst them. A few volumes, therefore, must contain all the polemical writings of pagan priests: And their whole theology must consist more of traditional stories and superstitious practices than of philosophical argument and controversy.

3 But where theism forms the fundamental principle of any popular religion, that tenet is so conformable to sound reason, that philosophy is apt to incorporate itself with such a system of theology. And if the other dogmas of that system be contained in a sacred book, such as the Alcoran, or be determined by any visible authority, like that of the ROMAN pontiff, speculative reasoners naturally carry on their assent, and embrace a theory, which has been instilled into them by their earliest education, and which also possesses some degree of consistence and uniformity. But as these appearances are sure, all of them, to prove deceitful, philosophy will soon find herself very unequally yoked with her new associate; and instead of

regulating each principle, as they advance together, she is at every turn perverted to serve the purposes of superstition. For besides the unavoidable incoherencies, which must be reconciled and adjusted; one may safely affirm, that all popular theology, especially the scholastic, has a kind of appetite for absurdity and contradiction. If that theology went not beyond reason and common sense, her doctrines would appear too easy and familiar. Amazement must of necessity be raised: Mystery affected: Darkness and obscurity sought after: And a foundation of merit afforded to the devout votaries, who desire an opportunity of subduing their rebellious reason, by the belief of the most unintelligible sophisms.

4 Ecclesiastical history sufficiently confirms these reflections. When a controversy is started, some people always pretend with certainty to foretel the issue. Whichever opinion, say they, is most contrary to plain sense is sure to prevail; even where the general interest of the system requires not that decision. Though the reproach of heresy may, for some time, be bandied about among the disputants, it always rests at last on the side of reason. Any one, it is pretended, that has but learning enough of this kind to know the definition of ARIAN, PELAGIAN, ERASTIAN, SOCINIAN, SABELLIAN, EUTYCHIAN, NESTORIAN, MONOTHELITE, *&c.* not to mention PROTESTANT, whose fate is yet uncertain, will be convinced of the truth of this observation. It is thus a system becomes more absurd in the end, merely from its being reasonable and philosophical in the beginning.

5 To oppose the torrent of scholastic religion by such feeble maxims as these, that *it is impossible for the same thing to be and not to be*, that *the whole is greater than a part*, that *two and three make five*; is pretending to stop the ocean with a bull-rush. Will you set up profane reason against sacred mystery? No punishment is great enough for your impiety. And the same fires, which were kindled for heretics, will serve also for the destruction of philosophers.

SECTION 12

With regard to Doubt or Conviction

1 WE meet every day with people so sceptical with regard to history, that they assert it impossible for any nation ever to believe such absurd principles as those of GREEK and EGYPTIAN paganism; and at the same time so dogmatical with regard to religion, that they think the same absurdities are to be found in no other communion. CAMBYSES entertained like prejudices; and very impiously ridiculed, and even wounded, APIS, the great god of the EGYPTIANS, who appeared to his profane senses nothing but a large spotted bull. But HERODOTUS judiciously ascribes this sally of passion to a real madness or disorder of the brain: Otherwise, says the historian, he never would have openly affronted any established worship. For on that head, continues he, every nation are best satisfied with their own, and think they have the advantage over every other nation.

2 It must be allowed, that the ROMAN CATHOLICS are a very learned sect; and that no one communion, but that of the church of ENGLAND, can dispute their being the most learned of all the CHRISTIAN churches: Yet AVERROES, the famous ARABIAN, who, no doubt, had heard of the EGYPTIAN superstitions, declares, that, of all religions, the most absurd and nonsensical is that, whose votaries eat, after having created, their deity.

3 I believe, indeed, that there is no tenet in all paganism, which would give so fair a scope to ridicule as this of the *real presence:* For it is so absurd, that it eludes the force of all argument. There are even some pleasant stories of that kind, which, though somewhat profane, are commonly told by the CATHOLICS themselves. One day, a priest, it is said, gave inadvertently, instead of the sacrament, a counter, which had by accident fallen among the holy wafers. The communicant waited patiently for some time, expecting it would dissolve on his tongue: But finding that it still remained entire, he took it off. "I wish," cried he to the priest, "you have not committed some mistake: I wish you have not given me God the Father: He is so hard and tough there is no swallowing him."

4 A famous general, at that time in the MUSCOVITE service, having come to PARIS for the recovery of his wounds, brought along with him a young TURK, whom he had taken prisoner. Some of the doctors of the SORBONNE (who are altogether as positive as the dervises of CONSTANTINOPLE) thinking

it a pity, that the poor TURK should be damned for want of instruction, solicited MUSTAPHA very hard to turn CHRISTIAN, and promised him, for his encouragement, plenty of good wine in this world, and paradise in the next. These allurements were too powerful to be resisted; and therefore, having been well instructed and catechized, he at last agreed to receive the sacraments of baptism and the Lord's supper. The priest, however, to make every thing sure and solid, still continued his instructions; and began the next day with the usual question, "How many Gods are there?" "None at all," replies BENEDICT; for that was his new name. "How! None at all!" cries the priest. "To be sure," said the honest proselyte. "You have told me all along that there is but one God: And yesterday I eat him."

5 Such are the doctrines of our brethren the CATHOLICS. But to these doctrines we are so accustomed, that we never wonder at them: Though, in a future age, it will probably become difficult to persuade some nations, that any human, two-legged creature could ever embrace such principles. And it is a thousand to one, but these nations themselves shall have something full as absurd in their own creed, to which they will give a most implicit and most religious assent.

6 I lodged once at PARIS in the same *hotel* with an ambassador from TUNIS, who, having passed some years at LONDON, was returning home that way. One day I observed his MOORISH excellency diverting himself under the porch, with surveying the splendid equipages that drove along; when there chanced to pass that way some *Capuchin* friars, who had never seen a TURK; as he, on his part, though accustomed to the EUROPEAN dresses, had never seen the grotesque figure of a *Capuchin*: And there is no expressing the mutual admiration, with which they inspired each other. Had the chaplain of the embassy entered into a dispute with these FRANCISCANS, their reciprocal surprize had been of the same nature. Thus all mankind stand staring at one another; and there is no beating it into their heads, that the turban of the AFRICAN is not just as good or as bad a fashion as the cowl of the EUROPEAN. "He is a very honest man," said the prince of SALLEE, speaking of de RUYTER, "It is a pity he were a CHRISTIAN."

7 *How can you worship leeks and onions?* we shall suppose a SORBONNIST to say to a priest of SAIS. *If we worship them*, replies the latter; *at least, we do not, at the same time, eat them. But what strange objects of adoration are cats and monkies?* says the learned doctor. *They are at least as good as the relicts or rotten bones of martyrs*, answers his no less learned antagonist. *Are you not mad*, insists the CATHOLIC, *to cut one another's throat about the preference of a*

cabbage or a cucumber? Yes, says the pagan; *I allow it, if you will confess, that those are still madder, who fight about the preference among volumes of sophistry, ten thousand of which are not equal in value to one cabbage or cucumber.*[58]

8 Every by-stander will easily judge (but unfortunately the by-standers are few) that, if nothing were requisite to establish any popular system, but exposing the absurdities of other systems, every votary of every superstition could give a sufficient reason for his blind and bigotted attachment to the principles in which he has been educated. But without so extensive a knowledge, on which to ground this assurance, (and perhaps, better without it) there is not wanting a sufficient stock of religious zeal and faith among mankind. Diodorus Siculus[59] gives a remarkable instance to this purpose, of which he was himself an eye-witness. While Egypt lay under the greatest terror of the Roman name, a legionary soldier having inadvertently been guilty of the sacrilegious impiety of killing a cat, the whole people rose upon him with the utmost fury; and all the efforts of the prince were not able to save him. The senate and people of Rome, I am persuaded, would not, then, have been so delicate with regard to their national deities. They very frankly, a little after that time, voted Augustus a place in the celestial mansions; and would have dethroned every god in heaven, for his sake, had he seemed to desire it. "Præsens divus habebitur Augustus," says Horace. That is a very important point: And in other nations and other ages, the same circumstance has not been deemed altogether indifferent.[60]

[58] It is strange that the Egyptian religion, though so absurd, should yet have borne so great a resemblance to the Jewish, that ancient writers even of the greatest genius were not able to observe any difference between them. For it is remarkable that both Tacitus and Suetonius, when they mention that decree of the senate, under Tiberius, by which the Egyptian and Jewish proselytes were banished from Rome, expressly treat these religions as the same; and it appears, that even the decree itself was founded on that supposition. "Actum & de sacris Ægyptiis, Judaicisque pellendis; factumque patrum consultum, ut quatuor millia libertini generis *ea superstitione* infecta, quis idonea ætas, in insulam Sardiniam veherentur, cœrcendis illic latrociniis; & si ob gravitatem coeli interissent, *vile damnum*: Ceteri cederent Italia, nisi certam ante diem profanos ritus exuissent." Tacit. ann. lib. 2. cap. 85. "Externas cæremonias, Ægyptios, Judaicosque ritus compescuit; coactis qui *superstitione ea* tenebantur, religiosas vestes cum instrumento omni comburere," *&c.* Sueton. Tiber. cap. 36. These wise heathens, observing something in the general air, and genius, and spirit of the two religions to be the same, esteemed the differences of their dogmas too frivolous to deserve any attention.

[59] Lib. 1.

[60] When Louis the XIVth took on himself the protection of the Jesuits' College of Clermont, the society ordered the king's arms to be put up over the gate, and took down the cross, in order to make way for it: Which gave occasion to the following epigram:

Sustulit hinc Christi, posuitque insignia Regis:
Impia gens, alium nescit habere Deum.

9 Notwithstanding the sanctity of our holy religion, says TULLY,[61] no crime is more common with us than sacrilege: But was it ever heard of, that an EGYPTIAN violated the temple of a cat, an ibis, or a crocodile? There is no torture, an EGYPTIAN would not undergo, says the same author in another place,[62] rather than injure an ibis, an aspic, a cat, a dog, or a crocodile. Thus it is strictly true, what DRYDEN observes,

> Of whatsoe'er descent their godhead be,
> Stock, stone, or other homely pedigree,
> In his defence his servants are as bold,
> As if he had been born of beaten gold.
>
> ABSALOM and ACHITOPHEL.

Nay, the baser the materials are, of which the divinity is composed, the greater devotion is he likely to excite in the breasts of his deluded votaries. They exult in their shame, and make a merit with their deity, in braving, for his sake, all the ridicule and contumely of his enemies. Ten thousand Crusaders enlist themselves under the holy banners; and even openly triumph in those parts of their religion, which their adversaries regard as the most reproachful.

10 There occurs, I own, a difficulty in the EGYPTIAN system of theology; as indeed, few systems of that kind are entirely free from difficulties. It is evident, from their method of propagation, that a couple of cats, in fifty years, would stock a whole kingdom; and if that religious veneration were still paid them, it would, in twenty more, not only be easier in EGYPT to find a god than a man, which PETRONIUS says was the case in some parts of ITALY; but the gods must at last entirely starve the men, and leave themselves neither priests nor votaries remaining. It is probable, therefore, that this wise nation, the most celebrated in antiquity for prudence and sound policy, foreseeing such dangerous consequences, reserved all their worship for the full-grown divinities, and used the freedom to drown the holy spawn or little sucking gods, without any scruple or remorse. And thus the practice of warping the tenets of religion, in order to serve temporal interests, is not, by any means, to be regarded as an invention of these later ages.

11 The learned, philosophical VARRO, discoursing of religion, pretends not to deliver any thing beyond probabilities and appearances: Such was his good sense and moderation! But the passionate, the zealous AUGUSTINE, insults the noble ROMAN on his scepticism and reserve, and professes the most thorough belief and assurance.[63] A heathen poet, however, contemporary

[61] De nat. Deor. lib. 1.

[62] Tusc. quæst. lib. 5.

[63] De civitate Dei, lib. 7. cap. 17.

with the saint, absurdly esteems the religious system of the latter so false, that even the credulity of children, he says, could not engage them to believe it.[64]

12 Is it strange, when mistakes are so common, to find every one positive and dogmatical? And that the zeal often rises in proportion to the error? "Moverunt," says SPARTIAN, "& ea tempestate, Judæi bellum quod vetabantur mutilare genitalia."[65]

13 If ever there was a nation or a time, in which the public religion lost all authority over mankind, we might expect, that infidelity in ROME, during the CICERONIAN age, would openly have erected its throne, and that CICERO himself, in every speech and action, would have been its most declared abettor. But it appears, that, whatever sceptical liberties that great man might take, in his writings or in philosophical conversation; he yet avoided, in the common conduct of life, the imputation of deism and profaneness. Even in his own family, and to his wife TERENTIA, whom he highly trusted, he was willing to appear a devout religionist; and there remains a letter, addressed to her, in which he seriously desires her to offer sacrifice to APOLLO and ÆSCULAPIUS, in gratitude for the recovery of his health.[66]

14 POMPEY's devotion was much more sincere: In all his conduct, during the civil wars, he paid a great regard to auguries, dreams, and prophesies.[67] AUGUSTUS was tainted with superstition of every kind. As it is reported of MILTON, that his poetical genius never flowed with ease and abundance in the spring; so AUGUSTUS observed, that his own genius for dreaming never was so perfect during that season, nor was so much to be relied on, as during the rest of the year. That great and able emperor was also extremely uneasy, when he happened to change his shoes, and put the right foot shoe on the left foot.[68] In short, it cannot be doubted, but the votaries of the established superstition of antiquity were as numerous in every state, as those of the modern religion are at present. Its influence was as universal; though it was not so great. As many people gave their assent to it; though that assent was not seemingly so strong, precise, and affirmative.

15 We may observe, that, notwithstanding the dogmatical, imperious style of all superstition, the conviction of the religionists, in all ages, is more affected than real, and scarcely ever approaches, in any degree, to that solid belief and persuasion, which governs us in the common affairs of life. Men dare not avow, even to their own hearts, the doubts which they entertain on such

[64] CLAUDII RUTILII NUMITIANI, iter. lib. 1. l. 387. [65] In vita ADRIANI.
[66] Lib. 14. epist. 7. [67] CICERO, de Divin. lib. 2. cap. 24.
[68] SUETON. AUG. cap. 90, 91, 92. PLIN. lib. 2. cap. 7.

subjects: They make a merit of implicit faith; and disguise to themselves their real infidelity, by the strongest asseverations and most positive bigotry. But nature is too hard for all their endeavours, and suffers not the obscure, glimmering light, afforded in those shadowy regions, to equal the strong impressions, made by common sense and by experience. The usual course of men's conduct belies their words, and shows, that their assent in these matters is some unaccountable operation of the mind between disbelief and conviction, but approaching much nearer to the former than to the latter.

16 Since, therefore, the mind of man appears of so loose and unsteady a texture, that, even at present, when so many persons find an interest in continually employing on it the chissel and the hammer, yet are they not able to engrave theological tenets with any lasting impression; how much more must this have been the case in ancient times, when the retainers to the holy function were so much fewer in comparison? No wonder, that the appearances were then very inconsistent, and that men, on some occasions, might seem determined infidels, and enemies to the established religion, without being so in reality; or at least, without knowing their own minds in that particular.

17 Another cause, which rendered the ancient religions much looser than the modern, is, that the former were *traditional* and the latter are *scriptural*; and the tradition in the former was complex, contradictory, and, on many occasions, doubtful; so that it could not possibly be reduced to any standard and canon, or afford any determinate articles of faith. The stories of the gods were numberless like the popish legends; and though every one, almost, believed a part of these stories, yet no one could believe or know the whole: While, at the same time, all must have acknowledged, that no one part stood on a better foundation than the rest. The traditions of different cities and nations were also, on many occasions, directly opposite; and no reason could be assigned for preferring one to the other. And as there was an infinite number of stories, with regard to which tradition was nowise positive; the gradation was insensible, from the most fundamental articles of faith, to those loose and precarious fictions. The pagan religion, therefore, seemed to vanish like a cloud, whenever one approached to it, and examined it piecemeal. It could never be ascertained by any fixed dogmas and principles. And though this did not convert the generality of mankind from so absurd a faith; for when will the people be reasonable? yet it made them faulter and hesitate more in maintaining their principles, and was even apt to produce, in certain dispositions of mind,

some practices and opinions, which had the appearance of determined infidelity.

18 To which we may add, that the fables of the pagan religion were, of themselves, light, easy, and familiar; without devils, or seas of brimstone, or any object that could much terrify the imagination. Who could forbear smiling, when he thought of the loves of MARS and VENUS, or the amorous frolics of JUPITER and PAN? In this respect, it was a true poetical religion; if it had not rather too much levity for the graver kinds of poetry. We find that it has been adopted by modern bards; nor have these talked with greater freedom and irreverence of the gods, whom they regarded as fictions, than the ancients did of the real objects of their devotion.

19 The inference is by no means just, that, because a system of religion has made no deep impression on the minds of a people, it must therefore have been positively rejected by all men of common sense, and that opposite principles, in spite of the prejudices of education, were generally established by argument and reasoning. I know not, but a contrary inference may be more probable. The less importunate and assuming any species of superstition appears, the less will it provoke men's spleen and indignation, or engage them into enquiries concerning its foundation and origin. This in the mean time is obvious, that the empire of all religious faith over the understanding is wavering and uncertain, subject to every variety of humour, and dependent on the present incidents, which strike the imagination. The difference is only in the degrees. An ancient will place a stroke of impiety and one of superstition alternately, throughout a whole discourse:[69] A modern often thinks in the same way, though he may be more guarded in his expression.

20 LUCIAN tells us expressly,[70] that whoever believed not the most ridiculous fables of paganism was deemed by the people profane and impious. To what purpose, indeed, would that agreeable author have employed the whole force of his wit and satire against the national religion, had not that religion been generally believed by his countrymen and contemporaries?

21 LIVY[71] acknowledges as frankly, as any divine would at present, the common incredulity of his age; but then he condemns it as severely.

[69] Witness this remarkable passage of TACITUS: "Præter multiplices rerum humanarum casus, cœlo terraque prodigia, & fulminum monitus, & futurorum præsagia, læta, tristia, ambigua, manifesta. Nec enim unquam atrocioribus populi Romani cladibus, magisque justis judiciis approbatum est, non esse curæ Diis securitatem nostram, esse ultionem." Hist. lib. 1. AUGUSTUS's quarrel with NEPTUNE is an instance of the same kind. Had not the emperor believed NEPTUNE to be a real being, and to have dominion over the sea, where had been the foundation of his anger? And if he believed it, what madness to provoke still farther that deity? The same observation may be made upon QUINTILIAN's exclamation, on account of the death of his children, lib. 6. Præf.

[70] Philopseudes. [71] Lib. 10. cap. 40.

And who can imagine, that a national superstition, which could delude so ingenious a man, would not also impose on the generality of the people?

22 The Stoics bestowed many magnificent and even impious epithets on their sage; that he alone was rich, free, a king, and equal to the immortal gods. They forgot to add, that he was not inferior in prudence and understanding to an old woman. For surely nothing can be more pitiful than the sentiments, which that sect entertained with regard to religious matters; while they seriously agree with the common augurs, that, when a raven croaks from the left, it is a good omen; but a bad one, when a rook makes a noise from the same quarter. Panætius was the only Stoic, among the Greeks, who so much as doubted with regard to auguries and divinations.[72] Marcus Antoninus[73] tells us, that he himself had received many admonitions from the gods in his sleep. It is true, Epictetus[74] forbids us to regard the language of rooks and ravens; but it is not, that they do not speak truth: It is only, because they can foretel nothing but the breaking of our neck or the forfeiture of our estate; which are circumstances, says he, that nowise concern us. Thus the Stoics join a philosophical enthusiasm to a religious superstition. The force of their mind, being all turned to the side of morals, unbent itself in that of religion.[75]

23 Plato[76] introduces Socrates affirming, that the accusation of impiety raised against him was owing entirely to his rejecting such fables, as those of Saturn's castrating his father, Uranus, and Jupiter's dethroning Saturn: Yet in a subsequent dialogue,[77] Socrates confesses, that the doctrine of the mortality of the soul was the received opinion of the people. Is there here any contradiction? Yes, surely: But the contradiction is not in Plato; it is in the people, whose religious principles in general are always composed of the most discordant parts; especially in an age, when superstition sate so easy and light upon them.[78]

[72] Cicero, de Divin. lib. 1. cap. 3 & 7. [73] Lib. 1. § 17. [74] Ench. § 17.

[75] The Stoics, I own, were not quite orthodox in the established religion; but one may see, from these instances, that they went a great way: And the people undoubtedly went every length.

[76] Eutyphro. [77] Phædo.

[78] Xenophon's conduct, as related by himself, is, at once, an incontestable proof of the general credulity of mankind in those ages, and the incoherencies, in all ages, of men's opinions in religious matters. That great captain and philosopher, the disciple of Socrates, and one who has delivered some of the most refined sentiments with regard to a deity, gave all the following marks of vulgar, pagan superstition. By Socrates's advice, he consulted the oracle of Delphi, before he would engage in the expedition of Cyrus. De exped. lib. 3. p. 294. ex edit. Leuncl. Sees a dream the night after the generals were seized; which he pays great regard to, but thinks ambiguous. Id. p. 295. He and the whole army regard sneezing as a very lucky omen. Id. p. 300. Has another dream, when he comes to the river Centrites, which his fellow-general, Chirosophus, also pays great regard to. Id. lib. 4. p. 323. The Greeks, suffering from a cold north wind, sacrifice to it; and the historian observes, that it immediately abated. Id. p. 329. Xenophon consults the sacrifices in

24 The same CICERO, who affected, in his own family, to appear a devout religionist, makes no scruple, in a public court of judicature, of treating the doctrine of a future state as a ridiculous fable, to which no body could give any attention.[79] SALLUST[80] represents CÆSAR as speaking the same language in the open senate.[81]

25 But that all these freedoms implied not a total and universal infidelity and scepticism amongst the people, is too apparent to be denied. Though some parts of the national religion hung loose upon the minds of men, other parts adhered more closely to them: And it was the chief business of the sceptical philosophers to show, that there was no more foundation for one than for the other. This is the artifice of COTTA in the dialogues concerning the *nature of the gods*. He refutes the whole system of mythology by leading the orthodox gradually, from the more momentous stories, which were believed, to the more frivolous, which every one ridiculed: From the gods to the goddesses; from the goddesses to the nymphs; from the nymphs to the fawns and satyrs. His master, CARNEADES, had employed the same method of reasoning.[82]

26 Upon the whole, the greatest and most observable differences between a *traditional, mythological* religion, and a *systematical, scholastic* one, are two:

secret, before he would form any resolution with himself about settling a colony. Lib. 5. p. 359. He was himself a very skilful augur. Id. p. 361. Is determined by the victims to refuse the sole command of the army which was offered him. Lib. 6. p. 372. CLEANDER, the SPARTAN, though very desirous of it, refuses it for the same reason. Id. p. 392. XENOPHON mentions an old dream with the interpretation given him, when he first joined CYRUS. p. 373. Mentions also the place of HERCULES's descent into hell as believing it, and says the marks of it are still remaining. Id. p. 375. Had almost starved the army, rather than lead them to the field against the auspices. Id. p. 382, 383. His friend, EUCLIDES, the augur, would not believe that he had brought no money from the expedition; till he (EUCLIDES) sacrificed, and then he saw the matter clearly in the Exta. Lib. 7. p. 425. The same philosopher, proposing a project of mines for the encrease of the ATHENIAN revenues, advises them first to consult the oracle. De rat. red. p. 932. That all this devotion was not a farce, in order to serve a political purpose, appears both from the facts themselves, and from the genius of that age, when little or nothing could be gained by hypocrisy. Besides, XENOPHON, as appears from his Memorabilia, was a kind of heretic in those times, which no political devotee ever is. It is for the same reason, I maintain, that NEWTON, LOCKE, CLARKE, &c. being *Arians* or *Socinians*, were very sincere in the creed they professed: And I always oppose this argument to some libertines, who will needs have it, that it was impossible but that these philosophers must have been hypocrites.

[79] Pro CLUENTIO, cap. 61. [80] De bello CATILIN.

[81] CICERO (Tusc. quæst. lib. 1. cap. 5, 6.) and SENECA (epist. 24.), as also JUVENAL (satyr. 2.) maintain that there is no boy or old woman so ridiculous as to believe the poets in their accounts of a future state. Why then does LUCRETIUS so highly exalt his master for freeing us from these terrors? Perhaps the generality of mankind were then in the disposition of CEPHALUS in PLATO (de rep. lib. 1.) who while he was young and healthful could ridicule these stories; but as soon as he became old and infirm, began to entertain apprehensions of their truth. This we may observe not to be unusual even at present.

[82] SEXT. EMPIR. advers. mathem. lib. 9.

The former is often more reasonable, as consisting only of a multitude of stories, which, however groundless, imply no express absurdity and demonstrative contradiction; and sits also so easy and light on men's minds, that, though it may be as universally received, it happily makes no such deep impression on the affections and understanding.

SECTION 13

Impious Conceptions of the Divine Nature in Popular Religions of Both Kinds

1 The primary religion of mankind arises chiefly from an anxious fear of future events; and what ideas will naturally be entertained of invisible, unknown powers, while men lie under dismal apprehensions of any kind, may easily be conceived. Every image of vengeance, severity, cruelty, and malice must occur and must augment the ghastliness and horror, which oppresses the amazed religionist. A panic having once seized the mind, the active fancy still farther multiplies the objects of terror; while that profound darkness, or, what is worse, that glimmering light, with which we are environed, represents the spectres of divinity under the most dreadful appearances imaginable. And no idea of perverse wickedness can be framed, which those terrified devotees do not readily, without scruple, apply to their deity.

2 This appears the natural state of religion, when surveyed in one light. But if we consider, on the other hand, that spirit of praise and eulogy, which necessarily has place in all religions, and which is the consequence of these very terrors, we must expect a quite contrary system of theology to prevail. Every virtue, every excellence, must be ascribed to the divinity, and no exaggeration will be deemed sufficient to reach those perfections, with which he is endowed. Whatever strains of panegyric can be invented, are immediately embraced, without consulting any arguments or phænomena: It is esteemed a sufficient confirmation of them, that they give us more magnificent ideas of the divine objects of our worship and adoration.

3 Here therefore is a kind of contradiction between the different principles of human nature, which enter into religion. Our natural terrors present the notion of a devilish and malicious deity: Our propensity to adulation leads us to acknowledge an excellent and divine. And the influence of these opposite principles are various, according to the different situation of the human understanding.

4 In very barbarous and ignorant nations, such as the Africans and Indians, nay even the Japonese, who can form no extensive ideas of power and knowledge, worship may be paid to a being, whom they confess to be wicked and detestable; though they may be cautious, perhaps, of pronouncing this

judgment of him in public, or in his temple, where he may be supposed to hear their reproaches.

5 Such rude, imperfect ideas of the Divinity adhere long to all idolaters; and it may safely be affirmed, that the GREEKS themselves never got entirely rid of them. It is remarked by XENOPHON,[83] in praise of SOCRATES, that this philosopher assented not to the vulgar opinion, which supposed the gods to know some things, and be ignorant of others: He maintained, that they knew every thing; what was done, said, or even thought. But as this was a strain of philosophy[84] much above the conception of his countrymen, we need not be surprized, if very frankly, in their books and conversation, they blamed the deities, whom they worshipped in their temples. It is observable, that HERODOTUS in particular scruples not, in many passages, to ascribe *envy* to the gods; a sentiment, of all others, the most suitable to a mean and devilish nature. The pagan hymns, however, sung in public worship, contained nothing but epithets of praise; even while the actions ascribed to the gods were the most barbarous and detestable. When TIMOTHEUS, the poet, recited a hymn to DIANA, in which he enumerated, with the greatest eulogies, all the actions and attributes of that cruel, capricious goddess: "May your daughter," said one present, "become such as the deity whom you celebrate."[85]

6 But as men farther exalt their idea of their divinity; it is their notion of his power and knowledge only, not of his goodness, which is improved. On the contrary, in proportion to the supposed extent of his science and authority, their terrors naturally augment; while they believe, that no secrecy can conceal them from his scrutiny, and that even the inmost recesses of their breast lie open before him. They must then be careful not to form expressly any sentiment of blame and disapprobation. All must be applause, ravishment, extacy. And while their gloomy apprehensions make them ascribe to him measures of conduct, which, in human creatures, would be highly blamed, they must still affect to praise and admire that conduct in the object of their devotional addresses. Thus it may safely be affirmed, that popular religions are really, in the conception of their more vulgar votaries, a species of dæmonism; and the higher the deity is exalted in power and knowledge, the lower of course is he depressed in goodness and benevolence; whatever epithets of praise may be bestowed on him by

[83] Mem. lib. 1.

[84] It was considered among the ancients, as a very extraordinary, philosophical paradox, that the presence of the gods was not confined to the heavens, but was extended every where; as we learn from LUCIAN. HERMOTIMUS sive de sectis.

[85] PLUTARCH. de superstit.

his amazed adorers. Among idolaters, the words may be false, and belie the secret opinion: But among more exalted religionists, the opinion itself contracts a kind of falsehood, and belies the inward sentiment. The heart secretly detests such measures of cruel and implacable vengeance; but the judgment dares not but pronounce them perfect and adorable. And the additional misery of this inward struggle aggravates all the other terrors, by which these unhappy victims to superstition are for ever haunted.

7 LUCIAN[86] observes, that a young man, who reads the history of the gods in HOMER or HESIOD, and finds their factions, wars, injustice, incest, adultery, and other immoralities so highly celebrated, is much surprized afterwards, when he comes into the world, to observe that punishments are by law inflicted on the same actions, which he had been taught to ascribe to superior beings. The contradiction is still perhaps stronger between the representations given us by some later religions and our natural ideas of generosity, lenity, impartiality, and justice; and in proportion to the multiplied terrors of these religions, the barbarous conceptions of the Divinity are multiplied upon us.[87] Nothing can preserve untainted the

[86] Necyomantia.

[87] BACCHUS, a divine being, is represented by the heathen mythology as the inventor of dancing and the theatre. Plays were anciently even a part of public worship on the most solemn occasions, and often employed in times of pestilence, to appease the offended deities. But they have been zealously proscribed by the godly in later ages; and the playhouse, according to a learned divine, is the porch of hell.

But in order to show more evidently, that it is possible for a religion to represent the divinity in still a more immoral and unamiable light than he was pictured by the ancients, we shall cite a long passage from an author of taste and imagination, who was surely no enemy to CHRISTIANITY. It is the Chevalier RAMSAY, a writer, who had so laudable an inclination to be orthodox, that his reason never found any difficulty, even in the doctrines which freethinkers scruple the most, the trinity, incarnation, and satisfaction: His humanity alone, of which he seems to have had a great stock, rebelled against the doctrines of eternal reprobation and predestination. He expresses himself thus: "What strange ideas," says he, "would an Indian, or a Chinese philosopher have of our holy religion, if they judged by the schemes given of it by our modern freethinkers, and pharisaical doctors of all sects? According to the odious and too *vulgar* system of these incredulous scoffers and credulous scribblers, 'The God of the Jews is a most cruel, unjust, partial and fantastical being. He created, about 6000 years ago, a man and a woman, and placed them in a fine garden of ASIA, of which there are no remains. This garden was furnished with all sorts of trees, fountains, and flowers. He allowed them the use of all the fruits of this beautiful garden, except one, that was planted in the midst thereof, and that had in it a secret virtue of preserving them in continual health and vigour of body and mind, of exalting their natural powers and making them wise. The devil entered into the body of a serpent, and solicited the first woman to eat of this forbidden fruit; she engaged her husband to do the same. To punish this slight curiosity and natural desire of life and knowledge, God not only threw our first parents out of paradise, but he condemned all their posterity to temporal misery, and the greatest part of them to eternal pains, though the souls of these innocent children have no more relation to that of ADAM than to those of NERO and MAHOMET; since, according to the scholastic drivellers, fabulists, and mythologists, all souls are created pure, and infused immediately into mortal bodies,

genuine principles of morals in our judgment of human conduct, but the absolute necessity of these principles to the existence of society. If common conception can indulge princes in a system of ethics, somewhat different from that which should regulate private persons; how much more those superior beings, whose attributes, views, and nature are so totally unknown to us? "Sunt superis sua jura."[88] The gods have maxims of justice peculiar to themselves.

so soon as the fœtus is formed. To accomplish the barbarous, partial decree of predestination and reprobation, God abandoned all nations to darkness, idolatry and superstition, without any saving knowledge or salutary graces; unless it was one particular nation, whom he chose as his peculiar people. This chosen nation was, however, the most stupid, ungrateful, rebellious, and perfidious of all nations. After God had thus kept the far greater part of all the human species, during near 4000 years, in a reprobate state, he changed all of a sudden, and took a fancy for other nations besides the JEWS. Then he sent his only begotten Son to the world, under a human form, to appease his wrath, satisfy his vindictive justice, and die for the pardon of sin. Very few nations, however, have heard of this gospel and all the rest, though left in invincible ignorance, are damned without exception, or any possibility of remission. The greatest part of those who have heard of it, have changed only some speculative notions about God, and some external forms in worship: For, in other respects, the bulk of Christians have continued as corrupt, as the rest of mankind in their morals; yea, so much the more perverse and criminal, that their lights were greater. Unless it be a very small select number, all other Christians, like the pagans, will be for ever damned; the great sacrifice offered up for them will become void and of no effect. God will take delight for ever in their torments and blasphemies; and though he can, by one *fiat*, change their hearts, yet they will remain for ever unconverted and unconvertible, because he will be for ever unappeasable and irreconcileable. It is true, that all this makes God odious, a hater of souls, rather than a lover of them; a cruel, vindictive tyrant, an impotent or a wrathful dæmon, rather than an all-powerful, beneficent Father of spirits: Yet all this is a mystery. He has secret reasons for his conduct, that are impenetrable; and though he appears unjust and barbarous, yet we must believe the contrary, because what is injustice, crime, cruelty, and the blackest malice in us, is in him justice, mercy, and sovereign goodness.' Thus the incredulous freethinkers, the judaizing Christians, and the fatalistic doctors have disfigured and dishonoured the sublime mysteries of our holy faith; thus, they have confounded the nature of good and evil; transformed the most monstrous passions into divine attributes, and surpassed the pagans in blasphemy, by ascribing to the eternal nature, as perfections, what makes the most horrid crimes amongst men. The grosser pagans contented themselves with divinizing lust, incest, and adultery; but the predestinarian doctors have divinized cruelty, wrath, fury, vengeance, and all the blackest vices." See the Chevalier RAMSAY's Philosophical Principles of natural and revealed Religion, Part II. p. 403.

The same author asserts, in other places, that the *Arminian* and *Molinist* schemes serve very little to mend the matter: And having thus thrown himself out of all received sects of CHRISTIANITY, he is obliged to advance a system of his own, which is a kind of ORIGENISM, and supposes the pre-existence of the souls both of men and beasts, and the eternal salvation and conversion of all men, beasts, and devils. But this notion, being quite peculiar to himself, we need not treat of. I thought the opinions of this ingenious author very curious; but I pretend not to warrant the justness of them.

[88] OVID. Metam. lib. 9. 500.

SECTION 14

Bad Influence of Popular Religions on Morality

1 HERE I cannot forbear observing a fact, which may be worth the attention of such as make human nature the object of their enquiry. It is certain, that, in every religion, however sublime the verbal definition which it gives of its divinity, many of the votaries, perhaps the greatest number, will still seek the divine favour, not by virtue and good morals, which alone can be acceptable to a perfect being, but either by frivolous observances, by intemperate zeal, by rapturous extasies, or by the belief of mysterious and absurd opinions. The least part of the *Sadder*, as well as of the *Pentateuch*, consists in precepts of morality; and we may also be assured, that that part was always the least observed and regarded. When the old ROMANS were attacked with a pestilence, they never ascribed their sufferings to their vices, or dreamed of repentance and amendment. They never thought that they were the general robbers of the world, whose ambition and avarice made desolate the earth, and reduced opulent nations to want and beggary. They only created a dictator,[89] in order to drive a nail into a door; and by that means, they thought that they had sufficiently appeased their incensed deity.

2 In ÆGINA, one faction forming a conspiracy, barbarously and treacherously assassinated seven hundred of their fellow-citizens; and carried their fury so far, that, one miserable fugitive having fled to the temple, they cut off his hands, by which he clung to the gates, and carrying him out of holy ground, immediately murdered him. "By this impiety," says HERODOTUS,[90] (not by the other many cruel assassinations) "they offended the gods, and contracted an inexpiable guilt."

3 Nay, if we should suppose, what never happens, that a popular religion were found, in which it was expressly declared, that nothing but morality could gain the divine favour; if an order of priests were instituted to inculcate this opinion, in daily sermons, and with all the arts of persuasion; yet so inveterate are the people's prejudices, that, for want of some other superstition, they would make the very attendance on these sermons the essentials of religion, rather than place them in virtue and good morals. The

[89] Called "Dictator clavis figendæ causa." T. LIVII, lib. 7. cap. 3. [90] Lib. 6.

sublime prologue of ZALEUCUS's laws[91] inspired not the LOCRIANS, so far as we can learn, with any sounder notions of the measures of acceptance with the deity, than were familiar to the other GREEKS.

4 This observation, then, holds universally: But still one may be at some loss to account for it. It is not sufficient to observe, that the people, every where, degrade their deities into a similitude with themselves, and consider them merely as a species of human creatures, somewhat more potent and intelligent. This will not remove the difficulty. For there is no *man* so stupid, as that, judging by his natural reason, he would not esteem virtue and honesty the most valuable qualities, which any person could possess. Why not ascribe the same sentiment to his deity? Why not make all religion, or the chief part of it, to consist in these attainments?

5 Nor is it satisfactory to say, that the practice of morality is more difficult than that of superstition; and is therefore rejected. For, not to mention the excessive penances of the *Brachmans* and *Talapoins*; it is certain, that the *Rhamadan* of the TURKS, during which the poor wretches, for many days, often in the hottest months of the year, and in some of the hottest climates of the world, remain without eating or drinking from the rising to the setting sun; this *Rhamadan*, I say, must be more severe than the practice of any moral duty, even to the most vicious and depraved of mankind. The four Lents of the MUSCOVITES, and the austerities of some ROMAN CATHOLICS, appear more disagreeable than meekness and benevolence. In short, all virtue, when men are reconciled to it by ever so little practice, is agreeable: All superstition is for ever odious and burdensome.

6 Perhaps, the following account may be received as a true solution of the difficulty. The duties, which a man performs as a friend or parent, seem merely owing to his benefactor or children; nor can he be wanting to these duties, without breaking through all the ties of nature and morality. A strong inclination may prompt him to the performance: A sentiment of order and moral obligation joins its force to these natural ties: And the whole man, if truly virtuous, is drawn to his duty, without any effort or endeavour. Even with regard to the virtues, which are more austere, and more founded on reflection, such as public spirit, filial duty, temperance, or integrity; the moral obligation, in our apprehension, removes all pretension to religious merit; and the virtuous conduct is deemed no more than what we owe to society and to ourselves. In all this, a superstitious man finds nothing, which he has properly performed for the sake of his deity, or which can peculiarly recommend him to the divine favour and protection. He considers not,

[91] To be found in DIOD. SIC. lib. 12.

that the most genuine method of serving the Divinity is by promoting the happiness of his creatures. He still looks out for some more immediate service of the Supreme Being, in order to allay those terrors, with which he is haunted. And any practice, recommended to him, which either serves to no purpose in life, or offers the strongest violence to his natural inclinations; that practice he will the more readily embrace, on account of those very circumstances, which should make him absolutely reject it. It seems the more purely religious, because it proceeds from no mixture of any other motive or consideration. And if, for its sake, he sacrifices much of his ease and quiet, his claim of merit appears still to rise upon him, in proportion to the zeal and devotion which he discovers. In restoring a loan, or paying a debt, his divinity is nowise beholden to him; because these acts of justice are what he was bound to perform, and what many would have performed, were there no god in the universe. But if he fast a day, or give himself a sound whipping; this has a direct reference, in his opinion, to the service of God. No other motive could engage him to such austerities. By these distinguished marks of devotion, he has now acquired the divine favour; and may expect, in recompence, protection and safety in this world, and eternal happiness in the next.

7 Hence the greatest crimes have been found, in many instances, compatible with a superstitious piety and devotion: Hence it is justly regarded as unsafe to draw any certain inference in favour of a man's morals from the fervour or strictness of his religious exercises, even though he himself believe them sincere. Nay, it has been observed, that enormities of the blackest dye have been rather apt to produce superstitious terrors, and encrease the religious passion. Bomilcar, having formed a conspiracy for assassinating at once the whole senate of Carthage, and invading the liberties of his country, lost the opportunity, from a continual regard to omens and prophecies. *Those who undertake the most criminal and most dangerous enterprizes are commonly the most superstitious*; as an ancient historian[92] remarks on this occasion. Their devotion and spiritual faith rise with their fears. Catiline was not contented with the established deities, and received rites of the national religion: His anxious terrors made him seek new inventions of this kind;[93] which he never probably had dreamed of, had he remained a good citizen, and obedient to the laws of his country.

8 To which we may add, that, after the commission of crimes, there arise remorses and secret horrors, which give no rest to the mind, but make it have recourse to religious rites and ceremonies, as expiations of its offences.

[92] Diod. Sic. lib. 20. [93] Cic. Catil. 1. Sallust. de bello Catil.

Whatever weakens or disorders the internal frame promotes the interests of superstition: And nothing is more destructive to them than a manly, steady virtue, which either preserves us from disastrous, melancholy accidents, or teaches us to bear them. During such calm sun-shine of the mind, these spectres of false divinity never make their appearance. On the other hand, while we abandon ourselves to the natural undisciplined suggestions of our timid and anxious hearts, every kind of barbarity is ascribed to the Supreme Being, from the terrors with which we are agitated; and every kind of caprice, from the methods which we embrace in order to appease him. *Barbarity, caprice*; these qualities, however nominally disguised, we may universally observe, form the ruling character of the deity in popular religions. Even priests, instead of correcting these depraved ideas of mankind, have often been found ready to foster and encourage them. The more tremendous the divinity is represented, the more tame and submissive do men become to his ministers: And the more unaccountable the measures of acceptance required by him, the more necessary does it become to abandon our natural reason, and yield to their ghostly guidance and direction. Thus it may be allowed, that the artifices of men aggravate our natural infirmities and follies of this kind, but never originally beget them. Their root strikes deeper into the mind, and springs from the essential and universal properties of human nature.

SECTION 15

General Corollary

1 THOUGH the stupidity of men, barbarous and uninstructed, be so great, that they may not see a sovereign author in the more obvious works of nature, to which they are so much familiarized; yet it scarcely seems possible, that any one of good understanding should reject that idea, when once it is suggested to him. A purpose, an intention, a design is evident in every thing; and when our comprehension is so far enlarged as to contemplate the first rise of this visible system, we must adopt, with the strongest conviction, the idea of some intelligent cause or author. The uniform maxims too, which prevail throughout the whole frame of the universe, naturally, if not necessarily, lead us to conceive this intelligence as single and undivided, where the prejudices of education oppose not so reasonable a theory. Even the contrarieties of nature, by discovering themselves every where, become proofs of some consistent plan, and establish one single purpose or intention, however inexplicable and incomprehensible.

2 Good and ill are universally intermingled and confounded; happiness and misery, wisdom and folly, virtue and vice. Nothing is pure and entirely of a piece. All advantages are attended with disadvantages. An universal compensation prevails in all conditions of being and existence. And it is not possible for us, by our most chimerical wishes, to form the idea of a station or situation altogether desirable. The draughts of life, according to the poet's fiction, are always mixed from the vessels on each hand of JUPITER: Or if any cup be presented altogether pure, it is drawn only, as the same poet tells us, from the left-handed vessel.

3 The more exquisite any good is, of which a small specimen is afforded us, the sharper is the evil, allied to it; and few exceptions are found to this uniform law of nature. The most sprightly wit borders on madness; the highest effusions of joy produce the deepest melancholy; the most ravishing pleasures are attended with the most cruel lassitude and disgust; the most flattering hopes make way for the severest disappointments. And in general, no course of life has such safety (for happiness is not to be dreamed of) as the temperate and moderate, which maintains, as far as possible, a mediocrity, and a kind of insensibility, in every thing.

4 As the good, the great, the sublime, the ravishing are found eminently in the genuine principles of theism; it may be expected, from the analogy of nature, that the base, the absurd, the mean, the terrifying will be equally discovered in religious fictions and chimeras.

5 The universal propensity to believe in invisible, intelligent power, if not an original instinct, being at least a general attendant of human nature, may be considered as a kind of mark or stamp, which the divine workman has set upon his work; and nothing surely can more dignify mankind, than to be thus selected from all other parts of the creation, and to bear the image or impression of the universal Creator. But consult this image, as it appears in the popular religions of the world. How is the Deity disfigured in our representations of him! What caprice, absurdity, and immorality are attributed to him! How much is he degraded even below the character, which we should naturally, in common life, ascribe to a man of sense and virtue!

6 What a noble privilege is it of human reason to attain the knowledge of the Supreme Being; and, from the visible works of nature, be enabled to infer so sublime a principle as its supreme Creator? But turn the reverse of the medal. Survey most nations and most ages. Examine the religious principles, which have, in fact, prevailed in the world. You will scarcely be persuaded, that they are any thing but sick men's dreams: Or perhaps will regard them more as the playsome whimsies of monkies in human shape, than the serious, positive, dogmatical asseverations of a being, who dignifies himself with the name of rational.

7 Hear the verbal protestations of all men: Nothing so certain as their religious tenets. Examine their lives: You will scarcely think that they repose the smallest confidence in them.

8 The greatest and truest zeal gives us no security against hypocrisy: The most open impiety is attended with a secret dread and compunction.

9 No theological absurdities so glaring that they have not, sometimes, been embraced by men of the greatest and most cultivated understanding. No religious precepts so rigorous that they have not been adopted by the most voluptuous and most abandoned of men.

10 *Ignorance is the mother of Devotion*: A maxim that is proverbial, and confirmed by general experience. Look out for a people, entirely destitute of religion: If you find them at all, be assured, that they are but few degrees removed from brutes.

11 What so pure as some of the morals, included in some theological systems? What so corrupt as some of the practices, to which these systems give rise?

12 The comfortable views, exhibited by the belief of futurity, are ravishing and delightful. But how quickly vanish on the appearance of its terrors, which keep a more firm and durable possession of the human mind?

13 The whole is a riddle, an ænigma, an inexplicable mystery. Doubt, uncertainty, suspence of judgment appear the only result of our most accurate scrutiny, concerning this subject. But such is the frailty of human reason, and such the irresistible contagion of opinion, that even this deliberate doubt could scarcely be upheld; did we not enlarge our view, and opposing one species of superstition to another, set them a quarrelling; while we ourselves, during their fury and contention, happily make our escape, into the calm, though obscure, regions of philosophy.

EDITOR'S ANNOTATIONS

Plan of the Annotations

The objective of the Annotations is to provide information about the text, not to interpret it. Each annotation serves one or more of eight purposes:

1. *Definition.* A few archaic, obsolete, or puzzling terms and phrases are defined or explained.

2. *Translation.* French, Latin, and Greek quotations supplied by Hume are always translated.

3. *Interpretation.* Interpretation of the text is avoided in so far as possible. However, the choice of passages to be annotated involves a judgement of what needs either explanation or additional information, and interpretation of works cited by Hume is not always avoidable. See 6 below.

4. *Amplification of a self-reference.* A few annotations identify a passage to which Hume is referring in his own text (a cross-reference).

5. *Information on related material written by Hume.* Related material in Hume's other published works and correspondence are identified, especially the location of passages in *THN* from which passages in *DP* descend. Further information concerning the derivation of passages in *DP* from *THN* is found in the Introduction to this volume, pp. l–cxvi.

6. *Information on passages in which authors are named.* Hume's footnote references are expanded to provide additional information (bk., ch., sect., verse, and the like). Brief summaries of cited passages are occasionally provided. A few annotations explain, summarize, or paraphrase the context or content of a work that Hume identifies or to which he alludes.

7. *Identification of passages in which authors are unnamed.* Annotations occasionally identify (or suggest) unnamed authors to whom Hume alludes. Full names and titles are often found in the Biographical Appendix, the Reference List, and the Catalogue.

8. *Information on the intellectual context.* Some annotations point to the intellectual and philosophical roots of Hume's concerns. Often, but not invariably, Hume's passages suggest an author known to have been read by him. However, most of the authors mentioned in these annotations should be understood as merely possible sources. The goal is usually to describe some of the available and relevant literature at the time Hume wrote the work under discussion.

Attention is not drawn in these annotations to critical commentary on these two works that appeared during Hume's lifetime. The Introduction to this volume (see esp. pp. cxvi–cxxxii) covers this material. Further information on Hume's sources is provided in the Catalogue of Hume's References, pp. 264–70.

References and Forms of Reference

All published materials mentioned in the Annotations are in the Reference List. Short titles are regularly used. Full bibliographical information is occasionally found only in the Catalogue. Page numbers are given only when needed for clarity or specificity; otherwise, divisions in the work (books, parts, chapters, sections, epistles, and the like) are provided.

Conventions in the field of classics are used for classical works. Titles in general scholarly use are preferred, whether English or Latin: for example, Tacitus, *Histories* (not *Historiæ*), Quintilian, *Institutes* (not *Institutio oratoria*), and Seneca, *Moral Essays* (not *Moralia*); but Cicero, *De natura deorum* (not *On the Nature of the Gods*), Lucretius, *De rerum natura* (not *On the Nature of the Universe*), and Horace, *Ars poetica* (not *The Art of Poetry*). Where both English and Latin titles are in general use, English is preferred. Parts or chapters are omitted whenever irrelevant or misleading. For example, in the case of Hobbes, *Leviathan* (and other works by Hobbes), only chapter and paragraph numbers (not parts) are cited. References to works by Hume (other than his *History of England*) use paragraph numbers rather than page numbers to specific editions. *Letters* refers exclusively to the 2-vol. Greig edition of Hume's letters.

Numbers to the left of each entry (the text material in the lemma) are *page and line* numbers in the text (e.g. 3.6 ***Good* or *Evil***]). However, references in the annotations to the text itself are to *section and paragraph* numbers (e.g. *NHR* 6.5).

The superscription [B] after a person's name indicates that a short biographical description of the person is found in the Biographical Appendix. These markers are used sparingly to avoid unnecessary distraction. All names cited by Hume are identified in the Biographical Appendix.

Sources of Translated Materials

All Greek and Latin words or passages presented by Hume are translated by M. A. Stewart. All French words or passages presented by Hume are translated by Tom L. Beauchamp. Translations of non-English texts quoted by the editor (and not quoted by Hume) are usually from the published translations included in the Reference List.

A DISSERTATION ON THE PASSIONS

SECTION 1

3.6 ***Good* or *Evil***] At *THN* 2.3.9.8, Hume equates 'good and evil' with 'pain and pleasure' (see also *THN* 1.3.10.2).

3.9 **good or evil . . . produces various passions**] It was a common thesis that the passions are states of mind (or soul) that present objects to individuals as good or evil (e.g. fear and hatred present objects as evil) *or* that the apprehension of good or evil produces passions (e.g. apprehension of a dangerous situation causes fear). In an influential account in *Tusculan Disputations* (3.11.24–5; 3.13.28; 4.7.14–15), Cicero discusses how passions arise from impressions of good and evil. For an early modern treatment, see Edward Reynolds (1599–1676; bishop of Norwich), *A Treatise of the Passions* 5, 12. René Descartes (1596–1650; French philosopher, mathematician, and scientist) characterizes the 'function of the passions' as consisting in disposing 'our soul to want the things which nature deems useful for us, and to persist in this volition' (*Passions of the Soul* 52). Walter Charleton (1620–1707; physician and philosopher) held that 'the first and *General Causes* of all Passions . . . is not the simple representation of *good* or *evil* in any object. . . . It is further required to the moving our affections, that the good or evil apprehended, be by us conceived to concern *ourselves* in particular, or our *Friends* at least' (*Natural History of the Passions* 4.6). William Ayloffe (fl. 1700) found a 'good use' for all passions. For example, fear, though 'look'd upon as the basest of all the Passions . . . is prudent in effect, only descrying Evils to shew us how to avoid them. . . . Fear then is a nature prudence, which delivers us from an Evil, by the very Apprehension alone she gives us of it' (*Government of the Passions*, pp. 102–3).

3.11 **Joy . . . Grief or Sorrow . . . Fear or Hope]** Aristotle noted some of the conditions mentioned by Hume when treating fear and confidence (for him the functional equivalent of hope), *Rhetoric* 1382^{a}2–1383^{b}11. His views were perpetuated by writers in the Aristotelian tradition, including Juan Luis Vives (1492–1540; philosopher and humanist of Spanish origins), *Passions of the Soul* 21–2, and Thomas Wright (British essayist; fl. 1604), *Passions of the Mind in General* 5.11. For a formulation that, like Hume's, uses probability, see Locke, *Essay* 2.20.7–10, and an earlier formulation in Reynolds, *A Treatise of the Passions* 5 (p. 40), 19–20, 23. In the writings of Isaac Watts (1674–1748; English hymn-writer, Dissenting minister, theologian), this approach to joy, sorrow, fear, and hope connects these passions to mirth, laughter, gaiety, melancholy, etc. (*A Plain and Particular Account of the Natural Passions* 10–11). In *Histoire naturelle de l'âme* 12 (esp. pp. 104–6), Julien Offray de La Mettrie (1709–51; French philosopher and physician) presents the passions as sentiments that develop from the senses and as comprised centrally of joy, sorrow, desire, love, hope, and the like (see ann. immediately below).

DP 1.4–10 was derived, with modifications, from *THN* 2.3.9.5–12.

3.15 **Desire . . . Aversion]** Descartes reports that this view of desire and aversion was common 'in the Schools' (*Passions of the Soul* 87). A comparable treatment of desire, appetite, and aversion is found in Thomas Hobbes (1588–1679; English philosopher), who reports that we acquired the language of appetite and aversion 'from the *Latins*' (*Leviathan* 6.2). Desire and aversion had long been paired opposites in many writings on the passions, which also connected the pair to other pairings, such as hope and fear.

3.16 **The Will exerts itself]** This passage is adapted from *THN* 2.3.9.7; *THN* 2.3 is entitled *Of the will and direct passions*. Philosophers commonly presented the will as a faculty of the mind, but at *THN* 2.3.1.2, Hume defines 'will' as 'nothing but *the internal impression we feel and are conscious of, when we knowingly give rise to any new motion of our body, or new perception of our mind*.'

3.19 ***Hope* and *Fear*]** On mixtures such as that of hope and fear (as suggested by the treatment below), cf. Descartes's reflections in *Passions of the Soul* 165–6; the conclusion of Baruch de Spinoza (1632–77; Dutch philosopher) that 'there is neither Hope without Fear, nor Fear without Hope' (*Ethics* 3, Def. Affects 13; 3.P50 (schol.)); and the thesis of Seneca[B] that hope and fear 'keep step together' (*Ad Lucilium epistulae morales* 5.7–8 ('On the Philosopher's Mean')). Others envisioned a derivative or causal connection between desire/aversion and hope/fear. For example, Alexander Forbes (1678–1762; Fourth Baron Forbes of Pitsligo) held that 'Hope and Fear issue from Desire and Aversion . . . [as] the Mind [meets] . . . with things agreeable or vexatious' (*Essays Moral and Philosophical on Several Subjects* 1.6 [48]).

3.20 **mixed passions]** Descartes maintained that '*There are only six primitive passions* . . . —namely, wonder, love, hatred, desire, joy and sadness. All the others are either composed from some of these six or they are species of them' (*Passions of the Soul* 69). Charleton followed Descartes: 'only six are simple; the rest mixed': wonder, love, hatred, desire, joy, and grief (or sadness)—while 'all the rest . . . are but various *species* of those Simple ones, or they result from divers *mixtures* and combinations of them' and are therefore '*Mixt* Passions' (*Natural History of the Passions* 5.65). See also Nicolas Malebranche (1638–1715; French philosopher and theologian), *Search after Truth* 5.7, on the combination of primitive passions; and two works by Marin Cureau de La Chambre (1596–1669; French man of letters), who maintained that there are eight simple passions (love, hate, pleasure, grief, audacity, fear, constancy, and consternation) and eleven mixed passions (hope, arrogance, impudence, emulation, anger, repentance, shame, jealousy, compassion, envy, and agony). See *Les charactères des passions*, 'Advis necessaire au lecteur'; and *L'Art de connoistre les hommes* 1.3 (pp. 81–9) or *The Art How to Know Men* 1.3.4 (pp. 88–95).

Other philosophers used a similar terminology, even if not the same analyses or conclusions. See Lord Shaftesbury (1671–1713; English philosopher, Third Earl of Shaftesbury), on how some passions mix with antithetical passions (*Characteristics*, 'An Inquiry concerning Virtue or Merit' 2.2 [321]); Henry More (1614–87; English philosopher, fellow of Christ's College, Cambridge) on how passions are compounded (*Enchiridion Ethicum* 1.10.4 ff.); Charles Le Brun [Lebrun] (1619–90; French historical painter and designer), on the mixed passions as interior motions connected to exterior parts of the body (*Conference of Monsieur Le Brun . . . upon Expression*, pp. 6, 9–17); Francis Hutcheson (1694–1746; Irish philosopher) on the mixture of sorrow and aversion and desire and joy (*Essay on the Nature and Conduct of the Passions and Affections* 3.2 (Treatise 1)); and Nicolas Coeffeteau (1574–1623; French theologian, poet, and historian) (*A Table of Humane Passions* 2).

See, further, in *THN* the doctrine of 'compound passions' and the 'mixture' of passions several times (e.g. 2.2.3.1; 2.2.11.1). The expression 'mixt passions' is used at 2.2.10.5 and 'mix'd passions' at 2.3.9.26. Mixed passions deriving from love and hatred, compassion, malice, envy, and the like are treated throughout *THN* 2.2. Among the most thorough treatments of the mixed passions is Henry Grove (1684–1738; tutor in ethics and pneumatology), *A System of Moral Philosophy* 2.9–10 (but beginning 2.8, p. 354). This work was published in 1749, ten years after *THN*, but before *DP*.

3.21 **Probability . . .]** This passage is adapted from *THN* 2.3.9.10. See also *THN* 2.3.9.12, where Hume says (in a passage not used in *DP*): 'the nature of probability is to cast a superior number of views or chances on one side; or, which is the same thing, a superior number of returns of one passion'. More generally on probability, see Hume's theories of probability and causal inference in *EHU* 4–6 and *THN* 1.3.11–13. See also *THN* 1.3.2 and the passages on probability beginning 1.3.6.4.

3.21 **opposition of contrary chances or causes]** See also *THN* 1.3.11 (*Of the probability of chances*) and *THN* 1.3.12 (*Of the probability of causes*). Hume thought that 'the very nature of chance' is 'to render all the particular events, comprehended in it, entirely equal' (*EHU* 6.2–3). At *THN* 1.3.12.5, 14, he notes that:

> The vulgar, who take things according to their first appearance, attribute the uncertainty of events to such an uncertainty in the causes. . . . But philosophers observing, that almost in every part of nature there is contain'd a vast variety of springs and principles, which are hid, by reason of their minuteness or remoteness, find that 'tis at least possible the contrariety of events may not proceed from any contingency in the cause, but from the secret operation of contrary causes. This possibility is converted into certainty by farther observation. . . .
>
> There is no probability so great as not to allow of a contrary possibility; because otherwise 'twou'd cease to be a probability, and wou'd become a certainty.

3.24 **imagination or understanding, call it which you please]** Hume's discussions of mental faculties ('the faculties of the mind'; see *THN* 1.4.2.33; 1.3.9.19 n.) sometimes suggest that their functions overlap. For example, the understanding is the faculty of probable inference, but Hume also suggests that at least some of the work of probable inference is the province of the imagination. At *THN* 1.3.12.22, he says that

> if the transference of the past to the future were founded merely on a conclusion of the understanding, it cou'd never occasion any belief or assurance. . . . The belief arises not merely from the transference of past to future, but from some operation of the *fancy* conjoin'd with it. This may lead us to conceive the manner, in which that faculty enters into all our reasonings.

3.33 **impression of joy or sorrow]** A passion *is* an impression in Hume's system. See *THN* 1.1.1.1; 1.1.2.1; 1.2.3.3; 1.4.2.7; 2.1.1.3. Malebranche also characterized passions as impressions, though his full formulation is 'impressions from the Author of nature' (*Search after Truth* 5.1).

4.1 **uneasiness]** Hume uses this term several times below. It is associated with pain. At *DP* 2.14, which is derived from *THN* 2.1.7.2, Hume substituted 'uneasiness' for 'a pain'. Locke closely associated 'uneasiness' with 'pain' in his discussion of the passions. See *Essay* 2.20.6, 15; 2.21.29–48 (and cf. *THN* 2.2.8.10 and 2.2.9.11).

4.3 **heart]** At *THN* 2.3.9.11, from which the present passage is derived, Hume uses the word 'affections' rather than 'heart'. From pre-Aristotelian thought through early modern theory, the heart was commonly considered the seat of the passions. For the persistence of this view in modern writings, see Wright, *Passions of the Mind in General* 1.9; Cureau de La Chambre, *L'Art de connoistre les hommes* 1.4; Le Brun, *Conference of Monsieur Le Brun . . . upon Expression*, pp. 6, 17; and Watts, *A Plain and Particular Account of the Natural Passions* 1.5 (p. 9). For a break with this theory, see Descartes, *Passions of the Soul* 31, 33, 36, 71. Shortly after Descartes, Charleton provided an engaging argument that concluded 'I cannot admit the *heart* to be the Seat of the Passions' (*Natural History of the Passions* 4.9).

4.18 **As this theory . . .]** *DP* 1.11–20 was derived from *THN* 2.3.9.18–29 (with modifications).

4.24 **superior degree of probability]** This passage is adapted from *THN* 2.3.9.19, but see also the background in *THN* 1.3.6.4 and 1.3.11.2 on knowledge, probability, and degrees of evidence. In *A Letter from a Gentleman* 26–7, Hume discusses 'degree of assurance' in a related context, and at *EHU* 10.4 he discusses degrees of probabilistic evidence.

4.31 **it changes insensibly into hope . . . by slow degrees, into joy]** The changeability, inconstancy, and restlessness of the passions was a recurrent topic of interest among philosophers of the seventeenth and eighteenth centuries.

4.35 **in optics . . . sun, passing through a prism . . . in the composition]** The reference is apparently to Newton's studies of colour. In 1666 Newton investigated the sun's light passing through a prism prior to its reflection by a coloured body. For years he developed and polished his theory of the coloured spectrum. See *Opticks*, esp. bk. 1, pt. 2, props. 4–5, 8, on 'the whiteness of the Sun's Light is compounded of all the primary Colours' and 'the discovered Properties of Light to explain the Colours made by Prisms'. Newton demonstrated that the colours can be mixed in various combinations, and that white is the presence of all colours mixed together. Cf. Hume's similar formulation at *THN* 2.3.9.19.

5.12 **fear . . . without trembling]** This example of fear and trembling was used by St Thomas Aquinas (*Summa Theologiæ* 1a2æ.44, art. 3) and also by Descartes, though for broader metaphysical and psychological purposes. Descartes maintained that movements that cause a passion in the soul may also cause bodily effects; for example, fear is accompanied by trembling, just as joy is accompanied by blushing, and sadness by pallor (*Passions of the Soul* 47, 114–18). See also the annotation immediately below; and *THN* 3.3.1.7.

5.16 **brink of a precipice . . . influences the imagination]** Hume uses this example of trembling on the brink of a precipice and the role of the imagination at *EPM* 5.14 and *THN* 1.3.13.10—as well as at *THN* 2.3.9.23, from which the present passage is derived. Blaise Pascal (1623–62; French philosopher, mathematician, and theologian) presented this example and linked the person's feelings directly to the role of the imagination (*Pensées* 78 (Levi no.)), but the example had been used earlier—in a version similar to that in *THN* and *DP*—by Michel de Montaigne (1533–92; French essayist and philosopher) in 'Apology for Raymond Sebond' (*Essays* 12, p. 671). Aristotle uses the example of the impossibility of suspending judgement when confronted with a precipice in *Metaphysics* 1008^{b}8–27, an example also used by Bayle (*Dictionary*, 'Pyrrho' [D]). Malebranche attempts to explain these phenomena in terms of 'traces in our brains' in *Search after Truth* 2.1.5.2.

6.4 **Horace has remarked]** Horace, *Epodes* 1, lines 19–22. See also the preceding lines in Horace, which are relevant to Hume's point. The quoted lines may be translated: 'As a bird that sits beside her unfledged young, deserting them, fears all the more the approach of snakes, but can bring them no further protection by staying at hand'. This verse had been cited by Hutcheson, *Essay on the Nature and Conduct of the Passions and Affections* 6.6 (Treatise 1), during a discussion of grievous anxiety about absent family members. Hume quotes the identical passage from Horace at *THN* 2.3.9.28. Hume apparently used the *THN* text in preparing *DP* and introduced an error in the handling of 'Serpentium' (although Hume's use in *DP* of 'præsentibus' is an improvement over the 'presentibus' of *THN*). Emendations in this quotation are reported in the Editorial Appendix below, p. 189.

6.13 **Concerning the mixture of affections . . . when contrary passions arise]** *DP* 1.21–5 is derived (with modifications) from *THN* 2.3.9.14–17.

6.30 **relations of ideas (which we shall explain more fully afterwards)]** See *DP* 5.1 and the related annotations at 24.4 below.

SECTION 2

7.1 **Besides those passions above-mentioned]** Hume's list of the particular passions corresponds closely to lists in works he is likely to have consulted. Compare, for example, the lists in Locke, *Essay* 2.20.3–14, 2.21.39; and Hobbes, *Leviathan* 6.13–48. Even in Renaissance and early modern writers influenced by medieval sources (primarily St Thomas), the list of particular passions (whatever precise name is chosen) is not vastly dissimilar. Compare Vives, *Passions of the Soul*,

Contents; and Wright, *Passions of the Mind in General* 1.6; 4.1A–3. Hume's list is particularly close to Locke's.

7.1 **direct pursuit of good and aversion to evil]** The introductory paragraphs in Section 2 contain the distilled essence of Hume's account of the direct and indirect passions in *THN*. (See the initial distinction in *THN* 2.1.1.4.) Hume recast this material for this summary in *DP*, but some parts were directly incorporated from *THN* 2.1.2.4. Pride and humility, the two indirect passions mentioned here in *DP*, are the subject of the remainder of *THN* 2.1. The direct passions are the subject of *THN* 2.3.9. See, further, the discussion in *THN* 2.3.1.1 and 2.3.9 of the distinction between direct passions—such as joy, sorrow, hope, and fear—and indirect passions—such as pride and humility, love and hate.

7.3 ***Pride* . . . satisfaction . . . *Humility* . . . dissatisfaction]** Pride and humility are discussed in numerous passages in *THN* 2–3. *THN* 2.1 is entitled *Of pride and humility*; see 2.1.2.1 on their 'definition' and 'description'. See also *DP* 2.3, where Hume connects pride to agreeable sentiment and humility to painful sentiment.

Pride (sometimes understood as self-esteem) and humility are briefly considered as opposites in Vives, *Passions of the Soul* 24; Descartes, *Passions of the Soul* 54 (and see the related discussion of esteem and contempt at 149–52); Hobbes, *Human Nature* 9.1–2; Charleton, *Natural History of the Passions* 5.9–10; Spinoza, *Ethics* 3, Def. Affects 18–19, 26, 28–9; and Malebranche, *Search after Truth* 5.7.

'Pride' and 'humility' are not univocal terms in these writings. Several philosophers pointed to ambiguities or saw connections between pride and humility and other passions. For example, Descartes associated 'pride' in Hume's sense of warranted esteem with both self-esteem and joy from self-love, and he associated 'humility' (in Hume's sense of a low opinion of oneself) with self-contempt, shame, and irresolution (*Passions of the Soul* 54, 66, 149–52, 157–60, 204–6; see also 155 and 159–60 for a treatment of humility as both a virtue and a vice). *Undue* self-esteem and vanity, by contrast, are forms of 'vice' for Descartes (*Passions of the Soul* 157, 190), as they are for Hume. Spinoza acknowledged legitimate self-esteem, but was quick to associate pride with undue self-esteem or vanity. (See his use of *gloriari*, carrying the sense of delight at being esteemed, and *superbia*, carrying the sense of arrogance or haughtiness.) 'Humility' and 'pride' generally carry a negative connotation for Spinoza (see *Ethics* 3.P26, 3.P55; 3, Def. Affects 26–9; 4.P48–9, 4.P53), whereas 'legitimate self-esteem' does not; see *Ethics* 4.P52 and his many assessments in *Short Treatise on God, Man, and his Well-Being*.

The confused and often conflicting meanings or connotations of 'pride', 'glory', 'humility', and the like had been treated in Hobbes, *Human Nature* 9.1–2; and see related observations (primarily on pride) in *Leviathan* 8.18–19; 15.19–21; and *De Cive* 3.13–14. He noted several favourable and unfavourable senses. Hutcheson observed that the term 'pride' can denote joy derivative from rightful honour, but also noted that it has a 'bad sense' when persons claim something to which they have no right (*Essay on the Nature and Conduct of the Passions and Affections* 3.3 (Treatise 1)). Some classic reflections on these themes (though not on humility) are found in Plutarch,[B] 'On Inoffensive Self-Praise' (in *Moralia*), which distinguishes between offensive and inoffensive self-praise. Hume himself noted that 'An excessive pride or over-weaning conceit of ourselves is always esteem'd vicious, and is universally hated; as modesty, or a just sense of our weakness, is esteem'd virtuous, and procures the good-will of every one' (*THN* 3.3.2.1).

Perhaps attuned to the distinctions drawn by these philosophers (and many Christian moralists), Hume once connected his thought to French sources and to controversies over self-love. He wrote in *EPM* (n. 66) that

> The term, *pride*, is commonly taken in a bad sense; but this sentiment seems indifferent, and may be either good or bad, according as it is well or ill founded, and according to the other circumstances which accompany it. The FRENCH express this sentiment by the term, *amour propre*, but as they also express self-love as well as vanity, by the same term, there arises thence a great confusion in ROCHEFOUCAULT, and many of their moral writers.

Although 'amour propre' is conventionally translated 'self-love' and 'self-regard', other apt translations in French writers, depending on the context, include 'pride', 'conceit', 'egotism', 'vanity', and 'boastfulness'. The expression was generally used with a connotation of selfishness, but also meant 'self-regard'.

7.7 ***Love . . . Hatred***] *THN* 2.2 treats *Of love and hatred*. These passions had been explored by virtually all previous writers on the passions. *Complacency* in this passage means satisfaction, and possibly calm pleasure or security. Cf. the usage in *THN* 2.1.11.2; *EPM* 2.22; 5.40; 6.3; n. 26; 7.2; Appx. 1.13; Appx. 2.4; Appx. 2.9; and 'Rise and Progress of the Arts and Sciences' 38.

7.9 **In these two sets of passion**] *DP* 2.3–9 is derived (with modifications) from *THN* 2.1.2.4; 2.2.1.3; and 2.1.4.2–5.

7.24 **certain principles**] This entire passage is derived from *THN* 2.1.4.2, where 'certain principles' appeared as 'certain properties of human nature'. In the 1757 edn. of *DP*, this wording in *THN* was simplified to 'certain properties'.

7.25 **not commonly much insisted on by philosophers**] In the final paragraph of his *Abstract* to *THN*, Hume states that 'if any thing can entitle the author to so glorious a name as that of an *inventor*, 'tis the use he makes of the principle of the association of ideas'. For the range of philosophers who discussed the topic, see the annotation immediately below.

7.26 ***association* of ideas . . . produced by it.[1]**] In n. 1 of *DP* (see also n. 3) Hume refers to his treatment of this topic in *EHU*. In particular, see Hume's characterization of the association of ideas in *EHU* 3.1 ff. For his earlier view, see *THN* 1.1.4–7 (*Of the connexion or association of ideas* and three sections following this section); see also *THN* 1.3.6.12–15 and 1.3.9.2. At *THN* 1.1.4.6, he likened the association of ideas in the mental world to attraction in the physical world: 'Here is a kind of ATTRACTION, which in the mental world will be found to have as extraordinary effects as in the natural, and to show itself in as many and as various forms. Its effects are every where conspicuous; but as to its causes, they are mostly unknown, and must be resolv'd into *original* qualities of human nature, which I pretend not to explain.'

Hume's discussion was informed by Locke's investigation (*Essay* 2.33), which bears a chapter title identical to Hume's. Hume appears to acknowledge Locke's influence in his Index to *ETSS* (see pp. 203, 272 in this volume). The precise target of Hume's reference to Locke in this Index is not clear, but the reference was found in all editions of *ETSS* that contained indexes. Several writers acknowledged Locke as the first to articulate an account of the association of ideas. (However, Locke knew the discussion in Hobbes, *Leviathan* 3.1–11, of association as a mechanistic function of the mind.) Another possible source of Hume's reflections is the account of natural connection in Malebranche, *Search after Truth* 2.1.5.1–2; 2.2.2. Hutcheson several times mentions the association of ideas in *Essay on the Nature and Conduct of the Passions and Affections*, but his theoretical framework is different.

English encyclopaedist Ephraim Chambers (d. 1740) (*Cyclopædia*, 'association: association of ideas') provides a general treatment of the philosophical meaning of the term, relying in part on Locke. Discussion that either supports or denies the existence of association and principles of connection appeared in George Turnbull (1698–1749; regent at Marischal College, Aberdeen), *Principles of Moral Philosophy*, 1: 81–96 (a post-*THN* work); John Gay (1699–1745; English clergyman and philosopher, fellow of Sidney Sussex College, Cambridge), *Preliminary Dissertation*, esp. pp. xxxi–xxxiii; and Edmund Law (1703–87; English minister; Master of Peterhouse, Cambridge), *An Enquiry into the Ideas of Space, Time, Immensity, and Eternity*, pp. 45–6.

8.18 **elegant writer . . . following manner:**[2]] Footnote reference: Joseph Addison, *Spectator* 412 (23 June 1712). *Spectator* 412 was quoted, but not cited by title or author, in *THN* 2.1.4.5; see also *EPM* 6.8—a clear allusion to Addison[B] as an 'elegant writer' (see Box, 'An Allusion'). In *THN* Hume apparently mistranscribed this passage from *Spectator* 412 in several places, and all transcriptions were carried into *DP*. This is clear evidence that, when composing his later works, Hume sometimes used pages from *THN* without returning to his original sources. These four apparent mistranscriptions ('is it' became 'it is'; 'water' became 'waters'; 'pleasures' became 'pleasure'; and 'their' became 'the') have not been corrected in the present edition because they did not deprive the passage of its sense or involve an unintelligible formal error.

9.9 **impressions or sentiments**] For impressions and ideas as the only types of perception in Hume's writings, see *EHU* 2.1 and *THN* 1.1.1–2 and 1.2.6.7. For sentiments and passions as instances of impressions, see the Advertisement to bk. 3 of *THN*.

9.13 **pride . . . pleasure . . . humility . . . uneasiness**] At *THN* 2.1.5.4, Hume says that 'pride is a pleasant sensation, and humility a painful. . . . Upon the removal of the pleasure and pain, there is in reality no pride nor humility.' Compare

Hume's comments here and in *THN* on the role of pleasure and pain with Locke, *Essay* 2.20.1–5.

9.18 **The double relation of ideas and sentiments]** In *THN* 2.1–2, Hume discusses the double relation(s) of impressions or sentiments and ideas more than thirty times. *DP* 2.13 appears to be derived in small measure from *THN* 2.1.5.1.

9.20 **personal merit and demerit]** Hume in this paragraph offers a condensed form of some themes in his theories of morals, personal merit, and virtue (see *EPM* and *THN* 3). *DP* 2.14–20 is derived (with modifications) from *THN* 2.1.7.2 and 2.1.7.5–2.1.8.6, where Hume used 'VICE and VIRTUE' rather than 'personal merit and demerit', a common change of terminology in his editing after 1760. In *EPM*, Hume defines 'virtue': 'It is the nature, and, indeed, the definition of virtue, that it is a quality of the mind agreeable to or approved of by every one, who considers or contemplates it' (n. 50). Cf. *THN* 2.1.7 (*Of vice and virtue*), as well as the characterizations of virtue at *THN* 3.2.6.7 and 3.3.1.29–30.

9.22 **examine the foundation of moral distinctions]** In a similar context at *THN* 2.1.7.2, Hume used the following language: 'the controversy, which of late years has so much excited the curiosity of the publick, *whether these moral distinctions be founded on natural and original principles, or arise from interest and education?*'. The latter reference to interest and education is likely an allusion to Hobbes and Bernard Mandeville (*c.*1670–1733; philosopher, physician, and economic theorist). The reference to natural or original principles is less clear, but presumably covers at least two groups of philosophers engaged in the controversy, and who were themselves at odds regarding whether the foundations of morality are in reason or in sentiment. Shaftesbury and Hutcheson are influential figures on the side of sentiment; other figures included Turnbull and, later, Lord Kames (1696–1782; Scottish lawyer and philosopher Henry Home). Samuel Clarke[B] and William Wollaston (1659–1724; English moral philosopher and theologian) were primary figures on the side of reason. Ralph Cudworth (1617–88; English philosopher, professor of Hebrew, and Master of Christ's College, Cambridge) is named in a similar capacity in *EPM* 3.34 and n. 12. Another candidate is John Balguy (1686–1748; English philosopher and theologian), who supported Clarke and criticized Hutcheson.

On moral distinctions, see *EPM* 1.2; *THN* 2.1.7.2; 3.1.1–2; 3.3.1.3, 11; 3.3.2.1. In the late seventeenth and eighteenth centuries several voluntarist philosophers and theologians believed that moral distinctions are fixed by the will of God, whereas rationalists (such as Clarke and Cudworth) held that distinctions of good and evil (and the like) are objective realities analogous to mathematical truths and knowable by reason. In the moral sense tradition, moral distinctions are real, but known through mental sentiments.

9.24 **The most probable system . . . to explain the difference between vice and virtue]** In *A Letter from a Gentleman*, Hume (or possibly his editor Lord Kames) described his position in the controversy over the foundation of morality:

He [Hume] hath indeed denied the eternal Difference of Right and Wrong in the Sense in which *Clark* and *Woolaston* maintained them, *viz.* That the Propositions of Morality were of the same Nature with the Truths of Mathematicks and the abstract Sciences, the Objects *merely* of Reason, not the *Feelings* of our internal *Tastes* and *Sentiments.* In this Opinion he concurs with all the antient Moralists, as well as with Mr. *Hutchison* Professor of Moral Philosophy in the University of *Glasgow*, who, with others, has revived the antient Philosophy in this Particular. (*Letter* 37)

For Hume's arguments in *THN* that morality is not founded on reason, but on passion, sentiment, or feeling, see *THN* 3.1; 3.3.1.

9.29 **To approve of a character . . . To disapprove]** For elaboration of this thesis, see *THN* 3.1.2.1–3 and *EPM* 9.12 and n. 50. The closest historical connection to Hume may be Hutcheson (see, e.g., *Inquiry*, Preface), though his account of the moral sense and moral approbation differ significantly from Hume's. For the language of 'delight upon its appearance', cf. Hobbes, *Leviathan* 6.11.

9.32 **blame or praise]** At *THN* 2.1.7.5, from which this passage is derived, Hume used 'vice and virtue' rather than 'blame or praise'.

10.2 **pride or self-satisfaction]** See the identical language at *DP* 2.41. At *Abstract* 30 Hume uses the language of 'pride or self-esteem' to make a related, but not identical, point. On the nature of pride, see ann. 7.3 (on *DP* 2.1).

10.6 **common systems of ethics]** These are called 'vulgar systems of ethicks' in the passage in *THN* 2.1.7.7 from which this passage descends. It is unclear precisely what Hume takes to count as a vulgar or common system, but the plural 'systems' suggests more than one.

10.11 **what *wit* is]** At *EPM* 8.3 Hume says that 'wit' is not 'easy to define' and links it to taste; at *THN* 2.1.8.1 (following on from 2.1.7.7), he says that wit 'cannot be defin'd, but is discern'd only by a taste or sensation'. When Hume says immediately below that he has located the 'very essence of true or false wit', he appears to be referring not to a definition but to psychological conditions. The nature of wit had been the subject of a series of articles in which Addison (*Spectator* 58–63) attempted to distinguish true wit from false wit. Addison began by saying that 'Nothing is so much admired and so little understood as Wit'. He maintained that no prior author had written directly on the subject, but then cited several writers who obliquely or indirectly had done so. He approvingly cited Locke and disapprovingly discussed a terse definition by John Dryden. Locke, who devoted a full section to wit and judgement (*Essay* 2.11.2), and Dryden (*An Essay of Dramatick Poesie*, passim) were more concerned than Addison to express 'what wit is'. Chambers (*Cyclopædia*, 'wit') used Locke as a basis for his discussion. Alexander Pope (1688–1744; English poet), in *An Essay on Criticism* (1711), offered influential observations about wit presented in verse, and Hobbes commented on wit in several works, esp. *Leviathan* 8.

10.15 **what is this *taste*]** Hume wrote about taste and the delicacy of taste in his essays 'Of the Delicacy of Taste and Passion' and 'Of the Standard of Taste' 16–17; and *EPM* 1.3–4; 1.10; 7.4; 7.28; Appx. 3.10. In 'Of the Standard of Taste', he said, 'Though it be certain, that beauty and deformity, more than sweet and bitter, are not qualities in objects, but belong entirely to the sentiment, internal or external; it must be allowed, that there are certain qualities in objects, which are fitted by nature to produce those particular feelings.... Where the organs are so fine, as to allow nothing to escape them; and at the same time so exact as to perceive every ingredient in the composition: This we call delicacy of taste.... [A] delicate taste of wit or beauty must always be a desirable quality; because it is the source of all the finest and most innocent enjoyments, of which human nature is susceptible.'

10.21 **vanity or mortification]** In the original passage in *THN* 2.1.7.7, the word 'pride' appears instead of 'vanity', and 'humility' appears instead of 'mortification'. Hume has omitted in *DP* a striking passage at *THN* 2.1.7.8 that originally followed this passage in *DP*: 'There may, perhaps, be some, who being accustom'd to the style of the schools and pulpit, and having never consider'd human nature in any other light, than that in which *they* place it, may here be surpriz'd to hear me talk of virtue as exciting pride, which they look upon as a vice; and of vice as producing humility, which they have been taught to consider as a virtue. But not to dispute about words, I observe, that by *pride* I understand that agreeable impression, which arises in the mind, when the view either of our virtue, beauty, riches or power makes us satisfy'd with ourselves: And that by *humility* I mean the opposite impression. 'Tis evident the former impression is not always vicious, nor the latter virtuous.'

10.23 **Beauty of all kinds . . .]** This passage is adapted from *THN* 2.1.8.1, which begins the section *Of beauty and deformity*. Hume's discussions of beauty—including what he calls in the next paragraph of *DP* 'the very essence of beauty'—are amplified in other sections of his works, especially *THN* (including the sparse comments on beauty in *THN* 3). See, further, the next annotation.

10.33 **the cause of pleasure]** *THN* 2.1.8.3 provides the following explanation and link between beauty and the theory of pride and humility: 'Now there is nothing common to natural and moral beauty, (both of which are the causes of pride) but this power of producing pleasure; and as a common effect supposes always a common cause, 'tis plain the pleasure must in both cases be the real and influencing cause of the passion. Again; there is nothing originally different betwixt the beauty of our bodies and the beauty of external and foreign objects, but that the one has a near relation to ourselves, which is wanting in the other. This original difference, therefore, must be the cause of all their other differences, and among the rest, of their different influence upon the passion of pride, which is excited by the beauty of our person, but is not affected in the least by that of foreign and external objects. Placing, then, these two conclusions together, we find they compose the preceding system betwixt them, *viz.* that pleasure, as a related or resembling impression, when plac'd on a related object, by a natural transition, produces pride; and its contrary, humility.' For some related early modern theories, see Berkeley, *Alciphron* 3.9–10; Addison, *Spectator* 412; Chambers, *Cyclopædia*, 'beauty'.

11.9 **But though pride and humility]** *DP* 2.21–32 is derived (with significant modifications) from *THN* 2.1.9.1, 2.1.9.6–2.1.10.3.

11.12 **houses, gardens, equipage]** This passage descends from *THN* 2.1.9.1; Hume had brought up the subject at *THN* 2.1.5.2, where he uses two of these three examples. Hutcheson uses exactly these three examples, in the order Hume uses them (adding also 'dress'), in *Essay on the Nature and Conduct of the Passions and Affections* 1.2 (Treatise 1); Hutcheson returns to the subject and the examples at 1.7 (Treatise 1) and 6.6 (Treatise 2).

11.18 **surprize and admiration]** Descartes treats the passion of admiration, using a word that may also be translated 'wonder' (one of only six primitive passions for Descartes), to account for the attached element of surprise or novelty (*Passions of the Soul* 53, 69–78, 99, 160): 'Wonder is a sudden surprise of the soul which brings it to consider with attention the objects that seem to it unusual and extraordinary' (70). In *Leviathan* 6.38 Hobbes defines 'admiration' as 'joy from apprehension of novelty'; he treats of 'Admiration and curiosity' in *Human Nature* 9.18; see also *Leviathan* 6.35, 38. For Descartes, admiration (or wonder) seems to arise when we recognize the significance of a new, novel, or surprising object. Charleton treated admiration similarly (*Natural History of the Passions* 5.3–7, with an acknowledgement of Hobbes on p. 89), as did Henry More (*Enchiridion Ethicum* 1.8.3–6) and Isaac Watts, who considered admiration one of the three 'most Primitive and Original Passions' (*A Plain and Particular Account of the Natural Passions* 4). Le Brun describes admiration as 'a Suprize which makes the Mind consider with Attention those Objects which seem rare and extraordinary' (*Conference of Monsieur Le Brun . . . upon Expression*, pp. 7–8). See also Malebranche's chapter on wonder and its related passions, *Search after Truth* 5.8.

11.23 **parish]** In British usage this term referred to a subdivision of a county or township.

11.33 **transition above explained]** See ann. 7.3 (on *DP* 2.1) for the explanation of pride (and humility), as resulting from a double relation.

12.12 **riches in ourselves . . . poor among our friends]** This passage is adapted from *THN* 2.1.9.10; see also the discussion of riches in *THN* 2.1.10 (*Of property and riches*) and 2.2.5 (*Of our esteem for the rich and powerful*).

12.20 **uninterrupted proprietors]** Hume's family had been the continuous proprietors of Ninewells (or Nine Wells) for two centuries, dating from 'George Hume of the Ninewells' (Mossner, *Life*, pp. 7–8). In 'My Own Life' 2, Hume reports that 'my father's family is a branch of the Earl of Home's, or Hume's; and my ancestors had been proprietors of the estate, which my brother possesses, for several generations'. See also Hume's more detailed comments on the family history at Ninewells in his letter of 12 April 1758, to Alexander Home of Whitfield, *Letters*, 1: 274–7.

12.24 **never passed through any female]** This phenomenon is explained, in part, in the next two paragraphs. The phenomena in question presumably include primogeniture, or the rule of inheritance whereby the real property of a deceased ancestor descends to the firstborn son. This reward of property involved a reciprocal expectation of military service. When no lineal descendants (male or female) existed, other rules in the system prevented females and junior male descendants at the next family level (the next degree of consanguinity) from inheriting. If only females survived, they divided the estate equally. Hume provides essentially the same discussion at *THN* 2.1.9.11–13; the explanation is expanded at 2.1.9.13.

12.26 **foregoing theory]** the theory of double relations.

13.3 **quality of human nature]** At *THN* 2.1.9.13 Hume provides a note stating that this quality is considered at 'Part 2. Sect. 2'—an apparent reference to *THN* 2.2.2.19–26.

13.10 **doctrine . . . explained afterwards]** The reference is to the discussion of '*general rules*' found at 2.46–7 below. Further on general rules, see *THN* 1.3.13.7–13 and 2.1.6.8–9.

13.20 ***property*, as it gives us the fullest power]** Cf. the more extensive comments on property (and riches) in *THN* 2.1.10 (*Of property and riches*), from which this passage in *DP* may have been partially adapted.

n. 3.1 **That property . . . to the mind.]** See the editor's Introduction, pp. lxxxi and cxvi, on the incorporation of n. 3 in 1760 and the connection of this passage to *THN*.

14.23 **love of fame]** See *THN* 2.1.11 (*Of the love of fame*) and *EPM* 9.10. For a satirical and poetic treatment of the subject by a student of the passions, see Edward Young (1673–1765; Fellow of All Souls College, Oxford), *Love of Fame, The Universal Passion*. Spinoza notes, writing on the passion of ambition, that, 'As Cicero says [*Pro archia poeta* 11.26–7], *Every man is led by love of esteem, and the more so, the better he is. Even the philosophers who write books on how esteem is to be disdained put their names to these works*' (*Ethics* 3, Def. Affects 44). A remarkably similar comment to Spinoza's is found in Archibald Campbell (Professor of Ecclesiastical History, St Andrews), *An Enquiry into the Original of Moral Virtue* 3, citing the identical passage in Cicero. See also *Spectator* 73 (Addison), 139 (Steele), and 255 (Addison).

In the 'Advertisement' to bks. 1 and 2 of *THN*, Hume wrote that '*The approbation of the public I consider as the greatest reward of my labours*'. In 'My Own Life' 3 and 21, he wrote that 'a passion for literature . . . has been the ruling passion of my life. . . . Even my love of literary fame, my ruling passion, never soured my temper, notwithstanding my frequent disappointments.'

14.29 **Though it be difficult]** *DP* 2.34–40 is derived (with modifications) from *THN* 2.1.11.11–13.

14.38 **suffrage]** approbation; support. See also *DP* 2.40.

15.9 **Thus few objects]** *DP* 2.41–3 is derived from *THN* 2.1.6.3, 2.1.6.7, and 2.1.6.4, respectively.

16.1 **As health and sickness]** *DP* 2.44–5 is derived almost directly from *THN* 2.1.8.8–9.

16.20 **epilepsy . . . gives a horror . . . itch; because it is infectious]** Those said to suffer from epilepsy were understood in the eighteenth century to have convulsions attended by a deprivation of understanding, grinding of teeth, foaming at the mouth, and violent shaking of the head (often with involuntary urination). Epileptics were commonly shunned and feared, and epilepsy was often associated with divine punishment and/or possession by evil spirits. The itch is a contagious skin disease (scabies) caused by a burrowing mite. It produces severe itching, chiefly at night. *THN* 2.1.8.9 contains an identical passage.

16.21 **king's evil]** scrofula, a lumpy swelling on the sides of the neck caused by a tuberculosis infection of the lymph glands. It was once thought curable by the touch of royalty, a touch sometimes attended with elevated ceremony. Hume mentions this disease and its history in *History of England* (chs. 3, 71); *THN* 2.1.8.9; and *EPM*, n. 33.

16.24 **A fourth circumstance]** *DP* 2.46–7 is derived (with modifications) from *THN* 2.1.6.8–9.

16.28 **Custom readily carries us beyond]** Compare *EHU* 5, pt. 1, and numerous passages in *THN*.

16.32 **principles or internal mechanism]** See ann. 29.5 (on *DP* 6.19, 'regular mechanism').

16.33 **person full-grown]** Cf. Hume's discussions of the model of the biblical Adam in *Abstract* 11–14; *NHR* 1.6; and *THN* 2.1.6.9. In eighteenth-century writings, Adam was a common paradigm of the person with fully rational powers.

16.35 **embarrassed]** perplexed; see also *DP* 1.20.

17.4 **here ascribe]** The language in the comparable passage of *THN* is 'shall hereafter ascribe'. Hume apparently is there referring to passages such as *THN* 2.1.10.9 and 2.2.5.6–7.

SECTION 3

18.3 **transferred from ourselves to another person . . . esteem or contempt]** Descartes mentions a related thesis about transfer, esteem, and begetting favourable sentiments, though his choice of passions is different (*Passions of the Soul* 61–2). 'Esteem' and 'contempt' are paired opposites in several writers—often used as interchangeable for 'love' and 'hatred'. See *THN* 2.2.2.10; 2.2.5.1; 3.3.4.2 n.; and compare Watts, *A Plain and Particular Account of the Natural Passions* 6.

n. 4.1 **affection of parents]** For this note Hume may have adapted a passage from the text of *THN* 2.2.12.5. See further the collation of *DP* n. 4 with *THN* 2.2.12.5 on 'the affection of parents' (editor's Introduction, p. cxvi). In *THN* 2.2.12, entitled *Of the love and hatred of animals*, Hume is discussing animals generally, not merely the human animal.

n. 4.1 **original instinct]** Appeals to original instinct (and, in some cases, denials of original instinct) are common in Hume's writings. At *Abstract* 6, he comments that 'all our passions are a kind of natural instincts, derived from nothing but the original constitution of the human mind'. See, further, the account at *THN* 2.3.9.8. The postulate that passions (of any sort) are given at birth had been fervently denied by Antoine Le Grand (1629–99; French Franciscan missionary and philosopher) throughout *Man without Passion: Or, The Wise Stoick* (see preface and pp. 69–71, 84, 118, 135 ff.).

18.30 **love and hatred are always followed by . . . benevolence and anger]** *DP* 3.6 is adapted from *THN* 2.2.6.3. Cf. other sections of *THN* 2.2.6 (*Of benevolence and anger*) and Hume's comment on love and benevolence in *EPM*, n. 67. Variants on Hume's point are in Descartes, *Passions of the Soul* 56, 79, 81; and Charleton, *Natural History of the Passions* 5.14–16 (tracing one form of this analysis to 'the Schools'). Hume's account of these four passions shows similarities to and differences from Hutcheson's *Essay on the Nature and Conduct of the Passions and Affections* 3.2 (Treatise 1).

18.33 **pure emotions in the soul]** Pure emotions, affections, or passions had been discussed by previous writers, though not with the same meaning or analysis as that found in Hume. For example, Hutcheson had maintained that '*Desire* and *Aversion* are the only pure Affections in the strictest Sense', and that 'other Affections differ from Sensations only, by including Desire or Aversion' (*Essay on the Nature and Conduct of the Passions and Affections* 3.2 (Treatise 1)).

19.10 **compassion is an uneasiness in the sufferings of another]** On the meaning of 'uneasiness', see anns. 4.1 (on *DP* 1.9) and 9.13 (on *DP* 2.13). For works that linked compassion to uneasiness, pain, or distress caused by the sufferings of (or by an evil present to) another, see Cicero, *Tusculan Disputations* 4.8.18 (also 3.10.21); Vives, *Passions of the Soul* 7; Descartes, *Passions of the Soul* 187; and Joseph Butler (1692–1752; English philosopher and bishop of Bristol and later of Durham), *Fifteen Sermons* 5.1–3, 6.5–8. *THN* 2.2.7 is entitled *Of compassion*, but is concerned with somewhat different issues than these lines in *DP*. See also 3.9 below. On sympathy, compassion, uneasiness, and pain, see *EPM* 5.18; n. 60; and Appx. 1.16.

19.16 **comparison of ourselves with others . . . source of envy and malice]** Cf. the conclusions and examples in Seneca, *Moral Essays*, 'De ira' ('On Anger') 3.31.1–3; 'De beneficiis' ('On Benefits') 2.28.1—and the more extreme conclusions delivered by his modern disciple, Le Grand, *Man without Passion* 4.4. See also

Plutarch, 'On Envy and Hate' (in *Moralia*); and Guillaume Du Vair (1556–1621; French politician and bishop), *Morall Philosophie of the Stoicks*, p. 65.

19.19 **compassion to that of benevolence]** Cf. *THN* 2.2.7 (*Of compassion*); 2.2.6 (*Of benevolence and anger*); and 2.2.9 (*Of the mixture of benevolence and anger with compassion and malice*).

19.20 **envy to anger]** Cf. *THN* 2.2.8 (*Of malice and envy*) and 2.2.6 (*Of benevolence and anger*). See *DP* 2.7 on the reverse sequence, namely, 'anger to envy'.

19.32 **Poverty, meanness, disappointment, produce contempt]** Cf. relevant antecedent theories of contempt and its sources in Vives, *Passions of the Soul* 12; and Descartes, *Passions of the Soul* 149–50. There is no direct predecessor of this paragraph in *THN*, but see *THN* 2.2.5.1, 14–16; 2.2.9.10–16; and *EPM*, n. 34.

20.6 **In respect . . . In contempt]** Cf. *THN* 2.2.10 (*Of respect and contempt*), where respect is treated as a mixture of love and humility, and contempt as a mixture of hatred and pride (see esp. 2.2.10.1–2).

20.8 **The amorous passion]** Cf. *THN* 2.2.11 (*Of the amorous passion, or love betwixt the sexes*), where the amorous passion is treated as a complex of three simpler 'impressions or passions, *viz.* the pleasing sensation arising from beauty; the bodily appetite for generation; and a generous kindness or good-will' (2.2.11.1).

SECTION 4

22.1 **The following are instances]** *DP* 4.6–11 is derived, with modifications, from *THN* 2.2.8.13–19.

22.4 **our proximity]** In the original of this passage, at *THN* 2.2.8.13, Hume supplies an example: 'A common soldier bears no such envy to his general as to his sergeant or corporal; nor does an eminent writer meet with so great jealousy in common hackney scriblers, as in authors, that more nearly approach him.'

22.13 **Flemish and a Welsh horse]** The Flemish (or Friesian) horse is large by comparison with the far smaller Welsh horse (or Welsh Mountain Pony). The same example is in Locke, *Essay* 2.26.5, and is found in identical form in *THN* 2.2.8.16.

22.19 **Guicciardin . . . the wars in ITALY]** In *History of Italy* 3.4, Guicciardini writes that 'it is a common human failing [ceding] to prefer serving foreigners to yielding to one's own people'. The passage from which Hume's paragraph is derived (*THN* 2.2.8.17) likewise lacks a specific reference. Guicciardini is frequently cited in vol. 3 of Hume's *History of England*. See also the mention of Guicciardini on the wars of Pisa, *EPM* 5.33.

22.27 **travellers . . . Chinese and Persians]** A large number of books were available to Hume about the reports of these 'travellers'. Voltaire and many other writers took note of these reports. In a work published in London in 1727, Voltaire wrote that 'Our European Travellers for the most Part are satyrical upon their neighboring Countries, and bestow large Praises upon the Persians and Chineses; it being too natural to revile those who stand in Competition with us, and to extol those who being far remote from, are out of the reach of Envy' ('Advertisement to the Reader' 2 (p. 76), in *An Essay upon the Civil Wars of France*).

One prominent body of reports centred on the so-called Chinese rites controversy (regarding whether Confucian practices of ancestor veneration were *social*, or rather, religious, and therefore whether converts were allowed to participate in these traditional practices). This controversy had been generated by Jesuit travellers who had found favour with the Chinese Imperial court, often taking a sympathetic view of its practices. For one such work, see the annotation concerning the travels and publications of Père Louis Daniel Le Comte, SJ, in China; this work is specifically mentioned by Hume at *NHR*, n. 6 (see ann. on n. 6). See also Richard Hakluyt's collection *The Principall Navigations, Voiages and Discoveries of the English Nation*, which is cited at ann. 82.20 below. For a different style of reports on Persian religious traditions, see the source Hume cites in *NHR* nn. 39 and 46 (Thomas Hyde, *Historia religionis veterum Persarum, eorumque Magorum*).

22.31 **serious and profound, another light and humorous]** See the annotation below on Matthew Prior's works and the classic statements on poetic licence and idle fancies in Horace, *Ars poetica*, lines 1–23. At *EPM* 3.18 Hume discusses problems of foreign elements inappropriately mixed or joined together.

22.33 **rules of art and criticism]** *DP* was originally published together with 'Of Tragedy' and 'Of the Standard of Taste' (in *Four Dissertations*). These essays examined the passions that the fine arts arouse and rules of art and criticism. However, it is unlikely that these essays affected the writing of this passage in *DP*, given that it is derived from *THN* 2.2.8.18. There Hume advances the following thesis: 'These rules of art are founded on the qualities of human nature; and the quality of human nature, which requires a consistency in every performance, is that which renders the mind incapable of passing in a moment from one passion and disposition to a quite different one.'

22.34 **Prior . . . *Alma* and *Solomon*]** The reference (carried over from *THN* 2.2.8.18) is to Matthew Prior,[B] who was known for his light verse and raillery, as well as his elegance and grace of language. As Hume suggests, 'Alma: or, the Progress of the Mind' is a humorous poem, 'Solomon on the Vanity of the World' a solemn work on moral duty and the meaning of life. In 'Solomon' Prior is concerned with how happiness is only partially obtained, inasmuch as the pleasures of life fail to compensate for the distresses. The life of King Solomon is illustrative. In the Preface, Prior writes that 'I had a Mind to collect and digest such Observations, and Apophthegms, as most particularly tend to the Proof of that great Assertion, laid down in the beginning of the ECCLESIASTES, ALL IS VANITY'. 'Alma', by contrast, is a light discussion between two men about philosophical problems regarding the soul and its relationship to the body and the brain. See Canto 1, lines 30–7, for typical examples of Prior's humour.

23.3 **An heroic and burlesque design . . . would be monstrous]** Though Hume mentions paintings here, a discussion of monstrous mixtures in other arts existed in literature of the period. See, e.g., Addison, *Spectator* 40, on the 'monstrous invention' of the tragi-comedy.

23.16 **For, not to repeat . . .]** This paragraph derives from *THN* 2.2.2.8–9.

SECTION 5

24.1 **reason . . . can never . . . be any motive to the will]** See *EPM* Appx. 1.21 (on mistaken views about reason as motivating action) and *THN* 2.3.3 (*Of the influencing motives of the will*). In the latter (at 2.3.3.1), Hume outlines his objectives: 'I shall endeavour to prove *first*, that reason alone can never be a motive to any action of the will; and *secondly*, that it can never oppose passion in the direction of the will.' An extensive literature existed on these topics. See e.g. the influential discussion in Locke, *Essay* 2.21.29–47. Hume cites this chapter in Locke ('Of Power') at *EHU*, n. 12 (during a discussion of causation and necessary connection).

24.4 ***Abstract relations* of ideas are the object of curiosity, not of volition. And *matters of fact*]** Cf. *EHU* 4.1 on *relations of ideas* and *matters of fact* as two functions or objects of reason. *THN* 2.3.10 (*Of curiosity, or the love of truth*), discusses curiosity as a passion and 'two kinds' of truth. Hume's choice of the term 'curiosity' may be mindful of literature on the passions, not merely an offhand equivalent of 'love of truth'. Several philosophers had recognized that although some passions thwart reason and the acquisition of knowledge, passions such as curiosity, wonder, and admiration stimulate knowledge acquisition. Hobbes wrote that '*Desire* to know why, and how, CURIOSITY, such as is in no living creature but *man*. . . is a lust of the mind that by a perseverance of delight in the continual and indefatigable generation of knowledge, exceedeth the short vehemence of any carnal pleasure. . . . ADMIRATION [is] proper to man, because it excites the appetite of knowing the cause' (*Leviathan* 6.35, 38; cf. *Human Nature* 9.18, 'Admiration and Curiosity'). Descartes (*Passions of the Soul* 88), Malebranche (*Search after Truth* 5.8, on wonder and related passions, and 4.3–4, on curiosity), and Addison (*Spectator* 237) all attribute a related role to the passions of curiosity, wonder, and admiration. See also the guarded appraisals of curiosity in Bernard Lamy (1640–1715; French ecclesiastic and scholar), *Entretiens sur les sciences* 2 (pp. 59–60).

24.9 **reason . . . is nothing but a general and a calm passion]** The distinction between calm passions and more intense passions is treated at *THN* 2.1.1.3; 2.3.3.8–10; 2.3.4; and 2.3.8.13. See also *DP* 5.4; 6.1; *EPM* 6.15; and correspondence of 10 Jan. 1743, to Francis Hutcheson, and 30 June 1743, to William Mure of Caldwell (*Letters*, 1: 46–7, 51). At *THN* 2.3.3.8 Hume maintains that the calm passions are frequently mistaken for reason. At *EPM* he uses the language of 'soft and gentle passions' in reference to love and friendship.

Literature on the passions had for centuries portrayed them as violent and impulsive, by contrast to reason. See the several sources mentioned in ann. 24.27 (on *DP* 5.4). Relevant background to Hume's distinction between calm and violent passions is found in Hutcheson's reflections on violent passions and calm desires and affections in *Essay on the Nature and Conduct of the Passions and Affections* 2.2–3 (Treatise 1); *An Inquiry into the Original of our Ideas of Beauty and Virtue* 7.9.3; 4.2; 6.3 (all in Treatise 2); and *Short Introduction* 1.1.5–7. Descartes (*Passions of the Soul* 46, 85) and Edward Young (*A Vindication of Providence*, p. 30) wrote about the 'lesser passions', by contrast to the 'violent' passions. See also Charleton, *Natural History of the Passions* 2.12, 15; 4.2; 6.10–11; Pierre Charron (1541–1603; French Roman Catholic theologian and philosopher), *Of Wisdome* (*De la sagesse*) 2.1; and Du Vair, *Morall Philosophie of the Stoicks*, p. 19.

Sometimes in this literature 'calm passion' referred to a type of passion that is always calm, such as fondness and desiring another's happiness; but in other cases it referred to the intensity of a passion on a particular occasion—e.g. fear might be calm at one time, violent at another. Some philosophers suggested that 'calm passion' is an oxymoron, on the grounds that all passions are violent agitations. See e.g. Thomas Reid (1710–96; Scottish philosopher), *Essays on the Active Powers of Man* 3.6, which comments on Hume's theory.

24.23 **The common error of metaphysicians . . . have no influence]** Some of these metaphysicians would presumably be among the philosophers engaged in the controversy over the foundations of morality discussed in ann. 9.22 (on *DP* 2.14). *DP* 5.4–6.19 (the end of *DP*) is derived from *THN* 2.3.3.10–2.3.6.9.

24.27 **counteract a violent passion]** The goal of counteracting inordinate appetites or passions, especially by the governance of right reason and virtue, is ancient, dating from Platonic, Aristotelian, Stoic, Epicurean, and Christian views that the passions are excessive impulses. See Plato, *Republic* 329C–D, 439C–41C, 444B–D; Seneca, *Moral Essays*, 'De ira' ('On Anger') 1.1.1–7, 1.8.1–6, 2.3.1–5, and 3.1.1–5; 'De beneficiis' ('On Benefits') 2.14.1; *Ad Lucilium epistulae morales* 85.6–27 ('On Some Vain Syllogisms') and 116.1–5 ('On Self-Control'); Plutarch, 'On the Control of Anger' 454B–D and 'On Tranquillity of Mind' 465C, 466D (in *Moralia*); Cicero, *Tusculan Disputations* 4.5.10–4.6.14. The Stoic model of overcoming the passions altogether was widely regarded in modern philosophy as an unattainable goal, although Le Grand held tenaciously to it throughout *Man without Passion* (see pp. 70, 85, 90–1, 96, 99–101, 115 ff., 135 ff.). He may have drawn from Du Vair, *Morall Philosophie of the Stoicks* (see esp. pp. 62–70, 100).

For a sample of early modern literature on counteracting violent, unruly, or animal passions, see Francis Bacon (1561–1626; English philosopher and statesman), *Advancement of Learning* 2.18.2, 4; Vives, *Passions of the Soul* 13–24; Wright, *Passions of the Mind in General* 1.2, 1.4, 2.1–3.3; Jean-François Senault (*c.*1601–72; French clergyman and philosopher), *The Use of the Passions* 1.1.1,

4, 1.2.5–1.3.5; Descartes, *Passions of the Soul* 46, 50, 148, 161, 211–12; Reynolds, *A Treatise of the Passions* 6; Charleton, *Natural History of the Passions* 3.7–9, 5.64, 6.11–13; Malebranche, *Search after Truth* 5.6; Louis de La Forge (1632–66; French physician and philosopher), *Traitté de l'esprit de l'homme* 21; Charron, *Of Wisdome* (*De la sagesse*), bk. 2, ch. 1; Bayle (*Dictionary*, 'Helen' [Y]); *Spectator* 408; Coeffeteau, *A Table of Humane Passions* 3; Ayloffe, *Government of the Passions*, pp. 38–45, 56–61, 122–3; Forbes, *Essays Moral and Philosophical on Several Subjects* 1.6; Watts, *A Plain and Particular Account of the Natural Passions* 14–15.

24.27 **violent passion . . . calm passions]** This passage is derived from *THN* 2.3.3.10; cf. also *THN* 2.3.4 (*Of the causes of the violent passions*). The term 'violent' often carried the meaning of intensity of influence and commanding effect (see *DP* 6.5 below). On the contrasting case of the calm passions, see ann. 24.9 (on *DP* 5.2).

24.32 ***strength of mind*]** 'Strength of mind', meaning firmness of purpose, appears several times in Hume's works. Under this category he places political resistance, withstanding intemperance, mitigation of natural propensities, even-tempered resistance in the face of disturbing events, and steady adherence to a distant interest. See *THN* 1.4.7.14 and 2.3.3.10; 'The Sceptic' 26; *EPM* 3.18, 4.1, and 6.15; and *History of England*, chs. 48–9. In *EPM* 6, Hume considers strength of mind among the 'qualities useful to ourselves' that lead us to classify persons as having personal merit.

SECTION 6

26.2 **passion calm or violent, which heighten or diminish any emotion]** For Hume's use of 'emotion' in his theory of the passions, see *THN* 2.2.2.5–6, 2.3.3.8–9, and 2.3.4.2–5. The word 'emotion' is used several times above in *DP*. *DP* 6.1–11 descends from *THN* 2.3.4.1–10.

26.7 **the theory above delivered]** At *THN* 2.3.4.2 (the original source of the present passage) Hume makes it clear that this theory is that of the 'double relation of impressions and ideas'. 'Above delivered' could refer to as many as seven previous passages in *DP* that mention a double relation.

26.10 **predominant passion swallows up the inferior]** Cf. Hume's discussions in 'Of Tragedy' 1, 6–10, 13, 19–20, and 27 of (1) why tragedy pleases and (2) the 'predominant' and 'subordinate' movements and emotions. See also the reference at *DP* 1.25 to the theory presented here.

26.20 **common artifice of politicians . . . delay as long as possible . . . before they give him a full insight]** In 'Of Tragedy' 13 Hume writes: 'Had you any intention to move a person extremely by the narration of any event, the best method of encreasing its effect would be artfully to delay informing him of it, and first to excite his curiosity and impatience before you let him into the secret. This is the artifice practiced by IAGO in the famous scene of SHAKESPEARE; and every spectator is sensible, that OTHELLO's jealousy acquires additional force from his preceding impatience, and that the subordinate passion is here readily transformed into the predominant one.'

27.3 **"Spes addita suscitat iras."]** Virgil, *Aeneid* 10, line 263. The Latin may be translated as 'Raised hope brings roused passions'. In Virgil's text the anger of warriors is roused ('blown up') by their hope of beating an enemy.

27.7 **direct passion of desire or aversion]** This passage derives from *THN* 2.3.4.4; the notion of a 'direct passion' is treated in detail at *THN* 2.3.9. (See above, ann. 7.1 at *DP* 2.1, on 'direct pursuit'.) The direct passions are immediate responses to good and evil (pleasure and pain) or to their expectation (see *THN* 2.3.1.1; 2.3.9.1 ff.)—of which desire and aversion are examples (along with grief and joy, hope and fear).

27.13 **encrease its violence]** See ann. 24.27 (on *DP* 5.4).

27.32 **despair . . . has a like influence]** Cf. parallels in *THN* 2.3.4.8–10, from which *DP* 6.9–11 derives. Hume held steadfastly to this view. In correspondence of 7 Jan. 1775, he wrote to the Comtesse de Boufflers that 'nothing extinguishes all passions so effectually as despair' (*Letters*, 2: 291).

28.1 **ROCHEFOUCAULT]** The reference is to the *Maximes* of La Rochefoucauld, max. 276. The maxim reads: 'L'absence diminue les médiocres passions, et augmente les grandes, comme le vent éteint les bougies et allume le feu.' (Absence diminishes the moderate passions and increases the great ones, just as the wind blows out candles and kindles fire.) This passage is derived from *THN* 2.3.4.10.

28.9 **spirits moving in their new direction]** apparently, though not unquestionably, a reference to animal spirits—a thin nerve fluid or humour inside narrow tubes and pores that makes sensation and voluntary motion possible. At *EHU* 7.14, Hume suggests a basis for his appeals: 'We learn from anatomy, that the immediate object of power in voluntary motion, is not the member itself which is moved, but certain muscles, and nerves, and animal spirits'. (See also *DP* 6.3; 6.7; 6.10.) See references and definitions in Chambers, *Cyclopædia*: 'animal spirits', 'brain', 'memory', 'passion', and 'spirits'. Explanations of the passions that appealed to brain traces and the animal spirits, or simply spirits, formed an important part of Descartes's account (*Passions of the Soul* 7–16, 21, 26–39, etc.), and were common in other writers. See Charleton, *Natural History of the Passions* 2.13–16, 4.4, 5.50; Malebranche, who understood the passions as arising from motions of the animal spirits and the blood (*Search after Truth* 2.1.5; 2.2.2; 5.1, 3, 7, 11—and related references throughout the work); and La Mettrie, *Histoire naturelle de l'âme* 12 (esp. pp. 103 ff.). George Cheyne (1671–1743; Scottish physician and philosopher), among others, maintained that the 'contriv'd' and 'dark' hypothesis of animal spirits was unconfirmed (*English Malady* 1.9).

28.10 **wonder, surprize . . . novelty]** Cf. the treatment of wonder and novelty in Descartes, *Passions of the Soul* 70, 72–3, 75; and Malebranche, *Search after Truth* 5.7–8. See also the dissent from their approach in Spinoza, *Ethics* 3, Def. Affects 4. See the related annotation above at *DP* 2.21 (11.18).

28.15 **foregoing principle]** See *DP* 6.2 and 6.6 for this principle. At *THN* 2.3.5.2, Hume, restating a principle first articulated at 2.3.4.2, says '*that every emotion, which precedes or attends a passion, is easily converted into it*'.

28.24 **particular and determinate idea]** *DP* 6.13 derives from *THN* 2.3.6.2 (although two-thirds of the latter was not carried into *DP*). In *THN* Hume writes: ''tis certain, that the more general and universal any of our ideas are, the less influence they have upon the imagination. A general idea, tho' it be nothing but a particular one consider'd in a certain view, is commonly more obscure; and that because no particular idea, by which we represent a general one, is ever fix'd or determinate, but may easily be chang'd for other particular ones, which will serve equally in the representation.'

28.31 **Nothing is more capable of infusing any passion . . . than eloquence]** The role of eloquence in arousing the passions was a common theme in philosophical and nonphilosophical writings of the period, and principles of eloquence and the importance of orators in exciting the imagination and the passions were closely studied. In 'Of Eloquence' and elsewhere Hume mentions the achievements of Demosthenes of Athens (4th century BC; Hellenic orator and statesman) and Cicero[B], as well as the writings of Quintilian[B] (*Institutes*) and 'Longinus'[B] (*On the Sublime*, a work of unknown authorship). Such recognition was common when Hume wrote; see Chambers, *Cyclopædia*, 'eloquence'.

An example of the infusion of which Hume speaks may be found in Cicero's *Against Verres*, a work cited at *EPM* Appx. 1.16 and in Hume's essay 'Of Eloquence'.

29.5 **regular mechanism]** Several of Hume's predecessors had proposed theories of the passions incorporating the idea of a regular mechanism. See 'The Intellectual Background: A Concise Account' (pp. 205–28 in this volume); Descartes, *Passions of the Soul* 7; Hobbes, *Leviathan* 3.1–11; Locke, *Essay* 2.21.3; Spinoza, *Ethics* 3, preface; and Malebranche, *Search after Truth* 5.3, 7. In a work Hume would likely have read, John Trenchard (1662–1723; English journalist and political writer) argued that 'our Passions are the Mechanical and necessary Effects of the Complexion, Constitution, and Distempers of our Bodies' (*The Natural History of Superstition*, p. 36; cf. p. 45). La Mettrie—in *L'Histoire naturelle de l'âme* (1745) and *Man a Machine (L'Homme machine*, 1748)—used mechanistic physiology and his medical training to offer materialistic and mechanical explanations of the passions. La Mettrie seems to have thought that the conclusion that *humans* are machines is a reasonable inference from the arguments in Descartes that *animals* are machines; he also concluded that 'man is exactly like animals both in his origin and in all points of comparison' as machines (*Machine Man*, ed. Thomson, pp. 34–5).

27.7 **natural philosophy]** Natural philosophy is the study of *physical* nature and history, whereas moral philosophy is the study of *human* nature and history. These labels can be confusing when applied to the passions. Hume's stated objective in *THN* (Introduction 6–7; cf. *Abstract* 1–3) of developing a science of human nature could be construed as making moral philosophy parallel to natural, as Hume himself suggested in *Abstract* 1: ''tis at least worth while to try if the science of *man* will not admit of the same accuracy which several parts of natural philosophy are found susceptible of.'

Natural philosophy had been associated by others with enquiry into the passions and human nature. For example, Reynolds, *Treatise of the Passions and Faculties of the Soule* 6, held that a *natural* discourse on the passions enquires into 'their essential *Properties*, their Ebbes and Flowes, their Springings and Decayes, the manner of their several *Impressions*, the Physical *Effects* which are wrought by them, and the like'; whereas a *moral* discourse enquires into the role of reason, the connection between the passions and good and evil, and how the passions are suppressed, slackened, and otherwise governed. Shortly after Reynolds's work was published, Descartes wrote a letter that was included in the 'Prefatory Letters' to *Passions of the Soul*, stating that 'My intention was to explain the passions only as a natural philosopher, and not as a rhetorician or even as a moral philosopher' (Letter, Egmont, 14 Aug. 1649; *Philosophical Writings*, 1: 327).

THE NATURAL HISTORY OF RELIGION

31.0 **NATURAL HISTORY]** Hume does not hereafter use or define the term 'natural history' (though he four times cites Pliny's *Natural History*). Eighteenth-century conceptions of natural history are discussed by the editor in an appendix to this volume ('The Intellectual Background: A Concise Account', pp. 215–20).

INTRODUCTION

33.3 **origin in human nature]** Scholars before and during Hume's period were concerned with the foundations of religion in human nature. They considered why, throughout history, persons had been driven to forms of religious belief, credulity, superstition, and zealotry. Theories of human nature were sometimes invoked to provide an answer. Two writers in this tradition were John Trenchard (1662–1723; English political writer), *The Natural History of Superstition*—the first natural history concerned with religious phenomena—and Bernard Fontenelle,[B] *De l'Origine des fables*, esp. pp. 11–17. For other relevant works, see the above mentioned appendix to this volume ('The Intellectual Background: A Concise Account', pp. 217 ff.).

33.10 **belief . . . in all ages]** Arguments from universal belief in God to the existence of God had long been found in theological writers. See the appendix to this volume on Gerard Vossius and Herbert of Cherbury ('The Intellectual Background: A Concise Account', 205–28).

33.13 **Some nations . . . entertained no sentiments of Religion, if travellers and historians may be credited]** It is unknown which nations, travellers, and historians Hume means (if any, in particular). However, at 'A Dialogue' 12 (placed at the end of *EPM*), Hume mentions one possible nation, viz. the 'TOPINAMBOUES' or Tupinamba Indians, who were considered primitive and without religion, based on the reports of travellers. A detailed account of this cannibalistic tribe of Brazil is found in the writings of Hans Staden, a Dutchman held captive by these people (in 1557) and later freed by the French. Staden depicts them as having beliefs in soothsayers, who help them devise rattles to which a tribe member prays 'for what he desires, just as we pray to the true God. These rattles are their gods, for they know nothing of the true God' (Staden, *True History*, ch. 22, pp. 148–51). Many of Staden's reports were confirmed by another traveller, Jean de Léry, who was in Brazil at the same time on a Huguenot expedition. In *History of a Voyage to the Land of Brazil* (1578), ch. 16, he presents the Tupinamba Indians as a rare exception to the general truth that all peoples have a sense that there is a divine being. He asserts categorically that they 'live without any religion at all', meaning that they neither confess nor worship idols or gods of any sort. He acknowledges that there is 'what one might call religion', but insists that it is controlled by charlatans ('false prophets') and exists in complete ignorance of the divine, sacred texts, accounts of creation, and the like. John Locke had also mentioned the customs of the Tupinamba Indians and listed several sources of his information (*Essay* 1.3.9).

33.17 **springs not from an original instinct]** At *Abstract* 6 Hume proposes that 'all our passions are a kind of natural instincts, derived from nothing but the original constitution of the human mind'. (Cf. his uses of 'natural instinct' in *EHU* 5.8; 9.3; 12.7; 12.16, 25.) See also Hume's letter of June 1743, to William Mure of Caldwell, *Letters*, 1: 51, where he observes that 'the Deity . . . is not the natural Object of any Passion or Affection'. A much discussed writer who held that religion is innate, natural, or instinctual in humans was Herbert of Cherbury, *De veritate* 5, 9 (esp. pp. 116–17, 289–304). He held that various religious principles are latent in human nature, though people need experience to deliver them to consciousness. See also George Turnbull (1698–1749; regent at Marischal College, Aberdeen), *Principles of Moral Philosophy* 7.

SECTION 1: That Polytheism Was the Primary Religion of Men

34.2 **polytheism or idolatry]** In the early editions of *NHR*, Hume used 'polytheism' and 'idolatry' synonymously. In the 1757–70 edns., the words 'idolatry' and 'idolatrous' appeared frequently; in the 1772 edn., they were systematically (but incompletely) replaced by the words 'polytheism' and 'polytheistic'. Hume moves freely in his writings between the two sets of words, as did other writers of the period. However, he appears not to assume that idolatry is always polytheistic. For example, in his *History of England* Hume writes that 'The protestants, far from tolerating the religion of their ancestors [Roman Catholicism], regard it as an impious and detestable idolatry', and that 'The general assembly importuned [Mary, Queen of Scots] anew to change her religion; to renounce the blasphemous idolatry of the mass' (ch. 37 [3: 434]; ch. 39 [4: 71]).

34.3 **most ancient religion]** This thesis drew as much discussion in commentaries on *NHR* during Hume's lifetime as any thesis in the work. See Sect. 9 of the editor's Introduction (pp. cxxii ff., cxxvii, and cxxix), which discusses relevant commentary by the Revd (later Bishop) William Warburton, Voltaire, and the anonymously published 'Remarks upon the Natural History of Religion by Mr. Hume'.

34.6 **1700 years ago all mankind were polytheists]** A similar thesis about common belief, with a qualification in the case of Judaism, had been discussed in considerable detail by Ralph Cudworth: 'All the Nations of the World heretofore (except a small and inconsiderable handful of the *Jews*) together with their Wisest men and greatest Philosophers, were generally look'd upon as *Polytheists*' (*True Intellectual System of the Universe* 1.4.11 ff.; Cudworth did not hold this belief himself, and indeed regarded it as 'irrational').

Though no commentator during Hume's lifetime mentioned his dating of '1700 years ago', more than one commentator pointed out that the relevant history of monotheism is 'Mosaic' (Jewish), and therefore that monotheism is of an older date than Hume seems to assume. The thesis that polytheism can be traced to events subsequent to the origins of the Mosaic tradition had often been discussed. See, e.g., Gerard Vossius, *De Theologia gentili*; Newton, *Chronology of Ancient Kingdoms Amended*; Herbert of Cherbury, *Pagan Religion* 14 (Herbert corresponded with Vossius on the subject); and Chevalier de Ramsay,[B] *The Philosophical Principles of Natural and Revealed Religion*, vol. 2.

A scheme of precise dating, according to traditional Christian beliefs, had been provided in Jacques Bossuet, *An Universal History: From the Beginning of the World*, pts. 1 and 2. Benoit de Maillet, in a treatise lauding natural history (published in 1748 in French; 1750 in English), scorned traditional biblical chronology and all forms of religion-induced dating, treating such schemes as fables and romances that were ill informed about originating causes. See his *Telliamed . . . relating to Natural History and Philosophy*, esp. Preface, pp. xiv–xv.

35.19 **causes of such objects . . . never strike our attention or curiosity]** Comparable observations on our lack of curiosity about the causes of familiar objects appear in Cicero, *De natura deorum* 2.38, where Cicero discusses the place of arguments that proceed from the order and frame of the universe to a transcendent and divine source.

35.22 **Adam . . . represented by Milton]** The reference is to John Milton, *Paradise Lost* 8, lines 250–82. Milton's character Adam reacts with wonder (lines 275–9):

> Ye Hills and Dales, ye Rivers, Woods, and Plaines,
> And yee that live and move, fair Creatures, tell,
> Tell, if ye saw, how came I thus, how here?
> Not of my self; by some great Maker then,
> In goodness and in power præminent.

Adam serves for Hume, in other works, as a model of the rational individual; see *THN* 2.1.6.9; *Abstract* 11–14; *EHU* 4.6; and *DP* 2.47.

35.26 **barbarous, necessitous animal]** Cf. the similar language and accounts of the necessitous condition or circumstance of humankind in *THN* 3.2.2.17–20 and *EPM* 3.4.

36.22 **Hercules, Theseus, Bacchus]** The historical origins of these legends are uncertain. Some evidence indicates that Hercules was a historical figure. The legend of Theseus also may have roots in a human person. Stories about Bacchus apparently did not. Hercules, according to some myths, was made a god by Zeus on his mortal death. As a cult figure, he was sometimes worshipped as a god. Theseus is the son of Poseidon, and founder-king of Athens. Legends about Theseus's traits were sometimes modelled on those of Hercules. Bacchus—god of wine, vegetation, and fertility—is among the most popular sources of myth and story in classical literature. The legends of Hercules and Theseus are discussed in ann. 63.15, on *NHR* 10.3. Hume mentions both Bacchus and Theseus in a related context in his essay 'Of Parties in General' 1.

36.35 **superstitions of the heathen world]** 'Superstition' commonly refers, in Hume's usage, to extravagant and unfounded religious beliefs and practices and beliefs related to such practices (including vain fears of a deity, idolatrous or excessive worship, and many silly or foolish beliefs). In his *History of England* Hume comments, during a discussion of the ancient Saxons, on how 'all' superstitions are viewed by other persons. He reports that the Saxons 'believed firmly in spells and inchantments, and admitted in general a system of doctrines, which they held as sacred, but which, like all other superstitions, must carry the air of the wildest extravagance, if propounded to those who are not familiarized to it from their earliest infancy' (ch. 1 [1: 27]). See, further, *NHR* 12.22; *EHU* 1.11 and 11.29; and 'Of Superstition and Enthusiasm'. For a classical discussion, see Plutarch, 'Superstition' (in *Moralia*); this work was influential on the treatments of superstition by Herbert of Cherbury (*Pagan Religion*), Shaftesbury (*Characteristics*, 'Miscellany 2'), and Anthony Collins (1676–1729; English philosopher) (*A Discourse of Free-Thinking*). For other relevant early modern views on superstition, see Spinoza, *Theologico-Political Treatise*, preface; Bayle, *Various Thoughts on the Occasion of a Comet*; Antonius van Dale, *Dissertationes de origine ac progressu idololatriae et superstitionum*;

John Toland (1670–1722; Irish-born British free-thinker), *Letters to Serena*; and Trenchard, *Natural History of Superstition.*

SECTION 2: Origin of Polytheism

37.2 **polytheism, the primitive religion]** See ann. 34.2 (on *NHR* 1.2).

37.7 **this vast machine]** Theses about the vast machine and hidden causes in the machine are found at *EHU* 7.8, 22; 8.14, 32; and *NHR* 2.2. For Hume's reflections on the 'whole machine'—i.e. the universe—and the adjustment of its parts, see *Dialogues* 2.5, 18; 7.14; 11.11; 12.5.

37.18 **statue of Laocoon . . . Pliny]** The reference is to Pliny the Elder, *Natural History* 36.4.37–8. Laocoön was a priest of Apollo. The statue, now in the Vatican, depicts Laocoön and his twin sons being killed by serpents. The statue has been attributed to Agesander, Athenodorous, and Polydorous. Pliny apparently believed that the statue was 'cut from one stone'. The statue known to Pliny may have been cut from one stone, but some scholars have proposed that the extant statue was constructed from as many as eight blocks.

37.22 **statuary]** sculptor, one who makes or carves images or statues in stone or wood (though in the eighteenth century this term also meant both *statues as a group* and *the art of making images or statues*).

38.16 **incessant hopes and fears]** See comparable themes about the rise of religion and superstition from hopes and fears (and their exploitation by priests) in Hobbes, *Leviathan* 12; Spinoza, *Theologico-Political Treatise*, preface, and *Ethics* 1, appx.; Fontenelle,[B] *De l'origine des fables*, pp. 13–17, 26; Trenchard, *Natural History of Superstition*, 9 ff., 33–4; and Toland, *Letters to Serena*, 3rd letter. A primitive but influential form of these themes is in Lucretius, *De rerum natura* 1.102–16, 146–58. See, further, the Appendix to this volume, 'The Intellectual Background: A Concise Account', pp. 224–5.

38.20 **Juno . . . Lucina . . . Neptune . . . Mars . . . Ceres . . . Mercury]** Roman names are used here, but only the Greek god or goddess possessed some of the particular attributes mentioned. (1) *Juno*: Hera is the Greek goddess of marriage, but the function is also assigned to Juno. (2) *Lucina*: Ilithyia is the Greek goddess of childbirth, but the function is assumed in Roman mythology by Juno. When invoked during childbirth, the name Lucina (light-bringer) is added to the name Juno to mark the particular function of making the child see the light of day. Whereas in Greek mythology Ilithyia and Hera are distinct personages, in Roman mythology Lucina is an aspect of Juno. (3) *Neptune*: In Roman mythology, Neptune is the god of water, whereas Poseidon is god of the sea and is worshipped on all navigational occasions. (4) *Mars*: Scholars have defended several interpretations of the function of Mars in Roman mythology, one of which is god of war. Ares was the Greek god of war. (5) *Ceres*: Roman Ceres is the goddess of agriculture, corn, and grain. Ceres and Demeter, her Greek equivalent, both protected the fields. (6) *Mercury*: As the god of commerce Mercury finds his Roman equivalent in Hermes.

n. 1.2 **Plin. lib. 2. cap. 7]** Pliny the Elder, *Natural History* 2.5.15. In the edn. of 1526 (see Cat.), the chapter cited by Hume is ch. 7; it is ch. 5 in modern editions. The passage from Pliny may be translated: 'Weak and toiling humanity, mindful of its own feebleness, has formed its gods into distinct divisions, so as to worship according to group the deity each most needs'.

n. 1.2 **Hesiod's . . . lib. 1]** Hesiod, *Works and Days*, lines 252–5. Hesiod reports that Zeus has 30,000 spirits on earth to keep watch on the judgements and deeds of mortals. Hume here cites 'lib. 1' of *Works and Days*. During Hume's period *Works and Days* was commonly divided into bk. 1 (1–380) and bk. 2 (381–762); modern editions do not follow this precedent.

n. 1.5 **Arist. Probl.]** Aristotle, *Problems* 33.7, 962^{a}21–4. The *Problems*, also published as *Problemata physica*, is considered by many scholars to be an Aristotelian work, but not a work by Aristotle. The cited passage queries why sneezing is considered of divine origin, while coughing and a runny nose are not.

39.4 **terror of death]** Related claims about the terror of death had been discussed by Hobbes, *Leviathan* 12.5–6, 11; and Trenchard, *Natural History of Superstition*, 9, 33–6, 45. Terror and fear of death played a larger explanatory role in some writings on the nature and origin of religion than they do for Hume. See Toland, *Letters to Serena*. See also ann. 38.16 (on *NHR* 2.4) regarding the role Hume gives to fear and hope, including fear of death.

Section 3: The Same Subject Continued

40.6 **secret and unknown causes]** Cf. *NHR* 8.1 and the discussion in *NHR* 4.1 of invisible intelligent power, as well as related themes at *NHR* 2.2; 2.5; 3.4; 5.2; 8.2; 15.5.

40.8 **hope and fear]** See ann. 38.16 (on *NHR* 2.4).

40.17 **ignorant multitude . . . *unknown causes*]** Central features of the thesis in this and the following paragraph are in Trenchard, *Natural History of Superstition*, pp. 9–13; and Fontenelle, *De l'origine des fables*, pp. 13–24.

40.26 **transfer to every object . . . natural propensity, if not corrected by experience and reflection]** In correspondence with Gilbert Elliot about his *Dialogues*, during the period he may have written *NHR*, Hume maintained that:

> [Strong & universal propensities to believe are] somewhat different from our Inclination to find our own Figures in the Clouds, our Face in the Moon, our Passions & Sentiments even in inanimate Matter. Such an Inclination may, & ought to be controul'd, & can never be a legitimate Ground of Assent. . . . As it is usual for us to transfer our own Feelings to

the Objects on which they are dependent, we attach the internal Sentiment to the external Objects. (10 Mar. 1751, *Letters*, 1: 155–6)

Hume mentions the mind's 'great propensity to spread itself on external objects' at *THN* 1.3.14.24–5.

Nicolas Malebranche (1638–1715; French philosopher and theologian) held that the mind has a tendency 'to spread itself onto the objects it considers by clothing them with what it has stripped from itself. . . . Thus, it judges not only that heat and cold are in fire and ice, but also that they are within its own hands' (*Search after Truth* 1.12.5; 5.6; also 1.11.1.1; *Elucidations* 15). Other philosophers had commented on the human tendency to project sentiments or ideas onto objects in the case of heat, sound, colour, and the like. For example, see the discussion of 'translating . . . our Passions to things without us' in Joseph Glanvill (1636–80; English philosopher and clergyman), *Scepsis scientifica* 12; Locke's celebrated discussion of primary and secondary qualities, *Essay* 2.8.8 ff.; and Antoine Arnauld (1612–94; French philosopher, theologian, and mathematician) and Pierre Nicole (1625–95; French theologian and writer on moral subjects) on transporting sensations to objects, *Logic or the Art of Thinking*, first part, ch. 9.

40.32 **sentiment and passion]** 'Sentiment' is an inner sensing, feeling, or emotion—e.g. anger, approval, disgust, sympathy, and compassion. The term was also used in Hume's period to refer to judgement and opinion. No later than 18 Feb. 1751, Hume was pondering the thesis that 'it was neither by Reasoning nor Authority we learn our Religion, but by Sentiment' (correspondence with Gilbert Elliot, *Letters*, 1: 151).

41.3 **river-god or hamadryad]** In classical mythology river-gods are rivers personified. For example, Achelous was god and namesake of the principal river in the south-western mainland of Greece. In this same mythology hamadryads are tree nymphs or the life spirits of trees. When the tree died, the hamadryad was believed to die as well. In ancient Egyptian religion 'hamadryad' refers to objects of veneration that are, in earthly form, animate (e.g. baboons and cobras), rather than inanimate objects like rivers. However, Hume's concern here is apparently with the personification of inanimate natural phenomena.

41.5 **particular *genius* or invisible power]** A *genius loci* ('genius of the place') was, in ancient belief, a minor god or spirit inhabiting or protecting a certain locality. Localities and institutions in which the Romans exercised authority had their own divine genius or tutelary and controlling spirit. Virgil mentions the 'geniumne loci' at *Aeneid* 5.95.

41.26 **Coriolanus in Dionysius,[2]]** Footnote reference: Dionysius of Halicarnassus, *Roman Antiquities* 8.2.2. This passage outlines a dialogue in which Marcius Coriolanus[B] insists that the gods are involved in all human activity. This involvement is said to hold in the case of wars, which are of urgent social importance and have uncertain results.

n. 3.1 **lines of EURIPIDES]** Euripides, *Hecuba*, lines 956–60. Euripides has the character Polymestor lament the destructive effects of the Trojan War. He ponders the transitory and uncertain nature of a life controlled by the whim of the gods. Polymestor maintains that the gods sow discord only to increase the reverence of mortals, who turn to the gods in times of flux and anguish. A literal translation of the passage Hume quotes is: 'There is nothing in which one can have confidence, whether the continuance of a good reputation, or the freedom from future misfortune of those who are successful now. On the contrary, the gods confound things, disorienting us this way and that, so that in our ignorance we may worship them.'

42.29 **says a GREEK historian,[4]]** Footnote reference: Diodorus Siculus, *Historical Library* 3.47.1. Diodorus recounts the story of an imperfect land in which exceptional happiness is experienced by the inhabitants, the Sabaeans ('the most numerous of the tribes of the Arabians', as reported at 3.46.1). Fortune combines harm with happiness and serves as a warning not to take the gods for granted. Hume cites Diodorus nine times in *NHR*, but see 'Of the Populousness of Ancient Nations', n. 115, where Hume warns of Diodorus's weaknesses as a historian.

43.7 **STRABO,[5] . . . the GETES]** Footnote reference: Strabo, *Geography* 7.3.4. The Getes, or Getae, were a stable tribal people of advanced material culture who inhabited a region corresponding roughly to a segment of modern Romania and Bulgaria. They were called 'Getae' in Hellenic culture, but 'Daci' or 'Dacians' by the Romans. Strabo reports on the Getean celibacy and religious fanaticism: '[These] people regard as wretched a life without many women, and yet at the same time regard as pious and just a life that is wholly bereft of women. . . . The interpretation that the wifeless men of the Getae are in a special way reverential towards the gods is clearly contrary to reason.' For further annotation on the Getes and Herodotus's reports on them, see ann. 57.6 and n. 41 (on *NHR* 7.3 and n. 41).

SECTION 4: Deities not Considered as Creators or Formers of the World

44.7 **before the revival of letters]** Hume apparently thought that philosophy and learning made little progress before the revival of letters. See his comments on the period before and after the Renaissance, with references to specific figures, in *History of England* (appx. 2 [1: 487]; ch. 12 [2: 72]; ch. 29 [3: 140]; appx. 4 [5: 150]).

44.10 **interposition]** intervention or stepping in.

44.16 **appellation of *atheism*]** The terms 'atheism' and 'atheist' were commonly used in the eighteenth century to indicate not only those who do not believe in God, but those who believe in God in an unacceptably unorthodox manner. The term was therefore applied to those who fail to accept some critical theistic belief, such as divine providence or the afterlife.

44.20 **invisible intelligent power]** Cf. Hume's use of the term 'invisible intelligent principle' at *EHU* 7.21; see also the related discussions at *NHR* 2.2; 2.5; 3.4; 5.2; 8.2; 15.5. Appeals to invisible intelligent agents are of central importance in Hobbes's treatment of religion in *Leviathan* 6.36 and 12.

n. 6.1 **Père Le Comte]** Footnote reference: Louis Daniel Le Comte, SJ, 'A Monseigneur le Cardinal de Bouillon. De la Religion ancienne & moderne des Chinois', in *Nouveaux mémoires sur l'état présent de la Chine* (see Cat.). Le Comte was among a group of Jesuits sympathetic to the Chinese. His favourable reports on Chinese culture, religion, and morality were translated into several European languages and widely read, but his writings were denounced by influential Christian theologians as impious and subversive of faith. In a discussion of idolatry, Le Comte notes that many idols are worshipped in China. He writes that 'If the people after worshipping them a great while do not obtain what they desire', they abandon the idols. He recounts a story of a person whose prayers were not answered and who retaliated by accusing the idol of deceitfulness, malice, and promise-breaking. After a formal trial, the idol was condemned, banished, and his temple destroyed. (See the translation, *Memoirs and Remarks . . . Made in Above Ten Years Travels through the Empire of China*, pp. 328–31.)

45.2 **Laplanders . . . extraordinary shape.[7]]** Footnote reference: Jean-François Regnard, *Voyage de Laponie* (*Journey to Lapland*). Lapland is a region of Scandinavia above the Arctic Circle that ranges over Finland, Sweden, Norway, and the Kola Peninsula of Russia. The Laplanders, or Lapps, are ancient inhabitants. Traditionally nomadic, they were often relatively isolated from the activities of national governments. Regnard's *Journey*, based on a 1681 tour, reported on diverse gods worshipped in Lapland. He describes Laplanders as addicted to magic, superstition, and paganism, and gives the following description of the primary gods: 'These gods are made of a long stone, without any other shape than that which nature has given it, and such as they find it on the borders of the lakes. So, every stone made in a particular manner, rough, or full of holes and concavities, is with them a god; and the more extraordinary the stone is, the greater is their veneration for it' (ed. Pinkerton, 1: 178–9).

45.3 **Egyptian mythologists . . . beasts.[8]]** Footnote references: Diodorus Siculus, *Historical Library* 1.86.1–3; Lucian, *On Sacrifices* 14; Ovid, *Metamorphoses* 5, lines 321 ff.; Manilius, *Astronomica* 4, lines 579–82, 800–1. Diodorus gives an explanation of the 'astonishing' Egyptian practice of animal worship: Because the gods who came into existence in the beginning were far outnumbered by mortals, they took on the forms of certain animals to save themselves from 'the savagery and violence of mankind'. In Lucian's explanation, the gods fled to Egypt to hide from their enemies. In their terror, each fled into a different animal. Ovid offers essentially the same explanation as Lucian, but credits Typhoeus with pursuing the gods until they fled into Egypt, where they took refuge in the form of animals. Manilius adds a tale about Venus, who changed herself into a fish. For more on

Egyptian practices and beliefs, see ann. 61.12 (at *NHR* 9.2, on Egyptian idolaters) and ann. 67.5 (on *NHR* 12.1, regarding Herodotus, Cambyses, and Apis).

45.6 **The CAUNII . . . foreign deities.**[9]] Footnote reference: Herodotus, *History* 1.172. The Caunii or Caunians were the people ('nation' or tribe) of Caunus, in South Asia Minor (called by Hume 'Lesser ASIA'). Herodotus reports that the Caunii disdained worship in foreign temples that had been erected in their land, preferring to return to the worship of their traditional gods. With this motivation, they performed the acts Hume mentions; but his claim that the Caunii conducted their ritual 'regularly, at certain seasons' goes beyond a literal reading of Herodotus's statements.

45.11 **the SUEVI."**[10]] Footnote reference: Gaius Julius Caesar, *Gallic War* 4.7. (Hume refers in this note to the full title of Caesar's *Gallic War—Commentariorum de bello Gallico* or *De bello Gallico comentarii*—but uses a shortened form of the title in n. 36 below.) 'Suevi' or 'Suebi' refers to the largest and most warlike of the German tribes. The term was used by Tacitus in *Germania* for a large group of peoples (roughly all Eastern and Northern Germanic peoples). However, Caesar's use of 'Suevi' is the common classical usage. Hume's report incorporates a close paraphrase of Caesar.

45.12 **DIONE in HOMER to VENUS . . . on the gods.**[11]] Footnote reference: Homer, *Iliad* 5, lines 381–4. Dione does not straightforwardly report that the gods have inflicted many ills on humans, but she comforts Venus, wounded by Diomedes, by saying that many of the gods 'have suffered at the hands of men, in bringing grievous woes one upon the other'.

45.15 **gross representations . . . LONGINUS**[12]] Footnote reference: Anonymous (generally, but erroneously, attributed to Longinus[B]), *On the Sublime* 9.7. The author is writing about Homer's depiction of the battle of the gods. He criticizes Homer for having made the men gods in the *Iliad*, and the gods men. Unless taken allegorically, he asserts, these passages from Homer are 'utterly irreligious'.

45.18 **Some writers**[13] **. . . impieties of ARISTOPHANES**] Footnote references: Pierre Brumoy, *Le théâtre des Grecs*, 'Discours sur le parallèle du théâtre ancien & du moderne'; and Bernard Le Bovier de Fontenelle, *Histoire des oracles* 8. Aristophanes used a satiric style to attack persons, politics, and practices. He ridiculed the gods as dishonest and absurd, using the same irreverence with which he lampooned the political and professional figures of Athens. However, Aristophanes did not challenge the commonplace belief that the community should worship the gods.

Brumoy remarks that it is difficult to reconcile the laughter of Athenians at Aristophanes' ridicule with either their reverence for the gods or their condemnation of the religious views of Socrates. Brumoy suggests that we may find a partial solution by distinguishing between 'serious religion' and 'fabulous religion' as represented in theatre. Fontenelle cites Aristophanes, and comments on the enjoyment some people obtain from seeing their religion treated amusingly.

45.26 **JUPITER in the AMPHITRYON . . . calamity.[14]]** Footnote reference: Arnobius, *Against the Heathen* 7.33. The *Amphitryon* (or *Amphitryo*) is a Greek play, adapted by Roman comic dramatist Titus Maccius Plautus (third–second century BC), in which Jupiter attempts to seduce a mortal woman by assuming the appearance of her husband, the Greek hero Amphitryo. She is tricked, and upon Amphitryo's return from fighting a war, a violent quarrel erupts. (Jupiter's sexual exploits and deceits are further discussed in ann. 73.6, on *NHR* 12.18.) Arnobius's seven books *Against the Heathen* have been given various titles, the most common being *Adversus gentes*. This book raises such questions as whether Jupiter sets aside his resentment when Plautus's play is acted.

45.32 **LACEDEMONIANS . . . XENOPHON,[15]]** Footnote reference: Xenophon, 'Constitution of the Lacedaemonians', 13.2–5. Xenophon writes of the Lacedaemonians' practice of offering sacrifices and prayers in the early morning to 'pre-engage' the gods in their favour.

46.1 **SENECA,[16] . . . votaries in the temples]** Footnote reference: Seneca, *Ad Lucilium epistulae morales* 41 ('On the God Within Us'). Seneca maintains that instead of relying on temples or prayer, we should look within ourselves for enlightenment: 'A holy spirit indwells within us' as our guardian. In saying 'We may *gather* from Seneca', Hume seems to be using Seneca's text to initiate his own ideas. Seneca does not discuss votaries (devoted followers and worshippers), beadles (minor parish officers), sextons (maintenance persons responsible for vessels, vestments, and the like), or a seat near the image of a deity. Seneca mentions only that 'We do not need . . . to beg the keeper of a temple to let us approach his idol's ear, as if in this way our prayers were more likely to be heard'.

46.4 **The TYRIANS, when besieged by ALEXANDER . . . enemy.[17]]** Footnote references: Quintus Curtius Rufus, *History of Alexander* 4.3.21–2; and Diodorus Siculus, *Historical Library* 17.41.8. Tyrians are the inhabitants of Tyre, an ancient maritime city of Phoenicia. The Phoenicians worshipped Baal and Astarte as principal divinities. The city fell to Alexander the Great in 332 BC. Quintus Curtius reports that even when Alexander's fleet encircled Tyrian territory, the Tyrians did not lose heart. However, when a Tyrian citizen reported having had a vision of the revered Apollo deserting the city, the Tyrians bound the statue of Apollo with a chain of gold and attached the chain to the altar of Hercules, supposing that Hercules had the strength to hold Apollo back. Diodorus Siculus reports only that 'the Tyrians were so credulous that they tied the image of Apollo to its base with golden cords, preventing, as they thought, the god from leaving the city'.

46.6 **AUGUSTUS . . . forbad NEPTUNE . . . that expedient.[18]]** Footnote reference: Suetonius, *Lives of the Caesars* 2, 'Augustus' 16. The pertinent part is 'Augustus' 16.1–2. Suetonius reports that Augustus twice lost his fleet by storms and then forbade Neptune to be carried in procession. One passage reads: 'Augustus has been taken to task for crying out, when he heard that his fleets were sunk: "I will win this war, whatever Neptune may do!" and for removing the god's image from the sacred procession.'

46.9 **enraged at their gods . . . allegiance to them.**[19]**]** Footnote reference: Suetonius, *Lives of the Caesars* 4, 'Gaius Caligula' 5. In Suetonius's account of stoning the gods in the temples, the stoning and overturning of altars illustrate the intense devotion of the supporters of Germanicus.[B] Hume's assertion that, on the death of Germanicus, the people were so enraged that they 'openly renounced all allegiance' to their gods requires interpretation of the central passage: 'Yet far greater and stronger tokens of regard were shown at the time of his death and immediately afterwards. On the day when he passed away the temples were stoned and the altars of the gods thrown down, while some flung their household gods into the street and cast out their newly born children' (*Lives of the Caesars*, 1: 408–9).

46.14 **canonical system of the heathens;**[20]**]** Footnote references: Herodotus, *History* 2.53; Lucian, *Zeus Catechized* 1, *On Funerals* 2, *Saturnalia* 5. Herodotus discusses how the Greeks learned when the gods came into being, and what outward shape they took. He and Lucian both credit Homer and Hesiod for these teachings.

46.15 **Hesiod . . . powers of nature.**[21]**]** Footnote reference: Hesiod, *Works and Days*, line 108. Hesiod recounts how the race of mortals came from the same source as various gods: namely from the gods who dwelt on Olympus. The translation of the passage cited by Hume is: '[I shall sketch] how gods and mortal men have come into being from the same source.'

46.17 **Pandora . . . Prometheus . . . celestial regions.**[22]**]** Footnote reference: Hesiod, *Theogony*, lines 570–2. Hesiod describes the creation by Zeus of the 'evil thing' Pandora. Pandora was created with the aid of the 'Limping God' (Hephaestus, or Vulcan) as a punishment for Prometheus's introduction of fire to mankind. Pandora is the only mythological example of a being divinely *created*, rather than generated by or evolved from existing beings.

46.23 **Ovid . . . "Quisquis fuit ille Deorum:"**[23] **. . . chaos]** Footnote reference: Ovid, *Metamorphoses* 1, line 32. This quotation is a fragment from Ovid, meaning 'Whichever of the gods it was'. In context the expression is declarative (not interrogative, as it was published in all editions of *NHR* after the 1st). The full passage in the *Metamorphoses* reads as follows: 'When he, whichever of the gods it was, had thus arranged in order and resolved that chaotic mass, and reduced it, thus resolved, to cosmic parts, he first moulded the earth into the form of a mighty ball so that it might be of like form on every side.' The 'chaos' here mentioned was understood in the eighteenth century as the doctrine of ancient philosophers that the world was first formed out of a disorderly or irregular mass of elements.

46.32 **Diodorus Siculus,**[24] **. . . origin of the world]** Footnote reference: Diodorus Siculus, *Historical Library* 1.6; 1.7.1–7. Diodorus appeals to natural physical causation to describe the earth's evolution. He reports that different chemical elements separated to form the sea and land, and that combinations of heat and cold, as well as moisture and aridity, created living creatures, presumably including the human species. Evidence of divine causation or influence is not mentioned as a factor. Hume made a similar, but not identical, notation about Diodorus's report in his 'Early Memoranda' (§ 203).

47.1 **passage,[25] ... Ichthyophagi]** Footnote reference: Diodorus Siculus, *Historical Library* 3.20.1–3. 'Ichthyophagi' derives from Greek for 'fish-eaters'. This term was applied by the ancients to various fish-eating peoples of Africa and Asia. Diodorus refers to 'one tribe of the Ichthyophagi'. His context suggests that the tribe is African, despite Hume's reference to a people of India. In n. 24, Hume cites bk. 1 in Diodorus and here in n. 25 writes 'ibid'; however, the proper reference to the Ichthyophagi is in bk. 3.

47.4 **physiologers]** students or practitioners of natural philosophy. Cudworth (*True Intellectual System of the Universe* 1.1.6–10, 13–16) uses this term (more narrowly) in contexts that are directly related to Hume's discussions of the ancients in *NHR*. Cudworth cites Democritus as a paradigm physiologer, but includes Leucippus and other ancient philosophers. He takes physiologers to be atomistic philosophers. See also the entry to 'theologers' at 47.13 below and Thomas Blount, *Glossographia: or a Dictionary Interpreting All Such Hard Words*, entries 'Physiology' and 'Physiologer'.

47.8 **specious]** plausible and seemingly allowable and just.

47.12 **zealous religionist![26]]** Footnote reference: Diodorus Siculus, *Historical Library* 15.48.1–4; tr. Laurentius Rhodomanus (1604 edn.), p. 364 (see Cat., p. 267 below). While discussing severe earthquakes and tidal waves, Diodorus notes that natural scientists provide a causal explanation different from the explanations given by persons who 'venerate the divine power'. The latter say that these disasters are occasioned by the anger of the gods. Diodorus discusses these issues further in bk. 16, chs. 61–4.

47.14 **theologers]** A 'theologue' or 'theologer' is a divine or professor of divinity. See Blount, *Glossographia*, entry 'Theologer'. In an alternative use, 'theologer' refers to a figure in theology in pagan traditions—possibly even a mythical figure. Cudworth regarded the 'Pagan Theologers' as monotheists rather than polytheists (*True Intellectual System of the Universe*, preface and 1.4.16–17, 29, 32), but he also used the term 'theologer' in reference to mythical figures such as Orpheus. Anthony Collins concluded that 'allegory was in use' among the pagan 'theologers' (*Discourse of the Grounds and Reasons of the Christian Religion* 1.11, pp. 83–4).

47.19 **Thales, Anaximenes, Heraclitus ... passed unquestioned]** Some interpreters believe these three pre-Socratic philosophers held cosmogonies built on naturalistic explanations, though theories of the gods or divine forces were sometimes merged with these explanations. The scope of these philosophers' commitments to Greek polytheism, theological explanation, and theism is disputed. Related observations about these three philosophers and about Anaxagoras[B] (see below) are in Toland, *Letters to Serena*, 2nd letter 3 (citing ancient sources different from those mentioned by Hume) and in passages in Cudworth mentioned in the annotations immediately below.

47.20 **ANAXAGORAS . . . first undoubted theist . . . accused of atheism.[27]]** Footnote reference: Plato, *Laws* 10. Anaxagoras was perhaps the first to hold that mind initiated the physical world, but his views were considered unorthodox, and he left Athens following a prosecution for impiety. The charge stemmed from his teaching that the heavenly bodies are not gods and that the sun and the moon are material bodies. See Cudworth's lengthy argument to the conclusion that 'Anaxagoras stopt th[e] Atheistick Current' in the cosmologies of his predecessors; *True Intellectual System of the Universe* 1.3.20, 24, 28; 1.4.20. See, further, Bayle, *Dictionary*, 'Anaxagoras'.

Hume's reference to *Laws* 10 is possibly in error, though 886A–E is distantly relevant, and Cudworth cites *Laws* 10 to make a similar point. See the annotations immediately below for references to Plato that appear more pertinent, including *Laws* 12 (also cited by Cudworth), 967A–D, as well as Plato's *Apology* 26C–D, and *Phaedo* 97B–D.

n. 27.1 **THALES, ANAXIMANDER, and those early philosophers . . . really were atheists]** Anaximander was commonly interpreted as having used entirely naturalistic explanations. Roughly the set of philosophers Hume here depicts as atheists had been reported by Cudworth to be 'Hylopathian Atheists' *in Aristotle's presentation* of their views. However, Cudworth cites other authorities who interpret Thales as a theist. Cudworth concludes that there is good reason 'why *Thales* should be acquitted from this Accusation of Atheism', but he insists that Anaximander was a 'physiologer', 'the First Atheistical Philosopher', and the founder of the atheistic, materialistic philosophy mistakenly attributed by Aristotle and others to Thales: '*Anaxagoras* . . . made *Mind* to be a Principle of the *Universe*. . . . *Anaximander* and the rest, supposed not *Infinite Mind*, but *Infinite matter*. . . . to have been the only Original of all things' (*True Intellectual System of the Universe* 1.3.19–21, 24). That Hume had read Cudworth on these philosophers and these issues is apparent from notations in his 'Early Memoranda' (§ 40) pertaining to 'four kinds of Atheists according to Cudworth'.

n. 27.2 **ANAXAGORAS and SOCRATES, . . . real theists . . . esteemed impious]** Hume gives an account similar to Cudworth's (see above passages) of both philosophers. By tradition, Anaxagoras had been, following the charge of impiety, protected by Pericles. Various accounts have been given of the outcome: Pericles may have helped Anaxagoras escape, but he also may have gone into voluntary exile. The life of Socrates is difficult to interpret on the matter of a commitment to theism, but his prosecution for impiety is not in doubt.

47.23 **Sextus Empiricus,[28] . . . Epicurus . . . Hesiod]** Footnote reference: Sextus Empiricus, *Against the Physicists* 2.18–19 (alternatively, and commonly, cited as *Adversus mathematicos* 10.18–19; or *Adversus dogmaticos* 4.18–19). Hume cited *Adversus mathematicos*, bk. 9. By traditional standards, this book number is incorrect. However, Hume apparently relied on the edition of Sextus edited by P. and J. Chouët (see Cat.), the only edition that uses numbering consistent with Hume's citations of Sextus (see Julia Annas, 'Hume and Ancient Scepticism').

Sextus describes the education of Epicurus. Under tutorial guidance, Epicurus read Hesiod's *Theogony* and raised questions about how the world was created from chaos. The tutor replied that philosophers teach such matters, whereupon young Epicurus turned to the philosophers to satisfy his curiosity. The verses cited by Hume are from *Theogony*, lines 116–17.

48.4 **philology]** In the eighteenth century philology was understood as an assemblage of sciences consisting of grammar, rhetoric, poetry, and criticism—and possibly also antiquities, history, and literary studies.

48.9 **penetration]** intellectual access to the inner content of something.

48.17 **Agrippa . . . gods must submit."[29]]** Footnote reference: Dionysius of Halicarnassus, *Roman Antiquities* 6.54.2. Dionysius reports that the Roman senator, Menenius Agrippa,[B] made the statement before the senate as a recommendation: 'And when you consider also how great is the power of necessity, the one thing to which even the gods yield, be not vexed at your misfortunes nor allow yourselves to be filled with arrogance and folly'.

48.18 **Younger Pliny,[30]]** Footnote reference: Pliny the Younger, *Letters* 6, letters 16, 20. In letters to Tacitus[B], Pliny reports on the eruption of Vesuvius. Pliny had witnessed the death of his uncle and adoptive father, Pliny the Elder,[B] in the eruption, which occurred 24 Aug. 79 AD. The Elder Pliny had sailed to get a closer view of the eruption. The Younger Pliny describes his uncle's courage and asphyxiation on the shore. In the second letter, Pliny the Younger relates his own experiences. He reports that many observers of the eruption believed that no gods survived. The passage quoted by Hume, in which Pliny is introspecting, may be translated: 'I might have boasted that amidst dangers so appalling, not a sigh or expression of fear escaped from me, had not my support been founded in that miserable, though strong consolation, that all mankind were involved in the same calamity, and that I was perishing with the world itself' (*Letters*, letter 20, 1: 496–7).

48.26 **Marcus Aurelius, Plutarch . . . Stoics and Academics]** These schools either rejected or reinterpreted indigenous religious beliefs. Many Stoics believed in an impersonal divine providence, depicted the Roman gods as powers of nature, and viewed the popular legends as parables. In his *Meditations*, Marcus left traces of a theory with a vague commitment to a moral and benevolent power in the universe. He was perhaps revising accounts of impersonal nature in Stoic orthodoxy. Plutarch and various Academics defended philosophies of religion indebted to Plato and

Platonism, often with borrowings from other schools. Plutarch, who had studied at the Academy and had been a priest at Delphi, used symbolism and allegory to situate popular beliefs within a Platonic framework.

48.28 **honourable appellation of *theism*]** 'Theism' here presumably refers to the monotheistic doctrine of a supreme, active, providential God, by contrast to polytheism, pantheism, and deism. The latter have etymological roots in theism, but they were considered by many in the eighteenth century to lack some condition(s) essential to genuine theism. See, further, ann. 71.14 (on *NHR* 12.13, 'imputation of deism').

SECTION 5: Various Forms of Polytheism: Allegory, Hero-Worship

49.23 **allegories . . . other mythologists]** Theagenes of Rhegium (6th century BC; Homeric critic) may have been the first scholar to interpret Homer's representations allegorically (though no work by Theagenes survives). He allegorized the gods and interpreted their quarrels as symbolizing conflicts of natural and psychological powers. Of notable historical influence was Euhemerus of Messene (4th–3rd century BC; mythographer and novelist of travel). From him descends Euhemerism, the doctrine that gods are representations of men whose capacities were inflated in stories that were magnified over time. He maintained that these men were heroic warriors and heroes deified after their deaths and that all such myth rests on historical decay of fact. Reports and observations on Euhemerus's theory are presented in Diodorus Siculus, *Historical Library* 6.1 ff. Cudworth says that the 'Atheistick' doctrine of Euhemerism is 'That all the Gods were really no other than Mortal Men' (*True Intellectual System of the Universe* 1.4.32, p. 478).

Many writers before Hume had emphasized the importance of allegory, not merely in polytheistic traditions, but in the dominant monotheistic traditions. For example, Thomas Woolston (1670–1733; English free-thinker) maintained that the biblical documents are fully allegorical (*Six Discourses on the Miracles of our Saviour*), and Nicolas Fréret (1688–1749; French secretary of l'Académie des belles-lettres) propounded allegorical theories in various contexts of miracle and myth (*Œuvres complettes*).

50.7 **MARS . . . VENUS?[31]]** Footnote reference: Hesiod, *Theogony*, lines 933–5. This passage recounts the birth of the gods Panic and Fear, which, according to Hesiod, are the children of Ares (Mars) and Cytherea (a name for Venus).

50.8 ***Harmony* . . . MARS?[32]]** Footnote references: Hesiod, *Theogony*, lines 936–7; Plutarch, *Lives*, 'Pelopidas' 19.2, 287F–288A. Hesiod attributes the parentage of Harmony to Ares (Mars) and Cytherea. Plutarch likewise presents Ares and Aphrodite (Venus) as the parents of Harmony.

50.10 **the Graces?[33]**] Footnote reference: Homer, *Iliad* 14, lines 263–76. 'Graces' in ancient mythology were minor goddesses who were personifications of grace, beauty, gentleness, and friendship. Traditionally presented as the three daughters of Zeus and Euronyme (though this parentage is disputed), they usually bore the names Aglaia (called Charis by Homer in the *Iliad*), Thalia, and Euphrosyne. In the passage cited by Hume, Homer introduces another Grace named Pasithea. Hera, wife of Zeus and queen of Heaven, wanted to lull Zeus to sleep in order that the gods could help the Greeks. She sought to achieve this end by the aid of Hypnos ('Sleep', the brother of Thanatos, 'Death'), to whom she promised the Grace Pasithea in marriage.

50.14 **Lucretius . . . appearance of allegory . . . popular religion**] The reference is to Lucretius, *De rerum natura* 1.1–43, where Venus is characterized as the guiding force behind the creation of everything joyous and lovely. Lucretius appeals to the goddess to instill in his poem some of her creativity and persuasive charm, and petitions Venus to end strife by working her charm on her mate, Mars. Lucretius does not discuss allegory and popular religion. *NHR* Sects. 13 and 14 have 'popular religions' in their titles. Hume also uses this term at *Dialogues* 1.17; 12.21, 23, 28. He is usually referring to prevailing indigenous religious traditions.

50.20 **as an Epicurean**] Epicurean theology was distanced from traditional Greek polytheism. Epicureans defended a deterministic causal chain in nature that excluded *particular providence*. (For the meaning of this expression, see ann. 52.22, on *NHR* 6.2, '*particular* providence . . . general laws'.) Humans were liberated in Epicurean theory from fears of harmful actions by the gods. See Epicurus, *Epicurus Reader*, texts 4.134; 16.43–56; 17.71–6; 18.103–10; Cicero, *De natura deorum* 1.7.17–1.8.18 ff.; 1.41.115–1.42.119; 2.17.45–7. The Stoics, in contrast, held that human affairs are governed providentially. See Lucian, *Zeus Rants* 3–4, 16–17, 36–51; and *Drinking Party, or Lapithae* 9, in which Zenothemis the Stoic ridicules the idea that an Epicurean could be a priest. The latter work is cited by Hume in *EHU*, n. 28, on a matter concerning the Epicureans and religion. Hume used Epicurus's theological views as the setting of *EHU* 11, and once commented to Gilbert Elliot that 'a profest Atheist' and 'an Epicurean' are 'little or nothing different' (*Letters*, 1: 155).

51.1 **statuary of Syria . . . Heliogabalus . . . solar deity.[34]**] Footnote reference: Herodian, *History* 5.3.3–5. A large, conic stone named Heliogabalus[B] was worshipped in the region of Syria as 'the solar deity'. According to Herodian, 'There was no actual man-made statue of the god, the sort Greeks and Romans put up; but there was an enormous stone, rounded at the base and coming to a point on the top, conical in shape and black. This stone is worshipped as though it were sent from heaven; on it there are some small projecting pieces and markings that are pointed out, which the people would like to believe are a rough picture of the sun.'

The Roman emperor Heliogabalus was descended from a family of the hereditary high priests of the sun-god Baal at Emesa, Syria. In Heliogabalus's local region, Baal was worshipped by the name Elah-Gabal, the root of 'Elagabalus' and 'Heliogabalus'. Hume briefly mentions Heliogabalus as emperor in 'Of the Populousness of Ancient Nations' 94 (and n. 114), citing Aelius Lampridius as the source of his information.

n. 34.1 **JUPITER AMMON is represented by CURTIUS]** Footnote reference: Quintus Curtius Rufus, *History of Alexander* 4.7.21–4. Quintus Curtius describes a shrine to Ammon found in the Ethiopian desert by Alexander's party. Three sets of walls enclose the shrine, making it a citadel for protection. In a 'grove of Ammon' a fountain known as the water of the sun flows, with its water growing progressively hotter throughout the day and night until it finally cools before daybreak, only to repeat the cycle again. The god has an image like that of a navel embedded in a mass of emeralds and other stones.

n. 34.2 **ARABIANS and PESSINUNTIANS . . . ARNOB. lib. 6.]** Footnote reference: Arnobius, *Against the Heathen* 6.11 (and also 3.15; 7.49–50). Arnobius depicts the worship of physical objects serving as idols. He discusses in bk. 6 the worship of unshapen stones and a flint worshipped by the people of Pessinus. In bk. 7 he questions the validity of attributing good fortune—e.g. military victory—to idols such as a rough, black stone.

51.5 **STILPO . . . MINERVA . . . workmanship of PHIDIAS, the sculptor.[35]]** Footnote reference: Diogenes Laertius, *Lives* 2.11, 'Stilpo' 116. Diogenes tells this story about the philosopher Stilpo of Megara, who was discussing the work of the sculptor Phidias:

> There is a story that [Stilpo] once used the following argument concerning the Athena of Phidias [Minerva being an Italian goddess regularly identified with Athena]: 'Is it not Athena the daughter of Zeus who is a goddess?' And when the other said 'Yes', he went on, 'But this at least is not by Zeus but by Phidias', and, this being granted, he concluded, 'This then is not a god'. For this he was summoned before the Areopagus; he did not deny the charge, but contended that the reasoning was correct, for that Athena was no god but a goddess; it was the male divinities who were gods. However, the story goes that the Areopagites ordered him to quit the city.

'MINERVA in the citadel' refers to Phidias's statue on the Acropolis. An Areopagite was a member of the council of the Areopagus, an aristocratic legislative and judicial council in Athens. The council met on a hill north-west of the Acropolis named Areopagus. Hume mentions the oratorical customs of the Areopagites in his essay 'Of Eloquence' 11.

51.20 **fabulous history and mythological tradition]** Many interpretations of fable and myth were published during the Enlightenment. Hume's views show some resemblance to theories that viewed myth and fable as the outgrowth of gullibility, superstition, curiosity, and imagination. Among those who ridiculed figures and stories in the ancient mythology, see Fontenelle, *De l'origine des fables*, pp. 13–17, 22–6, 33; and Bayle, *Dictionary*, articles 'Abel' (1: 22–4); 'Abraham'

(1: 44–6); 'Achilles' (1: 74–84); 'Adam' (1: 101–4); 'Cham' (2: 431–2); 'Juno' (3: 629–46); and 'Jupiter' (3: 646–54).

51.27 **all idolaters . . . not extremely different.**[36]] Footnote reference: Gaius Julius Caesar, *Gallic War* 6.17. Caesar describes particular characters and provinces that the Gallic people assigned to their deities. He says that, 'Of these deities they have almost the same idea as all other nations'. See ann. 61.12 (on *NHR* 9.2) for additional discussion of Roman and Egyptian idolaters.

51.30 **travellers and conquerors . . . found their own deities every where]** In the source listed in n. 36, Caesar writes that the Gauls 'most worship Mercury. . . . After him they set Apollo, Mars, Jupiter, and Minerva' (*Gallic War* 6.17). As suggested in the previous annotation, Caesar thought the Gauls had almost the same conceptions as did other nations. For Hume's somewhat different view of religion among 'the ancient Gauls and Britons', see his comments on their superstitions and idolatry in *History of England* (ch. 1 [1: 6]).

51.33 **Hertha . . . Tacitus,**[37] **. . . *Mater Tellus*]** Footnote reference: Tacitus, *Germania* 40. Tacitus gives a vivid portrayal of the northern deity Nerthus (another manuscript reading for Hertha) as mother earth (*Mater Tellus*): 'Then come the Reudigni and the Aviones, and the Anglii, and the Varini, the Eudoses and Suarines and Nuitones. These tribes are protected by forests and rivers, nor is there anything noteworthy about them individually, except that they worship in common Nerthus, or Mother Earth, and conceive her as intervening in human affairs, and riding in procession through the cities of men.'

Nerthus, or Hertha, is a nature-goddess or earth-goddess of the ancient Germans, whose name is similar to the Scandinavian 'Njörd', a Norse god of fertility, wealth, prosperity, and the sea. Though separated by forests and rivers, these tribes retained in common the worship of Hertha. Tacitus does not explicitly associate the 'goddess Hertha of our Saxon ancestors' with 'the *Mater Tellus* of the Romans'.

SECTION 6: Origin of Theism from Polytheism

52.22 ***particular* providence . . . general laws]** The subject of a particular providence is treated by Hume in *EHU* 11, 'Of a Particular Providence and of a Future State'. A *particular* providence is to be contrasted to a *general* providence. Particular providence is God's oversight of, and potential intervention in, the affairs of individuals; general providence is God's provision through the fixed general laws of nature. For a delineation of the distinction, see Richard Price (1723–91; British Nonconformist minister and philosopher), *Four Dissertations*, p. 7. Malebranche also assumes the distinction (using the language of 'general will' and 'particular will') in *Treatise on Nature and Grace* 1.43, 56–7; 2.3, 45; and illustration.

The term 'theist' was often used in the eighteenth century to refer to those who believe in a particular providence, by contrast to 'deists', who denied divine providential control of human affairs and emphasized fixed general laws. See ann. 44.16 (on *NHR* 4.1) regarding 'the appellation of *atheism*' and the editor's Introduction (pp. cxxii–cxxvi) on William Warburton's review of *NHR*. See also *NHR* 2.3 on 'particular providence'.

52.33 **Lord Bacon . . . atheists]** In 'Of Atheism' Bacon writes: 'Certainely, a little *Philosophie* inclineth mans minde to *Atheisme*, but depth in *Philosophy*, bringeth men about to Religion' (*Essays*, Essay 16 [6: 413]). In *Advancement of Learning* 1.1.3, Bacon says 'That a litle or superficiall tast [later translation: knowledge] of *Philosophy*, may perchance incline the Mind of Man to *Atheisme*, but a full draught [later translation: further proceeding] thereof brings the mind back againe to Religion'. Hume also mentions Bacon's views on this subject at *Dialogues* 1.18. In his *History of England*, Hume offers an assessment of Bacon's intellectual abilities and contribution (ch. 48 and Appendix to the Reign of James I [5: 86, 153]).

53.11 **Madness, fury, rage, and an enflamed imagination . . . immediate communication with the Deity]** This theme is reminiscent of the treatment of religion, superstition, and enthusiasm in Trenchard's *Natural History of Superstition*, pp. 46–8. Trenchard mentions madness and rage, in particular, as conditions of 'Enthusiasm, by which word is meant a strong and impetuous Motion, or extraordinary and transcendent Ardor, Fervency or Pregnancy of the Soul, Spirits or Brain, which is vulgarly thought to be Supernatural . . . [making Mankind] prone to believe some special Presence of God'.

53.20 **idolatrous nation]** 'Idolatrous' is here extensionally equivalent to 'polytheistic'. However, see ann. 34.2 (on *NHR* 1.1) on 'polytheism or idolatry'.

54.22 **St. Nicholas . . . Muscovites]** St Nicholas was the patron saint of Russia. Devout Russians invoked him frequently, and kept icons of him in their homes. They believed that he protected against evils such as sickness, famine, and dangers at sea. See also ann. 82.20 (on *NHR* 14.5–the four Lents of the Muscovites).

The term 'Muscovite' commonly referred to a native or inhabitant of Muscovy, or Moscow, but Hume here seems to use the term to refer to Russian Eastern Orthodox believers. Warrant for this usage is found in William Turner, *The History of All Religions in the World* (1695), pp. 210, 225; and James Debia (vicar of Walberton), *An Account of the Religion, Rites, Ceremonies, and Superstitions of the Moscovites* (1710), a work on the Russian Eastern Orthodox Church.

54.24 **to carry off Europa . . . Optimus Maximus of the heathens]** Jupiter was once enamoured of Europa, said by mythologists to be the daughter of Agenor, king of Phoenecia. In order to avoid the jealous wrath of his wife Juno, Jupiter concealed himself as a snow-white bull with gem-like horns and a striking black streak. Europa became fascinated with his beauty, and even in this unlikely form he was able to cast a spell over her. She played with the bull and then mounted his back, at which point he sped away and swam the sea to Crete. He later revealed himself as Jupiter, and she bore him three sons. This story had been disseminated in popular form in the 1694 work *Rape of Europa by Jupiter* (ed. Motteux and Eccles).

Jupiter was the son of Saturn and was identified with the Greek god Zeus, said to be the third son of Rhea and Cronus. In conspiracy with Hades and Poseidon, Zeus struck Cronus with a thunderbolt. According to Homer (in passages cited by Hume at *NHR* 6.11, on Homer and Hesiod), Zeus dispatched Cronus to live beneath the earth and sea (*Iliad*, lines 203–4).

As lord of heaven, Jupiter acquired the cult title Jupiter Optimus Maximus (the best and greatest). He was thus ranked above the other deities and above all Jupiters in other temples. Once enthroned in his temple in Rome as Optimus Maximus, Jupiter became central to Roman political life and patriotism, as its special protector.

54.28 **Jacobins . . . Cordeliers]** Jacobins were Dominican friars in France (or, more broadly, friars and sisters of the order of St Dominic). The term 'Les Jacobins' was originally applied to the French members of the order who came (as early as 1218) from the Church of St Jacques. Cordeliers were Franciscan friars in France. The name derives from the *cordelière*, the Franciscans' knotted-cord rope-girdle, worn around the waist.

54.32 **Boulainvilliers,[38] . . . Christ was interred]** Footnote reference: Henri, Comte de Boulainvilliers, *Abrégé chronologique de l'histoire de France*, in *Etat de la France* (1728 edn. [3: 499]). Boulainvilliers reported on a period of conflict between the Jacobins and Cordeliers: The Franciscans were defenders of the dogma of the Immaculate Conception, and the Dominicans were opponents. A conflict requiring papal intervention broke out during the period between the Council of Basel (1438) and the accession of Pope Sixtus IV (1471). Sixtus IV did not require the faithful to believe the dogma, but did require that there be no prejudice against those who believed either way. Further controversy led to further papal pronouncements, which increasingly favoured the dogma.

According to Boulainvilliers, a Cordelier preached against the hypostatic union (see the following annotation) at Bresse, Italy. This Cordelier maintained that when the blood of Jesus Christ was spilled at his passion, the hypostatic union was lost, and for a three-day period Jesus was neither divine nor the object of worship. This opinion was condemned as heresy by the Jacobins, leading to a controversy resolved by Pope Pius II. Boulainvilliers reports that even if the Cordeliers were rebuffed on this occasion, they gained revenge in disputes about the Immaculate Conception, which became a firm doctrine of the faith.

For Hume's early interests in Boulainvilliers's *Etat de la France*, see his 'Early Memoranda' (§§7–8, 11).

54.33 **hypostatic union . . . human nature]** In Christian theology the word 'hypostatic' has been used to refer to the substance or personhood of the divine. 'Hypostasis' means 'what stands under', hence 'substance' or 'subsistence'. The hypostatic union refers to either (1) the union of divine and human natures in the person of Christ, or (2) the consubstantial union of the three 'hypostases' or persons forming the Trinity. The three 'hypostases' of the Godhead are identical in substance; there is one nature or essence of God, but three hypostases, or persons. The doctrine of the hypostasis of Christ was developed by theologians to reconcile conflicting beliefs in separate, fully realized human and divine natures united inseparably in one person. Use of the Greek term 'hypostasis' and the Latin 'persona' provoked theological controversy, eventuating in various declarations of heresy; see ann. 66.18 ff. (on *NHR* 11.4).

55.3 **Homer . . . Oceanus and Tethys**] The reference is to Homer's *Iliad* 14, lines 200–4 and 301–4; see also *Iliad* 15, lines 12, 47, on Jupiter as 'the sire of gods and men'. (Hume Romanizes Homer's references to Zeus.) Oceanus and Tethys are parents from whom, in ancient mythology, the river-gods and Oceanids were sprung. Homer reports, through a 'lying tale' told by Juno, that it is Oceanus 'from whom all we gods proceed'. On the description of Jupiter as an upstart parricide and usurper, see ann. 54.24, on *NHR* 6.8. Hume's depiction of Jupiter (and others) as absurd and immoral figures resembles certain representations in Bayle. For examples, see the list of articles in ann. 51.19, on *NHR* 5.9 (fabulous history and mythological tradition).

55.9 **A like contradiction is observable in Hesiod**] The reference is to Hesiod's *Theogony*, lines 47–52, 73, and 176 ff. Hesiod mentions a song the goddesses sing, in which Zeus appears as the father of gods and men. Zeus is depicted as the 'most excellent' god.

55.12 **Mahometanism of this inconsistence**] Of this passage, religious controversialist William Warburton commented: 'We see what the man [Hume] would be at; through all his disguises . . . . an insinuation against the Jewish and Christian Religions' (*Remarks*, Remark 11). Whatever the merits of this interpretation, some traditional interpretations of Islamic monotheism do provide instances of the problem mentioned by Hume. The theological goal of not compromising God's omnipotence (prompted in part by Manichaeism) rests on firm Koranic premisses. These premisses led prominent Islamic interpreters to make God the creator of all evil as well as all good (and of all human actions as well as other events in nature). At the same time, the 'sublime colours' of God's infinite attributes (see the annotation immediately below) are joined with depictions of active qualities of divine will and speech, divine acts of punishment, and acts such as sitting on the throne and agreeing to a covenant. The eschatology of the faith also includes an account of the final judgement, in which the souls of unbelievers will stand trial and may be condemned to eternal punishment in hell—even if the underlying theology holds that reward and punishment are themselves predestined. However, not all Muslim theologians have accepted these interpretations; some have held, for example, that willing evil is evil and that an essential attribute of God is not to will evil. See Majid Fakhry, *Ethical Theories in Islam* 1–2, for a range of Islamic views.

55.13 **Deity in the most sublime colours]** Two nineteenth-century editors of Hume, T. H. Green and T. H. Grose, reported that 1756 proof-sheets of *NHR*, now lost, showed variant wording in this passage. An explanation of the changes Hume evidently made in the text is found in the editor's Introduction to this volume (pp. xxiv–xxvii). The representations of the deity discussed by Hume are found in Genesis 3 and 32 and Exodus 33. God is depicted in the Bible as speaking from the mouth, as having a countenance, as passing over the houses of the Israelites, etc.

SECTION 7: Confirmation of this Doctrine

56.15 **the MAGIANS]** A Magian (pl. Magi) is a member of a hereditary priestly class of Median origin (near western Iran) in the ancient Persian religion. Lucian somewhat misleadingly speaks of the Magi as 'the disciples and successors of Zoroaster' (*Menippus, or the Descent into Hades* 6). Some Magi resident in Persia merged their beliefs with the theology of Zoroastrianism, but other Magians had independent roots. See ann. 61.29 (on *NHR* 9.4, on the disciples of Zoroaster and the Magians).

56.17 **sun as his image]** An account of *the sun as God's image in the visible universe* appears in several passages in the book by Thomas Hyde (see ann. n. 39). This elaborate work contains the *Sadder* (or *Saddar* or *Sad Dar*), a holy text of the Zoroastrian religion that delineates a variety of religious duties, practices, penalties, rituals, and the like (translated in Hyde's edition into Latin, from the original Pahlavi). Although God cannot be represented by any human-created image, the Magians consider 'Water and Fire in their protected purity, to be the only Images of God on earth' (Hyde, *Historia religionis*, p. 139). Fire is almost always mentioned when the sun is mentioned in Hyde, and he seems to interpret the sun, as well as fire and water in their pure form, as visible images of God. Hyde distinguishes between the sun as image of God and the sun as God. He believes that there have been errors of interpretation by authorities who report that the Persians believe the sun is God (p. 138). Hyde also includes more esoteric references to the sun (and fire) as an image in the visible universe.

56.21 **bare foot upon the ground]** Regarding the admonition *never to set bare feet on ground*, the *Sadder* prescribes as follows: 'It is a precept for the religious man that he not place his bare foot upon the ground: because a bare foot on the ground is evil. . . . Therefore you must not place your bare foot on the ground, lest your body be carried down to Hell' (*Sadder*, porta 48, in Hyde, p. 461). Rules for women are also prescribed (with reference, in particular, to *pregnant* women): 'They must not look into the sky, *nor walk upon the ground on bare foot*' (*Sadder*, porta 75, in Hyde, p. 474; italics added).

56.21 **spit into a fire]** Regarding the prescription *not to spit in fire*, 'It is good to care well for fire because as it struggles not to die out, it is to you almost a soul. *That* *you would neither burn up soil or filth* nor leave alone any such thing (fire) in fields within three miles; and by caring faithfully for fire in home, you should not leave thorns or trash in it' (*Sadder*, porta XI, lines 1 ff., in Hyde, p. 442; italics added). The word 'spit', as used by Hume, may be his translation of the word 'spurcum', which is similar to the more direct word for spit, 'sputum'. 'Spurcum' is generally defined as that which is 'nasty, dirty, foul, or unclean', but can be read as 'saliva' or 'spit'.

56.21 **throw any water]** With regard to the admonition *not to throw water on fire*, the *Sadder* advises as follows: 'It is a precept, that when anything is cooked by a pot, only two [pots] must fill a third [pot] with water, so that if it will come to a boiling point, the water will not be poured into the Fire when it becomes hot. *For if you were not cautious in that part, so that water would not overflow into the Fire, the greatest sin will be on you, that you will receive torment until the day of reckoning*' (*Sadder*, porta 52, in Hyde, p. 463; italics added). In his 'Early Memoranda' (§187) Hume cited what appears to be this same passage in Hyde and the *Sadder*.

n. 39.1 **Hyde]** Footnote reference: Thomas Hyde, *Historia religionis veterum Persarum, eorumque Magorum*. Hyde's *Historia religionis*, also cited in n. 46, is apparently Hume's source for his several descriptions of Zoroastrian belief. Hume is apparently referring to Hyde's account as well as to the beliefs and prescriptions found in the *Sadder*. On the *Sadder*, see ann. 81.8 (on *NHR* 14.1). Hume cites a number of passages in Hyde, including principles in the *Sadder*, in his 'Early Memoranda' (§§184–92).

56.27 **bit of skin, about half the breadth of a farthing]** This reference to male circumcision could involve one of two bases of comparison. In the eighteenth century the term 'farthing' was commonly used to refer to the coin representing the value of one-fourth of a Saxon penny (until the seventeenth century a silver coin, subsequently made of copper or bronze). Occasionally, the term was used to refer to an ancient coin (farthing of gold), and the term could also mean simply a bit or an atom.

56.28 **two bits of cloth,[40]]** As indicated in n. 40, the reference is to 'the Scapulaire'. A scapular or *scapulaire* (French) was originally a cloak forming part of a religious habit adopted (no later than the eleventh century) by certain Roman Catholic religious orders and worn as a badge of affiliation. This material has a hole in the middle so that the head can pass through while the cloth hangs from the shoulders. The front and back portions were often arranged to present the form of a cross. A symbolic meaning thus became attached to the garment. It was viewed as a cross that one bears upon one's shoulders, reminiscent of the yoke of Christ (see Luke 9: 23). The friar was commanded to follow Christ by taking up this yoke and living in austerity and devotion.

'Small scapulars' began to be worn in the sixteenth century. These pieces of cloth were worn either as a single piece around the neck or as two pieces, one worn on the chest and the other on the back, joined by strings. The scapular commonly had an embroidered picture of the Virgin Mary or of a saint in whose honour it was worn. The purpose was to keep before the wearer's mind the ideals and traditions of the religious order. Some friars claimed that those who faithfully wore the scapular would not go to hell. This belief was controversial even among Roman Catholics, and highly controversial if not accompanied by a theory that made the believer's intention and will a relevant factor in salvation. Eventually the scapular was worn only as a fallible sign of one's interior commitment, which alone was believed to count as a condition of salvation.

57.6 **Zamolxis . . . Getes.**[41]] Footnote reference: Herodotus, *History* 4.93–4. Hume made a related observation about the Getae in his 'Early Memoranda' (§255). The Getae (see ann. 43.7 on *NHR* 3.6, on Strabo and the Getes) believed only in Zamolxis (also spelled *Zalmoxis*). Their doctrine of immortality affirmed that one who died went to Zamolxis. Thunder and lightning were regarded as threats from a rival god, and were answered by arrows shot into the sky.

Herodotus reports that Zamolxis may have been a man who lived before or during the time of Pythagoras and may have orchestrated a cult following. Herodotus recounts that the Getae were the bravest and most law-abiding of all Thracians. However, in 'Of the Populousness of Ancient Nations' 165, Hume describes Thracians as living 'by pasturage and plunder', with the Getes being 'still more uncivilized'. Hume there cites Ovid and Strabo as his sources of information. An observation about the Getes, Zamolxis, and immortality is found in Toland, *Letters to Serena* (2nd letter, pp. 42–3, also citing Herodotus and Strabo): 'The Getes learnt the Immortality of the Soul from their Countryman Zamolxis.'

SECTION 8: Flux and Reflux of Polytheism and Theism

58.0 **Flux and Reflux**] Beyond the meaning of the flowing and ebbing of the sea, this expression was used figuratively in various literatures. Examples include the flux and reflux of fortune, of nations, and of fears and hopes. See *Oxford English Dictionary*, 'flux', for distinctive uses of this expression in writers including Harvey, Shaftesbury, and De Foe.

58.14 **emergence**] an unexpected or sudden occurrence or development.

58.22 **the origin of idolatry or polytheism**] The title of the third of Toland's *Letters to Serena* is 'The Origin of Idolatry, and Reasons of Heathenism'. The enquiry in this letter shows some similarity to Hume's treatment of the subject (see esp. pp. 78, 129).

59.10 **Jews and Mahometans . . . banishing all the arts of statuary and painting**] Jews traditionally distinguish between the worship of strange gods (idols) and the use of images (icons). Both are condemned. The early history of Judaism was marked by struggles of biblical prophets to bring idolatrous cults in line with the second commandment: 'Thou shalt not make unto thee any graven image, or any likeness *of any thing* that *is* in heaven above, or that *is* in the earth beneath, or that *is* in the water under the earth: Thou shalt not bow down thyself to them, nor serve them' (Exod. 20: 4–5). Idolatry was present in the indigenous culture and enjoyed the allegiance of the reigning monarchs. The most popular cults were of Canaanite origin, and included those of Baal, Asherah, and Ashtaroth. Illegitimate iconolatry, of which the most famous is worship of the golden calf, was common and harshly criticized by the prophets.

During the advent of Islam, idolatrous beliefs pervaded the world of nomadic Arabs. The followers of Muhammad regarded idols, imagery, and symbols as distracting the mind from the true God, and as inconsistent with divine revelation. They condemned the stubborn pride found in those who adhered to traditional polytheism. The doctrinal basis for banning idolatry was that monotheism is the truth revealed by God. Muhammad declared that those who worship other gods are rebels who will be cast into hell. In the *Koran*, historical connections are established between the Jewish tradition, in figures such as Moses and Abraham, and Islamic commands to shun 'the filth of idols' (Mohammad, *Speeches & Table-Talk*, pp. 60, 62, 111; *Koran*, in *The Glorious Koran*, pp. 215, 436).

SECTION 9: Comparison of these Religions with regard to Persecution and Toleration

60.4 **knavery to impose on credulity]** At *EPM* 9.22 Hume discusses the 'sensible knave', who occasionally acts unjustly while concealing his immoral acts through deception. Hume also discusses knavery in his essay 'Of the Independency of Parliament' 1–2.

60.4 **humanity]** At *EPM* 5.46 Hume speaks of 'any such principle *in our nature* as humanity or a concern for others' (italics added). He also refers to the character trait of humanity as a virtue of concern and attention to others. 'Humanity' was a pivotal concept in moral treatises when Hume wrote and was sometimes associated with a capacity for sympathy and with fellow-feeling (see *EPM* 5.17, 20).

n. 42.1 **Verrius Flaccus . . . Pliny . . . Macrobius . . . Sammonicus Serenus]** Footnote references: Pliny the Elder, *Natural History* 28.4 (ch. 2 in older editions), §§18–19; Macrobius, *Saturnalia* 3.9.6–13. Verrius Flaccus was a freedman who became a distinguished writer. Hume's statement of Pliny's recounting appears to be a close paraphrase. Macrobius reports that bk. 5 of Sammonicus Serenus,[B] *Secret World* (*Res reconditæ*), supplies 'the two formulas' that (1) call forth the gods from a city and (2) commit the city to destruction or annihilation. Macrobius quotes both formulae.

60.24 **sects fall naturally into animosity . . . zeal . . . passions]** In his *History of England*, Hume offers many instances of animosity and zeal, especially with respect to differences within Roman Catholicism and within Protestantism. In one passage, he notes, in addition, that Catholics regarded Protestant sectarian disagreements as vindicating their own Catholic beliefs about the church universal: 'Differences among the protestants were matter of triumph to the catholics; who insisted, that the moment men departed from the authority of the church, they lost all criterion of truth and falshood in matters of religion, and must be carried away by every wind of doctrine' (ch. 35 [3: 385]). In another passage Hume is unsparing in his appraisal of the history of the denomination in which he had been raised: 'The Scots... had a near prospect of spreading the presbyterian discipline in England and Ireland.... Never did refined Athens so exult in diffusing the sciences and liberal arts over a savage world; never did generous Rome so please herself in the view of law and order established by her victorious arms; as the Scots now rejoiced, in communicating their barbarous zeal and theological fervour, to the neighbouring nations' (ch. 55 [5: 332–3]). Further examples are found in chs. 45, 47, 51–2, 57.

61.7 **replied the oracle.[43]]** Footnote reference: Xenophon, *Memorabilia* 1.3.1. The Delphic oracle became the leading shrine of Apollo. Oracular utterings were delivered by a young priestess in an ecstatic trance. A priest then mediated to a questioner what would otherwise be incoherent messages from the priestess. Though an oracle is a divine utterance made through a medium, 'consulting an oracle' could mean that one had consulted a god, a priest or priestess, or the shrine. Xenophon reports that the question 'What is my duty of sacrifice?' elicited the following response from the priestess of Delphi: 'Follow the custom of the State: That is the way to act piously.' Xenophon suggests that Socrates accepted this prescription and counselled others to do the same. A similar report is found at *Memorabilia* 4.3.16.

61.8 **The ROMANS commonly adopted the gods]** The religion of early Rome absorbed the poetry, ritual, and pantheon (deities) of the Greeks. The Romans also embraced religions of the Orient, such as Adonis of Syria, Isis and Osiris of Egypt (see n. 44), and Mithras of Persia. Elements of these religions were exported to Rome and incorporated into the practices and beliefs of a state religion controlled by secular officials. (Educated classes in Rome often preferred profane philosophical systems such as Stoicism and Epicureanism.)

61.11 **wars and persecutions of the EGYPTIAN idolaters... different sects]** The Romans did not consistently accommodate Egyptian theological beliefs. Several times between 58 and 48 BC the Romans destroyed Egyptian chapels and attempted to suppress the Egyptian cults. However, Egyptian gods were popular in the Roman Empire.

In early Egyptian idolatry, gods were presented either as animals, humans, inanimate objects, or (less commonly) plants. Although Greek and Christian interpreters attributed to Egyptians the belief that the animals are the gods, these images were widely regarded in Egypt as visible representations of divine spirits with whom the community wished to make contact. Each community had its own deity, often represented as an animal figure. For example, the city of Thebes worshipped Amon, depicted as a ram. Memphis had two protectors: Sekhmet, presented as a lioness, and Apis (or Hapis), depicted as a bull. Other adopted animals included the cobra, frog, baboon, mongoose, vulture, hippopotamus, cow, eel, and mouse. These figures were given human qualities and were often depicted as composite human-animals.

61.15 **worshippers of dogs . . . adorers of cats or wolves.**[44]**]** Footnote reference: Plutarch, *Moralia*, 'Isis and Osiris' 72, 379E–380C. Plutarch examines hypotheses that explain ancient Egyptian religious practices of animal worship. He notes that people were drawn into wars in order to protect their particular animal(s). Dogs, cats, and wolves are precisely the animals selected as examples by Trenchard, *Natural History of Superstition*, 15.

61.17 **EGYPTIAN superstition . . . HERODOTUS,**[45]**]** Footnote reference: Herodotus, *History* 2.180. Herodotus reports that the Delphians received a large donation from Amasis II[B] toward finishing the temple and also received a sum from Greeks living in Egypt. This pharaoh erected temples at Memphis and Sais and established alliances with the Greeks.

61.23 **MAHOMETANISM . . . bloody principles]** Hume is perhaps referring to the standard European view that Islam is a bloody, ruthless, vengeful, tyrannical, and intolerant religion—lacking in divine authority and viewing the sword as the route to heaven. Hume points to similar views at *EHU* 10.24 and 'Of the Standard of Taste' 4. He also explains the historical background of the Christian opinion of Islam in *History of England*. There the 'Turcomans or Turks' are characterized as having been particularly fierce and barbaric (ch. 5 [1: 235]). However, Hume also speaks of the Protestant–Catholic conflict in Britain as involving 'schemes the most bloody . . . that had ever been thought of in any age or nation' and of the 'bloody designs [that] . . . appeared every where' (chs. 39, 41 [4: 75, 211]). His vivid descriptions leave little doubt that he regarded much of British history as exhibiting bloody designs on the part of royalty, political leaders, religious officials, etc.

For a sample of the many writings available to Hume that reflect an estimate of Islam as a religion of bloody principles, see Isaac Barrow (1630–77; English mathematician and theologian), *Works*, sermon 14, 'Of the Impiety and Imposture of Paganism and Mahometanism' (2: 154–6); Humphrey Prideaux (1648–1724; lecturer at Christ Church, Oxford, and dean at Norwich), *True Nature of Imposture Fully Display'd in the Life of Mahomet*, esp. pp. viii–ix, 13, 26–7, 105, 199, 218; John Jackson (1686–1763; English religious writer and clergyman), *An Address to Deists*, pp. 80–5; Charles Wolseley (1630?–1714; British politician and theological writer), *The Reasonableness of Scripture-Belief*, pp. 167–71; Grotius, *Truth of the Christian Religion* 6.2, 5–8; Paul Rycaut, *Present State of the Ottoman Empire* 2.2 (pp. 102–3); (LACROZE), 'Historical and Critical Reflections upon Mahometanism and Socinianism'; Bayle, *Dictionary*, 'Mahomet' [K–P]; and Blaise Pascal (1623–62; French mathematician, philosopher, and theologian), *Pensées* 241–2 (Levi nos.).

Also influential was the translation and commentary of George Sale (1697?–1736; English lawyer and Arabic scholar), *Koran, Commonly called The Alcoran of Mohammed*; see his 'Preliminary Discourse', 49–50, 142–4. Hume's friend Edward

Gibbon (1737–94; British historian) offered a generally negative portrayal of Islam in ch. 50 of *Decline and Fall of the Roman Empire* (a post-*NHR* work). This chapter was later issued as an independent book entitled *Life of Mahomet*; see esp. pp. 48–51, 75, 122, 150.

61.25 **fire and faggot]** Both Catholics and Protestants used this expression to refer to acts of burning heretics alive. Protestants commonly used it to rebuke Catholics (e.g. with reference to the Inquisition), as is evident in the following condemnation of Catholics by Matthew Pool(e) (1624–79; Protestant biblical commentator): 'your Religion... is written in blood. I perceive you answer our Arguments with Fire and Faggot' (*A Dialogue Between A Popish Priest, and An English Protestant*, 114). Humphrey Prideaux went so far as to say that the 'Romanists' had learned to use 'Sword, Fire and Faggot' from 'the method which Mahomet took to establish' his religion (*True Nature of Imposture Fully Display'd*, p. 218).

In his *History of England* Hume several times uses the language of 'faggots'. He tells the following stories about English executions of Dutchmen (among other stories he tells involving faggots): 'four Dutch anabaptists, three men and a woman, had faggots tied to their backs at Paul's Cross, and were burned in that manner.... [A] Dutchman, called Van Paris, accused of the heresy, which has received the name of Arianism, was condemned to the [flames].... He suffered with so much satisfaction, that he hugged and caressed the faggots, that were consuming him; a species of frenzy, of which there is more than one instance among the martyrs of that age' (chs. 32, 34 [3: 264, 367]; see also ch. 31 [3: 216]).

The word 'faggot' (or 'fagot') meant, at the time Hume wrote, any of the following: (1) sticks or branches, as those used for fuel; (2) the punishment of burning alive; and (3) a badge worn on the sleeve of upper garments by persons who had recanted heretical views. 'To faggot' meant, among other things, to bind a person hand and foot.

61.29 **disciples of Zoroaster]** Zoroastrianism arose in ancient Persia as a monotheistic religion centring on *Ahura Mazdah*, 'the Wise Lord'. The century and location of its origins are unknown, but Zoroaster (or Zarathustra) may have lived before 1000 BC. After his death, the religion spread westward in Iran; see ann. 56.15 ff., on *NHR* 7.2.

61.29 **shut the doors... Magians.[46]]** Footnote reference: Thomas Hyde, *Historia religionis veterum Persarum, eorumque Magorum*. The classical Greek understanding of Zoroastrianism was largely limited to the depiction provided by the Magians. Hume seems to be following this conception, under guidance from Hyde's *Historia religionis*. A reference to *shutting the doors of heaven* is found in a passage in Hyde that discusses how the Persians diligently conceal their religion, because, 'by the religious precept of Zoroaster in the book *Sadder*', it is prohibited to teach and write to the outside (ch. 1, lines 9–15 (p. 5)). The *Sadder*, or 100 portae—'doors' in Latin—was not for public display; the doors were closed to anyone foreign to the religion. For more information on the Magians, Zoroaster, Hyde, and the *Sadder*, see anns. 56.15 ff. (on *NHR* 7.2); and 81.8 (on *NHR* 14.1, on the *Sadder*). (Caution is in order regarding Hyde's interpretations and his dating of the *Sadder*. Though a distinguished orientalist and scholar of Zoroastrianism, Hyde was a steadfast Christian who sometimes ridiculed other religious traditions.)

61.30 **PERSIAN conquests . . . temples and images of the GREEKS**] Herodotus (*History* 8.33–5, 51–4) relates stories of Persian plundering and burning of Greek temples to which Hume may be alluding. It appears that the temple burnings were part of a larger campaign of carnage, destruction, and plundering. It is historically unclear whether Persian zeal was directed specifically against temples and images and whether the Persian conquests were obstructed by these or other *anti-religious* actions.

61.33 **ALEXANDER . . . abolished.[47] . . . the BABYLONISH rites and ceremonies.[48]**] Footnote references: (n. 47) Arrian, *Anabasis* 3.16.4–5; 7.17.2; (n. 48) Arrian, *Anabasis* 3.16.4–5. Bks. 3 and 7 of Arrian's *Anabasis* depict Alexander's attitudes toward local deities after his invasion of Babylonia. In bk. 3 Arrian says that although the Persian Emperor Xerxes had previously destroyed a temple in Babylon, Alexander decided to rebuild it on the same site. Bk. 7 reports that upon entering Babylon, Alexander commanded the rebuilding of the temple of the chief deity in the Babylonian pantheon. The temple had also been destroyed by Xerxes. In nn. 47–8 Hume refers to a small part of Arrian's *Anabasis*. Also pertinent are *Anabasis* 3.1.5; 3.6.1.1; 3.7.6; 3.16.9; 3.25.1; 7.24.4, 7.25.3–6; 7.28.1–2.

62.3 **AUGUSTUS . . . CAIUS CÆSAR . . . by the PAGANS esteemed ignoble and barbarous.[49]**] Footnote reference: Suetonius, *Lives of the Caesars* 2, 'Augustus' 93. Suetonius reports that 'Augustus . . . not only refrained from taking a small detour to see Apis . . . when he was travelling in Egypt, but also greatly praised his grandson Gaius because he did not offer prayers at Jerusalem when passing by Judaea'. It was common for Gentiles to send offerings or make sacrifices upon the altar. Jews sometimes offered sacrifices for the Roman emperor, and the emperor sometimes contributed toward their cost.

n. 50 ***Corruptio optimi pessima***] This expression—'The worst state is a corruption of the best'—is not from any classical writer, but Aristotle's *Nicomachean Ethics* may have been a distant source. Aristotle asserts that tyranny is the worst of three forms of corruption (or perversion) of the best form of government, which is monarchy (*Nicomachean Ethics* $1160^{a}31$–$1160^{b}11$). Hume's expressions 'the corruption of the best things gives rise to the worst' (*NHR* 10.1) and 'the corruption of the best things begets the worst' (*NHR* 11.1) appear to be his translations of this same Latin expression. Hume begins his essay 'Of Superstition and Enthusiasm' by quoting and discussing the maxim 'That the corruption of the best things produces the worst', connecting the saying to 'corruptions of true religion' by superstition and enthusiasm.

62.10 **human sacrifices of the CARTHAGINIANS]** The Carthaginians (among others) practised royal sacrifices. The king was regarded as the source of sacred energy, which diminishes over time. The energy was believed renewable by sacrificing the king, who thereafter qualified as an object of worship. The Carthaginians sometimes substituted another person for the king, choosing an individual as close to royal status as possible. Commonly one of the king's sons was chosen, a custom that led to the Carthaginian practice of the sacrifice of children. Diodorus Siculus[B] reported that the Carthaginians sacrificed hundreds of children when they aspired to make amends to the gods. Their practice was to roll the children down from an image of Cronus into a pit filled with fire. See *Historical Library* 20.14.2–6. Diodorus also mentions connections between the Carthaginians and the Tyrians, to whom Hume refers in n. 51. Although various forms of sacrifice occurred in Tyre, little is known about human sacrifice.

62.11 **MEXICANS]** Evidence of practices in Mexico had been collected primarily from Spanish sources during the Spanish Conquest of 1518–21. The Aztecs, by these accounts, engaged in human sacrifices at festival commencements, usually sacrificing prisoners of war in the hope of inducing favours from the gods. The priests justified the practice by saying that the gods were famished and desirous of being worshipped, and that a victim had a path to the heavenly afterlife with the gods. The usual method of sacrifice involved a stone on which the victim was lain, nude and fully stretched. When the body cavity was cleaved, the heart was deftly removed by the priest and offered to the sun. The bodies of the dead were then distributed and eaten. Other forms of human sacrifice in Mexico involved pounding the head against a large rock in the temple, slitting the throat, beheading, and half-roasting the victim in a fire. After the sacrifice, the victims might be skinned and the skins worn as garments representing the divine. See Durán, *Book of the Gods and Rites*, pp. 91–5, 145–8, 175–80, 204–5, 212–16, 233–5, 242–4.

62.11 **inquisition and persecutions of ROME and MADRID]** Formal proceedings of the Inquisition began at least as early as 1184. Measures of suppression included excommunication, imprisonment, the death penalty, and confiscation or destruction of property. Those who did not recant their 'heresies' were brought to trial in secret hearings, with no right to counsel or legal assistance. Torture was common. Despite a long-standing papal denunciation of torture, Pope Innocent IV authorized its use in 1252. Unrecanted heresy often led to a sentence of burning at the stake or a similarly violent means of death. The Holy Office of the Inquisition was revived through a brief dated 14 Jan. 1542. Known as the Roman Inquisition, it was established primarily to combat Protestantism.

The Spanish Inquisition was established in 1478. The original purpose was to search for and punish heretics, but an underlying purpose was to end Jewish influence in Spain. Over 10,000 persons were burned, 100,000 imprisoned, and the Jews expelled in 1492. Hume (or his editor, Kames) cryptically ridicules the criteria used for accusations of atheism during the Spanish Inquisition in *A Letter from a Gentleman* 31.

62.17 **fatal vengeance of inquisitors]** 'Inquisitor' was commonly used to refer to a judge of the Spanish Inquisition.

62.21 **temple of DIANA . . . installed his successor.[52]]** Footnote references: Strabo, *Geography* 5.3.12; Suetonius, *Lives of the Caesars* 4, 'Gaius Caligula' 35.3. In early Roman religion there were several principal holy places or cult centres. Diana was worshipped in a temple in the Alban Hills in the grove of Aricia at the volcanic mountain Lake Nemi. The worship of spiritual powers included reading omens, charms, and taboos. The priest at the temple, who bore the title of king, could achieve that office only by killing the incumbent king in combat. Suetonius reports that Gaius Caligula secretly engaged a man willing to attack the king of Nemi. Volunteers for such a challenge were found among runaway, fugitive slaves. In order to succeed in the challenge, they were required to kill the reigning king with a sword. Strabo characterizes these religious traditions as barbaric. The temple's worshippers, he reports, once made a runaway slave the priest after he had killed his predecessor. Because of this incident, the priest was always armed with a sword lest another try to gain his office.

SECTION 10: With regard to Courage or Abasement

63.7 **monkish virtues]** Hume also mentions 'monkish virtues' at *EPM* 9.3. The list found there is somewhat different from the list here (and some terms on the lists carried somewhat different meanings, both within and outside Roman Catholic traditions, than they do today). Some of these 'virtues' had been defended by Blaise Pascal, whose views—along with those of St Dominic and St Ignatius of Loyola—drew comments from Hume in *EPM*, Dial. 54. See also Hume's comment on 'monkish historians' in his *History of England* (chs. 1–3, 5 [1: 14, 38, 132, 240]); and the treatment of monkish virtues in Adam Smith (1723–90; Scottish philosopher and economist), *The Theory of Moral Sentiments* 3.2 (pp. 229–31).

Hume's conception of monks, their proclaimed virtues, and their position in society is explored in his *History of England*. There he writes that 'The great encrease of monasteries, if matters be considered merely in a political light, will appear [will show] the radical inconvenience of the catholic religion. . . . Papal usurpations, the tyranny of the inquisition, the multiplicity of holidays; all these fetters on liberty and industry were ultimately derived from the authority and insinuation of monks, whose habitations, being established every where, proved so many seminaries of superstition and of folly. . . . Though monks were the true preservers, as well as inventors, of the dreaming and captious philosophy of the schools, no manly or elegant knowledge could be expected among men, whose lives, condemned to a tedious uniformity, and deprived of all emulation, afforded nothing to raise the mind, or cultivate the genius' (ch. 31 [3: 227, 229]).

63.15 **heroes in paganism]** These heroes figure in ancient pagan mythology. (1) HERCULES, or Heracles, was portrayed as prodigiously strong, adventuresome, good-humoured, generous, courageous, and compassionate (although also given to the vices of gluttony, lust, and a violent temper). (2) THESEUS, in Greek legend an Athenian hero and early king, was portrayed as an ideal athlete, as performing unique feats of strength, and as a military hero. In character, he is valiant, spirited, and highly intelligent. (3) HECTOR, the Trojan hero of the *Iliad*, is a figure of compassion and tenderness. He pursued peace in the war, yet was the bravest, most skilled, and noblest of the Trojan warriors. Aware that he was doomed to certain death, he faced his destiny with great courage. (4) ROMULUS, legendary founder of Rome made the city an asylum for fugitives. Although a spirited, peaceful, and wise ruler, Romulus was also at times quarrelsome, cunning, and even vindictive. Romulus and Theseus are mentioned in a related context in Hume's essay 'Of Parties in General' 1.

63.15 **saints in popery]** (1) DOMINIC, founder of the Dominican Order, preached against heresies, social evils, luxury, and clerical indolence. He is admired for his tenderness, devotion, compassion, humility, and obedience. (2) FRANCIS, founder of the Franciscan Order, devoted himself to service of the poor. He is venerated for his simplicity, moderation, spiritual devotion, charitable acts, and humility. (3) There are two St Antony's: (a) ANTONY OF EGYPT (3rd century AD) is celebrated for his austerity, humility, inner peacefulness, and dedication to prayer. (b) ANTONY OF PADUA (13th century AD), a Franciscan priest, was distinguished as a patron of the poor. The combination of his learning, eloquence, and charismatic presence attracted crowds for his preaching. (4) BENEDICT of Nursia founded the Benedictine Order. Both Romans and barbarians reportedly flocked to him because of his personal virtues and miraculous and prophetic powers. He was renowned for his holiness, devotion to monastic ideals, and authorship of a monastic code.

Hume discusses the early Dominicans and Franciscans in a different light in his *History of England*. He considers their 'perpetual rivalship with each other in promoting their gainful superstitions' and their 'pretending a desire of poverty and a contempt for riches' in order to gain 'a great dominion over the minds, and consequently over the purses of men'. 'Thus', he says, 'the several orders of monks became a kind of regular troops or garrisons of the Romish church; and though the temporal interests of society, still more the cause of true piety, were hurt, by their various devices to captivate the populace, they proved the chief supports of that mighty fabric of superstition, and, till the revival of true learning, secured it from any dangerous invasion' (ch. 12 [2: 71–2]).

63.16 **holy dervises in MAHOMETANISM]** These were figures of a Muslim religious order in the mystic tradition renowned for devotional exercises and austerity. Only a small number of Muslims were dervises. The word 'dervise' or 'dervish' derives from the Persian word for 'mendicant' (*darwesh* or *derwish*). The repetition of religious formulae accompanied by precisely structured bodily motions is common in the rituals. As the exercise develops, the motions become increasingly rapid (described as a 'whirling dance' by European travellers), ending in ecstasy and possibly a trance. Often performed using chants, the exercises may also be done in silence. A few orders use self-laceration. Some exercises involve austere acts, including long hours of prayer and meditation. In a book available to Hume, Turner refers to this tradition as a 'subordinate sect' (*History of All Religions in the World*, pp. 300–1).

The 'dervises of Constantinople' are mentioned below, at *NHR* 12.4. In *THN* 1.4.7.13, Hume mentions some dervises, monks, and Cynics as exhibiting 'great extravagancies of conduct'.

63.22 **Alexander . . . Hercules and Bacchus . . . excelled.**[53]] Footnote reference: Arrian, *Anabasis, passim*, esp. 4.10.5–7; 4.28.4; and 5.26.5. Arrian reports that the Macedonians deemed Alexander more worthy of divinity than Dionysus and Hercules, whose courage and ambition Alexander accepted as both a model and a personal challenge. Neither of these gods had direct connections with Macedon. In 'Of the Rise and Progress of the Arts and Sciences' 18, Hume discusses Alexander's conviction that he was *not* a god.

63.24 **Brasidas . . . defence he had embraced.**[54]] Footnote reference: Thucydides, *History* 5.10–11. Brasidas was honoured for heroic courage and military brilliance, as well as for honesty, moderation, discipline, and a sense of justice. He once captured the Athenian colony of Amphipolis, which he subsequently ruled and defended. Thucydides reports that after a mortal wound in a battle near Amphipolis, Brasidas was brought 'yet breathing into the city', where he died and was buried. The citizens of that city awarded him the honours of a hero and generously attributed the founding of the colony to him. Sacrifices were offered in his honour, and games were celebrated in his name annually thereafter.

63.29 **the observation of Machiavel,**[55]] Footnote reference: Niccolò Machiavelli, *Discorsi* 2.2.6–7 (see Cat.). Machiavelli comments on modernity's lack of devotion to liberty, as compared to the ancients. His premiss is that some differences are traceable to the pagan and Christian religions, with the latter placing more emphasis on humble, gentle, and contemplative values that ultimately lead to the exaltation of suffering and a weakening of resistance to authority.

64.4 **Brasidas . . . defend itself."**[56]] Footnote reference: Plutarch, *Moralia*, 'Sayings of Kings and Commanders', Brasidas 1, 190B. Plutarch quotes Brasidas as saying, upon catching a mouse (which bit him), that no living creature is too small to have the survival instinct or to attempt to defend itself from marauders.

64.6 **Bellarmine . . . present life."**[57]] Footnote reference: Pierre Bayle, *Dictionary*, 'Bellarmine', 1: 734–5, including note [Z]. Bayle reported that Bellarmine wished to live a simple life as a Jesuit, even to the point of giving flies 'the Liberty to fly, and light, where they pleased'. He mentions a source as follows:

> *Among the remarkable Virtues of Bellarmin, others place his wonderful Patience, in enduring Vexations, which* James Fuligatti *celebrates in the following Words*: 'He considered Gnats, a little flying Insect, and other small Vexations, . . . as sent by God, to exercise our Patience; and he suffered them so calmly, that he neither endeavoured to drive them away with his own Hand, nor permitted any one else to do it. . . . He would not drive the Flies from his Face, though they were extreamly troublesome, as is usual at *Rome*, in hot Weather; which when the Standers by expressed their Wonder at, he mildly told them, It was unjust to disturb those little Creatures, whose only Paradice is the Liberty of flying, and resting, where they please.'

SECTION 11: With regard to Reason or Absurdity

65.27 **the Alcoran]** The term is an archaic form of the Koran (or Qur'an, from Al-Qur'an), literally meaning 'The Reading'. Sale's influential translation of 1734 was entitled *The Koran, Commonly called The Alcoran of Mohammed*. The Koran is comprised of writings accepted in Islam as authentic revelations made to Muhammad by Allah (regarded as the same God who made revelations to Abraham, Moses, and Jesus), as delivered through the angel Gabriel. The book is sometimes said to be 'the reading of the man who knew not how to read', a metaphorical reference to Muhammad's 'reading' of God's word even though he could not read in the standard sense. The words came to Muhammad in a trance. The aim of the Koran is to re-establish the monotheistic tradition of the Semitic prophets and to detail a comprehensive system of morality.

Hume discusses moral precepts in 'the Alcoran' in 'Of the Standard of Taste' 4, and discusses the implications of the 'violent precepts' of the *Alcoran* in his *History of England* (ch. 5; cf. ann. at 61.23 (on *NHR* 9.3, Mahometanism . . . bloody principles)). Prideaux cast a negative light on the history and teachings of the *Alcoran* in *True Nature of Imposture Fully Display'd*, 16 ff., 37 ff., 116 ff.; see also disapproving depictions in (LACROZE), 'Historical and Critical Reflections Upon Mahometanism and Socinianism', Nathan Bailey's *Dictionarium Britannicum* (entry 'Alcoran'), and the later views of Gibbon in *Life of Mahomet* (from *Decline and Fall of the Roman Empire*), esp. 19–20. Sale's 'Preliminary Discourse' is more sympathetic. Numerous works specifically on the *Alcoran* were available to Hume in French, Latin, and English.

65.30 **education]** instruction by acculturation or habituation. See *THN* 1.3.9.17, which characterizes 'education' in terms of 'opinions and notions of things, to which we have been accustom'd from our infancy'.

66.4 **all popular theology . . . most unintelligible sophisms]**. The themes in this passage are explored many times in Hume's *History of England*, with special reference to Protestant and Catholic theologies. Context is given there for his saying here 'especially the scholastic'.

66.18 **the definition of** Arian . . . *&c.*] Each form of dissent listed has been denounced as a Christian heresy by an official Roman Catholic body (see the anns. below). In *A Letter from a Gentleman* 25, Hume (or his editor, Kames) writes that 'In Reality, whence come all the various Tribes of Hereticks, the *Arians, Socinians* and *Deists*, but from too great a Confidence in mere human Reason, which they regard as the *Standard* of every Thing, and which they will not submit to the superior Light of Revelation?' In his *History of England*, while discussing the Protestant reformers, Hume says: 'When men were once settled in their particular sects, and had fortified themselves in a habitual detestation of those who were denominated heretics, they adhered with more obstinacy to the principles of their education; and the limits of the two religions thenceforth remained fixed and unchangeable' (ch. 31 [3: 211]).

66.18 Arian] The Arian heresy dates from 318–20. Alexandrian priest Arius (3rd–4th century) maintained that the Godhead is indivisible and that the Father existed prior to and begot the Son, thus denying the Son's eternity and giving the Son a subordinate position. Arius maintained that Christ became divine at the Resurrection. His theology was interpreted as denying the divinity of both Christ and the Holy Spirit, beliefs for which Arius was excommunicated in 320 by the Alexandrian Synod. At the Council of Nicaea in 325 Arius's views were condemned as blasphemous, and the anti-Arian Creed of Nicaea was formulated. The final doctrine pronounced that the Father and Son are of one substance. See ann. 78.26 ff. (on *NHR* n. 78, on Newton, Locke, and Clarke as Arians or Socinians), and Bayle, *Dictionary*, 'Arius'.

66.18 Pelagian] Chambers provides one eighteenth-century perspective on the Romano-British monk Pelagius (4th–5th century): 'Pelagius, properly call'd Morgan, was an Irish Monk, Cotemporary with St Jerome, and St Augustin . . . . He absolutely denied all original Sin, which he held to be the mere Invention of St Augustin; and taught that Men are entire Masters of their Actions, perfectly free Creatures, in opposition to all Predestination, Reprobation, Election, &c' (*Cyclopædia*, 'Pelagians'). The Pelagian heresy rests on a doctrine of free will as the key element in human perfectibility and limits the role of divine grace and original sin. Divine grace is viewed as a facilitation of what the will can do on its own, and Adam's sin is not regarded as affecting other persons. St Augustine responded in vigorous opposition. There were several official condemnations of Pelagianism.

66.18 Erastian] The Erastian heresy refers to those who contest the supremacy of the Church over secular governors. Claims of heresy rest on affirmation of the doctrine of the rightful authority of the State over the Church even in ecclesiastical affairs. This 'heresy' is named after Thomas Erastus (1524–83; Swiss physician and Protestant theologian), who published his views in 1568. There has been controversy as to whether Erastus was an 'Erastian', because he held only the relatively weak thesis that under a Christian ruler there is no need for a corrective authority other than that of the State, and that there should not be a religious authority with coercive powers independent of the State's powers.

66.18 SOCINIAN] The Socinian heresy derives from Protestant anti-trinitarian teachings developed in Italy, Poland, Germany, Holland, and Great Britain in the sixteenth and seventeenth centuries. The heresy is named after two Italian theologians named Sozzino (or Sozini), but known by their Latin names: Laelius Socinus (1525–62) and Faustus Socinus (1539–1604). Both associated with Protestant reformers and both left the Roman Catholic Church. Laelius insisted on free theological enquiry, but did not hold radical anti-trinitarian views. Faustus maintained that the ascended Christ was not divine by *nature* but was divine by *office*. Unitarians were influenced by various Socinian views, and many thinkers in the late seventeenth century were publicly accused of Socinianism. The term 'Socinian' sustained an array of connotations in seventeenth-century theological disputes. The term was often used pejoratively in reference to free-thinkers and those of unorthodox views. See ann. n. 78.26 ff. (on *NHR* n. 78, on Newton, Locke, and Clarke (as Arians or Socinians)); and Bayle, *Dictionary*, 'Socinus (Faustus)'.

66.18 SABELLIAN] The Sabellian heresy is a trinitarian heresy named after the Roman Christian prelate and theologian Sabellius (fl. 3rd century). It emphasizes the unity of God the Father to the point of making the Son's subsistence and person dependent on that of the Father. Sabellius was excommunicated *c.* 217–20 on grounds of Monarchianism—the doctrine of the essential unity and indivisible substance of the deity (a doctrine intended to reinforce monotheism). Sabellianism, Arianism, and Socinianism were widely discussed forms of non-trinitarian theology, and the label 'Sabellian' came to be attached to various Monarchian doctrines.

66.19 EUTYCHIAN] The Eutychian heresy is a form of Monophysitism, a Christological heresy insisting on one nature in Christ, which is divine and not human. The heresy is linked to the Byzantine monk Eutyches (4th–5th century), who held that after the joining of the divine with the human in Christ there were no longer two natures. This heresy consists in the belief that Christ's flesh is not consubstantial with human flesh, which seemed to Eutyches' critics to entail that the Word never truly became flesh. Eutyches refused to recant before the Council of Constantinople in 448, and was deposed from his position in a monastery. After a brief restoration, he was condemned and exiled in 451 by the Council of Chalcedon, which unequivocally supported the two-natures doctrine.

66.19 NESTORIAN] The Nestorian heresy derives from unorthodox views about Christ and the Virgin Mary defended by archbishop of Constantinople, Nestorius (4th–5th century). In opposition to Arianism, he held a Christology of two natures or substances in Christ: a divine nature and a human nature. Nestorius refused to attribute to the divine nature the human acts and suffering of Jesus. He also held that the Virgin Mary was the mother of Christ but not the mother of God. On this latter premiss, he reasoned, divine nature would be born of a human woman, whereas

Mary had begotten only a man. In 431 Nestorius was condemned as a heretic and driven out of the Byzantine Empire. (See Bayle, *Dictionary*, 'Nestorius'.)

66.19 **Monothelite**] The Monothelite heresy was a seventh-century Incarnation heresy advocating that Christ had two natures, divine and human, but that the two natures are manifested as one will. As Christ has only one will and is divine, he never performed distinctly human acts. The doctrine was initially promulgated in 624 by Byzantine emperor Heraclius in an attempt to end theological controversy. However, exponents of the view that Christ had no human will were condemned by several papal pronouncements between 640 and 649. At an ecumenical council in 680–1, Monothelitism was condemned, and Christ was officially proclaimed to have both a divine will and a free human will, which function in harmony.

66.23 **scholastic religion**] 'Scholastic religion' refers to Roman Catholic teachings integrated and supported by philosophy and theology in schools and universities. Chambers provides this perspective: 'School Divinity, is that Part of Divinity which clears and discusses Questions, by means of Reason, and Arguments: In which Sense, it stands, in good measure, opposed to positive Divinity, which is founded on the Authority of Fathers, Councils, &c' (*Cyclopædia*, 'Scholastic'). The term 'scholasticism' was often used to refer to philosophical and dogmatic theologies promulgated during the period from approximately the tenth through the fifteenth centuries. Hume several times refers to Scholastic doctrines in his writings. In his Index to *ETSS* (see p. 277 in this volume), Hume phrased his entry as 'Scholastic Religion, its usual Absurdity'.

SECTION 12: With regard to Doubt or Conviction

67.5 **Cambyses . . . Apis**] Apis was an Egyptian bull-god of Memphis, where the reigning bull occupied an extravagant residence with walkways and courts. In the artistic representation of Apis the body is typically black, with a square or triangular white spot on the forehead. Cambyses, upon entering Memphis, found the inhabitants of the city engaged in a festival celebrating the reappearance of Apis. Apparently convinced that he was the subject of ridicule in the celebration, Cambyses had the sacred bull brought before him and killed with a dagger. He ordered punishment of the priests. In the passage from Suetonius cited earlier by Hume (n. 49), the worship of Apis is briefly mentioned.

67.8 **Herodotus**] Hume inserted an additional footnote at this point in the 1757–70 edns. of *NHR*. The note read (in the edn. of 1770, p. 295): 'Lib. iii. c. 38'. The reference was to Herodotus, *History* 3.38, a passage that Hume here partially paraphrases; however, only *History* 3.27–30 explains the particular story to which Hume here refers. In these four chapters Herodotus presents the historical information that Hume reviews, relating, first, the incident involving the bull and, second, the evidence for the attribution of madness to Cambyses.

67.14 **communion**] union of persons joined by a commonly held religious faith and set of rites.

67.16 Averroes] Averroës held many views in opposition to Christian beliefs. Hume's attribution to Averroës of this remark about the doctrine of transubstantiation (referred to at *NHR* 12.3 as the 'real presence') likely derives from Bayle, *Dictionary*, 'Averroës', 1: 552–61. Bayle presents precisely the statement Hume here attributes to Averroës and cites specific sources of the quote.

The first source mentioned by Bayle is Jean Daillé (1594–1670; theologian), who, in his *Réplique aux deux livres que Messieurs Adam et Cottiby* 1.16 relates that Jacques Davy (Cardinal) Du Perron (1565–1618) reports in his *Traitt du sainct sacrement de l'Eucharistie . . . refutation du livre du Sieur du Plessis Mornay* 3.29 (p. 973) that a Jesuit named Sarga (also 'Scarga') had said that Averroës '*found no sect worse, or weaker, than That of the* Christians, *who, themselves, eat, and break to pieces, the God, whom they adore*'. Bayle says that the original source that quoted Sarga appears to be 'De Plessis'—i.e. Philippe de Mornai [Mornay], seigneur du Plessis-Marly (1549–1623; also referred to as Du Plessis-Mornay and Du Plessis-Marly), in his *De l'institution, usage et doctrine du sainct sacrement de l'Eucharistie* (p. 1106; also available to Hume in an English translation). Du Plessis had a celebrated public disputation at Fontainebleau with Du Perron in 1600 regarding the Roman Catholic eucharistic doctrine.

Another source cited by Bayle is Charles Drelincourt (1595–1669; minister of the Calvinist Church at Paris), who often wrote in opposition to Roman Catholic theology. His statement, as reported by Bayle, seems closest to Hume's paraphrase. Drelincourt is said to have reported that Averroës, 'having seen the Sacrament eaten, which had before been adored, said, *That he had never seen a more foolish, or more ridiculous Sect, than That of the* Christians, *who adore That, which they eat*' (*Dialogues familiers sur les principales objections des missionnaires de ce temps*, pp. 305–6).

67.20 ***real presence***] This term (used by Catholics and non-Catholics alike) refers to that into which the substance of the bread and wine of the sacrament of Holy Communion are allegedly transformed. Their accidental properties do not change, but their substance does. St Thomas Aquinas offered a detailed analysis (*Summa theologiæ* 3a.75–7); and several Councils (Fourth Lateran Council, 1215; Council of Constance, 1414–18; Council of Florence, 1439; Council of Trent, 1562) published influential accounts of the real presence. They agree that the whole substance of bread and the whole substance of wine are converted by divine power into the whole substance of the body and blood of Christ—so that the presence is real, not symbolic or metaphorical.

In his *History of England*, Hume several times discusses the historical importance of this doctrine and what he takes to be the absurd and superstitious beliefs of Roman Catholics that produced it. He writes that 'the real presence [is the] . . . doctrine, . . . among the numberless victories of superstition over common sense, [whose] triumph is the most signal and egregious. . . . It was the last doctrine of popery, that was wholly abandoned by the people [during the course of the Protestant Reformation]. . . . The chief cause was really the extreme absurdity of the principle itself, and the profound veneration, which of course it impressed on the imagination. The priests likewise were much inclined to favour an opinion, which attributed to them so miraculous a power; and the people, who believed, that they participated of the very body and blood of their Saviour, were loth to renounce so extraordinary, and as they imagined, so salutary a privilege' (chs. 32 and 34 [3: 261, 365]). In *EHU* 10.1, Hume discusses criticisms of the doctrine by John Tillotson (1630–94; English preacher and theologian). See also the annotation immediately above on Averroës.

67.24 **counter]** a round piece of wood, metal (often stamped brass), or ivory. The term derived from use of the item in counting, keeping accounts, and arithmetical operations, but generally referred to imitation coins or tokens.

67.32 **doctors of the Sorbonne]** professors at the theological college in the University of Paris. The college was founded c. 1257, and gained distinction in the late Middle Ages and early modern period, when Sorbonne professors rendered influential opinions on theological and ecclesiastic controversies. The faculty came to be called the Sorbonne in the sixteenth century. See also ann. 68.33 at *NHR* 12.7 below.

67.33 **dervises of Constantinople]** On 'dervise' generally, see ann. 63.16 at *NHR* 10.3, dervises in Mahometanism. In 1668 Paul Rycaut published the book *The Present State of the Ottoman Empire containing . . . The Most Material Points of the Mahometan Religion*. In it he stated his official position as 'Embassador Extraordinary for his Majesty Charles the Second . . . to Sultan Mahomet Han the Fourth, Emperour of the Turks' (title-page). During his five years in Constantinople, Rycaut gathered information pertaining to religious practices, and devoted a chapter of his book to religious men and dervises, also called '*Mevelevee*'. He describes them as aspiring to 'great Patience, Humility, Modesty, Charity and Silence'. He reports that after sermons and other parts of religious services, the dervises 'begin to turn round, some of them with that swift motion that their faces can scarce be seen'. Rycaut describes the dervises of Constantinople as being (contrary to Islamic prohibitions) addicted to strong wine, intoxicating liquors, and opium, which raise their spirits and foster devotion. (Ch. 13, 'Of the Dervises'.) Perhaps coincidentally, during his discussion of dervises, Rycaut also mentions Capuchin friars (p. 138); see second ann. below.

68.19 **ambassador from Tunis]** Hume was more than once lodged in hotels in Paris. He is probably referring to a time before 1753, perhaps while on a diplomatic mission during the last half of 1748.

68.23 **some *Capuchin* friars . . . Franciscans]** Capuchins are friars of an austere branch of the order of St Francis dedicated to missionary work. They wear the same type of clothes that St Francis wore, including the *capuche*, or *capuccio*, a long, pointed cowl or hood. Capuchins were prominent in attending to, and popular among, the uneducated masses in Europe.

68.31 **prince of Sallee, speaking of de Ruyter**] In 1641, while occupied as a trader, Admiral Michel de Ruyter[B] stopped in Morocco, where he journeyed inland to show his samples to the prince of Sallee, Sidi Ali ben Mohammed ben Moussa.[B] The following transaction allegedly occurred: The prince offered a price well below the value of a cloth that de Ruyter was trading. When de Ruyter declined the offer, the prince threatened to confiscate the cloth; but de Ruyter said he would rather give the merchandise to the prince than trade at such a low price. The prince departed, but said to his attendants upon leaving that it is a pity that *such a man* is a Christian. Later the prince returned and commented that de Ruyter's honesty and determination should set an example for everyone. This story is presented by de Ruyter's biographer, P. Blok (*Life of Admiral de Ruyter*, pp. 26–8). However, Gerard Brandt's *La Vie de Michel de Ruiter* may have been Hume's source for the story. Brandt gives an account closely resembling Hume's (here translated, with the spelling 'Ruiter' retained):

> 'I cannot', said Ruiter, 'part with my master's goods for a price that is below their value.' At this there were strong words between them, so Ruiter judged it appropriate to tell him that because he was not able to sell the piece of cloth at such a bargain price, he preferred to make him a present of it. 'What,' responded the Sultan, 'you have the power to give away the goods of your master for nothing, and you don't have the power to sell them for the price I am offering you?' Ruiter responded, 'I cannot sell it at such a low price without incurring a loss on the sale of my other merchandise; but I can without any consequence make a present in the case of a necessity, and to avoid bigger trouble.' The Sultan, not wanting to go on in this fashion, began to make threats. 'Do you know', he said 'that I can arrest you, and detain your vessel with all of its cargo?' 'I know it well,' replied Ruiter, 'but if you abuse me in such a way, you will show the world that one cannot trust your words'; to this he added, 'if I am your prisoner, put me up for ransom, and I will try to pay you'. At that the Sultan, entering into an extreme fury, redoubled his threats, and Ruiter, angry in turn, said to him, 'If I were on my vessel, you wouldn't threaten me like that.' The Sultan thus retired to another room, clenching his teeth, and stomping his feet, and said in his language, 'Isn't it too bad that such a man is a Christian?' (pp. 12–13)

68.33 ***worship leeks and onions***] In the work Hume cites in n. 81 (but in a different section), Juvenal reports that the leek and the onion were objects of sanctity and worship in a few places in Egypt: 'None adore Diana, but it is an impious outrage to crunch leeks and onions with the teeth. What a holy race to have such divinities springing up in their gardens!' (Juvenal, *Satires* 15.1–13). The worship and deification of leeks and onions by the ancients was an example used by Hobbes (*Leviathan* 12.16; 44.11) and by Malebranche in a discussion of religion and the cause of good and evil (*Search after Truth* 6.2.3). At Num. 11: 5 there is a biblical reference to the Jews' remembrance of leeks and onions as a food of Egypt, but without reference to Egyptian religious practices.

68.33 SORBONNIST] See ann. 67.32 (on *NHR* 12.4). Sorbonnists are 'those Doctors and Batchelors of Divinity of the Colledge of *Sorbon* in *Paris*' (Blount, *Glossographia*, 'Sorbonists'). The faculty at the Sorbonne maintained a conservative theological curriculum.

68.34 **priest of SAIS]** In the ancient Egyptian city of Sais, the chief deity and proclaimed foundress was Neith, Net, or Nit, an ancient goddess with pre-dynastic origins. She was worshipped at all temples in Sais, including those of other gods. Neith was considered the mother of Osiris, and Sais was also referred to as the 'City of Osiris'. (Plato reported that the Egyptians said that Neith is identical to the Hellenic Athena, and that the inhabitants of Sais believed themselves in some way related to Athenians (*Timaeus* 21E).) Many animals, birds, and reptiles were worshipped at Sais.

n. 58.1–5 **EGYPTIAN religion . . . resemblance to the JEWISH . . . EGYPTIAN and JEWISH proselytes were banished from ROME]** Footnote references: Tacitus, *Annals* 2.85; Suetonius, *Lives of the Caesars* 3, 'Tiberius' 36. Tacitus and Suetonius, as well as Dio Cassius Cocceianus (2nd–3rd century AD; politician and historian of Rome) and Josephus (1st century AD; governor of Galilee and Jewish historian), are the four classical sources for the account of the senate decree under which the proselytes were banished. *Suetonius* asserts that 'Tiberius suppressed foreign religious practices, such as the Egyptian and Jewish rites, and compelled those who subscribed to that superstition to burn the apparel and all the trappings of their religion.' *Tacitus* asserts that 'They discussed the expulsion of the Egyptian and Jewish religions, and there was a senate decree that four thousand freedmen of a suitable age, who had been tinged with that superstition, should be transported to the island of Sardinia, there to suppress piracy; and if they died from the unhealthy climate, it was a trifling loss. The rest were to leave Italy unless they had renounced their profane rites before the stated day.'

Tacitus and Suetonius lump together the Jewish and Egyptian rites, suggesting that they are 'the same' religion. However, the two rites may have been grouped together by the Romans for reasons such as the need to prevent the spread of both Isis worship and Judaism. The accounts found in Josephus and Dio Cassius are probably more reliable. They treat the expulsion of the Jews as independent of the expulsion of Egyptians. See Dio Cassius, *Roman History* 57.5a (7: 162–3); Josephus, *Jewish Antiquities* 18.81–4 (9: 58–61).

69.7 **blind and bigotted attachment]** Hume is perhaps referring to the uncharitable, but common, practice of attempting to defend one religion or sect by pointing to the most unattractive features of others. This form of argument had been used against Islam and other religions by European writers. See the authors named at ann. 61.23 ff. (on *NHR* 9.3).

69.11 **DIODORUS SICULUS[59] . . . killing a cat]** Footnote reference: Diodorus Siculus, *Historical Library* 1.83.8–9. Diodorus describes the cult of the cat in ancient Egypt, and observes that the Egyptian superstition affected Ptolemaic

Egypt's political relations with Rome. The Egyptians were eager to court Rome's favour, but the accidental killing of a cat by a visiting Roman diplomat precipitated punishment by a frenzied Egyptian mob.

69.18 **voted Augustus . . . Præsens divus habebitur Augustus**] The clause is from Horace, *Odes* 3, ode 5, lines 2–3. It may be translated 'Instantly will Augustus be judged divine'. This clause means that Augustus will be deemed a presently existing god, without implying that he resides in a particular location or has an overriding, supreme authority. Horace often wrote in praise of the gods and showed devotion to Augustus. In this passage, he addresses both Jove and Augustus. That Augustus was deemed a god is unmistakable in Horace. However, that he wielded such power as to cause the people to dethrone every god in heaven must be conjectured on the basis of the passage or learned from another source.

n. 60.1 **Louis the XIVth . . . College of Clermont**] The Latin in n. 60 may be translated: 'They carried from thence the insignia of Christ and set up those of the king: impious people, who cannot recognize any other God.' Different versions of the Latin wording have been handed down, but they have substantially the same meaning.

Initial donations were insufficient to sustain the Collège de Clermont, and its existence was threatened by a devalued currency and poor financial management. Louis XIV rescued the institution through royal patronage and declared himself financial benefactor. These royal initiatives led some to believe that a change of name was warranted to Collège Louis-Le-Grand, thereby acknowledging the college's second 'founder'. The Jesuits agreed to the renaming. Louis' name was engraved in gold letters above the entrance to the college in October 1682. In the archives of the Jesuit fathers, the following is recorded: *Ludovici Magni nomen, aureis literis, in Collegii fronte, inscripsimus.* ('The Name of Ludwig the Great we have inscribed in gold letters on the façade of the College'.)

The name 'Clermont' did not need to be erased from the façade of the college's entrance because it had never been displayed there. Only the words 'Collegium Societatis Jesus' had been so placed, despite the fact that the name 'Clermont' had become the traditional name of the college. Those who opposed the change of name regarded it as scandalous and sacrilegious, because, in place of the name of Jesus, the Fathers were substituting the name of the king. However, some Jesuits pointed out that the college had originally been named by persons who persecuted the Jesuit order. (Dupont-Ferrier, *Du Collège de Clermont*, 1: 7–11.)

70.1 **Tully,[61] . . . author in another place,[62]**] Footnote references: n. 61: Cicero, *De natura deorum* 1.29.81–2; n. 62: Cicero, *Tusculan Disputations* 5.27.78. In *De natura deorum* Cicero (Tully) writes on sacrilege and Egyptian respect: 'For we have often seen temples robbed and images of gods carried off from the holiest shrines by our fellow-countrymen, but no one ever even heard of an Egyptian laying profane hands on a crocodile or ibis or cat.' In *Tusculan Disputations* Cicero writes about Egyptian superstitions: 'Who does not know of the custom of the Egyptians? Their minds are infected with degraded superstitions and they would sooner submit to any torment than injure an ibis or asp or cat or dog or crocodile.' In *De natura deorum* 1.36.100–1 Cicero notes that the Egyptians deified animals for their utility—e.g. by worshipping the ibis, which destroyed snakes.

70.6 **Dryden . . . Absalom and Achitophel**] The reference is to John Dryden, 'Absalom and Achitophel', lines 100–3. This satirical poem discusses the oppression of the heathens and sacrilege against their gods under David's reign in Jerusalem: 'This [their gods having been disgraced under David's government] set the Heathen Priesthood in a flame;/For Priests of all Religions are the same' (lines 98–9).

70.24 **Petronius . . . parts of Italy**] The reference is to Petronius, *Satyricon*, §17. In his story, a character named Quartilla makes the following observation about gods in Italy: 'The gods walk abroad so commonly in our streets that it is easier to meet a god than a man.'

70.33 **Varro . . . Augustine . . . belief and assurance.[63]**] Footnote reference: Augustine, *City of God* 7.17. In *On the Latin Language* 5.10.57–74, Marcus Terentius Varro explains the naming of the gods. He discusses names related to sky, earth, fire, water, male, and female. In *City of God* Augustine rebukes Varro: 'Varro himself preferred to be sceptical about everything. . . . Thus he renders uncertain not only what he says about the uncertain gods, but also what he says about the certain gods.' Augustine's criticisms are expanded in *City of God* 3.4, 17; 4.31–2; 6.2.

70.37 **A heathen poet . . . believe it.[64]**] Footnote reference: Claudius Rutilius Namatianus, *Itinerarium* 1, lines 387–94. (For this title, see Cat., p. 269. The title is translated in the Loeb edn. as *A Voyage Home to Gaul*.) Rutilius writes: 'We pay the abuse due to the filthy race that infamously practices circumcision: a root of silliness they are: chill Sabbaths are after their own heart, yet their heart is chillier than their creed. Each seventh day is condemned to ignoble sloth, as 'twere an effeminate picture of a god fatigued. The other wild ravings from their lying bazaar methinks not even a child in his sleep could believe.' Rutilius is speaking of Jews, which he mentions by name (Judaeus); Hume's use of 'religious system' therefore may refer to the foundations of Christianity in Judaism.

Hume gives the title of Rutilius' work as 'iter'. The title on the edition he used would likely have been *Itinerarium*, meaning roughly 'Of the Journeys', though the work was also published under other titles (*De redito suo* and *De reditu suo itinerarium*).

71.6 **Spartian . . . genitalia."[65]**] Footnote reference: Spartian, *Life of Hadrian* 14.2. The Latin may be translated as 'It was at this time also that the Jews started a war, because they were not being permitted to mutilate their genitals' (i.e. circumcision was forbidden). According to Dio Cassius—probably a more reliable authority on this subject than Spartian—the beginning of the war was caused by the Jews' vexation over the transplantation of an alien religion into their city and the dedication of a temple to Jupiter Capitolinus on the site of the Jewish Temple of Jehovah (*Roman History* 69.12).

71.14 **imputation of deism]** Hume once noted that the 'cry of Deism' was brought against him when he was placed in candidacy as library-keeper to the Faculty of Advocates (4 Feb. 1752, to John Clephane, *Letters*, 1: 165; see also the letter of Mar. 1755, to William Strahan, *Journal of the History of Philosophy* 29 (1991)). 'Deism' is briefly mentioned in Hume's *Dialogues* 1.19.

71.15 **wife TERENTIA . . . his health.[66]]** Footnote reference: Cicero, *Epistulae ad familiares* [*The Letters to His Friends*] 14, ep. 7.1. In his letter (of 49 BC) to his wife Terentia[B] and cherished daughter Tullia, Cicero depicts undiluted bile as the cause of his ill health. After he quickly recovered, he fancied that some god had 'doctored him'. He asked Terentia and Tullia to pay tribute in their praise and worship to Apollo and Aesculapius. For pertinent texts that express Cicero's views on religion, freedom of belief, and the philosophical theologies of his predecessors, see *De natura deorum*, esp. 1.1–14, and *De divinatione* (and annotations immediately below). In general, Cicero seems opposed to superstition rather than religion.

71.19 **POMPEY's devotion . . . to auguries, dreams, and prophesies.[67]]** Footnote reference: Cicero, *De divinatione* 2.9.24; and see also 1.14.24–6. Hume's condensed reference (in the original) to Cicero—de Divin. lib. 2 c. 24—may be a reference, in common modern numbering, to 2.24 (or 2.9.24 in full numbering). This chapter mentions Pompey in the following context: 'Assuming that men knew the future it cannot in any wise be said—certainly not by the Stoics—that Pompey would not have taken up arms, that Crassus would not have crossed the Euphrates, or that Caesar would not have embarked upon the civil war. If so, then, the deaths that befell these men were not determined by Fate.' This passage is not precisely on Hume's topic, and does not discuss Pompey's devotion to auguries or whether his devotion was more sincere than Cicero's (as Hume states). However, *De divinatione* 1.14.24–6 also contains relevant material, and other passages in bk. 2—e.g. 36–7 (§§76–9) and 47 (§99)—help support the interpretation that Pompey was associated with soothsayers, trusted auguries, and the like. At one point, Quintus says to Cicero, 'Indeed how trustworthy were the auspices taken when you were augur!' (1.15.25). These passages suggest that Pompey trusted auguries, but not that his trust was more robust than Cicero's.

71.21 **reported of MILTON]** The report was made by Milton's nephew, pupil, and translator, Edward Phillips,[B] in 'The Life of Mr. John Milton', published in 1694. Phillips says of Milton 'That his Vein never happily flow'd, but from the *Autumnal Equinoctial* to the *Vernal*, and that whatever he attempted was never to his satisfaction' (*Letters of State*, p. xxxvi; cf. *Complete Poems and Major Prose*, p. 1035).

71.23 **AUGUSTUS . . . left foot.[68]]** Footnote references: Suetonius, *Lives of the Caesars* 2, 'Augustus' 90–2; Pliny the Elder, *Natural History* 2.5.24 (2.7 in older edns.). Suetonius reports that Augustus was superstitious, and took preventive measures to guard himself against the unusual and unknown. He was sensitive to thunder and lightning, and scrutinized his dreams. Suetonius adds that 'All through the spring his own dreams were very numerous and fearful, but idle and unfulfilled; during the rest of the year they were less frequent and more reliable'. Suetonius notes that Augustus regarded certain events as infallible omens: e.g. if he put his shoes on the wrong feet, he considered this action a bad sign. Pliny observes that some people venerate or fear fortune more than the divine. He points to Augustus as representative of this tendency, and recounts that Augustus told a story about how, on the day his army almost mutinied, he had put his left boot on the wrong foot.

72.1 **implicit faith . . . disbelief and conviction**] For other uses of the common expression 'implicit faith' in Hume's writings, see *Letters*, 1: 473 (to Gilbert Elliot of Minto); *History of England* (chs. 4, 40 [1: 188; 4: 152]); *THN* 1.4.2.56; 'Of Parties in General' 13; and 'Of National Characters', n. 2. For related philosophical and theological uses of the notion, see Hobbes, *Leviathan* 32.2; Locke, *Essay* 1.4.22; 2.33.17; 4.12.6; 4.17.4; François de la Mothe Le Vayer (1588–1672; French man of letters), *De la vertu des payens*, 'De Pyrrhon' (p. 298); Toland, *Christianity not Mysterious* 2.1 (p. 35); and Chambers, *Cyclopædia*, 'faith'. See also the use in George Campbell (1719–96; Aberdeen Professor of Divinity) in *A Dissertation on Miracles*, p. 77 (in commenting on Hume).

73.6 **the loves of MARS and VENUS**] Mars (or Ares), the impetuous and quarrelsome god of war and son of Jupiter and Juno, loved Venus (or Aphrodite), goddess of love and beauty, and became the father of her three children. This affair involved deception, as Venus was already married to Hephaestus, who discovered the duplicity and concocted a scheme to trap the two lovers in a hunting-net in his marriage-bed. After netting them, he invited all the gods as his witnesses to the affair. Venus had numerous romances. Some involved tender passion, especially her time with the lovely Adonis. See, further, ann. 38.20 (on *NHR* 2.4), regarding Mars, and ann. 50.7 (on *NHR* 5.4), regarding Mars and Venus.

73.6 **amorous frolics of JUPITER and PAN**] Although married to the jealous Juno, Jupiter had numerous love affairs with both goddesses and mortals. His female loves and the forms of concealment taken to hide from Juno included Danae (shower of gold), Alcmena (the impersonation of her husband), Leda (swan), Io (dark cloud), Callisto (Artemis), Europa (bull), and Antiope (satyr). Each love eventuated in offspring. The story of Io is illustrative: Jupiter assumed the form of a dark cloud to conceal his activities from Juno. When Jupiter sensed Juno's approach, he turned Io into a heifer, but Juno asked for the heifer as a gift. To avoid suspicion, Jupiter agreed, thereby initiating a series of attempts to conceal her identity and restore her true form. (See, further, on Jupiter's power and role, ann. 45.26 and 54.24, on *NHR* 4.5 and 6.8.)

Pan, the god of wood and fields, flocks and shepherds, enjoyed the dances and revels of the nymphs, several of whom he seduced. In a story told by Mercury, Pan wooed a chaste nymph named Syrinx. She darted away and called for help from her friends the water-nymphs near the bank of the river. When Pan put his arms around what he thought to be her form, he found that he had embraced a tuft of reeds. Pan's foremost amorous frolic was the successful seduction of Selene, which he achieved by disguising his black, goat-like appearance with white fleeces.

73.15 **prejudices of education]** See ann. 65.30 (on *NHR* 11.3). The term 'education' is often used by Hume to refer to the imbibing of second-hand opinion, with the consequence that a bias is transmitted or that proper learning is obstructed. See *NHR* 15.1; *THN* 1.3.9.17–19–1.3.10.1; *EHU* 8.11; 9.3; n. 20; 10.15; 12.4; *EPM* 3.36; 5.3–4. Cf. the strongly worded discussion of the 'prejudice of Custom and Education' in Glanvill, *Scepsis scientifica* 16–17; the less strongly worded statement in Robert Boyle (1627–91; English natural philosopher), *Reconcileableness of Reason and Religion* 4 (*Works*, 4: 164); and the more guarded presentation in Locke, *Essay* 1.2.27; 1.3.20; 2.21.69; 4.20.9.

73.18 **spleen]** Plausible meanings here are hatred, malice, and spite.

n. 69.1 TACITUS] Footnote reference: Tacitus, *Histories* 1.3. The passage from Tacitus may be translated: 'Besides the various misfortunes that affected human life, there were prodigies in the sky and on the earth, warning thunderbolts, and presages of things to come—joyful, grievous, doubtful, certain. Never has the Roman people been subject to greater devastation, or received more decisive signs, in proof that the gods' concern is not for our safety but for their vengeance.' Tacitus notes that Rome was once devastated by decline in personal virtue, religious observance, and social order, although many examples of virtue and personal strength were present in his age.

n. 69.4 **AUGUSTUS's quarrel with NEPTUNE]** See ann. 46.6 (on *NHR* 4.6, on 'AUGUSTUS . . . forbad NEPTUNE').

n. 69.8 **QUINTILIAN's exclamation, on account of the death of his children]** Footnote reference: Quintilian, *Institutes* 6, preface. Quintilian laments the loss of his wife and two sons. Although he blames fortune for the deaths and for his partial loss of the will to live, he reports that this twist of fortune instilled a powerful motivation to continue his life's work. Several of Quintilian's references to fortune involve impiety, whereas other references express a belief in the decrees of fate.

73.26 **LUCIAN tells us expressly,[70]]** Footnote reference: Lucian, *Lover of Lies* [*Philopseudes*] 3. Lucian cites religious beliefs of the Cretans, the Athenians, and the Thebans as examples of foolishly entertained falsehoods. Belief in these lies is so pervasive, he suggests, that those who do not believe them are subject to ridicule by their peers.

73.31 **LIVY[71] . . . incredulity of his age]** Footnote reference: Livy, *History* 10.40. In bks. 3 and 10 of this history, Livy refers to the religiousness of former times. In bk. 10, which alone is mentioned by Hume, the story is told of a young man solemnly considering a dispute over a day's chicken omens. Livy observes that the youth had been born in an age before it was popular to make light of the gods.

In *History* 3.20.5–6, Livy contrasts previous attitudes of respect for the gods with modern attitudes, in which persons hold the gods in contempt and use oaths and laws for personal benefit.

74.3 **STOICS . . . sage]** For relevant comments on the ideal wise person or sage, see Seneca, esp. 'On Tranquillity of Mind' 2.4 (in *Moral Essays*), and Epicurus (*Epicurus Reader*, texts 3.85–7; 4.128–31; 9; 16.53). For more on Hume's views, see *EHU* 5.1; *EPM* 7.16; and 'The Stoic' 5, 12–13, 18.

74.6 **nothing can be more pitiful . . . religious matters]** Stoicism provided many moral and religious guidelines, and offered a robust view of divine providence. While objecting to superstition and anthropomorphism, the Stoics restructured the traditional gods as powers of nature, and treated traditional legends as parables imparting truths about nature. For critical comments by Hume on the Stoics and religion, see ann. 48.26 (on *NHR* 4.14); *NHR* n. 75; and 'The Stoic'.

74.10 **PANÆTIUS . . . auguries and divinations.[72]]** Footnote reference: Cicero, *De divinatione* 1.3.6; 1.7. Panaetius wrote on the subject of divine providence. He was praised by Cicero, who reports that Panaetius differed with other Stoics on several central issues about divination, including those involving omens, prophecy, and astrology. Cicero comments that 'Panaetius . . . dared not say that there was no efficacy in divination, yet he did say that he was in doubt' (1.3.6). Cicero also reports (subsequent to the passages Hume cites) that Panaetius 'was the only one of the Stoics to reject the prophecies of the astrologers' (*De divinatione* 2.42.88). Cicero acknowledges that his treatment in *De divinatione* 2.41–7 derives from Panaetius.

74.12 **MARCUS ANTONINUS[73] . . . admonitions from the gods in his sleep]** Footnote reference: Marcus Aurelius, *Meditations with Himself* 1.17.8. (This title is translated *The Communings with Himself* in the Loeb edn.) Marcus Aurelius succeeded as emperor under the name Marcus Aurelius Antoninus. He is referred to by Hume here (but not elsewhere), as Marcus Antoninus. Like Epictetus, he maintained a Stoicism that provided for a close relation between the human and the divine. The passage cited in n. 73 contains this sentiment, and includes a description of certain remedies that were given or suggested in dreams. Marcus regarded loyalty to the imperial religion as a duty to the state. *Meditations with Himself* 7.54 and 10.1, 6 express similar views.

74.13 **EPICTETUS[74] . . . nowise concern us]** Footnote reference: Epictetus, *The Manual* (*Encheiridion*) 18. (Hume refers to ch. 17, the appropriate number in his edition; see Catalogue of Hume's References.) Epictetus, as presented by Arrian, held that God has given to all persons the means to become happy, but that life's events, including its disappointments and hardships, are expressions of the will of God. The chief matter is to have right opinions about the gods, and then to obey them. In ch. 18, Epictetus discusses the faint croak of a raven and how to interpret omens. The suggestion is made that one need not interpret a message as applying to one's *person*, but rather as it pertains to one's body, one's estate, one's wife, and the like.

74.17 **philosophical enthusiasm]** Elsewhere Hume mentions philosophers other than the Stoics when discussing philosophical enthusiasm and religious superstition. In *EPM*, 'A Dialogue', at its conclusion, Hume speaks of a philosophical enthusiasm such as that found in Diogenes of Sinope (4th century BC; Greek philosopher). When revising the *Treatise* to 'give as little Offence as possible', Hume reported that 'I was resolv'd not to be an Enthusiast, in Philosophy, while I was blaming other Enthusiasms' (2 Dec. 1737, to Henry Home, *New Letters*, 3).

For his comments on enthusiasm generally, see *EPM* 3.7; 3.24; 'Of Superstition and Enthusiasm' 3, 6–8; *Dialogues* 12; and *History of England*, chs. 40, 55, 57–62. In the latter, he writes that 'All enthusiasts, indulging themselves in rapturous flights, extasies, visions, inspirations, have a natural aversion to episcopal authority, to ceremonies, rites, and forms, which they denominate superstition, or beggarly elements, and which seem to restrain the liberal effusions of their zeal and devotion' (ch. 40 [4: 123]).

Commentary in the eighteenth century concentrated on religious enthusiasm. Trenchard defines 'enthusiasm' as quoted above, at ann. 53.11 (on *NHR* 6.3). Publications and sermons that cautioned about the follies of enthusiasm, understood as forceful but misguided pretence to inspiration, were common before and during Hume's lifetime. In his influential *Enthusiasmus Triumphatus*, Henry More called for reliance on reason and the development of a criterion to distinguish genuine from false inspiration in religion. Sect. 42 of this work treats 'Philosophical Enthusiasm'; see also sects. 1–8, 18–24, 28–32, 48–51, 55–61, 67. See also Locke's chapter 'Of Enthusiasm' (*Essay* 4.19).

74.20 **PLATO[76] . . . SOCRATES . . . rejecting such fables]** Footnote reference: Plato, *Euthyphro* 6A–D. Euthyphro observes that Zeus, who was believed to be 'the best and most just of the gods', prosecuted his own father. Socrates asks, 'Is not this, Euthyphro, the reason why I am being prosecuted, because when people tell such stories about the gods I find it hard to accept them?'

74.23 **subsequent dialogue,[77] . . . mortality of the soul]** Footnote reference: Plato, *Phaedo* 64A–65A, 68B–D, 70A–B, 80D–E. Socrates comments: 'We believe, do we not, that death is the separation of the soul from the body' (64C). Faced with the question whether the soul lives after this separation, as some believed, Socrates avoids giving a direct answer. Cebes asserts, in response to Socrates, that 'men are very prone to disbelief' about immortality (70A).

n. 78.1–6 **XENOPHON's conduct . . . ex edit. Leuncl.]** Footnote references: Xenophon, *Opera*, trans. Joannes Leunclavius (1625 edn.). *Anabasis*: (1) bk. 3, ch. 1, §§5–8; (2) bk. 3, ch. 1, §§11–14; (3) bk. 3, ch. 2, §9; (4) bk. 4, ch. 3, §§8–9; (5) bk. 4, ch. 5, §§3–4; (6) bk. 5, ch. 6, §§16–17; (7) bk. 5, ch. 6, §29; (8) bk. 6, ch. 1, §§19–24; (9) bk. 6, ch. 6, §36; (10) bk. 6, ch. 1, §§22–4; (11) bk. 6, ch. 2, §2; (12) bk. 6, ch. 4, §§12–22; (13) bk. 7, ch. 8, §§1–3. 'Ways and Means', 6.2–3. *Memorabilia*, *passim*. All page numbers given by Hume in n. 78 refer to the standardized numbers in the Leunclavius edn. Hume's original references were mistaken in two cases, both corrected in the present edn.: He listed p. 273 for what is either 372 or 373 or both; and after the 1st edn. an error was introduced when 932 was changed to 392 (and retained in all subsequent edns.). Hume here mentions the *Memorabilia* without listing specific pages or passages. He may be referring to passages such as that found in bk. 4, ch. 8, where Xenophon defends Socrates against charges that he was deluded to think that he had been divinely forewarned about his death. Xenophon's defence ignores Socrates' apparent claim to have been visited by a deity. In his essay 'Of the Populousness of Ancient Nations', n. 115, Hume praises the *Anabasis* as one of 'the two most authentic pieces of all Greek history', the other being Demosthenes' orations.

n. 78.18 **the Exta**] the bowels or entrails (organs in the abdominal cavity) of the victim sacrificed, which soothsayers used as the basis of auguries.

n. 78.26 NEWTON] On the nature of the Socinian and Arian 'heresies', see ann. 66.18 (on *NHR* 11.4). These labels were used to imply atheism, free-thinking, or unorthodox appeals, no less than heresy. Newton challenged orthodox interpretations of the Trinity and exhibited an acquaintance with Arian and Socinian writings. Although he maintained secrecy about his views so far as possible during his lifetime, Newton's work on 'the corruption of two texts of scripture' was revealing. He argued that passages in 1 John and 1 Timothy that had been used as a scriptural basis of the Trinitarian doctrine are corrupt texts. Newton explained his ideas in a letter of Nov. 1690 (*Correspondence*, 3: 129–44). He does not specifically propound the essentials of a Unitarian theology or explicitly commit himself to Arianism or Socinianism, but he concludes that the trinitarian corruptions of the scripture occurred in the fourth century while the Arian controversy persisted. He also finds that 'Catholicks are here found much more guilty of these corruptions than the hereticks' (*Correspondence*, 3: 138).

William Whiston (1667–1752), Newton's friend and successor at Cambridge in the Mathematical Chair (Lucasian Professor), resisted the label Arian, but it became difficult to escape, and he was, as a result, relieved of his university chair. It became increasingly difficult to protect Newton against the charge of Arianism, inasmuch as Whiston had publicly aligned his views with Newton's. In *A Collection of Authentick Records Belonging to the Old and New Testament*, Whiston commented on the 'pretended *Arian Heresy*' for which he was 'Banished and Persecuted'. He maintained that he had been banished for 'the very same Christian Doctrines which the great Sir *I. N.* had discovered and embraced many Years before me' (2: 1080).

n. 78.26 LOCKE] Locke was labelled a Socinian (and deist) shortly after publication of his *Essay*. In his formulations of basic Christian doctrines, the Trinity does not appear to be essential. He maintains that 'Son of God' in the gospels stands for *Messiah*, and that the fundamentals of Christian belief are that there is one supreme creator God, that Jesus is the Messiah, and that obedience is owed to the laws of

God, as transmitted through Jesus. Locke notes that the first of these fundamentals is shared with Judaism, whereas the other two express the new covenant.

Innumerable publications pertaining to Locke's Socinianism, Arianism, and deism had been issued by the time Hume wrote *NHR*. Edward Stillingfleet (1635–99; English theologian and bishop of Worcester) and John Edwards (1637–1716; Calvinistic divine) attacked Locke in prominent exchanges, on grounds that he compromised the doctrine of the Trinity. Edwards accused Locke of Socinianism in 1695 in the first published work to advance the charge (*Some Thoughts concerning the Several Causes and Occasions of Atheism*, which criticized Locke's *The Reasonableness of Christianity*). Locke replied with *A Vindication of the Reasonableness of Christianity, &c. from Mr. Edwards's Reflections* (1695), and Edwards responded in 1696 with *Socinianism Unmask'd*. Locke then published *A Second Vindication of the Reasonableness of Christianity, &c.* in 1697 (the same year in which Stillingfleet criticized Locke). In both works Locke protested Edwards's line of interpretation, and denied in firm and caustic terms that he was a Socinian: 'Socinianism then is not the fault of the book, whatever else it be. For I repeat it again, there is not one word of socinianism in it' (*A Vindication of the Reasonableness of Christianity*, 7: 167).

Nonetheless, Edwards's attack was influential, and Locke was regarded as a Socinian by diverse interpreters for many years thereafter (see John C. Higgins-Biddle (ed.), Locke, *Reasonableness of Christianity*, introduction, pp. xlii ff.). For example, John Milner devoted Part 2 of his *An Account of Mr. Lock's Religion* (1700) to the question of 'whether Socinianism be justly Charged upon Mr. Lock' (title-page). Noting Locke's rejection of the charge, Milner decided to leave the answer to his question to the reader, but came to the firm conclusion that 'when he alledges any place where Christ is said or confess'd to be the *Son of God*, he interprets it of his being the Messiah' (pp. 183–4).

n. 78.26 CLARKE] Two years after Whiston was stripped of his chair, Samuel Clarke, a friend of both Newton and Whiston, published *The Scripture Doctrine of the Trinity* (1712). He declared the Athanasian Creed to be unscriptural, a conclusion he reached by analysing more than 1,250 texts of the New Testament pertaining to the Father, the Son, and the Holy Spirit. He determined that only 'God' and 'Father' are used synonymously. Clarke argued that the Father alone is self-existent, underived, unoriginated, and independent; the Son is divine only in so far as divinity is derivative from the Father, and the Holy Spirit is subordinate in both dominion and authority. Issues surrounding Arian and Socinian ideas are discussed by Clarke throughout *Scripture Doctrine of the Trinity* (see esp. pt. 2, §§ 2, 5, 9–12, 14, 18, 23, 34–43). He argues that many theological notions are compatible with Arianism, and that some theologians have fallen into Sabellianism or Socinianism (Clarke seems to equate the two) by being too eager to avoid Arian errors.

Clarke's work was sternly criticized as Arian and Latitudinarian. He was arraigned before the Lower House of Convocation, where he was condemned in 1714 for assertions about the doctrine of three persons that were contrary to the faith, as received by the Reformed Church of England. A partial recantation that mentioned the need to avoid heresy saved him from condemnation by the Upper House. These events embroiled him in trinitarian controversies for the remainder of his life.

75.3 **doctrine of a future state]** The connection between providence and a future state (immortality) had been treated by many writers of Hume's period. The two topics are ostensibly treated together in *EHU* 11. For Hume's views on the possibility of a future state, see his essay 'Of the Immortality of the Soul' 11, where he writes that, 'if any purpose of nature be clear, we may affirm, that the whole scope and intention of man's creation, so far as we can judge by natural reason, is limited to the present life'. In *Dialogues* 12.10, Hume has his characters debate the proposition that 'a future state is so strong and necessary a security to morals, that we never ought to abandon or neglect it'.

75.3 **give any attention.[79]]** Footnote reference: Cicero, *Pro Cluentio* 61.171. In this 'Defence of Cluentius', Cicero comments that death for a scoundrel might be a gift, relieving a misery more painful than death. Death has not done the person harm 'unless perhaps we are led by silly stories to suppose that he is enduring the torments of the damned in the nether world'.

75.4 **SALLUST[80] . . . CÆSAR . . . same language in the open senate]** Footnote reference: Sallust, *War with Catiline* 51.20. Sallust writes about an oration of Caesar before the Senate in which he portrayed death as putting 'an end to all mortal ills' and as leaving 'no room either for sorrow or for joy'. Caesar notes that death in certain circumstances of grief and wretchedness is a relief. There is no specific mention of a future state.

n. 81.1 **CICERO . . . SENECA . . . JUVENAL . . . accounts of a future state]** Footnote references: Cicero, *Tusculan Disputations* 1.5–6; Seneca, *Ad Lucilium epistulae morales* 24 ('On Despising Death', esp. §18); Juvenal, *Satires* 2, esp. lines 149–52. In *Tusculan Disputations*, the figures *A* and *M* discuss whether death is wretched. Stories such as that of the three-headed Cerberus in the lower world are recounted. *A* asserts that he is not so deranged as to believe these stories and does not understand why philosophers treat them at length. Seneca's epistle 'On Despising Death' also discusses the foolishness exhibited by Epicurus when harping upon tales of the world below, such as those of Cerberus. Seneca maintains that the fear of death can be conquered, although he refuses to agree that 'the terrors of the world below are idle'. Juvenal asserts that even most boys do not believe in these tales.

n. 81.3 **LUCRETIUS . . . his master]** The mention of Lucretius exalting his master (Epicurus) is an allusion to *De rerum natura* 1 (lines 62–79) and possibly 2 (lines 55–61).

n. 81.4 **CEPHALUS in PLATO . . . became old and infirm]** Footnote reference: Plato, *Republic* 1, 330D–331A. Cephalus is presented as an older man who realizes that, as one draws nearer death, new fears and cares enter the mind. He expresses concern that there might be truth in the tales of a world below and punishment for deeds done in this life.

75.9 **chief business of the sceptical philosophers . . . artifice of COTTA]** In *De natura deorum* 3.17–20 (see also 1.6.15–1.7.17; 3.8.20–1), Cicero presents Gaius Aurelius Cotta as a proponent of the Academic school who criticizes other theologies as worthless or fatal to religion. 'Artifice' here refers to a manœuvre or device of debate—a 'method of reasoning'—that is rhetorically skilful, but not necessarily a proper means for reaching truth. It is a device used to prove that the gods do not exist (or, possibly, if they do exist, that they are not just). Cotta starts with major deities in the pantheon such as Jupiter and Neptune, and argues that if they are gods, then their relatives must also be gods. If these relatives are gods, then their relatives too must be gods. Cotta then proceeds to discuss the lowest deities, who were not commonly accepted as authentic by learned persons. He argues that if one rejects the lower deities, one must reject the higher as well. See the annotation immediately below.

75.16 **CARNEADES . . . method of reasoning.[82]]** Footnote reference: Sextus Empiricus, *Against the Physicists* 1.182–90 (alternatively, and commonly, cited as *Adversus mathematicos* 9.182–90). Hume cites *Adversus mathematicos*, bk. 8; but by both traditional and contemporary standards, his bk. nos. for Sextus are incorrect. An explanation of the problem is provided in ann. on *NHR* n. 28. Carneades' reasoning, which is closely related to the artifice of Cotta, is described by Sextus: 'If Zeus is a God, . . . Poseidon also, being his brother, will be a God. And if Poseidon is a God, Achelous, too, will be a God; and if Achelous, Neilos; and if Neilos, every river as well; and if every river, the streams also will be Gods; and if the streams, the torrents; but the streams are not Gods; neither, then, is Zeus a God. But if there had been Gods, Zeus would have been a God. Therefore, there are no Gods.' Sextus reports that Carneades propounds other arguments of the same form. Cicero discusses Carneades' objectives in the parts of *De natura deorum* 3.17.43 ff. mentioned in the previous annotation: 'These arguments were advanced by Carneades, not with the object of establishing atheism, . . . but in order to prove the Stoic theology worthless.'

75.19 ***scholastic* one]** See ann. 66.23 (on *NHR* 11.5), regarding scholastic religion.

SECTION 13: Impious Conceptions of the Divine Nature in Popular Religions of Both Kinds

77.1 **primary religion . . . from an anxious fear of future events]** See anns. 38.16 and 39.4 (on *NHR* 2.4 and 2.5, on the role of hopes, fears, and terror).

78.5 **XENOPHON,[83] in praise of SOCRATES]** Footnote reference: Xenophon, *Memorabilia* 1.1.19. Xenophon presents Socrates as differing from his contemporaries in asserting that the gods are omniscient, ubiquitous, and communicative with humans.

78.9 **strain of philosophy[84] much above the conception of his countrymen]** Footnote reference: Lucian, *Hermotimus* 81. Lucian does not discuss Socrates' view of the gods as a strain of philosophy above his countrymen's conception (see the previous annotation), but he does discuss the hypothesis that the gods are ubiquitous. Lycinus the Sceptic tells a story of a boy in philosophical training who spoke of God as not being in heaven, but as pervading everything. The view was commonly considered laughable.

78.12 **HERODOTUS . . . *envy* to the gods]** For a passage in Herodotus that attributes envy to the gods, see *History* 7.46: 'The god is seen to be envious therein, after he has given us but a taste of the sweetness of living.' A similar ascription is found in *History* 1.32.

78.16 **TIMOTHEUS . . . hymn to DIANA . . . celebrate."[85]]** Footnote reference: Plutarch, *Moralia*, 'On Superstition' 10, 170A–B. Plutarch reports that Timotheus, in the song (or hymn) sung at Athens, called Artemis (Diana to the Romans) an 'ecstatic Bacchic frantic fanatic'. The song-writer Cinesias then stood up and exclaimed, 'May you have a daughter like that'. Plutarch submits that the superstitious tremble at and dread the gods.

79.8 **LUCIAN[86] observes, that a young man, who reads the history of the gods]** Footnote reference: Lucian, *Menippus, or the Descent into Hades* 3. In this dialogue, Menippus discusses his decision to descend into the underworld:

> While I was a boy, when I read Homer and Hesiod about wars and quarrels, not only of the demigods but of the gods themselves, . . . I thought that all these things were right. . . . But when I came of age, I found that the laws contradicted the poets and forbade adultery, quarrelling, and theft. So I was plunged into great uncertainty, . . . for the gods would never have committed adultery and quarrelled with each other, I thought, unless they deemed these actions right, and the lawgivers would not recommend the opposite course unless they supposed it to be advantageous.

n. 87.8 **no enemy to CHRISTIANITY . . . the Chevalier RAMSAY]** Footnote reference: Andrew Michael Ramsay, *Philosophical Principles of Natural and Revealed Religion*, 2: 403–6. (Hume mistranscribed or altered several features of Ramsay's text. However, no item deprived Ramsay's text of its sense or made an unintelligible formal error. See n. 6 in the Editorial Appendix to this volume, p. 177.)

Ramsay's ambitious two-volume work was, he said, an attempt to establish two primary theses:

> [1] That the great principles of *Natural Religion* are founded upon the most invincible evidence; and that the essential doctrines of *Revealed Religion* are perfectly conformable to *Reason*. . . .
>
> [2] That vestiges of all the principal doctrines of the Christian religion are to be found in the monuments, writings, or mythologies of all nations, ages, and religions; and that these vestiges are emanations of the primitive, antient, universal religion of mankind, transmitted from the beginning of the world by the Antidiluvians to the Postdiluvian

patriarchs, and by them to their posterity that peopled the face of the earth. (*Philosophical Principles*, 1: iv–v)

In the preface to his other major work, *Travels of Cyrus*, Ramsay says that he intends to prove 'two principal points':

The first is to prove against the Atheists the existence of a supreme Deity, . . . [and] to shew that the earliest [theological] opinions of the most knowing and civiliz'd nations come nearer the truth than those of latter ages. . . . The second point is to shew, in opposition to the Deists, that the principal doctrines of reveal'd religion, concerning the states of innocence, corruption and renovation, are as ancient as the world. (*Travels of Cyrus*, 1: xvii–xix)

Hume's estimate of Ramsay's views is given in more than one item of correspondence. See esp. his letter of 26 Aug. 1737, to Michael Ramsay, in T. Kozanecki, 'Dawida Hume's nieznane listy w zbiorach Muzeum Czartoryskich [Polska]'.

n. 87.10 **doctrines which freethinkers scruple]** Bayle, Shaftesbury, Collins, Toland, and Charles Blount were principal free-thinkers. Des Maizeaux, Bayle's intellectual heir, may have been viewed by Hume as a promoter of free-thinking. The term itself had gained notoriety from Collins's *Discourse of Free-Thinking* (1713). It was applied to deists as well as heretics and atheists. Religious free-thinking was attacked by Richard Bentley (1662–1742; English classical scholar and Master of Trinity College, Cambridge), *Remarks Upon a Late Discourse of Free-Thinking*; Jonathan Swift (1667–1745; Anglo-Irish poet and satirist, dean of St Patrick's Cathedral, Dublin), *Mr. C----ns's Discourse of Free-Thinking* (esp. pp. 3–19); and Benjamin Hoadly (1676–1761; English bishop and pamphleteer), *Queries Recommended to the Authors of the late* Discourse of Free-Thinking. Berkeley, who disapproved of Collins, attacked free-thinking in contributions to the *Guardian* and in *Dialogues between Hylas and Philonous*; later he used these materials as a basis for a criticism of free-thinking in *Alciphron* 1. Related issues arose in France, often as a result of clandestine philosophical literature; see John S. Spink, *French Free-Thought from Gassendi to Voltaire*, and Ira O. Wade, *The Clandestine Organization and Diffusion of Philosophic Ideas in France from 1700 to 1750*.

n. 87.15 **pharisaical]** like the Pharisees in being rigid and strict in doctrine and ritual, emphasizing outward displays of religion; hypocritical.

n. 87.60 ***Arminian* and *Molinist* schemes]** Arminianism was initially formulated *c.* 1610 by the Protestant clerical followers of Jacobus Arminius (1560–1609; Dutch Reformed theologian, properly Jakob Hermandszoon). Arminian theology teaches that Calvinist theories of predestination, irresistible grace, and election are false. Adherents, including Hugo Grotius, emphasize human free will and hold that grace is won by human co-operation and can be lost. God is said to have foreknowledge of all human sin, but neither to will nor to predestine the sin. Various Protestant groups were widely regarded as Arminian in the seventeenth and eighteenth centuries.

Molinism derives from the theology of Luis de Molina (1535–1600; Spanish Jesuit theologian). His theological reflections on divine grace and human free will were controversial, and stimulated a response from the Dominicans. There ensued a protracted conflict between the two orders. Molinism attempted to reconcile human free will with doctrines of divine grace, providence, prerogative, and foreknowledge. Molinists held that God has comprehensive foreknowledge, but that grace is made effective by the assent of the recipient's will.

Ramsay touches only briefly on the two theologies mentioned by Hume. He maintains that they misunderstand human freedom: 'The Molinist, Arminian and mitigated scheme about prescience leads to fatality, and is destructive of liberty, as well as that of the Thomists, Jansenists, and predestinarians' (*Philosophical Principles*, 1: 175).

Hume devotes parts of ch. 46, the Appendix to the Reign of James I, and ch. 51 of his *History of England* to the topic of 'Arminianism'. He discusses (1) 'Vorstius, the disciple of Arminius', who was burned by the king as a heretic 'for his blasphemies and atheism'; (2) the social reception of Arminianism in Britain; and (3) the impact of the fact that James I came 'towards the end of his reign, to favour the milder theology of Arminius' (5: 46, 131).

n. 87.62 **a kind of ORIGENISM**] Ramsay rejects central doctrines in virtually every major school or system of theology, including Origenism, Molinism, and Arminianism. 'Origenism' should probably be understood here, in light of Hume's comments, as (1) a cosmology of the 'pre-existence of the souls of men and beasts', (2) an interpretation of the nature of the voluntary fall of both angels and humans, and (3) a theology of divine transformation and restoration. From this perspective, Ramsay could be said to defend 'a kind of Origenism': He shares some of Origen's beliefs regarding the fall of the angels, the pre-existent souls of humans and their redemption, Adam's transgression, and human freedom. Ramsay also shares with Origen the conviction that Christian belief was compatible with Greek pagan belief and philosophical thought. In addition, Ramsay quotes a lengthy passage from Origen's *Contra Celsum* on 'the truly wise in all religions' (*Philosophical Principles*, 2: 55).

However, Ramsay also rejects many doctrines in Origenism, even within the slice of the theory he retains. For example, he rejects critical features of the 'Origenian sense' of the nature and condition of the pre-existent souls and of restitution. He condemns this Origenist thesis as an 'absurd system' that destroys 'articles of faith' (*Philosophical Principles*, 2: 245, and appendix on 'the condemnation of Origen'). In the preface to *Travels of Cyrus* (1: xxii), Ramsay considers accusations by his critics that he follows Origen: 'The Author introduces in his last book two persons of very different characters, a Philosopher and a Prophet; the one employs the powers of reason against incredulity, the other imposes silence on all reasonings by a supernatural authority. This is the only use which the Author would make of the opinions of Origen.'

80.6 **"Sunt superis sua jura."[88]**] Footnote reference: Ovid, *Metamorphoses* 9, line 500. Ovid observes that the gods have been incestuous, and then offers the statement quoted by Hume, which means 'but the gods are a law unto themselves'. It is thus futile, Ovid says, to compare human and divine customs.

SECTION 14: Bad Influence of Popular Religions on Morality

81.0 **Bad Influence of Popular Religions on Morality**] James Boswell (1740–95; Scottish man of letters) reported that Hume said on his deathbed that 'the morality of every religion was bad' (*Boswell in Extremes, 1776–1778*, p. 11). However, questions have been raised about Boswell's report. On the reliability of the story, see Schwartz, 'Boswell and Hume: The Deathbed Interview'.

Hume's comments on the monkish virtues at *NHR* 10.2 and *EPM* 9.3 have been widely quoted, and he elsewhere offers sundry observations on the bad influence of religion on morality: e.g. see *Dialogues* 12.12 on 'the proper office of religion'.

81.8 **the *Sadder***] The *Sadder* (or *Saddar, Sad Dar*, or *Sad-der*) sets forth the religious precepts of Zoroaster. The name 'Sadder' refers to 'a hundred subjects', or topics—called doors—that treat a variety of religious duties, practices, penalties, rituals, and explanations. Each section provides a separate, elementary guidance in religious understanding and observation. For example, the text covers, in five of its 100 sections, the necessity of unwavering faith in the religion, the prohibition of sin, the nature of good works, why high-priests must be obeyed, and reasons for wearing the sacred thread-girdle. In nn. 39 and 46 (see anns. above), Hume cites as his source of information Thomas Hyde, *Historia religionis veterum Persarum . . . Atque Magorum liber Sad-der*. The title of the *Sadder* in Hyde is *The Sadder book of the Magians, Containing the Precepts and Canons of Zoroaster: For the use of the Religion of the Magians and of all those Faithful*; however, the *Sadder* is probably a relatively late compilation, well after Magian influence. For Hume's youthful notes on the *Sadder* in Hyde, see his 'Early Memoranda' (§§191–2).

81.8 **the *Pentateuch***] the first five books of the Bible, which contain numerous precepts of morality. At *EHU* 10.40 Hume also cites the Pentateuch for its reports of miracles.

81.15 **They only created a dictator,[89] in order to drive a nail**] Footnote reference: Livy, *History* 7.3.3–9. The translation of 'Dictator clavis figendæ causa' (n. 89) is 'the dictator for the driving in of the nail'. Livy reports that 'The elders recollected that a pestilence had once been allayed by the dictator's driving a nail. Induced thereto by this superstition, the senate ordered the appointment of a dictator to drive the nail. Lucius Manlius Imperiosus was appointed.' Livy is likely reporting events in 363 BC. The first act of driving a nail may have occurred under the dictator Quintus Servilius Priscus in 435 BC.

81.18 **In ÆGINA . . . HERODOTUS,[90]**] Footnote reference: Herodotus, *History* 6.91. Aegina was a leading commercial state until its eclipse by Athens. Herodotus reports how a faction of the wealthier Aeginetans defeated a revolt of the common people led by Nicodromus. Hume's recounting of the story of the 'miserable fugitive' closely follows Herodotus.

81.31 **The sublime prologue of ZALEUCUS's laws[91] ... LOCRIANS]** Footnote reference: Diodorus Siculus, *Historical Library* 12.20–21. Zaleucus,[B] the lawgiver in Locri and a student of Pythagoras, won fame for authoring the Locrian Code. According to Diodorus, Zaleucus declared in the Prologue that it is necessary for the inhabitants to accept the view that the gods are responsible for cosmic order and the goods of life, and that citizens should keep their souls untainted by evil because the gods most highly prize just and honourable practices (and not sacrifices or costly gifts).

82.15 **excessive penances of the *Brachmans* and *Talapoins*]** 'Brachman', 'brahman' (as it was spelled in the 1757 edn. of *NHR*), 'brachmin', or 'brahmin' refers to the hereditary class of priests and the teachers of the Vedas. They enjoyed high prestige in religious and secular affairs, yet lived austere and solitary lives, sometimes in caves and deserts (living only on herbs, roots, and fruits). They often had poor apparel, were under mandates to abstain from carnal pleasures, and were required to engage in fasts. Vedism or Brahminism dominated parts of the subcontinent of India in the second and first millennium BC. When early Vedism combined with other spiritual movements in India into what is now commonly called Hinduism, traditions of brachmans as priests survived. Several books on brachmans were available in Britain during Hume's lifetime, and many writers on religious subjects punctuated their work with references to brachmans.

Talapoins are Buddhist priests or monks who lead exemplary and devout lives. Well-respected Talapoins go with bare feet and bare heads at all times—and follow rigid standards of temperance and rules of chastity. The most rigorous lived like mendicant friars, partially surviving on gifts from others. European travellers to India, Siam, Burma, and other countries with Buddhist adherents had reported on the Talapoins. Two contributions to the *Guardian* of 1713 mention Talapoins: no. 39, by George Berkeley, and no. 3, by either Richard Steele (1672–1729; Irish essayist) or Berkeley. Both contributions rely on comments on the Talapoins found in Collins, *A Discourse of Free-Thinking*. The contribution in *Guardian* no. 3 gives the following description: 'The *Talapoins* of *Siam* have *a Book of Scripture* written by *Sommonocodom*, who, the *Siamese* say, was *born of a Virgin*, and was *the God expected by the Universe*' (*Guardian*, ed. Stephens, p. 49); see further, Bayle, *Dictionary*, 'Sommona-Codom'.

Cudworth, a writer Hume had read on matters of religion when making notes in his 'Early Memoranda', mentions a discussion in Strabo of the 'ancient Indian Brachmans' (*True Intellectual System of the Universe* 1.4.32 [1: 504]). Strabo treats Brachmans as one of two groups within the philosopher caste; he gives descriptions of their life-style, course of studies, and role in the state (*Geography* 15.1.39, 59, 61, 66, 70). Thomas Burnet discusses brachmans and even refers to '*Siamese*

Brachmans' ('Brachmanes Siamenes'). Burnet is presuming a Siamese Empire that assimilated Indian Brachmans. His discussion points to the various understandings of both 'Brachmans' and 'Siamese religion' at work in European discussions of the seventeenth and eighteenth centuries (*Archæologiæ philosophicæ* 1.3 and Appendix, which includes a list of sources).

82.16 ***Rhamadan* of the TURKS . . . more severe than the practice of any moral duty]** The Ramadân is the ninth month of the year in the Moslem lunar calendar. It is of sacred value because the Koran (or Qur'ân) was reported to have been revealed during this month. In commemoration of the revelation, the faithful adhere throughout the month to a fast during daylight hours (exempting soldiers and the ill). Drinking, eating, smoking, and marital relations are not permitted during these hours. Acts of observance have merit only if undertaken willingly and are free of self-interest. Intentional breaking of the fast carries penalties. However, the period need not be gloomy or sombre. Ramadân nights can be joyous occasions during which family and friends gather for food, singing, and light entertainment. In the 'Preliminary Discourse' to his *The Koran, Commonly called The Alcoran of Mohammed*, Sale presented a meticulous discussion of the obligation to fast and its roots in 'the express command of the *Koran*' (sect. 4, p. 112).

82.20 **four Lents of the MUSCOVITES]** See ann. 54.22 (on *NHR* 6.7, on 'Muscovites'). Unlike those Christians who engaged in the practice of Lent once a year, the Muscovites (or Russian Eastern Orthodox) recognized four Lents in which priests played a leading role. Associated with the Lent recognized in the West were the fast of the Assumption of the Virgin or the Lent of the Mother of God, which lasted two weeks, the fast before St Peter's Day or St Peter's Lent, and the fast before Christmas, from 14 November until the night before Christmas. Some travellers reported protracted church services and demanding practices of fasting. English seaman Richard Chancelor reported first-hand on the four fasts of the Muscovites: 'The first beginnes with them, at the time that our Lent beginnes. The second is called amongst them, the fast of S. Peter. The third is taken from the day of the Virgin Marie. And the fourth, and last, beginnes upon S. Philips day. But as we begin our Lent upon Wensday, so they begin theirs upon the Sunday' (in Richard Hakluyt, *The Principall Navigations*, pp. 290–1).

83.26 **BOMILCAR . . . historian[92] remarks]** Footnote reference: Diodorus Siculus, *Historical Library* 20, esp. 43–4. Bomilcar negotiated a treaty between Agathocles and some Sicilian cities. He attempted to exploit a situation created by Agathocles' invasion of Carthage (310–308 BC). Hoping to make himself tyrant in Carthage, Bomilcar attempted a revolution and was supported by approximately 500 confederates and 1,000 mercenaries. However, he received no popular support, and the Carthaginians successfully resisted the attempt. Whether Bomilcar had legitimate grievances or attempted revolution from sheer ambition is uncertain, as is whether he failed in some of his plans because of delays and postponements that he chose out of superstition. Diodorus reports on how the Carthaginians put down Bomilcar's attempt to become tyrant, and also that Bomilcar was among those who, when acting lawlessly, are superstitious and tend to delay rather than take decisive action.

83.31 **Catiline . . . terrors made him seek new inventions of this kind;[93]]** Footnote references: Cicero, *Against Catiline* 1.6.16 and 1.9.24; Sallust, *War with Catiline* 22. Catiline entered into a conspiracy to plunder Rome and assassinate the consuls. Cicero helped foil the plan, assailing Catiline in the Senate and the Forum. Both Cicero and Sallust refer cryptically to religious innovations by Catiline. The clearest example is Sallust's description of Catiline as conducting solemn rites for the purpose of inducing faithfulness and requiring that an oath be taken among the conspirators. One ritual compelled those who participated to taste bowls of human blood mixed with wine.

SECTION 15: General Corollary

85.1 **stupidity]** incomprehension (from insensitivity or lack of awareness). Cf. the usage at *NHR* 6.1; and *EPM* 6.16 and Appx. 4.3.

85.20 **draughts of life, according to the poet's fiction . . . each hand of Jupiter]** This account is found in Homer, *Iliad* 24, lines 528–33. Two urns are said to stand on the floor of the palace of Zeus, one filled with his allocation of ills (evils) and the other filled with his allocation of blessings (goods). Plato mentions these lines in Homer as he discusses the role of the gods as causes of good and evil (*Republic* 2, 379d–f). At *THN* 1.3.10.5, Hume discusses the thesis that poets 'tho' liars by profession . . . endeavour to give an air of truth to their fictions'.

85.31 **mediocrity]** middle or mean state or condition between two extremes (possibly alluding to Aristotle's doctrine of the mean); middle course in action.

86.5 **universal propensity . . . human nature]** Cf. Hume's Introduction in *NHR* to this passage.

86.21 **sick men's dreams]** possibly an allusion to Horace, *Ars poetica* 1–23, where the same expression appears. Horace's context—comparing idle fancies in books that join disparate elements to 'sick men's dreams'—may be related to Hume's discussion in *THN* 2.2.8.17 and *DP* 4.10–14 on foreign elements inappropriately conjoined.

87.4 **The whole is a riddle, an ænigma, an inexplicable mystery . . . the frailty of human reason]** Cf. the penultimate paragraph in Hume's *Dialogues* and his comment on mysteries at *EHU* 8.36. In *THN* and *EHU*, Hume suggests that human understanding is not fitted for such abstruse subjects. The language of 'mystery' could possibly be an oblique reference to the mysteries of pagan religion, church doctrine about mysteries and revealed truth, philosophical enquiry into the mysteries of religion, and the like. Toland, in addressing such issues in *Christianity not Mysterious*, used the language of mystery beyond reason.

EDITORIAL APPENDIX: EMENDATIONS AND SUBSTANTIVE VARIANTS

Hume regularly modified *DP* and *NHR* as he issued new editions from 1757 until his death in 1776. This Appendix explains and records substantive variations in the editions of these two works—that is, changes in the exact wording of the text from the 1757 edition to the 1777 edition. It also explains how these changes have been used by the editor to create the critical text of this edition.[1]

Hume's many formal, or 'accidental', changes are recorded only as necessary for a particular purpose. They are listed in full in an electronic edition to be published separately. These accidentals involve changes in typographic convention, spelling, and punctuation, and are recorded in this Appendix whenever their history has a bearing on the editor's emendation of Hume's text. This Appendix records all editorial changes, whether substantive or accidental, that have been made in the copytext—that is, the basic document for the construction of the edited critical text. Interested readers can therefore determine exactly how the critical text differs, both substantively and formally, from the copytext on which it is based. They can also trace every substantive variation between the original text and every other edition authorized by Hume.

This Appendix is divided into three parts. Part 1 contains a brief explanation of the kinds of changes made in constructing the critical text. Part 2 lists 'unreported' changes and systematic emendations. Part 3 is a combined register of non-systematic emendations and substantive variants. This classification of emendations as either systematic or non-systematic creates three (imperfectly distinguishable) forms of textual change, each reported separately:

1. Systematic changes of form made silently.
2. Systematic changes of form made collectively and reported by kind.
3. Non-systematic changes made individually and reported individually in the Register of Non-Systematic Emendations and Substantive Variants.

[1] A text is critical if and only if one or more editors has exercised principled and systematic judgement about each word and every form of words and punctuation in the text, in light of the historical and textual evidence that can be marshalled. A critical edition includes appropriate supplementary material such as an argued explanation of the choice of copytext(s), a history of the text(s), a complete list of substantive (and critical accidental) variants, and a list of and defence of textual emendations.

Part 2 of this Appendix, on systematic changes handled as a group, treats (1) and (2). Part 3 (non-systematic changes handled individually) treats (3).

Systematic changes involve groups of identical or very similar changes that occur at more than one place. As a rough rule, systematic changes—by comparison to non-systematic changes—are of no importance in interpreting the text. All non-systematic emendations are reported in the Register in the form of shaded entries. Full information about modifications made by Hume (or his printer) is supplied in the Register for each non-systematic change. Reference numbers are to page (or note no.) and line in the text, not to section and paragraph.

PART 1

THE RATIONALE OF THE CRITICAL TEXT

Hume prepared nine editions of *NHR* and *DP*. An editor must select one among these as the copytext. As the copytext is emended, it is converted into the critical text. The resultant text normally resembles the copytext more than it resembles any other text of the same work, but in principle an eclectic critical text can deviate widely from the copytext.

No edition of a work in Hume's corpus is sufficiently flawless that corrections are unnecessary. Even if an edition were flawless by the standards operative at the time it was produced, printing practice evolved throughout Hume's lifetime in ways of which he was undoubtedly aware. An editor must be alert to this evolution as well as to Hume's judgements about it.

Choice and Treatment of the Copytext

Bibliographical scholars have often attached great weight to the difference between substantive and accidental variants. If it is known that an author carefully attended to the text in its progressive editions, it can be assumed that substantive changes are authorial. However, changes in accidentals can often be attributed to the printer or some other non-authorial source. From this perspective, it is advisable to make the first or another early edition the copytext. An editor is then free, in the absence of contrary evidence, to incorporate changes in substantives while excluding changes in accidentals.

However, there are justified exceptions to this editorial strategy. The primary exception is a work whose substantives and accidentals are known to have been extensively revised by the author. The two works in this volume fit this description. Hume took extraordinary care, exhibiting the commitment of a devoted hobbyist, in modifying his substantives, accidentals, and style. As the work matured, he removed archaic spellings and made many changes that it would be inappropriate for an editor to dismiss as if they had never transpired (see the Register below).

Even if some changes in accidentals were made at the press, Hume had ample opportunity through the later editions to correct such changes. We can therefore assume that he sanctioned, or at least condoned, these modifications.

There is no reason in Hume's case to make a virtue of retaining accidentals that he clearly wished to avoid or to alter. As bibliographical scholars now recognize, the appropriate standard for scholarly modification of the text is evidence to warrant the changes made, not a theory that predetermines the changes.

The copytext for *NHR* and *DP*—and for almost all titles in Hume's *Essays and Treatises on Several Subjects* (*ETSS*) in the Clarendon Hume—is the 1772 edition. The general editors selected it for several reasons. This edition is the culmination of more than two decades of diligent attention by Hume, his printer, and even his booksellers. Hume's correspondence regarding the 1772 edition provides a record of his attention to, and satisfaction with, this edition that is unparalleled for any other edition of *ETSS*. He wrote to his printer, William Strahan, shortly before publication of this edition, that 'my philosophical Pieces' have been 'perusd . . . carefully five times over'. During this same period he pointed to the meticulous and likely the final nature of the improvements he had made: 'This [work] . . . is now brought to as great a degree of accuracy as I can attain.'[2]

While correcting the sheets of this edition, he wrote to Strahan one of his most memorable comments about his revisions:

> I thank you for your Corrections, which are very judicious; and you see that I follow them for the greatest part. I shall be obligd to you for continuing them as far as your Leizure will permit. For tho' I know, that a man might spend his whole Life in correcting one small Volume, and yet have inaccuracies in it, I think however that the fewer the better, and it is a great Amusement to me to pick them out gradually in every Edition.[3]

Immediately upon the publication of the 1772 edition, Hume wrote to his bookseller, Thomas Cadell, that 'I have carefully perusd the Essays [*ETSS*], and find them very correct, with fewer Errors of the Press, than I almost ever saw in any book.'[4]

Despite his sense of finality and accuracy, Hume prepared additional corrections for the posthumously published edition of 1777. This edition introduced various uses of accidentals and modest word shifts (chiefly commas, spelling, verb–adverb order, and subjunctive verb-forms) that are atypical of Hume's previous editions. The present critical edition gives greater credence to substantive changes in the posthumous 1777 edition than to its changes in accidentals, but a few changes of both types introduce inconsistencies or defects that are most plausibly attributed

[2] 25 Mar. 1771, to William Strahan, *Letters*, 2: 239.

[3] 18 Sept. 1771, to William Strahan, *Letters*, 2: 250. This letter was about the *History*. Strahan was sending to Hume up to five proof-sheets, or eighty pages, per week during the period when the *History* was printed.

[4] 3 June 1772, to Thomas Cadell, *Letters*, 2: 262.

to the compositors.[5] Hume did not live to see the proofs, and the compositor's changes could more easily have gone undetected than in an edition that Hume himself corrected.

Previous editions of works in *ETSS* by other editors have commonly, though not without exception, used the 1777 edition as the primary text. This edition was authorized by Hume before he died, and therefore has a strong claim as the copytext. It would have been the copytext for this edition had it not been for the following. First, Hume did not see the 1777 edition through the press, whereas in all previous editions he had the opportunity to oversee publication. Second, there appear to have been questionable modifications in the 1777 edition. Third, the 1772 edition is basically consistent with that of the 1777 edition, and can easily be emended to incorporate Hume's authentic changes in 1777. On balance, then, the 1772 edition is a relatively clear choice.

However, the 1772 edition, like all late editions, is not perfect. Some deterioration in foreign language quotations and bibliographical references went uncorrected in all late editions, and many formal inconsistencies persisted throughout the editions. These problems are manageable, and do not provide a sufficiently strong basis for overriding the ample evidence that Hume oversaw his later editions with as much or more care than the early editions. He was pleased with his investment in correcting the editions of *ETSS*, and justifiably so. Overall, the later editions are stylistically enriched and formally more accurate than the earlier editions.

[5] Based on what is known about the journeyman printers of London, it is possible that distinct compositorial forms were introduced during the typesetting of a single work. The possibilities were increased when an edition of several works was under production. This hypothesis may account for the pockets or sections of single works in *ETSS* in which different spellings are introduced and thereafter vanish. Many examples suggest that compositors, rather than Hume, were the source of inconsistencies. The terms 'connexion' and 'connection' provide a representative example. Hume wrote and indexed using the spelling 'connexion', and in the copytext there are no occurrences of 'connection'. In the first editions of *ETSS* (those closest to his manuscripts), there are 122 occurrences of 'connexion' and only one of 'connection'. However, in two middle editions—the 1764 and 1768 editions—there are ten and twenty-one occurrences, respectively, of 'connection'. (These figures change in significant ways if *The History of England*, the correspondence, and the *Dialogues* are taken into consideration.) That Hume himself made these spelling changes is improbable. Similarly, in his own writing Hume virtually always uses 'choose' (not 'chuse') and 'show' (not 'shew'); but in the printed texts 'chuse' forms appear slightly more often than 'choose' forms, and 'shew' forms appear with almost the same frequency as 'show' forms (in the *Treatise*, 'shew' forms are used in the overwhelming majority of cases). It appears, then, that compositors introduced multiple inconsistencies.

More generally, as Hume worked with his printer, Strahan, Hume's manuscript habits and preferences became intermixed with print-shop practices. Changing sets of compositors brought different standards to the work, and conventions varied across the editions. Hume's text progressively became a joint and evolving product of the writing–printing–bookselling industry. Hume acknowledged this fact by pointing to the skills that Strahan and his workers exhibited in composition, correcting proofs, helping with indexing, and the like. See correspondence of 1 Feb. 1757, 18 Apr. 1757, and 3 Sept. 1757, all to William Strahan (*Letters*, 1: 241, 247, 267), and 22 July 1771 and 22 Feb. 1772, to Strahan (*Letters*, 2: 246–7, 259); and Burton (ed.), *Letters of Eminent Persons*, 86.

The State of Hume's Editions and the Need for Repair

Despite the many corrections and improvements made in Hume's editions, anyone intimately familiar with the history of the changes made in *ETSS* might reasonably conclude that, in every edition in which these individual works were published, both its author and its printer were muddled and casual about some matters of orthography, punctuation, capitalization, italics, case, and quotation marks. Neither Hume nor his printer was meticulous about the implementation of these conventions. Hume's authorized editions contained inconsistent forms from the beginning and through all later editions, and they have not been rendered consistent by subsequent editors.

Hume's editors have usually corrected blatant typographical errors while leaving subtle errors (such as 'an' misprinted as 'any', commas inadvertently dropped, and plural forms incorrectly made singular), formal inconsistencies, and some substantive errors (such as incorrect references in footnotes). In this edition, every effort has been made to determine which words and forms need correction in the light of Hume's preferred or uncorrupted forms, abbreviations, and the like. There is good reason to believe that the printed texts are more inconsistent than Hume's manuscript practices, and therefore suspicion falls on the compositors as a source of some, perhaps most, of the inconsistencies in the texts. The evidence from manuscript analysis is presented in another volume of the Clarendon Hume—*A Treatise of Human Nature*—which reports on the results of a study of Hume's early correspondence and manuscript practices. This evidence indicates that Hume had settled, and reasonably consistent, preferences that were not always reflected in his published texts (though Hume's manuscript practices were not in every respect uniform).

Many compositorial preferences and constraints that introduced inconsistencies in *A Treatise of Human Nature* introduced similar problems in *ETSS*. Analysis of the copytext as regards orthography, punctuation, upper and lower case, the use of italic, and the like (supplemented by the previously mentioned evidence of Hume's manuscript practices) indicates that several inconsistencies in the copytext were the joint product of the compositors' forms and preferences in collision with Hume's competing predilections. Faced with an unavoidable choice of preserving or eliminating pointless inconsistencies, their elimination was usually the reasonable course.

The elimination of errors and several types of inconsistency, in light of a justified policy, is a fundamental objective of the Clarendon Hume editions. The general guideline used by the editor of the present volume has been to follow the copytext in substance and form unless an authoritative practice, *bona fide* error, inconsistency, or instruction from Hume to his printer or bookseller warrants a change. The justifying conditions for deviations from the copytext are authoritativeness, removal of unwarranted inconsistency, and elimination of error. So far as substantive changes are concerned, the editing is exceptionally conservative. Hard choices occasionally had to be made when the editor was not satisfied that a single most defensible reading could be determined; but these cases were few in number for the two works in this volume.[6] The only difficult case of a possibly significant editorial change in *NHR* is discussed in the Introduction, pp. xxiv–xxvii.

The various principles used for the editing of Hume's works in *ETSS* and the *Treatise of Human Nature*, and a defence of those principles, are found in the Clarendon editions of *EHU* and the *Treatise*.

PART 2

SYSTEMATIC CHANGES

The remaining two parts of this appendix record the differences between the copytext and the critical text. As a general rule, all instances of modification of

[6] Also rare are *errors* in the copytext. The principles of the Clarendon Hume call for genuine errors to be corrected, but editors must struggle with the question, 'What counts as an error?' Errors are usually typographical and conspicuous, but some are more subtle, and editorial verdicts of error, made by less than conservative editors, generate questionable changes. The problem of incorrect quotation is an example. (On the related problem of incorrect *references*, see 'A Note on the Text'.) Each of Hume's direct quotations has been checked for this edition against the first edition and all other editions of Hume's text and also against the (or a principal) published source of the work cited. If it is known which source or edition Hume used (or an authoritative, reliable source or edition of the cited work is available), and it is determined that the passage became corrupt in some edition of Hume's text subsequent to Hume's first edition, then the text has been corrected to the wording or forms in Hume's first—or otherwise most correct—edition. That is, the copytext has (in rare instances) been restored to the forms that Hume or his printer used in his original (or most correct) transcription of the passage, which the evidence indicates is his most faithful transcription. Only if Hume's quotation in all of his editions deprived the passage of its sense or made an unintelligible formal error has it been restored to a form other than that found in Hume's own editions. In the latter (very rare) event, the text has been corrected to the wording or forms in the source cited by Hume (the original publication).

An example of a range of problems about quotation is found in the lengthy, direct quotation from the Chevalier Ramsay in n. 87 of *NHR*. There was only one published edition of this work, and Hume cites it by page. Hume or his compositor edited Ramsay's punctuation liberally (and even some of the substantive wording), to bring his text in to line with the style of Hume's edition (and perhaps to make it more readable). In Hume's first edition (1757), the quotation was only modestly changed from Ramsay's original. Over the course of the subsequent eight editions of *NHR*, the passage was progressively edited in style and modestly in substance. In the present edition this quotation has not been restored to conform in every respect to Ramsay's original. The editor accepts the copytext unless a clear corruption internal to Hume's own editions appears. In this case, the editor has used the presentation that is least corrupt in the history of Hume's editions. As it turns out, no aspect of Hume's transcription deprived Ramsay's text of its sense or made an unintelligible formal error, and therefore this criterion was not applicable in this case. (Ramsay's original text served only to determine when Hume was correct in his original quotation in the 1757 edition or in some other edition.) For a case in which Hume's transcription did deprive a quoted text of its sense or made an unintelligible formal error (thereby warranting emendation), see the example of Horace in n. 8 below on p. 189.

the copytext are reported by page and line number, either in block reports (in the last half of Part 2) or in the Register (comprising Part 3). Exceptions to this general rule are changes of form that are made silently. The latter changes will now be explained.

Systematic Changes of Form Made Silently

Changes made silently—i.e. without further notice—are limited to the following.

1. Single quotation marks have sometimes been exchanged for double quotation marks, or vice versa, thereby silently correcting an oversight or printing error.

2. No effort has been made to retain certain typographical publishing and formal practices that were commonly used in the eighteenth century. Practices eliminated include:

a. Pointing ('.') following section and part titles.
b. The long 's' ('ſ').
c. Catchwords.
d. Booksellers' advertisements (announcements).
e. Typographical or decorative ornaments.
f. Roman numerals (presented as arabic in this edition).
g. Unnumbered note markers, including asterisks (*), daggers (†), double daggers (‡), and the like. These are replaced with superscripted numbers.
h. Inverted commas or quotation marks running along the margin that distinguish quoted material.
i. Concluding a work or volume with 'FINIS'.

3. Footnote markers have been placed to the right, rather than to the left, of punctuation marks, reversing the practice in the copytext. Whereas the copytext uses both footnotes and endnotes, the critical text prints all notes as footnotes, as Hume and his printer had done in every edition until 1770.[7] These footnotes are numbered consecutively, whereas Hume and his printer had used asterisks, daggers, and the like.

4. Missing French accents have occasionally been added (e.g. Père BRUMOY, *Théâtre des GRECS*), following some relevant precedent in Hume's publications.

5. This edition continues a practice standard in Hume's editions, the capitalization of whole words (capital/small capital combinations) in the beginning line of parts such as sections. However, no two-line capitals have been used in these lines. (See 6 below for a related and abandoned practice.)

6. The typographical practice of capitalizing whole words in introducing footnotes was executed with remarkable inconsistency throughout *ETSS*, and has been discontinued.

[7] Hume once, in a letter to his printer, stated a preference for on-page notes over endnotes. Commenting on Gibbon's *History*, he wrote, 'All these Authorities ought only to be printed at the Margin or the Bottom of the Page' (8 Apr. 1776, to William Strahan, *Letters*, 2: 313).

7. The practice of capitalizing in full the first word under each letter in Hume's Index has been continued. Thus, capitals have been *added* to each first entry under a letter if the entry was not already capitalized. Some of the words capitalized in the critical edition were not capitalized in the copytext or in any other edition. Hume's comprehensive Index to *ETSS* has been divided into the proper entries for this volume so that only the entries for *DP* and *NHR* are included. The remaining entries in Hume's Index are published in other volumes of the Clarendon Hume Edition. Numbering of sections and paragraphs, capitalization, and punctuation have been made consistent.

In the Register, changes to three forms in Hume's Indexes have not been considered variants to be reported: (1) page numbers (which are converted to section and paragraph numbers), (2) commas to set off entries (which were used inconsistently in Hume's Index), and (3) lines of the form '————' used to repeat an entry found on an immediately previous line. (The third type of change was required in this edition because some lines had to be eliminated in order to pare the Index down to *NHR* and *DP* entries.) In addition, no report is made of new capitals for the opening entries under several letters, as the abridging required. (The function of the capitalization practices in the Index other than for opening entries under each letter is not well understood. It may have been Hume's way of giving emphasis, as it is elsewhere.)

Systematic Changes of Form Reported by Kind

Systematic changes of form reported by kind derive largely from formal inconsistencies eliminated from the copytext. These emendations have no effect on substantive meaning. They are classified under seven headings:

1. Orthography (spelling and abbreviation).
2. Punctuation.
3. Italic and roman type.
4. Upper and lower case.
5. Errors in typography (misprints).
6. Errors in alphabetization (in the Index).
7. Errors in Greek (mistranscriptions).

Emendations of forms in the copytext (items 1–4) are reported using the abbreviation *displ.* (for 'displaces'). Misprints in the copytext (item 5), are reported using the abbreviation *mispr.* (for 'misprinted'). Any apparent misprint that conceivably might be classified as a substantive change is reported in the Register, rather than in this block form. Emendations not resulting from the elimination of a problem of form in the copytext are reported in the Register, not by kind. Either page and line numbers or footnote numbers (and their lines) are supplied for each change. Both alphabetical order and numerical order by page or note number are used, as appropriate to a particular list.

1. Orthography

Inconsistent orthography has been eliminated by adopting the principal forms in the copytext, other *ETSS* editions (1758–70, 1777, as well as *Four Dissertations*), and other publications and manuscripts, as explained in Part 1 of this Appendix. Orthography is never modernized; the goal has been to restore Hume's preferred or conventional spellings, abbreviations, use of hyphens, and the like.

Primary Spelling or Abbreviation Displaces Secondary Spelling or Abbreviation (1) ARRIAN *displ.* ARIAN *NHR* n. 53. (2) cap. *displ.* c.: *NHR* n. 49, *NHR* n. 58 (twice), *NHR* n. 63, *NHR* n. 67, *NHR* n. 89. (3) HESIOD *displ.* Hes.: *NHR* n. 21. (4) lib. *displ.* l.: *NHR* n. 61, *NHR* n. 63, *NHR* n. 89. (5) PLUTARCH. *displ.* PLUT.: *NHR* n. 32, *NHR* n. 56. (6) quæst. *displ.* Quest.: *NHR* n. 62. (7) Section *displ.* Sect.: *DP* n. 1, *NHR* n. 1, and in the title of each section in *DP* and *NHR*. (8) SUETON. *displ.* Suet.: *NHR* n. 18.

Spelling or Nomenclature Modified: Proper Names and Titles (1) AUGUSTINE *displ.* AUGUSTIN: 70.35. (2) AMPHITRYON *displ.* AMPHITRION: 45.26. (3) COMTE *displ.* Compte: *NHR* n. 6. (4) QUINTILIAN *displ.* QUINCTILIAN *or* Quinctilian: *NHR* n. 69, Index (Q) at 276.25.

Spelling or Alternative English Form Modified: Other than Proper Names and Titles (1) ambassador *displ.* embassador: 68.19. (2) burdensome *displ.* burthensome: 82.24. (3) *Capuchin displ.* Capucin: 68.23, 68.25. (4) dependence *displ.* dependance: 40.11. (5) enflamed *displ.* inflamed: 53.11. (6) enlist *displ.* inlist: 70.16. (7) enquiry *displ.* inquiry: 34.29. (8) foretel *displ.* foretell: 66.12. (9) hamadryad *displ.* hama-dryad: 49.11. (10) implicit *displ.* implicite: 68.17. (11) incoherencies *displ.* incoherences: 66.3. (12) merchandize *displ.* merchandise: 49.22. (13) passed *displ.* past: 47.20. (14) penances *displ.* pennances: 82.15. (15) practice(d) *displ.* practise(d): 43.12, 43.16, *NHR* n. 42. (16) recall *displ.* recal: 36.21, 59.2. (17) resolvable *displ.* resolveable: *DP* n. 3. (18) show *displ.* shew: 10.12. (19) tossed *displ.* tost: 4.23. (20) Whichever *displ.* Which ever: 36.31. (21) yoked *displ.* yoaked: 65.33.

Hyphenated Word Displaces Unhyphenated Form (1) above-mentioned *displ.* above mentioned: 15.20. (2) before-hand *displ.* beforehand: 34.30, 45.33. (3) full-grown *displ.* full grown: 16.33. (4) sun-shine *displ.* sunshine: 84.4.

Unhyphenated Word Displaces Hyphenated Word (1) hamadryad *displ.* hama-dryad: 49.11. (2) overbalanced *displ.* over-ballanced: 60.15.

Apostrophe Added or Deleted till *displ.* 'till: 4.27, 4.31, 5.31.

2. Punctuation

Inconsistent punctuation that is governed by a clear rule has been eliminated by adopting the principal usage in the copytext, the other *ETSS* editions, and other publications and manuscripts, as explained in Part 1 of this Appendix. The bulk of the changes occur in the footnotes, which appear to have been hastily prepared or hastily typeset, and not scrupulously validated (in most editions). The apparent *ETSS* rule was to use a comma after an unabbreviated name and a period (not followed by a comma) after an abbreviated name. Correction of inconsistencies of punctuation under this rule has occasionally required an editorial decision about whether there is a principal usage or fixed rule in Hume's writings and about what constitutes inconsistency in the use of abbreviation.

Comma or Period Added before a Title, after a Title, or after an Author or Number in the Notes (1) CICERO,: *NHR* n. 67, *NHR* n. 72. (2) de luctu,: *NHR* n. 20. (3) HYDE,: *NHR* n. 39, *NHR* n. 46. (4) CLAUDII RUTILII NUMITIANI,: *NHR* n. 64. (5) 24.),: *NHR* n. 81. (6) ARRIAN.: *NHR* n. 53.

Comma Displaces Period after a Title or Author in the Notes (1) Opera & dies,: *NHR* n. 1. (2) HESIOD,: *NHR* n. 21, *NHR* n. 31. (3) Iliad,: *NHR* n. 33.

Question Mark Deleted. Deorum: *displ. Deorum?*: 46.26.

3. *Italic and Roman*

Inconsistent use of italic and roman type has been eliminated by adopting the principal usage in the copytext, all relevant *ETSS* editions, and other of Hume's publications and manuscripts. Roman forms sometimes replace italic equivalents, and vice versa. Most of these inconsistencies consist of small oversights, such as incorrectly italicizing a question mark. A few cases, however, involve a larger inconsistency of presentation, such as failing to italicize a title, question, or statement of the form typically italicized in ETSS. The normal but not uniform practice of Hume's writings was to print mentioned words or terms in italic. This practice has been here made as consistent as possible, but changes have been introduced in the text if and only if the context is undoubtedly one of mentioning rather than using; changes have not been introduced in borderline cases.

Italics Removed from Names, Titles, and Latin Wording (1) JUPITER confutatus, de luctu, SATURN.: *NHR* n. 20. (2) Opera & dies: *NHR* n. 1. (3) Probl.: *NHR* n. 1. (4) Ut assidens . . . plus præsentibus: 6.5.

Roman Small Capitals for Group Names Displace Italic Equivalents See below, in section 4, under '*Small Capitals Displace Lower Case*'.

Quotation Marks Added or Displace Italics for Quotations In the reports below, words in Hume's text that appear in small capitals are replaced by ellipses whenever these words were not italicized in the original; these words were never italicized and therefore in no respect undergo a change. (1) "Spes addita suscitat iras.": 27.3. (2) "Fortune has never liberally, without envy," . . . "bestowed an unmixed happiness on mankind; but with all her gifts has ever conjoined some disastrous circumstance, in order to chastize men into a reverence for the gods, whom, in a continued course of prosperity, they are apt to neglect and forget.": 42.28.

(3) "The leaders and examples of every kind of superstition," . . . "are the women. These excite the men to devotion and supplications, and the observance of religious days. It is rare to meet with one that lives apart from the females, and yet is addicted to such practices. And nothing can, for this reason, be more improbable, than the account given of an order of men among the . . . who practiced celibacy, and were notwithstanding the most religious fanatics.": 43.6. (4) "Not even the immortal gods," . . . "are a match for the . . . ": 45.10. (5) "Quisquis fuit ille Deorum:": 46.26. (6) "And chaos whence?": 48.1. (7) "Think of the force of necessity," . . . "that force, to which even the gods must submit.": 48.16. (8) "A little philosophy," . . . "makes men atheists: A great deal reconciles them to religion.": 52.32. (9) "Those which are legally established in each city,": 61.6. (10) "There is nothing so contemptible," . . . "but what may be safe, if it has but courage to defend itself." . . . "We shall have heaven," . . . "to reward us for our sufferings: But these poor creatures have nothing but the enjoyment of the present life.": 64.4. (11) "I wish," . . . "you have not committed some mistake: I wish you have not given me God the Father: He is so hard and tough there is no swallowing him.": 67.27. (12) "How many Gods are there?" "None at all," . . . "How! None at all!" . . . "To be sure," . . . "You have told me all along that there is but one God: And yesterday I eat him.": 68.8. (13) "He is a very honest man," . . . "It is a pity he were a . . . ": 68.31. (14) "Præsens divus habebitur . . . ,": 69.20. (15) "Moverunt," . . . "& ea tempestate, Judæi bellum quod vetabantur mutilare genitalia.": 71.6. (16) "May your daughter," . . . "become such as the deity whom you celebrate.": 78.19. (17) "Sunt superis sua jura.": 80.6. (18) "By this impiety," . . . "they offended the gods, and contracted an inexpiable guilt.": 81.22.

Italics Added to Questions and Reported Statements (1) *What rites or worship was most acceptable to the gods?*: 61.5. (2) *How can you worship leeks and onions? . . . If we worship them . . . at least, we do not, at the same time, eat them. But what strange objects of adoration are cats and monkies? . . . They are at least as good as the relicts or rotten bones of martyrs. . . . Are you not mad . . . to cut one another's throat about the preference of a cabbage or a cucumber? Yes . . . I allow it, if you will confess, that those are still madder, who fight about the preference among volumes of sophistry, ten thousand of which are not equal in value to one cabbage or cucumber.*: 68.33.

Italics Added to Mentioned Words and to &c. (1) *atheism*: 44.16. (2) *theism*: 48.28. (3) *&c.*: 15.36, *NHR* n. 20, 66.19, *NHR* n. 58, *NHR* n. 78.26.

4. Upper Case and Lower Case

Inconsistent upper and lower case has been eliminated by adopting the principal usage in the copytext, all relevant *ETSS* editions, and other publications and manuscripts, as explained in Part 1 of this Appendix. The conventions in the copytext governing lower case and upper case (both large and small capitals) were commonly violated in the notes, but rarely in the text.

Initial Lower-Case Letter Displaces Upper-Case (1) but *displ.* But: 48.2. (2) de *displ.* De: *NHR* n. 36, *NHR* n. 84. (3) dies *displ.* Dies: *NHR* n. 21. (4) epist. *displ.* Epist.: *NHR* n. 81. (5) ex *displ.* Ex: *NHR* n. 26. (6) exped. *displ.* Exped.: *NHR* n. 47. (7) god *displ.* God: *NHR* n. 1. (8) mathem. *displ.* MATHEM.: *NHR* n. 28, *NHR* n. 82. (9) oracles *displ.* Oracles: *NHR* n. 13. (10) quæst. *displ.* Quest. *and* Quæst.: *NHR* n. 62, *NHR* n. 81. (11) quoted *displ.* Quoted: Index (D) at 274.26. (12) rep. *displ.* Rep.: *NHR* n. 15, *NHR* n. 81. (13) sacrificiis *displ.* Sacrificiis: *NHR* n. 8. (14) superstit. *displ.* Superstit.: *NHR* n. 85.

Lower Case Displaces Small Capitals (1) Iliad *displ.* ILIAD: *NHR* n. 33. (2) mathem. *displ.* MATHEM.: *NHR* n. 28, *NHR* n. 82.

Initial Upper-Case Letter Displaces Lower-Case (1) Creator *displ.* creator: 44 title. (2) Deity *displ.* deity: 52.1, 60.11, 60.22, 63.4, 86.11. (3) Divinity *displ.* divinity: 79.17, 83.1. (4) Lents *displ.* lents: 82.21. (5) Lord *displ.* lord: 52.33. (6) Object *displ.* object: Index (B) at 272.9. (7) Object *displ.* object: Index (M) at 273.3. (8) *Philosophical Principles of natural and revealed Religion displ.* philosophical principles of natural and revealed religion: *NHR* n. 87. (9) Section *displ.* sect.: *NHR* n. 1. (10) Supreme *displ.* supreme: 41.34, 83.3, 84.7, 86.17. (11) The *displ.* the: 48.1. (12) *What displ.* what: 61.5. (13) Titles in the Contents and in section titles were occasionally modified to render capitalization consistent.

Small Capitals Displace Lower Case (1) ACADEMICS *displ. Academics*: 48.27. (2) ADRIANI *displ.* Adriani: *NHR* n. 65. (3) ARNOB. *displ.* Arnob.: *NHR* n. 14. (4) ARRIAN *displ.* Arrian: *NHR* n. 47, *NHR* n. 53. (5) AUG. *displ.* Aug.: *NHR* n. 18, *NHR*, n. 49, *NHR* n. 68. (6) BAYLE *displ.* Bayle: *NHR* n. 57. (7) BRUMOY *displ.* Brumoy: *NHR* n. 13. (8) CÆS. *displ.* Cæs.: *NHR* n. 10. (9) CAL. *displ.* Cal.: *NHR* n. 19, *NHR* n. 52. (10) CATHOLIC(S) or ROMAN CATHOLICS *displ.* Catholic(s) or ROMAN Catholics or *Roman catholics* or *Roman Catholics*: 56.29, 67.13, 67.23, 68.12, 68.38, 82.21. (11) CHRISTIAN(ITY)(S) *displ. Christian* or Christian(ity)(s): 55.22, 67.15, 68.2, 68.32. *NHR* n. 87 (twice). (12) CICERO *displ.* Cicero: *NHR* n. 67, *NHR* n. 72. (13) CLAUDII RUTILII NUMITIANI *displ.* Claudii Rutilii Numitiani: *NHR* n. 64. (14) DIOD. SIC. *displ.* Diod. Sic.: *NHR* n. 8, *NHR* n. 17. (15) EUTYPHRO *displ.* Eutyphro: *NHR* n. 76. (16) GRECS *displ.* Grecs: *NHR* n. 13. (17) HERMOTIMUS *displ.* Hermotimus: *NHR* n. 84. (18) HERODOT. *displ.* Herodot.: *NHR* n. 9, *NHR* n. 20. (19) HESIOD *displ.* Hes.: *NHR* n. 21. (20) HYDE *displ.* Hyde: *NHR* n. 46. (21) ISID. & OSIRIDE *displ.* Isid. & Osiride: *NHR* n. 44. (22) JESUITS *displ.* Jesuits: *NHR* n. 60. (23) JUPITER *displ.* Jupiter: *NHR* n. 20. (24) LACED. *displ.* Laced.: *NHR* n. 15. (25) LAPONIE *displ.* Laponie: *NHR* n. 7. (26) LE COMTE *displ.* le Compte: *NHR* n. 6. (27) LUCIAN *displ.* Lucian: *NHR* n. 8, *NHR* n. 20. (28) MAHOMETAN(ISM)(S) *displ.* Mahometan(ism)(s): 55.12, 56.23. (29) ORIGENISM *displ. Origenism: NHR* n. 87. (30) PERSARUM *displ.* Persarum: *NHR* n. 46. (31) PHÆDO *displ.* Phædo: *NHR* n. 77. (32) PLIN. *displ.* Plin.: *NHR* n. 68. (33) PLUTARCH. *displ.* Plut.: *NHR* n. 56. (34) PLUTARCH *displ.* Plutarch: *NHR* n. 44. (35) QUINT. CURTIUS *displ.* Quint. Curtius:

NHR n. 17. (36) REGNARD *displ.* Regnard: *NHR* n. 7. (37) SATURN. *displ.* Saturn.: *NHR* n. 20. (38) STOICS *displ. Stoics* or Stoics: 48.27, *NHR* n. 75. (39) STRABO *displ.* Strabo: *NHR* n. 52. (40) SUETON. *displ.* Suet. *or* Sueton.: *NHR* n. 18, *NHR* n. 49, *NHR* n. 52, *NHR* n. 68. (41) THUCYD. *displ.* Thucyd.: *NHR* n. 54. (42) XENOPH. *displ.* Xenoph.: *NHR* n. 43.

5. *Typographical Errors (Misprints in the Copytext)*

(1) is in *mispr.* is: 3.11. (2) accomplishments *mispr.* accompishments: 10.34. (3) ourselves *mispr.* ourseves: 19.18. (4) solution. The *mispr.* solution, the: 33.5. (5) goddess *mispr.* goodess: 49.29. (6) PESSINUNTIANS *mispr.* PERSINUNTIANS: *NHR* n. 34. (7) DIOG. *mispr.* DIOD.: *NHR* n. 35. (8) denominated *mispr.* denomiated: 51.32. (9) profanos *mispr.* profanus: *NHR* n. 58. (10) p. *mispr.* P.: *NHR* n. 78. (11) knowledge *mispr.* knowlege: 77.30. (12) extraordinary *mispr.* extraodinary: *NHR* n. 84. (13) interests *mispr.* interest: 84.1. (Note: Some changes mentioned elsewhere in this Editorial Appendix may be corrections of typographical errors. See, e.g., the section on 'Hyphenated Word Displaces Unhyphenated Form'.)

6. *Errors of Alphabetization*

The following entries were in improper alphabetical order in the Index of the copytext (1772) and have been placed in proper order in this edition: (1) ARNOBIUS; (2) EPICURUS; (3) Jewish Religion and Egyptian resembling; (4) Morality hurt by popular Religions; (5) ROME.

7. *Errors in Greek*

The use of accents and breathings in Greek type has been normalized, but wording and spelling judged acceptable in the printed editions of Hume's day has been retained. Errors in foreign languages other than Greek are reported in the Register.

NHR n. 3: *αὖ displ. αν.*

PART 3

NON-SYSTEMATIC CHANGES: A REGISTER OF NON-SYSTEMATIC EMENDATIONS AND SUBSTANTIVE VARIANTS

This final part contains the Register of non-systematic editorial changes in the text reported individually, together with a list of all substantive variants. Emendation is infrequent, but typically is substantive. The changes, with few exceptions, derive from the authority of an edition of *ETSS*, most often the 1777 edition. No overlap or redundancy between lists in prior sections has been permitted unless a report in Part 3 happens to incorporate a change of the sort mentioned in Parts 1 or 2.

Terms, Symbols, and Practices in the Register

Each entry in the Register begins with a page and line reference to the critical text. These numbers are followed by the relevant portion of the critical text, hereafter referred to as the *lemma*. The lemma is followed by a bracket (]), which is followed by one or more additional portions of text, each portion separated by a vertical line (|). The abbreviations and symbols used in this string are as follows:

] separates the critical text (printed to the left of the ']') from variants in the collated editions (printed to the right of the ']'). The first entry (in order of years) that shows a difference from the lemma entry is always reported in full.

| separates a variant (or other unit) from other variants (or units) of the same entry.

Abbreviated dates. The editions of *DP* and *NHR* authorized by Hume were published between 1757 and 1777. The relevant dates are abbreviated to 57, 58, 60, 64, 67, 68, 70, 72, 77. Items of the form '67' indicate that a variant reading is found in the 1767 edition. Items of the form '57–60' indicate that a particular variant reading is found in all editions published from 1757 to 1760. (See the editor's Introduction for a history of the editions.)

~ means identical in all respects, accidental and substantive. This sign is always followed by an abbreviated date. For example, '~ 64–77' indicates that the text of all editions appearing from 1764 to 1777 are in every respect identical to the lemma.

In accordance with the above, an entry of the form

62.1 antipathy] aversion 57–70 | ~ 72–77

indicates that at page 62, line 1, the critical text reads 'antipathy', and that from 1757 to 1770 the text found at that part reads 'aversion'.

* denotes an otherwise unregistered difference *in accidentals* in the listed editions. Thus, items of the form 57*60 indicate that a variant substantive reading from 57 to 60 is accompanied by a variant accidental not revealed in the record shown here. 'Belief 57*68' indicates that whereas the 57 edition includes the word 'Belief' in precisely that form, at least one later edition appearing by 1768 includes in the same location this same substantive, but in a different accidental form.

In any entry following the ']' or '|' symbols, the accidentals printed at that point in the Register are those found in the *first year* in the string of dates. If material is not in the copytext, but is in one or more of Hume's other editions, the same first-year rule applies. For example, if the material appears in 57*60, the 57 edition is the text displayed. The reason the earliest form is shown first is to display the original form of publication.

Although accidentals are not directly reported in the Register, accidental differences in otherwise identical substantives are *always* noted by the marker '*'. These variant accidentals typically involve differences in capitalization or punctuation. The asterisk is not used in a manner that masks either a substantive or an accidental in the copytext; the reason such obscuring is impossible is explained under the next entry on shading (or redlining).

Shading (or redlining). Entries are shaded whenever they contain *emendations* of the copytext that have not already been reported by kind above. The lemma (the critical text) displays the corrections made to the 1772 copytext. Unshaded entries record variations between editions and contain no emendation (other than those already reported by kind in block). Changes in accidentals are often relevant to understanding and evaluating an emendation. Accordingly, the use of the asterisk (*) is not permitted in any shaded entry, and the form of the accidentals in the copytext can never be obscured as to differences in accidental forms. The form '~' is preserved for pure identity, accidental and substantive, so that the reader can easily see which editions have served as sources for any emendation to the copytext.

Er refers to an entry made by Hume in the errata of an edition. Items of the form '58*Er*' indicate that the errata of an edition (58 in this example) is the source generating a particular variant. The year of a single edition is always specified next to the *Er* form. Thus, 'foretel 57*Er*' means that the errata in 57 instructs the reader that the correct reading is 'foretel' (and not that 'foretel' is the incorrect reading). A report of the form 'corrupt] corrupted 57| ~ 57*Er*–77' means that the printed text in 57 reads 'corrupted', that the errata in 57 instructs the reader that the correct reading is 'corrupt', and that all subsequent editions read 'corrupt'.

. . . Ellipses indicate that material has been omitted from the span of text presented as the lemma. Ellipses are used only in lemmas.

¶ designates the beginning of a paragraph. Though changes of paragraph are accidental variants, they are always reported by the use of this symbol.

{ } Material inside these braces indicates a relevant source or authority (other than routine judgements made by the editor of this volume) for an emendation of the copytext. The following are types of relevant authority: (1) the *person* responsible for suggesting the need for a change, (2) the *publication* in which the change was first made, (3) an *authoritative published text* of an author quoted by Hume. Items of the form {AWC} and {GG} indicate that in emending the text the editor has concurred with particular previous editors known to have made the same emendation; {TXT} indicates that a check of an authoritative publication quoted by Hume supports a change in the copytext. (For an explanation of the conditions under which such a change is warranted, see 'A Note on the Text' and n. 6 in this Editorial Appendix.) Such emendation is rare, and almost always supported by a printed quotation found in one or more of Hume's early editions or in *A Treatise of Human Nature* (from which Hume extracted some quotations in his later work). 'TXT' thus does not indicate that a source external to Hume's writings is the sole or primary reason for the modification of his text. If available, several editions of an author's work have been consulted. The following abbreviations have been used:

{AWC} signifies the edition of *The Natural History of Religion* prepared by A. Wayne Colver, as given in the Reference List.

{GG} signifies the edition of Hume's *Philosophical Works* prepared by T. H. Green and T. H. Grose, as given in the Reference List.

{TLB} signifies the editor of this volume, Tom L. Beauchamp.

Only a few shaded (redlined) entries in the Register specify such an individual source when there has been an emendation of the copytext. The reason is that the bulk of the substantive changes derive from the authority of the 77 edition or, occasionally, some edition prior to 72. Whenever a shaded (or redlined) string contains a form such as '~ 77' or '~ 58–68', the reader can assume that the edition(s) listed are the main source(s) of authority for the change. These authorities are usually supported by other evidence. Often other editions contain the same form, and commonly there is evidence internal to the copytext that the change reflects a standard form.

Authorities are also listed for emendations involving punctuation changes, but authorities are not necessarily listed for the following types of change:

1. Spelling and abbreviation.
2. Italic and roman.
3. Upper and lower case.
4. Arabic and roman numerals.

These changes derive almost entirely from inconsistencies in the texts or in printing conventions. With the exception of arabic and roman numerals, these changes are reported in the block reports in Part 2 above. They are, in a few cases, reported more than once, because they are intrinsic to other variants that are reported in the register. These changes have rarely been introduced by previous editors (none of whom used the 1772 as copytext).

No exhaustive search of all posthumous editions of the works of Hume by his various editors has been undertaken in order to locate possible authorities for these changes. However, it has been established that all previous editions of these works are inconsequential for purposes of systematic emendation of types 1–4 listed immediately above.

Entries of text in the Register do not include an item of punctuation unless the punctuation itself is a variant or is needed to locate or make sense of the variant. If there is no contrasting punctuation in another edition, the punctuation is irrelevant to a display of variation. Misprints in editions of *DP* and *NHR* other than the copytext are not included in the list of variants.

Some passages in Hume's writings appeared first as main text and then, in later editions, as notes or appendices (or vice versa). This material is printed and collated as text material if it is text in the 72 edition and as note material if it appears in one of the notes in the 72 edition. The general rule on note material is that the location in the Register is determined by the location in the 72 edition.

The editor has attempted to simplify the forms used in the list below to make it as readable as possible. Preference is given to short, simple entries, avoiding longer strings of text. This general rule favouring simplicity and atomic units is occasionally overridden, usually by placing two short variants together as a larger and more meaningful unit. A few entries are explained in prose, without employing the above abbreviations.

Front Matter

The front matter in *ETSS* is collated in the Clarendon Hume Edition of *An Enquiry concerning Human Understanding*. That collation is augmented below to include: (1) the front matter in the 1757 edition of *Four Dissertations* and (2) changed titles in the Contents of *DP* and *NHR* in editions after 1757. There are no section titles in the Contents or the text of the 1757 edition.

Half-titles of a work or a collection of works appear in the front matter in 57, 64, 67, and 72 only. There are no substantive variants between versions of the same title; but there are title changes, as shown below.

Every volume except 57 contains a title-page.

Every volume except 57 contains a table of contents with titles of sections; 57 presents only a list of the titles of the four essays (dissertations) that comprise the volume.

vii.5 A DISSERTATION ON THE PASSIONS] II. OF THE PASSIONS. 57 | A DISSERTATION on the PASSIONS 58–77

viii.1 in] ~ 58| in most 64–70 | ~ 72–77

viii.4 Corollary] Corollary from the Whole 58–64 | ~ 67–77

Errata are located in the back matter only in 57 and 58.

A Dedication to 'The Reverend Mr. Hume' (John Home) appears only in some copies of 57 (see editor's Introduction, pp. xxxii–xxxiv).

A Dissertation on the Passions

3.0 *A DISSERTATION ON THE PASSIONS*] *DISSERTATION II. Of the Passions. 57* | *~ 58–77*

Section 1

3.9 arises] ~ 57–67 | rises 68 | ~ 70–77

3.14 degree] degrees 57–70 | ~ 72–77

3.23 is determined, one moment,] in one moment is determined 57–68 | ~ 70–77

3.24 another] in another 57–68 | ~ 70–77

3.25 between] betwixt 57–58 | ~ 60–77

3.30 destroys] utterly destroys 57–68 | ~ 70–77

3.31 produces] ~ 57–64 | produce 67–68 | ~ 70–77

4.2 between] betwixt 57–58 | ~ 60–77
4.3 between] betwixt 57–58 | ~ 60–77
5.1 it is] is it 57–60 | ~ 64–77
5.4 namely] to wit 57–68 | ~ 70–77
5.13 of] ~ 57–70 | on 72–77
6.4 phænomenon.] phænomenon: 57 | ~ 58–67 | phænomena. 68 | ~ 70–77
6.5 pullis] {TLB,TXT} | pullus 57–77
6.7 Serpentium] {TLB,TXT} | Serpentûm 57–77[8]
6.14 nowise] no way 57–60 | ~ 64–77
6.18 between] betwixt 57–58 | ~ 60–77
6.26 case,] ~ 57–58 | case 60–72 | ~ 77
6.30 explain more fully afterwards] afterwards explain more fully 57–70 | ~ 72–77
6.34 and] or 57 | ~ 58–77
6.35 consist] 57–72 consists | ~ 77
6.39 explained] ~ 57–64 | explain 67 | ~ 68–77

Section 2

7.2 which are of] of 57 | ~ 58–77
7.9 passion] passions 57–70 | ~ 72–77
7.10 between] betwixt 57–58 | ~ 60–77
7.17 ourselves] ourself 57–70 | ~ 72–77
7.24 principles] properties 57–60 | ~ 64–77
n. 1 *Enquiry concerning Human Understanding*, Section 3] philosophical Essays. Essay iii 57 | Enquiry concerning Human Understanding, Sect. III 58–77
8.11 any] ~ 57–72 | an 77
8.11 received from] from 57–60 | ~ 64–77
8.12 a] ~ 57–67 | an 68 | ~ 70–77
8.23 continued] {TXT} | ~ 57 | continual 58–77
8.29 when] {TXT} | where 57–77
9.4 between] betwixt 57–58 | ~ 60–77
9.10 previously excites] produces antecedently 57–72 | ~ 77
9.16 which] that 57–68 | ~ 70–77

[8] An explanation of this quotation as it appears in the *Treatise* is provided in the Clarendon Hume Edition of the *Treatise* (ed. Norton and Norton). The first emendation in the present edition (pullis] pullus) is required for reasons of sense, syntax, and metre. Although in Horace the adult bird is panicking over the fate of the young, Hume's representation of the passage would have a chick panicking over the fate of the young. The second emendation (Serpentium] Serpentûm) follows the text presented in the second book of Hume's *Treatise* and in eighteenth-century editions of Horace. The short 'i' of 'serpentium' is required by the metre, whereas a circumflex accent normally represents a contraction or long vowel. (Information for this note has been kindly supplied by Brian Hillyard.)

9.25 between] betwixt 57–58 | ~ 60–77
11.7 between] betwixt 57–58 | ~ 60–77
11.21 one] ~ 57 | the one 58 | ~ 60–77
11.21 the other] ~ 57–67 | another 68 | ~ 70–77
11.27 happy temperature] temperature 57–58 | ~ 60–77
11.31 sense] the senses 57–70 | ~ 72–77
11.37 between] betwixt 57–58 | ~ 60–77
12.3 met] have met 57–58 | ~ 60–77
12.7 ourselves] ourself 57–70 | ~ 72–77
12.15 regarded] conceived 57–72 | ~ 77
13.18 rule] rules 57–58 | ~ 60–77
n. 3 **Note 3 occurs only from 60 to 77.**
n. 3.3 to whom it belongs] whom it belongs to 60–64 | ~ 67–68 | whom it belongs to 70 | ~ 72–77
n. 3.5 only] sole 60–64 | ~ 67–77
n. 3.11 person] ~ 60–64 | persons 67–68 | ~ 70–77
13.29 to] in 57 | ~ 58–77
15.1 delicate] nice 57–60 | ~ 64–77
15.5 suffrages of the world] opinions of others 57–68 | ~ 70–77
15.7 the opinions of others] they 57–68 | ~ 70–77
15.7 in] ~ 57 | on 58–60 | ~ 64–77
15.16 brilliancy] brilliant 57 | ~ 58–77
15.23 durableness] duration 57–68 | ~ 70–77
15.35 good weather] weather 57–58 | ~ 60–77
15.35 a happy climate] climate 57–58 | ~ 60–77
16.5 hope] hopes 57–70 | ~ 72–77
16.20 a horror] ~ 57–67 | horror 68 | ~ 70–77
16.25 suitably] suitable 57–68 | ~ 70–77
16.33 that,] ~ 57–64 | that 67–68 | ~ 70 | that 72 | ~ 77
16.35 much] very much 57–68 | ~ 70–77

Section 3

18.3 ourselves] ourself 57–70 | ~ 72–77
18.6 poverty,] ~ 57 | poverty 58–72 | ~ 77
18.12 contempt towards us] contempt 57–60 | ~ 64–77
18.13 our hatred] hatred 57–60 | ~ 64–77
18.13 our friendship] friendship 57–60 | ~ 64–77
18.14 ourselves] ourself 57–70 | ~ 72–77
19.16 seems to be] seems 57–70 | ~ 72–77
19.20 between] betwixt 57–58 | ~ 60–77
19.21 which was insisted] insisted 57–70 | ~ 72–77
19.25 or] ~ 57–67 | and 68 | ~ 70–77

20.1 A bankrupt, at first, . . . compassion and contempt.] **This paragraph occurs in 77 only.**

20.6 with] along with 57 | ~ 58–77

Section 4

21.6 pleasing] pleasant 57–68 | ~ 70–77

21.7 as they have] having 57–58 | ~ 60–77

21.7 or] ~ 57–67 | and 68 | ~ 70–77

21.13 all along] ~ 57–64 | along 67 | ~ 68–77

21.21 who are related] related 57–70 | ~ 72–77

21.24 easy] very easy 57–68 | ~ 70–77

22.1 operation] ~ 57–67 | operations 68 | ~ 70–77

22.3 between] betwixt 57–58 | ~ 60–77

22.20 between] betwixt 57–58 | ~ 60–77

22.27 praise] praises 57–68 | ~ 70–77

22.35 perfectly succeeded] succeeded perfectly 57–70 | ~ 72–77

23.9 between] betwixt 57–58 | ~ 60–77

23.10 only know] know only 57–72 | ~ 77

23.11 between] betwixt 57–58 | ~ 60–77

23.27 are] ~ 57–67 | were 68 | ~ 70–77

23.28 derived] proceeding 57–60 | ~ 64–77

Section 5

24.11 a distant] distant 57 | ~ 58–77

24.15 regard to public good, or] regard 57–58 | ~ 60–77

25.2 affection] affections 57–68 | ~ 70–77

25.2 desire] desires 57–68 | ~ 70–77

25.3 with regard to] concerning 57–70 | ~ 72–77

Section 6

26.9 in] ~ 57–67 | to 68 | ~ 70–77

26.14 between] betwixt 57–58 | ~ 60–77

26.14 between] betwixt 57–58 | ~ 60–77

26.23 of it] it 57–70 | ~ 72–77

26.25 this] his 57 | ~ 58–77

27.5 be] are 57–72 | ~ 77

27.5 same time] ~ 57–67 | time 68 | ~ 70–77

27.7 this] that 57–67 | that the 68 | ~ 70–77

27.18 effect] influence 57–60 | ~ 64–77

27.20 arise] arises 57–72 | ~ 77

27.27 emotion] agitation 57–58 | ~ 60–77
27.27 emotion] agitation 57–58 | ~ 60–77
28.4 affection] passion 57–70 | ~ 72–77
28.12 agreeable] very agreeable 57–70 | ~ 72–77
28.30 desire] desires 57–68 | ~ 70–77
28.30 appetite] appetites 57–68 | ~ 70–77
28.37 in others] others 57–68 | ~ 70–77
28.38 and] or 57 | ~ 58–77
29.3 to have here] here to have 57–70 | ~ 72–77

The Natural History of Religion

31.0 *THE NATURAL HISTORY OF RELIGION*] *DISSERTATION I. The Natural History of Religion. 57* | ~ *58–77*

Introduction

33.2 attention] principal attention 57–70 | ~ 72–77
33.4 is exposed to] admits of 57 | ~ 58–77
33.12 exception] exceptions 57–70 | ~ 72–77
33.18 between] betwixt 57–58 | ~ 60–77

Section 1

34.0 SECTION 1 That Polytheism was the Primary Religion of Men] I. 57 | SECT. I. *That Polytheism was the primary Religion of Men.* 58–77
34.6 incontestable] uncontestable 57 | ~ 58–77
34.7 polytheists] idolaters 57–70 | ~ 72–77
34.11 polytheism] idolatry 57–70 | ~ 72–77
34.12 that system] polytheism 57–70 | ~ 72–77
34.13 creed] system 57–70 | ~ 72–77
34.27 sciences] ~ 57–70 | science 72–77
34.31 scarcely] scarce 57–68 | ~ 70–77
35.10 own frame] frame 57–60 | ~ 64–77
35.14 between] betwixt 57–58 | ~ 60–77
35.19 such objects, as] objects, which 57–60 | ~ 64–77
35.21 in] may be in 57–68 | ~ 70–77
35.27 man] ~ 57–72 | a man 77
35.27 society),] society) 57–72 | ~ 77
35.29 those objects] objects 57–70 | ~ 72–77
36.8 polytheism] idolatry 57–70 | ~ 72–77
36.9 reason] reasoning 57–68 | ~ 70–77

36.11 much] infinitely 57–68 | ~ 70–77
36.12 retaining of] retaining 57–70 | ~ 72–77
36.13 between] betwixt 57–58 | ~ 60–77
36.23 founded in] ~ 57–64 | derived from 67–68 | ~ 70–77
36.25 on] in 57–70 | ~ 72–77
36.29 apprehension] apprehensions 57–68 | ~ 70–77
36.31 be buried] buried 57 | ~ 57*Er*–77
36.34 polytheism] idolatry 57–70 | ~ 72–77
36.35 when] when very 57–68 | ~ 70–77
36.37 principle or opinion] principles, or opinions 57*70 | ~ 72–77

Section 2

37.0 SECTION 2 Origin of Polytheism] II. 57 | SECT. II. *Origin of Polytheism.* 58–77
37.1 in enquiring] ~ 57–60 | enquiring 64 | and enquire 67–68 | ~ 70–77
37.2 polytheism] idolatry or polytheism 57–70 | ~ 72–77
37.11 merely] mere 57–68 | ~ 70–77
37.14 throughout] thro' 57–60 | through 64 | ~ 67–77
37.18 The statue of LAOCOON . . . obvious supposition.] **These sentences occur as a footnote from 57 to 68 and as text from 70 to 77.**
37.20 imagined] concluded 57*70 | ~ 72–77
37.32 by land] ~ 57–60 | land 64–70 | ~ 72–77
38.14 polytheism] polytheism or idolatry 57–70 | ~ 72–77
n. 1.3 dies,] {TLB} | *Dier.* 57–77
n. 1.3 252] {AWC} | 250 57–77
n. 1.5 suitably] suitable 57–70 | ~ 72–77
n. 1.6 among] amongst 57 | ~ 58–77
38.28 present] visible 57 | ~ 58–77
39.7 various and] ~ 57 | various 58–60 | ~ 64–77

Section 3

40.0 SECTION 3 The Same Subject Continued] III. 57 | SECT. III. *The same subject continued. 58–77*
40.2 event] event, 57–72 | ~ 77
40.2 concealed from] unknown to 57–70 | ~ 72–77
40.4 between] betwixt 57–58 | ~ 60–77
40.5 among] amongst 57–64 | ~ 67–68 | amongst 70–77
40.21 researches] research 57–70 | ~ 72–77
40.24 some] some seeming 57–68 | ~ 70–77

40.25 among] amongst 57–64 | ~ 67–68 | amongst 70 | ~ 72–77
40.29 or] and 57–70 | ~ 72–77
41.6 and] ~ 57 | or 58–70 | ~ 72–77
41.15 fortune] fortunes 57–70 | ~ 72–77
41.25 reflection] meditation 57–68 | consideration 70 | ~ 72–77
42.3 together] along 57 | ~ 58–77
42.7 polytheism] idolatry 57–70 | ~ 72–77
42.15 begets] engenders 57 | ~ 58–77
42.22 secret] secret, 57*68 | sacred 70 | ~ 72–77
43.12 among] amongst 57–64 | ~ 67–68 | amongst 70 | ~ 72–77
43.14 bad] very bad 57 | ~ 58–77

Section 4

44.0 SECTION 4 Deities Not Considered as Creators or Formers of the World] IV. 57 | SECT. IV. *Deities not considered as creators or formers of the world.* 58–67 | SECT. IV. *Deities not considered as creators or reformers of the world.* 68 | SECT. IV. *Deities not considered as creators or formers of the world.* 70–77
44.4 among] amongst 57 | ~ 58–77
44.9 was yet] yet was 57–58 | ~ 60–77
44.18 one] ~ 57 | other 58–60 | ~ 64–77
44.18 between] betwixt 57–58 | ~ 60–77
44.20 between] betwixt 57–58 | ~ 60–77
44.25 polytheists] polytheists or idolaters 57–70 | ~ 72–77
45.7 among] amongst 57 | ~ 58–77
n. 11 5. 381] {AWC and TLB} | ix. 382 57–77
45.22 do not consider] consider not 57–70 | ~ 72–77
45.26 in the] ~ 57–68 | in 70 | ~ 72–77
45.26 represented] ~ 57–67 | represents 68 | ~ 70–77
45.30 recital] rehearsal 57–70 | ~ 72–77
45.30 prowess and vigour] activity and vigour 57*64 | vigour 67–68 | ~ 70–77
45.31 vanity] pride and vanity 57–68 | ~ 70–77
46.2 beadle or sexton, that they might] beadles or sextons, in order to 57–60 | beadles or sextons, that they might 64–68 | ~ 70–77
46.3 in order to] that they might 57–60 | ~ 64–77
46.14 with] along with 57 | ~ 58–77
46.16 throughout] thro' 57–60 | through 64–68 | ~ 70–77
46.27 Deorum:] ~ 57 | *Deorum?* 58–77
46.35 he was much more prone] that author had a much greater proneness 57–68 | he had a much greater proneness 70 | ~ 72–77
n. 26.3 tempests;] ~ 57 | tempest; 58 | ~ 60–72 | tempests: 77
47.15 kind] nature 57–68 | ~ 70–77

n. 27.8	for] of 57–68 | ~ 70–77
n. 27.9	namely his] viz. his 57–64 | his 67–68 | viz. his 70–72 | ~ 77
n. 28	10] {TLB} | ix 57–77
48.9	scarcely] scarce 57–68 | ~ 70–77
48.9	And even] ~ 57–64 | Even 67–68 | ~ 70–77
48.12	from] ~ 57–67 | and from 68 | ~ 70–77
48.15	Throughout] Thro' 57–60 | Through 64–68 | ~ 70–77
48.18	agreeably] suitable 57–60 | agreeable 64–67 | ~ 68–77
48.19	thinking] reasoning 57–70 | ~ 72–77
48.21	gods] ~ 57–67 | the gods 68 | ~ 70–77
48.24	later] latter 57–70 | ~ 72–77
48.26	scarcely] scarce 57–68 | ~ 70–77
48.26	even of] ~ 57–67 | of 68 | ~ 70–77
48.27	much] infinitely 57–68 | ~ 70–77
48.28	appellation] denomination 57–70 | ~ 72–77

Section 5

49.0	SECTION 5 Various Forms of Polytheism: Allegory, Hero-Worship] V. 57 | SECT. V. *Various Forms of Polytheism; Alegory, Hero-Worship.* 58*77
49.1	polytheism] polytheism and idolatry 57–70 | ~ 72–77
49.24	often been] been often 57–72 | ~ 77
49.25	production] product 57–60 | ~ 64–77
50.5	productions] products 57–70 | ~ 72–77
n. 31	933] {AWC} | 935 57–77
50.7	why] ~ 57–67 | what 68 | ~ 70–77
n. 33	263] {AWC} | 267 57–77
50.11	palpable] obvious 57–70 | ~ 72–77
50.14	LUCRETIUS was . . . admit of.] **These sentences occur as a footnote from 57 to 68 and as text from 70 to 77.**
50.16	renews,] ~ 57–58 | renews 60–72 | ~ 77
50.25	among] amongst 57–64 | ~ 67–68 | amongst 70 | ~ 72–77
50.27	The] And the 57–64 | ~ 67–77
51.7	must] may 57–60 | might 64–68 | ~ 70–77
51.8	in] ~ 57–64 | among 67–68 | ~ 70–77
51.12	bestow] bestow on us 57–68 | ~ 70–77
51.12	little known] unknown 57–60 | ~ 64–77
51.13	very uncertain] uncertain 57–60 | ~ 64–77
51.20	together] along 57 | ~ 58–77
n. 36	6] vi 57–70 | xi 72–77
51.32	titles] ~ 57–68 | title 70–77
51.32	might] may 57–60 | ~ 64–77

Section 6

52.0 SECTION 6 Origin of Theism from Polytheism] VI. 57 | SECT. VI. *Origin of Theism from Polytheism*. 58–77
52.3 men] persons 57–70 | ~ 72–77
52.31 interposition] interposal 57–60 | ~ 64–77
52.33 Lord] my lord 57*64 | lord 67*68 | my lord 70 | lord 72–77
53.5 design] ~ 57–64 | a design 67–68 | ~ 70–77
53.12 to the] the 57–70 | ~ 72–77
53.17 principles] opinions 57–70 | ~ 72–77
53.20 that,] ~ 57–70 | that 72 | ~ 77
53.21 is there] may there be 57–68 | ~ 70–77
53.30 art] act 57–60 | ~ 64–77
53.35 predecessor] predecessors, 57*70 | ~ 72–77
53.36 successor] successors, 57*70 | ~ 72–77
54.26 the God of ABRAHAM, ISAAC, and JACOB, became the supreme deity or JEHOVAH of the JEWS] notwithstanding the sublime ideas suggested by *Moses* and the inspired writers, many vulgar *Jews* seem still to have conceived the supreme Being as a mere topical deity or national protector 57*60 | ~ 64–77 **(See the editor's Introduction to this volume, pp. xxvi–xxvii, for a history of the early drafting of this passage.)**
54.28 The JACOBINS, . . . immaculate conception.] **This paragraph occurs as a footnote from 57 to 68 and as text from 70 to 77.**
n. 38.1 Histoire] See Histoire 57–68 | ~ 70–77
n. 38.1 **A note occurs (immediately prior to the reference) from 57 to 68 that occurs as text in 70–77.**
55.4 conformably] conformable 57–68 | ~ 70–77
55.11 as] that 57–60 | ~ 64–77

Section 7

56.0 SECTION 7 Confirmation of this Doctrine] VII. 57 | SECT. VII. *Confirmation of this Doctrine*. 58–77
56.2 limited] very limited 57–68 | ~ 70–77
56.29 a] ~ 57 | an 58–70 | ~ 72–77
57.1 and the] ~ 57–64 | the 67–68 | ~ 70–77

Section 8

58.0 SECTION 8 Flux and Reflux of Polytheism and Theism] VIII. 57 | SECT. VIII. *Flux and reflux of polytheism and theism*. 58*77
58.7 far as] as 57–72 | ~ 77

58.14 to on] to, at 57–60 | to, 64–68 | ~ 70–77
58.23 begets] engenders 57 | ~ 58–77
58.31 their] ~ 57–64 | the 67–68 | ~ 70–77
58.32 which] ~ 57–64 | who 67–68 | ~ 70–77
58.32 between] betwixt 57–60 | ~ 64–77
59.17 between] betwixt 57–60 | ~ 64–77
59.17 infirmity] ~ 57–58 | infirmities 60 | ~ 64–77

Section 9

60.0 SECTION 9 Comparison of these Religions, with regard to Persecution and Toleration] IX. 57 | SECT. IX. *Comparison of these Religions, with regard to Persecution and Toleration.* 58–77
60.4 given,] left 57–72 | ~ 77
60.5 from the] ~ 57–70 | the 72–77
60.8 to a] ~ 57–58 | to 60 | ~ 64–77
n. 42.2 tutelar] ~ 57–64 | tutelary 67–68 | ~ 70–77
n. 42.3 greater] equal or greater 57–70 | ~ 72–77
60.20 pretence] pretext 57–60 | ~ 64–77
60.21 objects] subjects 57 | ~ 58–77
61.6 *was*] were 57 | ~ 58–77
61.6 which are legally] legally 57–70 | ~ 72–77
n. 43.1 1] {GG}| ii 57–77
61.10 local] topical 57–72 | ~ 77
61.13 singular] very singular 57–68 | ~ 70–77
61.14 sects among] sects of 57 | ~ 58–77
61.17 But] And 57–60 | ~ 64–77
61.22 of] in 57–60 | ~ 64–77
61.25 among] amongst 57–68 | ~ 70–77
62.1 antipathy] aversion 57–70 | ~ 72–77
62.2 scarcely] scarce 57–68 | ~ 70–77
62.4 when this latter prince] when 57*68 | ~ 70–77
62.4 deigned] he deigned 57–68 | ~ 70–77
62.5 the] ~ 57–67 | the custom of 68 | ~ 70–77
62.9 society] political society 57–70 | ~ 72–77
n. 51.1 guilt of human sacrifices; though,] guilt; tho' 57*68 | ~ 70–77
n. 51.4 their] the 57–72 | ~ 77
62.11 scarcely] scarce 57–68 | ~ 70–77

Section 10

63.0 SECTION 10 With regard to Courage or Abasement] X. 57 | SECT. X. *With regard to courage or abasement.* 58*77

63.18 Instead] And instead 57–68 | ~ 70–77
63.18 subduing of] subduing 57–68 | ~ 70–77
63.18 the] ~ 57–67 | and the 68 | ~ 70–77
63.19 whippings] celestial honours are obtained by whippings 57–68 | ~ 70–77
63.19 cowardice] by cowardice 57–68 | ~ 70–77
63.20 abject] by abject 57–68 | ~ 70–77
63.20 obedience, are become the means of obtaining celestial honours among mankind] obedience 57–68 | ~ 70–77
63.26 And in] ~ 57–64 | In 67–68 | ~ 70–77
63.27 among] amongst 57–70 | ~ 72–77
64.1 An observation, which] And this observation 57–64 | This observation 67–68 | ~ 70–77
64.5 said] says 57–70 | ~ 72–77
64.7 said] says 57–70 | ~ 72–77
64.9 between] betwixt 57–60 | ~ 64–77

Section 11

65.0 SECTION 11 With regard to Reason or Absurdity] XI. 57 | SECT. XI. *With regard to reason or absurdity*. 58*77
65.4 at first be apt] be apt at first 57–70 | ~ 72–77
65.5 in] of 57–70 | ~ 72–77
65.10 among] amongst 57–64 | ~ 67–77
65.17 by] by the 57–68 | ~ 70–77
65.21 And their] ~ 57–64 | Their 67–70 | ~ 72–77
65.32 are sure] do often 57–60 | ~ 64–77
65.32 to prove] prove 57–60 | ~ 64–77
66.8 to the] the 57–70 | ~ 72–77
66.12 always pretend] pretend always 57–70 | ~ 72–77
66.12 foretel] conjecture 57| ~ foretel 57*Er* | foretell 58–67 | fortell 68 | foretell 70–77
66.16 among] amongst 57–64 | ~ 67–77
66.21 It is] And 57–64 | 'Tis 67–68 | ~ 70–77
66.24 *same thing*] ~ 57–60 | *same* 64–70 | ~ 72–77

Section 12

67.0 SECTION 12 With regard to Doubt or Conviction] XII. 57 | SECT. XII. *With regard to doubt or conviction*. 58*77
67.5 communion] communions 57–68 | ~ 70–77
67.8 But HERODOTUS] **The following note occurs at this point only from 57 to 70:** Lib. iii. c. 38.

67.9 the] ~ 57–67 | his 68 | ~ 70–77
67.9 never would] would never 57 | ~ 58–77
67.21 all] almost all 57–68 | ~ 70–77
67.27 cried] cries 57–60 | ~ 64–77
68.6 sacraments] ~ 57–64 | sacrament 67–68 | ~ 70–77
68.8 began the] began his catechism 57 | began his catechism the 58–68 | ~ 70–77
68.19 PARIS] *Paris* 57 | PARIS, 58–72 | ~ 77
68.28 Thus] And thus 57–68 | ~ 70–77
68.29 into] out of 57–70 | ~ 72–77
69.2 those] all those 57–68 | ~ 70–77
n. 58.3 between] betwixt 57–68 | ~ 70–77
n. 58.3 remarkable] very remarkable, 57*68 | ~ 70–77
n. 58.9 profanos] ~ 57–70 | profanus 72 | ~ 77
n. 58.12 comburere," *&c.*] {TLB}| comburere, *&c.*" 57–77
n. 58.13 differences] ~ 57–67 | difference 68 | ~ 70–77
69.5 few] very few 57–68 | ~ 70–77
69.6 exposing] the exposing 57–68 | ~ 70–77
69.8 principles] principles, 57–72 | ~ 77
69.10 among] amongst 57–64 | ~ 67–68 | amongst 70 | ~ 72–77
69.15 the] their 57 | ~ 58–60 | their 64 | ~ 67–77
69.20 Præsens] {TXT}| ~ 57 | Presens 58–77
69.22 deemed] esteemed 57–70 | ~ 72–77
n. 60.2 the] their 57–68 | ~ 70–77
70.2 heard of] heard 57–60 | ~ 64–77
70.16 Crusaders] *Croises* 57–64 | *Crusaders* 67*77
70.20 systems of that kind] systems 57–70 | ~ 72–77
70.26 that this] that that 57–68 | ~ 70–77
70.30 And thus] ~ 57–64 | Thus 67–68 | ~ 70–77
70.32 later] latter 57–70 | ~ 72–77
n. 63.1 7] {TLB}| iii 57–77
n. 64.1 387] {TLB}| 386 57–77
71.5 rises] ~ 57–70 | arises 72 | ~ 77
71.13 take] use 57–72 | ~ 77
71.34 scarcely] scarce 57–68 | ~ 70–77
72.6 their] the 57–70 | ~ 72–77
72.7 between] betwixt 57–58 | ~ 60–77
72.8 to the] the 57–72 | ~ 77
72.8 to the] the 57–72 | ~ 77
72.11 texture] contexture 57–70 | ~ 72–77
72.30 assigned] found 57–60 | ~ 64–77
72.32 nowise] no way 57–60 | ~ 64–77
73.5 object] objects, 57*70 | ~ 72–77

73.11 ancients] antient 57–64 | antients 67–68 | ancient 70–72 | ~ 77

73.21 every variety] all varieties 57–68 | ~ 70–77

73.24 throughout] thro' 57–67 | through 68 | ~ 70–77

n. 69.3 unquam] *umquam* 57 | umquam 58 | ~ 60–77

n. 69.8 exclamation] exclamations 57–60 | ~ 64–77

73.25 expression] expressions 57–70 | ~ 72–77

73.27 deemed] esteemed 57–68 | ~ 70–77

73.29 that] ~ 57–64 | the 67–68 | ~ 70–77

74.2 ingenious] great 57–70 | ~ 72–77

74.7 religious matters] all popular superstitions 57–68 | ~ 70–77

74.8 seriously] very seriously 57–68 | ~ 70–77

74.11 among] amongst 57–68 | ~ 70–77

74.17 nowise] no way 57–60 | ~ 64–77

n. 78.9 CENTRITES,] *Centrites*, 57 | ~ 58–68 | CENTRITES; 70–72 | ~ 77

n. 78.11 observes,] ~ 57–68 | observes; 70–72 | ~ 77

n. 78.13 He was] He 57–68 | ~ 70–77

n. 78.14 372] {TLB} | 273 57–77

n. 78.18 lead them] lead 57–68 | ~ 70–77

n. 78.22 932] ~ 57 | 392 60–77

n. 78.28 these] these great 57–68 | ~ 70–77

75.3 ridiculous] most ridiculous 57–68 | ~ 70–77

n. 81.1 quæst. lib. 1. cap. 5, 6.)] Quæst. lib. i. cap. 5, 6.) 57 | Quæst.) lib. i. cap. 5, 6. 58–77

n. 81.6 This] This, 57–72 | ~ 77

n. 81.6 observe] observe, 57–72 | ~ 77

75.9 chief] great 57–70 | ~ 72–77

n. 82.1 9] {GG} | viii 57–77

75.18 between] betwixt 57–58 | ~ 60–77

75.19 *scholastic*] ~ 57 | *scholastical* 58–70 | ~ 72–77

76.3 minds] ~ 57–72 | mind 77

76.4 happily makes] makes 57–68 | ~ 70–77

Section 13

77.0 SECTION 13 Impious Conceptions of the Divine Nature in Popular Religions of Both Kinds] XIII. 57 | SECT. XIII. *Impious conceptions of the divine nature in most popular religions of both kinds.* 58*70 | SECT. XIII. *Impious conceptions of the divine nature in popular religions of both kinds.* 72–77

77.4 must augment] augment 57 | ~ 58–77

77.5 ghastliness] ~ 57–64 | affright 67–68 | ~ 70–77

77.17 will be deemed] be esteemed 57–60 | be deemed 64–68 | ~ 70–77

77.19 phænomena: It] phænomena. And it 57–68 | ~ 70–77

77.21 objects] object 57–72 | ~ 77
77.22 between] betwixt 57–58 | ~ 60–77
77.24 adulation] praise 57–70 | ~ 72–77
77.25 And the] ~ 57–64 | The 67–68 | ~ 70–77
78.5 that this] that that 57–68 | ~ 70–77
n. 84.1 was] ~ 57–72 | were 77
78.17 in which] where 57–70 | ~ 72–77
78.21 their] ~ 57–64 | the 67–68 | ~ 70–77
78.21 their] often their 57–70 | ~ 72–77
78.30 that conduct] these measures 57–58 | ~ 60–77
78.31 Thus] And thus 57 | ~ 58–77
78.32 popular] many popular 57–60 | most popular 64–68 | ~ 70–77
78.34 depressed] frequently deprest 57*68 | ~ 70–77
79.1 Among] Amongst 57–68 | ~ 70–77
79.2 among] amongst 57–68 | ~ 70–77
79.3 contracts] often contracts 57–70 | ~ 72–77
79.6 struggle] ~ 57–64 | contest 67–68 | ~ 70–77
79.13 between] betwixt 57–60 | ~ 64–77
79.14 later] latter 57–70 | ~ 72–77
n. 87.4 later] latter 57–70 | ~ 72–77
n. 87.7 and unamiable] unamiable 57 | ~ 58–77
n. 87.7 he was pictured by the ancients] the antient 57 | the antients 58–68 | ~ 70–77
n. 87.13 a Chinese] ~ 57–64 | Chinese 67–68 | ~ 70–77
n. 87.14 freethinkers] {TXT} | ~ 57–58 | free-thinkers 60–77
n. 87.16 scribblers] {TXT} | scriblers 57–72 | ~ 77
n. 87.16 partial] {TXT} | ~ 57–60 | partial, 64–77
n. 87.18 garden of] ~ 57–67 | garden in 68 | ~ 70–77
n. 87.27 drivellers] ~ 57 | driveller 58 | ~ 60–77
n. 87.30 idolatry] {TXT} | ~ 57–60 | idolatry, 64–67 | ~ 68 | idolatry, 70–77
n. 87.32 rebellious,] {TXT} | ~ 57–68 | rebellious 70–77
n. 87.34 a] ~ 57–64 | the 67–68 | ~ 70–77
n. 87.40 corrupt,] {TXT} | ~ 57–60 | corrupt 64–77
n. 87.43 effect.] {TXT} | ~ 57–68 | effect; 70–77
n. 87.44 ever] {TXT} | ~ 57–68 | ever, 70–77
n. 87.44 *fiat*,] {TXT} | ~ 57–68 | *fiat* 70–77
n. 87.48 Father] {TXT} | ~ 57–68 | father 70–77
n. 87.51 freethinkers] {TXT} | ~ 57–58 | free-thinkers 60–77
n. 87.53 thus,] {TXT} | ~ 57–60 | thus 64–77
n. 87.59 403] {TLB} | 401 57–77
n. 88.1 500] {AWC} | 501 57–77

Section 14

81.0 SECTION 14 Bad Influence of Popular Religions on Morality] XIV. 57 | SECT. XIV. *Bad influence of most popular religions on morality.* 58*70 | SECT. XIV. *Bad influence of popular religions on morality.* 72–77
81.2 such as] those, who 57–68 | ~ 70–77
81.7 and] ~ 57–64 | or 67–68 | ~ 70–77
81.9 also be assured] be assured 57–60 | be assured also 64–72 | ~ 77
81.12 thought] ~ 57–68 | thought, 70–77
81.18 forming] entering into 57–68 | ~ 70–77
81.25 never] seldom 57–70 | ~ 72–77
82.18 setting] setting of the 57–68 | ~ 70–77
82.30 obligation] beauty 57–70 | ~ 72–77
82.34 pretension] pretence 57–70 | ~ 72–77
82.35 deemed] esteemed 57–68 | ~ 70–77
82.37 his] ~ 57–72 | this 77
83.8 because] that 57–64 | ~ 67–77
83.12 nowise] no way 57–60 | ~ 64–77
83.20 Hence] HENCE 57–60 | ~ 64–68 | Hence, 70–72 | ~ 77
83.21 Hence] ~ 57–68 | Hence, 70–77
n. 92.1 20] xx 57–60 | xv 64–77
83.32 the] his 57–58 | ~ 60–77
83.36 after] even after 57–70 | ~ 72–77
84.11 form] to form 57–60 | ~ 64 | from 67 | ~ 68–77
84.17 Thus] And thus 57–64 | ~ 67–77
84.18 artifices] ~ 57–64 | artificers 67 | ~ 68 | artificers 70 | ~ 72–77

Section 15

85.0 SECTION 15 General Corollary] XV. 57| SECT. XV. *General Corollary from the whole.* 58–64 | SECT. XV. *General Corollary.* 67–77
85.3 scarcely] scarce 57–68 | ~ 70–77
85.9 throughout] thro' 57–58 | through 60–64 | ~ 67–77
85.19 not] scarce 57–68 | ~ 70–77
86.3 equally discovered] discovered equally 57–72 | ~ 77
86.7 may] it may 57 | ~ 58–77
86.9 other] the other 57–70 | ~ 72–77
86.9 creation] ~ 57–64 | universe 67–68 | ~ 70–77
86.10 universal] ~ 57–64 | supreme 67–68 | ~ 70–77
86.11 appears] commonly appears 57–68 | ~ 70–77
86.18 supreme Creator] ~ 57–64 | sovereign Author 67–68 | ~ 70–77
86.21 any thing but] other than 57–70 | ~ 72–77

86.25 so certain] they are so certain of 57–70 | ~ 72–77
86.29 secret] ~ 57–67 | sacred 68 | ~ 70–77
86.30 that they] as 57–70 | ~ 72–77
86.32 that they] as 57–70 | ~ 72–77
86.35 destitute] devoid 57 | void 58–70 | ~ 72–77
86.39 corrupt] corrupted 57 | ~ 57*Er*–77
87.8 scarcely] scarce 57–68 | ~ 70–77

Hume's Index
(Editions: 58, 64, 67, 68, 70, 72, 77)

A Dissertation on the Passions

Lead Entry

DESIRE	and Aversion, whence] Aversion 58–67 | ~ 68 | Aversion 70–77
FAME	**There may be a mistake in the listing of the page of this entry (printed as p. 199 in the 1772 edn.). It is possible that Hume intended to refer to 2.22 ff. or 2.33, rather than 2.25 ff.**
JOY	and GRIEF] Grief 58–67 | ~ 68 | Grief 70–77
LOCKE, Mr.	**The conclusion, reached by the editor of this volume, that Hume is referring to *DP* 2.6 (the 1st par. in Hume's no. 3 of sect. 2) requires inference; but the page number given by Hume corresponds to *DP* 2.6, and Hume's reference is consistent throughout all of his indexes to the editions of *ETSS*.**
PASSIONS	Objects] ~ 58–70 | Objections 72–77

The Natural History of Religion

Lead Entry

ARNOBIUS	**This entry was not in correct alphabetical order in the copytext.**
EGYPTIAN	Religion resembling] ~ 58–67 | resembling, each other 68 | ~ 70–77
EPICURUS	took] ~ 58–67 | betook 68 | ~ 70–77
EPICURUS	**In the index of 1772, the printed reference to p. 426 appears to be a misprint; the correct page is 429.**
Heresy	Appellation] ~ 58–67 | The Appellation 68 | ~ 70–77
Hero-worship	**Hume perhaps meant 5.3 rather than 5.1 ff.; p. 428 in the index of 1772 appears to have been misprinted as 429.**

Hesiod	**Hume originally included the reference to Hesiod at 4.11 in his first index (1758), then apparently lost the reference in the subsequent editions. The 1758 original is correct, and is here restored.**
Mary	became] ~ 58–67 | become 68 | ~ 70–77
Newton	Arians, and sincere] ~ 58–67 | sincere Arians 68 | ~ 70–77
Nicholas	became] ~ 58–67 | become 68 | ~ 70–77
Persecution	**In the index of 1772, the printed reference to p. 443 appears to be a misprint that should have been printed 442.**
Personify	Personify, to] ~ 58–67 | Personification 68 | ~ 70–77
Religion	**In the index of 1772, the printed reference to p. 507 is a misprint that should have been printed 407.**
Scholastic	usual] ~ 58–67 | useful 68 | ~ 70–77

THE INTELLECTUAL BACKGROUND: A CONCISE ACCOUNT, WITH BIBLIOGRAPHY

The Biographical Appendix (pp. 229–40) describes all persons specifically mentioned by Hume in the two works in this volume.[1] Many authors, in addition to those Hume himself mentions, were influential in the eighteenth century for writings on the passions, natural history, or religion; and many of their writings were on topics of interest to Hume. This Intellectual Background is a compact historical and bibliographical catalogue of the most prominent such figures and their works. The goal is to present the principal features of the intellectual context of Hume's reflections on the passions and the natural history of religion, starting with the passions.

A DISSERTATION ON THE PASSIONS

Many philosophers known to Hume had discussed the nature, classification, origins, and causal role of the passions. Though limited information is available on the works that Hume consulted while developing his views in *Treatise* 2 and *A Dissertation on the Passions*, several authors whom he mentions in other writings and in his correspondence had contributed to literature on the passions. Other seventeenth- and eighteenth-century figures were also widely recognized for their writings on the passions.

This section itemizes notable contributors to this literature, and emphasizes issues that cut across their writings. No attempt is made to provide either a comprehensive list of writers who treated the passions or a detailed inventory of the issues under investigation. No suggestion is made that Hume read each of the mentioned works or was influenced by them. However, he is known to have been familiar with many of these works and could have encountered all of them.

Ancient, Medieval, and Early Modern Writers

Several ancient and medieval philosophers identified, classified, or explained the passions. Leading contributors include:[2]

[1] See also, on the passions, several parts of the Clarendon Hume Edition of *A Treatise of Human Nature*.

[2] Plato's dialogues might seem a questionable omission, but Plato paid scant attention to what would become the primary areas of interest in the philosophy of the passions. He concentrated on

Aristotle (384–322 BC), *Rhetoric*[3]
Cicero (106–43 BC), *Tusculan Disputations*[4]
Seneca (4 BC–65 AD), *Moral Essays* and *Ad Lucilium epistulae morales*[5]
Plutarch (46–*c.*120 AD), *Moralia*[6]
St Thomas Aquinas (1225–74), *Summa Theologiæ*[7]

Hume often mentions Aristotle, Plutarch, Seneca, and Cicero. Although he never cites St Thomas, whose theory of the passions may have been the most influential account carried into early modern philosophy, Hume would have encountered Thomistic treatments of the passions through the chain of scholarly transmission. (St Thomas's analysis of the passions was arguably the most comprehensive philosophical account available to Hume.) However, the primary influences on Hume's thinking about the passions seem to be early modern theories of human nature and conduct such as those of Descartes, Hobbes, Malebranche, Locke, and Hutcheson.

Study of the passions was linked to issues in metaphysics and moral philosophy in early modern philosophy. Prominent writers and works published prior to Hume's investigations in the *Treatise*—all mentioned or discussed in the Annotations in this volume—include:[8]

the competition between reason and the passions and the different parts of the soul. See *Republic* 329C–D; 439D–444E; 571B–572B; 580D–581E; *Laws* 863A–864B.

[3] *Rhetoric* 1378ª18–1388ᵇ31. Aristotle described this portion of the *Rhetoric* as a 'discussion of the emotions' (1378ª19). See also *On the Soul* 433ª–ᵇ30 (on mind and appetite) and *Nicomachean Ethics* 1111ª22–ᵇ3 (on voluntariness and passion). The latter work contains a moral psychology that occasionally treats the passions.

[4] *Tusculan Disputations*, bks. 3–4. See also *De finibus bonorum et malorum* (e.g. 1.18.58–61; 3.10.35) for additional passages on Stoic, Epicurean, and Academic views; and *De oratore* (esp. 1.51.219–1.54.233; 2.44.185–2.45.190; 2.51.206–2.53.216) on the orator's control of the emotions of audiences.

[5] *Moral Essays*, esp. 'De ira' ('On Anger') and 'De beneficiis' ('On Benefits'); *Ad Lucilium epistulae morales*, esp. 'On the Diseases of the Soul' and 'On Self-Control'.

[6] *Moralia*, esp. 'On the Control of Anger', 'On Tranquillity of Mind', 'On Affection for Offspring', 'On Envy and Hate', 'On Praising Oneself Inoffensively', and 'The Dialogue on Love'.

[7] *Summa Theologiæ*, 1a2æ.22–32, 35, 39–48. In his analysis of the passions St Thomas draws heavily on Aristotle, using material in addition to the three works by Aristotle cited above. Approximately half of St Thomas's references in the core sections on the passions are to Aristotle's *Rhetoric*. He also cites Cicero's *Tusculan Disputations* several times; Cicero is the only Latin pagan author he consults. The early 'fathers of the Church' had little to say about the passions, but St Augustine, St John Damascene, and Nemesius all had a place in St Thomas's understanding of the subject.

[8] English titles and spellings are not modernized in this edition for books published in English, even if the spellings were long ago abandoned. These titles do not always correspond to entries in the Annotations or the Reference List. English translations of books that were published after Hume's lifetime are not listed in the notes below. The year in parentheses following each title is the year of first publication in the original language. Additional bibliographical information is supplied in footnotes, as appropriate. For available information on the particular editions used by either the editor or Hume, see the Reference List and the Catalogue.

No works on the passions published after *THN* and before *DP* are on the lists in this Intellectual Background because Hume's intellectual indebtedness in writing *DP* is essentially identical to

Juan Luis Vives, *The Passions of the Soul* (1538)[9]
Guillaume Du Vair, *The Moral Philosophy of the Stoics* (1585)[10]
Pierre Charron, *Of Wisdom* (1601)[11]
Thomas Wright, *The Passions of the Mind* (1601)[12]
Nicolas Coeffeteau, *A Table of Human Passions. With their Causes and Effects* (1620)[13]
Edward Reynolds, *A Treatise of the Passions and Faculties of the Soul of Man* (1640)[14]
Marin Cureau de la Chambre, *The Characters of the Passions* (1640)[15]
Jean-François Senault, *The Use of Passions* (1641)[16]
René Descartes, *The Passions of the Soul* (1649)[17]
Thomas Hobbes, *Leviathan* (1651)[18]
Antoine Le Grand, *Man without Passion: Or, the Wise Stoic According to the Sentiments of Seneca* (1662)[19]
Henry More, *Enchiridion Ethicum* (1666)[20]
Walter Charleton, *Natural History of the Passions* (1674)[21]

that of *THN*. This conclusion does not presume a lack of new work on the passions during this near 20-year period.

[9] *De anima et vita* (Basel, 1538), bk. 3.

[10] *Philosophie morale des Stoïques* (Paris, 1585). Eng. trans. Thomas James: *The Morall Philosophie of the Stoicks* (London, 1598). Du Vair also reflects on the passions in *De la sainte philosophie*; see esp. pp. 24, 33.

[11] *De la sagesse* (Bordeaux, 1601). Eng. trans. Samson Lennard: *Of Wisdome* (London, 1608).

[12] *The Passions of the Minde* (London, 1601); corrected edn. published as *The Passions of the Minde in Generall* (London, 1604).

[13] *Tableau des passions humaines: de leurs causes, et de leurs effets*. Eng. trans. E. Grimeston: *A Table of Humane Passions. With their Causes and Effects* (London, 1621).

[14] *A Treatise of the Passions and Faculties of the Soule of Man. With the Severall Dignities and Corruptions Thereunto Belonging* (London, 1640).

[15] *Les caractères des passions*, 5 vols. (Paris, 1640–62). Eng. trans.: *The Characters of the Passions*, part 1. (London, 1650; Part 2, 1661). Cureau de la Chambre's *L'Art de connoistre les hommes* (Paris, 1659) also treats modestly of the passions (see 1.3.1.6; 1.3.2–6; 1.4; 2.6.3–4). Eng. trans. John Davies: *The Art How to Know Men* (London, 1665).

[16] *De l'usage des passions* (Paris, 1641). Eng. trans. Henry Earle of Monmouth: *The Use of Passions* (London, 1649).

[17] *Les passions de l'âme* (Paris, 1649). Eng. trans.: *The Passions of the Soule* (London, 1650).

[18] *Leviathan, or the Matter, Forme, & Power of a Commonwealth, Ecclesiasticall and Civil* (London, 1651), esp. ch. 6.

[19] *Le sage des Stoiques ou l'homme sans passions. Selon les sentiments de Sénèque* (The Hague, 1662). Eng. trans.: *Man without Passion: Or, the Wise Stoick, According to the Sentiments of Seneca* (London, 1675). Le Grand subsequently came under the influence of Descartes's account of the passions and modified his earlier Stoic principles.

[20] *Enchiridion Ethicum* (London, 1666), in Latin. Eng. trans.: *An Account of Virtue* (London, 1690). Esp. chs. 6–13.

[21] *Natural History of the Passions* (London, 1674), published anonymously. This book has been incorrectly described in the British Museum Catalogue, and databases dependent on it, either as authored by Jean François Senault or as descended from Senault's *De l'usage des passions*.

Nicolas Malebranche, *Search after Truth* (1674–5)[22]
Baruch Spinoza, *Ethics* (1677)[23]
John Locke, *An Essay concerning Human Understanding* (1690)[24]
William Ayloffe, *The Government of the Passions According to the Rules of Reason and Religion* (1700)[25]
Charles Le Brun [Lebrun], *The Conference of Monsieur Le Brun . . . upon Expression* (1698)[26]
The Earl of Shaftesbury (Anthony Ashley Cooper), *Characteristics of Men, Manners, Opinions, Times* (1711)[27]
Bernard Mandeville, *Fable of the Bees* (1714)[28]
Joseph Butler, *Fifteen Sermons Preached at the Rolls Chapel* (1726)[29]
Francis Hutcheson, *An Essay on the Nature and Conduct of the Passions and Affections. With Illustrations on the Moral Sense* (1728)[30]
Isaac Watts, *A Plain and Particular Account of the Natural Passions* and *The Doctrine of the Passions Explained and Improved* (both 1729)[31]

Cross-Cutting Areas of Interest

Several distinctions, topics, and typologies cut across ancient, medieval, and early modern theories of the passions. They are addressed by most of the authors mentioned above, but are not investigated or understood in the same way by every writer. Some traditional topics—such as the distinction between concupiscible and irascible passions—play no role in *A Dissertation on the Passions*, and therefore are not considered here. The discussion below is confined to six areas that are covered in virtually every comprehensive theory of the passions, including Hume's (in the *Treatise* if not in the *Dissertation*).

1. Nature of the Passions. Many writers on the passions have discussed their nature. Some writers assumed a fundamental difference between action

[22] *De la recherche de la verité* (Paris, 1674–5). Eng. trans.: *Malebranch's Search after Truth*, 2 vols. (London, 1694–5). Esp. bk. 5, 'The Passions'.

[23] *Ethica*, in *Opera posthuma* (Amsterdam, 1677). Esp. 'Third Part', 'On the Origin and Nature of the Affects'.

[24] *An Essay concerning Humane Understanding* (London, 1690), esp. 2.20.3–18.

[25] *The Government of the Passions According to the Rules of Reason and Religion* (London, 1700).

[26] *Conférence de monsieur le Brun, premier du roi . . . sur l'expression générale et particulière* (Amsterdam, 1698). Eng. trans.: *The Conference of Monsieur Le Brun . . . upon Expression, General and Particular* (London, 1701).

[27] *Characteristicks of Men, Manners, Opinions, Times* (n.p., 1711).

[28] *The Fable of the Bees: Or, Private Vices, Publick Benefits* (London, 1714).

[29] *Fifteen Sermons Preached at the Rolls Chapel* (London, 1726).

[30] *An Essay on the Nature and Conduct of the Passions and Affections. With Illustrations on the Moral Sense* (London, 1728).

[31] *Discourses of the Love of God and the Use and Abuse of the Passions in Religion. . . . To which is prefix'd, A Plain and Particular Account of the Natural Passions, with Rules for the Government of Them* (London, 1729); and *The Doctrine of the Passions Explained and Improved* (London, 1729). Watts altered the title(s) and contents of his work on the passions in later editions.

(or agent) and passion (or patient). As Isaac Watts stated the view, 'The word *Passion* . . . denotes the *receiving of the Action of some Agent*: As if an Archer bend his Bow, the Archer is the *Agent*; the Bow is the *Patient*'.[32] This distinction incorporated the proposition, challenged by the Stoics,[33] that the passions include no volitional or judgemental element, and that the soul is not acting when affected by passions—just as persons are not acting when they receive sensory perceptions. As Spinoza put it, a passion is an affection that arises if someone is acted upon, by contrast to acting.[34]

However, the proposition that the passions are purely passive features of human nature has not been widely promulgated in the history of philosophy. Even Aristotle and his followers linked passion to active states of mind, including cognition.[35] Following Aristotle's lead, St Thomas suggested that passions are not purely passive. Of anger, he said that 'anger . . . involves a consideration of inflicting punishment. . . . Now inference and deduction are acts of reason. Hence anger in some sense involves reason. . . . [T]he act may be commanded by reason . . . [and] the act may be motivated by reason.'[36] Passions are, from this perspective, intimately connected to forms of apprehension and involve active responses to objects or states apprehended.

A few philosophers suggested that the passions are distinctive feelings analogous to sensory perceptions,[37] and others regarded the passions as confused ideas or perceptions, twisted judgements, or conditions that distort true understanding or reason (see 5 below). For example, Spinoza, in his 'General Definition of the Affects', said: 'An Affect that is called a Passion of the Mind is a confused idea . . . which, when it is given, determines the Mind to think of this rather than that. . . . [T]he Mind is acted on only insofar as it has inadequate, *or* confused, ideas.'[38]

Some philosophers treated assorted passions on the model of madness, disease, or disorder in the soul. The Stoics and Spinoza used disease analogies, and regarded the passions as rooted in misunderstandings that can and should be corrected and

[32] Watts, *a Plain and Particular Account* 1.1 (p. 1). Watts himself dismisses this 'logical sense' of 'passion' as outmoded.

[33] Cicero writes of the Stoics: 'All disorders are, they think, due to judgment and belief. Consequently they define them more precisely, that it may be realized not only how wrong they are but to what extent they are under our control' (*Tusculan Disputations* 4.7.14–15). For classic models of the Stoic teaching, see Seneca, *Moral Essays*, 'De ira' ('On Anger') 1.1.1–7; 1.7.2–4; 1.8.1–6; 2.1–2; 2.3.1–5; 2.12.3–6; and 3.1.1–5; 'On Tranquillity of Mind' 10.5–6; 'De beneficiis' ('On Benefits') 2.14.1; *Ad Lucilium epistulae morales* 75.11–18 ('On the Diseases of the Soul'); 116.1–5 ('On Self-Control'). See also Le Grand, *Man without Passion*, pp. 69–72.

[34] Spinoza, *Ethics* 3, Defs. 2–3; 3.P1; 3.P3.

[35] Aristotle, *Nicomachean Ethics* 1149^{b}1: 'Emotion follows reason in a way, but appetite does not.'

[36] St Thomas Aquinas, *Summa Theologiæ* 1a2æ.40, art. 2; 1a2æ.46, art. 4.

[37] See More, *Enchiridion Ethicum* 1.7.7: '*Passion* is rightly called *Sensation*.' Malebranche, by contrast, maintained that a distinction should be drawn between passions and the distinctive sensations that accompany them (*Search after Truth* 5.3).

[38] Spinoza, *Ethics* 3, 'General Definition of the Affects'.

controlled. Some philosophers viewed fear, love, hate, and other passions as phobias or sicknesses of the soul.[39] However, these reductions of the passions to feelings, confused ideas, or disorderly states have been minority views in the history of philosophy.

Finally, many philosophers were interested in precise definitions or conceptual conditions of specific passions. They wanted both to understand those passions and to distinguish them from related passions. Aristotle, for example, addressed definitional questions such as the following:

Let *shame* then be defined as a kind of pain or uneasiness in respect of misdeeds, past, present, or future, which seem to tend to bring dishonour; and *shamelessness* as contempt and indifference in regard to these same things. . . . Let *pity* then be a kind of pain excited by the sight of evil, deadly or painful, which befalls one who does not deserve it. . . . Now what is called *indignation* is the antithesis to pity; for the being pained at undeserved good fortune is in a manner contrary to being pained at undeserved bad fortune and arises from the same character; . . . *Envy* is a kind of pain at the sight of good fortune in regard to the goods mentioned, in the case of those like themselves, and not for the sake of a man getting anything, but because of others possessing it.[40]

2. Typology. Some philosophers appealed to a distinction between *basic* and *derived* passions or between *primitive* and *mixed* passions. They attempted to establish a typology. Lists and categories differed from one author to the next, as did their accounts of how the passions mix. Cicero's fourfold typology of the basic passions ('with numerous subdivisions') was influential:

there are two [passions] proceeding from an idea of good, one of which is exuberant pleasure, that is to say, joy excited beyond measure by the idea of some great present good; the second is the intemperate longing for a supposed great good . . . rightly termed desire or lust. . . . [They] disturb the soul just as the two remaining [passions], fear and distress, cause disturbances by the idea of evil. For fear is the idea of a serious threatening evil and distress is the idea of a serious present evil.[41]

The most influential typology by an early modern philosopher was Descartes's schema of 'six primitive passions . . .—namely, wonder, love, hatred, desire, joy, and sadness'. All others, he held, are 'either composed from some of these six or they are species of them'.[42] Descartes discussed how diverse passions derive from these primitive passions. For example, he maintained that love is the source of several

[39] Plato, *Republic* 329D, 439D, 444E; Seneca, *Ad Lucilium epistulae morales* 116.1 ('On Self-Control') and 75.10–14 ('On the Diseases of the Soul'); Cicero, *Tusculan Disputations* 3.4.7–8; 4.5–7; 4.11.24–6; Coeffeteau, *A Table of Humane Passions* 1; and Spinoza, *Ethics* 3.P26 (schol.); 4.P44 (schol.); 4.Appendix (18).

[40] Aristotle, *Rhetoric* 1383^{b}15–1387^{b}24.

[41] Cicero, *Tusculan Disputations* 3.11.24–5; cf. 3.13.28; 4.5.11–12; 4.7.14–15. These are the only basic passions for Cicero. For his treatment of the *subdivisions* of these classes, see 4.7.16–19. Along the way, Cicero assesses Stoic, Peripatetic, and Epicurean views. See also Senault, *Use of Passions* 1.3 (pp. 24–5); Le Grand, *Man without Passion*, pp. 8–10.

[42] Descartes, *Passions of the Soul* 69. The bulk of this classification scheme agrees with Aquinas's list of the concupiscible passions.

passions and expanded the analysis to distinguish different kinds of love. Charleton, Malebranche, More, and others followed the main lines of Descartes's typology. Charleton, for example, held that 'only six' passions (wonder, love, hatred, desire, joy, and sadness) 'are simple.... All the rest... are but various *species* of those simple ones, or they result from divers *mixtures* and combinations of them', and therefore are '*Mixt* Passions'.[43]

A few writers were interested in what Henry More called the 'kinds and species' of the *particular* passions. For example, More analysed the passions that 'fall under the Head of *Cupidity*': 'The Kinds and Species of *Cupidity* are, in the First Rank, *Hope, Fear, Jealousie, Security*, and *Despair*: In the next [rank] are *Irresolution, Animosity, Courage, Emulation, Cowardise, and Consternation*.'[44] However, no writer claimed to have provided an exhaustive list of all the passions. Nicolas Coeffeteau even warned that 'there are an infinite number [of passions whose names] we know not'.[45]

3. Causal Inquiry. Another objective of those who investigated the passions was to explain them causally. Terms such as *origins, creation, causes, effects*, and *motions* of the passions expressed this objective.[46] Alexander Forbes (1678–1762) envisioned a vast philosophical potential: 'Numberless Observations might be made on the Passions, each whereof would require a Book, if one was to consider their Rise, their Progress, their Decay, their Extinction, their Rising again, their giving way to other Passions quite opposite, their Combinations, their Force, their Subtilty, their Enhancement, *&c.* All which are but the different turnings of Human Nature.'[47]

The conditions under which particular passions arise, become modified, or are extinguished was a recurrent topic of discussion. An elementary example is a thesis that Plutarch plucked from a lost work of Aristotle: 'anger ceases when cold water is sprinkled on it, as Aristotle says, but... it is also extinguished when a poultice of fear is applied to it.'[48] A typical example of how one passion may causally affect another is Guillaume Du Vair's conclusion that 'one of the worst effects of fear is that it makes us hate the object of our fear'.[49]

Some analyses of how one or more passions cause, or causally affect, one or more other passions were intricate. For example, a complex theory of human

[43] Charleton, *Natural History of the Passions* 5.65; cf. More, *Enchiridion Ethicum* 1.7.3 ff.; Malebranche, *Search after Truth* 5.7, 10. Malebranche concludes that love and hatred are the two parent impressions, and that the only general passions they produce are desire, joy, and sadness. More 'contracts' Descartes's list of six into three. Descartes spoke of the passions as mixing in various ways, but did not use precisely the language of 'mixed passions'. In *DP* Hume uses the notions of 'mixed passions' and 'pure passions' (his account is more elaborate in *THN*).

[44] More, *Enchiridion Ethicum* 1.10.1; cf. the roots of the analysis at 1.7.5 ff.

[45] *A Table of Humane Passions*, p. 30. See also Alexander Forbes, *Essays Moral and Philosophical on Several Subjects* 1.6, p. 49.

[46] See Descartes, *Passions of the Soul* 27–8; Malebranche, *Search after Truth* 5.1–3 [337–8].

[47] Forbes, *Essays Moral and Philosophical on Several Subjects* 1.6, p. 50.

[48] Plutarch, 'On the Control of Anger' 454D.

[49] Du Vair, *Morall Philosophie of the Stoicks*, p. 30.

nature underlies St Thomas's conclusion that 'where the objective is some good, orectic movement [that of appetite] begins with love, passes into desire and ends in hope; where it is some evil, it begins with hatred, passes into aversion, and ends in fear'.[50]

Several philosophers were interested in how passions cause or influence either physical or mental states in persons. For example, Cureau de La Chambre argued that the passions have two primary effects: movements in the body and intentions in the soul.[51] He pointed to specific instances, such as how sparkling eyes and a terrified voice are indicative of anger and how certain passions foster moral intentions. Many writers were intrigued with the idea that the passions are closely, perhaps necessarily, associated with corresponding bodily expressions or states. For example, Descartes held that there are 'many external signs which usually accompany the passions—signs which are much better observed when several are mingled together, as they normally are, than when they are separated. The most important such signs are the expressions of the eyes and the face, changes in colour, trembling, listlessness, fainting, laughter, tears, groans and sighs.'[52]

4. Functional Explanation. It was often said in early modern philosophy either that the passions function to present objects to individuals as good or evil (for example, fear presents objects as evil) or that the apprehension of circumstances as good or evil produces passions (for example, apprehension of a dangerous situation causes fear).[53] Descartes, who held the latter view, described the 'function of the passions' as follows:

> the objects which stimulate the senses do not excite different passions in us because of differences in the objects, but only because of the various ways in which they may harm or benefit us, or in general have importance for us. The function of all the passions consists solely in this, that they dispose our soul to want the things which nature deems useful for us, and to persist in this volition.[54]

Malebranche offered another sanguine interpretation of the purpose of the passions: 'The *passions* of the soul . . . incline us toward loving our body and all that might be of use in its preservation.'[55]

[50] St Thomas asked and answered a series of questions about the causal foundations of love and the effects of love on other passions (*Summa Theologiæ* 1a2æ.25, art. 4; 1a2æ.27–9, 43).

[51] Cureau de La Chambre, *Characters of the Passions* 1.

[52] Descartes, *Passions of the Soul* 112; also 113 ff. Cf. the many different effects of interest to two commentators on the Cartesian theory: Julien Offray de La Mettrie (1709–51; French philosopher and physician), *Histoire naturelle de l'âme* 12 (esp. pp. 108–13), and Cartesian commentator Charles Le Brun, *Conference of Monsieur Le Brun*, pp. 1–38.

[53] See Cicero, *Tusculan Disputations* 3.11.24–5; 3.13.28; 4.7.14–15; Reynolds, *A Treatise of the Passions* 5, 12; Charleton, *Natural History of the Passions* 4.6; Watts, *A Plain and Particular Account* 13.

[54] Descartes, *Passions of the Soul* 52; see 40, 79, 85–7, 89, 94, 137 for his broader functional analysis.

[55] Malebranche, *Search after Truth* 5.1. Cf. Watts, *A Plain and Particular Account of the Natural Passions* 13 (on service to both body and mind).

Jean-François Senault apparently chose the title *The Use of Passions* because his book considered (in Part 2, 'Of Passions in Particular') what he called 'the good use' and 'the bad use' of the passions. He treated the good and bad uses of love, hatred, hope, despair, desire, eschewing, audacity, fear, anger, pleasure, and sorrow. In the instance of love, he maintained that its bad uses include being excessively attracted to others and being enticed to form illicit friendships, whereas its good uses include charity and licit friendships.[56] Six decades later Senault's list was appropriated by William Ayloffe to analyse 'the good use' of each passion, suitably moderated. Even hatred and anger were held to have good uses.[57]

Several philosophers discussed the distinctive functions of *particular* passions. For example, Charleton defended the engaging thesis that '*Glory* and *Shame*, tho directly opposite each to other, doe yet agree in their End, which is *to incite us to Virtue*.'[58] A no less charming hypothesis about hope and fear was offered by Henry More: 'The Use of *Hope* is to have Delight in acting; and of *Fear* to proceed with Circumspection and Diligence.'[59]

Other functions were discussed in literature on the passions. Prominent were those of (1) motivating persons to perform actions and (2) hindering reason and rational control. The latter function received sufficient attention that it warrants independent consideration as a cross-cutting area of interest.

5. Control of the Passions. The idea that agents are acted upon when passions are active was sometimes connected to the idea that agents are active only when governed by reason and the will. In the *Treatise* 2.3.3.1, Hume wrote that:

> Nothing is more usual in philosophy, and even in common life, than to talk of the combat of passion and reason, to give the preference to reason, and assert that men are only so far virtuous as they conform themselves to its dictates. Every rational creature, 'tis said, is oblig'd to regulate his actions by reason; and if any other motive or principle challenge the direction of his conduct, he ought to oppose it, 'till it be entirely subdu'd, or at least brought to a conformity with that superior principle. On this method of thinking the greatest part of moral philosophy, antient and modern, seems to be founded.

The need to replace disruptive, inordinate, or violent passions with rational control or calm dispositions has a history dating from Platonic, Aristotelian, Stoic, Epicurean, and Christian ideas that many passions are unruly appetites that render persons their victims.[60] Plato's defence of reason in the face of a 'civil war in the soul'[61] between reason and the passions reverberated throughout later centuries,

[56] Senault, *Use of Passions* 2.1–6. See p. 7 for a functional theory directed against Stoic views.

[57] Ayloffe, *Government of the Passions*, pp. 68–123. Ayloffe held that the 'design' of all passions is that of 'assistants or servants to virtue', p. 41.

[58] Charleton, *Natural History of the Passions* 5.49.

[59] More, *Enchiridion Ethicum* 1.10.2.

[60] See Seneca, 'De ira' ('On Anger') 1.1.1–2; 1.8.1–6; 2.3.1–5; 3.1.1–2; Du Vair, *Morall Philosophie of the Stoicks*, pp. 62–70, 100; Charron, *Of Wisdome* (*De la sagesse*) 2.1; Wright, *Passions of the Mind* 1.4; 2.1–3.3; Senault, *Use of Passions* 1.2.5–1.3.5; Le Grand, *Man without Passion*, pp. 70, 85, 90–1, 96, 99–101, 115 ff., 135 ff.; Charleton, *Natural History of the Passions* 3.7–9; 5.64; 6.11–13; Malebranche, *Search after Truth* 5.6.

[61] Plato, *Republic* 440E, 444B.

as did a Stoic–Peripatetic disagreement cryptically formulated by Seneca: 'The question has often been raised whether it is better to have moderate emotions, or none at all. Philosophers of our school reject the emotions; the Peripatetics keep them in check.'[62]

The regulation of the passions by reason—regarded as the proper master over the potential slavery of the passions—was of considerable interest to early modern writers. Spinoza, who entitled the fourth part of his *Ethics* 'On Human Bondage, or the Powers of the Affects', sought to understand the power of reason to control the affects: 'For our purpose, which is to determine the powers of the affects and the power of the Mind over the affects, it is enough . . . for us to understand the common properties of the affects and of the Mind, so that we can determine what sort of power, and how great a power, the Mind has to moderate and restrain the affects.'[63]

Though recommendations of rational control were common, the Stoic ambition of altogether overcoming the passions was generally regarded as an unattainable ideal. Anthony Le Grand was an exception: 'Man cannot serve himself of [passions] without becoming their Slave. . . . *Passion* then in *Stoick* terms, is nothing else but a violent motion of the Soul against Reason, caused by the apprehension of good or evil. . . . No man is more miserable than he that is subject to Passions. . . . A Wise man may live without Passion.'[64] The common metaphors of *slavery* and *bondage*[65] perhaps motivated Hume's famous statement in the *Treatise* 2.3.3.4 that 'Reason is, and ought only to be the slave of the passions.'

6. Role in the Moral Life. Certain passions were widely regarded as dangerous to moral judgement, virtuous conduct, and a healthy soul. For example, Thomas Wright held that the passions 'trouble wonderfully the soul, corrupting the judgement and seducing the will, inducing, for the most part, to vice, and commonly withdrawing from virtue; and therefore some call them maladies or sores of the soul. . . . [P]assions and sense are like two naughty servants who ofttimes bear more love one to another than they are obedient to their Master [reason].'[66]

[62] Seneca, *Ad Lucilium epistulae morales* 116.1 ('On Self-Control'). Cf. *Moral Essays*, 'De ira' ('On Anger') 1.19.1–2 and later parts of this work pertaining to the difficulty of governing anger.

[63] Spinoza, *Ethics* 3.P56 (schol.); cf. 4.Preface and 4.P1–5.

[64] Le Grand, *Man without Passion*, preface, pp. 69–70, 107, 115. See further the neo-Stoic view of Du Vair, *Morall Philosophie of the Stoicks*, pp. 32–3. For Spinoza's adoption of features of the Stoic teaching, see *Ethics* 4, preface and props. 24, 34–5, 44, 46.

[65] In addition to the sources mentioned in the previous footnote, see Charron, *Of Wisdome* 2.1.5, 9; Bayle, *Dictionary*, 'Helen' [Y]; Ayloffe, *Government of the Passions*, pp. 23–4.

[66] Wright, *Passions of the Mind in General* 1.2 (pp. 94–5). Wright was influenced by St Thomas, who had sorted out a range of issues concerning what he called 'the morality of the emotions' (*Summa Theologiæ* 1a2æ.24). However, St Thomas's conclusions are not as negative as those of Wright. Thomas wrote that, 'intrinsically of course the emotions are simply movements of the non-rational orexis; one cannot therefore ascribe to them moral good or evil, which we have shown to involve the reason' (1a2æ.24, art. 1; see also art. 4).

Several writers observed that passions such as jealousy, malice, envy, anger, spitefulness, hatred, and pride bear some kind of intimate connection to vices, perversities, or blameworthy conduct. For example, Hobbes noted that passions such as *covetousness* are 'used always in signification of blame'.[67] However, few modern philosophers held the Stoic view defended by Le Grand: 'Passions [are] opposed to Vertues. . . . Passions are mans domestick enemies, . . . [and they] corrupt his Reason, disorder his Will, and throw confusion into all the powers of his Soul.'[68] Several philosophers argued that certain passions, properly moderated, are allies of moral judgement or otherwise positively influence judgement or behaviour. They cited love, humility, charitableness, benevolence, compassion, sympathy, and kindness. Some noted that humility and other passionate states could be either a virtue or a vice, depending on the circumstances.[69] For example, Senault argued the striking thesis that some passions are the seeds of virtues and others the seeds of vice, but that all passions may, under the right circumstances, be 'changed into virtues'.[70]

The role of the passions in morality was often the motivating force behind published work on the passions. Disputes ran deep in this literature, and many controversies turned on competing theories of human nature.

THE NATURAL HISTORY OF RELIGION

Before he completed the *Natural History of Religion*, Hume published discussions of revealed and natural religion in Sections 10–11 of *An Enquiry concerning Human Understanding*. He had also published assorted essays pertaining to religion and drafted his *Dialogues concerning Natural Religion*. These writings are treated in other volumes of the Clarendon Hume. This section considers them, and their intellectual context, only in so far as they contain references or ideas that shed light on the intellectual context of *NHR* as a natural history of religion.

The Notion of a Natural History

Hume does not in his extant works and correspondence discuss the notion of a 'natural history'. Except in the title, he never uses this term throughout the *Natural History*. In choosing this title, Hume may have been declaring that his history is *natural* by contrast to *supernatural* or *theological*; or he may have been signalling

[67] Hobbes, *Leviathan* 6.23. See, further, Descartes, *Passions of the Soul* 182; Watts, *A Plain and Particular Account* 12, 14.

[68] Le Grand, *Man without Passion*, pp. 80, 85; cf. pp. 108–11.

[69] See, e.g., Charleton, *Natural History of the Passions* 5.10–11; Forbes, *Essays Moral and Philosophical* 6. Spinoza maintained that passions such as humility that are commonly believed to be virtues are not virtues at all; they are simply passions (*Ethics* 4.P53).

[70] Senault, *Use of Passions* 2.4, 'Of the Commerce of Passions with Virtue and Vice'. Cf. Ayloffe, *Government of the Passions*, pp. 41, 58–60, 78, 122–3.

that religion has its origins in human nature. These interpretations are speculative. More secure is the proposition that Hume presumed his audience to be familiar with the meaning of 'natural history' in the many works that had been published with this term in their titles. Major writers in science and philosophy had used the term and commented on the nature and significance of some type of natural history.

The Scientific Context. Most published materials on natural history were in the natural sciences and would today be categorized neither as philosophical nor historical. Nonetheless, they provide a critical background for understanding Hume's title and the way it would have been received.

A natural history was understood in the eighteenth century as a work that presented the properties and historical development of natural phenomena. Natural histories grew up around the study of the animal, vegetable, and mineral kingdoms. In some areas of investigation the proper goals and methods of natural history were unsettled. Those sympathetic to the work of scientists such as Hume's contemporary Carolus Linnaeus (Carl von Linné, 1707–78)[71] concentrated on the description, order, and classification of phenomena of similar and different kinds. Others viewed natural history as engaged in classification only to prepare the way for causal explanations of the historical development of items under investigation, revealing the causal order of phenomena.[72] Unfortunately, the idea of a causal, not merely descriptive, natural history was poorly explained in writings prior to Hume, and the nature and methodology of such a history (including the respects in which it is *natural* and is a *history*) were ill formulated.[73]

Temporal and causal forms of study gradually gained pre-eminence over classification schemes—e.g. in the study of minerals and the earth's history (eventually geology) and the study of fossil forms and the history of life forms (eventually

[71] *Systema naturae* (1735). Linnaeus produced a method of arranging plant and animal species. He incorporated a rudimentary natural history of the human species by placing it among the mammals in the order of primates.

[72] See the attack on Linnaeus by French naturalist Georges Louis Leclerc Buffon (1707–88), *Histoire naturelle, générale et particulière*, and the reviews and critical reception of this influential work, as collected in *From Natural History to the History of Nature*, ed. Lyon and Sloan. Buffon's early pages (in his discourse 'on the manner of studying and treating natural history') contain discussion of an inductive methodology for science congenial to Hume's apparent assumptions in the *Natural History*. Buffon makes cryptic suggestions about a natural history of the human animal, as an animal understandable in terms of its natural properties and environment. Hume owned a copy of Buffon's volumes; see Hume's letter to Adam Smith, Aug. 1766, *Letters*, 2: 82; and the entry '*Histoire Naturelle, Génerale et Particulière. Avec Supplement.* 20 vols. ... Paris, 1749–75' (a presentation copy from the author to Hume when he was in Paris as secretary to the British ambassador) in Norton and Norton, *The David Hume Library*, pp. 24, 27, 79.

Although Hume suggests some ways of ordering and classifying popular religions, his *Natural History* does not conform to criteria of a natural history in the description–classification tradition.

[73] For examples, see Benoit de Maillet, *Telliamed: or, Discourse between an Indian Philosopher and a French Missionary ... relating to Natural History and Philosophy*, Preface; and Noël-Antoine Pluche, *Le spectacle de la nature; ou Entretiens sur le particularités de l'histoire naturelle*, preface.

palaeontology). Though these areas of investigation have not typically been treated by historians as leading fields in the scientific revolution,[74] and may have had little or no direct influence on Hume, they were at the frontier of the evolving idea of natural history when Hume wrote his *Natural History*.

The Philosophical Context. Several philosophers prior to Hume had paid tribute to the place of natural history in the understanding of phenomena. For example, Francis Bacon (1561–1626) had proposed a model of an inductive natural history structured to order and classify natural phenomena. He hypothesized that this form of investigation would supply the foundation for scientific (causal) explanation; that is, the beginnings of scientific explanation are in description, ordering, and classification.

Whereas Bacon's concerns were methodological and focused on scientific investigation, Hobbes had commented, in his *Leviathan*, on natural history as a type of history:[75]

> The register of knowledge of fact is called history. Whereof there be two sorts: one called natural history; which is the history of such facts, or effects of nature, as have no dependence on man's will; such as are the histories of metals, plants, animals, regions, and the like. The other, is civil history; which is the history of the voluntary actions of men in commonwealths.

Use of the distinction between civil history and natural history had declined by Hume's lifetime, in part the result of an appreciation that voluntary actions in commonwealths were themselves influenced by natural conditions such as climates. The idea of a natural history had undergone a corresponding broadening of scope (under the influence, to some degree, of Bacon's model of description and experimentation).[76] Locke presumed a broader meaning,[77] and writers of natural histories had, by Hume's time, begun to investigate aspects of the human mind and human social institutions. Their objective was to transcend local histories and beliefs in order to discover underlying natural causes of some human phenomenon. Development through history was examined in terms of what was natural, rather than in terms of ordinary or civil history, in Hobbes's sense.

Charleton's *Natural History of the Passions* (discussed in the previous section) is exemplary. Charleton appeals to physical as well as psychological explanations of

[74] See Joseph M. Levine, 'Natural History and the History of the Scientific Revolution', esp. 61 ff.

[75] Hobbes, *Leviathan* 9.2, 'Of the Several Subjects of Knowledge'. Cf. Berkeley's mention of 'facts in civil or natural history', *Alciphron* 7.

[76] For additional data and historical discussion, see Michel Malherbe, 'Hume's *Natural History of Religion*', 257–62.

[77] Locke, *Essay concerning Human Understanding* 3.11.24: 'To define [the] names [of things themselves] right, natural history is to be inquired into; and their properties are, with care and examination, to be found out. For it is not enough . . . to have learned from the propriety of the language, the common but confused, or very imperfect idea, to which each word is applied, and to keep them to that idea in our use of them: But we must, by acquainting ourselves with the history of that sort of things, rectify and settle our complex idea belonging to each specific name.'

the passions—for example, motions, spirits, blood, and solid body parts.[78] Another writer influenced by the natural history paradigm was Julien Offray de La Mettrie, who had offered as his first published philosophical work *L'Histoire naturelle de l'âme*, a work that included a discussion of the passions and that was criticized for a materialistic philosophy of the human mind.[79] This book was published at approximately the time Hume pursued the writing of his *Natural History*.

There had not been a natural history of religion *in general* prior to Hume's, but John Trenchard (1662–1723) had published *The Natural History of Superstition* in 1709. This natural history was the first to concentrate on a particular aspect of religion, and Trenchard offered an array of ideas pertinent to Hume's interests. In particular, Trenchard held that superstitious human beliefs are effects to be explained by tracing them to the kinds of causes that Hume, among others, found credible:

> it is incumbent upon us, first of all to examine into the frame and constitution of our own Bodies, and search into the Causes of our Passions and Infirmities.... I take [our lack of knowledge] wholly to proceed from our ignorance of Causes, and yet curiosity to know them.... There must be causes in Nature for every thing that does or will happen.... [O]ur Passions are the Mechanical and necessary Effects of the Complexion, Constitution, and Distempers of our Bodies.[80]

The first objective in a natural history, Trenchard suggested, is to state the descriptive facts about the historical phenomena under investigation (superstitious behaviour and beliefs, in his study), and the second objective is a causal explanation (psychological or physiological) of the phenomena. Trenchard appealed to causes such as human ignorance, curiosity, anxiety, and the desire for happiness as conditions contributing to the development of superstitious forms of religious belief and practice (though Trenchard did not assume that these conditions are solely sufficient to produce superstition).

[78] Charleton, *Natural History of the Passions*. See p. 3 on methods and goals, and throughout the book for states of the passions expressed in physical categories.

[79] La Mettrie, *Histoire naturelle de l'âme* (1745; seized immediately by the police and condemned in 1746 by the Paris Parlement; 2nd edn. 'purged...of errors', 1747). This work was directed against abstruse metaphysics and views of mind and body in Descartes, Malebranche, Leibniz, and others. Invoking the empirical commitments of Aristotle and Locke, among others, La Mettrie argued that the mind is dependent upon and reducible to the physical world. His use of the medical sciences and mechanistic physiology, in which he had been trained, may underlie the language of 'natural history' in the title, which was changed in 1751 to *Traité de l'âme* (see Kathleen Wellman, *La Mettrie: Medicine, Philosophy, and Enlightenment*, esp. ch. 6). This change of title does not indicate a dissatisfaction with the term 'histoire naturelle'. In the first and later editions of his *Œuvres philosophiques* (1751), the collected texts are arranged under a title placed on the whole: 'Mémoires pour servir à l'histoire naturelle de l'homme' ('Memoirs to Serve the Natural History of Man'). This collected edition included La Mettrie's *L'Homme machine* (1748), which had been reprinted several times before Hume completed the drafting of *Four Dissertations*. The 'Preliminary Discourse' in the *Œuvres* derives from part of *Histoire naturelle de l'âme*. La Mettrie did not explicitly define or analyse the nature or method of a 'natural history'.

[80] Trenchard, *Natural History of Superstition*, pp. 9–10, 36.

In the light of publications such as Trenchard's, the project of a natural history of religion was not remarkably innovative by the time Hume commenced his dissertation on the subject. Nonetheless, one of Hume's critics, Duncan Shaw, determined in 1776 that

'The Natural History of Religion' [is a] title that *naturally* attracts attention, and which (let me say so without offence) it is probable was given as much for this reason, as for any propriety there is in it.

The Epithet of *Natural History*, when applied to the account given of the natural productions of a country, . . . we can easily see, and must at first admit the propriety of, but when applied to Religion, we must be excused, if we say it is not so apparent.[81]

Shaw submits that Hume's title could be expected to be startling and provocative.

Bishop Warburton was openly suspicious of the choice of title:

[Hume's] very *title-page* . . . demands our attention. It is called,THE NATURAL HISTORY OF RELIGION.

You ask, why he chuses to give it this title. Would not the *Moral history of Meteors* be full as sensible as the *Natural history of Religion*? Without doubt. Indeed had he given the history of what he himself would pass upon us for the only true Religion, namely, NATURALISM, or the belief of a God, the Creator and Physical Preserver, but not moral Governor of the world, the title of *Natural* would have fitted it well, because all *Morality* is excluded from the Idea.

But this great Philosopher is never without his Reasons. It is to insinuate, that what the world calls Religion, of which he undertakes to give the history, is not founded in the JUDGMENT, but in the PASSIONS only.[82]

These observations by Shaw and Warburton notwithstanding, the term 'natural history' was associated by 1750 with discovery of the origins and historical development of phenomena of many types: minerals, metals, plants, fossils, animals, human blood, the human soul, human passions, political empires, and the Bible.[83] Charleton, La Mettrie, and Trenchard, among others, had maintained that a natural history could guide investigation into human nature, the human soul, and phenomena such as religious superstition. Their objective of finding underlying causes in human nature presumed that a human phenomenon has developed by a natural process, and that there is a discoverable movement from primitive origins to present

[81] Shaw, *A Comparative View of the Several Methods of Promoting Religious Instruction from the Earliest Down to the Present Time*, Appendix 2, pp. 270–1. (This appendix is discussed in section 7 of the editor's Introduction to this volume.)

[82] Warburton, *Remarks on Mr. David Hume's Essay on the Natural History of Religion*, Remark 1 (also discussed in editor's Introduction, Sect. 7).

[83] The following are illustrative of the many and diverse sources that were available to Hume: Benoit de Maillet, *Telliamed: or, Discourse . . . relating to Natural History and Philosophy*; John Woodward, *An Essay toward a Natural History of the Earth*; Claude Perrault *et al.*, for the Académie des sciences (France), *Memoir's* [sic] *for a Natural History of Animals*; Johannes Goedaert, *Histoire naturelle des insectes, selon leurs differentes metamorphoses*; Robert Boyle, *Memoirs for the Natural History of Humane Blood*; Engelbert Kaempfer *et al.*, *Histoire naturelle, civile, et ecclesiastique de l'empire du Japon*; Johann Jakob Scheuchzer *et al.*, *Physique sacrée, ou histoire-naturelle de la Bible*.

conditions (though Charleton did not claim quite this sort of movement in his analysis). A natural history of an aspect of the human mind or of a human social institution such as religion, then, was an explanation of its natural course of development.

'Natural History' in Hume's Philosophy. Hume's project in his *Natural History* appears to be guided by the above-mentioned models, which he assimilates to his grand project of a science of human nature. In the Introduction to *NHR*, Hume presents two principal questions concerning religion:

> As every enquiry, which regards Religion, is of the utmost importance, there are two questions in particular, which challenge our principal attention, to wit, that concerning its foundation in reason, and that concerning its origin in human nature. . . . What those principles are, which give rise to the original belief, and what those accidents and causes are, which direct its operation, is the subject of our present enquiry.

The first of these two questions is presumably the subject of Hume's *Dialogues* (and *EHU* 11), the second, the subject of his *Natural History*. It is the principles of human nature, he says, that explain the origin and development of religious belief and religious phenomena, though a comprehensive explanation also requires knowledge of cultural and environmental conditions (*NHR* Introduction; 5.1, 9–10; 13.3). The following appears to be one expression in *NHR* of the connection, as Hume saw it, between the objectives of natural history and the science of human nature: 'It is chiefly our present business to consider the gross polytheism of the vulgar, and to trace all its various appearances, in the principles of human nature, whence they are derived.'[84]

Whether Hume succeeded in writing a natural history in any of the senses outlined in this section remains an open question, and one decidable only by an informed interpretation of his text as well as his context.

Hume's Familiarity with Religious and Theological Writings

Many publications by European scholars of religion and theology were available for Hume to consult. This section presents an inventory of early modern figures whose works on religion and philosophical theology *Hume himself* cites either in his correspondence or in writings published prior to the *Natural History*. No attempt is made here to develop a comparable list of ancient writers, few of whom dedicated works specifically to a religious or theological topic.[85] No suggestion is made that

[84] *NHR* 5.1; cf. 5.9.

[85] This restriction is not proposed on grounds that Hume ignored the ancients. Classical works such as Cicero's *De natura Deorum* and *De divinatione* were major influences on Hume, as his texts and footnotes show. See the several references in the text (*NHR* 12.13 and 12.24) and notes (*NHR* nn. 61, 62, 66, 67, 72, 79, 81, 93) to works by Cicero, including *De natura Deorum* and *De divinatione*.

Moreover, Hume adopted the prevailing eighteenth-century practice of addressing issues by referencing classical literature. In *ETSS* Hume acknowledges 109 different authors. Statistically,

the works referred to were considered natural histories or that any of these works informed Hume in his writing of *NHR*.

In *A Treatise of Human Nature* and the two works pertaining to the *Treatise* (the *Abstract* of *THN* and *A Letter from a Gentleman*[86]), Hume cites the following early modern works for their commentary on religion:

Antoine Arnauld and Pierre Nicole, *Logic or the Art of Thinking*[87]
Pierre Bayle, *Historical and Critical Dictionary*[88]
Samuel Clarke ('and others'), *Discourse concerning the Being and Attributes of God*[89]
Gottfried Wilhelm Leibniz, *Theodicy*[90]
Nicolas Malebranche ('and other Cartesians'[91]), *The Search after Truth*[92]
Charles Rollin, *The Ancient History of the Egyptians, Carthaginians, Assyrians, Babylonians, Medes and Persians, Macedonians and Grecians*[93]
John Tillotson, sermon 'The Wisdom of Being Religious'[94]
William Wollaston, *The Religion of Nature Delineated*[95]

he most often cites Cicero, Homer, Lucian, Plutarch, and Suetonius. Of course, whether an acknowledged source exerted a significant influence on Hume's thought requires investigation beyond the mere fact of the acknowledgement.

[86] In *A Letter from a Gentleman* Hume mentions, without reference to specific works, the 'Systems of *Spinoza* [and]... the Theologians'; Bishop Huet's work of '*Scepticks* or *Pyrrhonians*' (see the entry under Hume's *Dialogues*, below); 'metaphysical Arguments for a Deity' in Clarke and Descartes; and occasional causes and the deity in Descartes, Cudworth, Locke, Clarke, and Newton. The subtitle of this work is 'CONTAINING Some OBSERVATIONS ON A Specimen of the Principles concerning RELIGION and MORALITY, *said to be* maintain'd in a Book lately publish'd, intituled, *A Treatise of Human Nature*, &c.'

[87] *La Logique, ou L'art de penser* (1st pub. 1662). Eng. trans. 1685, as *Logic, or, The Art of Thinking*.

[88] *Dictionnaire historique et critique* (1st pub. 1697). Eng. translations date from 1709, 1710, and 1734.

[89] From the Boyle lectures delivered 1704–5. See below for Clarke's *A Discourse Concerning the Unchangeable Obligations of Natural Religion* and *Scripture Doctrine of the Trinity*.

[90] *Essais de Theodicée sur la bonté de Dieu, la liberté de l'homme, et l'origine du mal* (1st pub. 1710), a 1720 copy of which is listed in Norton and Norton, *David Hume Library*, pp. 32, 109. In his *Abstract* (par. 4) of *THN*, Hume repeats a remark from Leibniz's *Theodicy*; see also *Dialogues* 10.6, where Hume mentions a theme in the *Theodicy*, but does not mention that work specifically.

[91] 'Other Cartesians' could include, e.g., Louis de La Forge, *Traitté de l'esprit de l'homme* (1st pub. 1666); Gerauld [Géraud] de Cordemoy, *Six discours sur la distinction et l'union du corps et de l'ame* (1st pub. 1666); and Johann Clauberg, *Opera omnia philosophica* (1st pub. 1691).

[92] *De la recherche de la verité* (1st pub. 1674). An authentic David Hume bookplate is on the 3rd edn. of 3 vols. (Lyon, 1684). See Norton and Norton, *David Hume Library*, pp. 16–18.

[93] *Histoire ancienne des Aegyptiens, des Carthaginois, des Assyriens, des Babyloniens, des Medes et des Perses, des Macedoniens, des Grecs* (1st pub. 1730–8). Eng. trans. 1730 (in part), 1734–6 (the whole). Hume may have owned a copy; see Norton and Norton, *David Hume Library*, pp. 32, 125. This general history treats ancient religions as one among many other topics.

[94] In *The Works of the Most Reverend Doctor John Tillotson* (1st pub. 1696), sermon 1.

[95] 1st pub. 1722.

In *Essays and Treatises on Several Subjects* (in particular, *EHU*, *EPM*, *NHR*, and the *Essays*[96]) Hume mentions several other authors or works on religious subjects:[97]

Anonymous [attributed to Richard Allestree], *The Whole Duty of Man*[98]
Anonymous, *Collection of the Miracles Performed at the Tomb of the Deacon, Monsieur de Pâris*[99]
Francis Bacon, 'Of Atheism'[100]
George Berkeley, *A Treatise concerning the Principles of Human Knowledge. Wherein the Chief Causes of Error and Difficulty in the Sciences, with the Grounds of Scepticism, Atheism, and Irreligion, are inquired into*[101]
Samuel Clarke, *A Discourse concerning the Unchangeable Obligations of Natural Religion, and the Truth and Certainty of the Christian Revelation* and *The Scripture Doctrine of the Trinity*[102]
René Descartes, passages on the efficacy of the Deity[103]
Bernard Le Bovier de Fontenelle, *History of Oracles*[104]
Thomas Hyde, *History of the Religion of the Ancient Persians, and of their Priestly Class*[105]
Louis Daniel Le Comte, *New Reports on the Present Condition of China*[106]

[96] Hume's numerous references in these works are primarily to classical sources, with few citations to modern authors.

[97] Duplications from the *Treatise* are omitted in this list, as are unclear references in Hume's text. For example, Locke, Newton, and Clarke are mentioned in n. 78 of *NHR*. All had written on a topic or issue having to do with some aspect of religious history. Ralph Cudworth, who is elsewhere cited by Hume, had invested heavily in comparative religion and the history of religion. However, Hume's references are too vague to place these figures on the present list. See the Annotations and Reference List in this volume for further details on their published works.

[98] 1st pub. 1657 or 1658 (anon.) under the title *The Practice of Christian Graces, or, the Whole Duty of Man*.

[99] *Recueil des miracles operés au tombeau de M. de Paris Diacre* (n.p., 1732).

[100] In *Essays* (1st pub. 1597). Bacon's *Opera moralium et civilium tomus* of 1638 contains his *Essays*, and is listed in Norton and Norton, *David Hume Library*, pp. 42, 73.

[101] 1st pub. 1710. The full title of the 1734 edn., which Hume mentions at *EHU* (n. 32), is *A Treatise concerning the Principles of Human Knowledge. Wherein the Chief Causes of Error and Difficulty in the Sciences, with the Grounds of Scepticism, Atheism, and Irreligion, are inquired into. To which are added Three Dialogues Between Hylas and Philonous, In Opposition to Scepticks and Atheists.*

[102] *Discourse*, 1st pub. 1706 (cited at *EPM*, n. 12); *Scripture Doctrine*, 1st pub. 1712 (cited at *NHR*, n. 78).

[103] Hume does not specify a particular work by Descartes. He mentions only that Descartes 'insinuated' the doctrine of 'the universal and sole efficacy of the Deity' (*EHU*, n. 16). Such a doctrine is insinuated in *Principles of Philosophy* 1.21; 2.36, 39, 42 (1st pub. 1644); and *Objections and Replies* to *Meditations* 5 and 6 (*Philosophical Writings*, 2: 253–5, 293–4). (See also 'Letter to Princess Elizabeth', 6 Oct. 1645, in *Philosophical Writings*, 3: 272.)

[104] *Histoire des oracles* (1st pub. 1687), in *Œuvres*, 6 vols. (Paris, 1742–51), which is listed in Norton and Norton, *David Hume Library*, pp. 32, 91. Eng. trans. 1699, as *The History of Oracles*.

[105] *Historia religionis veterum Persarum, eorumque Magorum* (1st pub. 1700).

[106] *Nouveaux mémoires sur l'état présent de la Chine* (1st pub. 1696). Eng. trans. 1697, as *Memoirs and Observations . . . Made in a Late Journey through the Empire of China*.

Louis Basile Carré de Montgeron, *The Truth of the Miracles Brought About by the Intercession of M. de Pâris*[107]
Jean Racine, *Brief History of Port-Royal*[108]
Andrew Michael Ramsay, *The Philosophical Principles of Natural and Revealed Religion*[109]

In his *Dialogues* (posthumous, but drafted near the time of the writing of *NHR*), Hume cites:[110]

Bishop Pierre-Daniel Huet, *A Philosophical Treatise concerning the Weakness of Human Understanding*[111]
William King, *An Essay on the Origin of Evil*[112]

In the so-called 'Early Memoranda',[113] Hume lists three additional works[114] from which he made notes on religious subjects:

Pierre Bayle, *Various Works*[115]
Ralph Cudworth, *The True Intellectual System of the Universe*[116]
François de Salignac de La Mothe Fénelon, *Demonstration of the Existence of God*[117]

In extant correspondence prior to 1752, Hume mentions several other authors and works on religious subjects:[118]

Joseph Butler, *Sermons* and *Analogy of Religion, Natural and Revealed*[119]
Jean Claude, *The Catholic Doctrine of the Eucharist in All Ages* [in Response to Arnauld (and Nicole)][120]
Lord Kames (Henry Home), *Essays on the Principles of Morality and Natural Religion*[121]

[107] *La verité des miracles operés par l'intercession de M. de Paris* (1st pub. 1737).

[108] *Abrégé de l'histoire de Port-Royal* (1st pub. 1742). [109] 1st pub. 1748–9 (2 vols.).

[110] Duplications from the above lists for the *Treatise* and *ETSS* are omitted from this list.

[111] *Traité philosophique de la foiblesse l'esprit humain* (1st pub. 1723). Eng. trans. 1725, as Peter Huet, *A Philosophical Treatise concerning the Weakness of Human Understanding*.

[112] *De origine mali* (1st pub. 1702). Eng. trans. 1731, as *An Essay on the Origin of Evil*.

[113] 'Hume's Early Memoranda, 1729–1740', ed. Mossner.

[114] Duplications from the above lists for the *Treatise, ETSS*, and *Dialogues* are here omitted.

[115] *Œuvres diverses* (1st pub. 1725). Hume may have owned a copy; see Norton and Norton, *David Hume Library*, pp. 32, 107.

[116] 1st pub. 1678 (2 vols.). [117] *Démonstration de l'existence de Dieu* (1st pub. 1713).

[118] Duplications from the above lists for the *Treatise, ETSS*, and the 'Early Memoranda' are omitted from this list.

[119] *Fifteen Sermons Preached at the Rolls Chapel* (1st pub. 1729); *The Analogy of Religion, Natural and Revealed, to the Constitution and Course of Nature* (1st pub. 1736). Hume may have owned a copy; see Norton and Norton, *David Hume Library*, pp. 42, 80.

[120] *Réponse aux deux traitez intitulez La Perpétuité de la foy de l'Eglise Catholique touchant l'Eucharistie* (1st pub. 1665). Eng. trans. 1684, as *The Catholick Doctrine of the Eucharist in All Ages; in Answer to What M. Arnaud, Doctor of the Sorbon Alledges.*

[121] 1st pub. 1751. Listed in Norton and Norton, *David Hume Library*, pp. 34, 42, 107.

William Leechman, *The Nature, Reasonableness, and Advantages of Prayer: With an Attempt to Answer the Objections Against It: A Sermon*[122]
Pierre Nicole, *The Perpetuity of the Faith of the Catholic Church concerning the Eucharist, Defended Against the Book of M. Claud, Minister of Charenton*[123]
Thomas Sherlock, Pastoral Letter[124]

Some degree of familiarity with these works was a fact of Hume's history by the time he published the *Natural History of Religion*. Though evidence about the depth of his learning in writings on religion is fragmentary, it is reasonable to presume that he had been exposed to the principal philosophical treatises by British and French writers of the period.

Psychological Explanation

Hume's natural history includes psychological explanations of religious phenomena. He probes for features of human nature that explain the expansive, but not universal, belief in invisible, intelligent, hallowed agents. He inquires into the role of passions such as fear and hope in stimulating human responses to unknown causes in nature, religious attitudes that spring from anxiety about the future, and the psychology of superstition and zealotry. A representative psychological explanation occurs at *NHR* 2.5:[125]

> What passion shall we here have recourse to, for explaining [inferences about invisible intelligent power]? . . . Not speculative curiosity surely. . . . [Consider] the ordinary affections of human life; the anxious concern for happiness, the dread of future misery, the terror of death, the thirst of revenge, the appetite for food and other necessaries. Agitated by hopes and fears of this nature, especially the latter, men scrutinize, with a trembling curiosity, the course of future causes, and . . . they see the first obscure traces of divinity. . . . *Unknown causes*, then, become the constant object of our hope and fear; and while the passions are kept in perpetual alarm by an anxious expectation of the events, the imagination is equally employed in forming ideas of those powers, on which we have so entire a dependence.

Learned writers before Hume had offered rudimentary psychological explanations of religious beliefs in terms of curiosity, fear, anxiety, and other passions. Exemplary is Hobbes's *Leviathan*, a book cited several times in Hume's works. Hobbes explained the origin and perpetuation of religion in terms of passions and affective responses. He saw curiosity about invisible causes in nature as the causal origin of religion; humans want to know how and why events occur, especially when they affect 'their own good and evil fortune'.[126] Religion is the result of 'fear

[122] 1st pub. 1743.
[123] *La Perpétuité de la foi de l'Eglise Catholique touchant l'Eucharistie, défendue contre le livre du sieur Claude, ministre de Charenton*, 1st pub. 1669–74 (3 vols. in 4).
[124] 'A Letter from the Lord Bishop of London to the Clergy and People of London and Westminster; on Occasion of the Late Earthquakes', 1st pub. 1750.
[125] See also the preparatory work at *NHR* 2.4 on the role of the passions of hope and fear.
[126] *Leviathan* 6.35; 12.1–5; cf. 11.26.

of power invisible, feigned by the mind or imagined from tales publicly allowed'.[127] Hobbes offered a causal analysis of the 'seeds' of religion:

And they that make little, or no inquiry into the natural causes of things, yet from the fear that proceeds from the ignorance it self, of what it is that hath the power to do them much good or harm, are inclined to suppose, and feign unto themselves, several kinds of powers invisible; and to stand in awe of their own imaginations; and in time of distress to invoke them; as also in the time of an expected good success, to give them thanks; making the creatures of their own fancy, their gods.... And this fear of things invisible, is the natural seed of that, which every one in himself calleth religion; and in them that worship, or fear that power otherwise than they do, superstition....

[M]an observeth how one event hath been produced by another; and remembereth in them antecedence and consequence; and when he cannot assure himself of the true causes of things, (for the causes of good and evil fortune for the most part are invisible,) he supposes causes of them, either such as his own fancy suggesteth; or trusteth to the authority of other men.[128]

Psychological explanations of the origin of religion were also scattered throughout Baruch Spinoza's *Theologico-Political Treatise*, which, on matters of religious superstition, shows similarities to Hobbes's account of religion and the passions:

Anything which excites their [most people's] astonishment they believe to be a portent signifying the anger of the gods or of the Supreme Being, and, mistaking superstition for religion, account it impious not to avert the evil with prayer and sacrifice.... Such is the unreason to which terror can drive mankind! Superstition, then, is engendered, preserved, and fostered by fear.[129]

Hume would have encountered these, and other, psychological accounts of religious belief. Trenchard's *Natural History of Superstition* has already been mentioned; noteworthy are his accounts of the passions and enthusiasm. Fontenelle's succinct *Origin of Fables* (1724) was a study in the psychology of religion congenial to Hume's assessments in *NHR*. Fontenelle, an author well known to Hume (and cited in n. 13 of *NHR*), stressed the use of imagination to aggrandize experiences, the birth of the gods in human ignorance and human needs for strength and assistance, and the human tendency to explain events in nature by analogy to personal feelings and experiences.[130] Fontenelle also wrote on the psychology of superstition and reflected on other subjects of interest to Hume, including religious impostures and the role of the passions in religious experience.[131]

Historical Explanation

Hume's term 'natural history' together with his thesis regarding the evolution of monotheism from polytheism may suggest that his objective was a *history of religion.*

[127] *Leviathan* 6.36; see, similarly, *De cive* 16.1. [128] *Leviathan* 11.26, 12.4.

[129] *Tractatus theologico-politicus*, preface, pp. 3–4.

[130] *De l'origine des fables*, 13, 17–20, 26. It is unknown whether Hume had read this work. However, in both *NHR* (n. 13) and 'The Populousness of Ancient Nations' (n. 263), Hume cites Fontenelle's *History of Oracles* (*Histoire des oracles*).

[131] *History of Oracles*, esp. pp. 110–11.

This assumption seems attractive in light of the possibility that Hume was planning or writing parts of his *History of England* as he was polishing the *Natural History*.

The *Natural History*, however, is not a history of religion in any conventional sense. Hume does not concentrate on historical evidence about religious traditions; nor does he write narratively or chronologically. His interests are in philosophical reflection, causal explanation, and illustrative anecdote. Collections of evidence about the history of religion and historical studies published by others are not basic to his work; and the few historical facts that he requires for his conclusions do not appear to derive from historical writings, archives, or documentary materials. Hume also does not undertake to explain religion historically. Instead, religion and its history are to be understood in terms of natural features of human nature, including the naturalness of belief in religion.

Nonetheless, some of Hume's contentions and examples pertain to the history of religion. In particular, he reflects on historical connections between polytheism and monotheism. Among his best-known theses in *NHR* is that polytheism, not monotheism, was the historical source of religion: 'The most ancient records of human race still present us with that system [polytheism] as the popular and established creed. The north, the south, the east, the west, give their unanimous testimony to the same fact' (*NHR* 1.2). This thesis was framed in opposition to the received views of the period, which took monotheism to be the first and basic religion and polytheism to be a derivative body of beliefs resulting from the deterioration or adulteration of monotheism.[132]

These concerns with history prompt questions about whether Hume consulted sources of information about the history of religion. A number of historical, comparative, and documentary works were available to him (though, in general, the scholarship and information in these works is thin and often guided by apologetic goals). There existed an abundance of material on Greek, Roman, and Egyptian religion, the historical relation of Judaism and Christianity, comparative religion, the history of superstition, the origins of polytheism, and other subjects treated in the *Natural History*. Also available were accounts of non-Christian religious practices in many cultures, as well as translations of the sacred scriptures of several religions.[133] Whether Hume read widely in these published works is not known,

[132] See Herbert of Cherbury, *Pagan Religion* 14; Ralph Cudworth, *True Intellectual System of the Universe*, Preface and 1.3–4 (especially the thesis stated on p. 507); Chevalier Ramsay, *Philosophical Principles of Natural and Revealed Religion*, vol. 2; William Rose, Review of 'Remarks upon the Natural History of Religion By Mr. Hume. With Dialogues on Heathen Idolatry, and the Christian Religion By S.T.', 532–3; Voltaire, *Philosophical Dictionary*, 'Religion'.

[133] For an indication of the abundance of historical, documentary, and comparative sources—and their possible connections to Hume—see Alan Charles Kors, *The Orthodox Sources of Disbelief* and 'The French Context of Hume's Philosophical Theology'; Michel Malherbe, 'Hume's *Natural History of Religion*'; Frank E. Manuel, *The Eighteenth Century Confronts the Gods*; C. J. Betts, *Early Deism in France*; and David Berman, *A History of Atheism in Britain: From Hobbes to Russell*. Some of these authorities advance speculative conclusions; all contain a rich body of references.

For a volume available to Hume that contained general information about religions of the world, see William Turner, *The History of All Religions in the World*.

but even if he did, there is no reason to think that this literature was a substantive basis for his conclusions in the *Natural History*.

More likely to have attracted Hume's attention, though no documentation exists, was a body of writings that display reflective interests in the nature and historical development of religion. Several such works enjoyed sufficient standing among European scholars of religion that Hume would have been familiar with their goals and reputation. Two writers are exemplary, though neither is known to have influenced Hume.[134]

(1) Gerardus Johannes Vossius (Gerard Jan Vos (or Voss), 1577–1649), a Dutch professor of history and Protestant humanist theologian, published *De theologia gentili et physiologia christiana, sive de origine ac progressu idolatricae* in 1641 (a work that followed his *Historia Pelagiana, De historicis Latinis*, and *De historicis Graecis*). Vossius presented erudite but unsystematic views on several theological and historical issues addressed by Hume, with massive attention devoted to the Greek gods, sun cults in ancient religions, the origins and development of religion, and natural philosophy. *De theologia gentili* is an imposing collection of data intended, in part, to demonstrate the diversity of ancient idolatries and to explain how they developed. Vossius traced their growth and pointed to similarities between pagan gods and biblical figures, occasionally suggesting that pagan polytheists drew from the earlier Judaeo-Christian tradition.[135]

(2) Herbert of Cherbury (1583–1648), a philosopher and historian well known for his metaphysical treatise *De veritate*, also wrote *Pagan Religion* (*De religione gentilium*; pub. 1663, written by 1645). In both he argued that, despite the many superstitions and absurdities in pagan religion, there is a universally affirmed core of true religious propositions. This core is expressed by five 'common notions' or 'principles of religion' that are instinctive—that is, latent in human nature and stimulated by suitable experiences. These principles are recognized as true by all impartial persons in all religions and all ages.[136]

In *Pagan Religion* Herbert assembled from ancient religions, primarily Graeco-Roman, what he took to be empirical evidence for his claim. Much of his scholarly information derived, as he acknowledged, from Vossius. He sometimes used data about historical traditions to support his five notions and to agree with Vossius. For example, he used this data to find the primal religion in humanity's original circumstances to be monotheistic, without exception. However, Herbert also

[134] Among other noteworthy scholars is Antonius van Dale, whose *De oraculis veterum ethnicorum* was the primary source and inspiration of Fontenelle's *History of Oracles*. Van Dale was also known for his *Dissertationes de origine ac progressu idololatriæ et superstitionum*.

[135] See, e.g., *De Theologia gentili* 1.18 (1: 142–3). Vossius is discussed in Bayle's *Dictionary*. Hume had examined a less well-known work (*Variarum observationum liber*, 1685) by Vossius's son, Isaac (1618–89), a biblical scholar; for Hume's references to the latter source, see 'The Populousness of Ancient Nations' 3, 135 (nn. 146 and 193); Hume's 'Early Memoranda', ed. Mossner, p. 514, §§216–17; and correspondence of Apr. 1750, to John Clephane, *Letters*, 1: 140.

[136] *Pagan Religion*, pp. 52, 304; *De veritate* 5, 9 (esp. pp. 139–41, 289–304). One of the five common notions is that 'There is a Supreme God'.

frequently disagreed with Vossius, even using Vossius's data to reach opposed conclusions.

Herbert's treatise critically assesses the history of superstition and priestcraft, but occasionally reads almost as if it were a justification of pagan beliefs. There is a detachment from the Christian tradition as well as an insistence that Judaism and the Old Testament were not the origins of religion (and had borrowed from more ancient monotheistic traditions).[137] By contemporary standards, Herbert developed theories of the reasonable origins of religion, the fundamentals of the religion of nature, and the difference between superstition and true religion; his work was not a history of religion.[138] In this attempt, Herbert appears to have had both scholarly and religious goals.[139]

Other prominent works on religion contained some form of historical thesis or material of potential interest to Hume. Many are best classified as studies in *natural religion* rather than *history of religion*. For example, English deist Matthew Tindal (1657–1733) wrote *Christianity as Old as the Creation* in part to consider whether pagan religions had captured true religion. Tindal says in his preface that he 'builds nothing' on historical tradition, and that he aims primarily at making a distinction 'between *Religion*, and *Superstition*'.[140] Most of his book is noteworthy for its absence of references to historical evidence or events.

Hume's footnotes in the *Natural History* include Fontenelle's *Histoire des oracles*, Hyde's *Historia religionis veterum Persarum, eorumque Magorum*, and Bayle's *Dictionnaire historique et critique*. Each offers a model of how enquiry into historical questions about religion—for example, in Fontenelle's case, whether oracles ceased when Christianity began[141]—can be conducted without writing either a conventional history or a religious apologetics. However, and notably, none of the three works is similar in form, method, or content to Hume's *Natural History*.

137 *Pagan Religion* 1–3, 14–16, esp. pp. 285, 302, and 325.

138 See his statements in *Pagan Religion* 15.

139 *Pagan Religion* 1–2, 16.

140 Preface, p. iii.

141 *History of Oracles*, preface and pp. 1, 132–7, 141–3. Fontenelle states in the opening line of the book (p. 1): 'My Design is not to give you directly an History of *Oracles*; I only intend to argue against that common Opinion, which attributes 'em to *Daemons*, and will have 'em to cease at the coming of Jesus Christ.'

BIOGRAPHICAL APPENDIX

This Appendix contains biographical sketches of all individuals mentioned by Hume in the text and the notes to *DP* and *NHR*.[1] Hume refers to most by name, but occasionally uses an indirect, yet definite, reference, such as 'the poet who said'. Biographical data are not supplied in this Appendix for persons mentioned by the editor and not mentioned by Hume. Basic facts on editor-introduced persons are presented upon their first appearance in the editor's Annotations and the editor's Introduction. Titles such as 'Count' and 'Duke' have been used only if essential for a proper presentation of the name.

The abbreviations RL (Reference List) and Cat. (Catalogue) are placed at the end of each biographical portrait if the person's works are cited in one or both of these bibliographical appendices (found on pp. 241–70). The abbreviation 'q.v.' refers the reader to another entry in the Biographical Appendix. The form 'c.' abbreviates 'century'.

ABRAHAM (*c.* 20th–15th c. BC), traditional patriarch of the Hebrew people, father of Isaac (q.v.) and Ishmael. By tradition he is the founder of Judaism as a religion of covenant.

ADDISON, JOSEPH (1672–1719), English essayist, poet, dramatist, and politician. Addison held several government posts, and became a Member of Parliament. He contributed regularly to the *Tatler*, the *Guardian*, the *Spectator*, and other journals. His 274 numbers of the *Spectator* were acclaimed for their style and humour. (RL; Cat.)

AELIUS SPARTIANUS. See SPARTIAN.

AGRIPPA, MENENIUS. See MENENIUS AGRIPPA.

ALEXANDER III (known as ALEXANDER THE GREAT) (4th c. BC), Macedonian king and military leader, student of Aristotle (q.v.). He led his forces to victory against the Persian empire. His own empire extended through North Africa to the Middle East and the eastern Mediterranean coasts. His rule eventuated in a Hellenization of territories beyond the Hellenic city-states.

AMASIS II, or AHMOSE II (6th c. BC), pharaoh attracted to Hellenic culture. He maintained Hellenic alliances, made gifts to Hellenic shrines, and married a woman from Cyrene. A peaceful ruler, he brought prosperity and Hellenic culture to Egypt.

ANAXAGORAS of Clazomenae (5th c. BC), pre-Socratic philosopher. While resident in Athens, he was a close associate of Pericles, who may have helped him escape after he had been indicted on a charge of impiety. The facts of his life and of

[1] The innumerable sources consulted for this Appendix cannot be individually acknowledged. However, *The Oxford Classical Dictionary* was especially serviceable for classical figures.

his philosophy have proved elusive, but he enjoyed a substantial reputation in antiquity.

ANAXIMANDER of Miletus (6th c. BC), cosmologist, mathematician, and by tradition an inventor. He was a companion and student of Thales (q.v.).

ANAXIMENES of Miletus (6th c. BC), cosmologist and, by tradition, a friend and pupil of Thales (q.v.) and Anaximander (q.v.). He reputedly taught that everything in nature is composed of air with different degrees of density.

ANTHONY, ST, or ST ANTONY. See Annotations, 63.15.

ARISTOPHANES of Athens (5th–4th c. BC), comic playwright. He wrote satiric comedies, including *The Clouds, The Birds, Lysistrata*, and *The Frogs*. He satirized the gods and a variety of social classes and vocations.

ARISTOTLE of Stageira (4th c. BC), Macedonian philosopher, student of Plato (q.v.) at the Academy, and the teacher of Alexander the Great (Alexander III, q.v.). When he returned to Athens after tutoring Alexander, he opened the Lyceum. His lifelong and deep connections in Macedonia led him to leave Athens during a period of rising anti-Macedonian feeling. He left Theophrastus in charge of his school, which became known as the Peripatetic School. (RL; Cat.)

ARNOBIUS (known as ARNOBIUS AFER) (3rd–4th c. AD), Christian apologist in Numidia, Northern Africa. His seven books of the *Adversus gentes* were both an attack on ancient pagan beliefs and a rebuttal of charges that the Christian religion was impious and had created social disturbances. He had earlier held pagan beliefs himself. (RL; Cat.)

ARRIAN (FLAVIUS ARRIANUS) of Nicomedia, Bithynia (2nd c. AD), historian of Alexander the Great (Alexander III, q.v.) and Roman governor of Cappadocia under Hadrian, and consul under Antoninus Pius. He was a pupil and friend of Epictetus (q.v.), whose *Discourses* he preserved. (RL; Cat.)

ATTICUS, TITUS POMPONIUS (2nd–1st c. BC), Roman historian and bibliophile. He is known for his editing and preservation of a collection of letters from his friend Cicero (q.v.). He preserved the writings of his contemporaries by having his slaves copy their work.

AUGUSTINE, ST (AURELIUS AUGUSTINUS) (4th–5th c. AD), teacher of rhetoric, Neoplatonic philosopher, and bishop of Hippo. He often wrote as a critic of ancient philosophies and heresies such as those of the Manichaeans and the Pelagians. His prodigious output was directed at a celebration and defence of Church authority and teachings. (RL; Cat.)

AUGUSTUS, title for GAIUS OCTAVIUS (GAIUS JULIUS CAESAR OCTAVIANUS) (known as OCTAVIAN) (1st c. BC–1st c. AD), first emperor of Rome. He was nephew of Julius Caesar. His defeat of Mark Antony and Cleopatra in 31 BC left him sole ruler of the realm.

AURELIUS, MARCUS, surnamed ANTONINUS (2nd c. AD), Roman emperor (161–80) and Stoic philosopher. His reign was consumed largely by military defence against rebellion and external attack. His Stoic philosophy is found in his *Meditations* (or *Communings with Himself*), an unarranged series of aphorisms and reflections apparently transcribed from a notebook or diary that was planned for personal recollection and guidance. (RL; Cat.)

Averroës (*Arabic* Ibn Rushd) (12th c. ad), Spanish-Muslim philosopher, theologian, and physician. He is known in philosophy primarily for his commentaries on Aristotle (q.v.), which influenced medieval scholastic philosophers and theologians.

Bacon, Francis, Baron Verulam, Viscount St Albans (1561–1626), philosopher, essayist, barrister, and Lord Chancellor of England. He devised a plan of research designed to organize the sciences on a grand scale. His *Novum organum* and *Advancement of Learning* were distinct parts of this research plan. (RL; Cat.)

Bayle, Pierre (1647–1706), French philosopher, encyclopaedist, and critic. His controversial *Dictionnaire historique et critique* had a deep influence on eighteenth-century thought in France and Great Britain, although he had eminent detractors. (RL; Cat.)

Bellarmine, Robert Francis Romulus (1542–1621), Jesuit theologian and Italian cardinal. Bellarmine is known for his criticisms of King James I of England and Scottish theologian William Barclay over the divine right of kings and the authority of the Pope in political affairs.

Benedict, St (5th–6th c. ad), Roman founder of Benedictine Order and author of a set of rules for monastic life.

Bomilcar (4th c. bc), Carthaginian military commander and attempted usurper. He commanded the Carthaginians against Agathocles, tyrant of Syracuse. Later, assisted by mercenaries, he attempted in a bloody engagement to make himself tyrant of Carthage. A citizen uprising foiled his plans, and he was crucified.

Boulainvilliers, Henri de (1658–1722), French historian and commentator on philosophical and religious figures. He held aristocratic views about government and admired the feudal system. He published his *Abrégé chronologique de l'histoire de France* (1733) with his larger and more influential *État de la France*. (RL; Cat.)

Brasidas of Sparta (5th c. bc), Spartan commander during the first decade of the Peloponnesian War between Athens and Sparta. He earned the confidence and admiration of several Athenian allies and defeated the Athenians at Amphipolis.

Brumoy, Pierre (1688–1742), Jesuit, Church historian, and figure in French literature and drama. His three-volume work *Le théâtre des Grecs* contains his translations and analyses of Greek tragedies and discourses, including remarks about the Greek theatre. (RL; Cat.)

Caesar, Gaius Julius (1st c. bc), Roman commander, author, orator, and statesman. Noted for his military conquests, he formed the first triumvirate with Pompey (q.v.) and Crassus, and later became dictator. His commentaries on the Gallic War provide a chronicle of the first seven years of the war and a history of the civil war. Brutus, Cassius, and other conspirators assassinated him. (RL; Cat.)

Cambyses II (6th c. bc), Persian ruler, eldest son and successor of Cyrus I (q.v.), and father of Cyrus II. He conquered Egypt and considered further conquests, but died in Syria.

CARNEADES of Cyrene (3rd–2nd c. BC), sceptical philosopher. He became head of the New Academy when anti-dogmatic scepticism achieved perhaps its greatest strength. He left no writings, but his students transmitted his teachings and reputation as a controversialist.

CATILINE (LUCIAS SERGIUS CATILINA) (1st c. BC), Roman politician, praetor, and governor of Africa. He organized a conspiracy against the republic that Cicero (q.v.) thwarted through vigilant opposition. Cicero's Catilinian orations register his formal denunciation.

CEPHALUS (5th c. BC), wealthy Syracusan convinced by Pericles to resettle in Athens. The scene in Plato's (q.v.) *Republic* is set in the Piraeus at the house of Cephalus. Plato depicts him as an honourable person of experience who is at 'the threshold of old age'. His sons are Polemarchus, who has a significant role in the dialogue, Euthydemus, and Lysias, who ran a business with their father as manufacturers of shields.

CHEIRISOPHUS, or CHIROSOPHUS, of Sparta (5th–4th c. BC), military commander. He served with Xenophon (q.v.) in Cyrus's expedition against his brother Artaxerxes. The rise and fall of Chirosophus as commander-in-chief and the subsequent course of a partitioned army are described in Xenophon's *Anabasis* and in Diodorus Siculus's (q.v.) *Historical Library*.

CHEVALIER RAMSAY. See RAMSAY, ANDREW MICHAEL.

CICERO, MARCUS TULLIUS (also known as TULLY) (lst c. BC), Roman orator, statesman, poet, and philosophical writer. As consul, Cicero suppressed Catiline's (q.v.) conspiracy, but later fled and was declared an exile for activities against Catiline's group. Recalled by Pompey (q.v.), Cicero sided with him against Caesar (q.v.). He also opposed Antony and the second triumvirate. In addition to orations and correspondence, he wrote poetry and works on rhetoric, epistemology, moral philosophy, political theory, and theology. (RL; Cat.)

CLAUDIUS RUTILIUS NAMATIANUS. See RUTILIUS.

CLARKE, SAMUEL (1675–1729), English philosopher and translator. Clarke was a Fellow at Cambridge, served in several parishes as rector, and became chaplain to Queen Anne. She appointed him rector of St James, Westminster. He published many sermons, as well as treatises on metaphysics and ethics. His *Scripture Doctrine of the Trinity* was criticized as an anti-trinitarian, and therefore heretical, tract. He also engaged in controversies over physical theory. In a famous body of correspondence, he debated Leibniz on questions of human freedom and physical theory. (RL; Cat.)

CLEANDER of Sparta (5th–4th c. BC), military commander and governor (Harmost) at Byzantium during Spartan supremacy over subject cities and islands. He engaged in military campaigns with both Cheirisophus (q.v.) and Xenophon (q.v.).

CORIOLANUS, GNAEUS MARCIUS (5th c. BC, legendary), according to tradition a Roman commander and hero. By legend he gained the name 'Coriolanus' for his remarkable courage, feats, and leadership during the capture of Corioli from the Volscians. He was later prosecuted by the tribunes as an aspiring tyrant. As an exile he became a commander for the Volscian army, then resigned upon the pleas of his mother and wife, only to be murdered by the Volscians.

COTTA, GAIUS AURELIUS (1st c. BC), Roman consul and orator. His speeches have not survived, but he had a reputation for honed and penetrating reasoning. Cicero (q.v.) depicts him in *De natura deorum* as a proponent of Academic scepticism.

CURTIUS RUFUS, QUINTUS (1st c. AD), rhetorician and historian of Alexander the Great (Alexander III, q.v.). His history of Alexander contained 10 books, but several portions have been lost. His method is dramatic narrative. (RL; Cat.)

CYRUS I (known as CYRUS THE GREAT and CYRUS THE ELDER) (6th c. BC), king and founder of the Archaemenid Persian empire. His defeat of Croesus of Lydia and other victories gave him vast new territories, where citizens sometimes greeted him as an honoured liberator from the previous regimes.

DIODORUS SICULUS of Agyrium (Agira) (1st c. BC), historian. He composed his *Historical Library* as a world history in 40 books, covering the earliest times to Caesar's (q.v.) Gallic Wars. Only the first five and the eleventh through the twentieth books have survived. (RL; Cat.)

DIOGENES LAERTIUS (2nd c. AD), Hellenic biographer and historian of ancient philosophers. His work in 10 books on the lives, opinions, and apophthegms of famous philosophers from the earliest times has provided source material for biographical information about ancient philosophers. (RL; Cat.)

DIONYSIUS of Halicarnassus (1st c. BC), historian and rhetor. He investigated artistic word order, Attic oratory, prose style, and the interpretation of historical texts. He wrote a 20-book history of early Rome (only the first 10 books and fragments remain). (RL; Cat.)

DOMINIC, ST (12th–13th c. AD), Spanish priest, founder of the Dominican Order, and *Magister sacri palatii* (The Pope's Theologian).

DRYDEN, JOHN (1631–1700), poet, essayist, playwright, and translator of poetry. His work *Absalom and Achitophel* (1681) was one piece in a famous series of satires. (RL; Cat.)

EPICTETUS of Hierapolis (Phrygia) (1st–2nd c. AD), Stoic philosopher. A former slave, his teachings on ethics and theology attracted many pupils, among them Arrian (q.v.), who recorded and preserved notes of his lectures published as the *Discourses* and the *Manual*. (RL; Cat.)

EPICURUS of Samos (4th–3rd c. BC), philosopher and founder of Epicureanism. He established a school in Athens intended to rival the Academy. Only fragments of his reputedly extensive writings remain, but Diogenes Laertius (q.v.) recorded information about his life and teachings.

EUCLEIDES, or EUCLIDES (5th–4th c. BC), Phliasian augur and son of Cleagoras, the painter of the murals in the Lyceum in Athens. Euclides advised Xenophon (q.v.) about proper religious sacrifice to the gods, as Xenophon records in his *Anabasis*.

EURIPIDES, possibly of Salamis (5th c. BC), dramatic poet, one of the most renowned writers of Greek tragedy. He wrote approximately 92 plays, of which 19 are extant, including *Medea*, *Alcestis*, and *Electra*. (RL; Cat.)

FLACCUS, MARCUS VERRIUS (1st c. AD), Roman scholar, grammarian, and teacher of the grandsons of Augustus (q.v.). He wrote several works on antiquities, but his chief work (now lost, but abridged by Festus) was *Libri de significatu verborum*, a storehouse of information in which Latin classics are quoted extensively.

FONTENELLE, BERNARD LE BOVIER DE (1657–1757), French figure of letters, playwright, and leading Cartesian thinker. Among his many works are *Dialogues des morts*, which imitates the style of Lucian (q.v.), *Entretiens sur la pluralité des mondes*, which attempts to popularize Copernican and Cartesian astronomy, and *Histoire des oracles* and *De l'origine des fables*, which criticize certain forms of superstition and orthodox religious belief. (RL; Cat.)

FRANCIS of Assisi, ST (12th–13th c. AD), Italian friar and preacher, founder of the Franciscan Order.

GERMANICUS (GERMANICUS JULIUS CAESAR) (1st c. BC–1st c. AD), nephew and adopted son of Tiberius (q.v.). In direct line of succession as emperor, he died while a military commander in Syria, possibly poisoned by the governor of Syria.

GUICCIARDINI, FRANCESCO (1483–1540), Florentine historian and statesman in the pontifical and Medicean service. His influential *Della istoria d'Italia* chronicles events from the last decade of the 15th century to 1534. (RL; Cat.)

HELIOGABALUS, or ELAGABALUS (byname of CAESAR MARCUS AURELIUS ANTONIUS AUGUSTUS, born VARIUS AVITUS BASSIANUS) (3rd c. AD), emperor of Rome from 218 to 222. Known primarily for eccentric behaviour and religious commitments, he imposed the religion of Baal on the Roman Empire.

HERACLITUS of Ephesus (6th–5th c. BC), cosmologist and epistemologist. He appears to have been preoccupied with the phenomenon of change.

HERODIAN (2nd–3rd c. AD), minor official in Rome and historian of Rome. His history covers the period from Marcus Aurelius (q.v.) to Gordian III (180–238 AD). (RL; Cat.)

HERODOTUS of Halicarnassus (5th c. BC), historian of Persia and the Hellenic world. His history in 9 books covers the Persians and the Persian invasion of the Hellenic states. He provides biographical detail and narrative reports. (RL; Cat.)

HESIOD of Boeotia (8th–7th c. BC), early poet in the ancient Hellenic world. Details of his life and dates are obscure. His most important works are *Theogony*, which deals with the origins and genealogies of the gods in mythology, and *Works and Days*, a body of moral maxims in hexameter verse about a life of honest work. (RL; Cat.)

HOMER (8th c. BC), poet assigned by ancient tradition as the author of the *Iliad* and the *Odyssey*. These works are considered paradigms of epic poetry. (RL; Cat.)

HORACE (QUINTUS HORATIUS FLACCUS) (1st c. BC), Latin poet and satirist. Horace flourished under the emperor Augustus (q.v.), his friend and supporter. His works are *Satires*, ten discourses in hexameter verse, *Epodes*, seventeen poems often in iambics, *Odes*, four books of 103 short poems in lyric meters, *Epistles*, which are personal letters in hexameter to his friends, and *Art of Poetry*, his epistles on poetry and poetic criticism. (RL; Cat.)

Hyde, Thomas (1636–1703), English orientalist with a speciality in Persian religion. He held a series of academic positions at Cambridge and Oxford as Professor of Hebrew and Professor of Arabic. He was also chief librarian of the Bodleian Library. In the *Historia religionis veterum Persarum* he attempted to correct misunderstandings of Persian religion presented in Hellenic and Roman sources. (RL; Cat.)

Ibn Rushd. See Averroës.

Isaac (20th–15th c. bc?), biblical son of Abraham (q.v.) and Sarah, and father of Jacob (q.v.).

Jacob (20th–15th c. bc?), biblical son of Isaac (q.v.) and Rebecca. His sons became the ancestors of the twelve tribes of Israel.

Juvenal (Decimus Junius Juvenalis) (1st–2nd c. ad), Roman satiric poet. His satires of indignation are protests directed against forms of moral degeneration, criminal behaviour, and folly in Rome. In them he exhibits an intense loathing of the emperor Domitian. (RL; Cat.)

La Rochefoucauld, François de (1613–80), French classical moralist. He is known for his appraisals of human motivation expressed in the form of brief epigrams, as found in his *Maximes*. (RL; Cat.)

Le Comte, or Le Compte, Louis Daniel (1655–1728), French Jesuit and missionary to China. He taught and travelled for ten years in China. His *Nouveaux Mémoires sur l'état présent de la Chine* was criticized and in some instances officially condemned as an overly favourable view of the Chinese people and culture. Objections focused on his laudatory assessment of Chinese religion and morality. (RL; Cat.)

Livy (Titus Livius) (1st c. bc–1st c. ad), Paduan historian of Rome. He composed his history in 142 books. Only 35 books and fragments are extant. His stated purpose for the work was to reveal the lessons of the past. The work was an immediate and enduring popular success. (RL; Cat.)

Locke, John (1632–1704), English philosopher, physician, and political figure. His *Essay concerning Human Understanding* and *Two Treatises on Civil Government* were both first published in 1690. Shortly thereafter he engaged in controversies over his alleged anti-trinitarian views. These discussions are reflected in his *Letters concerning Toleration, The Reasonableness of Christianity, A Vindication of the Reasonableness of Christianity*, a second *Vindication*, some epistolary pamphlets, correspondence with Isaac Newton (q.v.), and his commentary on the epistles of St Paul. (RL)

Longinus (1st c. ad?), the name assigned by tradition to the unknown author of *On the Sublime*, which contains internal evidence of being written in the 1st c. ad. There was a long but incorrect attribution of this treatise to Cassius Longinus (3rd c. ad), from whom the name was derived. The book discusses style and literary criticism in antiquity. (RL; Cat.)

Louis XIV (known as Louis Le Grand) (1638–1715), French king through a 73-year reign (1643–1715). He was the first child of Anne of Austria and Louis XIII, and became king at age 4, under his mother's regency. He sought to expand the domain of the French monarchy, which led him into European wars. The wars drained the treasury and the resources of the French people.

LUCIAN of Samosata (2nd c. AD), Hellenic satirist, rhetorician, and poet. He satirized the religious beliefs of his period as well as the pretensions of the various schools of philosophy. He wrote biographical and rhetorical works, but his development of the satiric dialogue is commonly regarded as his major contribution. (RL; Cat.)

LUCRETIUS (TITUS LUCRETIUS CARUS) (1st c. BC), philosophical poet. Little has been confirmed about his life other than his authorship of *De rerum natura*, a didactic poem in six books that presents the physical, psychological, metaphysical, and moral theories of Epicurus (q.v.). (RL; Cat.)

MACHIAVELLI, or MACHIAVEL, NICCOLÒ (1469–1527), Florentine statesman, political theorist, and historian. He held several government posts until dismissed from office after the fall of the Florentine republic (1512). He soon published on themes of political power in *The Prince* and *Discourses on the First Ten Books of Livy* (1513). (RL; Cat.)

MACROBIUS, AMBROSIUS THEODOSIUS (5th c. AD), Roman grammarian and Neoplatonist philosopher whose extant works are his *Saturnalia* and commentary on Cicero's *Dream of Scipio*. (RL; Cat.)

MANILIUS, MARCUS (1st c. BC–1st c. AD), author of a Latin didactic poem on astrology entitled *Astronomica*. His work describes the origin and structure of the heavens, the signs of the zodiac, and methods of determining horoscopes. (RL; Cat.)

MENENIUS AGRIPPA (6th–5th c. BC, legendary), by tradition Roman consul in 503 BC. He mediated a split between patricians and plebeians when the latter had seceded. Reports circulated that he brought the plebeians back to Rome in 493 BC. The origin and dates of the legend are uncertain.

MILTON, JOHN (1608–74), English poet. He abandoned a potential career as a clergyman in favour of poetry. In addition to *Paradise Lost*, he wrote prose works in the cause of liberty and liberation. His *Letters of State* was written while serving as Latin secretary to the Commonwealth and to Cromwell. (RL; Cat.)

MOSES (*Hebrew* MOSHE; *c.* 13th c. BC?), by tradition the founder of ancient Israel, the author of the Pentateuch, and a Jewish lawgiver. According to Exodus, he led the Israelites out of slavery in Egypt through the wilderness into Canaan.

NAMATIANUS, CLAUDIUS RUTILIUS. See RUTILIUS.

NERO (NERO CLAUDIUS CAESAR DRUSUS GERMANICUS) (1st c. AD), Roman emperor. Nero's mother, Agrippina, poisoned his stepfather, Claudius, and made it possible for Nero to gain the throne. He installed his former teachers Seneca (q.v.) and Burrus as heads of government. When they retired, Nero's reign turned tyrannical. He murdered both his mother and his wife.

NEWTON, ISAAC (1642–1727), English mathematician, natural philosopher, experimental scientist, and writer on biblical and theological subjects. He published the Latin edition of *Mathematical Principles of Natural Philosophy* in 1687. After almost another twenty years he published his *Opticks* (1704). Newton was also intensely interested in theology and biblical criticism and scholarship. (RL)

NICHOLAS, ST (4th c. AD), Christian prelate, bishop of Myra in Licia, Asia Minor, and patron saint of Russia.

OCTAVIANUS, or OCTAVIAN. See AUGUSTUS.

ORIGEN of Alexandria (2nd–3rd c. AD), Christian theologian. He was head of the catechetical school in Alexandria, and wrote exegetical, doctrinal, devotional, apologetic, and recensional treatises.

OVID (PUBLIUS OVIDIUS NASO) (1st c. BC–1st c. AD), Roman poet. Among his chief works is *Metamorphoses*, which involves a chain of stories about change of shape and includes a rich body of mythology. Although immensely popular in Rome, he was banished for an unknown offence against political authorities. (RL; Cat.)

PANAETIUS of Rhodes (2nd c. BC), Stoic philosopher. He succeeded Antipater as head of the Stoa in Athens, a position Panaetius held for twenty years.

PETRONIUS ARBITER, GAIUS (1st c. AD), Roman satirist and consul who fell from Nero's (q.v.) favour. The *Satyricon* attributed to him is a prose-and-verse presentation of Roman life in his time. (RL; Cat.)

PHIDIAS (5th c. BC), Athenian sculptor. He sculpted several statues of Minerva, or, more properly, Athena. One, the Athena Parthenos, was made for the Parthenon. He also made a large Zeus for the temple at Olympia. His marble sculptures of the Parthenon are the main source of contemporary knowledge.

PHILLIPS, or PHILIPS, EDWARD (1630–96?), poet, novelist, writer, editor, and lexicographer. He was the nephew of John Milton (q.v.) who housed and educated him. He maintained a close relationship to Milton despite major differences of viewpoint. He provided an English translation of Milton's *Letters of State*, to which he prefixed a short biographical memoir. (RL; Cat.)

PLATO of Athens (5th–4th c. BC), philosopher, founder of the Academy, and teacher of Aristotle (q.v.). His dialogues often featured the life and philosophy of Socrates (q.v.). Teaching at the Academy and writing his dialogues occupied him for approximately the last forty years of his life. (RL; Cat.)

PLINY, THE ELDER (GAIUS PLINIUS SECUNDUS) (1st c. AD), Roman politician, commander, scholar, and natural historian, uncle of Pliny the Younger (q.v.). He authored works on diverse subjects, but only his *Natural History* survived. He assembled this ambitious compilation of the natural science of his time from the work of prior authorities. (RL; Cat.)

PLINY, THE YOUNGER (GAIUS PLINIUS CAECILIUS SECUNDUS) (1st–2nd c. AD), Roman governor and consul, nephew and adoptive son of Pliny the Elder (q.v.). He studied law in the schools of Quintilian (q.v.) and had a career as a public servant. He had relationships with several Roman emperors. He published many of his literary letters. (RL; Cat.)

PLUTARCH of Chaeronea (1st–2nd c. AD), biographer, moral philosopher, and historical scholar. His lives of leading figures in the Graeco-Roman world are basic sources of biographical data. He also wrote short essays on moral philosophy, defences of Platonism, and treatises in opposition to Stoicism and Epicureanism. A priest of Apollo at Delphi for the last thirty years of his life, he adhered to the ancient religious beliefs. (RL; Cat.)

POMPEY (GNAEUS POMPEIUS MAGNUS) (1st c. BC), Roman military commander and statesman. He formed the first triumvirate with Julius Caesar (q.v.) and Crassus. After differences with Caesar erupted, a civil war broke out, and Pompey was decisively defeated.

PRINCE OF SALLEE. See SIDI ALI BEN MOHAMMED BEN MOUSSA.

PRIOR, MATTHEW (1664–1721), English poet, epigrammatist, and diplomat. Prior had an early career of public service. However, upon Queen Anne's death and the accession of the Whig ministry of George I, Prior, a Tory, was ruined politically. He was impeached by Sir Robert Walpole and imprisoned for two years by the Whigs. (RL; Cat.)

QUINTILIAN (MARCUS FABIUS QUINTILIANUS) (1st c. AD), rhetor and teacher. He taught and wrote about oratory in Rome for twenty years, and was patronized by Vespasian and Domitian. His *Institutionum Oratoriarum* prescribes the training of an orator from childhood and serves as a description of a proper education in the liberal arts. (RL; Cat.)

QUINTUS CURTIUS RUFUS. See CURTIUS.

RAMSAY, ANDREW MICHAEL (known as THE CHEVALIER DE RAMSAY) (1686–1743), philosophically inclined theologian and writer on diverse subjects. Although of Scottish origin, he lived in France after 1710 and often wrote in French. Under the influence of his friend Fénelon, he converted to Roman Catholicism after becoming disaffected with Anglicanism. His chief works were *Travels of Cyrus* and *Philosophical Principles of Natural and Revealed Religion*. (RL; Cat.)

REGNARD, JEAN-FRANÇOIS (1655–1709), French comic dramatist. He wrote short plays in verse as well as prose works. He travelled extensively and recorded many of his experiences. His *Voyage de Laponie* is an account of his trip to Lapland in 1681. This work is a set of notes that the author never prepared for publication. After posthumous publication in 1731, the work was widely read. (RL; Cat.)

ROCHEFOUCAULD. See LA ROCHEFOUCAULD.

RUTILIUS (CLAUDIUS RUTILIUS NAMATIANUS) (5th c. AD), Roman poet. His major work is a lengthy poem and itinerary in two books. It describes a coastal voyage from Rome to Gaul, although the poem breaks off before Gaul is reached. (RL; Cat.)

RUYTER, MICHEL ADRIAANSZOON DE (1607–76), Dutch naval officer and hero. He commanded several large fleets against the forces of various European nations. He also spent time in command of merchant vessels. While occupied as a trader, he reached the coast of Morocco, where he encountered the Prince of Sallee, Sidi Ali ben Mohammed ben Moussa (q.v.).

SALLUST (GAIUS SALLUSTIUS CRISPUS) (1st c. BC), Roman historian and politician. He was elected tribune in 52 and became a partisan of Caesar (q.v.). He retired to write histories of political affairs. His *War with Catiline* dealt with the conspiracy of Catiline (q.v.). Only fragments remain of his *History*. (RL; Cat.)

Seneca, Lucius Annaeus (known as Seneca the Younger) (1st c. AD), Roman Stoic philosopher, literary writer, and political figure. He wrote philosophy, a comedy, a treatise on natural science, and several tragedies. He was tutor to Nero (q.v.), who eventually entrusted to him, together with Burrus, effective control of government. He was suspected of a Stoic plot against Nero, who commanded him to commit suicide. (RL; Cat.)

Serenus, Sammonicus (2nd–3rd c. AD), Roman scholar during the period of Emperor Septimius Severus. He was reputed to have an enormous library of possibly 62,000 books. His only known work is *Res reconditae*.

Sextus Empiricus (2nd–3rd c. AD), physician, philosopher, and recorder of the Pyrrhonian tradition. His works contain the most comprehensive statement of the ancient sceptical tradition, and include criticisms of many other philosophers. (RL; Cat.)

Sidi Ali ben Mohammed ben Moussa (17th c. AD), the Prince of Sallee, vassal of the sultan of Morocco.

Socrates of Athens (5th c. BC), philosopher. Although immortalized as the primary figure in Plato's dialogues, Socrates wrote no philosophy, and little is known about his life until the events surrounding his death. According to Plato (q.v.) and Xenophon (q.v.), he was indicted and sentenced to death for theological innovation and for teachings that corrupted the youth of Athens.

Spartian (Aelius Spartianus) (*c.* 3rd–6th c. AD), one of six alleged biographers of Roman emperors, Caesars, and usurpers found in the *Scriptores historiae Augustae*. Scholarship has been divided over the purpose, date, and authorship of the work. Little is known of its six alleged authors. (RL; Cat.)

Stilpo, or Stilpon, of Megara (4th c. BC), third head of the Megarian school. Stilpo's dialogues have not survived, save for a few fragments drawn from passages quoted by others.

Strabo of Amaseia, Pontus (1st c. BC–1st c. AD), historian and geographer. The 47 books of his *Historical Studies* have been lost, but the 17 books of his *Geography* have survived. His geographical observations were based on travel in Europe, Asia, and North Africa. (RL; Cat.)

Suetonius (Gaius Suetonius Tranquillus) (1st–2nd c. AD), Roman lawyer, biographer, and historian. His *Lives of the Caesars* contains portraits and entertaining anecdotal material of the first twelve caesars, including intimate details of their private lives. He held several government posts, and became Hadrian's private secretary and Imperial librarian. (RL; Cat.)

Tacitus, Cornelius (1st–2nd c. AD), Roman orator, politician, and historian. He was praetor, consul, and proconsul in Asia. His *Germania* is an ethnological report on the behaviour of tribes north of the Rhine and the Danube. His *Histories*, from the reign of Galba to that of Domitian, and the later *Annals*, from Tiberius (q.v.) to the death of Nero (q.v.), are histories of various rulers of the Roman empire. (RL; Cat.)

TERENTIA (lst c. BC), wife of Cicero (q.v.). They were close companions until after his exile, when a growing chill in the relationship eventuated in divorce.

THALES of Miletus (7th–6th c. BC), astronomer and philosopher of the physical world. Stories circulated that he was a sage versatile in many fields of knowledge, but few teachings and no writings have survived.

THUCYDIDES of Athens (5th c. BC), military commander and historian of the early wars between Athens and Sparta. He commanded an expedition sent to Amphipolis to defend it against Brasidas (q.v.), but he failed to prevent the city's capture. His history stops in the middle of the narrative of events. (RL; Cat.)

TIBERIUS (TIBERIUS JULIUS CAESAR AUGUSTUS) (1st c. BC–1st c. AD), Roman emperor. He served as military commander, consul, and tribune before becoming the adopted son of Augustus (q.v.). After Augustus died, Tiberius reigned from 14 to 37 AD. His rule has often been depicted in terms of severe vice, cruelty, and abuse, as well as mental instability; but scholarly opinion has been divided.

TIMOTHEUS of Miletus (5th–4th c. BC), poet and musician. He composed in several styles, and claimed for himself revolutionary advances in music.

TULLY. See CICERO.

VARRO, MARCUS TERENTIUS (1st c. BC), versatile author, tribune and praetor, librarian, and philologist. Quintilian (q.v.) refers to him as the most learned of the Romans. Although a partisan of Pompey (q.v.), he remained in favour with Julius Caesar (q.v.), who appointed him to assemble a public library of Hellenic and Latin literature. Only two of his many works survived: *De lingua Latina* (books 5–10) and *Rerum rusticarum*. (RL; Cat.)

VERRIUS FLACCUS. See FLACCUS.

VIRGIL, or VERGIL (PUBLIUS VERGILIUS MARO) (1st c. BC), Roman epic, didactic, and idyllic poet. He wrote, in order of composition, the *Eclogues* (or *Bucolics*), the *Georgics*, and the *Aeneid*. (RL; Cat.)

XENOPHON of Athens (5th–4th c. BC), military leader, historian, and essayist. He became a follower of Socrates (q.v.) and recorded events surrounding Socrates' death in *Memorabilia* and *Apology*. Xenophon left Athens in 401 to join the expedition of Cyrus the Younger against Artaxerxes, which Xenophon records in his *Anabasis*. Xenophon wrote other works on history, polity, financial management, and the command of a cavalry unit. (RL; Cat.)

ZALEUCUS of Locri (7th c. BC), reputed author of the first codification of laws in the ancient city-states. These laws were severe, but Zaleucus's abilities as a conciliator were renowned.

ZOROASTER (*Persian* ZARATHUSTRA; 10th–6th c. BC?), Persian founder of Zoroastrianism. Little has been documented about his life, but he has commonly been depicted as a reformer who protested against nature worship and priestly cults. Through a commitment to monotheism, he and his followers seem to have transformed the popular nature gods into archangels.

REFERENCE LIST

The authors and works listed here all derive from one or both of the following two sources: (1) works cited by Hume in *DP* and *NHR* and (2) works cited by the editor in the Annotations, Introduction, and other parts of this volume.

Entries for Latin, French, and other foreign-language sources generally follow today's forms for these languages. However, inconsistencies in language and publishing conventions were commonplace in early modern publishing. These inconsistencies—in accents, capitalization, spelling, and punctuation—are not always eliminated in the reference list below, in order to remain faithful to the forms used on title-pages.

Loeb Classical Library editions (abbreviated 'Loeb Library') are used for classical works wherever possible. The dates listed are printing dates for the volumes consulted, not original dates of publication or dates of revised editions. Printing dates vary widely in some multi-volume editions.

If an author has been established for a work that was originally published anonymously (for example, Hume's *Treatise* and early essays), the author's name is used, rather than the category 'anonymous' or the convention of using brackets around the name of the author.

ADDISON, JOSEPH, *Cato*, in vol. 1 of *The Miscellaneous Works of Joseph Addison*, ed. A. C. Guthkelch, 2 vols. (London: Bell, 1914). (See also *The Guardian* and *The Spectator*.)

—— *The Spectator*, no. 412 (June 1712). In *The Spectator*, ed. Donald F. Bond, 5 vols. (Oxford: Clarendon Press, 1965).

ANNAS, JULIA, 'Hume and Ancient Scepticism', in J. Sihvola (ed.), *Ancient Scepticism and the Sceptical Tradition*, Acta Philosophica Fennica, 66 (Helsinki, 2000), 271–85.

ANONYMOUS, *Recueil des miracles operés au tombeau de M. de Paris Diacre* [*Collection of the Miracles Performed at the Tomb of the Deacon, Monsieur de Pâris*] (n.p., 1732).

ANONYMOUS, Review of *Four Dissertations, The Critical Review: or, Annals of Literature*, 3 (1757), 97–107 (Feb., art. 1); 209–16 (Mar., art. 2).

ANONYMOUS, Review of *Four Dissertations, The Literary Magazine: or, Universal Review*, 2 (Dec. 1757), 32–6.

ANONYMOUS, Review of 'Remarks upon the Natural History of Religion, by Mr. Hume. With dialogues on heathen idolatry, and the christian religion', *The Critical Review: or, Annals of Literature*, 6 (Nov. 1758), art. 7, 411–18. (Remarks on Stona, as below.)

APPIAN, *Roman History*, trans. Horace White, 4 vols., Loeb Library (1912–13).

AQUINAS. See Thomas Aquinas.

ÁRDAL, PÁLL S., *Passion and Value in Hume's* Treatise, 2nd edn. (Edinburgh: Edinburgh University Press, 1989).

ARISTOTLE, *The 'Art' of Rhetoric,* trans. John H. Freese, Loeb Library (1959).

—— *The Complete Works of Aristotle*, ed. Jonathan Barnes, 2 vols. (Princeton: Princeton University Press, 1984).

—— *The Metaphysics*, trans. Hugh Tredennick, 2 vols., Loeb Library (1933–5).

—— *Nicomachean Ethics*, trans. H. Rackham, Loeb Library (1947).

—— *On the Soul*, trans. J. A. Smith, in vol. 2 of *The Complete Works of Aristotle.*

—— *Problems*, trans. W. S. Hett, 2 vols., Loeb Library (1937).

ARNAULD, ANTOINE, and NICOLE, PIERRE, *Logic or the Art of Thinking*, ed. and trans. Jill Vance Buroker (Cambridge: Cambridge University Press, 1996).

ARNOBIUS, *The Seven Books of Arnobius Against the Heathen*, trans. Hamilton Bryce and Hugh Campbell, in vol. 6 of *The Ante-Nicene Fathers*, ed. Alexander Roberts and James Donaldson, 10 vols. (New York: Scribner, 1926).

ARRIAN (FLAVIUS ARRIANUS), *Anabasis Alexandri* [*Anabasis of Alexander*], trans. P. A. Brunt, 2 vols., Loeb Library (1976–83).

AUGUSTINE, *The City of God Against the Pagans*, trans. George E. McCracken *et al.*, 7 vols., Loeb Library (1957–72).

AURELIUS ANTONINUS, MARCUS, *The Communings with Himself* [*The Meditations*], trans. C. R. Haines, Loeb Library (1930).

AYLOFFE, WILLIAM, *The Government of the Passions According to the Rules of Reason and Religion* (London, 1700).

BACON, FRANCIS, *Advancement of Learning*, in vol. 3 of *The Works of Francis Bacon.*

—— *Essays*, in vol. 6 of *The Works of Francis Bacon.*

—— *The Works of Francis Bacon*, ed. James Spedding, Robert Leslie Ellis, and Douglas Denon Heath, 14 vols. (London 1858–74; repr. Stuttgart: Frommann, 1961–3).

BAHR, FERNANDO A., 'Pierre Bayle en los "Early Memoranda" de Hume', *Revista Latinoamericana de Filosofía*, 25 (1999), 7–38.

BAILEY, NATHAN (ed.), *Dictionarium Britannicum* (1730; fac. Hildesheim: Olms, 1969).

BALFOUR, JAMES, *A Delineation of the Nature and Obligation of Morality. With Reflexions upon Mr. Hume's Book, intitled*, An Inquiry concerning the Principles of Morals (Edinburgh, 1753; fac. Bristol: Thoemmes, 1989).

BALGUY, JOHN, *The Foundation of Moral Goodness* (London, 1728–9; fac. 2 vols. in 1, New York: Garland, 1976).

BARFOOT, MICHAEL, 'Hume and the Culture of Science in the Early Eighteenth Century', in M. A. Stewart (ed.), *Studies in the Philosophy of the Scottish Enlightenment* (Oxford: Clarendon Press, 1990), 151–90.

BARROW, ISAAC, *The Works of the Learned Isaac Barrow*, ed. John Tillotson, 3rd edn., 3 vols. (London, 1716).

BAXTER, RICHARD, *The Reasons of the Christian Religion* (London, 1667).

Bayle, Pierre, *The Dictionary Historical and Critical of Mr Peter Bayle*, ed. and trans. Pierre Des Maizeaux, 2nd edn., 5 vols. (London, 1734–8; fac. New York: Garland, 1984).

—— *Œuvres diverses* [*Various Works*] (The Hague, 1727; fac. Hildesheim: Olms, 1970; introduced by Elisabeth Labrousse).

—— *Various Thoughts on the Occasion of a Comet*, trans. Robert C. Bartlett (Albany, NY: State University of New York Press, 2000).

Bentley, Richard, *Eight Boyle Lectures on Atheism* (London, 1692–3; fac. New York: Garland, 1976). (The general subject is 'A Confutation of Atheism'. The first lecture was delivered from the pulpit of St Martin's Church, 7 Mar. 1692.)

—— *Remarks Upon a Late Discourse of Free-Thinking: In a Letter to F.H. D.D.* (London, 1713; fac. New York: Garland, 1978). (The facsimile is bound with Anthony Collins, *A Discourse of Free-Thinking*.)

Berkeley, George, *Alciphron*, in vol. 3 of *The Works of George Berkeley, Bishop of Cloyne*.

—— *Three Dialogues between Hylas and Philonous*, in vol. 2 of *The Works of George Berkeley, Bishop of Cloyne*.

—— *A Treatise concerning the Principles of Human Knowledge*, in vol. 2 of *The Works of George Berkeley, Bishop of Cloyne*.

—— *The Works of George Berkeley, Bishop of Cloyne*, ed. A. A. Luce and T. E. Jessop, 9 vols. (Edinburgh: Nelson, 1948–57).

Berman, David, *A History of Atheism in Britain: From Hobbes to Russell* (London: Croom Helm, 1988).

Betts, C. J., *Early Deism in France: From the So-Called 'Déistes' of Lyon (1564) to Voltaire's 'Lettres philosophiques' (1734)* (Boston: M. Nijhoff, 1984).

Bible, *The Holy Bible . . . The Authorized Version Published in the Year 1611* (Oxford: Oxford University Press, 1985).

Blok, P., *The Life of Admiral de Ruyter*, trans. G. J. Renier (Westport, Conn.: Greenwood Press, 1975).

Blount, Thomas, *Glossographia: or a Dictionary Interpreting All Such Hard Words* (London, 1656).

Bossuet, Jacques Benigne, *An Universal History: From the Beginning of the World, to the Empire of Charlemagne*, trans. James Elphinston, 13th edn. (Dublin, 1785).

Boswell, James, *Boswell in Extremes, 1776–1778*, ed. Charles McC. Weis and Frederick A. Pottle (New York: McGraw-Hill, 1970). Yale Editions of the Private Papers of James Boswell.

Boulainvilliers, Henri de, *Abrégé chronologique de l'histoire de France* [*Chronological Summary of the History of France*], in vol. 3 of *Etat de la France*, 3 vols. (London, 1727–8).

Box, M. A., 'An Allusion in Hume's *An Enquiry concerning the Principles of Morals* Identified', *Notes & Queries*, 231 (Mar. 1986), 60–1.

Boyle, Robert, *Memoirs for the Natural History of Humane Blood* (London, 1684).

BOYLE, ROBERT, *Some Considerations about the Reconcileableness of Reason and Religion*, in vol. 4 of *The Works of the Honourable Robert Boyle*, ed. Thomas Birch, 6 vols. (London, 1772; fac. Hildesheim: Olms, 1966). (Birch died six years before this edition appeared; it was based on Birch's 1744 edition.)

BRANDT, GERARD [GEERAERT], *La vie de Michel de Ruiter: Duc, Chevalier, Lieutenant Amiral Général de Hollande & de Oüest-Frise* [*The Life of Michel de Ruiter: Duke, Knight, Lieutenant Admiral General of Holland and of West Frisia*] (Amsterdam, 1698).

BRUMOY, PIERRE, *The Greek Theatre of Father Brumoy*, trans. Charlotte Lennox, 3 vols. (London, 1759). (See also Cat. entry of the 1730 edn.)

BUFFON, GEORGE LOUIS LECLERC, *Histoire naturelle, générale et particulière* [*Natural History, General and Particular*], 20 vols. (Paris, 1749–67) (with others, in 44 vols., 1749–1804).

—— *Natural History, General and Particular*, in *From Natural History to the History of Nature: Readings from Buffon and His Critics*, ed. John Lyon and Phillip R. Sloan (Notre Dame, Ind.: University of Notre Dame Press, 1981).

BURNET, THOMAS, *Archaeologiæ Philosophicæ: sive doctrina antiqua de rerum originibus* [*Philosophical Archaeology: or the Ancient Teaching on the Origins of Things*] (London, 1692).

BURTON, J. H. (ed.), *Letters of Eminent Persons Addressed to David Hume* (Edinburgh, 1849; fac. Bristol: Thoemmes, 1989).

—— *Life and Correspondence of David Hume*, 2 vols. (Edinburgh, 1846; fac. New York: Burt Franklin, 1967; New York: Garland, 1983).

BUTLER, JOSEPH, *The Analogy of Religion, Natural and Revealed, to the Constitution and Course of Nature*, in vol. 1 of *The Works of Joseph Butler*.

—— *Fifteen Sermons Preached at the Rolls Chapel*, in vol. 2 of *The Works of Joseph Butler* (under the title *Fifteen Sermons*).

—— *The Works of Joseph Butler*, ed. W. E. Gladstone, 2 vols. (Oxford, 1896; fac. Bristol: Thoemmes, 1995).

CAESAR, GAIUS JULIUS, *The Gallic War*, trans. H. J. Edwards, Loeb Library (1946).

CAMPBELL, ARCHIBALD, *An Enquiry into the Original of Moral Virtue* (Edinburgh, 1733). (Published fraudulently in 1728 by Alexander Innes under a different title.)

CAMPBELL, GEORGE, *A Dissertation on Miracles: Containing an Examination of the Principles Advanced by David Hume* (Edinburgh, 1762; 3rd edn. Edinburgh, 1796 and 1797).

CHAMBERS, EPHRAIM, *Cyclopædia: or, An Universal Dictionary of Arts and Sciences*, 5th edn., 2 vols. (London, 1741–3).

CHARLETON, WALTER, *Natural History of the Passions* (London, 1674).

CHARRON, PIERRE, *Of Wisdome*, trans. Samson Lennard (London, 1612). (This work is sometimes catalogued as *De la sagesse* even for an English translation.)

CHEYNE, GEORGE, *The English Malady* (London, 1733; fac. Delmar, NY: Scholars' Facsimiles & Reprints, 1976).

CHUO UNIVERSITY LIBRARY, *David Hume and the Eighteenth Century British Thought: An Annotated Catalogue*, ed. Sadao Ikeda, 2 vols. (Tokyo: Chuo University Library, 1986–8).

CICERO, MARCUS TULLIUS, *Academica* [*The Academy*], in *De natura deorum, Academica*.

——*De divinatione* [*On Divination*], in *De senectute, de amicitia, de divinatione*, trans. William Armistead Falconer, Loeb Library (1959).

——*De finibus bonorum et malorum* [*On the Chief Good and Evil*], trans. H. Rackham, Loeb Library (1921).

——*De natura deorum* [*On the Nature of the Gods*], in *De natura deorum, Academica*.

——*De natura deorum, Academica*, trans. H. Rackham, Loeb Library (1972).

——*De oratore* [*On the Orator*], trans. E. W. Sutton and completed by H. Rackham, 2 vols., Loeb Library (1942).

——*In Catilinam* [*Against Catiline*], in *The Speeches: In Catilinam I–IV, Pro Murena, Pro Sulla, and Pro Flacco*, trans. Louis E. Lord, Loeb Library (1967).

——*In Verram* [*Against Verres*], in *The Verrine Orations*, trans. L. H. G. Greenwood, 2 vols; Loeb Library (1928–35).

——*The Letters to His Friends*, trans. W. Glynn Williams, 3 vols., Loeb Library (1927–9). (Translation of *Epistulae ad familiares*.)

——*Pro Cluentio* [*In Defence of Cluentius*], in *The Speeches: Pro Lege Manilia, Pro Caecina, Pro Cluentio, Pro Rabirio, and Perduellionis*, trans. H. Grose Hodge, Loeb Library (1927).

——*Tusculan Disputations*, trans. J. E. King, Loeb Library (1966).

CLAIR, COLIN, *A History of Printing in Britain* (London: Cassell, 1965).

CLARKE, SAMUEL, *A Discourse concerning the Being and Attributes of God*, in vol. 2 of *The Works of Samuel Clarke*.

——*A Discourse concerning the Unchangeable Obligations of Natural Religion*, in vol. 2 of *The Works of Samuel Clarke*.

——*The Scripture Doctrine of the Trinity*, in vol. 4 of *The Works of Samuel Clarke*.

——*The Works of Samuel Clarke, D.D.*, 4 vols. (London, 1738; fac. New York: Garland, 1978).

CLAUBERG, JOHANN, *Opera omnia philosophica* (Amsterdam, 1691).

CLAUDE, JEAN, *The Catholick Doctrine of the Eucharist in All Ages; in Answer to What M. Arnaud, Doctor of the Sorbon Alledges* (London, 1684).

CLAYTON, ROBERT, *Some Thoughts on Self-Love, Innate-Ideas, Free-Will, Taste, Sentiment, Liberty and Necessity, etc. Occasioned by Reading Mr. Hume's Works...* (Dublin and London, 1753).

COCHRANE, J. A., *Dr. Johnson's Printer: The Life of William Strahan* (London: Routledge; Cambridge, Mass.: Harvard University Press, 1964).

COEFFETEAU, NICOLAS, *A Table of Humane Passions. With their Causes and Effects*, trans. E. Grimeston (London, 1621).

COLLINS, ANTHONY, *A Discourse of Free-Thinking* (London, 1713; fac. New York: Garland, 1978).

COLLINS, ANTHONY, *A Discourse of the Grounds and Reasons of the Christian Religion* (London, 1724; fac. New York: Garland, 1976).

COLVER, A. WAYNE, 'A Variant of Hume's Advertisement Repudiating the *Treatise*', *Papers of the Bibliographical Society of America*, 67 (1973), 66–8.

—— 'The "First" Edition of Hume's Essays and Treatises', *Papers of the Bibliographical Society of America*, 68 (1974), 39–44.

CORDEMOY, GERAULD [GÉRAUD] DE, *Six discours sur la distinction et l'union du corps et de l'âme* [*Six Discourses on the Distinction and the Union of the Body and the Soul*—the later title of *Le discernement du corps et de l'âme* (*The Distinction between the Body and the Soul*) (1666)], in *Œuvres philosophiques*, ed. Pierre Clair and François Girbal (Paris: Presses Universitaires de France, 1968).

CUDWORTH, RALPH, *The True Intellectual System of the Universe*, 2 vols. (London, 1678; fac. New York: Garland, 1978).

CUNNINGHAM, IAN C., 'The Arrangement of the Royal Society of Edinburgh's David Hume Manuscripts', *The Bibliotheck*, 15 (1988), 8–22.

CUREAU DE LA CHAMBRE, MARIN. See LA CHAMBRE.

CURTIUS RUFUS, QUINTUS, *History of Alexander*, trans. John C. Rolfe, 2 vols., Loeb Library (1946).

DAILLÉ, JEAN, *Réplique aux deux livres que Messieurs Adam et Cottiby ont publiez contre luy* [*Reply to the Two Books that Messrs. Adam and Cottiby Published Against Him*] (Geneva, 1662; 2nd edn., 1669).

DALE, ANTONIUS VAN, *De oraculis veterum ethnicorum dissertationes duae* [*Two Essays on the Oracles of Diverse Peoples*] (Amsterdam, 1683).

—— *Dissertationes de origine ac progressu idololatriae et superstitionum* [*Treatises on the Origin and Progress of Idolatry and Superstition*] (Amsterdam, 1696).

DAVID, MADELEINE, 'Histoire des religions et philosophie au XVIIIe siècle: le président de Brosses, David Hume et Diderot' ['History of the Religions and Philosophy of the 18th Century: The Premier de Brosses, David Hume, and Diderot'], *Revue philosophique*, 164 (1974), 145–60.

—— 'Lettres inédites de Diderot et de Hume écrites de 1755 à 1763 au président de Brosses' ['Unedited Letters from Diderot and Hume Written from 1755 to 1763 to Premier de Brosses'], *Revue philosophique*, 156 (1966), 135–44.

—— 'Le Président de Brosses historien des religions et philosophie' ['Premier de Brosses: Historian of Religions and Philosophy'], in Jean-Claude Garreta (ed.), *Charles de Brosses, 1777–1977* (Geneva: Slatkine, 1981), 123–40.

DEBIA, JAMES, *An Account of the Religion, Rites, Ceremonies, and Superstitions of the Moscovites, Extracted from Several Writers of the Best Character and Authority* (London, 1710).

DESCARTES, RENÉ, *Letters*, in vol. 3 of *The Philosophical Writings of Descartes*.

—— *The Passions of the Soul*, in vol. 1 of *The Philosophical Writings of Descartes*.

—— *The Philosophical Writings of Descartes*, ed. and trans. John Cottingham, Robert Stoothoff, and Dugald Murdoch, 3 vols.; vol. 3 also trans. Anthony Kenny (Cambridge: Cambridge University Press, 1984–91).

Dio Cassius Cocceianus, *Roman History*, trans. Earnest Cary, 9 vols., Loeb Library (1924–7).

Diodorus Siculus, *The Library of History*, in *Diodorus of Sicily*, trans. C. H. Oldfather, Francis R. Walton, and Russel M. Geer, 12 vols., Loeb Library (1933–67). A better translation of *Bibliotheca historica* is *Historical Library*. The latter is used in this edition.

Diogenes Laertius, *Lives of Eminent Philosophers*, trans. R. D. Hicks, 2 vols., Loeb Library (1925–70).

Dionysius of Halicarnassus, *Roman Antiquities*, trans. Earnest Cary, 7 vols., Loeb Library (1943–5).

Drelincourt, Charles, *Dialogues familiers sur les principales objections des missionnaires de ce temps* [*Familiar Dialogues on the Principal Objections of Contemporary Missionaries*] (Geneva, 1648).

Dryden, John, 'Absalom and Achitophel', in vol. 2 of *The Works of John Dryden*.

——*An Essay of Dramatick Poesie and Shorter Works*, in vol. 17 of *The Works of John Dryden*.

——*The Works of John Dryden*, 20 vols. (Berkeley: University of California Press, 1956–).

Du Perron, Jacques Davy, *Traitt du sainct sacrement de l'Eucharistie.... Livrese contenant la refutation du livre du Sieur du Plessis Mornay* [*Treatise on the Sanctity of the Sacrament of the Eucharist.... Books containing the Refutation of the Book by Sieur du Plessis Mornay*] (Paris, 1622).

Du Vair, Guillaume, *De la sainte philosophie* [*On the Holy Philosophy*] *and Philosophie morale des Stoïques* [*Moral Philosophy of the Stoics*], ed. G. Michaut (Paris: J. Vrin, 1945).

——*The Morall Philosophie of the Stoicks*, trans. Thomas James (London, 1598; fac. New Brunswick, NJ: Rutgers University Press, 1951).

Dupont-Ferrier, Gustave, *Du Collège de Clermont au Lycée Louis-le-Grand [Of the Collège de Clermont at the Lycée Louis-le-Grand]*, 3 vols. (Paris: Boccard, 1921–5).

Durán, Diego, *Book of the Gods and Rites*, ed. and trans. Fernando Horcasitas and Doris Heyden (Norman, Okla.: University of Oklahoma Press, 1971). (Published with Durán's *The Ancient Calendar*.)

Edwards, John, *Socinianism Unmask'd. A Discourse Shewing the Unreasonableness of a Late Writer's Opinion Concerning the Necessity of only One Article of Christian Faith; And of his other Assertions in his late Book, Entitled, The Reasonableness of Christianity as deliver'd in the Scriptures, and in his Vindication of it. With a Brief Reply to another (professed) Socinian Writer* (London, 1695; fac. New York: Garland, 1984).

——*Some Thoughts Concerning the Several Causes and Occasions of Atheism, Especially in the Present Age. With some Brief Reflections on Socinianism: And on a Late Book Entituled The Reasonableness of Christianity as deliver'd in the Scriptures*

(London, 1695; fac. New York: Garland, 1984). (Published with *Socianianism Unmask'd.*)

EMERSON, ROGER L., 'The "Affair" at Edinburgh and the "Project" at Glasgow: The Politics of Hume's Attempts to Become a Professor', in M. A. Stewart and John P. Wright (eds.), *Hume and Hume's Connexions* (Edinburgh: Edinburgh University Press, 1994), 1–22.

EPICTETUS, *The Manual*, in *The Discourses as Reported by Arrian, The Manual, and Fragments*, trans. W. A. Oldfather, 2 vols., Loeb Library (1926–8).

EPICURUS (and the testimony of others), *The Epicurus Reader*, ed. and trans. Brad Inwood and L. P. Gerson (Indianapolis: Hackett, 1994).

EURIPIDES, *Hecuba*, in *Iphigeneia at Aulis, Rhesus, Hecuba, The Daughters of Troy, Helen*, trans. Arthur S. Way, Loeb Library (1966).

FAKHRY, MAJID, *Ethical Theories in Islam* (New York: E. J. Brill, 1991).

FÉNELON, FRANÇOIS DE SALIGNAC DE LA MOTHE, *Demonstration de l'existence de Dieu* [*Demonstration of the Existence of God*] (Amsterdam, 1713).

FIESER, JAMES (ed.), *Early Responses to Hume's Moral, Literary and Political Writings*, vols. 1–2 of the series Early Responses to Hume (Bristol: Thoemmes, 1999).

—— (ed.), *Early Responses to Hume's Metaphysical and Epistemological Writings*, vols. 3–4 of the series Early Responses to Hume (Bristol: Thoemmes, 2000).

FLEMING, CALEB, *Three Questions Resolved . . . Wherein Popery is Proved to Have no Claim . . . With A Postscript on Mr.* Hume's *Natural History of Religion* (London, 1757). (The Postscript appears on pp. 50–6, but the title appears only on the title-page of the larger work.)

FLEW, ANTONY (ed.), *David Hume: Writings on Religion* (La Salle, Ill.: Open Court, 1992).

FONTENELLE, BERNARD LE BOVIER DE, *Histoire des oracles*, nouvelle edn. (Paris, 1707).

—— *The History of Oracles and the Cheats of the Pagan Priests* (London, 1688); fac. in *The Achievement of Bernard le Bovier de Fontenelle*, ed. Leonard M. Marsak (New York: Johnson, 1970).

—— *De l'origine de fables* [*On the Origin of Fables*], ed. Jean Raoul Carré (Paris: Félix Alcan, 1932).

FORBES, ALEXANDER, *Essays Moral and Philosophical on Several Subjects* (London, 1734; fac. New York: Garland, 1970).

FRÉRET, NICOLAS, *Œuvres complettes de M. Freret* [*Complete Works of Mr. Fréret*], 4 vols. in 1 (London, 1775; fac. Westmead: Gregg International, 1972).

GASKIN, J. C. A., *Hume's Philosophy of Religion*, 2nd edn. (Atlantic Highlands, NJ: Humanities Press International, 1988).

GAWLICK, GÜNTER, and KREIMENDAHL, LOTHAR, *Hume in der deutschen Aufklärung. Umrisse einer Rezeptionsgeschichte* [*Hume in the German Enlightenment: Outline of the History of His Reception*] (Stuttgart, 1987).

GAY, JOHN, *Preliminary Dissertation concerning the Fundamental Principle of Virtue and Morality* (London, 1731; fac. New York: Garland, 1978). (This work is 'prefix'd' to William King's *Essay on the Origin of Evil* in the 1731 edition.)

GERARD, ALEXANDER, *The Influence of the Pastoral Office on the Character Examined; with a View, especially, to Mr. Hume's Representation of the Spirit of that Office* (Aberdeen, 1760).

GIBBON, EDWARD, *Life of Mahomet* (Philadelphia, 1805). (This volume is based on ch. 50 of *The Decline and Fall of the Roman Empire*.)

GLANVILL, JOSEPH, *Scepsis scientifica: or Confest Ignorance, the Way to Science* (London, 1665; fac. New York: Garland, 1978).

GOEDAERT, JAN [JOHANNES], *Histoire naturelle des insectes, selon leurs differentes metamorphoses* [*Natural History of Insects, according to their Different Metamorphoses*] (The Hague, 1700).

GROSE, THOMAS HODGE, 'History of the Editions', in vol. 3 of *The Philosophical Works of David Hume*, ed. T. H. Green and T. H. Grose, 4 vols. (London, 1875, as in the edn. of 1882–6; fac. Aalen: Scientia, 1964), 15–84.

GROTIUS, HUGO, *The Truth of the Christian Religion*, trans. John Clarke (London, 1827).

GROVE, HENRY, *A System of Moral Philosophy*, ed. and partially completed by Thomas Amory, 2 vols. (London, 1749).

The Guardian, by Joseph Addison *et al.*, ed. John Calhoun Stephens (Lexington, Ky.: University Press of Kentucky, 1982).

GUICCIARDINI, FRANCESCO, *La storia d'Italia* [*The History of Italy*], in *History of Italy and History of Florence*, ed. John R. Hale, trans. Cecil Grayson (New York: Twayne, 1964).

HAKLUYT, RICHARD (ed.), *The Principall Navigations, Voiages and Discoveries of the English Nation* (London, 1589; fac. Cambridge: Cambridge University Press, 1965).

HANDOVER, P. M., *Printing in London: From 1476 to Modern Times* (Cambridge, Mass.: Harvard University Press, 1960).

HERBERT OF CHERBURY (EDWARD HERBERT), *Pagan Religion: A Translation of* De religione gentilium, ed. John Anthony Butler (Ottawa: Dovehouse, 1996).

—— *De veritate* [*On Truth*], ed. Meyrick H. Carré (Bristol: University of Bristol, 1937; fac. London and Bristol: Routledge/Thoemmes, 1992).

HERNLUND, PATRICIA, 'William Strahan's Ledgers: Standard Charges for Printing, 1738–1785', *Studies in Bibliography*, 20 (1967), 89–111.

—— 'William Strahan's Ledgers II: Standard Charges for Papers, 1738–1785', *Studies in Bibliography*, 22 (1969), 179–95.

HERODIAN, *History of the Empire from the Time of Marcus Aurelius*, trans. C. R. Whittaker, 2 vols., Loeb Library (1969–70).

HERODOTUS, *History*, trans. A. D. Godley, 4 vols., Loeb Library (1928–38).

HESIOD, *The Homeric Hymns and Homerica*, trans. Hugh G. Evelyn-White, Loeb Library (1936).

HESIOD, *Theogonia*, in *The Homeric Hymns and Homerica.*

—— *Works and Days*, in *The Homeric Hymns and Homerica.*

HILLYARD, BRIAN, 'The Keepership of David Hume', in P. Cadell and A. Matheson (eds.), *For the Advancement of Learning: Scotland's National Library 1689–1989* (Edinburgh: HMSO, 1989), 103–9.

—— and NORTON, DAVID FATE, 'The Hume Bookplate: A Cautionary Note', *The Book Collector*, 40 (1991), 539–45.

HIPPOCRATES, *Nature of Man*, in *Hippocrates*, trans. W. H. S. Jones, Loeb Library (1931). Bound with Heracleitus, *On the Universe*.

HOADLY, BENJAMIN, *Queries Recommended to the Authors of the late* Discourse of Free-Thinking (London, 1713).

HOBBES, THOMAS, *De Cive* [*Of the Citizen*], ed. Howard Warrender (Oxford: Clarendon Press, 1983).

—— *Human Nature, or the Fundamental Elements of Policy* ['Hobbes Tripos . . . The first, *Human Nature*'], in vol. 4 of *The English Works of Thomas Hobbes*, ed. William Molesworth, 12 vols. (London, 1839–45; fac. London: Routledge/Thoemmes, 1994, as *The Collected Works of Thomas Hobbes*).

—— *Leviathan*, ed. Edwin Curley (Indianapolis: Hackett, 1994).

HOMER, *The Iliad*, trans. A. T. Murray, 2 vols., Loeb Library (1976–8).

—— *The Odyssey*, trans. A. T. Murray, 2 vols., Loeb Library (1966).

HORACE (QUINTUS HORATIUS FLACCUS), *Ars poetica* [*The Art of Poetry*], in *Satires, Epistles and Ars poetica*, trans. H. Rushton Fairclough, Loeb Library (1947).

—— *Epodes*, in *The Odes and Epodes.*

—— *Odes*, in *The Odes and Epodes.*

—— *The Odes and Epodes*, trans. C. E. Bennett, Loeb Library (1924).

HUET, PIERRE-DANIEL, *Traité philosophique de la foiblesse de l'esprit humain* [*A Philosophical Treatise concerning the Weakness of the Human Spirit*] (Amsterdam, 1723).

HUME, DAVID, *An Abstract of a Book lately Published; Entituled, A Treatise of Human Nature, &c.*, in *A Treatise of Human Nature*, ed. David Fate Norton and Mary J. Norton (as below).

—— *Disertación sobre las pasiones y otros ensayos morales* [*Dissertation on the Passions and Other Moral Essays*], ed. and trans. José Luis Tasset Carmona (Barcelona: Anthropos, 1990).

—— *An Enquiry concerning Human Understanding*, ed. Tom L. Beauchamp (Oxford: Oxford University Press, 1999). (Two different editions exist: One is in the Clarendon Hume, and the other is a student edition in Oxford Philosophical Texts.)

—— *An Enquiry concerning the Principles of Morals*, ed. Tom L. Beauchamp (Oxford: Oxford University Press, 1998). (Two different editions exist: One is in the Clarendon Hume, and the other is a student edition in Oxford Philosophical Texts.)

——*Essays: Moral, Political, and Literary*, ed. Eugene F. Miller, 2nd edn. (Indianapolis: LibertyClassics, 1987).

——*Four Dissertations*, ed. John Immerwahr (London, 1757; fac. Bristol: Thoemmes, 1995).

——*The History of England: From the Invasion of Julius Caesar to the Revolution in 1688*, 6 vols. (Indianapolis: LibertyClassics, 1983–5). (Based on the edition of 1778.)

——'Hume's Early Memoranda, 1729–1740', ed. Ernest C. Mossner, *Journal of the History of Ideas*, 9 (1948), 492–518.

——*A Letter from a Gentleman to his Friend in Edinburgh*, ed. Ernest C. Mossner and John V. Price (Edinburgh, 1745; fac. Edinburgh: Edinburgh University Press, 1967). (Pub. anonymously; though now commonly ascribed to Hume, it was heavily edited by Henry Home, Lord Kames.)

——*A Letter from a Gentleman to his Friend in Edinburgh*, in *A Treatise of Human Nature*, ed. David Fate Norton and Mary J. Norton (as below).

——*The Letters of David Hume*, ed. J. Y. T. Greig, 2 vols. (Oxford: Clarendon Press, 1932).

——*Letters of David Hume to William Strahan*, ed. G. Birkbeck Hill (Oxford, 1888).

——'The Life of David Hume, Esq. Written by Himself', in *The Letters of David Hume*, 1:1–7.

——*The Natural History of Religion*, ed. James Fieser (New York: Macmillan, 1992). (Library of Liberal Arts, later acquired by Prentice-Hall.)

——*The Natural History of Religion* and *Dialogues concerning Natural Religion*, ed. A. Wayne Colver and John Valdimir Price (Oxford: Clarendon Press, 1976).

——*New Letters of David Hume*, ed. Raymond Klibansky and Ernest C. Mossner (Oxford: Clarendon Press, 1954).

——*The Philosophical Works of David Hume*, ed. Thomas Hill Green and Thomas Hodge Grose, 4 vols. (London, 1882–6; fac. Aalen: Scientia, 1964).

——*A Treatise of Human Nature*, ed. David Fate Norton and Mary J. Norton (Oxford: Oxford University Press, 2000, 2007). (Two different editions exist: One is in the Clarendon Hume (2007), and the other is a student edition in Oxford Philosophical Texts (2000).)

Hurd, Richard, *A Discourse, By Way of General Preface to the Quarto Edition of Bishop Warburton's Works; containing some Account of the Life, Writings, and Character of the Author* (London, 1794), as reprinted in vol. 1 of Warburton, *The Works* (London, 1788–94; fac. Hildesheim: Olms, 1980).

Hutcheson, Francis, *Collected Works of Francis Hutcheson*, 7 vols., fac. edn. by Bernhard Fabian (Hildesheim: Olms, 1969–71).

——*An Essay on the Nature and Conduct of the Passions and Affections. With Illustrations on the Moral Sense* (London, 1728), in vol. 2 of *Collected Works of Francis Hutcheson*.

HUTCHESON, FRANCIS, *An Essay on the Nature and Conduct of the Passions and Affections. With Illustrations on the Moral Sense*, 3rd edn. 1742; fac. edn. by Paul McReynolds (Gainesville, Fla.: Scholars' Facsimiles & Reprints, 1969).

—— *An Inquiry into the Original of our Ideas of Beauty and Virtue*; In *Two Treatises* (London, 1725), in vol. 1 of *Collected Works of Francis Hutcheson.*

—— *A Short Introduction to Moral Philosophy* (London, 1747), in vol. 4 of *Collected Works of Francis Hutcheson.*

HYDE, THOMAS, *Historia religionis veterum Persarum, eorumque magorum* [*History of the Religion of the Ancient Persians, and of their Priestly Class*] (Oxford, 1700). (See the Annotations, at nn. 39 and 46, for a fuller statement and explanation of this title.)

IMMERWAHR, JOHN, 'Hume's *Dissertation on the Passions*', *Journal of the History of Philosophy*, 32 (1994), 225–40.

JACKSON, JOHN, *An Address to Deists, Being a Proof of Reveal'd Religion from Miracles and Prophecies* (London, 1744).

JAMES, SUSAN, *Passion and Action: The Emotions in Seventeenth-Century Philosophy* (Oxford: Clarendon Press, 1997).

JESSOP, T. E., *A Bibliography of David Hume and of Scottish Philosophy from Francis Hutcheson to Lord Balfour* (London: A. Brown & Sons, 1938; fac. New York: Garland, 1983).

JOSEPHUS, *Jewish Antiquities*, trans. H. St. John Thackeray, Ralph Marcus, A. P. Wikgren, and L. H. Feldman, 10 vols., Loeb Library (1926–65).

JUVENAL (DECIMUS JUNIUS JUVENALIS), *Satires*, in *Juvenal and Persius*, trans. G. G. Ramsay, Loeb Library (1930).

KAEMPFER, ENGELBERT, *et al.*, *Histoire naturelle, civile, et ecclesiastique de l'empire du Japon* (The Hague, 1729). ('Naturelle' added in the French title, which was adapted from an English translation of 1727 by J. G. Scheuchzer that did not use 'Natural History' in the title.)

KAMES, LORD (HENRY HOME), *Essays on the Principles of Morality and Natural Religion* (Edinburgh, 1751; fac. New York: Garland, 1976).

KERNAN, ALVIN, *Printing Technology, Letters, & Samuel Johnson* (Princeton: Princeton University Press, 1987).

KING, WILLIAM, *An Essay on the Origin of Evil* (London, 1731; fac. New York: Garland, 1978).

Koran, in *The Glorious Koran*, trans. Muhammad Marmaduke Pickthall (London: Allen & Unwin, 1976).

KORS, ALAN CHARLES, *The Orthodox Sources of Disbelief*, in vol. 1 of *Atheism in France 1650–1729* (Princeton: Princeton University Press, 1990).

—— 'The French Context of Hume's Philosophical Theology', *Hume Studies*, 21 (1995), 221–36.

KOZANECKI, TADEUSZ, 'Dawida Hume's nieznane listy w zbiorach Muzeum Czartoryskich [Polska]', *Archiwum Historii Filozofii i Myśli Spolecznej*, 9 (1963), 127–41, as published in Richard Popkin, 'So Hume did Read Berkeley'.

Kreimendahl, Lothar, 'Humes frühe religionsphilosophische Interessen im Lichte seiner "Early Memoranda"' [*Hume's Early Interest in the Philosophy of Religion in Light of his 'Early Memoranda'*], *Zeitschrift für philosophische Forschung*, 53 (1999), 553–68.

Kuehn, Manfred, 'Hume in the *Göttingische Anzeigen*', *Hume Studies*, 13 (1987), 46–73.

La Chambre, Marin Cureau de, *L'Art de connoistre les hommes* [*The Art of Knowing Humans*] (Amsterdam, 1660).

—— *The Art How to Know Men*, trans. John Davies (London, 1665).

—— *The Characters of the Passions* (London, Part 1, 1650; Part 2, 1661).

—— *Les charactères des passions* (Paris, 1662).

La Forge, Louis de, *Traitté de l'esprit de l'homme* [*Treatise on the Mind of Man*] (Amsterdam, 1666; fac. Hildesheim: Olms, 1984).

La Mettrie, Julien Offray de, *Histoire naturelle de l'âme* [*Natural History of the Soul*], augmented edn. [2nd or 'Nouvelle Edition'] (Oxford, 1747). (First published in The Hague, 1745.)

—— *Machine Man*, in *Machine Man and Other Writings*, ed. and trans. Ann Thomson (Cambridge: Cambridge University Press, 1996).

—— *Man a Machine: Translated from the French* (London, 1749).

—— *Œuvres philosophiques* (Paris: Fayard, 1987).

La Mothe Le Vayer, François de, *De la vertu des payens* [*On the Virtue of the Pagans*], in vol. 1 of *Œuvres* (Dresden, 1756–9; fac. Geneva: Slatkine Reprints, 1970, 14 vols. in 2).

La Rochefoucauld, François de, *Maximes* [*Maxims*], ed. Jacques Truchet (Paris: Garnier Frères, 1967).

—— *Maxims*, trans. John Heard, jun. (New York: Mifflin, 1917).

Lamy, Bernard, *Entretiens sur les sciences* [*Discourses on the Sciences*] (Paris: Presses Universitaires de France, 1966).

Law, Edmund, *An Enquiry into the Ideas of Space, Time, Immensity, and Eternity* (London, 1734; fac. New York: Garland, 1976).

Le Brun, Charles, *Conference of Monsieur Le Brun . . . upon Expression, General and Particular*, 'Translated from the French' (London, 1701).

Le Comte, Louis Daniel, *Memoirs and Remarks . . . Made in Above Ten Years Travels through the Empire of China* (London, 1737). (French title: *Nouveaux mémoires sur l'état présent de la Chine*. In the 1770–7 editions of *NHR*, the spelling of 'Comte' was changed to 'Compte'. A possible explanation of Hume's spelling is that Hume or his printer saw an edition of Comte's book in which his name was spelled 'Compte'. Such an edition was published in English in London in 1697 (*Memoirs and Observations . . . Made in a Late Journey through the Empire of China*). However, the bookseller, Benjamin Tooke, corrected the improper spelling by dropping the 'p' in the editions of 1698 and 1699.) (See also Cat.)

(Lacroze, Mathurin V.,) 'Historical and Critical Reflections upon Mahometanism and Socinianism', in *Four Treatises Concerning the Doctrine, Discipline and Worship of the Mahometans* (London, 1712). (This collection of essays gives no indication of an editor.)

LE GRAND, ANTHONY, *Man without Passion: Or, the Wise Stoick, According to the Sentiments of Seneca* (London, 1675).

LEECHMAN, WILLIAM, *The Nature, Reasonableness, and Advantages of Prayer: With an Attempt to Answer the Objections Against It: A Sermon* (Glasgow and London, 1743).

LEIBNIZ, GOTTFRIED WILHELM, *Discourse on Metaphysics*, in *Philosophical Essays*, ed. and trans. Roger Ariew and Daniel Garber (Indianapolis: Hackett, 1989).

—— *New Essays on Human Understanding*, ed. and trans. Peter Remnant and Jonathan Bennett (Cambridge: Cambridge University Press, 1996).

—— *Theodicy: Essays on the Goodness of God, the Freedom of Man, and the Origin of Evil*, ed. Austin Farrer, trans. E. M. Huggard, from C. J. Gerhardt's edn. (New Haven: Yale University Press, 1952).

LÉRY, JEAN DE, *History of a Voyage to the Land of Brazil*, trans. Janet Whatley (Berkeley: University of California Press, 1990).

LEVI, ANTHONY, *French Moralists: The Theory of the Passions 1585–1649* (Oxford: Clarendon Press, 1964).

LEVINE, JOSEPH M., 'Natural History and the History of the Scientific Revolution', *Clio*, 13 (1983), 57–73.

LINNAEUS, CAROLUS, *Systema naturae*, 10th edn. (Holmiae, 1758; fac. London: British Museum, 1956).

LIVY (TITUS LIVIUS), *Ab urbe condita*, trans. B. O. Foster, F. G. Moore, E. T. Sage, and A. C. Schlesinger, 14 vols., Loeb Library (1919–59). (Livy's *History*, trans. in Foster's edition as *From the Founding of the City*.)

LOCKE, JOHN, *An Essay concerning Human Understanding*, ed. Peter H. Nidditch (Oxford: Clarendon Press, 1975).

—— *Letters concerning Toleration*, in vol. 6 of *The Works of John Locke*.

—— *The Reasonableness of Christianity*, ed. John C. Higgins-Biddle (Oxford: Clarendon Press, 1999).

—— *A Second Vindication of the Reasonableness of Christianity, &c.*, in vol. 7 of *The Works of John Locke*.

—— *A Vindication of the Reasonableness of Christianity &c., from Mr. Edwards's Reflections*, in vol. 7 of *The Works of John Locke*.

—— *The Works of John Locke*, 10th edn., 10 vols. (London, 1801; corrected 1823).

LONGINUS. See *On the Sublime*.

LUCIAN, *The Carousal, or the Lapiths* [*The Drinking Party, or Lapithae*], trans. A. M. Harmon, Loeb Library (1921).

—— *Hermotimus*, trans. K. Kilburn, Loeb Library (1959).

—— *The Lover of Lies*, trans. A. M. Harmon, Loeb Library (1921).

—— *Menippus, or the Descent into Hades*, trans. A. M. Harmon, Loeb Library (1925).

—— *On Sacrifices*, trans. A. M. Harmon, Loeb Library (1921).

——*Zeus Catechized*, trans. A. M. Harmon, Loeb Library (1929).

——*Zeus Rants*, trans. A. M. Harmon, Loeb Library (1929).

LUCRETIUS CARUS, TITUS, *De rerum natura* [*On the Nature of the Universe*], trans. W. H. D. Rouse, rev. Martin Ferguson Smith, Loeb Library (1975).

MACHIAVELLI, NICCOLÒ, *Discourses on the First Ten Books of Livy*, in *The Discourses*, ed. W. Stark, trans. Leslie J. Walker, 2 vols. (London: Routledge & Kegan Paul, 1950).

MACROBIUS, AMBROSIUS THEODOSIUS, *The Saturnalia*, trans. Percival Vaughan Davies (New York: Columbia University Press, 1969).

MAILLET, BENOIT DE, *Telliamed: or, Discourses between an Indian Philosopher and a French Missionary . . . relating to Natural History and Philosophy* (London, 1750). (The Original, in French, was published in Amsterdam in 1748. *Telliamed* is an anagram of *de Maillet*.)

MALEBRANCHE, NICOLAS, *De la recherche de la vérité* [*The Search after Truth*], ed. Geneviève Lewis (Paris: Librairie Philosophique J. Vrin, 1945).

——*The Search after Truth*, trans. T. M. Lennon and P. J. Olscamp (Columbus, Oh.: Ohio State University Press, 1980).

——*Treatise on Nature and Grace*, trans. Patrick Riley (Oxford: Clarendon Press, 1992).

MALHERBE, MICHEL, 'Hume's *Natural History of Religion*', *Hume Studies*, 21 (1995), 255–74.

MANDEVILLE, BERNARD, *The Fable of the Bees: OR, Private Vices, Publick Benefits*, ed. F. B. Kaye, 2 vols. (Oxford: Clarendon Press, 1924; repr. Indianapolis: LibertyClassics, 1989).

MANILIUS, MARCUS, *Astronomica*, trans. G. P. Goold, Loeb Library (1977).

MANUEL, FRANK, *The Eighteenth Century Confronts the Gods* (Cambridge, Mass.: Harvard University Press, 1959).

MASLEN, KEITH, *An Early London Printing House at Work: Studies in the Bowyer Ledgers* (New York: The Bibliographical Society of America, 1993).

——*The Bowyer Ornament Stock*, Oxford Bibliographical Society Occasional Publication, 8 (Oxford: Oxford Bibliographical Society, 1973).

——and LANCASTER, JOHN (eds.), *The Bowyer Ledgers: The Printing Accounts of William Bowyer, Father and Son, Reproduced on Microfiche with a Checklist of Bowyer Printing, 1699–1777, a Commentary, Indexes, and Appendixes* (London: The Bibliographical Society; New York: The Bibliographical Society of America, 1991; distributed by Oxford University Press, Oxford).

MCLEOD, RANDALL, 'Collator in a Handbag' (Toronto: Graduate Department of English, University of Toronto, 1986).

MILNER, JOHN, *An Account of Mr. Lock's Religion, Out of His Own Writings, and in His Own Words* (London, 1700).

MILTON, JOHN, *Paradise Lost*, ed. Merritt Y. Hughes (New York: Macmillan, 1985). (See also Phillips, 'The Life of Milton'.)

MOHAMMAD, *Speeches & Table-Talk*, ed. and trans. Stanley Lane-Poole (London, 1882).

MONTAIGNE, MICHEL DE, *The Complete Essays*, ed. and trans. M. A. Screech (London: Penguin Books, 1993).

MONTGERON, LOUIS BASILE CARRÉ DE, *La verité des miracles operés par l'intercession de M. de Paris* [*The Truth of the Miracles Brought about by the Intercession of M. de Pâris*] (Utrecht, 1737).

MORE, HENRY, *Enchiridion Ethicum: The English Translation of 1690* (London, 1690, published as *An Account of Virtue*; fac. New York: Facsimile Text Society, 1930).

—— *Enthusiasmus Triumphatus*, in vol. 1 of *A Collection of Several Philosophical Writings of Dr. Henry More*, 2 vols. (London, 1662; fac. New York: Garland, 1978).

MORNAI [MORNAY], PHILIPPE DE, *De l'institution, usage et doctrine du sainct sacrement de l'Eucharistie en l'Eglise ancienne* [*On the Institution, Usage, and Doctrine of the Holy Sacrament of the Eucharist in the Ancient Church*] (La Rochelle, 1598).

MOSSNER, ERNEST CAMPBELL, *The Life of David Hume*, 2nd edn. (Oxford: Clarendon Press, 1980).

—— 'Hume's *Four Dissertations*: An Essay in Biography and Bibliography', *Modern Philology*, 48 (Aug. 1950), 37–57.

MOTTEUX, PETER ANTHONY, and ECCLES, JOHN (eds.), *The Rape of Europa by Jupiter* (London, 1694; fac. Los Angeles: Augustan Reprint Society, UCLA Clark Library, 1981).

NEWTON, ISAAC, *Chronology of Ancient Kingdoms Amended* (London, 1728).

—— 'Newton to a Friend [?John Locke]', no. 359, in vol. 3, ed. H. W. Turnbull, *The Correspondence of Isaac Newton*, 7 vols., ed. Turnbull *et al.* (Cambridge: Cambridge University Press, 1959–77). (Regarding Newton's *Account of Two Notable Corruptions of Scripture*.)

—— *Opticks* (New York: Dover, 1952). (Based on the 4th ed., London, 1730.)

NICHOLS, JOHN, *Literary Anecdotes of the Eighteenth Century; comprizing Biographical Memoirs of William Bowyer, Printer, F.S.A, and Many of His Learned Friends*, 6 vols. (London, 1812).

NICOLE, PIERRE, *La Perpétuité de la foi de l'église catholique touchant l'Eucharistie, défendue contre le livre du sieur Claude, ministre de Charenton* [*The Perpetuity of the Faith of the Catholic Church concerning the Eucharist, Defended Against the Book of M. Claud, Minister of Charenton*] (3 vols. in 4; Paris, 1669–74).

NORTON, DAVID FATE, and NORTON, MARY J., *The David Hume Library* (Edinburgh: Edinburgh Bibliographical Society, 1996).

On the Sublime (incorrectly attributed to Longinus), trans. W. Hamilton Fyfe, Loeb Library (1927). Bound with Aristotle and Demetrius.

OSWALD, JAMES, *An Appeal to Common Sense in Behalf of Religion*, 2 vols. (Edinburgh, 1766, 1772).

OVID (PUBLIUS OVIDIUS NASO), *Metamorphoses*, trans. Frank Justus Miller, 2 vols., Loeb Library (1960–4).

PASCAL, BLAISE, *Pensées and Other Writings*, trans. Honor Levi (New York: Oxford University Press, 1995). (*Pensées* was first published in 1670 by Arnauld, Nicole, *et al.*)

PERRAULT, CLAUDE, *et al.*, for the Académie des sciences (France), *Memoir's* [sic] *for a Natural History of Animals containing the Anatomical Descriptions of Several Creatures Dissected by the Royal Academy of Sciences at Paris* (London, 1688). (Annotation: Translation of *Mémoires pour servir à l'histoire naturelle des animaux*. Paris, 1676.)

PETRONIUS ARBITER, GAIUS, *Satyricon*, trans. Michael Heseltine, Loeb Library (1951). Bound with Seneca, *Apocolocyntosis*.

PHILLIPS, EDWARD, 'The Life of Milton', in John Milton, *Complete Poems and Major Prose*, ed. Merritt Y. Hughes (New York: Odyssey, 1957), Appendix.

PITTION, JEAN-PAUL, 'Hume's Reading of Bayle: An Inquiry into the Source and Role of the Memoranda', *Journal of the History of Philosophy*, 15 (1977), 373–86.

PLATO, *Apology*, in *Euthyphro, Apology, Crito, Phaedo, Phaedrus*.

—— *Cratylus*, in *Cratylus, Parmenides, Greater Hippias, Lesser Hippias*, trans. Harold North Fowler, Loeb Library (1926).

—— *Crito*, in *Euthyphro, Apology, Crito, Phaedo, Phaedrus*.

—— *Euthyphro*, in *Euthyphro, Apology, Crito, Phaedo, Phaedrus*.

—— *Euthyphro, Apology, Crito, Phaedo, Phaedrus*, trans. Harold North Fowler, Loeb Library (1923).

—— *Laws*, trans. R. G. Bury, 2 vols., Loeb Library (1926).

—— *Phaedo*, in *Euthyphro, Apology, Crito, Phaedo, Phaedrus*.

—— *Republic*, trans. Paul Shorey, 2 vols., Loeb Library (1946).

—— *Timaeus*, in *Timaeus, Critias, Cleitophon, Menexenus, Epistles*, trans. R. G. Bury, Loeb Library (1952).

PLAUTUS, TITUS MACCIUS, *Amphitryon*, in *Amphitryon, The Comedy of Asses, The Pot of Gold, The Two Bacchises, The Captives*, trans. Paul Nixon, Loeb Library (1937).

PLINY THE ELDER (GAIUS PLINIUS SECUNDUS), *Natural History*, trans. D. E. Eichholz, W. H. S. Jones, and H. Rackham, 10 vols., Loeb Library (1938–86).

PLINY THE YOUNGER (GAIUS PLINIUS CAECILIUS SECUNDUS), *Letters*, trans. William Melmoth, rev. W. M. L. Hutchinson, 2 vols., Loeb Library (1961–3).

PLOMER, H. R., BUSHNELL, G. H., and DIX, E. R. McC., for the Bibliographical Society, *A Dictionary of the Printers and Booksellers who were at Work in England, Scotland and Ireland from 1726 to 1775* (Oxford: Oxford University Press, 1932).

PLUCHE, NOËL-ANTOINE, *Le spectacle de la nature; ou Entretiens sur les particularités de l'histoire naturelle* [*The Spectacle of Nature; or, Discussion of the Particularities of Natural History*], 2nd edn., 8 vols. (Paris, 1732–52).

PLUTARCH, *Lives*, trans. Bernadotte Perrin, 11 vols., Loeb Library (1914–28).

—— *Moralia* [*Moral Essays*], trans. Frank Cole Babbitt, Harold Cherniss, and William C. Helmbold, 16 vols., Loeb Library (1927–2004).

POOL, MATTHEW, *A Dialogue between A Popish Priest and An English Protestant* (London, 1672).

POPE, ALEXANDER, *An Essay on Criticism* (London, 1711; fac. London: Scolar Press, 1970).

POPKIN, RICHARD, 'So, Hume Did Read Berkeley', *Journal of Philosophy*, 61 (1964), 773–8.

PRICE, RICHARD, *Four Dissertations*, 2nd edn. (London, 1768; fac. Bristol: Thoemmes, 1990).

PRIDEAUX, HUMPHREY, *The True Nature of Imposture Fully Display'd in the Life of Mahomet*, 8th edn. (London, 1723).

PRIOR, MATTHEW, *Alma: or, The Progress of the Mind*, in vol. 1 of *The Literary Works of Matthew Prior*.

—— *The Literary Works of Matthew Prior*, vol. 1, ed. H. Bunker Wright and Monroe K. Spears, 2nd edn., 2 vols. (Oxford: Clarendon Press, 1971).

—— *Solomon on the Vanity of the World*, in vol. 1 of *The Literary Works of Matthew Prior*.

QUINTILIAN (MARCUS FABIUS QUINTILIANUS), *The Institutio oratoria* [*Oratorical Institutes or The Education of an Orator*], trans. H. E. Butler, 4 vols., Loeb Library (1921–53).

RACINE, JEAN, *Abrégé de l'histoire de Port-Royal* [*Brief History of Port-Royal*] (Cologne, 1742).

RAMSAY, ANDREW MICHAEL, *The Philosophical Principles of Natural and Revealed Religion. Unfolded in a Geometrical Order*, 2 vols. (Glasgow, 1748–9).

—— *The Travels of Cyrus*, 2 vols. (London, 1730). (Originally published in French; Paris, 1727.)

REGNARD, JEAN-FRANÇOIS, *Journey to Lapland*, in vol. 1 of *A General Collection of the Best and Most Interesting Voyages and Travels in all Parts of the World*, ed. John Pinkerton, 6 vols. (London, 1808).

REID, THOMAS, *Essays on the Active Powers of Man* (Edinburgh, 1788; fac. New York: Garland, 1977).

REYNOLDS, EDWARD, *A Treatise of the Passions and Faculties of the Soule of Man. With Severall Dignities and Corruptions Thereunto Belonging* (London, 1640).

ROCHEDIEU, CHARLES ALFRED, *Bibliography of French Translations of English Works 1700–1800* (Chicago: University of Chicago Press, 1948).

ROLLIN, CHARLES, *The Ancient History of the Egyptians, Carthaginians, Assyrians, Babylonians, Medes and Persians, Macedonians and Grecians*, 4 vols. (New York, 1864).

ROSE, WILLIAM, Review of *Four Dissertations, The Monthly Review, or, Literary Journal*, 16 (Feb. 1757), 122–39. (Published anonymously.)

—— Review of *Essays on Suicide and Immortality, The Monthly Review, or, Literary Journal*, 70 (June 1784), 427–8.

——Review of 'Remarks upon the Natural History of Religion By Mr. Hume. With Dialogues on Heathen Idolatry, and the Christian Religion By S.T.', *The Monthly Review, or, Literary Journal*, 19 (1758), 532–3. (Reply to Stona.)

RUTILIUS NAMATIANUS, CLAUDIUS, *A Voyage Home to Gaul*, in *Minor Latin Poets*, trans. J. Wright Duff and Arnold M. Duff, Loeb Library (1935).

RYCAUT, PAUL, *The Present State of the Ottoman Empire. Containing . . . The Most Material Points of the Mahometan Religion* (London, 1668).

SALE, GEORGE (trans.), *The Koran, Commonly called The Alcoran of Mohammed*, to which is prefixed 'A Preliminary Discourse' (London, 1734).

SALLUST (GAIUS SALLUSTIUS CRISPUS), *The War with Catiline* in *Sallust*, trans. J. C. Rolfe, Loeb Library (1960).

SCHEUCHZER, JOHANN JAKOB, *et al.*, *Physique sacrée, ou histoire-naturelle de la Bible* [*Sacred Physics, or Natural History of the Bible*], 8 vols. (Amsterdam, 1732–7).

SCHWARTZ, RICHARD B., 'Boswell and Hume: The Deathbed Interview', in Greg Clingham (ed.), *New Light on Boswell* (Cambridge: Cambridge University Press, 1991), 116–25.

SENAULT, JEAN-FRANÇOIS, *De l'usage des passions* [*The Use of the Passions*] (Paris, 1641).

——*The Use of Passions*, trans. Henry [Carey], earl of Monmouth (London, 1671).

SENECA, LUCIUS ANNAEUS, *Ad Lucilium epistulae morales* [*Moral Letters to Lucilius*], trans. Richard M. Gummere, 3 vols., Loeb Library (1917–67).

——*Moral Essays*, trans. John W. Basore, 3 vols., Loeb Library (1935–65).

SEXTUS EMPIRICUS, *Against the Physicists*, trans. R. G. Bury, Loeb Library (1936).

SHAFTESBURY, ANTHONY ASHLEY COOPER, THIRD EARL OF, *Characteristics of Men, Manners, Opinions, Times*, ed. John M. Robertson, 2 vols. in 1 (London, 1900; repr. Indianapolis: Bobbs-Merrill, 1964).

SHAW, DUNCAN, 'Number 2' (Appendix 2), in vol. 2 of *A Comparative View of the Several Methods of Promoting Religious Instruction from the Earliest Down to the Present Time*, 2 vols. (London, 1776), 268–302.

SHER, RICHARD, 'The Book in the Scottish Enlightenment', in Roger Emerson, Richard Sher, Stephen Brown, and Paul Wood (eds.), *The Culture of the Book in the Scottish Enlightenment* (Toronto: Thomas Fisher Rare Book Library, 2000), 40–60.

——'Professors of Virtue: The Social History of the Edinburgh Moral Philosophy Chair in the Eighteenth Century', in M. A. Stewart (ed.), *Studies in the Philosophy of the Scottish Enlightenment* (Oxford: Clarendon Press, 1990), 87–126.

SHERLOCK, THOMAS, 'A Letter from the Lord Bishop of London to the Clergy and People of London and Westminster; on the Occasion of the Late Earthquakes' (London, 1750).

SMITH, ADAM, *The Theory of Moral Sentiments*, ed. A. L. Macfie and D. D. Raphael (Oxford: Clarendon Press, 1976).

SPARTIAN (AELIUS SPARTIANUS), *Life of Hadrian*, in *Scriptores Historiae Augustae*, trans. David Magie, 3 vols., Loeb Library (1921).

The Spectator, by Richard Steele, Joseph Addison, *et al.*, ed. Donald F. Bond, 5 vols. (Oxford: Clarendon Press, 1965).

SPINK, J. S., *French Free-Thought from Gassendi to Voltaire* (London: Athlone Press, 1960).

SPINOZA, *The Collected Works of Spinoza*, vol. 1, ed. and trans. Edwin Curley (Princeton: Princeton University Press, 1985).

—— *Ethics*, in *The Collected Works of Spinoza*, vol. 1.

—— *Short Treatise on God, Man, and His Well-Being*, in *The Collected Works of Spinoza*, vol. 1.

—— *Theologico-Political Treatise*, in vol. 1 of *The Chief Works of Benedict de Spinoza*, trans. R. H. M. Elwes (New York: Dover Publications, 1951), 1–278.

STADEN, HANS, *The True History of his Captivity*, ed. and trans. Malcolm Letts (London: Routledge & Sons, 1928).

STEWART, M. A., 'The Dating of Hume's Manuscripts', in Paul Wood (ed.), *The Scottish Enlightenment: Essays in Reinterpretation* (Rochester: University of Rochester Press, 2000), 267–314.

—— *The Kirk and the Infidel: An Inaugural Lecture* (Lancaster: Lancaster University, 1994).

STONA, THOMAS, *Remarks upon the Natural History of Religion By Mr. Hume. With Dialogues on Heathen Idolatry and the Christian Religion* 'By S.T.' (London, 1758). (Published anonymously 'by S.T.'. Authorship is attributed to Stona in Nichols, *Literary Anecdotes of the Eighteenth Century* (see above), vol. 2, p. 717.)

STRABO, *Geography*, trans. Horace Leonard Jones, 8 vols., Loeb Library (1924–60).

STRAHAN LEDGERS, London: British Library, Department of Manuscripts. William Strahan, Printer. Receipts and Payments Accounts. Add. MS 48800 (1739–68; credits and payments to 1773), 48801 (1768–85), 48815 (later entries).

SUETONIUS TRANQUILLUS, GAIUS, *Lives of the Caesars*, trans. J. C. Rolfe, 2 vols., Loeb Library (1930–9).

SWEDIAUR, F. X., *Philosophical Dictionary: or the Opinions of Modern Philosophers on Metaphysical, Moral, and Political Subjects*, 4 vols. (London, 1786).

SWIFT, JONATHAN, *Mr. C-----ns's Discourse of Free-Thinking, Put into plain English* (London, 1713).

TACITUS, CORNELIUS, *The Annals*, trans. John Jackson, in *The Annals Books I–III*, Loeb Library (bound with *The Histories Books IV–V*) (1979), and *The Annals Books IV–VI, XI–XII, The Annals Books XIII–XVI*, Loeb Library (1981).

—— *Germania*, trans. M. Hutton, rev. E. H. Warmington, in *Agricola, Germania, Dialogus*, Loeb Library (1980).

—— *The Histories*, trans. Clifford H. Moore, in *The Histories Books I–III*, Loeb Library (1980); and *Histories Books IV–V, Annals Books I–III*, Loeb Library (1979).

THOMAS AQUINAS, *Summa theologiæ*, 60 vols. (Blackfriars, in conjunction with New York: McGraw-Hill and London: Eyre & Spottiswoode, 1964–).

with precision, even when an author is directly quoted.[4] In these cases, only titles and basic bibliographical information about publication dates and editions are provided.

Titles in both original languages and translations into English are provided for classical and non-classical works. Greek titles are followed by a transliteration, a Latin version, and an English translation. An attempt has been made to supply more accurate translations than those found on the title pages of many published sources in English. The reader therefore should not expect the translation to follow conventional English renderings. Edition titles for collections and more inclusive works—such as *Quae exstant opera*—are not translated. Hume himself did not cite the titles of collected works, though he did use such works.

Spelling, punctuation, and accents in this Catalogue sometimes vary from forms that are now customary. This Catalogue remains faithful to the prevailing forms in the eighteenth century, or earlier, as appropriate.[5]

The names of translators and editors of texts have been supplied wherever possible. Their names are reported as displayed on the title pages, except that Latin syntax has been altered as necessary. As a result of this rule, the Catalogue contains some inconsistency in the presentation of names and titles. The names of cities, as printed on title-pages, have occasionally been translated into modern forms.

The date of first publication and facts about whether there were other lifetime or posthumous editions are supplied. In a few cases, conclusive evidence could not be obtained regarding the date of first publication of essays or short works that were later published as parts of books. The first documented date of publication is provided in these cases.

A DISSERTATION ON THE PASSIONS

Addison, Joseph. *The Spectator* (no. 412, 23 June 1712). First comprehensive edn. 1712–15, other lifetime and posthumous edns. *DP* n. 2.
°*The Spectator*, 5th edn., 8 vols. (London, 1720).

Guicciardini, Francesco. *Della historia d'Italia / The History of Italy*. First pub. 1561 (first 16 books) and 1564 (last 4 books), all edns. posthumous. *DP* Sect. 4.9.
°*Della istoria d'Italia*, 2 vols. (Venice, 1738–9).

Horace (Quintus Horatius Flaccus). *Epodi / Epodes*. *DP* Sect. 1.19.
°*Opera*, ed. Usher Gahagan (London, 1744).

[4] If no specific edition is traceable to Hume, the editor has not cited an edition that was available for Hume to use even if it seems plausible that he might have used that edition. Also, Hume generally does not specify whether he used an existing English translation in the case of foreign-language works that had been translated.

[5] The fact that two or more inconsistent forms appeared during the century has on several occasions forced a judgement about which form to use. In this Catalogue, French accents have not been modernized, but if the preferred seventeenth- or eighteenth-century form could not be determined, an appropriate rule consistent with modern usage has been followed.

La Rochefoucauld, François de. *Maximes / Maxims*. First pub. 1664, other lifetime and posthumous edns. *DP* Sect. 6.11.

Prior, Matthew.

'Alma: or, The Progress of the Mind'. First pub. 1719, other posthumous edns. *DP* Sect. 4.10.

'Solomon on the Vanity of the World'. First pub. 1719, other posthumous edns. *DP* Sect. 4.10.

Virgil (Publius Vergilius Maro). *Aeneis / Aeneid. DP* Sect. 6.4.

°*Opera* (London, 1744). (Hume may have owned more than one relevant edition of Virgil. See Norton and Norton, *The David Hume Library*.)

THE NATURAL HISTORY OF RELIGION

Aristotle. Προβλήματα (*Problēmata*) / *Problemata / Problems. NHR* note 1.

Arnobius. *Adversus gentes / Against the Heathen. NHR* nn. 14, 34.

Arrian (Flavius Arrianus). Περὶ ἀναβάσεως Ἀλεξάνδρου (*Peri anabaseōs Alexandrou*) / *De expeditione Alexandri Magni / Anabasis* or *The Expedition of Alexander. NHR* nn. 47, 48, 53.

°*De expeditione Alexandri Magni*, ed. Nicolaus Blancardus, trans. Bonaventura Vulcanius (Amsterdam, 1668).

Augustine. *De civitate Dei / The City of God. NHR* n. 63.

Aurelius Antoninus, Marcus. Τὰ εἰς ἑαυτόν (*Ta eis heauton*) / *De seipso et ad seipsum / Meditations with Himself. NHR* n. 73.

°*Eorum quae ad seipsum libri XII* (Oxford, 1704).

°*Commentaries of the Emperor Marcus Antoninus. Containing his Maxims of Science, and Rules of Life. Wrote for his own Use, and address'd to Himself*, trans. James Thomson (London, 1747).

Bacon, Francis. *Essays*. First pub. 1597, other lifetime and posthumous edns. *NHR* Sect. 6.2.

°*Opera, moralium et civilium*, ed. Guilielmus Rawley (London, 1638).

Bayle, Pierre. *Dictionnaire historique et critique / Historical and Critical Dictionary*. First pub. 1697, other lifetime and posthumous edns. *NHR* n. 57.

Boulainvilliers, Henri de. *Abrégé chronologique de l'histoire de France / Chronological Summary of the History of France*. First pub. 1728, other posthumous edns. *NHR* n. 38.

+*Abrégé chronologique de l'histoire de France*, in vol. 3 of *Etat de la France*, 3 vols. (London, 1727–8).

Brumoy, Pierre. *Le théâtre des Grecs / The Theatre of the Greeks*. First pub. 1730, other lifetime and posthumous edns. *NHR* n. 13.

°*Le théâtre des Grecs* (Paris, 1730).

Caesar, Gaius Julius. *De bello Gallico / On the Gallic War. NHR* nn. 10, 36.

°*De bello Gallico*, in *Quae extant* (London, 1744).

CICERO, MARCUS TULLIUS.

De divinatione / On Divination. NHR nn. 67, 72.

De natura deorum / On the Nature of the Gods. NHR n. 61; *NHR* Sect. 12.25.

Epistulae ad familiares / Letters to his Friends. NHR n. 66.

In Catilinam / Against Catiline. NHR n. 93.

Pro Cluentio / In Defence of Cluentius. NHR n. 79.

Tusculanae disputationes / Tusculan Disputations. NHR nn. 62, 81.

°*Opera*, ed. Pierre Joseph Olivet, 9 vols. (Paris, 1740–2).

CLARKE, SAMUEL. *The Scripture Doctrine of the Trinity.* First pub. 1712, other lifetime and posthumous edns. *NHR* n. 78.

CURTIUS RUFUS, QUINTUS. *Historiae Alexandri Magni / History of Alexander the Great. NHR* nn. 17, 34.

°*Quintus Curtius*, ed. Usher Gahagan, 2 vols. (London, 1746).

DIODORUS SICULUS. Βιβλιοθήκη ἱστορική (*Bibliothēkē historikē*) / *Bibliotheca historica / Historical Library. NHR* nn. 4, 8, 17, 24, 25, 26, 59, 91, 92.

°*Bibliothecae historicae libri XV*, trans. Laurentius Rhodomanus, 2 vols. in 1 (Hanover, 1604).

DIOGENES LAERTIUS. Περὶ βίων δογμάτων καὶ ἀποφθεγμάτων τῶν ἐν φιλοσοφίᾳ εὐδοκιμησάντων (*Peri biōn dogmatōn kai apophthegmatōn tōn en philosophiai eudokimēsantōn*) / *De vitis dogmatibus et apophthegmatibus eorum qui in philosophia claruerunt / On the Lives, Teachings, and Sayings of the Famous Philosophers. NHR* n. 35.

DIONYSIUS OF HALICARNASSUS. Ῥωμαϊκὴ ἀρχαιολογία (*Rōmaikē archaiologia*) / *Antiquitates Romanorum / Roman Antiquities. NHR* nn. 2, 29.

DRYDEN, JOHN. *Absalom and Achitophel. A Poem.* First pub. 1681, other lifetime and posthumous edns. *NHR* Sect. 12.9.

EPICTETUS. Ἐγχειρίδιον (*Encheiridion*) / *Enchiridion / Manual. NHR* n. 74.

°*Omnia Graece et Latine: Epicteti Enchiridion, Cebetis Tabula, Prodici Hercules, et Cleanthis Hymnus* (Glasgow, 1744).

EURIPIDES. Ἑκάβη (*Hekabē*) / *Hecuba / Hecuba. NHR* n. 3.

FONTENELLE, BERNARD LE BOVIER DE. *Histoire des oracles / History of Oracles.* First pub. 1687, other lifetime and posthumous edns. *NHR* n. 13.

°*Œuvres*, 6 vols., Paris (1742–51).

HERODIAN. Ἱστορίαι (*Historiai*) / *Historiae / Histories. NHR* n. 34.

°*Historiarum libri VIII*, trans. Angelus Politianus (Edinburgh, 1724).

HERODOTUS. Ἱστορίαι (*Historiai*) / *Historiae / Histories. NHR* nn. 9, 20, 41, 45, 90.

HESIOD.

Θεογονία (*Theogonia*) / *Deorum generatio / Theogony. NHR* nn. 22, 31, 32; *NHR* Sect. 6.11.

Ἔργα καὶ ἡμέραι (*Erga kai hēmerai*) / *Opera et dies / Works and Days. NHR* nn. 1, 21; *NHR* Sect. 4.11.

Homer.

Ἰλιάς (*Ilias*) / *Ilias* / *Iliad*. *NHR* nn. 11, 33; *NHR* Sect. 6.11.

Ὀδύσσεια (*Odusseia*) / *Odyssea* / *Odyssey*. *NHR* Sect. 15.2.

Horace (Quintus Horatius Flaccus). *Carmina* / *Odes*. *NHR* Sect. 12.8.

°*Opera*, ed. Usher Gahagan (London, 1744).

Hyde, Thomas. *Historia religionis veterum Persarum, eorumque magorum* / *History of the Religion of the Ancient Persians, and of their Priestly Class*. First pub. 1700, one posthumous edn. 1760. *NHR* nn. 39, 46.

+*Historia religionis veterum Persarum, eorumque magorum* (Oxford, 1700).

Juvenal (Decimus Junius Juvenalis). *Satyrae* / *Satires*. *NHR* n. 81.

°*Decii Junii Juvenalis et A. Persii Flacci satyrae*, ed. Usher Gahagan (published with the *Satyrae* of A. Persius Flaccus) (London, 1744).

Le Comte, Louis Daniel. *Nouveaux mémoires sur l'état présent de la Chine* / *New Reports on the Present Condition of China*. First pub. 1696, other lifetime edns. *NHR* n. 6.

Livy (Titus Livius). *Historiae ab urbe condita* / *Histories since the Founding of the City*. *NHR* nn. 71, 89.

°*Historiarum ab urbe condita*, ed. Arn. Drakenborch, 7 vols. (Amsterdam and Leiden, 1738–46).

[Longinus]. Περὶ ὕψους (*Peri hupsous*) / *De sublimitate* / *On the Sublime*. *NHR* note 12. (This work was incorrectly attributed to 'Longinus' in the eighteenth century.)

°*De sublimitate commentarius*, ed. Zacharias Pearce (Amsterdam, 1733).

Lucian.

Ἑρμότιμος ἢ περὶ αἱρήσεων (*Hermotimos ē peri hairēseōn*) / *Hermotimus, sive de sectis* / *Hermotimus, or On Sects*. *NHR* n. 84.

Ζεὺς ἐλεγχόμενος (*Zeus elenchomenos*) / *Jupiter confutatus* / *Zeus Catechized*. *NHR* n. 20.

Μένιππος ἢ νεκυομαντεῖα (*Menippos ē Nekuomanteia*) / *Necyomantia* / *Menippus, or the Descent into Hades*. *NHR* n. 86.

Περὶ θυσίων (*Peri thusiōn*) / *De sacrificiis* / *On Sacrifices*. *NHR* n. 8.

Περὶ πένθους (*Peri penthous*) / *De luctu* / *On Funerals*. *NHR* n. 20.

Τὰ πρὸς Κρόνον (*Ta pros Kronon*) / *Saturnalia* / *Saturnalia*. *NHR* n. 20.

Φιλοψευδής (*Philopseudēs*) / *Philopseudes* / *The Lover of Lies*. *NHR* n. 70.

Lucretius Carus, Titus. *De rerum natura* / *On the Nature of the Universe*. *NHR* n. 81; *NHR* Sect. 5.5.

°♦*De rerum natura*, ed. Sigebertus Havercampus, 2 vols. (Leiden, 1725).

Machiavelli, Niccolò. *Discorsi sopra la prima deca di Tito Livio* / *Discourses on the First Ten Books of Livy*. First pub. 1531, other posthumous edns. *NHR* n. 55.

°*Opere*, 4 vols. (The Hague, 1726).

Macrobius, Ambrosius Theodosius. *Saturnalia* / *Saturnalia*. *NHR* n. 42.

Manilius, Marcus. *Astronomica* / *Astronomical Studies*. *NHR* n. 8.

Milton, John. *Paradise Lost*. First pub. 1667, other lifetime and posthumous edns. *NHR* Sect. 1.6.

Ovid (Publius Ovidius Naso). *Metamorphoses / Metamorphoses*. *NHR* nn. 8, 23, 88.
°*Opera quae extant*, 5 vols. (London, 1745).

Petronius Arbiter, Gaius.
Satyricon / Satyricon. *NHR* Sect. 12.10.

Phillips, Edward. 'The Life of Mr. John Milton'. First pub. 1694, other posthumous edns. *NHR* Sect. 12.14.
+In John Milton, *Letters of State . . . To Which is Added, An Account of His Life* (London, 1694).

Plato.
Εὐθύφρων (*Euthuphrōn*) / *Euthyphro / Euthyphro*. *NHR* n. 76.
Νόμοι (*Nomoi*) / *De legibus / Laws*. *NHR* n. 27.
Πολιτεία (*Politeia*) / *De republica / Republic*. *NHR* n. 81.
Φαίδων (*Phaidōn*) / *Phaedo / Phaedo*. *NHR* n. 77.
+*Opera quae extant omnia*, ed. Henr. Stephanus, trans. Ioannes Serranus, 3 vols. (Geneva, 1578). (There is more than one Serranus edn., but this is the translation used by Hume. The edn. listed here is an example.)

Plautus, Titus Maccius. *Amphitryon / Amphitryon*. *NHR* Sect. 4.5.

Pliny the Elder (Gaius Plinius Secundus). *Historia naturalis / Natural History*. *NHR* nn. 1, 42, 68; *NHR* Sect. 2.2.
♦*Historia naturalis* (Paris, 1526).

Pliny the Younger (Gaius Plinius Caecilius Secundus). *Epistolae / Epistles*. *NHR* n. 30.

Plutarch.
Βίοι (*Bioi*) / *Vitae / Lives*. *NHR* n. 32.
Ἠθικά (*ēthika*) / *Moralia / Moral Essays*. *NHR* nn. 44, 56, 85.

Quintilian (Marcus Fabius Quintilianus). *Institutiones oratoriae / Oratorical Institutes*. *NHR* n. 69.
°*Institutionum oratoriarum libri duodecim*, ed. Carolus Rollin (London, 1738). (The Hume Library lists this work edited by Rollin in an edn. of 1735, but this date is in doubt because no copies have been discovered or listed elsewhere. A 1736–7, 2-vol. Rollin edn. does exist.)

Ramsay, Andrew Michael. *The Philosophical Principles of Natural and Revealed Religion. Unfolded in a Geometrical Order*. *NHR* n. 87.
+*The Philosophical Principles of Natural and Revealed Religion. Unfolded in a Geometrical Order*, 2 vols. (Glasgow, 1748–9).

Regnard, Jean-François. *Voyage de Laponie / Journey to Lapland*. First pub. 1731, all edns. posthumous. *NHR* n. 7.
°*Œuvres*, 4 vols. (Paris, 1742).

Rutilius Namatianus, Claudius. *Itinerarium / Journey*. *NHR* n. 64.

SALLUST (GAIUS SALLUSTIUS CRISPUS). *Bellum Catilinae / The War of Catiline. NHR* nn. 80, 93.

°*Quae extant*, ed. Usher Gahagan (London, 1744).

SENECA, LUCIUS ANNAEUS. *Ad Lucilium epistulae morales / Moral Letters to Lucilius. NHR* nn. 16, 81.

SEXTUS EMPIRICUS. Πρὸς φυσικούς *(Pros phusikous) / Adversus physicos / Against the Physicists. NHR* nn. 28, 82.

+♦*Opera*, trans. H. Stephanus and G. Herveto (Geneva, 1621). (An edn. by P. and J. Chouët, using a rare numbering system that was employed by Hume. *Adversus physicos* is commonly cited as *Adversus mathematicos* 9, 10, or *Adversus dogmaticos* 3, 4.)

SPARTIAN (AELIUS SPARTIANUS). *Vita Hadriani Caesaris / Life of Hadrian. NHR* n. 65.

STRABO. Γεωγραφικά *(Geōgraphika) / Res geographicae / Geography. NHR* nn. 5, 52.

SUETONIUS TRANQUILLUS, GAIUS. *Vitae Caesarum / Lives of the Caesars. NHR* nn. 18, 19, 49, 52, 58, 68.

TACITUS, CORNELIUS.

Annales / Annals. NHR n. 58.

Germania / Germania. NHR n. 37.

Historiae / Histories. NHR n. 69.

THUCYDIDES. Ἱστορίαι *(Historiai) / Historiae / Histories. NHR* n. 54.

VARRO, MARCUS TERENTIUS. *De lingua Latina / On the Latin Language. NHR* Sect. 12.11.

XENOPHON.

Ἀπομνημονεύματα *(Apomnēmoneumata) / Memorabilia / Memorabilia. NHR* nn. 43, 78, 83.

Κύρου ἀνάβασις *(Kurou anabasis) / De Cyri minoris expeditione / The Expedition of Cyrus. NHR* n. 78.

Λακεδαιμονίων πολιτεία (*Lakedaimonion politeia*) */ De Lacedaemoniorum republica / The Constitution of the Lacedaemonians. NHR* n. 15.

Περὶ πόρων *(Peri porōn) / Rationes redituum / On Ways and Means. NHR* n. 78.

+*Quae exstant opera*, ed. Antonius Stephanus, trans. Joannes Leunclavius, 2 vols. in 1 (Paris, 1625). (There is more than one Leunclavius edn. It is unknown which among the Leunclavius folios Hume used. The above edition is listed as an example.)

HUME'S INDEX

This Index is Hume's,[1] except for the substitution of sections, paragraphs, and note numbers for his pages and note markers. Footnotes are the editor's. The Index is based on the entire index for *Essays and Treatises on Several Subjects*, but that index is here reduced in size to include all and only *DP* entries (placed first) and *NHR* entries (placed second). The remaining entries in the full index of *ETSS* are published in other volumes of the Clarendon Hume.

This Index follows the copytext's typographical convention of small capitals for the first word of the first entry under each letter. Inconsistent capitalization of first words in the entries in the copytext (using small capitals in some instances and lower case in parallel instances) has been corrected and standardized throughout the Index; the conventions of the copytext itself have been followed in eliminating these inconsistencies. Otherwise, the capitalization is Hume's. Hume's spellings are retained in all entries unless a spelling inconsistency was discovered, in which case Hume's most common spelling is used. Incorrect alphabetical ordering has been corrected. The now archaic combination of I and J entries is Hume's; it is here retained, as are lines of a specific length used to show what is repeated from the immediately prior entry. These lines were occasionally printed with an incorrect length and with inconsistent use of commas; these lines have been adjusted to conform to Hume's principal convention.

[1] Hume first compiled his Index for the 1758 *ETSS* edn., which was published in a single volume. This edition brought all previous essays and treatises together. The Index was compiled seven times, from 1758 through 1777 (though pagination in the 1777 edn. was not under Hume's control). The Index was always compiled for the whole of *ETSS*. Few changes were introduced after the 1758 original. In the critical edition, the Index has been separated into discrete units corresponding to each particular volume and work in the Clarendon Hume.

Hume not infrequently missed pages that probably should have been indexed under one of his chosen terms. When an oversight occurred in indexes in all of his editions, no attempt has been made here to correct the text. For example, Cicero appears to have been overlooked at three points relevant to the Index, but this apparent oversight is not here corrected. By contrast, Hume's failure to cite Hesiod at *NHR* 4.11 has been corrected because this reference is correct and is found in his original 1758 index.

Caution is required in interpreting Hume's frequent use of the term 'quoted', as he commonly uses it in a broader sense than is common today. He means, roughly, 'to take note of or to notice'. See n. 2 below.

Hume evidently played an active role in the indexing. On 3 Sept. 1757, he wrote to his bookseller, Andrew Millar (*Letters*, 1: 265): 'I have finish'd the Index to this new Collection of my Pieces. This Index cost me more Trouble than I was aware of when I begun it. I am oblig'd to Mr Strahan for the uncommon Pains he has taken in making it correct.'

For further evidence of Hume's involvement in creating the original Index of 1758, see correspondence of 18 Jan. 1757, to Andrew Millar; and 15 Feb. 1757, to William Strahan (*Letters*, 1: 239, 245).

Hume's Index was published in the editions of 1758, 1764, 1767, 1768, 1770, 1772, and 1777. Variants are reported in the 'Editorial Appendix: Emendations and Substantive Variants', as are all emendations. All footnotes in the Index are the editor's.

A DISSERTATION ON THE PASSIONS

[2] This reference to Locke as 'quoted' may appear to be a mistake, yet it occurs in all of Hume's indexes to *ETSS*. See the statement in n. 1 above that Hume commonly uses the term 'quoted' in

M

N–P

Q–R

S–Z [NO ENTRIES FOR *DP*]

THE NATURAL HISTORY OF RELIGION

A

the now antiquated sense of 'to take note of or to notice'. In this reference Hume may be subtly recognizing Locke's contribution to the theory of association of ideas. For the record, as David Norton pointed out to me, Addison is the only figure quoted, in today's sense, in Sect. 2. Nonetheless, Hume is not likely to be here, in any way, referring to Addison, because earlier in the Index he enters 'ADDISON quoted' with the correct page. Of course, he still could have made a mistake in the Locke entry. For example, it is possible that he saw the nearby reference to his own *An Enquiry concerning Human Understanding* and confused it with Locke's title *An Essay concerning Human Understanding* (when constructing the original index of 1758). We need not suppose that he repeatedly made this mistake in later editions when adjusting the page numbers of his index, because some printing-house apprentice might have been assigned the task.

F

G

H

I & J

K–L

M

N

O

P

Q

R

[3] The copytext was printed as p. 507 at this point—a typographical error for p. 407; p. 507 contained notes for *EPM*.

S

T

U–V

W

X

Y–Z [NO ENTRIES FOR *NHR*]

EDITOR'S INDEX

This index contains entries from almost all parts of this volume, but names, titles, and concepts in Hume's texts and index are given priority. Entries for titles of books and other publications are generally restricted to titles mentioned or alluded to by Hume (see the Catalogue of Hume's References, pp. 264–70), Hume's own works, and publications that reviewed or advertised the two works in this volume during Hume's lifetime. *Not indexed* are the following: variants and errors listed in the Editorial Appendix (on pp. 180–204); items in the Reference List; publishers of books (other than Hume's booksellers) and cities of their publication; and bibliographical and technical data that are located in a concise section of the Editor's Introduction (pp. xxxii–l). Many published works mentioned in the Editor's Introduction and Annotations are not indexed by title; however, names of the authors of these works are included in the index.

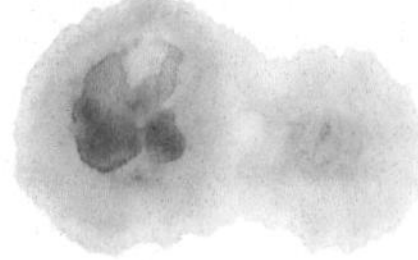

Printed in Great Britain
by Amazon